Preface

The retailing industry is experiencing major changes. (See *Update 2020: The Pandemics Lasting Impact on Retailing*). To stay relevant retailers must recognize trends and adapt. The main goal for retail managers should be to provide customers excellent products and experiences while meeting company goals. Every person is involved in the process of retailing throughout his or her lifetime. As consumers, we interact with retailers every day of the week. We visit retail outlets, shop online with our favorite e-tailers, and see ads for our favorite retailers across different communication platforms. Given the importance of retailing to world economies, it is essential that we understand the processes involved in retailing and their implications for those students who study this important business activity.

Retailing is more complex than it seems. The study of retailing encompasses all areas of business study. To be a successful retail manager, one must understand accounting, finance, management, information technology, marketing, and other business activities involved in the effective planning and execution of retail plans. The more you understand these processes, the better retail professional you will be.

Because retailing encompasses all areas of business, it is sometimes difficult to see the "big picture" as it relates to retailing. Most retailing texts present students with a series of chapters that provide useful information but fail to explain how the various activities involved in retailing affect each other. The approach of *Retailing: Integrated Retail Management* is to offer the student an overview of the retail process through the use of an integrated retail management (IRM) plan. The steps involved in retailing as presented in the text are tied together through the IRM plan. The flowchart depicting the IRM plan appears on every chapter opener, so that students can retain the big picture of the flow of operations at a typical retail establishment.

Of the many retailing texts to choose from, we hope that you will prefer this updated *Retailing: Integrated Retail Management 3e*, with its integrated approach, clear organization, and comprehensive, up-to-date coverage. We are confident that after browsing through this text, you will find that the organization and topic coverage is current, easy to follow, and accessible to students.

Content and Organization

As mentioned earlier, this retailing text relies on an integrative approach to help the reader see the big picture regarding the retailing process. Through the integrated retail management (IRM) flowchart provided at the onset of each chapter, the reader will be able to see where each of the various concepts fit in to the overall retail management process. In other words, instead of teaching students chapter material, this text reinforces the teaching of "subject" areas. This approach allows students to utilize critical thinking instead of chapter memorization. As one of the book's reviewers commented, "…the organization of the textbook is logical and student-friendly in approach, which enhances the user's learning and the emphasis on the role and importance of strategy in retailing."

Part 1 of the text, which includes Chapters 1 and 2, offers the reader an overall, macro view of the world of retailing. Each of the environments that have an impact on retail decision making is presented. Retail decision makers rely on their understanding of the macro environment to make the best possible decisions with regard to their operations.

Chapter 1, "The World of Retailing," presents a definition of retailing and takes an in-depth look at the macro environment surrounding the retail decision maker. The IRM flowchart is presented, and a brief overview of each step in the process is given, providing an outline of the text's framework. Careers in retailing are discussed to give the student a quick picture of what jobs typically exist within a retailing operation.

Chapter 2, "Customer Value, Services, and Retailing Technologies," continues to explore the external retail environment by providing an in-depth look at three environments that are important to the retail decision maker. Chapter 2 covers important concepts such as quality, service, price, and equity development for retailers. The area of services retailing is presented and systems used for creating retail relationships are explored. The chapter ends with full coverage of technology in retailing and e-tailing; e-tailing and e-commerce; and finally laws, ethics, and corporate social responsibility.

Part 2, consisting of Chapters 3 through 5, deals with the creation of effective retail strategies. The coverage of each chapter relates back to the importance of an effective retail strategy and how this strategy provides a guide for the development of retail tactics. Chapter 3, "An Overview of the Retail Planning and Management Process," gives an overview of the retail planning and management process. Each of the steps in the management process is introduced in this chapter and expanded upon later within the text. Chapter 4, "The Retail Environment: A Situational and Competitive Analysis," explains the process of creating a situational and competitive analysis and explains retail institutions. Chapter 5, "Evaluation and Identification of Retail Customers," concludes the part with extensive coverage on evaluating and identifying retail customers. This coverage includes the application of demographic, psychographic, geographic, geodemographic, and behavioristic data in retail problem solving.

Part 3 of the text, encompassing Chapters 6 through 10, is concerned with internal planning and management. It includes information about research, retail information systems, market and location selection, operations management, merchandise buying and selling, and human resource management. Chapter 6, "Retail Information Systems and Research," provides an in-depth look at changes in retail information systems—systems such as radio frequency identification (RFID), POS terminals, and self-checkout. In addition, a method of gathering marketing and market research is provided and reinforced at the end of the chapter. This chapter provides the reader with tools and skills that are easily transferable to other classes. A particular area of emphasis is on resources useful in undertaking the research process. One of the text's reviewers commented: "Three cheers for the excellent coverage of secondary data and internet research." Chapter 7, "Selecting the Appropriate Market and Location," provides coverage of the processes used in selecting a market and a physical--or cyber--location for a retailer. Chapter 8, "Financial Aspects of Operations Management," presents the different methods of managing retail operations, with a focus on financial analysis. Merchandise buying and handling is covered in Chapter 9, "Merchandise Buying and Handling," and finally, in Chapter 10, "Human Resource Management," discussion centers on the human resource management function.

Part 4 of the text, covering Chapters 11 through 15, deals with the issues of retail tactical executions and ends with coverage of laws, ethics, diversity, and trends in retailing. Chapter 11, "Pricing in Retailing," is an introduction to retail tactics, focusing on pricing in retailing--namely pricing objectives and policies. The student is provided information about both setting a price and adjusting the price once it is set. Chapter 12, "Developing an Effective Integrated Marketing Communications Mix," presents an integrated marketing communications process, including the use of various media to assist the retailer in communicating with stakeholders. This chapter also integrates the concepts of store layout and design with customer communications. Because it has been proven that is cheaper to keep a current customer than to get a new one, Chapter 13, "Customer Service in Retailing," offers suggestions on creating superior customer service. Chapter 14, "Laws and Ethics," provides information on laws and ethics specifically related to retail management. Chapter 15, "Retailing Trends and Best Practices," ends the text with a discussion of trends in the retail environment as well as best practices.

Acknowledgments

We are very excited to be part of an outstanding team at Textbook Media. A special thanks to Tom Doran and Ed Laube, co-founders of Textbook Media, for their support and constructive feedback. The energy and dedication of the Textbook Media team was great. We would also like to thank our family (David, Anne, Kari, their spouses, Kerrie, Anthony and Marcus and three grandchildren, Kaleb, Kaden and Frankie) who have been supportive of our work throughout our lives. Thanks to our moms, Ninfa Alarid and Marianne Ogden, and our dads, Diego Alarid and Dr. Russell L. Ogden (deceased), for their inspiration. Finally thanks to all our former and current students who continue to inspire us.

The quality of this book has been enhanced through the insights and helpful comments of all our reviewers. Even for the third edition we looked back at their comments. Specifically, we would like to thank:

Chad W. Autry, Bradley University
Anne L. Balazs, Mississippi University for Women
Gayle Brown-Litwin, Hofstra University
James W. Camerius, Northern Michigan University
W. Peter Cornish, University of South Carolina Upstate
Judith Grenkowicz, Kirtland Community College
Kathleen Gruben, Georgia Southern University
Mary A. Higby, University of Detroit Mercy
Dexter Hinton, New York University--Stern
Patricia Holman, Montana State University--Billings
Terence L. Holmes, Murray State University
Rhea Ingram, Columbus State University
Ruth Krieger, Oklahoma State University
Cathy Martin, University of Akron
Carolyn Predmore, Manhattan College
James Rakowski, University of Memphis
Jill Slomski, Mercyhurst College
Robert. L. Stephens, Macon State College

About the Authors

Denise T. Ogden, Ph.D.

Professor, Marketing

Penn State Lehigh Valley

President, The Doctors Ogden Group, LLC

Dr. Ogden is in her sixteenth year as a Professor of Marketing at Penn State University's Lehigh Valley Campus. Prior to pursuing a career in academia, Dr. Ogden worked in Public Relations for the U.S. Bureau of Reclamation, Alamosa, Colorado. Upon arriving to Pennsylvania in 1989 she joined D&B (formerly the Dun & Bradstreet Corporation) where she gained experience in various positions. There her accomplishments included development and implementation of a diversity training program and two national awards for outstanding performance. While at D&B she also delivered marketing training (consultative selling).

In 2003 and 2013, Dr. Ogden was the recipient of the Lehigh Valley Campus Teaching Excellence Award. She was also awarded the Penn State University Atherton Award for excellence in teaching in 2017. Her research interests include retailing, integrated marketing communication (IMC), and multicultural elements of business. In addition to diversity consulting, her consulting firm, The Doctors Ogden Group LLC, specializes in retailing, marketing research, and entertainment retailing. She is also active as newsletter editor and college liaison for the Center for Retailing Solutions

Dr. Ogden holds a Ph.D. (Business Administration/Marketing) from Temple University, an M.B.A. from DeSales University (Marketing and Quality Systems), and a B.S. (Business Administration/Marketing) and B.A. (Psychology) from Adams State College (CO). She is the co-author of texts in retailing, marketing, and integrated marketing communication and has published articles in many academic journals.

James R. (Doc) Ogden, Ph.D.

Emeritus Professor of Marketing

Kutztown University of Pennsylvania

CEO, The Doctors Ogden Group, LLC

Dr. James R. Ogden (Doc) is an Emeritus Professor of Marketing at Kutztown University as well as CEO of the consulting firm The Doctors Ogden Group, LLC (T-Dog). He is in demand as a public and motivational speaker, having given presentations during the last few years all over the world. In addition, Dr. Ogden has published in leading journals and is the author of nine books on business and integrated marketing communications (IMC). Notably, he and his consulting partner and wife (Dr. Denise T. Ogden) have co-authored textbooks on retailing, marketing and IMC. Doc's academic training includes a Ph.D. with concentrations in research and statistical methodology, psychology and business; a Master's in Marketing and a Bachelor's in General Business and Business Education with minors in English, Language and Literature

Doc has sat/sits on the board of directors for numerous corporations and has worked for an array of corporations including General Motors, Meijer, Martin Guitar and D&B, to name just a few. He has consulted for many others in the areas of advertising and marketing. Ogden has been listed in over 40 "Who's Who" publications and has been given Outstanding Educator awards on numerous occasions. Ogden has been cited for "Excellence in Marketing Education" and has received the prestigious *Freedom's Foundation at Valley Forge* Award for "Excellence in Economic Education". He is currently the Chairman of the Board for the Center for Retailing Solutions.

3e Format Options for Students

eBook

eBook + PDF Chapters Bundle

eBook + Loose-Leaf (3-hole punched, Black & White) Bundle

eBook + Paperback Bundle (Black & White)

eBook + Paperback Bundle (Color)

eBook with Café Learn ™ Interactive Applications (with Web Assignments and Gradebook)

3e Supplements

For Instructors:

Instructor Resource Guide

Test Bank (4000 + questions)

PowerPoint® Slides (650 lecture slides)

Video Lab with Student Assignments

Café Learn ™ Web-based Assignments and Grade Book Application

For Students:

Range of Media and Price Options

Video Labs (gratis)

Lecture Guide

Café Learn Web-based Assignments and Additional Applications

Quizlet ™ Learning Tools and Flash Cards

Update 2020

The Pandemic's Lasting Impact on Retailing

"The only constant in the universe is change." With the recent outbreak of the COVID pandemic, this saying has never been truer. A common complaint of retailers is they don't have time to plan. The response to that is simply, You don't have time *not* to plan. Retailers must be constantly planning, evaluating, and controlling their integrated retail management plans in order to respond to change. Consumer and customer wants and needs change regularly. Other environmental factors and variables also impact a retailer's business. Changes in the environment have a lasting effect on sales. Chapter 4 provides an overview of the overall situational analysis process, and Chapter 3 provides an overview of the environmental scanning process.

Importance of Environmental Scanning

As part of the *retail planning and management function*, retailers create a system for environmental scanning. As defined in Chapter 3, environmental scanning is a process that progressive retailers use to monitor changes in their retail environments. Retailers are looking for changes in their business environments that can have an impact on their business. Retailers can no longer afford to ignore international changes. As seen by the recent pandemic (COVID-19) outbreak in 2019/2020, retailers can be damaged by not having plans in place that respond to important environmental changes.

Environmental scanning can be used to identify and respond to changes in the retail organization's market. Numerous variables might cause this change. It's important to identify those variables, determine the nature and rate of change of the variables, and then respond to the changes. Once the variables have been identified, a response can be infused with market forecasting techniques to get a better picture of what the market is going to look like. As mentioned, there must be a response to those changes.

Overview

In this chapter we examine changes in retailing and the impact the COVID-19 pandemic has had and will have on the retail industry. We break down the environmental scanning process and provide a more in-depth look at responding to changes in retailers' environments, particularly during a crisis or pandemic. Also covered are forecasting levels and demand analysis during a crisis. Finally, we provide suggestions for marketing and retailing responses during a crisis.

Changes in Retailing: 2017- 2019

The retail industry has experienced such turmoil over the past few years that the term "retail apocalypse" became popular. The trend away from big box stores to boutique stores and the growth of online retail led to closures of traditional brick-and-mortar stores. 2017 was a record-breaking year as more than 8,000 stores closed including locations from major retailers such as Charming Charlie, Sears, Kmart, J.C. Penney, Macy's, and Payless. Designer brands such as True Religion, Ascena Retail Group (Ann Taylor, Justice, Loft), Michael Kors, Abercrombie and Fitch, J Crew and Bebe stores were not immune to closures.

Despite improvements in technology, personalization, and reimagined brick-and-mortar stores, in 2018, traditional brick-and-mortar retailers closed about 5,900 locations. Several retailers closed permanently including Toys "R" Us, Henri Bendel, Dress Barn, Charlotte Russe, Charming Charlie, Avenue, and Performance Bicycle.

2019 was another record-breaking year as over 9,300 stores closed, a 63% increase from 2018. Retailers closing stores included Game Stop, Signet stores (Jared, Kay Jewelers and Zales), Dollar Store, Chicos, Gap, Walgreens, Things Remembered, Pier 1 Imports, Office Depot, Barneys New York, J.C. Penney, Bed Bath Beyond, and Party City. The stores that survived offered unique experiences and high levels of customer service.

While some viewed the retail landscape as apocalyptic, others viewed it as in transition. According to a 2019 report from IHL Group (Holman & Buzek 2019), the press tends to focus on negative news. The IHL report shows that although stores were closing in record numbers, since January 2017 the industry actually increased sales by $565.7 billion and 8,575 stores. Of the retail segments examined, the apparel and department store chains experienced the most net closures. From 2017 to 2019 there were net closures of 9,651 stores. In 2019 there were more than five retail chains opening stores for every store closing. Most of the growth came from food/drug/convenience/mass merchants (+9.5) and restaurants (+6.3).

In 2019, unemployment was low and, while many retailers closed branches, overall retailing was up. The traditional formats were no longer working as people purchased items from multiple channels.

The Shift from Brick and Mortar to Online Retail

Prior to the pandemic, online retailing was growing at a steady pace. This led many retailers to invest more heavily in technology and knowledge acquisitions concerning ecommerce. Figure 1 shows U.S. ecommerce sales compared to total sales from 2017 to 2019. Online sales for 2019 were up 14.9% over 2018 and 2018 sales were up 12% from 2017.

U.S. ECOMMERCE VS. TOTAL RETAIL* SALES
In $billions, 2017-2019

2017 — $3,484 B

2018 — $3,626 B

2019 — $3,763 B

Source: Digital Commerce 360 (formerly Internet Retailer) analysis of U.S. Department of Commerce data
*Total retail figures exclude sales of items not normally purchased online such as spending at restaurants, bars, automobile dealers, gas stations and fuel dealers

In 2017, Cyber Monday sales hit a record of $6.59 billion, the largest shopping day recorded. In comparison, that same year, Black Friday sales were $5.03 billion and Thanksgiving day brought in $2.87 billion (Su, 2017). Cyber Monday was promoted by retailers to increase sales after the Thanksgiving holiday.

In the online realm, because people can't touch the merchandise, other indicators become more important. Several studies suggest that brand names and brand loyalty are more important in online retail (Anesbury, Nenycz-Thiel, Dawes, & Kennedy, 2016). In some categories, brand names are more important online than offline and price promotions have stronger effects online (Degeratu, Rangaswamy & Jianan, 2000; Chu, Arce-Urriza, Cebollada-Calvo, & Chintagunta, 2010).

This shift of consumer purchases to online retail from brick-and-mortar stores was further exacerbated when many retailers were forced to close due to COVID-19. Even after stores reopen, many consumers will be uneasy about exposure to other shoppers and store employees.

Here Comes the Pandemic: COVID-19

Coronaviruses are a large family of viruses, some of which cause illness. COVID-19 is a new type of coronavirus that causes respiratory illness and can be spread from person to person (Centers for Disease Control, 2020). In the Fall of 2019, the novel SARS-CoC-2 coronavirus emerged in Wuhan, China (Scripps Research Institute, 2020). On December 31st, 2019, spokespeople from China told the World Health Organization (WHO) of an outbreak of a novel strain of coronavirus causing severe illness (Ibid, 2020). This was the beginning of a pandemic that has caused harm to both human health and world economies. On March 11, 2020, the World Health Organization declared the coronavirus outbreak a pandemic. It was determined that the virus was natural and not lab manufactured.

During 2014-2015, the United States government under President Barack Obama recognized the danger of worldwide pandemics. Coming off issues with the Ebola outbreak, the U.S. government decided it must act. A document was developed called the "Playbook for Early Response to High-Consequence Emerging Infectious Disease Threats and Biological Incidents" (Knight, 2020). The goal was to have a plan in place for the United States in case there were further outbreaks of worldwide disease, such as was the case with Ebola and Zika. A pandemic playbook was needed. Although environmental scanning identified a potential issue and the government developed a response, further utilization of the planned response was scrapped when a new administration decided to pursue a different course.

COVID-19 Timeline

Retail Customer Experience (2020) tracked the environmental impact of the virus on retailers. The following highlights are adapted and modified from Retail Customer Experience (Mottl, 2020):

January 31, 2020: Coronavirus likely to impact airport travel, retail worldwide

February 3, 2020: Apple shuts stores in China

March 12, 2020: Apple shuts stores in Italy

March 13, 2020: Questions surface about payment methods for retailers, digital versus cash

March 16, 2020: Retailers close stores for worker safety and customer safety

March 17, 2020: Amazon is hiring 100k workers to keep up with online sales increases

March 19, 2020: Grocers begin to hire more to meet demand

March 24, 2020: Retail industry begin lobbying for federal support

March 25, 2020: Retailers begin to set up 'special' shopping times for seniors

March 27, 2020: Stimulus package to offer $350 Billion in small business loans. $2 Trillion rescue package offered to businesses and employees

Match 30, 2020: Federal CARES Act provides relief

April 1, 2020: Walmart begins checking employee temperature before shifts

April 2, 2020: J.C. Penney furloughs workers

April 6, 2020: Amazon begins to deploy masks and taking workers temperatures

April 7, 2020: Target workers get masks, gloves...customers get more space. Wayfair gets a stock boost

April 8, 2020: Self-service grows

April 14, 2020: Amazon continues hiring to meet demand

April 16, 2020: Some retailers prepare to open; The Nebraska Mall gets ready to reopen. Walmart sets special pickup hours for their COVID high-risk customers

April 21, 2020: COVID-19 drives ecommerce upward 'big time.' Treatment of essential workers impacting consumer decision making

April 24, 2020: Target extends worker pay enhancements and benefits

April 27, 2020: The U.S. House approves an additional $484 Billion in relief funds for small businesses, testing, and hospitals

April 28, 2020: Requiring masks is difficult because of customers. Digital shopping increases Target sales

April 30, 2020: Social distancing drives changes in the way consumers spend their money

May 5, 2020: Consumer mindsets shift during the virus outbreak

May 7 and 8, 2020: The Gap will open 800 stores by month's end. Nordstrom is shuttering stores

May 11, 2020: The NRF says the retail recovery will be gradual

May 15, 2020: J.C. Penney files Chapter 11 bankruptcy

May 27, 2020: Tuesday Morning files Chapter 11 bankruptcy

June 8, 2020: The National Bureau of Economic Research announces the United States is in a recession, which began in February, 2020

Many retail experts predict more retail closures in the months and years ahead. Camilla Yanushevsky, a retail stock analyst for CFRA Research, states that "The companies that are most at risk are the ones that were already distressed before the crisis." (Bomey, 2020, para 13).

ENVIRONMENTAL SCANNING IN PRACTICE

Environmental scanning is important to ensure awareness of trends and threats. Retailers that have a risk/crisis management program in place have a better chance of surviving. Environmental scanning programs allow a company to better adapt to changes occurring in the retail environment. This section looks at (a) environmental scanning in more detail, (b) forecasting methods, and (c) responses to changes in the retailer's environment.

Environmental scanning programs must be set up to be flexible and allow for continual input. In good economic times, retailers often fail to look to their future, allowing their scanning to fall behind. Programs should ensure that environmental changes can be shared by all decision makers in a timely manner. Employees involved in environmental scanning must have strong communication skills, patience, and flexibility.

Retailers need to identify environmental forces that will affect the organization. Any change in the retailer or marketer's environment that could affect marketing strategies or marketing opportunities creates an environmental force. This force may be positive (new technological advances that create production savings) or negative (COVID 19).

In early 2019, retailers had reason to be optimistic. Unemployment was low and, while many retailers closed branches, overall retailing rose. The hospitality and travel industries were at their highest revenue levels in more than 16 years and consumer spending was at a record $13.2 trillion (Repko, Josephs, Wayland & Lucas, 2020). The traditional retail formats were no longer working as people purchased items from multiple channels. Very few could have predicted that retail employees would become essential workers as a pandemic hit the world.

COVID-19 has, in many ways, crippled economies around the world. As governments scrambled to create policies that would protect their citizens, countries' economies were shut down. Nobel Prize-winning economist Joseph Stiglitz summed it up when he stated on the CBS show *Sunday Morning (2020)* in connection to the recent COVID-19 crisis, "We are shutting down the economy to protect our health." Fed Chairman Jerome Powell, echoed, Stiglitz's words, "It is worth remembering that the measures we are taking to contain the virus represent an investment in our individual and collective health." He added, "As a society, we should do everything we can to provide relief for those who are suffering for the public good" (Powell, 2020).

The pandemic, other crises (scandals, natural disasters, consumer boycotts), and environmental forces will push the retailer to make needed changes. The more prepared retailers are, the faster they can adapt and make changes. In these situations, it's important to generate as much data and information as possible and make the best decision. This can only happen if the retailer continually monitors its retail environment.

Retail Environments

The retail environment, simply, is any *external* change or force that impacts the retailer. The retailer's environment is largely uncontrollable, which increases the complexity of responding to changes. Every retailer scans the specific environments that are most important. Primary environments affecting retail include social, governmental, technological, economic, and natural.

In the following section we look at the main environments affecting retailers and how COVID-19 has impacted them. Keep in mind that these environments are related to each other and often overlap. A combination of these environments could also provide threats and/or opportunities for retailers.

The Social Environment

The social environment includes consumer behavior and insights as well as how the social environment may be changing.

Retailing, and in particular brick-and-mortar retailing, is a social activity. When the pandemic hit the United States in February and March of 2020, stay-at-home and shelter-in-place orders shocked the operations of brick-and-mortar retailers. Most people stayed home except for essential trips. Those people who were required to go to work during this time were deemed "essential." Essential businesses like grocery stores, banks, and drug stores remained open. Especially hit were service retailers such as restaurants and bars, salons, and entertainment venues. The orders to stay home were lifted region by region based on guidelines issued by the CDC.

Even when stay-at-home orders were lifted, retailing changes were apparent. Social distancing, fewer people in stores, protections for employees, food shortages and purchase limits, increased credit card usage, reduced hours, and curbside pickup changed consumer behaviors.

According to a University of Southern California study, the pandemic has created significant shifts in people's behavior. People are washing their hands more than ever and adhering to social distancing guidelines. People also cancelled or postponed travel and avoided public spaces. Many stockpiled essentials out of fear (Hedt, 2020). The fear and stockpiling led to a widely publicized nationwide shortage of toilet paper.

Retailers still have a need to connect their products and services with consumers, but the COVID-19 pandemic fundamentally, at least in the short-term, has changed the way consumers interact with products and their physical surroundings. At the very least, the pandemic has accelerated the already changing retail dynamic. Although the way consumers buy is changing, why they buy -- their motivations -- change little.

Impact of COVID-19 on the Consumer Psyche

When asked about potential changes in consumer motivations, retail guru Paco Underhill, author of the books *Why We Buy* and *Call of the Mall*, responds, "The monster of consumption is intact" (2020, personal interview). While consumer demand for some products and categories may ebb and flow over the next few years, like durable luxury goods, it is probable that consumer desire to consume will change very little post COVID-19. This desire for products and services resides deep within the human psyche, which seeks to maintain stable levels of psychological assets related to the self, such as self-esteem, belongingness, feelings of power, and feelings of control over one's environment (Crocker & Park, 2004; Kay, Wheeler, & Smeesters, 2008; Leary, Tambor, Terdal, & Downs, 1995; Whitson & Galinsky, 2008).

How long will the effects of the coronavirus remain in consumers' psyches? It's unclear. Products serve as psychological salve to reduce distress (Mandel, Rucker, Levav, & Galinsky, 2017). To maintain stable human psyche levels, individuals often monitor the congruence between their present state (or actual self) and a goal state (or ideal self) (Carver & Scheier, 1990; Higgins, 1987). When a person perceives a self-discrepancy, or an inconsistency between one's ideal and actual self, she seeks to correct the discrepancy (Higgins, 1987). For many consumers this results in altered consumer behavior. This cerebral hard wiring is an important consideration for the U.S. retailer as consumer spending in some industries (healthcare services, transportation, recreation, food services, accommodations) showed considerable losses in sales (Council of Economic Advisers, 2020). It is evident that the pandemic is affecting psychological functioning. A study by NORC at the University of Chicago (2020) reports that people's happiness is the lowest it's been in fifty years. The study, conducted in May, 2020, reports that only 14 percent of American adults say they are very happy compared to 31 percent in 2018, a 17 percent drop.

Social Unrest

Over the course of a month, many demonstrations worldwide were held to protest the killing of George Floyd, who died on May 25, 2020, when a police officer held a knee to his neck for 8 minutes and 46 seconds. Of course this happened against the backdrop of the frustration of the Coronavirus pandemic. For many, the knee to the neck is a metaphor for how many black people are treated. Many retailers made statements supporting the protests or donated to the Black Lives Matter movement or other organizations that stand for racial equality. Retailers who donated monies include Apple, Amazon, Lululemon, McDonalds, Wendy's, Walmart, Warby Parker, Target, Etsy, H&M, Gap Brands and Home Depot. Coupled with additional changes in the social environment, such as the Black Lives Matter movement, retailers must have a thorough understanding of their market. Consumer insights become more and more important and must be incorporated into any analysis.

The Government/Political Environment

The government and political environment includes information on laws and how political decisions are affecting retail operations. The goal of government is to help consumers and businesses. With unemployment at record highs, the government is playing a key role in information and aid.

To help the economy, Congress passed a $1.7 trillion economy relief package called the CARES Act (Coronavirus Aid, Relief and Economic Security). The money provided financial assistance for Americans, small businesses, and low- and middle-income citizens. As part of the package, the federal government issued economic impact checks. While amounts varied, eligible taxpayers received a payment of $1,200 for individuals ($2,400 for married couples) and up to $500 for each qualifying child. As of June, 2020, a second stimulus check had been proposed by Congress.

Early on, both major political parties politicized the virus outbreak. The Pew Research Center (Green & Tyson, 2020) described five facts about partisan responses to the pandemic:

1. Majorities in both parties agree that a range of restrictions were necessary, although a greater percentage of Democrats agree with this as the table below shows:

Majorities of Republicans and Democrats see restrictions as necessary to address outbreak

% who say each of the following has been a necessary step to address the coronavirus outbreak

	Dem/ Lean Dem	Rep/ Lean Rep	Total
Restricting international travel to the U.S.	94	96	95
Canceling major sports and entertainment events	87	95	91
Closing K-12 schools	85	94	90
Asking people to avoid gathering in groups of more than 10	82	92	87
Limiting restaurants to carry-out only	78	91	85
Requiring most businesses other than grocery stores and pharmacies to close	61	81	71
Postponing upcoming state primary elections	66	73	70

Source: Survey of U.S. adults conducted March 19-24, 2020.

PEW RESEARCH CENTER

2. There was a wide partisan gap on views of President Trump's response to the outbreak. 83% of Republicans and people who lean Republican rated Trump's response as either excellent or good, while only 18% of Democrats and Democratic leaners agreed.

3. Democrats/Democratic leaners were more likely than Republicans/Republican leaners to see the coronavirus in the most serious terms. 78% of Democrats and people who lean Democrat believed the outbreak was a major threat to the U.S. population, while 52% of Republicans and people who lean Republican felt the same.

4. Both parties (Democrats, 36% and Republicans, 30%) said that someone in their household had either lost a job or taken a pay cut due to the coronavirus outbreak.

5. The two major parties differed on how people across the country reacted to the outbreak. Republicans/Leaners were more likely to say that people in the U.S. are overreacting to the outbreak (39%) than Democrats/Leaners (25%). 31% of Republicans/Leaners believed that people in the U.S. were not taking the virus seriously enough while 48% of Democrats/Leaners believed this.

2020 is an election year, so political ads and issues are prevalent. As many have said, the coronavirus does not care about a person's political stance. Yet one's political stance does impact retailing. According to retailing expert Erin Jordan, politics plays a role in changing people's perspectives on the economy, and this may affect consumer spending. She says that consumers look at brands as extensions of themselves and are more aware of retailers' social stances as they represent their own lifestyle (Danziger, 2018).

The Technological Environment

The technological environment includes changes and improvements in technology that help consumers and/or retailers.

The World Economic Forum (2020) lists technology trends that have emerged during the pandemic. Trends that affect retailing include:

1. The growth of online shopping and contactless delivery, including using robots for delivery. Companies got creative when enticing people to purchase. Innovative ideas included online happy hours and lunch with strangers via Zoom.

2. Digital and contactless payments. Because cash carries germs, many consumers increased the use of digital payments such as Apple Pay, Google Pay, Paypal, and Venmo.

3. Remote work. As more people throughout the world were forced to work from home, technologies to make work more efficient were increasingly adopted including virtual private networks (VPNs), remote virtual meeting programs such as Zoom, GoToMeeting, Google Hangouts and Skype and facial recognition technology. The downside to using these technologies is the concern about information security and privacy.

4. Telehealth. The rise in health care organizations providing telehealth services skyrocketed during the pandemic. In addition, there was an increase in wearable technology that tracks health statistics. Chatbots are being used to triage patients prior to allowing a face-to-face visit.

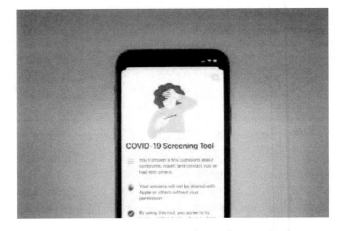

5. Online entertainment. Internet and streaming technology allowed many types of technology to move online. Museums and zoos offered virtual tours, online concerts and theatre were live streamed. As movie theaters closed, studios released movies on various streaming and on-demand platforms. One of the biggest movie streaming success stories was *Trolls World Tour*, making over $100 million in three weeks. The success of the movie led to a dispute with AMC theaters, who said it would stop streaming films from Universal (Alexander, 2020).

6. Supply Chain 4.0. The pandemic created havoc on supply chains as demand increased for some products and fell dramatically for others. Some factories were shut down as COVID-19 outbreaks spread among the workforce. The usage of technologies increased including cloud computing, Big Data, Internet-of-Things (IoT), circular economy, and blockchain (electronic ledger used to record cryptocurrency transactions).

7. 3-D Printing. As the supply chain broke down, shortages of products, especially medical protective gear, were common. Several individuals and companies began using 3-D printing technology to make items such as nasal swabs, face shields, face masks and even ventilators.

8. Robotics and drones. To protect people from contacting COVID-19, the use of robotics and drones increased. Uses included cleaning, food delivery and walking dogs. Some municipalities used talking drones to remind people to keep the recommended social distancing.

9. 5G and other communication technology. 5G is the fifth generation mobile network that is faster, more reliable and promises higher connectivity and a more uniform experience for users. With 5G a movie can be downloaded 500 percent faster than with 4G . The technology will allow retailers to better use technologies such as augmented reality and virtual reality. With families working from home, reliable Internet technology becomes more important. Experts predict the need for better, faster, and more reliable wireless technology will increase the adoption of 5G technology. All major U.S. carriers have 5G technology, but it takes a while to roll out technology nationwide. In addition, smart phones must have 5G capability.

Retail innovations such as improvements in POS (point of sale) systems, augmented shopping, staff-free stores, and the use of artificial intelligence will continue to evolve as consumers navigate the new normal.

The Economic Environment

The economic environment includes information on employment, sales and trends. As a result of shutting down, world economies were faced with two big problems. On the supply side, supply chains became fractured as producers closed to protect their workers. Manufacturers struggled to find product sources and transportation was interrupted. On the demand side, consumer spending dropped sharply. During the first quarter of 2020, millions of people lost their jobs and consumer confidence plunged to historic lows.

The Consumer Confidence Index (CCI) is based on answers from consumers about their financial situation, unemployment, and capability of savings. An indicator above 100 means consumers are confident about the future economic situation and are more inclined to spend. An indicator below 100 means that consumers are pessimistic about the future economy and tend to save more and consume less (OECD Data, 2020). The Conference Board noted that in April, 2020, its confidence index tumbled to a reading of 86.9, the lowest level in nearly six years and down from 118.8 in March of the same year (CNBC, 2020).

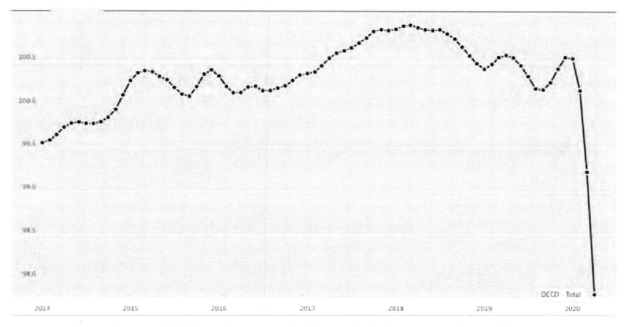

Source: OEDC Data: Consumer Confidence Index (Jan 2014 - May 2020).
Retrieved from https://data.oecd.org/leadind/consumer-confidence-index-cci.htm

Low consumer confidence and, in some instances, constrained supply channels during the first quarter of 2020 had a profound negative effect on the U.S. economy. According to the Bureau of Economic Analysis (2020), consumer spending dropped a record 13.6% in April, 2020. The unemployment rate went from one of the lowest on record at 3.8% in February, 2020 to one of the highest on record at 14.4% in April, 2020. Due to the pandemic, the number of unemployed Americans grew from 6.2 million in February, 2020 to 20.5 million in May, 2020 (Kochhar, 2020).

Recession Hits

On June 8, 2020, The National Bureau of Economic Research announced the United States is in a recession, which began in February, 2020. Economists are unsure if the economic recovery from the recession will take a "V-shape" or a "U-shape." A V-shaped recovery is a short period between decline and economic recovery. A U-shaped recovery is where a longer period is spent in a recession before recovery occurs. If the coronavirus resurges, a "W-shape" may emerge where the economy is in recession, improves, then falls into another recession, followed by a quick improvement. An economic depression is depicted by an L-shaped recovery where there is a sharp decline in the economy followed by a long recovery that could take a decade or more.

The economy and consumer behavior are intertwined. S&P credit analyst Sarah Wyeth states, "We believe the economic shutdown and lingering social distancing behaviors will trigger a broad shakeout of retail as the industry will be forced to meaningfully reduce its physical footprint and rapidly evolve to reach the post-pandemic consumer" (Bomey, 2020, para 6). Retailers are hoping that pent-up demand will result in a return to pre-pandemic sales levels. Others fear that people will realize they don't need as much, especially with the possibility of unemployment looming. It is clear that people are more likely to return to brick-and-mortar shopping if they feel safe. In response, retailers have developed plans around how to disinfect stores and how to communicate safety measures to customers. Until a vaccine is developed, social distancing and wearing masks in public spaces may become the norm.

The Natural Environment

The natural environment includes things like natural resources, terrain, physical barriers for customers, the climate, disease and pandemics, pollution, and other areas.

This is not the first infectious outbreak experienced in North America. Other outbreaks include:

- Smallpox (1633-1634)
- Yellow fever (1793)
- Cholera (1832-1866)
- Scarlet fever (1858)
- Typhoid fever (1906-1907)
- H1N1 Flu aka Spanish Flu (1918)
- Diphtheria (1921-1925)
- Polio (1916-1955)
- H2N2 flu (1957)
- Second Measles Outbreak (1981-1991)
- H1N1 flu (2009)
- HIV/AIDS (1980s – present)

Any time there is a worldwide pandemic, retail is affected. Based on past experience, scientists have learned much about disease spread, hygiene, and treatments that is helping people and businesses navigate the changing environment.

Currently the pandemic is getting the most attention due to its far-reaching impact, but other disasters occurred in 2020 that also affected retailing including wildfires, flooding, and earthquakes. An unexpected benefit of the pandemic was the cleaner air that resulted from fewer cars on the road and the shutdown of many pollution-causing businesses. Early in April, 2020 daily global carbon emissions were down by 17% compared to 2019. The gains may be short-lived as the economy opens again. Corinne Le Quéré, professor of climate change at the University of East Anglia (Britain), fears that the carbon output could exceed pre-COVID-19 levels because, during the 2007/08 financial crisis, emissions bounced back after the crisis ended (Gardiner, 2020).

ENVIRONMENTAL SCANNING STEPS

The importance of environmental scanning becomes clear during a worldwide pandemic. Environmental scanning systems, environments and techniques must be continually monitored. The information and data generated must be transmitted to all decision makers. There are numerous techniques for undertaking environmental scanning. In Chapter 3, a five-step process for the undertaking of environmental scanning is presented.

Step 1: Identify Relevant Environments

Retailers should look for any changes that may have an impact on their marketing operations. These changes might come from internal as well as external environments. It is best to also look for international changes. Changes in the international environment affect retailers even if they only operate domestically. Think about the World Health Organization and changes in the world's health that impact retailing.

Retailers also examine their country environments such as changes in competition, supply chains, and consumer behavior. From the domestic markets, more specific environments such as legal, technological, and other macro-environments should be monitored. From the macro-environmental view, move to micro-environment including the task/mediating environments such as markets, intermediaries, competitors, etc. Finally, end with an assessment of intraorganizational environments (changes in departments, personnel, etc.).

Within those environments, look at the outside forces (external to the marketing function) and the relationship those forces have (or could potentially have) on the retailing operations. Once identified, the retailer must strive to create an understanding of the impact of the social market (think about anything within the social environment that could affect retailing such as changes in age of the market, pandemics, shortages of raw materials, and interruption of the supply chain).

In summary, when identifying relevant environments, the retailer is: a.) collecting needed information and data in order to analyze outside forces, b.) looking at all events occurring within the identified environments, and c.) looking at the relationships between the change and the retailer's business Then, d.) try to avoid crisis by undertaking advanced planning – i.e., be proactive, not reactive, and e.) have a clear understanding of the social, technological, legal, political, economic, natural and any other environment(s) that will affect the retail operations.

Step 2: Identify Changes in the Retailer's Environments

When searching for and identifying change, the retailer should be looking for movements in their markets, movement by competitors and changes in the macro environment that could be causing the changes.

During a crisis, this step is difficult, yet critical. It is difficult because many do not know what will happen tomorrow, much less a year from now. It is critical because changes occur very quickly; it's important to be proactive in the response. It is also necessary for the retailer to look at the probability of changes and potential impact. It may be helpful to analyze different scenarios looking at the best, worst, and moderate scenarios.

Two researchers (Klein and Neuman, 1980) developed a system for identifying important environments called SPIRE (A Systematic Procedure for Identifying Relevant Environments for Strategic Planning). SPIRE is an effective tool because it combines data with computer analysis to identify environmental factors that are likely to affect a company's strategic operations. Retailers have a variety of other computer analytic tools to help identify changes.

Depending upon the speed of the movement of the change, differing types of scanning may be required. Some retailers use continuous scanning, which creates a new cost. Others use intermittent scanning, which can create a 'crisis-response' situation that is not preferred. Some type of regular scanning is highly recommended. In terms of creating a scanning technique, often ad hoc studies are undertaken, structured data-collection systems are used and crisis-avoidance or response systems or models are also used. Once the change in the environment has been identified, the retailer must determine if it is necessary to keep an eye on that change. Some questions to ask are: What's the nature of the change? What's the direction of change? How fast is the change occurring? What is the magnitude of the change? What will be the impact of the change on the retail industry?

Step 3: Monitor the Change

During this step, retailers attempt to understand the changes in terms of their *nature*, *direction,* and *magnitude.* Monitoring change is a function of marketing or business research. Although larger corporations create models to monitor the change, smaller retailers utilize already-published data (secondary data) such as newspapers, internet sites, business magazines, non-business magazines, trade associations, chambers of commerce, the Conference Board, and others. The government is a great source of data and information to assist in monitoring change. Trade sources and the government offer some of the best (and often free) sources of information to allow for change monitoring. The United States Department of Commerce, Bureau of Labor Statistics, Data Resources, Inc., Yankelovich, Inc. D&B, IRI, Nielsen and others are great sources for information and data that will allow the monitoring of environmental change.

While monitoring the change, the retailer must pay attention to what could occur in the future. Remember, the future is unknown, so the retailer may have to guess as to what will occur (or perhaps utilize research). Thus, the next step is to forecast.

Step 4: Forecast the Impact, the Timing, and the Consequences of the Change

Because they want to be ready when the change occurs, retailers may have to project what will occur in the future by using historical trends and data. The better the monitoring system, the better the identification of relevant environments, the better the forecast. The objective is to estimate the timing of the change or force and its impact on the retail operation. The techniques presented below are popular with retailers:

- *SWAGs* or *guesstimates*. Often called individual judgment. It's very hard to initiate cause and effect studies (called causal modeling) because the actual cause of the change may not be known. Therefore an expert might create a best guess. In practice, best guesses are often called SWAGs (or Scientific Wild Ass Guess) based on any/all information and data available. There are, obviously, validity and reliability issues with this method.

- *The Delphi Method,* developed by the Rand Corporation, utilizes a panel of knowledgeable people or experts. The experts are individually questioned without a group discussion. The individual responses from the panel members are brought together and summarized. The most popular responses are then re-sent to the panel until the panel has some degree of consensus regarding the forecast or responses.

- If specific causes of change can be identified, and those causes can be correlated and expressed in equation or econometric modeling form, modeling can be undertaken. *Modeling* typically regresses thousands of pieces of data and forecasts outcomes as changes in the environments occur. Judgment is often used to help modify the models as time progresses.

- *Trend Extrapolation* came about because of the intuitive nature of the Delphi Technique forecasting. Trend extrapolation does not consider causes of change in the environment. Trend extrapolation, rather, projects historical trends into the future. It assumes the factors causing the change will be like those causing change in the past. It is typically used when the nature of the change is not very well understood.

- *Scenarios* are cases, or verbal pictures, of a potential future. An in-depth account of events that created the situation or scenario described should also be included. Usually more than one scenario is developed. By developing more than one scenario, different strategic directions for response can be tested and evaluated. By looking at the various scenarios, retailers can develop more realistic-based responses to the environmental changes.

- *Cross-Impact Matrices* are tools for assessing retailers' environments and estimating their collective impact. *These tools* are used to search for integrated and consistent visions or descriptions of the future of the retailer after the environmental force hits. Each force is assigned a score (often between -10 and +10) in a table based on its own strength and the strength of interactions with other forces. When adding up the scores, they separate to determine driving versus inhibiting forces. Cross-impact matrices can help to identify interactions among other forecasting techniques that are consistent. The cells can then be looked at to see if the occurrence or nonoccurrence of change will have an impact on the retailer by (1) altering the likelihood of another event; (2) having a strong or weak influence on another event or (3) speeding up or delaying another event. The overall concern of the

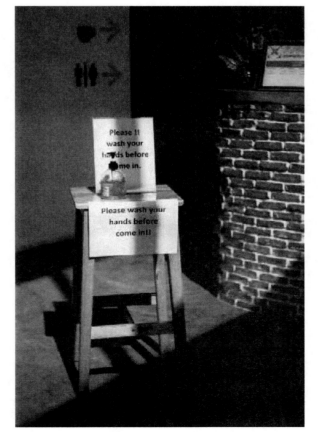

cross-impact matrix becomes the complexity as additional events (or large numbers of events) are placed into the equation.

Chapter 6 of the text focuses on the processes used for the creation and understanding of market and marketing research. Statistics and research methodologies are a great tool in helping to generate data that will help assess the impact, timing and consequences of action or inaction.

A thorough understanding of the market and retail operations is required to develop effective strategic responses to environmental changes. Numerous strategies should be developed and studied in order to select the best response strategy.

Step 5: Developing Strategic Responses to Changes in the Environment

A decision on how to react to change is both a fact-based and intuitive process. The idea is to match the retailer's strength with the changing marketplace. Retailers access the retail information system to help provide additional data and information that will be used to deal with the external environmental change. Remember, retailers often have limited funds, skills and other limitations. There must be a creative and fact-based response. What needs to be done and when it needs to be accomplished should be delineated. Use the following guidelines:

- *Focus on Probability, Consequences and Timing.* The goal is to balance the probabilities of occurrences with the consequences of those occurrences as potential strategies are evaluated. If there are dangerous outcomes or consequences, the situation must be dealt with even if the probability of occurrence is low. Alternatively, if there is a great marketing opportunity with great rewards, that outcome is given attention even if the probability of occurrence is low. Efforts should be focused on prioritizing events that are most likely to occur and that have the most significant outcomes or consequences. The objective is to exploit positive outcomes and tamp down negative consequences. Finally, it's important to concentrate on those occurrences that are likely to occur soon. Timing is extremely important!

- *Stay Flexible* in order to be able to change quickly. Remember, the only constant in the universe is change. Forecasts are based on historical sampling data and probabilities, so there must be flexibility in the strategic response. Employees who are entrepreneurial or who have an entrepreneurial spirit are good candidates.

- *Develop Counterforces* in order to modify or slow the force. When a retailer responds to an environmental force, they either try and modify the force or they change their response strategy. It is often impossible to modify a force (such as a natural disaster) and attempts to modify the force may be unsuccessful. If the force can't be modified, retailers must adapt to the change.

- Create an *"If you can't beat them, join them"* or *reposition strategy*. Alter your marketing strategy to reduce or eliminate the force. If you can reposition away from the trajectory the force is taking, the retailer can reduce the impact. Or, the retailer may want to reposition in order to join the force's potential path. In any case it should reduce the impact of the environmental force.

DEMAND ANALYSIS AND FORECASTING

After changes in the environment are identified and after the retailer has created a strategic response to the change, it's time to look to the future. Any type of environmental change will have an impact on demand, sales and revenue. Disruptions in the supply chain should also be considered. At this point the retailer must ask where the best marketing opportunities exist. A revisit to the market opportunity analysis (MOA) will help reduce losses and take advantage of potential markets that will increase revenues and sales.

Retailers need to look at all potential markets and assess each market's value by looking at the market's size, the market's requirements, and the typical behaviors of competitors. For example, Melitta is a popular brand of coffee filters. The company has been in business over 100 years. When the coronavirus hit, safety masks were in short supply in Germany. The company realized that making masks and making coffee filters had a similar process. The company also had a division that made vacuum cleaner bags. After quickly assessing the situation, the company used their knowledge and equipment to make medical-grade masks. In the first month, the German company produced over 10 million masks. While the company had considered making masks in the past, the company considered the market too small, until the pandemic caused exponential market growth (Schuetze, 2020).

A funnel approach in trying to identify market opportunities is useful.

A. Identify the market area's population.

B. Subtract out the Generic Class Market

C. Subtract the Product Market

D. Subtract the Brand or Niche Market

   = Demand and/or Revenue

Each of these steps is based on consumer buying decisions. When the consumer wants to know:

- Which needs or wants to satisfy, it creates *Generic Product Demand.*
- Which type of product will best satisfy needs or wants creates *Product Demand.*
- Which specific brand of the product will best satisfy wants and needs creates *Brand Demand.*

The retailer must assess demand potential and make a forecast at each level of demand (generic, product and brand). In addition, retailers and demand analysis specialists forecast upper limits, lower limits and expected demand for each level mentioned above. The upper limit represents demand (and/or revenue) if the retailer sells the entire category. The expected forecast is what the retailer can expect to happen (based on input variables). For each level of demand there will be a market profile, industry profile and a demand potential (selling the entire market) and forecast.

Generic Market Profile + The Industry Profile = Aggregate Demand Potential and Forecast

Product Market Profile + Product Industry Profile = Market Demand Potential and Forecast

Brand Demand Profile + Competitor Profile + Retailer's Brand Positioning Position/Strategy/Tactical Executions = Sales Demand Potential and Forecast

In building the forecasts make sure to include all outside influences on the markets such as market composition, market requirements, the economy, population growth, key competitors and other variables that could affect demand for a market.

Next, we take a closer look at the impact of the pandemic on retail employees, how some retailers are thriving during the pandemic and the future.

RETAIL EMPLOYEES DURING COVID-19

Incentives for Essential Workers

With the increase in sales, more employees were needed. Many retailers rewarded and incentivized their employees with temporary pay hikes under the monikers of Service Pay, Hero Pay and Hazard Pay. Kroger initiated a "hero bonus" of $2 per hour for frontline and other "essential workers." Albertsons granted a $2 "Appreciation Pay" bonus to its 230,000 employees' checks. Walmart provided two bonuses: $300 for full time and $150 for part-time and temporary employees. Amazon paid a bonus of $2/hour and doubled overtime pay. All good things come to an end and that is the case with the temporary pay hikes that many retailers instituted. By the end of May and June 2020 many of the bonus pay programs were ending as states lifted the stay-at-home orders. United Food and Commercial Workers International Union (UFCW) called on retailers to reinstate essential pay until protective gear is no longer needed.

Much of the retail grocery growth was due to online shopping. According to Coresight Research (Redman, 2020b), online grocery sales are projected to grow about 40 percent from 2019 levels.

Safety and Health Concerns

Since the start of the pandemic, front line retail workers have been spat on by disgruntled customers, suffered physical violence from angry customers and have been greeted by irate customers who blame employees for empty shelves.

According to the United Food and Commercial Workers International Union (UFCW) (2020), at least 68 grocery workers have died and more than 10,000 have become infected or exposed to the virus. This is a conservative number as many retailers, including Walmart, Trader Joes, Whole Foods and Kroger, did not release information on deaths and infections.

According to one retail employee (as cited from the UFCW website 2020, para 9):

"There is a lot of fear in my store because of the virus. Every day, we prepare like we're going into battle with the virus. We are exposed to thousands of people every day for hours and the reality is it only takes one person to expose an entire store. Kroger ended our 'hero pay,' but the crisis is not over. I face each day with anxiety and it gets worse when I see customers refuse to wear masks. I am a mother and my children need me to stay healthy," - a Kroger meat department worker in Lansing, Michigan.

Early in the pandemic retail employees protested the lack of personal protection provided by employers. Protests at Amazon's facilities led to changes in warehouse policies, including screening for sickness and mandating social distancing (Dzieza, 2020). United for Respect, an advocacy group, says that retail employees should have a seat on the board of directors. Walmart's employees are attempting to exert more influence and to have a bigger seat at the table, including board representation. This step would require investor support and support from the Walton family, who own half of the company. Still, the concern for worker safety may be the tipping point for employee representation on the board (Jones, 2020).

In March, 2020, Remish and Mercer/Sirota conducted an online focus group with 256 retail employees from various organizations. When asked how retailers can help, many had financial concerns and wanted assurances that employees would keep their jobs and receive paid leave if they became sick. Employees wanted straightforward communication with daily updates. Safety and health for themselves and other employees were essential. They felt people should be able to stay home when sick. Finally, employees called for better emotional and psychological resources and support (Caputo & Hyland, 2020). Retailers who listen and respond to employees' concerns are more likely to retain them during this uncertain time.

Retailers that Are Thriving During the Pandemic

Despite all of the negative impact retailers face in a worldwide pandemic, some retailers are not only surviving but have benefited from a revenue and company value perspective. Those retailers who were strong before the pandemic fared better during the pandemic. For example, the largest retailers (Walmart, Amazon, Costco, Target) are positioned for record sales and profits. Walmart reported a 74% surge in online sales from February to April 2020 (Bhattarai, 2020) and Target's ecommerce surged 141% (Davis and Toney, 2020).

RV (recreational vehicle) retailers experienced a surge in demand as vacations were canceled and the fear of staying in hotels or rentals increased. People were tired of staying home and the RV provided them more control over their environment. A survey by MMGY Travel Intelligence (2020) showed that 67% of respondents are likely to travel by personal car in the next six months. This is more than twice the percentage of respondents who reported planning to travel by air during the same period. Other segments experiencing an increase in sales include home pool installation and home exercise equipment and products.

While sales for some companies are rising, so are customer complaints. The Federal Trade Commission (2020) reports that complaints related to COVID-19 surged. Top areas of complaints include cancellation and refunds for travel, and problems with online shopping. Scams related to the coronavirus were also a concern as consumers reported losses of $4.77 million due to fraud. Amazon's customers alone left 800,000 negative reviews during April, 2020, twice the number from 2019 for the same month (Newton, 2020).

Retailers who adopted an omnichannel strategy are also more likely to survive. Smaller retailers often do not have an integrated omnichannel strategy and struggled to compete after the pandemic hit. Small retailers account for about 40% of overall retail sales (pre-pandemic). Small business closings result in substantial job losses, especially for rural communities.

Grocery Industry Sales Rise Significantly

The retail grocery industry did very well during the midst of the Coronavirus. As an industry (NAISC 4451), revenues rose 14.4% the first four months of 2020 over the same time period in 2019 (U.S. Census, 2020). The Kroger Co., the largest grocery retailer in the U.S., noted that customer behavior began changing in the last few days of February, 2020 as shoppers stocked up on sanitizer, cleaning products, water, paper goods, boxed meals and health-related products in preparation for stay-at-home orders. The company experienced a 30% year-over-year growth in the online and brick-and-mortar combined business. Increases in grocery sales are attributed to restaurant closures, stay-at-home orders, increased caring for children in the home, fear of going out, and stockpiling (Redman, 2020a).

During the beginning of fiscal 2020, the Albertsons Companies (2020), the second largest U.S. grocery chain that also operate the Safeway, Jewel-Osco, and Acme chains, reported that identical sales increased 47% during the first four weeks of fiscal 2020 (ending March 28, 2020) and increased 21% during the second four weeks of fiscal 2020 (ending April 25, 2020)

Grocers were not the only retail winners. Retail giants like Walmart and Home Depot reported boosts in the first half of 2020, due to panic buying as Americans stayed home. Walmart's online sales surged 74%, lifting overall sales by nearly 9% from February to April of 2020. Meanwhile, Home Depot said its revenue rose 7 percent. Walmart provided free masks and gloves to employees and, like many other brick-and-mortar retailers, installed sneeze guards at its checkouts. Walmart spent nearly $900 million on employee bonuses and other COVID-19 related costs (Bhattarai, 2020).

The Future

So where does retailing go from here? During the COVID-19 pandemic, phrases like, "unprecedented," "new normal," and "we'll get through this together" were ubiquitously used throughout media and became the mantra for several marketing campaigns. Marketers paused their overt sales messages to, instead, convince people how much they cared for their customers, their communities, and the world.

Radical Changes in Retailing

According to McGahan (2014, para 10), radical transformation of an industry is unusual and occurs when "both core activities and core assets are threatened with obsolescence." There has to be new technology, regulatory changes, changes in consumer tastes or some crisis that forces transformation. For the retailing industry, the crisis may be COVID-19.

There are many areas of concern for the retail industry including insurance, travel, automotive and department stores. Many businesses are operating in a limited capacity or have ceased operations permanently. By May, 2020, 260,000 U.S. retailers had temporarily closed their stores during the coronavirus outbreak (Bhattarai, 2020).

Of particular concern are regional shopping centers. The demise of malls has been forecasted for years. Mall expert and consultant, Paco Underhill (personal interview, 2020) is far more optimistic. He posits that there are many strategies that, although not often utilized within the U.S., could breathe life and foot traffic into the malls. For example, bringing a day-care center into a mall would not only attract young parents, but would be appealing for a mall tenant selling children's goods. Underhill suggests malls consider leasing space for offices, apartments, churches, schools, medical practices, upscale grocers, and libraries. Underhill goes on to state that the most underused asset for malls is the crumbling parking lot. One could imagine seasonal pop-up shops or mobile food and retail trucks.

While a world-wide pandemic will make recovery slow and painful, changes in the shopping model are not new. The Sears catalog, now defunct, was seen as a great innovation as it allowed customers to purchase products they could not physically examine. In 1916, a Memphis, Tennessee Piggly Wiggly store was the first self-service supermarket and allowed customers to choose what they wanted and then pay at a central checkout area. When customers can see and touch their own items, they buy more (Turrow, 2017). This idea caught on and is still present today (Strasser, 1989). In 2002, Apple changed retailing when they sold digital goods directly to consumers via iTunes. In 1994 a major disrupter entered the scene. Amazon became a one-stop shop for the masses and in 2005 developed a membership program called Amazon Prime which gave users free two-day shipping, access to music and movies and other perks. Today there are over 100 million Prime members.

Changing Consumer Behavior

According to a May, 2020 survey by *Salesforce Research*, due to the convenience and the positive experience during the stay-at-home orders, many customers will continue to buy items online even after the pandemic. To return to stores, consumers need assurance of safety precautions such as social distancing measures and use of personal protection equipment for employees and customers. Many consumers indicate they won't return until there is wide-spread availability of COVID-19 testing and/or a vaccine. Older people tend to more cautious with return to in-store interactions.

Experts predict that COVID-19 will significantly change our lives. Shown below are some of their predictions that impact retailing (Hochman, 2020):

Expert	Prediction
Eric Toner, M.D., Senior Scholar, Johns Hopkins Center for Health and Security	Mask wearing may draw political and generational lines.
Rami el Samahy, Boston Architect	"'Clean' is the new 'green'" (p. 10) as businesses make clear their elevated hygiene efforts.
Tim Wu, *New York Times* opinion columnist and author of "The Curse of Bigness"	The distance economy will grow as people are using online to buy things never considered before the pandemic
Ken Doctor, Media Analyst	The pandemic is an "extinction event" for the newspaper industry
Jeffrey Cole (2020), Director for the Center for the Digital Future	Going to the movies may be replaced by streaming at home. If movie theaters survive, the industry will be much smaller.
Abraham Madkour, Publisher and Executive Editor of *Sports Business Journal*	The Fear of Going Out (FOGO) will grow as people avoid large crowds. Sports events will operate at 25 – 30% capacity with strict attendance standards such as segmented arrival times.
Bert Sperling, Founder of BestPlaces.net	Society will rethink commuting as fewer people opt to take mass transportation.
Brian Kelly, The Points Guy founder	Rental shares such as Airbnb will face less consumer demand as staying in someone's house becomes less appealing during a pandemic.
Nora Super, Senior Director of the Milken Institute's Center for the Future of Aging	People are considering moving to less populated cities. Older people considering downsizing may stay put as space is more desirable.

Retailer Activities to Move Forward

McKinsey and Co. suggest that companies must act across five stages to emerge from the pandemic (Sneader & Singhal, 2020):

1. **Resolve** is the need to determine the scale and depth of action required at the business, state, and national levels.
2. **Resilience** refers to the need to stay the course despite uncertainty.

3. **Return** refers to actions needed to return businesses to operational health after shutdowns.

4. **Reimagination** is about reinventing oneself and businesses to leverage the opportunities that will emerge.

5. **Reform** refers to improvements and flexibility to weather future crises.

Waldron and Wetherbe (2020) describe five key strategies they call the "HEART framework of sustained crisis communication" (para 6):

1. **Humanize the company** – Retailers should let customers know they understand the changing environment and that they care. Communicate the value that the company creates for customers.

2. **Educate about change** – Retailers need to communicate to their stakeholders the changes to the operation and their responsiveness to concerns.

3. **Assure stability** – Retailers should let customers know that the business will continue to provide products and services (now or upon reopening) and how the retailer will maintain their value propositions.

4. **Revolutionize offerings** – Retailers need to adapt to changes and invent new ways to provide value.

5. **Tackle the future** – Retailers should be proactive and determine how and when the business will reevaluate changes in operations; they should learn from the crisis and keep the changes that improve the customer experience.

The implications on in-store merchandising and hygiene will also be critical to successful retailing. Underhill (personal interview, 2020) points out the need for retailers to consider hygiene from two perspectives – design and operationally. The design of the space, the interaction with products, traffic flow, signage, furniture, employee engagement, entrances and exits are all considerations that retailers must now address. Operationally, stores must be cleaned and disinfected more often and will likely require greater expense in terms of equipment, cleaning products, and labor.

Summary

Retailing will be forever defined as before COVID-19 and after COVID-19. We do not yet know how different the before and after will be. Even after the economic fallout is calculated, there will be questions that remain unanswered. The use of planning, technology, employees, and information security could play a large role as retailers move forward. Retailers are being asked to perform under extraordinary uncertainty. The new normal may not include small businesses and some iconic brands that were unable to recover. Still, there will be entrepreneurs who leverage the changes to create new retail establishments.

The challenge for retailers will be to consistently perform environmental scanning and to keep customers and employees safe while providing engaging, efficient, and even fun shopping experiences.   Brands must continue to improve the customer experience and better connect with their customers if they want to remain relevant. Retailers of all sizes need to gain a deeper understanding of their markets to better connect with their customers.

The pandemic shutdown may provide opportunities for retailers to examine their brands in terms of brand promise, brand message, and brand attributes. Doing so will empower retailers to better understand and align their own purpose, mission, and vision for their stakeholders.

Discussion Questions

1.   Give two examples of retailers that perform environmental scanning well. Provide a rationale for your choices.

2.   What retailers did well during the outbreak? How could they improve?

3.   What impact does a pandemic have on a retailer's supply chain?

4.   In what ways does customer behavior affect the supply chain?

5.   Suggest ways retailers can lessen the impact of the pandemic on business.

6.   What types of changes in consumer behavior that occurred during the pandemic do you think will continue? Explain.

Exercises

1.   Choose a major retailer and discuss their response to the COVID-19 outbreak.

2.   Research a major retailer that closed during the COVID-19 outbreak. What environments impacted their business operations?

3.   What would retailers have to do to make you feel more comfortable shopping in a physical store? How about entertainment retailers, like movie theaters and music venues?

4.   What advice would you give to retailers to retain employees during the pandemic? Research a company that is treating their employees well and one that is not treating employees well and explain their actions.

Acknowledgement

The authors would like to thank Dr. Timothy L. Schauer, Associate Professor, College of Business, University of Lynchburg, Virginia for his contributions to this chapter.

Case

Sherwin-Williams Adapting to Change During COVID-19

Based in Cleveland, Ohio, Sherwin-Williams (symbol: SHW) was founded in 1866 and is dedicated to innovating and distributing paints, coatings, and related products to professional, industrial, commercial, and retail customers. The company is vertically integrated, which means that the company controls the supply chain, including manufacturing, development, production, transportation, and sales.

There are 4,900 company-operated stores and facilities where Sherwin-Williams branded products are exclusively sold. Brands include Valspar, HGTV HOME®by Sherwin-Williams, Dutch Boy, Krylon, Minwax, Thompson's Water Seal, Cabot and many more. These brands are sold through various retailing venues including home centers, mass merchandisers, independent paint companies and automotive retailers and detailers.

To remain competitive and nimble in their environments, many retailers and organizations adjust their strategy to capitalize on their brand successes and adapt to the changing environment. The purpose is to broaden the retailers' customer bases by developing products and services that allow them to capture new markets or expand their current market base. However, 2020 has been a challenging year for many retailers, including Sherwin-Williams.

At the end of their first quarter financial reporting, Sherwin-Williams initially predicted that the rapid decline in the world economy due to COVID-19 would carry through to the second quarter. They did not see an improvement in their markets and could not predict when improvements would be seen. They predicted second quarter 2020 consolidated net sales to decrease by a low-to-mid-teen percentage versus the second quarter of 2019.

Sherwin-Williams' company-owned brick-and-mortar stores were closed during the pandemic shut down orders. The stores were able to complete some sales with curbside pick-up. This change in operations strikes at the heart of Sherwin-Williams' core values: customer service and to provide expert product knowledge of its products from store personnel.

A challenging market did not discourage Sherwin-Williams. According to the website (www.sherwin-williams.com), in June 2020, the company announced an improvement in all three of their business segments during the second quarter. This improvement was due to the quick change in business operations and included curbside pick-up, utilizing their fleet of over 3,000 delivery vehicles, and leveraging their e-commerce platform. They gradually opened nearly all of their sales floors and ensured safety measures were implemented to protect employees and customers. Safety measures included enhanced cleaning and sanitizing procedures, establishment of a COVID-19 Intranet Resource Center (for employees), cancellation of large events, temperature checks and social distancing policies, and limiting the way customers can order and receive products.

The Do-It-Yourself (DIY) segment remained strong while the residential repaint and new residential segments improved at a faster rate than other segments of the business. In the Consumer Brands Group, the demand from their retail partners remained strong. The demand was driven by consumers who were stuck at home and decided to tackle DIY projects.

Questions:

1. What activities made Sherwin-Williams successful during the pandemic?
2. Do you believe Sherwin-Williams will be outperformed by a competitor? Explain. What can Sherwin-Williams do to prevent the competition from capturing their customers?
3. What are ways Sherwin-Williams can leverage the process of customers ordering online and picking up at a local store and still maintain customer service levels?
4. What are the advantages and disadvantages of Sherwin-Williams manufacturing their own products and selling them through a variety of channels?
5. What are the characteristics of a strong brand name that will help the brand through a crisis?

This case was prepared by Jeremy Schmoyer, Director of Account and Project Development at GGA Global and Part-Time faculty member at Penn State and DeSales Universities.

Sources: Sherwin-Williams website; Press Release (June 22, 2020). Sherwin-Williams Increases Second Quarter 2020 Sales Guidance. Retrieved from https://investors.sherwin-williams.com/press-releases/press-release-details/2020/Sherwin-Williams-Increases-Second-Quarter-2020-Sales-Guidance/default.aspx

References

Albertsons Companies (2020). Albertsons Companies, Inc. Reports Fourth Quarter and Full Year Results. Company press release (Apr 30). Retrieved from https://www.globenewswire.com/news-release/2020/04/30/2025276/0/en/Albertsons-Companies-Inc-Reports-Fourth-Quarter-and-Full-Year-Results.html#:~:text=Fiscal%202019%20Results,(%22fiscal%202018%22).

Alexander, J. (2020). Trolls World Tour Made Nearly $100 Million Without Theaters, but Theaters Aren't Obsolete. *The Verge* (Apr 29). Retrieved from https://www.theverge.com/2020/4/29/21239703/trolls-world-tour -amc-digital-streaming-theaters-nbcuniversal-disney-warnerbros

Anesbury, Z., Nenycz-Thiel, M., Dawes, J., & Kennedy, R. (2016). How Do Shoppers Behave Online? An Observational Study of Online Grocery Shopping. *Journal of Consumer Behaviour, 15*(3), p. 261.

Bhattarai, A. (2020). Sales Soar At Walmart and Home Depot During the Pandemic. *The Washington Post* (May 19). Retrieved from https://www.washingtonpost.com/business/2020/05/19/walmart-earnings-economy-coronavirus/

Bomey, N. (2020). Can These 13 Retailers Survive Coronavirus? Permanent Store Closings, Bankruptcies Coming. *USA Today* (May 8). Retrieved from https://www.usatoday.com/story/money/2020/05/08/store-closings-chapter-11-bankruptcy-coronavirus-covid-19/3090235001/

Bureau of Economic Analysis (2020). Consumer Spending. Retrieved from https://www.bea.gov/data/consumer-spending/main

Caputo, A. and Hyland, P. (2020). Employee Concerns About COVID-19. Marsh & McLennan Companies. Retrieved from https://www.mmc.com/insights/publications/2020/march/employee-concerns-about-covid-19.html

Carver, C. S., & Scheier, M. F. (1990). Origins and Functions of Positive and Negative Affect: A Control-Process View. *Psychological Review, 97*(1), p. 19.

CBS Sunday Morning (2020). The Economic Fallout of the Coronavirus (Video, March 22.) Retrieved from https://www.cbsnews.com/video/the-economic-affect-of-the-coronavirus/#x

Centers for Disease Control (2020). Fact Sheet: What You Should Know about COVID-19 to Protect Yourself and Others. Retrieved from https://www.cdc.gov/coronavirus/2019-ncov/downloads/2019-ncov-factsheet.pdf

CNBC (2020). Economy: Consumer Confidence Plunges in April as Millions Lose Jobs. Online (April 28). Retrieved from https://www.cnbc.com/2020/04/28/us-consumer-confidence-april-2020.html?

Cole, J. (2020). Jeffrey Cole: Perspectives on the Digital Realm (April 22). Center for the Digital Future. Retrieved from https://www.digitalcenter.org/cole/

Crocker, J. & Park, L. E. (2004). The Costly Pursuit of Self-Esteem. *Psychological Bulletin*, 130 (May), 392-414. DOI: 10.1037/0033-2909 .130.3.392.

Chu, J., Arce-Urriza, M., Cebollada-Calvo, J., & Chintagunta, P. K. (2010). An Empirical Analysis of Shopping Behavior Across Online and Offline Channels for Grocery Products: The Moderating Effects of Household and Product Characteristics. *Journal of Interactive Marketing, 24*(4), 251-268.

Council of Economic Advisers (2020). An In-Depth Look at COVID-19's Early Effects on Consumer Spending and GDP. Press release (April 29). Retrieved from https://www.whitehouse.gov/articles/depth-look-covid-19s-early-effects-consumer-spending-gdp/#:~:text=Falling%20consumer%20spending%20has%20major,roughly%2068%20percent%20of%20GDP.

Danziger, P. N. (2018). Trump Economy Has Powered Consumer Spending, But Politics Affect Where People Shop. *Forbes* (June 8). Retrieved from https://www.forbes.com/sites/pamdanziger/2018/06/08/trump-economy-has-powered-consumer-spending-how-retailers-can-make-it-sustainable/#d93c98a59bf0

Davis, S. and Toney, L. (2020). How Coronavirus Is Impacting Ecommerce (June). ROI Revolution Blog. Retrieved from https://www.roirevolution.com/blog/2020/06/coronavirus-and-ecommerce/

Degeratu, A. M., Rangaswamy, A., & Wu, J. (2000). Consumer Choice Behavior in Online and Traditional Supermarkets: The Effects of Brand Name, Price, and Other Search Attributes. *International Journal of Research in Marketing, 17*(1), 55-78.

Dzieza, J. (2020). An Amazon Warehouse Worker in New York Has Died of COVID-19. *The Verge* (May 5). Retrieved from https://www.theverge.com/2020/5/5/21248427/amazon-warehouse-worker-coronavirus-death-new-york-covid-19

Federal Trade Commission (2020). FTC Data Shows Jump in Coronavirus-related Complaints from Consumers. Press release (Mar 31). Retrieved from https://www.ftc.gov/news-events/press-releases/2020/03/ftc-data-shows-jump-coronavirus-related-complaints-consumers

Gardiner, B. (2020). Why COVID-19 Will End Up Harming the Environment. *National Geographic* (June 18). Retrieved from https://www.nationalgeographic.com/science/2020/06/why-covid-19-will-end-up-harming-the-environment/

Green, T.V. and Tyson, A. (2020). 5 Facts About Partisan Reactions to COVID-19 in the U.S. Pew Research Center. Retrieved from https://www.pewresearch.org/fact-tank/2020/04/02/5-facts-about-partisan-reactions-to-covid-19-in-the-u-s/

Hedt, S. (2020). Survey Results Suggest the Importance of Clearly Communicating Coronavirus Risk and Behavior — Including as States Re-Open (press release). USC Leonard D. Schaeffer Center for Health Policy & Economics. Retrieved from https://healthpolicy.usc.edu/article/usc-survey-results-suggest-the-importance-of-clearly-communicating-coronavirus-risk-and-behavior-including-as-the-country-re-opens/

Higgins, E. T. (1987). Self-discrepancy: A Theory Relating Self and Affect, *Psychological Review*, 94, 319-340.

Hochman, D. (2020). What Comes Next. Experts Predict How the Pandemic Will Change Our Lives. *AARP Bulletin* (June), 10-12.

Holman, L and Buzek, G (2019). Retail's Renaissance: The True Story of Store Openings/Closings. IHL Group.

Jones, S. (2020). Walmart Workers Are Dying From the Coronavirus. Now They Want a Seat at the Table. *Intelligencer* (May 26). Retrieved from https://nymag.com/intelligencer/2020/05/as-the-pandemic-rages-walmart-workers-bid-for-power.html

Kay, A. C., Wheeler, S. C., & Smeesters, D. (2008). The Situated Person: Effects of Construct Accessibility on Situation Construals and Interpersonal Perception. *Journal of Experimental Social Psychology*, 44(2), 275-291.

Klein, H., & Newman, W. (1980). How to Use SPIRE: A Systematic Procedure for Identifying Relevant Environments for Strategic Planning. *Journal of Business Strategy (Pre-1986)*, 1(000001), 32. Retrieved from http://ezaccess.libraries.psu.edu/login?url=https://search-proquest-com.ezaccess.libraries.psu.edu/docview/209891879?accountid=13158

Knight, V. (2020). Obama Team Left Pandemic Playbook for Trump Administration, Officials Confirm, PBS Newshour, (May 23). Kaiser Health News, Retrieved from https://www.pbs.org/newshour/nation/obama-team-left-pandemic-playbook-for-trump-administration-officials-confirm.

Kochhar, R. (2020). Unemployment rose higher in three months of Covid 19 than it did in two years of the Great Recession. Pew Research Center (2020). Retrieved from https://www.pewresearch.org/fact-tank/2020/06/11/unemployment-rose-higher-in-three-months-of-covid-19-than-it-did-in-two-years-of-the-great-recession/

Leary, M.R., Tambor, E.S., Terdal, S.K., & Downs, D.L. (1995). Self-esteem as an Interpersonal Monitor: The Sociometer Hypothesis, *Journal of Personality and Social Psychology*, 68(3), 518-30.

Mandel, N., Rucker, D. D., Levav, J., & Galinsky, A. D. (2017). The Compensatory Consumer Behavior Model: How Self-discrepancies Drive Consumer Behavior. *Journal of Consumer Psychology*, 27(1), 133-146. doi:http://dx.doi.org.ezaccess.libraries.psu.edu/10.1016/j.jcps.2016.05.003

McGahan, A. M. (2020). How Industries Change. *Harvard Business Review* (Oct 2004). Retrieved from https://hbr.org/2004/10/how-industries-change

MMGY Travel Intelligence (2020). Travel Intensions Pulse Survey (TIPS): Impact of Covid-19 (June 15). Retrieved from https://www.mmgyintel.com/travel-intentions-pulse-survey-tips-impact-covid-19/

Mottl, J. (2020). Following COVID-19: How Coronavirus Pandemic Is Impacting Retail, *Retail Customer Experience* (May 12). Retrieved from https://www.retailcustomerexperience.com/articles/following-covid-19-how-coronavirus-pandemic-is-impacting-retail/?style=print

Newton, C. (2020). How Amazon is Growing its Power During the Pandemic. *The Verge* (May 14). Retrieved from https://www.theverge.com/interface/2020/5/14/21257313/amazon-delivery-times-worker-raises-price-gouging-liability-pandemic

NORC at the University of Chicago (2020). Issue Brief: Historic Shift in Americans' Happiness Amid Pandemic. Retrieved from https://www.norc.org/PDFs/COVID%20Response%20Tracking%20Study/Historic%20Shift%20in%20Americans%20Happiness%20Amid%20Pandemic.pdf

OEDC Data: Consumer Confidence Index (Jan 2014 - May 2020). Retrieved from https://data.oecd.org/leadind/consumer-confidence-index-cci.htm

Powell, J.H. (2020). Covid 19 and the Economy. At the Hutchins Center on Fiscal and Monetary Policy. The Brookings Institute, Washington, D.C. (via webcast). (April 9). Retrieved from https://www.federalreserve.gov/newsevents/speech/powell20200409a.htm

Redman, R. (2020a). Kroger sees March Identical-store Sales Jump 30% Due to Coronavirus. *Supermarket News* (Apr 1). Retrieved from https://www.supermarketnews.com/retail-financial/kroger-sees-march-identical-store-sales-jump-30-due-coronavirus

Redman, R. (2020b). Online Grocery Sales to Grow 40% in 2020. *Supermarket News* (May 11). Retrieved from https://www.supermarketnews.com/online-retail/online-grocery-sales-grow-40-2020

Repko, M., Josephs, L. Wayland, M. & Lucas, A. (2020). American Companies Spent Years in an Economic Boom. Then the Coronavirus Hit. CNBC (Economy), (May 11). Retrieved from https://www.cnbc.com/2020/05/10/american-companies-spent-years-in-an-economic-boom-then-the-coronavirus-hit.html

Salesforce Research (2020). A Survey of 3,500+ Consumers Shows How COVID-19 Will Transform Shopping for the Long Haul. *Salesforce* website. Retrieved from https://www.salesforce.com/company/news-press/stories/2020/5/salesforce-research-results/

Schuetze, C. (2020). "A Gift from Heaven": The Company Turning Coffee Filters into Face Masks. *Independent* (May 22). Retrieved from https://www.independent.co.uk/life-style/coronavirus-coffee-filters-face-mask-melitta-a9522821.html

Scripps Research Institute (March 17, 2020), COVID-19 Coronavirus Epidemic has a Natural Origin. *Science Daily*. Retrieved May 13, 2020 from www.sciencedaily.com/releases/2020/03/200317175442.htm

Sneader, K. and Singhal, S. (2020). Beyond Coronavirus: The Path to the Next Normal. McKinsey & Company (Mar). Retrieved from https://www.mckinsey.com/industries/healthcare-systems-and-services/our-insights/beyond-coronavirus-the-path-to-the-next-normal#

Strasser, S. (1989). *Satisfaction Guaranteed: The Making of the American Mass Market*. New York, NY: Pantheon.

Su, J. (2017). Cyber Monday Hits New Record At $6.6 Billion, The Largest Online Shopping Day In U.S. History. *Forbes* (Nov 28). Retrieved from https://www.forbes.com/sites/jeanbaptiste/2017/11/28/report-cyber-monday-hits-new-record-at-6-6-billion-over-1-billion-more-than-2016/#2021de593662

Turrow, Joseph. (2017). The Aisles Have Eyes: How Retailers Track Your Shopping, Strip Your Privacy, and Define Your Power. Yale University Press: New Haven & London

Underhill, P. (2020). Personal interview conducted via Zoom on May 23, 2020 by Timothy Schauer, Associate Professor of Business, University of Lynchburg, VA.

United Food and Commercial Workers International Union (2020) In National Coronavirus Press Conference, America's Largest Food & Retail Calls on Top Supermarket Companies to Reinstate Hazard Pay (May 2020). Retrieved from http://www.ufcw.org/tag/coronavirus/

U.S. Census (2020). Monthly Retail Trade report. Retrieved from https://www.census.gov/retail/index.html

Waldron, T. and Wetherbe, J. (2020). Ensure that your Customer Relationships Outlast Coronavirus. *Harvard Business Review* (Apr 1). Retrieved from https://hbr.org/2020/04/ensure-that-your-customer-relationships-outlast-coronavirus

Whitson, J. A., & Galinsky, A. D. (2008). Lacking Control Increases Illusory Pattern Perception. *Science*. 322 (5898), 115-117.

World Economic Forum (2020). 10 Technology Trends to Watch in the COVID-19 Pandemic, (Apr 27). Retrieved from https://www.weforum.org/agenda/2020/04/10-technology-trends-coronavirus-covid19-pandemic-robotics-telehealth/

Part 1

An Introduction to Retailing

Source: TK Kunikawa/Shutterstock.com

Chapter 1: The World of Retailing
Chapter 2: Customers, Customer Value, and Retailing Technologies

Part 1 examines the external, or macro, environment that affects all retail decision making. Because decisions aren't made in a vacuum, retail decision makers must have a clear understanding of their environments. Chapter 1, "The World of Retailing," provides a definition of retailing and describes the world in which retailers operate. Chapter 2, "Customers, Customer Value, and Retailing Technologies," introduces the reader to those three external environments: customers, customer value, and technology.

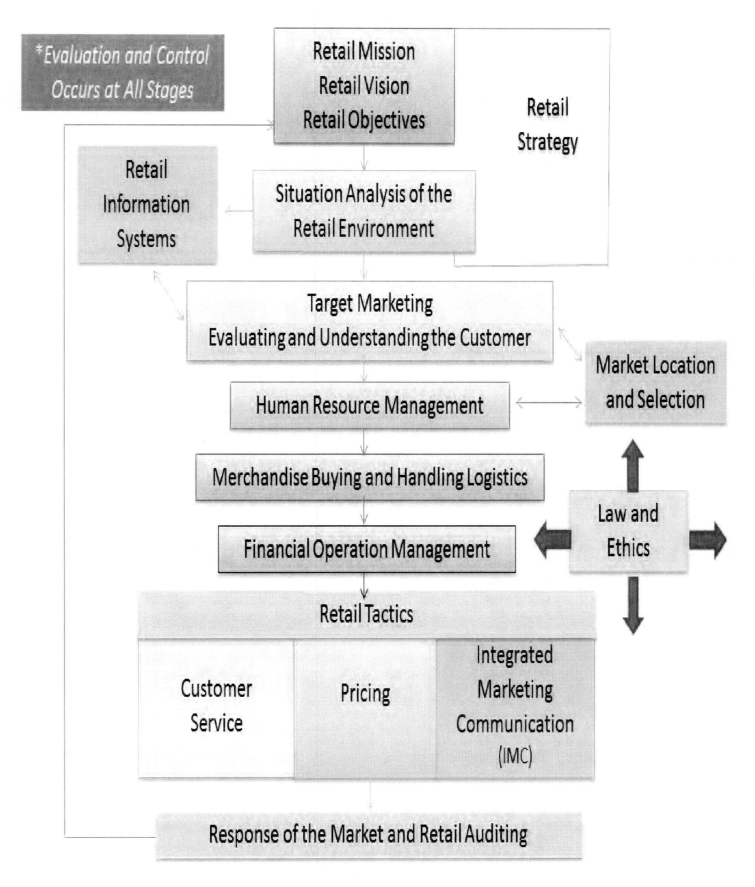

Chapter 1

The World of Retailing

"It was always my endeavor to do everything I could to establish a good reputation by giving good measure and quality, to avoid every trick that would save a penny at the expense of the other fellow."
~ Henry A. Sherwin

Source: Rawpixel.com/Shutterstock.com

CHAPTER OBJECTIVES

After completing this chapter you will be able to:

- Describe activities involved in retail management and explain how retailing fits into the overall marketing program.
- Explore the difference between e-tailing and retailing, and describe how e-tailing can be integrated into the overall retailing function.
- Provide an overview of career opportunities available in the retailing field.
- Identify the text organization and understand the importance of integrated retail management for retailing success.

Source: Tooykrub/Shutterstock.com

Toys "R" Us Shuts Down

When Toys "R" Us started business in 1948, the company's mission was to be the "worldwide authority on kids, families and fun" (Toys "R" Us Website, www.toysrus.com, 2013). For many years Toys "R" Us lived up to its mission and expanded its retail operations in ways that industry experts felt would ensure continued success. For example, Toys "R" Us partnered with American Girl®, a subsidiary of Mattel that carries premium dolls and accessories. Through the partnership, Toys "R" Us featured American Girl shop-in-shops in select stores (Toys R Us Press Release, 2016). Unfortunately, Toys "R" Us did not recognize the changing retail environment and the company filed for bankruptcy protection in September, 2017. After a disappointing holiday season, the company decided to close or sell its remaining stores.

In addition to its 880 stores under Toys "R" US and Babies "R" Us brands, the company had a strong online presence. Toys "R" Us is a good illustration of how quickly the retail environment changes. Even iconic retailers are not safe in the fast-paced and volatile retail industry. Changing consumer desires, online competition, and debt are some of the things that led to their downfall.

Introduction

Retailing is undergoing dramatic changes that present opportunities and challenges. The Internet has allowed new entrants and has transformed retailing. While Walmart is still the biggest brick and mortar retailer in the world, Amazon.com is a dominant force in online retail and technological advances. Department stores are closing many anchor stores, which impacts the viability of malls in the U.S. The retail environment is extremely dynamic and is demanding increasing skills and education.

To succeed in retailing, current and future retailers must be able to adapt to a constantly changing environment. This book will give you a basic understanding of the functions of retailing, along with a framework you can use to help you become a more knowledgeable and effective member of a retail organization. Successful retailers can anticipate and adapt to change. They also have theoretical and pragmatic training that provides them with the tools that help make businesses and organizations successful.

To effectively adapt to environmental change, it is imperative that the retail manager have a good grasp of the *macro retail environment* prior to developing a retail plan. An understanding of retailing's external environments and collection of appropriate data on those environments provides useful information for the retailer and is the starting point for the development of effective integrated retail management (IRM) plans.

Source: mama-mia/Shutterstock.com

In this chapter, we look at retailing's role in the business environment, channels of distribution, multi-channel and omni-channel retailing, the importance of the customer in retailing, a brief history of retailing, and service retailing. To provide an overall picture of the components involved in retailing, a flow chart is presented. Finally, ethical and legal considerations are discussed.

What Is Retailing?

Retailing is defined as the sale of goods and services, in small quantities, directly to consumers (Ogden and Ogden, 2005). Thus, a *retailer* is a company or an organization that purchases products from individuals or companies with the intent to resell those goods and services to the ultimate, or final, consumer. The U.S. federal government considers a retailer a business that sells more than 50 percent of its products to the ultimate consumer. *Ultimate consumers*, or *end users*, are families, individuals, and households that plan to consume the products or services themselves. The toothpaste you used this morning, the shampoo you used last night, and the gasoline that powers your vehicle are all products that were purchased for personal consumption from a retailer.

e-Tailing is selling retail goods and services through the Internet. E-tailing is a specialized form of e-commerce. *e-Commerce* is "the conduct of selling, buying, logistics, or other organization-management activities via the Web" (Schneider, 2002). Examples of e-tailers, both service and product, include eBay.com and Amazon.com. Although e-tailers conduct business online, they re-

Source: mama-mia/Shutterstock.com

quire the same planning processes that brick-and-mortar retailers use. One key to successful e-tailing is to achieve high gross margins for products. Simply stated, a *gross margin* is the revenue remaining from the sales of products after subtracting production costs. The larger the margin, the more money there is to spend on advertising and brand development. Successful e-tailers, such as Amazon.com, have high gross margins. One partner of Rosewood Capital, a venture capital fund, stated, "If gross margins are 40% to 50%, the company has a shot of surviving. . ." (Sparks, 1999).

In this text there is a focus on *omni-channel retailing*, which is an integrated approach to multi-channel retailing in which company managers strive to create a consistent and seamless shopping experience for the customer. This approach has also been called *unified commerce*, which emphasizes the connection of all channels in real time. *Multi-channel retailing* is selling through several channels to reach customers where they buy.

Retailers sell commodities to ultimate consumers. Retail supports 42 million jobs and represents $2.6 trillion of annual GDP in the U.S. (National Retail Federation, 2017). Retailing is America's largest private sector employer, and it is likely that you have worked or will work in a retailing-related job. There are different types of retailers. Those that might come to mind immediately are sellers of physical goods such as Walmart, Macy's, Target, Kroger and Wegman's. However, retailers also include service providers such as Netflix, Verizon, or home-delivered Domino's Pizza. There are also entertainment retailers such as Rave Motion Pictures, the Detroit Tigers events, and Knott's Berry Farm that offer services at a retail level. Many retailers may offer both goods and services. For example, Home Depot, the home improvement retailer, sells thousands of products. In addition to these products, the company

also offers services such as installation, tool rental, and workshops that help homeowners learn how to complete projects themselves. The company even has experts that post home improvement tips in blogs.

The National Retail Federation launched a campaign in 2012 called "Retail Means Jobs" to advance policies that support the creation of new jobs, encourage continued innovations that drive commerce, and fight against higher costs for consumers (National Retail Federation launches…, 2011). Retail spurs the travel and freight industry, engages consumers and merchants, powers manufacturing and services, grows the agriculture industry, anchors main street businesses, and drives research and innovation.

Integrated Retail Management

Integrated retail management is an approach that involves coordinating all functions of a retailer so that different areas deliver consistent messages and service to customers. In order for retailers to control changes in their retailing environments that affect the sales of goods and services to customers, they create integrated retail management plans (IRM). IRM plans help guide retailers in their business operations to achieve their business goals.

Retailing leverages marketing in planning and communication. Therefore, prior to the development of the IRM, it is desirable to have an understanding of controllable aspects of marketing. These variables are known as the marketing mix (aka marketing tactics) (see Figure 1.1) and are described below:

The Product – anything that is produced and sold

The Price - the amount of money set for a product

Channels of Distribution (aka place) - the network that directs the flow of products used to get the products and services from the point of production to the final consumer of the good or service.

Integrated Marketing Communication (aka promotion) - methods to promote and generate awareness of retailers and their products (includes advertising, sales promotion, direct marketing, personal selling, Internet marketing and public relations).

Figure 1.1: Marketing Mix (aka Marketing Tactics)

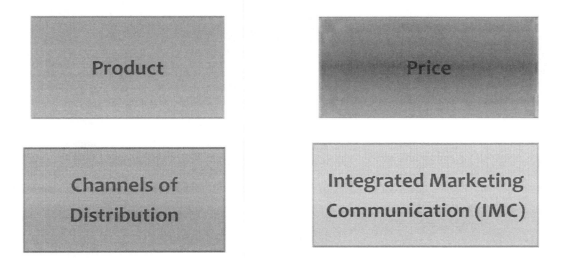

To effectively manage and integrate all of the many retailing functions, it is necessary to develop an overall plan for the retail organization. Although planning is essential to success in retailing, the first two chapters of this book focus on acquiring the requisite knowledge of retailing and of the environments that affect the retailer and the many retail institutions Figure 1.2. represents the *integrated retail management (IRM) flow chart*. This chart can be used as a guide for retail decision making. In addition, it will serve as a framework for the future retailer. Each chapter discusses one or more of the elements that make up the flow chart. This chapter is dedicated to the macro retail environment.

The retail environment is represented at the top of the flow chart to highlight the importance of the macro environment for all areas of retail management. The following topical areas relate to the external environment.

Figure 1.2 - Integrated Retail Management (IRM) Flow Chart

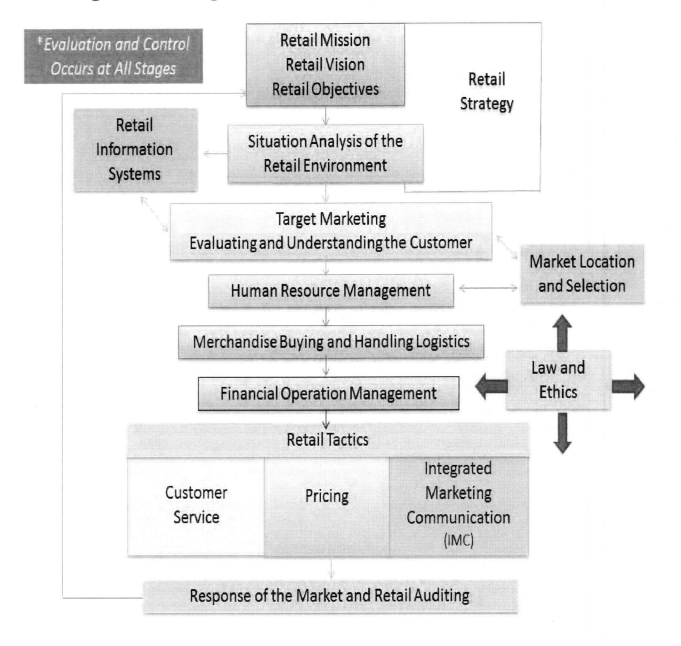

In addition to selling to end users, some retailers sell products to other intermediaries, such as other businesses, universities, hospitals, and so on. These transactions are considered nonretail transactions. Nonretail transactions, or *business sales* (or *business to business*, also referred to as *b-to–b* or *B2B*), are sales in which the purchasers plan to use the products or services in their business operations or to resell them. The vast majority of retailing occurs in stores throughout the world. Other venues for retailing include vending machines, door-to-door sales, online (or e-tailing), cart sales (such as hot dog or pretzel stands), party sales (such as Tupperware parties), point-of-consumption sales (such as purchasing drinks on an airplane), telephone sales, infomercial sales, and other creative methods.

Source: Dmitry Kalinovsky/Shutterstock.com

Retailers are often referred to as *intermediaries, middlemen,* or *in-betweens* because of the positions they hold in the marketing process. A **marketing intermediary (middleman)** "links producers to other middlemen or to ultimate consumers through contractual arrangements or through the purchase and reselling of products" (Pride and Ferrell, 2003). Wholesalers are also intermediaries. A **wholesaler** is "an individual or organization that facilitates and expedites exchanges that are primarily wholesale transactions." (Pride and Ferrell, 2003). In other words, wholesalers buy products and resell them to reseller, government, and institutional users. Some wholesalers, although limited, also sell to final consumers (but not more than fifty percent of their total sales).

Although there are exceptions, retailers generally do not produce the goods they sell; rather, they are a part of the channel of distribution that facilitates the flow of goods and services to the ultimate consumer. The channel helps direct the flow of goods and services from the producer to the end user, or ultimate consumer. A channel of distribution may include producers, logisticians, transportation specialists, warehousers, wholesalers, and retailers, among others. Because retailers have the most frequent contact with the consumers of their goods and services, they are the "front line" in marketers' attempts to successfully capture and develop markets. Figure 1.3 graphically depicts where the retailer falls within the channel of distribution.

Figure 1.3: The Retailer in the Channel of Distribution

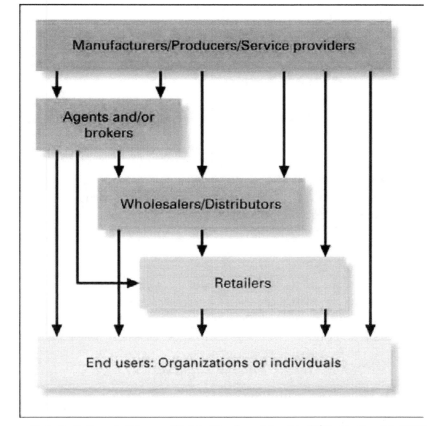

Source: Marketing's Powerful Weapon, "Point of Purchase Advertising" (Washington, DC: POPAI, 2001).

A problem for retailers is communicating with the large number of publics---individuals, groups, organizations, and institutions---with which they come in contact. Because retailers interact with the ultimate consumer, they must communicate with their customers to ensure that they know their customers' needs and wants. Because retailers purchase products from producers, wholesalers, and other groups or individuals, they must also develop good communications systems for those groups.

To provide customers with the products they need and want and to effectively manage all of the retail functions, retailers must also deal with additional "facilitators." *Facilitators* are external individuals or groups that help the retailer make a sale. American Express, Visa, Discover, and Master-Card are all facilitators because they help consumers purchase retail products by providing them with credit, or payment systems. Store-based retail credit cards, owned and managed by organizations external to the retailer (such as Target or JCPenney), are also facilitators. Shipping companies and installers are facilitators because they help ensure that products get to retailers and consumers. Banks are facilitators because they allow the retail-

Source: Ollig/Shutterstock.com

er to borrow money to help its operations run smoothly. Advertising agencies and other IMC tactics facilitate sales of products by communicating with the consumer via some medium such as television, radio, newspapers, or the Internet. Retailers must develop effective communication channels for all their facilitators.

Finally, retailers must have a good working relationship with other businesses and producers because they need to select product lines to place in their stores for sale to the ultimate consumer. A *product line* is a group of related products that satisfy a class of need, serve a particular market, have similar methods of distribution, or fall within a specific range of prices.

Multi-Channel and Omni-Channel Retailing

Most retail sales throughout the world are still made in brick and mortar stores. Nevertheless, many retailers use multi-channel and omni-channel retailing. The basic idea of multi-channel retailing is to have a sales channel available wherever the customer is and wants to buy. Therefore, retailers rely on a variety of channels such as catalogs, email campaigns, kiosks, the Internet, smartphone sales, infomercial sales, party sales, vending machines, door-to-door, and social networking, to reach their customers. A problem with multi-channel retailing is that many retailers do not have the channels integrated due to differing infrastructures and profit models. This means customers can get confused when, for example, an online price of an item differs significantly from the in-store price. Omni-channel retailing solves problems associated with multi-channel retailing by focusing on the creation of a seamless experience across channels for the customer. According to marketing consultants Frost & Sullivan, omni-channel retailing is "seamless and effortless, high-quality customer experiences that occur with and between contact channels" (Butte, 2015). Omni-channel retailing focuses on a single channel with multiple touch points. *Touch points* are contacts between the retailer and the target market. Consistency across channels is paramount with Omni-channel retailing. According to Pat Bakey, Global General Manager Consumer Industries SAP SE, customers don't think in terms of channels, just brand experiences (Omnichannel Reality in Retail, 2015). While there is a difference between multi- and omni-channel retailing, often the terms are used interchangeably.

Innovative technologies have hastened the trend toward omni-channel retailing and have revolutionized the way business is conducted. Technology has pushed many retailers to add channels to stay competitive. More and more retailers have Twitter accounts, Snapchat accounts, Facebook pages, Instagram and other emerging social media and mobile retail applications. While technology has made it easier to integrate brand information across channels, it is still a challenge to get it right all of the time. Consumers are active producers of online content, and retailers need to find ways to engage consumers in multiple formats while providing a seamless and consistent experience.

Most successful retailers use a multi-channel or omni-channel strategy. Amazon.com's success has been due, in large part, to its early success in multi-channel retailing and its ability to embrace omni-channel retailing. Amazon, the world's largest online retailer, started in 1995 as an

online bookstore. It soon expanded into selling music, games, food, apparel, and even furniture. The website attracts over 186 million visitors per month (Statista, 2017). Amazon's multi-leveled strategy allows almost anyone to sell products using its platform. This allows customers access to more products and services and increases Amazon's reach. Although the company is known for sales through its website, in 2016 it announced plans to open pop up stores in U.S. malls. The stores will sell hardware devices including Echo home speakers and Kindle e-readers. The stores will complement and drive sales from their online stores. The effort is part of Amazon's strategy to reach their customers through a variety of channels (Kim, 2016).

Source: Zapp2Photo/Shutterstock.com

Consumers seek different experiences when it comes to buying products and services, and retailers must be flexible and adapt to consumer desires. One way to do so is to have a physical, online, and mobile presence through omni-channel retailing. Omni-channel retailing is multi-channel retailing done better. The goal is to increase customer touch points through a seamless experience across channels. A *target market* is all those individuals toward whom the retailer plans to aim its marketing efforts. Technology has improved social and mobile retailing activity. Retailers who are not in the social and mobile retailing world may be missing out on potentially lucrative channels. According to IDC research, in 2010 smartphones outsold personal computers (Wollman, 2011). It is projected that smart phones and tablets will replace personal computers (Lohrmann, 2016). According to *Wired*, "With each passing season, another wave of mobile devices is released that's more capable and more powerful than the generation preceding it. We're at the point where anyone armed with a current model smartphone or tablet is able to handle almost all of their at-home—and even at-work—tasks without needing anything else..." (Bonnington, 2015).

Smart retailers use social media and mobile media to engage and involve consumers. IBM released a study that showed consumers are willing to tell retailers about their media consumption, demographic information (race, income, age, gender), and lifestyles, and even provide their name and address in exchange for a better, more personalized shopping experience. The study showed that consumers want to receive more communication from a retailer if it can be delivered in a relevant way through preferred media (Henschen, 2012). Retailers can use this information to customize solutions in an omni-channel environment. To better serve its customers, Guess, the clothing retailer, launched an application that allows users to see their loyalty points, look up purchase history, see the latest products via a "Look Book," and share their likes with friends in social media sites such as Facebook (Henschen, 2012). 2016 updates to the app include personalized shopping recommendations, VIP access to campaigns, and an improved messaging and notification system to alert users of sales and new styles.

Retailing Spotlight – Pop-Ups are Popping Up

At the beginning of the fall 2010 college season, Walmart made a decision to develop pop-up stores that would be located at many of the colleges and universities around the United States. Walmart knew that their venture might not produce additional revenue, but would have the impact of "helping" students and their families as they move into their new homes (i.e., dorms). The pop-ups were well received by the students and their families, and Walmart deemed their new venture a "success" based upon products moved and exposure received. The best-performing pop-up store was at Kutztown University of Pennsylvania. Kutztown University has about 10,000 students but is in a rural, Amish area of Pennsylvania. Walmart felt that a pop-up store in a rural campus would have a better impact than those erected at urban campuses. They were correct.

Because pop-up stores are temporary and occupy a smaller retailer space, there can be more creativity in the merchandising. For example, eyewear retailer Warby Parker turned a school bus into a traveling eyewear store. Leather couches and wood paneling were used to create an inviting space. The company took the bus for a road trip to promote its brand and sell their eyewear. Of course, an optician was available to provide prescriptions (Parmley, 2016)!

Source: Source: Parmley, S. (2016). Warby Parker's latest store is a classic school bus across from the Rocky Steps. _The Inquirer Daily News_ (July 16).

Source: Razvan Iosif/Shutterstock.com

The Retail Management Process

As mentioned earlier, an essential element in becoming an effective and successful retailer is planning. Each major function of retailing must strive for the same goals. It is important that all retail functions become integrated so that there is little overlap in work to be performed by retail employees. Although external environmental factors will have an impact on the end-of-year bottom line for retailers, those who plan can overcome many external problems.

Take a look at the largest retailers in the U.S./World listed in table 1.1. What have they done well? What areas could they improve on?

Table 1.1 - Largest Retailers by Sales

Rank	Top Retailers – U.S. (2016)	Top Retailers – World (2015)
1	Walmart	Walmart (U.S.)
2	The Kroger Co	Costco Wholesale Crop (U.S.)
3	Costco Wholesale Corp	The Kroger Co (U.S.)
4	The Home Depot	Schwarz Unternehmenstreuhand KG (Germany)
5	CVS Caremark	Walgreens Boot Alliance (U.S.)
6	Walgreens Boot Alliance	Home Depot (U.S.)
7	Amazon.com	Carrefour S. A. (France)
8	Target	Aldi Einkauf GmbH & Co. oHG (Germany)
9	Lowe's Companies	Tesco PLC (United Kingdom)
10	Albertsons Companies	Amazon.com (U.S.)
Rank is based on sales. Sources: NRF Retrieved from https://nrf.com/resources/annual-retailer-lists/top-100-retailers and https://nrf.com/2017-global-250-chart		

During the recession in 1990, Walmart surpassed all other retailers to become the retail leader in the United States (Millman, 2001). Today, Walmart maintains its retail dominance. The key to Walmart's success? A thorough understanding of its customers and superior strategic planning. Walmart's sales have continued to grow in all economic climates, even when the retailer faced bad press, such as coverage of the sex discrimination in pay and promotions lawsuit filed in 2001 by six women, which by 2003 grew to a class-action suit on behalf of 1.5 million women (Egelko, 2003). In 2011, the Supreme Court ruled in favor of Walmart that the women did not have enough in common to constitute a class action suit (Jamieson, 2012). Successful retail management begins and ends with an outstanding retailing mission and vision that engenders superior retail strategies.

It is the job of retail owners and managers to make sure the entire retail operation is running under a "seamless" integrated effort. *Seamless* means the business functions as one cohesive unit, with no "seams," or vulnerabilities, in the strategy that may weaken the company. The concept of striving toward a seamless organization refers to early manufacturers. When placing two units together, such as drywall in building a house, the consumer does not want to see the spot where the two units were joined; rather, he or she wants the wall to appear as one unit. The same principle applies to retailing: The consumer does not want to "see" the individual units such as accounting, selling, and finance. Customers don't think in terms of different channels. Each time the customer has as experience they think of the brand. Consequently, the retailer must strive to be consistent with brand messages and appear as a cohesive unit to its customers.

In a retail organization that has achieved *integration*, all parts of the organization have the information necessary to carry out their function, and the strategic philosophies are incorporated consistently throughout the plan. To better illustrate the components and inter-relationships of an Integrated Retail Management (IRM) Plan, a flow chart was developed in Figure 1.2 to help us illustrate the components and interrelationships in such a plan. The flow chart illustrates the big picture of the IRM plan and is used as a planning aid for retailers. Let's look at the parts of the IRM plan.

Components of the IRM Plan

The following list briefly describes the components of the IRM plan.

- *Retailer Mission, Vision and Objectives.* The flowchart starts with mission and vision statements and development of retail objectives. The mission statement declares the purpose of the business. The vision statement articulates where the retailer sees the operation going over the next several years. In order to assess the effectiveness of an integrated retail management plan, there must be performance measures in place. The retail objectives provide those measures.

- *The Situation Analysis.* Because customer-centered retailing is based on research, the retailers document facts and data about their history, the industry, market, competitors, etc. These data are placed within the situation analysis in categories such as company history, competitors, demographic market analysis, and objectives.

- *Retail Strategy.* A strategy is the guiding force behind an IRM. The *strategy* provides the big picture and overall direction that will be used to achieve the IRM objectives. The retail strategy is composed of the mission, vision, and objectives, and is developed after a thorough situation analysis is completed.

- *Retail Information Systems.* Retail information systems (RIS) help a retailer collect and analyze information. Information collected in the situation analysis can be added to the RIS. The information in the RIS helps with target market selection. Retailers must consider the type of research available and the best ways to develop and disseminate research findings to retail managers. Information in the RIS is also used to identify and understand customers.

- *Target Marketing and Evaluating and Understanding the Customer.* In this step, retailers identify their target customers. Some questions to answer are: Who are the customers? Are all customers the same in terms of product preferences? Will all customers respond to marketing communications in the same manner? Is the retailer adopting a customer-centric approach? Information collected is also fed back into the RIS.

- *Market and Location Selection.* Information about the target market is used to make decisions about the market and where the business should be located. Managers must determine which markets and locations provide the greatest competitive advantage. Information gathered here also helps a retailer to better understand their customer and is also used in making decisions concerning human resources.

- *Human Resources Management. Human resources* is a function that involves finding the right mix of skilled people to perform activities within an organization. All employee decisions are determined in this step. Retailers will consider the types of employees needed, pay, supervision, benefits, and how to improve or remove underperforming employees.

- *Merchandise Buying and Handling – Logistics.* In this step retailers decide how to build and maintain a supply chain and select the most effective logistic system to get products through the channel of distribution. A *supply chain* is all the people and companies involved in getting products/services from the manufacturer to the final consumer. *Logistics* are the processes used as an interface between the consumer, the marketplace and the consumer (Christopher and Peck, 2003).

- *Financial Operations Management.* With financial operations, retailers must consider the types of accounting systems to use. Financial managers will determine how to account for inventory, how to finance the operation, and the types of financial records to use.

- *Retail Tactics* are the short-term decisions that drive the organization's day-to-day activities. Tactics are what needs to occur in pricing, marketing communication (integrated marketing communications) and customer service to make sure objectives are reached that are consistent with the strategy the organization is pursuing.

- *Customer Service.* In this step a retailer considers its customers' service expectations as well as what can be done to improve service offerings.

- *Pricing.* Decisions regarding how to price products and service are made in this step.

- *Integrated Marketing Communication.* This step defines the types of communication used by a retailer to convey its messages to consumers. Areas considered may be the combination of advertising, sales promotion, direct selling and personal selling that will be used. Also considered are the most effective methods and the content and time that messages should be communicated.

- *Ethical and Legal Considerations.* Ethical and legal considerations affect all areas of the IRM plan. Considered in this step are the laws that will limit or protect the operations and whether a code of ethics is needed.

- *Response of the Market and Retail Auditing.* In this step the retailer measures the response of its target market to its marketing efforts. Surveys, online blogs and other methods of feedback are developed and monitored. Sometimes a company performs a *retail audit*, which is a comprehensive evaluation of the retail plan.

- *Evaluation and Control.* Evaluation and control of the IRM plan occurs at all stages and is important for maximum return and effectiveness. A manager must determine how and when changes should be made and how to control problems that occur during execution of the plan.

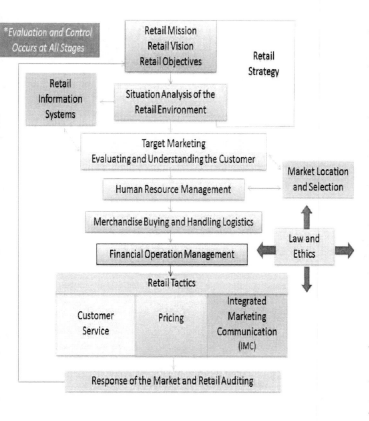

The box around the flowchart represents the border between the internal and external environment. Managers are more in control of the internal environment. The external environment includes all aspects that the manager has little or no control over such as politics, the weather, and competitors. Although there are steps in the IRM plan, many times these steps are not sequential. Depending on the situation a manager may be evaluating financial operations before market and location selection, for example. The arrow from the "response of the market and retail auditing" to the top of the flowchart, shows that the process is repetitive and often managers must re-evaluate their plan to ensure relevance of the retailer's actions.

To illustrate the importance of developing an IRM, let's consider how it affects pricing. Pricing is one challenge multi-channel retailers face. Imagine going online to search for a new pair of jeans. You purchase the jeans and then you go into that store to discover that the price of the jeans is much lower than the online price. When you call customer service, yet another price is quoted for the jeans. The retailer may have a business rationale for the different prices. Perhaps because it is often less expensive to sell a product online than in a store, some retailers offer lower prices for goods and services online. Other retailers offer lower-priced products to drive customers to their online stores.

However, customers don't always understand differences in price for the same product across channels. Lower online prices can make some consumers feel that retailer is trying to cheat them when they encounter the higher store price. Some consumers feel that prices should be the same online and in the store.

To avoid upsetting customers and losing business, retailers should consider omni-channel retailing where the marketing communication is integrated across channels. When prices are different across channels the retailer can offer an explanation to help the customer understand why there are differences. Often companies will have sales that are only available online. When this is clearly stated, consumers are less likely to defect. Today's customers are using apps in-store as well as out of store to make purchase decisions. A customer may use her smart phone to compare prices or to send a picture of an outfit to a friend. Later she may go to the store website to make a purchase. Mobile retail is an extension of the physical and online store fronts. An integrated and seamless experience across channels will increase satisfaction with the process and enhance the experience.

Adapting to the Changing Environment

As we look at all of the activities involved in the creation of an effective and integrated retail plan, we must keep in mind that markets change quickly and retailers have to adapt quickly as well. Many methods are being developed, and there is new research daily that provides additional information for retail planners. Retailers conducting a situation analysis found that in the mid-to-late

Marketing Blunder

The following retailing story has been passed around from person to person and via the Internet. In 1987, a retail entrepreneur wanted to create and sell T-shirts to commemorate the Pope's visit to Miami. Because his target market was primarily Catholic and Hispanic, the entrepreneur decided to use the Spanish language on the shirts. On the backs of the shirts he placed the phrase "I Saw the Pope." This phrase was translated into Spanish but for some reason, no matter how hard he tried, he couldn't sell any. What was the cause for this lack of sales? He soon learned that instead of writing "I Saw the Pope" (*El Papa*), he had mistranslated and written "I Saw the Potato" (*la papa*).

This example serves as a lesson on the importance of understanding the retail markets in which one operates.

Source: Famous Marketing Blunders. Retrieved 2013 from Digital Dreams at http://www.digitaldreams.com.ar/english/empresa/marketing_blunders.htm

2000s there was a movement toward the use of social media in the execution of integrated marketing communication. Advertisers and retailers embraced the technologies, but found it very time-consuming to learn and understand how to best use the new tools.

One of the technologies having an impact on retailing is the Open Graph protocol (http://opengraphprotocol.org/). This protocol allows people to indicate what web content they like or recommend, thus creating a search engine based on likes instead of links (Ingram, 2010). Because Open Graph may be a part of the retail information system, retail managers wanted to understand how this new technology would help them in their business endeavors. As web pages are *Open Graph enabled*, they will show up in web searches when a user wants them. Facebook developed the open graph web search feature to compete with Google. Retailers who adopt Open Graph use the new search feature to connect with their consumer groups as well as to research potential and current product offerings. The idea is to have the Open Graph feature serve as a conduit between search engines and social media. Open Graph assists in the charting of customer behaviors, preferences and connections via social networks and the World Wide Web. Facebook suggests that the Open Graph feature will help make sense out of all the demographic and psychographic data currently available (The Facebook Fallacy: Open Graph..., 2010). This helps retailers in several areas of the IRM plan, including evaluating and understanding customers and retail information systems.

Often retailers will modify their retail tactics to improve sales and profits. To buck the trend of deep price cutting, Talbots stores decided not to follow this industry trend, but rather they decided to create tighter controls over their pricing, and not to discount. This move brought Talbots' back into the black for the last quarter of 2010 (Talbots' Passes..., 2010).

In 2015, Whole Foods Market announced a smaller format store concept called 365 by Whole Foods Market. The name comes from the company's belief that fresh healthy food can be readily available to more people every day (Turnas, 2015). The stores are about 30,000 square feet. In 2017 Amazon.com acquired Whole Foods, which expands Amazon's physical presence. It will be interesting to see how Amazon changes Whole Foods to fit with their business model.

Target is another example of a company that tries new strategies. Target tailors their merchandise mix to meet the needs of their customer groups and better suit the needs of their local communities. Target created an online offering that includes a consumer-customizable electronic version of Target's weekly advertising flier. This allows users to create sales alerts for their favorite products (Big-box chains think smaller..., 2010).

Source: TK Kunikawa/Shutterstock.com

Global Growth

One of the changes that retailers have adjusted to is the global growth of the industry. Although most sales come from large international retailers, only a very small percentage of the world's retailers pursue global expansion with brick and mortar stores. Many are reaching an international market with e-commerce. It is difficult to expand physical locations due to the numerous issues involved with going global, with the most important including legal, organizational, language, monetary and exchange issues. Often retailers must create new or modified business models to allow them to exploit local or regional international markets. In deciding

Source: NEGOVURA/Shutterstock.com

to become an international retailer, a company needs to make sure that the nation they wish to target for expansion has an adequate number of customers that will buy their offering. Just because there is a large population, doesn't mean that it will translate into retail sales. International retailers must conduct extensive research studies to create a better understanding of the marketing environment in which they will operate. Retailers should focus on the generation of global branding and brand awareness. Retailers can create brand positioning within their home country, and then use this in other countries, reducing one of the barriers to international retail entry. Finally, the global retailer should gain country-specific or local expertise. The easiest method of gaining this expertise is through the creation of strategic alliances, joint ventures, or hiring retail personnel from the local area.

Today, retailers are concentrating on their traditional products, locations and services, but they are also creating new and exciting methods of reaching their customers. The worldwide consumer is becoming more demanding, and retailers are responding by developing new advertising and promotional methods of reaching their customers.

Careers in Retailing

In the United States and around the world, retailers make up a significant portion of all employers. If you want to work with customers, there is not a better field of study. Retail graduates work for large companies such as Target, Disney, or The Gap. They also work for smaller retailers

Source: Rawpixel.com/Shutterstock.com

such as regional airlines or small, mom-and-pop retailers. Some even prefer to take a chance and open their own businesses.

Because retailing is labor intensive, there will always be open positions within the industry. With thousands of retailers opening every year and with many retailers becoming international, the number of employment opportunities is growing rapidly.

Appendix A offers hints on securing positions within the retail industry. Figure 1.4 (next page) outlines selected retail positions.

Figure 1.4 – Help Wanted: Retail Positions

Accountant Responsibilities include auditing, recording, and summarizing transactional information.

* * *

Advertising Specialist Works with outside advertising agencies to develop communication methods and promotional strategies.

* * *

Buyer (Assistant Buyer or Senior Buyer) Responsibilities include acquisition of merchandise, controlling sales, forecasting profits, and optimizing the product mix. Opportunity to specialize in specific product lines (such as women's sportswear). Also works with suppliers through product acquisition, negotiation, and evaluation. May be asked to assist in development of point-of-purchase displays, in conjunction with corporate merchandisers.

* * *

Catalog Manager Responsibilities include managing the operations for the catalog, including merchandise acquisition and customer fulfillment.

* * *

Commercial Artist/Visual Director Duties include creating the illustration of advertisements and handling the package design. May also be asked to communicate divisional merchandising directives to stores and to partner with the Merchandise Team Manager in organizing and executing selling-floor fixture/merchandise moves.

Collections and Credit Specialist Assists with the develoment of credit terms, types of credit accepted, credit eligibility, and collections of delinquent accounts.

* * *

Department Manager/Assistant Manager Responsibilities include ensuring that displays are effective and illustrate the retailer's mission. Must train, lead, control, and evaluate departmental sales staff. Also assists buyers in merchandising purchase decisions.

* * *

District Manager Responsible for maximizing sales volume and profits for assigned stores through effective management; development of field and store staff; and execution of company programs, policies, and procedures.

* * *

Line Manager Works with other line managers. Responsible for either the "hard lines" or the "soft lines" of the store, to provide leadership on all sales-floor processes, ensuring that merchandising and floor events conform to high standards of quality. Plans and directs all sales events for maximum profits, sales, guest service, team spirit, and team development.

* * *

Merchandise Manager Assists buyers and departmental managers with merchandise buying to ensure that all departments are offering an integrated product mix. Works closely with a team of associates to ensure accuracy and timeliness of the markdown process. May be asked to act as a liason between buyers and store managers.

* * *

Operations Manager Ensures that all store operations are running smoothly and profitably by inspecting, marking, and distributing merchandise.

* * *

Personnel Manager Recruits and helps retain employees. Performs various training functions and outlines benefits and compensation for employees. Must provide all human resource needs and engage in personnel forecasting.

* * *

Store Manager Oversees all operations of a specific store. Develops creative plans to increase store sales and decrease losses. Provides training and development for Assistant Store Manager and Associates. Ensures consistency of store presentation with company standards. Maintains communication with district/regional management to stay abreast of company initiatives.

* * *

Miscellaneous Positions Positions available for e-tail managers, warehouser/warehouse specialists, salespersons, site location specialists, or merchandise analysts.

Depending on the areas you wish to work in, salaries in retailing are competitive. Entry-level management trainee positions can pay in the upper $40,000 range, with liberal benefits. It is not uncommon for managers of large stores to make more than $100,000 a year, with generous benefits.

Retail careers offer all individuals the chance to succeed. Great opportunities abound for women and men of all races. Retailing also offers a good deal of geographic mobility; retail outlets exist in every city of every state in the United States and worldwide.

A retailing career also poses many challenges. Workweeks can be long, particularly during holiday seasons. Retail professionals may have to manage temporary employees as well as perform many different activities in a day. Therefore, a strong work ethic is essential for success in retail management. In addition, retail employees must be flexible and creative in their positions, and they must have analytical skills. The universal functions of management---planning, organizing, leading, and controlling---are imperative for success in a retail career.

In summary, retailing is a very dynamic field and needs dynamic individuals to implement programs that will generate a significant return to store owners. Individuals who desire success, both personal and financial, are in high demand. If you have the enthusiasm necessary for success, integrated retail management will offer you a satisfying career and quality of life.

Source: Jacob Lund/Shutterstock.com

Text Organization

As you read through the textbook, you will notice that the major focus is on the integration of the retail management functions necessary for successful retailing. You need to understand the flows and processes that go into the retailing function and how these flows and processes fit into the big picture of retailing.

As a student of integrated retail management, you will encounter each process or variable needed for effective retailing and see the strategy that goes into the use of all tactical areas. Retailers must be aware of the environments in which they do business. They must understand what environments will affect their retail operations and have plans that take those environments into account. In other words, retailers must be proactive rather than reactive in their retail operations.

This text follows the integrated retail management plan presented earlier in this chapter. By following this outline, you will understand the importance of each step in the plan.

This chapter began by looking at the retail macro environment. It provided an outline and a general understanding of retailing and e-tailing. The chapter outlined a flow, or system, for retail planning. Chapter 2 also concentrates on the external, or macro, environment by looking at the all-important environment of customers. The chapter discusses the importance of developing an understanding of customers, customer value, and retailing technology. It provides hints on how to create relationships with customers to encourage loyalty.

Chapter 3 provides a detailed overview of the retail management flow chart. In this chapter, the book begins to take a more micro approach to retail management. The chapter provides an in-depth insight into each element of the IRM plan. Chapters 4 through 13 look at each of these elements in detail and offer suggestions for implementation.

In Chapter 14, the book returns to a more macro view of the retail environment. This chapter discusses laws that affect retailers and explores principles of ethics in retailing. Chapter 15 covers trends in retailing, diversity, and an example of the IRM process.

To further engage the student in analytical thinking, each chapter concludes with a case featuring selected companies. Appendix A offers guidelines for breaking into and succeeding in the field of retailing. Appendix B is an in-depth case study of Z-Coil, a manufacturer and retailer of specialty footwear. Ideally this text will serve both as a point of reference and a pragmatic manual. Keep it for future use in other classes and as an on-the-job resource.

Summary

The field of retailing is dynamic, challenging, and exciting! The retail environment has seen many changes and will continue to do so. Retailing encompasses all business activities that provide customers with goods and/or services that satisfy or exceed their needs. Successful retailers today are integrating all their functions to return an investment to their owners and at the same time provide wanted goods and services to their customers.

Retailers serve two groups of customers: the ultimate consumer, or end user, of products and the companies that produce products and services to sell to end users (business-to-business, or B2B). Retailers provide a critical function in the distribution channel. Retailing offers numerous employment opportunities, including managers, accountants, merchandisers, and buyers. The world of retailing entails demanding work, but it also offers many rewards.

Terms

business sales	Sales from one business organization to another business organization; also called *business to business* or *B2B*.
channel of distribution	A network that includes all members of a team of businesses and organizations that help direct the flow of goods and services from the producer to the end user, or ultimate consumer.
e-commerce	The conduct of selling, buying, logistics or other organizational management activities via the Web.
e-tailing	A form of retailing utilizing the Internet to take the place of or supplement a physical retail location.
facilitators	External individuals or groups that help the retailer make a sale.
gross margin	The revenue remaining from the sales of products once the production costs have been subtracted.
human resources	A function that ensures that a company has the right mix of skilled people to perform its value creation activities effectively.
integrated marketing communication (IMC)	The process and methods used to integrate and coordinate all a firm's marketing communication activities.
integrated retail management	An approach that involves coordinating all functions of a retailer so that different areas deliver consistent messages and service to customers.
integrated retail management (IRM) flow chart	A chart that provides a framework to guide retail decision making.
integration	The condition wherein all parts of the retail organization have the information necessary to carry out their functions and the strategic philosophies are incorporated consistently throughout the plan.
logistics	Every action taken to ensure that products and services get from the point of origin to the final customer.
macro retail environment	The external environments that affect retailers.
marketing intermediary (middleman)	A business that links producers to other middlemen or to ultimate consumers through contractual arrangements or through the purchase and reselling of products.
multi-channel retailing	Retailing through several channels to reach customers where they buy.
omni-channel retailing	An integrated approach to multi-channel retailing which strives to create a consistent and seamless shopping experience for the customer.
pop-up retail	A temporary retail space.
price	The amount of money set for a product.
product	Anything that is produced and sold.
product line	A group of related products that satisfy a class of need, serve a market, have similar methods of distribution, or fall within a specific range of prices.
retail audit	A comprehensive evaluation of the retail plan.
retailer	A company or an organization that purchases products from individuals or companies with the intent to resell those goods and services to the ultimate, or final, consumer.
retailing	To sell goods and services in small quantities directly to consumers.
seamless	Functioning as one cohesive unit, with no "seams," or vulnerabilities.
strategy	Planning that provides the total directional thrust of the retail plan.
supply chain	All the people and companies involved in getting products/services from the manufacturer to the final consumer

tactics	The actual executions of the plan; provide for short-term (less than one year) actions.
target market	All the people toward whom the retailers plans to aim its marketing efforts.
touch points	Contacts between a company and a consumer or group of consumers.
ultimate consumers	Families, individuals, and/or households that plan to consume the products or services themselves. AKA end users.
unified commerce	An approach to multi-channel retailing that emphasizes the connection of all channels in real time.
wholesaler	An individual or organization that facilitates and expedites exchanges that are primarily wholesale transactions.

Questions

1. In your own words, define the term "retailing." What differences are there in your definition as opposed to the definitions found in the chapter? What part of the retailing process excites you the most? Why? Which aspect of retailing does not appeal to you? Why?

2. Identify four different retailers for which you would consider working. Look up their websites, and answer the following questions.

   · Based on the information on the websites, rank the retailers in order of their attractiveness as a potential employer.

   · What characteristics helped you rank your choices in question 1?

   · In what ways could each retailer make its website more user friendly for potential employees?

3. Find an online retailer that is customer-centered. What items on their website signal their customer-centered orientation?

4. How do you think the retailing industry will change over the next ten years? Twenty years? Fifty years?

5. Why is it so important to follow an integrated retail management plan (IRM)?

Exercises

1. Write about an experience where you were disappointed in a retailer and one in which your expectations were surpassed. What attributes did each retailer possess that formed your impressions about the experience?

2. Research the history of one of the following: department stores, malls, or online auctions. Write a summary of the history and how the development affected retail practices.

3. Choose three products from an e-tailer that also has a physical store close to you. Compare the price of the products from the website to the prices found in the physical store. Did they match? Write a summary of the experience.

4. Go to the National Retail Federation career center to learn more about retailing careers:

   https://nrf.com/career-center

   Navigate through the following websites and find a job that might interest you

   http://retail.management.jobs.topusajobs.com/

   http://www.allretailjobs.com/cgi-local/search.cgi?action=SendForm&TypeOfUser=browse

·   What are the responsibilities of the position?

·   Why does the position interest you? What might you not like about the position?

·   Look up the position (or closest to it) in the occupational outlook handbook. What did you find out? The census publication (occupational outlook handbook) website: http://www.bls.gov/oco/

Case

eBay: Growth of an e-Tail Business

Founded in September 1995, eBay was the first online auction site. eBay paved the way for individuals and businesses to sell goods through auction or fixed price to a worldwide audience. Pierre Omidyar, a software developer from California, started eBay when he ran into a dead end after trying to help his girlfriend connect with other Pez candy dispenser collectors. His girlfriend, who later became his wife, was frustrated because, like other collectors, she was bound by geography. Omidyar's interest in the Internet, coupled with his desire to help his girlfriend, pushed him to develop a software program that allowed people from all parts of the globe to post information about items for sale in one location. Other people could then visit the website and bid for the goods listed. Originally eBay's mission was --"to help practically anyone trade practically anything on earth." Over the years eBay has grown and revised their mission as: "We give sellers the platform, solutions, and support they need to grow their businesses and thrive. We measure our success by our customers' success... Our mission is to be the world's favorite destination for discovering great value and unique selection." The company is a leading commerce platform for buyers and sellers.

eBay generates revenue by charging fees to sellers. The first 50 listings are free. After that, when a seller posts an item for sale eBay charges an insertion fee. The fee depends on the price that is set for an item being sold. eBay can enhance a listing (bigger photo or bold text) for extra fees. When the item sells, eBay gets a part of the selling price (called a final value fee).

In 2015, eBay celebrated its 20th anniversary. They also completed the separation from their online money transfer service (PayPal). The company also owns StubHub (www.stubhub.com), an online secondary market ticket exchange service which was acquired in 2007. In addition, the company owns several websites they categorize as Classified platforms. Brands included under this category include Mobile.de, Kijiji, Gumtree, Marktplaats and eBay Classifieds. These platforms help people find items in their local communities. Collectively the company connects buyers and sellers throughout the world.

To provide a seamless experience for customers, eBay invested in improvements to their existing mobile technology. The goal was to simplify mobile selling and enhance the user experience. As of 2015, the company employed 11,600 people globally with 6,200 of those in the U.S. 2015 revenue was $8.59 billion with a net income of $1.72 billion.

The search for a Pez dispenser ballooned to a way for geographically diverse people to come together, share goods, and trade stories. Thus, a small idea sparked a great enterprise. eBay had forged into new territory and, despite some growing pains, is today a highly successful enterprise. According to their annual report, "We are driven by the notion of persistent reinvention — that for a company to succeed over time and through generations, it must be resilient, embrace change and be willing to challenge its own conventional wisdom with courage and conviction" (2015 annual report, pg. 5).

Questions:

- Why has eBay been so successful?

- When should a company revise their mission statement? Is eBay's mission statement effective? Explain.

- How can eBay reduce the threat of new entrants?

- If you were Amazon.com how would you respond to eBay as a competitive threat?

- Visit the eBay site (www.ebay.com). What do you like and/or dislike about the site?

References

Sources: Woo, S., & Letzing, J. (2012, Jan 19). Corporate news: EBay turnaround picks up steam. *Wall Street Journal*, pp. B.3-B.3; 2015 Annual Report

http://www.annualreports.com/HostedData/AnnualReports/PDF/NASDAQ_EBAY_2015.pdf

Big-box Chains Think Smaller as They Seek to Serve the Masses (2010,). In NRF *SmartBrief*, (Sep 9).

Bonnington, C. (2015). *Wired*. (Feb 10). In Less than Two Years a Smartphone Could be Your Only Computer. Retrieved from https://www.wired.com/2015/02/smartphone-only-computer/

Butte, B. (2015). Cloud: The Engine of the Omni-channel Customer Experience. *Network World* (Dec 4). http://www.networkworld.com/article/3011910/cloud-computing/cloud-the-engine-of-the-omni-channel-customer-experience.html

Christopher, M. and Peck, H. (2003). *Marketing Logistics, 2nd Edition*. Burlington, MA: Butterworth-Heinmann, pp.1-2.

Egelko, B. (2003). Sex Discrimination Cited at Walmart: Women Accuse Walmart/Lawyers Seek OK for Class Action Suit. *San Francisco Chronicle*, (April 29), p. B1.

Henschen, D. (2012). Social, Mobile Meet Shopping: Retailers Must Scramble. *Informationweek - Online*, (19383371), Retrieved from http://search.proquest.com/docview/916677353?accountid=13158

Ingram, M. (2010). Is Facebook's Social Search Engine a Google Killer? (June 25, 2010). Retrieved from http://gigaom.com/2010/06/25/is-facebooks-social-search-engine-a-google-killer/

Jamieson, D. (2012). Betty Dukes, Renowned Dukes v. Walmart Plaintiff, Takes Her Fight Back to Capitol Hill. *The Huffington Post*, (June 20). Retrieved from http://www.huffingtonpost.com/2012/06/20/betty-dukes-walmart-supreme-court_n_1613305.html

Kim, E. (2016). Amazon Is Doubling Down on Retail Stores with Plans to Have up to 100 Pop-up Stores in US shopping Malls. *Business Insider* (Sept 9).

http://www.businessinsider.com/amazon-big-expansion-retail-pop-up-stores-2016-9

Lorhmann (2016). Will a Smartphone Replace Your PC? Retrieved from http://www.govtech.com/blogs/lohrmann-on-cybersecurity/will-a-smartphone-replace-your-pc.html

Marketing's Powerful Weapon, Point of Purchase Advertising (2001). Washington, DC: POPAI.

Millman, C. (2001). Stores Still Sell in Downturn. *The Morning Call*, (July 22), pp. D1, D4.

National Retail Federation (2017).   Retrieved from https://nrf.com/who-we-are/retail-means-jobs

National Retail Federation Launches Major, Multifaceted Campaign to Push Jobs, Innovation and Consumer Value Agenda (2011). Businesswire (Sept 20). Retrieved from http://www.businesswire.com/news/home/20110920005475/en/National-Retail-Federation-Launches-Major-Multifaceted-Campaign

Ogden, J. R. and Ogden, D. T. (2005). *Retailing: Integrated Retail Management,* Boston: Houghton Mifflin, p.6.

Ogden, J. R. and Ogden, D. T. (2010). *Marketing Basics: Cutting Through the Clutter*, Dubuque, IA: Kendall Hunt Publishing Company, pp. 1-7.

Omnichannel reality in Retail: Omni- vs Multi-channel - What They Mean for Retailers and Customers (2015). You Tube video (Mar 27). https://www.youtube.com/watch?v=Q3HmC-ueafs&feature=youtu.be

Pride, W. M. and Ferrell, O.C. (2003). *Marketing (12th ed.)* Boston: Houghton Mifflin, p. 352.

Schneider, G. P. (2002). *New Perspectives on E-Commerce*. Boston: Course Technology, a division of Thomson Learning, p. 1.04.

Statista (2017, January). Statista.com. Retrieved from https://www.statista.com/statistics/271412/most-visited-us-web-properties-based-on-number-of-visitors/

Sparks, D. (1999). Who Will Survive the Internet Wars? *Business Week*, December 27, 1999, p. 98.

Talbots Passes Up Deep Discounting to Boost Bottom Line (2010). NRF *SmartBrief*, (Sept 9).

The Facebook Fallacy: Open Graph = Google killer (2010). OneUpWeb.com, (whitepaper) Traverse City, MI.

Toys "R" Us Website (2013). About Toys'R' Us. Accessed from http://www.toysrusinc.com/about-us/

Toys "R" Us Press Release (2016). American Girl® Announces Exclusive Multi-Year Partnership with Toys "R" Us® (Aug 31).   https://www.toysrusinc.com/press/american-girlannounces-exclusive-multi-year-partnership-with-toysrus#sthash.2ATUPL74.dpuf

Turnas, J. (2015). Introducing Our New Store Concept: 365 by Whole Foods Market™ http://www.wholefoodsmarket.com/blog/introducing-our-new-store-concept-365-whole-foods-market

Wollman, D. (2011). Smartphones Outsell PCs for the First Time Ever. *Huff Post Tech*, (Feb 8) Retrieved from http://www.huffingtonpost.com/2011/02/08/smartphones-outsell-pcs-f_n_820454.html

Chapter 2

Customer Value, Services, and Retailing Technologies

"An organization that is strong and stable and is ready to commit time, money, and patience will be more apt to reap rewards than the quick-hitting opportunist."
~ Richard Miller, Market Response International

Source: Daniel Krason/Shutterstock.com

CHAPTER OBJECTIVES

After completing this chapter you will be able to:

- Explain how retail decisions are impacted by the marketing concept and the extended marketing concept in order to create customer value.
- Define value and explain its importance to the retailer.
- Compare and contrast customer service and services retailing.
- Identify the dimensions that are important to the customer in building a relationship.
- Differentiate between e-commerce and e-tailing
- Define and explain the importance of ethics and corporate social responsibility in building strong relationships with customers.

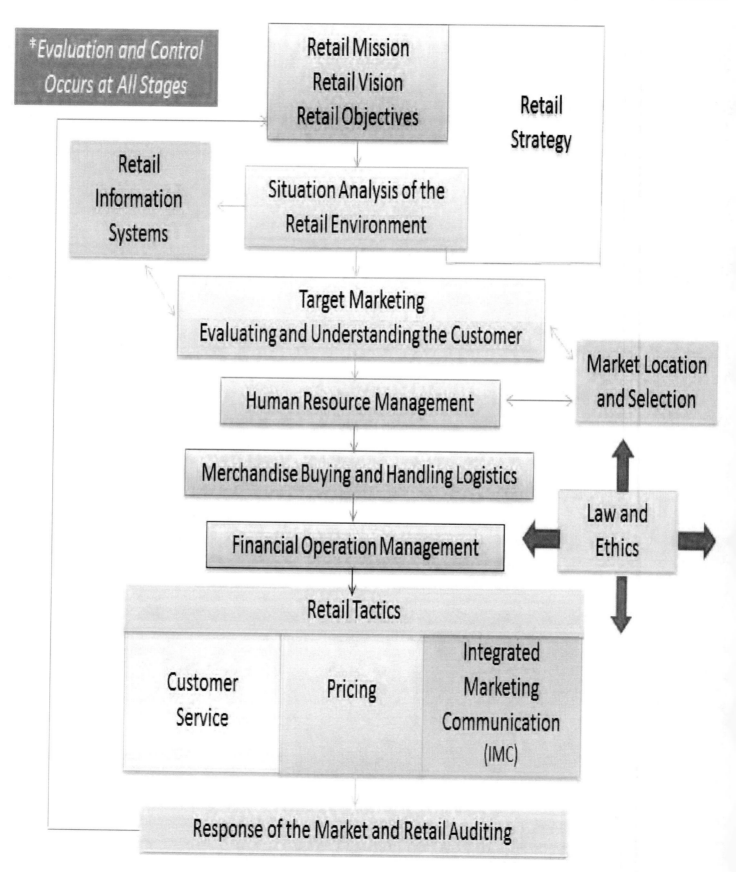

Source: ESB Professional/Shutterstock.com

Dillard's Focus on the Customer

Dillard's Incorporated was started by William T. Dillard in 1949. Dillard's philosophy was to focus on giving customers value. In 1964, Dillard realized that malls offered a great deal of potential to reach a large number of the rapidly growing suburban populations. As a result, he opened a Dillard's department store in a mall in Austin, Texas (Kaufman, 2002). As the mall format grew, so did Dillard's department stores. In 2017 there were 273 stores and 24 clearance centers in 29 states. The company earns about $6.5 billion in yearly sales (Dillard's website, www.dillards.com) from the physical locations and Internet site.

Dillard's sells brand-name and private-label merchandise with a focus on apparel and home furnishings. Some of the ways in which the company has built value are based on William Dillard's philosophies. He placed service and quality as top priorities. His department stores were among the first to use technology to improve their efficiency. The company used computerized checkout systems and inventory tracking systems and sought innovation to improve value.

William Dillard passed away in February 2002, but he remains one of the visionaries in retailing who early on realized that customers add value and equity to retail operations. His son, William Dillard II, has succeeded him and continues to employ his father's retail philosophies.

Introduction

This chapter continues our focus on the external environment as it relates to retailing. Chapter 1 dealt with the overall nature of retailing. This chapter examines who retail customers are and how their buying decisions and purchase behaviors affect the retailer. In addition, it covers important aspects of the technological environment and that environment's relationship to retail management. The chapter concludes with a discussion of ethics and social responsibility in retailing. This topic is covered at length later in the text but is touched on in this chapter as it relates to customer value, services, and retailing technologies.

Over the past five decades, marketing has become more sophisticated, and marketers have relied upon the *marketing concept* to guide their marketing initiatives. According to the marketing concept, marketers should attempt to satisfy customer needs and wants at a profit. The philosophy places the customer in the center of marketing planning (Wright et al., 1997). Because the emphasis of the marketing concept is on the customer, marketers must know as much as possible about their customers. Once information is gathered, managers can form *market segments*, which are groups of customers that share one or more characteristics and respond similarly to marketing efforts. Gap, Inc. has several retailers that appeal to different segments: Old Navy appeals to the young, budget-conscious consumer. Banana Republic is an upscale retailer targeted to the 25-35 demographic, and Gap-

Source: Jacob Lund/Shutterstock.com

Source: William Perugini/Shutterstock.com

Kids is targeted to the parents of children who want stylish fashion at affordable prices. Once managers know something about each market segment, they can use that information to create strategies and tactics that will be effective in reaching the individual groups. The most important part of the research process is to determine who the customers are and to define their wants and needs.

Although the marketing concept provides a good basis for developing marketing programs, many organizations have expanded the concept. In implementing the *extended marketing concept,* marketers do not stop at only satisfying the customers' needs and wants, but rather, they take the concept one step further and "wow" or excite the customer base. Thus, the extended marketing concept says that marketers should *exceed* the needs and wants of consumers while making a profit (Ogden and Ogden, 2009). Today's customers are in control of how they research, shop, and select retailers. Those retailers that provide customers with a positive experience will be winners. Accordingly, retailers must make the shopping experience a memorable event (Pine and Gilmore, 1999).

To exceed customer wants, the retailer must understand its customers and what they offer the retailer. An excellent way to gain an understanding of the customer is to develop an understanding of the "value" of a customer. Thus, the first part of this chapter focuses on the development of customer value. What economic value does the customer provide for the retailer?

Understanding customer value is not the only important issue in dealing with customers. A retailer must also engage in *relationship marketing* -- that is, build long-lasting relationships with customers. The next section of the chapter discusses the many ways to develop this relationship, whether for a brick-and-mortar business, an e-tailing business, or a combination of each (bricks-and-clicks). Next, the chapter explores services retailing and the differences between the concepts of customer service and services retailing. Advances in technology assist retailers and e-tailers in the relationship-building process. These are discussed in detail later in the chapter and in Chapter 13.

Think of your relationships with retailers. Are they positive or negative? What makes them good or bad? To gain insight into these questions, you first need to understand customer service and the value the customer brings to the retail organization.

Customer Service

Customer service is "a series of activities designed to enhance the level of customer satisfaction – that is, the feeling that a product or service has met the customer expectation" (Turban 2003, p. 165). The philosophy of L.L. Bean, a popular retailer of outdoor apparel and equipment, is typical of a company that uses the extended marketing concept. According to the company founder, "A customer is not an interruption of our work...he is the purpose of it. We are not doing a favor by serving him...he is doing us a favor by giving us the opportunity to do so" (www.llbean.com). L.L. Bean is well-known for providing outstanding customer service. It is one of a few companies that offer free shipping and a 100% satisfaction guarantee. Customer-centered integrated retail management plans are based upon the extended marketing concept and developing customer service policies that meet or exceed customer expectations.

Source: Michael G McKinne/Shutterstock.com

To focus on the customer, retail managers should conduct research to determine who their customers are, where they live, where they shop, their attitudes, how they shop, and what they purchase when they shop. The more data that can be converted to useful information the better the retailer can meet the needs of its target audience. The *customer-centered retailing approach* places the customer at the center of all decisions. It applies user-centered design to make retail processes more user-friendly. Information collected about the consumer can be used to stock the right products and to create stores that interest and excite customers. The concept is to create a retail design that provides benefits for the merchant, the customer, and the suppliers so that everyone benefits. Customers get their desired products and services, the retailer achieves greater profitability by selling more products and creating a desirable shopping experience, and suppliers increase their sales volumes as well. When retailers have strong reputations they attract customers who are not as concerned about price. Customers who focus only on price are not as valuable to retailers compared to customers who are willing to spend more for customer service and merchant trust (Chandler and Hyatt, 2003). Therefore, research provides information on a customer's overall retail value in addition to helping retailers target how, why, and where they prefer to shop.

In the past, retailers used the mantra, "the customer is always right," which was successful until competitors began to focus on profitability. The move toward a focus on profitability required retailers to shift to a different approach to doing business: They set shorter-term goals that were intended to boost sales and profits. Retailers must earn profits to remain in business, but these short-term goals caused many retailers to lose customers as they switched from "the customer is always right" to "sell, sell, sell" with little regard for the customer. Customers are now required to take more responsibility for their shopping services, which in the past were provided by retail merchants. It is not unusual for today's customers to unload their carts, mark prices, scan their purchases, and place their purchases in their own vehicles to transport home. Customers prefer to shop where they know they can find the products and services they want quickly and effortlessly. They want to shop in stores where they can enjoy their shopping experience. They welcome added service and perceived value.

A *value proposition* is a "short, clear, simple statement containing the reasons for choosing one brand over another. It includes what the target market is for a particular product, what key benefits will be delivered, and how much will be charged. It provides the rationale (tangible and intangible) for choosing one brand over another" (Swystun, 2007, p.122). In customer-centered retailing, a value proposition integrates the right products with the right customer experience. Utilizing the value proposition increases sales, generates greater customer loyalty, and provides for customer return visits. Many customers focus on time constraints, convenience, ease of pur-

Source: Rawpixel.com/Shutterstock.com

chase, and value for the money they've spent. To balance the needs of customers with the needs of retailers, the retailer must have intimate knowledge of the customer. Because customers want to find what they need quickly and be entertained as they do so, the main goal of customer-centered retailing is to create a value proposition that attracts and retains a loyal customer base. Successful retailers create and build relationships by making the retailer's goals the same as the consumer's goals.

Customer Value

Excellent retailers understand that their job is not to merely satisfy their customers but to *excite* them and induce them to return to the store. To exceed customers' expectations and excite them, the retailer must be flexible and able to continually force change the store environment. New shopping experiences should be created to stimulate the customer's return to the store or online site to make additional purchases. Thus, value becomes the basis for the customer's differentiation between one retailer and another.

Think about your experiences with service retailers such as banks. What makes one bank different from another? They all offer the same basic products (checking accounts, savings accounts, CDs, money market funds, and so on), but you prefer to do business with a specific bank or branch. Telephone companies offer the same services, yet you choose one over another. What entices you to make those selections? The answer is your perception of the value that the company provides to you, the customer. Value is a concept that the customer defines. What one customer considers valuable, another may not.

So how can retailers create value in customers' minds? First, the retailer must understand the variables that make up the concept of value. *Value* is defined as "an amount, as of goods, services, or money, considered to be a fair and suitable equivalent for something else" (American Heritage Dictionary, 2002). The retailer must decide not only on the value of products and services but also on the value of customers. The premise for overall customer value is elementary; however, the executions needed to create this value are not. To keep these related concepts clear, see Table 2.1, which lists four important areas related to value.

Table 2.1 – Customer Value

The following four areas are important concepts related to the creation of value:

1. The customer's perception of the value provided by the retailer
2. The equity, both financial and informational, that the customer provides to the retailer
3. The importance of developing strong relationships with customers
4. The integration and utilization of technology to support customer relationships and increase customer equity

Source: Rido/Shutterstock.com

How does a customer determine value? Earl Naumann (1995b), who has written extensively on customer service, suggests that the concept of value can be seen within a "customer value triad." The triad consists of three separate variables: value-based prices, product quality, and service quality (see Figure 2.1 on next page). Product and service quality provide the "pillars" of the triad and are the bases for value-based pricing. When retailers provide poor service or have products of poor quality, value-based pricing fails. If the price line is set in an inconsistent manner, sales will decline. High product quality is important, but not enough to ensure total customer value. The quality of the products or services, additional services provided, and the pricing strategy all influence value perceptions. All three variables must be in place to achieve true integration in customer value.

Figure 2.1 – The Customer Value Triad

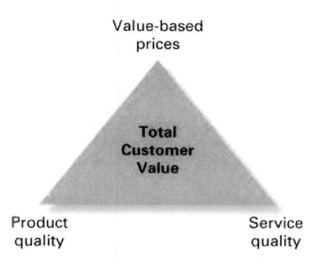

Source: Adapted from Naumann, E. (1995). *Customer Value Toolkit*. Cincinnati, Ohio: Thompson Executive Press, 1995, p. 17.

To achieve true value within the organization, the retailer should integrate value into the overall strategy. Integrating value into the strategy results in 10 essential retailing outputs (see Table 2.2).

Table 2.2 – Retailing Value Outputs

1. Understanding customer choices
2. Identifying customer segments
3. Increased competitive options (e.g., increased product lines or products)
4. Avoidance of price wars
5. Improved service quality
6. Strengthened retail communications
7. A focus on what is meaningful to customers
8. Customer loyalty
9. Improved brand success
10. Stronger customer relationships

Source: S. MacStravic, "Questions of Value in Health Care," *Marketing Health Services*, Winter 1997, pp. 50–53. Reprinted by permission of the American Marketing Association.

Quality, Service, and Price (QSP)

The concepts shown in Table 2.1 help create additional differentiation for the retailer. An understanding of the outputs helps the retailer integrate overall customer value into the IRM plan. It is often difficult to represent, or express, customer value because it is hard to measure. One suggestion for expressing customer value is to categorize the value by quality, service, and/or price (QSP). Customer value can be expressed in terms of a combination of the retailer's overall service, quality, and price (Tucker, 1995). As such, a retailer needs to understand that a combination of these three variables will affect how much value customers believe they have gained by shopping at a particular retail outlet. Because of the high costs associated with trying to be a leader in all three areas, retailers often concentrate on one or two manageable areas to create value differentiation.

It would be very expensive, and strategically unwise, for example, for Saks Fifth Avenue to try to compete on price when the basis for its strategy and differentiation is quality products and service. Likewise, for a discount retailer such as Walmart to try to offer high-end services would mean a price increase to cover their costs. Since the strategy of both of these retailers is to provide quality, low-cost goods, an increase in customer service to a level equivalent to Saks would be inconsistent with their strategy and could possibly have a negative impact on sales. This is not to say that these retailers should not try to maintain a minimal level of QSP; rather, they should concentrate on the areas in which they have the greatest competitive advantage (price for Walmart; quality products and services for Saks).

Equity

An understanding of customer value helps develop a long-term, loyal customer base. The underlying theme is to create equity in the retail operation by making customers want to return to the store or online site. *Equity* is simply the marketing and financial value that the customer provides for the retailer. Retailers attempt to develop *name equity* -- that is, the value of the organization's name as well as equity for the brands they sell (brand equity). *Customer equity* is "the value of the complete set of resources, tangible and intangible, that customers invest in a firm" (Dorsch and Carlson, 1996). Retailers must seamlessly incorporate equity in all of the activities they perform.

Brand Equity

Brand equity refers to the consumer's perceived level of quality for the retailer's product lines. Often consumers cannot make a quantitative judgment on the actual quality of the retail organization and the products it carries, so they use the brand as an indicator of the organization's overall quality (Pride and Ferrell, 2003). That is, if the consumer has a positive perception of the brand, this may translate into a highly positive perception of the store. Four elements, or variables, are essential in the development of brand equity: brand-name awareness, brand loyalty, perceived brand quality, and brand associations (Aaker, 1991).

Source: Ritu Manoj Jethani/Shutterstock.com

Brand Associations

The concepts of brand-name awareness, brand loyalty, and perceived brand quality are self-explanatory. *Brand associations* refer to the attributes or personality that the owners of the brand wish to convey to their current or potential customers. In other words, marketers often connect some type of lifestyle, or personality, to a brand. Hallmark suggests that you will send a Hallmark card "When you care enough to send the very best."

Applying the Concepts of Value and Equity

Let's look at the value and equity a customer may represent to the retailer by examining buying habits. Think of a retailer you visit at least once a week on average. This might be a gas station, a convenience store, a local "watering hole," your school's bookstore, or a fast-food restaurant. Write down the average amount of money you spend at that retail outlet for each week. Then multiply that amount by the number of weeks in a year, or 52. Next, multiply that figure by 5 (years), then by 10 (years). Finally, multiply that figure by 20 years. That final number is your value to the retailer. For example, by purchasing just an average of $30 worth of gasoline a week, you generate a value to that gas station of $1,560 per year, $7,800 for 5 years, $15,600 for 10 years, and $31,200 over a 20-year period. In this example, if you multiply $1,560, the amount generated to the gas station by one person in one year, by 10,000 happy customers, you will see that this retailer earns more than $15 million a year in sales. Imagine keeping these customers over their lifetimes! Indeed, customers are valuable.

Customer value must be integrated into all retail operations and channels. Retailers provide value when they adopt a customer-centered approach. Value must be present when creating customer service. The retailer must create value when communicating price to customers. In addition, value must be communicated to customers through effective integrated marketing communication (IMC). Perhaps the greatest need for the concept of value is through the use of relationship marketing. Finally, remember that value must be communicated to *all* members of the retailer's channel of distribution.

Services Retailing

The services industry comprises a diverse range of retail businesses. Banks, credit unions, airlines, hotels and motels, many transportation companies, lawn care companies, restaurants, and even your university are services retailers. According to the Bureau of Labor Statistics, the services sector employed more than 125 million people in the United States (www.bls.gov) and the average wage was about $31/hour (includes benefits) in 2016. Although service retailers do not sell products in the typical sense, most are heavily involved in logistics systems and transport, distribute, and utilize various types of physical goods. Governments and charities often describe themselves as being in the services industry. Organizations set up as not for profit, as well as those set up for profit, are involved in the acquisition and distribution of services to end users.

Source: Monkey Business Imagesl/Shutterstock.com

Services Retailing Defined

Because of the large numbers of individuals and businesses involved in services retailing, it is beneficial to operationally define what we would consider a service business. An abridged definition would deal with the actual ownership of the outputs from service retailers. In *services retailing*, customers rarely take permanent ownership of anything tangible; rather, needs satisfiers are generated from the performance of the retailer.

Suppose you are in Manhattan (New York City) and want to get from Greenwich Village to midtown. You have several options, but a taxi seems like the quickest way. The taxi company that owns the taxi you hire is a service retailer allowing you to have temporary ownership in the length of the ride. You don't want to buy the cab just to travel 25 to 30 blocks; rather, you want to use the

Source: Tom Wang/Shutterstock.com

taxi temporarily. The value you receive is the relatively fast trip down Broadway into midtown and the fact that you don't have to expend your energy by walking. Thus, services offer customers value that usually perishes once the service is completed.

Services retailing should not be confused with customer service that is provided to customers. The difference is that in the case of services retailing, the "product" being sold is actually a service. Thus, the customer derives value from the "service product" that was provided. As an example, consider gift wrapping. Although the physical act of gift wrapping is a service, what the consumer is really buying is the physical gift enclosed in the wrapping, not the wrapping itself. Another example is home installation of an air-conditioning unit. The consumer is actually buying the unit, not the installation. The installation is a value-added (or profit-generating) service that complements the physical good. On the other hand, if a consumer goes to Holiday Hair for a haircut, the primary motive for the trip is the haircut itself; thus, the "product" is the service performed.

Tangibility versus Intangibility

To observe the differences between products and services, it is useful to utilize a continuum, or spectrum, based on the degree of tangibility. G. Lynn Shostack (1977) proposed such a model, presented in Figure 2.2.

Figure 2.2 – Continuum of Tangible and Intangible Elements in Products and Services

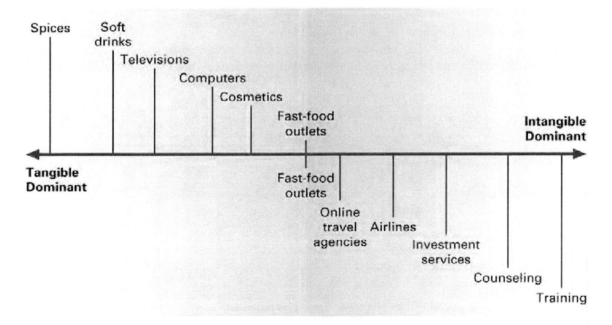

Source: Shostack, G.L. (1977). Breaking Free from Product Marketing. *Journal of Marketing*, 41 (April), pp. 73-80.

The products and services are positioned on the spectrum based on their level of tangibility. The more tangible the products and services are, the higher they are placed on the tangible, dominant end of the spectrum. The lower the tangibility, the closer the products and services fall toward the intangible dominant area. Thus, very tangible products, such as soft drinks and spices, would be perceived as highly tangible dominant, whereas teaching and investment management would be seen as highly intangible dominant.

Although services are not new to consumers, the academic study of services retailing is relatively young. Early researchers in services marketing created four main differences between service and product marketing. The researchers focused on the *intangibility of services*, the *heterogeneity of services*, the *perishability of output,* and the *simultaneity of production and consumption* of the service (Sasser, Olsen and Wyckoff, 1978). In this regard, one could look back at the Shostack model for intangibility of the product (or service) offering. The more intangible the offering, the more likely that it is a service. Similarly, with the heterogeneity of the service, the more variable (or heterogeneous) the offering, the more likely that it is a service.

Perishability refers to how long the offering lasts. In services retailing, the product begins to perish almost immediately.

Finally, services are produced and consumed at (relatively) the same time. Once a plane takes off and begins to make its way to its final destination, the consumption of that service has started. Thus, services provide for production and consumption of the offering almost simultaneously.

Differences between Products and Services

Recent work in this area has increased the number of variables that help differentiate between services and physical products. Christopher Lovelock (1996) proposes eight areas of differentiation between physical goods and services (see Table 2.3).

Table 2.3
Lovelock's Differentiation between Physical Goods and Services

1. The nature of the product
2. Customer/Retailer interaction and involvement in the production process
3. People as part of the product
4. Greater difficulties in maintaining quality control standards
5. Harder for customers to evaluate
6. Absence of inventories
7. Relative importance of the time factor
8. Structure and nature of distribution channels

Source: Services Marketing 3e by Lovelock, ©1996. Reprinted by permission of Pearson Education, Upper Saddle River, NJ.

The *nature of the product* refers to a product being a physical object, whereas a service is seen more as a performance (Berry, 1980). With services, there is often more *interaction between the retailer and the customer* because the *customer is involved in the actual production of the service.*

In services retailing, the customer becomes *part of the product.* For example, it is the customer's money that is actually loaned to a bank; the bank provides a secure place for the deposit of the money. The customer, in turn, states preferences as to where to place the money, such as in a certificate of deposit (CD) account, a checking with savings account, a money market account, or a savings account. The customer thus develops the product in conjunction with the bank's personnel.

Because the customer is involved and often is part of the service offering, and because the service is created at the time of delivery, there are many *quality control problems* for the retailer. The service cannot be checked or regulated prior to being sold. On the airline flight discussed earlier, the customer may have one or more unpleasant experiences, such as air turbulence, surly flight attendants, a cold meal, or delay or even cancellation of the flight. However, the customer does not know how the flight will turn out prior to boarding and actually consuming the service.

It is often *hard for the consumer to evaluate the service* received from a service retailer. Think of the last time you used a repair person. The only way you could evaluate the service provided was by operating the unit to verify that it worked after the repair. You probably knew little about the replacement parts you paid for. You also had no way of knowing if someone else could have done a better job (and perhaps charged a lower price). Because of such factors, services involve some risk to the customer.

Source: latsenko Olga/Shutterstock.com

In services retailing, the retailer *keeps no inventory* since the service is intangible. The problem this creates in the retailing of services is the possibility of stockouts. For example, customers in Buffalo, New York, may have a hard time finding someone to shovel their driveways after a heavy snowfall because all snow removal personnel are tied up with other customers. In this case, the snow removal service experiences a temporary stockout, resulting in a displeased or even angry customer.

Conversely, there are times when the services retailer may have too many employees "on the clock" with nothing to do. Suppose a drought in Indiana has slowed down growth of people's lawns. In this situation, providers of lawn-cutting services are likely to find themselves with too many employees, because the lawns need to be cut less often than normal.

Today's customers are demanding and do not like to wait to receive a service. Therefore, the *time factor* becomes extremely important. Because services are performed in real time, the retailer must understand that there are limits to the customer's patience and willingness to wait. For example, when people go out to eat, they are typically willing to wait only about 10 minutes for a table. If many restaurants with similar offerings are available, the need to wait is lessened. Thus, service retailers must provide the service expeditiously to retain their customers.

Finally, services use *different channels of distribution.* Often services can be distributed electronically, such as e-tickets at an airport kiosk or hotel reservations via a personal computer or smart phone.

The Servicescape

With the differences between physical products and services in mind, retailers need to create unique strategies and tactics to ensure that they are meeting customers' needs and wants. Although services retailing follows the same basic flow that product retailing does, some modifications are necessary in the actual execution of the IRM plan.

Bitner (1992) suggests that the design of the services retailer's physical environment will play a major role in differentiating that retailer from competitors. This physical environment design is called a servicescape. Much like a landscape, a *servicescape* encompasses all the variables of the service operation that are visible to consumers, including facilities, personnel, equipment, and the service's customers.

Services Retailing Adjustments

Due to the differences between retailing a physical good and retailing a service, some adjustments to operations are suggested in the areas of human resource supervision, customer involvement, pricing, and control and evaluation.

Human Resources. Services retailing requires a greater emphasis on human resources than does product retailing. Closer supervision of sales and service personnel is necessary. Because of the specialized nature of performing services (think of professions such as airline pilots and computer technicians), minimizing employee turnover is more important. Although not always practiced, the salary of service personnel usually should be higher. To maintain control and ensure quality, the service retailer needs to conduct employee performance reviews more frequently. Finally, employee scheduling needs to be flexible; thus, more time needs to be spent on this function in services retailing than in product retailing.

Customer Involvement in the Production of Services. One of the differentiating aspects of services retailing is that at times the customer is part of the service output. Think of an amusement park. Part of the fun is the hustle and bustle of the park. Participating with other patrons in the rides, games, and other attractions heightens one's experience. In this way, customers become part of the service experience. Because of this, there must be more involvement by customers in the production of the service. Customers must be continually evaluated for their level of satisfaction with the offered service. Frequent customer feedback helps ensure that the quality of the service is acceptable.

Pricing of Services. The pricing of services is somewhat harder than the pricing of physical goods. Many service retailers provide estimates of what the service will cost. A related concern is that services generally are based not on price but on one of the other controllable marketing variables, such as the channel of distribution, location, and service value. It is difficult to calculate the value of a service (quality of the service relative to the price). Therefore, value is often defined by the customer: The customer establishes the real value by choosing to patronize or not patronize a particular retailer.

Closely tied to pricing is the retailer's integrated marketing communication (IMC). Because services are intangible, customers have a hard time identifying service value. In that regard, it may be important to link the service with physical goods. This is a good argument for cross-selling services and products. Many service providers, such as portrait photographers, house painters, and hair salons, offer "before" and "after" pictures to help create value in their customers' minds. An additional determinant of value in services retailing is the prestige associated with the service itself or the service domain.

Service Price Adjustments. Complaints about services need special attention. Customers cannot return a service once it has been performed. Because of this, many service retailers offer fairly liberal price adjustments for unsatisfactory service performance. The service retailer must have *specific,* written information about these types of service price adjustments. Many offer to re-do the service if it is not satisfactory. For example, when a plumber comes to the house to fix a leaking faucet and gets the dripping to stop, the customer is satisfied. But what if the faucet starts leaking again a few months later? Should the plumber provide a second repair job at no charge to the customer? Should the plumber offer to make a follow-up visit to make sure the faucet is still working properly? The solution is up to the plumber service. Services retailers must keep in mind that an unhappy customer is likely to talk to others about the unsatisfactory service experience, and the retailer's reputation could be jeopardized if the problem is not addressed and fixed.

Control and Evaluation of Services. Control and evaluation is difficult for services retailers. Because employees represent the services retailer, the service provider has a greater chance of losing good employees to its competitors. Likewise, in services retailing it is easier to steal customers than in product retailing. For example, a new airline may exploit the weaknesses of other airlines in an attempt to lure leisure travelers. Therefore, services retailers can achieve success with both employee and customer loyalty programs. An example of a customer loyalty program is the Plenti program (https://www.plenti.com/), launched in 2015 by American Express. The loyalty program lets consumers earn points at one place and use them at another one of the partner companies. Customers can use the points they earn at Macy's or to defray the cost of renting a car at Enterprise. Macy's, AT&T, Rite Aid, Enterprise Rent-A-Car and Hulu are a few of the companies in the program. Examples of employee loyalty programs include gifts based on service anniversaries and trips awarded for outstanding performance.

Source: Rawpixel.com/Shutterstock.com

The overall IRM program set up by the services retailer must be evaluated. Although the services retailer can use some of the same evaluative tools that product retailers use, certain problems are unique to services retailing. For example, there are no (or limited) inventories; thus, inventory turn cannot be measured. In addition, services are labor intensive; thus, personnel costs are generally higher. Services retailers should use cost accounting, which allows them to assign costs for services performed. Using a costing system along with a return on net worth ratio provides the services retailer with better information than do many of the other techniques used for product retailing.

A services retailer's profit should be generated after the costs of labor are factored in (thus replacing the gross margin for products). Recordkeeping for each job performed is essential. It allows the retailer to see how much profit was generated from each job and makes estimations of costs quoted to customers more accurate. Finally, records for sales support personnel, a non-revenue-generating function, should be kept separate from records used to record revenue production.

As we have seen, although services retailers can use a generic IRM flow chart to develop their retail plans, they must be aware of the differences in the ways they execute their tactics, manage, and evaluate and control.

Creating and Building Relationships

According to Earl Naumann (1995a), a consultant specializing in customer satisfaction:

> Customers are not targets! Customers are probably a firm's most valuable asset, and they should be nurtured, developed, and treated accordingly. Each and every customer should be the objective of proactive, bonding relationships. And customers, in person, should be integrated into the firm's decision-making processes. (pp. 17 and 163)

To develop and keep a loyal customer base, retailers must focus on relationship marketing to build relationships with their customers. When developing a relationship strategy, the customer must be integrated into the retailer's overall strategic direction. Thus, objectives and strategies must be customer focused.

Solid customer relationships provide long-term, loyal customers. "The longer a customer stays with a company, the more that customer is worth. Long-term customers buy more, take less of a company's time, are less sensitive to price, and bring in new shoppers. Best of all, they have no acquisition or start-up cost" (Reichheld, 1996). A major concern to retailers should be customer retention. According to Lois Geller, partner and president of Mason & Geller LLC/Direct Marketing in New York City, some large companies report that 95 percent of profits come from long-term customers (Geller, 1997). Geller believes that customer retention is important to retailers because when a customer leaves, it costs the retailer three to seven times more money to get a new customer than to retain the current customer. Table 2.4 lists the fifteen elements that Geller believes should be incorporated into customer-retention strategies.

Table 2.4 – 15 Elements to Increase Customer Retention

1. Deliver a high-quality, high-value product
2. Make every single contact count
3. Know your customers
4. Know when customers defect
5. Keep the company at the top of customer's minds
6. Modify your product-service mix
7. Always close the loop in marketing programs
8. Deliver excellent customer service
9. Keep customer retention programs human
10. Use partnerships to build customer retention
11. Do the unexpected
12. Use databases to maximize the personalization of offers
13. Identify the timing and frequency of customer promotions
14. Utilize retail and catalog synergies
15. Incorporate online marketing into the strategy

Source: Geller, L. (1997). Customer Retention Begins with the Basics. *Direct Marketing*, (Sept), pp. 58-62.

Retailers must also strive to create positive working relationships with suppliers. Effective management of the supply chain translates into increased retailer productivity and greater profitability. Supply chain management is discussed in more detail in Chapter 9 when the concept of logistics is explored.

Many other methods can be utilized to create long-term relationships with customers; we will discuss some of these methods in Chapter 13 when we integrate customer retention and customer service. For now, bear in mind that long-term relationships are essential in developing and adding value to the retail organization.

Source: Rawpixel.com/Shutterstock.com

Retailing Technology

Technology is any tool that helps one succeed in a given endeavor. *Retail technology* is any tool that helps a retailer succeed in carrying out strategy. Advances in the technological environment are important to retailers for many reasons, one of which is customer value. Retail technology can be used to create customer relationships and to integrate and develop effective retailing operations. Although technology is covered throughout the textbook, there are some general concepts of technology that we should address at this time.

Technology in retailing can manifest itself in many areas. For example, integrated marketing communications (IMC) benefit by allowing for, among other things, digital photography, direct marketing, database use, mobile applications, and in-store telecommunications. In addition, technologies can help develop and monitor the retailer's customer value and retention strategies and executions.

Technology is used for forecasting and the development of financial and accounting systems. In addition, technology can be used for service retailing, e-tailing, omni-channel strategies, franchising, and market segmentation. Other uses of technology include electronic data interchange (EDI), electronic fund transfers, point-of-sale information, and perpetual inventory systems.

Technology has been developed for many areas of logistics, including inventory replenishment, inventory management, customer relationships, and geographic information systems. Optimal store atmospheres as well as retail audits can be managed with the assistance of technology. In short, technology offers the retailer new and exciting ways to expand on existing or future market opportunities.

E-commerce and E-tailing

E-commerce is short for electric commerce and means buying and selling over electronic systems such as the Internet. E-commerce activities include e-tailing, inventory management, automated data collection and *electronic data interchange* (EDI), which is the exchange of information between businesses. E-tailing differs from e-commerce in that e-tailing is a subset of e-commerce that deals only with the retailing function online. Because of the changing consumer environment, retailers have been forced to add additional channels of distribution. In the past, some retailers expanded their channels with catalogs. More recently, they have used the Internet and m-commerce, which includes leveraging the mobile technology available for smart phones and computer tablets.

The growth of e-commerce and e-tailing is due to the rising amount of Internet usage. As of March 2017, there were over 320 million users in North America, representing 88.1% of the North American population. Although Asia had the highest number of users (about 1.9 billion), the percent of their population using the Internet was only 45%. Worldwide, the number of Internet users has risen 933% from 2000 – 2017 (Internet World Stats, 2017).

Companies that have both a brick and mortal store and an Internet site are called *bricks and clicks.* E-tail divisions often felt they were in competition with the brick-and-mortar divisions. Thus, retail organizations developed silos that acted independently and didn't communicate or share information with each other. Silo syndrome is the biggest barrier to success of omni-channel retailing.

Silo is a metaphor for how different parts of an organization work separately from one another. As grain silos segregate one type

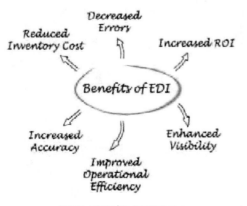

Source: arka38/Shutterstock.com

of grain from another, so do organizations keep separate departments, resulting in silo syndrome (Rosen, 2010). Silo syndrome leads to redundancies and suboptimal decision making because each silo had its own goals and profit-and-loss component. Silos prevent retail organizations from developing productive and effective retail systems that could create additional sales, profits and revenues. For example, a retailer might have an Internet division and a division for brick-and-mortar stores. Silos are created and these channels compete against each other for sales, resources, and overall power. Top-level management often doesn't provide support so that there is no reason or incentive to share strategies, information, resources, or best practices within the organization. There is no incentive to create cross-promotions or to leverage any type of promotional activity.

Breaking Down Silos

Rosen (2010) identified five steps to eliminating silos:

1. Eliminate needless formality and hierarchy – this could involve the removal of some middle management positions and improving communication

2. Provide "One-Click" access to the entire organization – this means giving anyone in the organization the ability to contact anyone else

3. Design dedicated physical spaces for collaboration – it's important to have physical spaces where team members can discuss services, opportunities, and create solutions to problems

4. Adopt common systems and processes – this includes giving everyone the same rights over information and data

5. Establish cross-functional mentoring – this involves encouraging employees to have mentors in functions other than the ones in which they work

Retailers understand the importance of breaking down silos and focusing on integration to create more revenue and customers. Integration allows retailers to maximize their marketing, sales, consumer experiences, the infrastructure and their supply chains, resulting in more productivity at less cost. In order to achieve integration, competition between functions must be removed, assuring that different parts of the company are working together to better serve the customer.

These retailers are creating new business models that recognize that the whole is greater than the sum of individual parts. Every touch point with customers is an opportunity to communicate messages in a coordinated, clear, and consistent manner. Multiple impressions result in more customer traffic and more sales. Thus, integration of a retailer's business practices across channels maximizes the retailers' brand and marketing initiatives.

Sephora, the cosmetic retailer, is an example of a company that is successful in integrating commu-

Source: Daniel Krason/Shutterstock.com

nication messages across channels. Sephora has a site that is compatible with smart phones and other mobile devices, an iPhone app that integrates with an in-store retail experience, and an iPad app that contains videos on how to apply their products. An *app* (short for application) is software that can run on computers or mobile devices.

In 2016 Sephora was labeled a "genius" specialty retail brand by the L2 consulting company because of their digital efforts. According to L2, the Sephora to Go app has several tools valued by customers, such as a virtual lipstick assistant, a reward system, and notifications. The app makes it easy for people to share links and product ideas through social media (L2 Inc, 2016)

A Brief History of E-commerce and E-tailing

The Internet started out in 1969 as a private communications system created for the U.S. Department of Defense. Since its initial development, the Internet has evolved into a communications medium used by individuals and companies for research and to convey company and product information as well as to sell products and services. During the 1970s and 1980s, the system increased in power, convenience, and speed. The latter half of the 1990s saw the Internet erupt into an economic platform that began to alter business strategies and business development. The Internet gave a platform to e-commerce that had never existed before.

Electronic commerce, or e-commerce, allegedly started about 125 to 130 years ago with the use of Western Union's money transfer system. It expanded with the development of credit cards during the late 1900s. In the early to mid-1980s, the ATM (automated teller machine) was developed and gave e-commerce another large push.

On the supply side, e-commerce evolved from two movements facilitated by the Internet. The first was the decrease in costs of long-distance calling. The second was the increased use of database management software and corporate intranets that streamlined the purchasing process for many large, progressive companies. On the demand side, the development of e-mail increased access to business and e-tailer networks. Because most customer service contact activities had become routine, e-tailers found this service could be provided effectively with a computerized process, saving time and money for both consumer and e-tailer. Thus, electronic systems have changed the way we do business in the 21st century.

Laws, Ethics and Corporate Social Responsibility

In developing an understanding of customer value and retention, the retailer must be aware that ethics and corporate social responsibility have an impact on the customer-retailer relationship. It is very hard to repair the bond between customer and retailer once that trust is broken.

Source: jdwfoto/Shutterstock.com

Because retailers are always in the public eye, ensuring that they operate in an ethically and socially responsible manner is a challenge.

Ethical behavior helps develop relationships and trust, and increases profits and sales. In addition, by operating ethically, managers and employees feel positive about themselves and about their companies. Think about people you know who treat you fairly and with respect, and those whom you feel you can't trust. With whom would you more likely want to do business? The same principles hold for retailing. Customer trust means long-term, loyal customers, which means greater sales and stability.

Laws and Ethics

Although laws and ethics are covered in detail in Chapter 14, the topic has great importance for customer value. The many corporate scandals that have dominated the news have made business ethics more prominent. Add to this the pressure retailers face in generating same-store sales and increased profit reports, and an environment is created that lends itself to questionable retail practices. Although very few retailers are known to engage in unethical practices, the actions of just a few affect many employees, consumers, and other companies. To make it through tough financial times, a company can opt to file for bankruptcy, a form of which provides a retailer protection from its creditors.

Retail organizations must ensure they follow sound ethical standards. In the long run, ethical retail practices pay off both financially and in the creation of customer value. A strong example of ethics in retailing is JCPenney Company, founded on James Cash Penney's work ethic and social philosophy of taking good care of the customers and the community (Anthony, 2002). The stores' employees still follow this work ethic. Ethics may be even more important to e-tailers and those engaged in e-commerce activities that do not involve sales. Conducting business over the Internet creates many opportunities to engage in questionable business practices or even fraud.

Corporate Social Responsibility (CSR)

The World Business Council for Sustainable Development defines *corporate social responsibility (CSR)* as "the commitment of business to contribute to sustainable economic development, working with employees, their families, the local community and society at large to improve their quality of life" (Corporate Social Responsibility…, 2002). In essence, corporate social responsibility is about managing a business to improve society (Baker, 2004). Strong CSR actions strengthen the relationship between the retailer and its customers and increase the value of the firm.

Figure 2.3 illustrates the relationship of businesses in society. The figure shows that businesses must answer to two primary aspects of their operations: (1) the quality of their management and (2) their impact on society in the marketplace, workplace, environment, and community.

Figure 2.3 – The Business in Society

Source: Baker, M. (2004). Corporate Social Responsibility – What Does It Mean?
Retrieved from http://www.mallenbaker.net/csr/definition.php

More and more companies are realizing that they improve their company image when they work to improve their communities. By recognizing the interdependence of businesses and society, retailers can make a positive impact. According to Brad Hecht, chief research officer at Reputation Institute (2015), "Consumers want to engage with companies that are good corporate citizens"

The Reputation Institute ranked the firms with the best CSR reputations in the world which are presented in Table 2.5 (Strauss, 2016).

Table 2.5 2016 – Top-Ranked Companies in the World for Corporate Social Responsibility

1. Google	6. Daimler
2. Microsoft	7. Apple
3. Walt Disney Co	8. Rolls-Royce Aerospace
4. BMW	9. Rolex
5. LEGO	10. Intel

Source: Strauss, K. (2016). The Companies with the Best CSR Reputations in the World in 2016. Forbes. Retrieved from http://www.forbes.com/sites/karstenstrauss/2016/09/15/the-companies-with-the-best-csr-reputations-in-the-world-in-2016/#5245d04f7b83

Microsoft has a Citizenship Team at the corporate level with Citizenship Leads throughout the world that work with communities on a range of issues. In September 2012, the company launched Microsoft YouthSpark, an initiative that connects hundreds of millions of young people with opportunities for education, employment and entrepreneurship. In 2012, the company reached a $1 billion milestone for employee giving (Smith, 2012). In 2015 alone, Microsoft employees raised $125 million for more than 18,000 nonprofits and schools worldwide. The employee participation rate was 71%, which included employees volunteering and donating money (Microsoft.com, 2017). Corporate social responsibility can help ensure that customers view companies as empathetic and understanding of societal needs.

Summary

The marketing concept means satisfying customers' wants and needs at a profit. Retailers are finding that to maintain competitive advantage, they must exceed customer expectations. Thus, when extending the marketing concept from merely satisfying customer wants and needs, integration of all retailing functions becomes paramount.

Because the world of retailing is constantly changing, retail professionals must be up to date on the latest techniques and theories that affect (both positively and negatively) the retail firm. Understanding customer value allows retailers to incorporate consumers' wants and needs into their integrated retail management plans. Without this understanding, a retailer is at a competitive disadvantage.

It is important to distinguish between providing services and being a service retailer. In services retailing, the product being sold is a service. Most retailers provide some type of service beyond their core offerings, but they are not services retailers if their core offerings are tangible as opposed to intangible.

Because customers are demanding more and more service from retailers, an understanding of the customer base can help the retailer create long-term, mutually beneficial relationships with customers. Developing customer relationships builds customer equity, the value that customers provide to the retailer.

Technology has created capabilities that were never imagined possible. From online banking to buying groceries and other products online, the Internet is becoming an increasingly important channel. It is important for retailing professionals to stay current with all the changing technologies and to understand the difference between selling tangible products versus intangible services (services retailing) as well as the impact of technology on their retail businesses.

As we move forward into the 21st century, ethics and social responsibility will play an increasing role in retailers' visions and missions. The development and implementation of a sound work ethic for employees and stakeholders will become paramount for success. Ethics and social responsibility build stronger communities, increase profits and sales, and develop positive, long-term relationships. They also make retail employees feel positive about themselves and the firms they work for.

Key Terms

app	Short for application; software that can run on computers or mobile devices.
brand associations	Attributes or personality that the owners of a brand wish to convey to their current or potential customers.
brand equity	The consumer's perceived level of quality for the retailer's product lines.
bricks and clicks	Companies that have both a brick-and-mortar store and an Internet site.
corporate social responsibility (CSR)	The commitment of business to contribute to sustainable economic development, working with employees, their families, the local community, and society at large to improve their quality of life.
customer equity	The value of the complete set of resources, tangible and intangible, that customers invest in a firm.
customer service	Activities designed to enhance the level of customer satisfaction.
customer-centered retailing	An approach to retailing that places the customer at the center of all decisions.
electronic data interchange (EDI)	The exchange of information between businesses using an electronic system.
encryption system	A system that codes data so that the data can be understood only by the intended user.
equity	The marketing and financial value that the customer provides for the retailer.
extended marketing concept	The concept of exceeding customer wants and needs at a profit.
market segments	Groups of customers that share one or more characteristics and respond similarly to marketing efforts.
m-commerce (mobile commerce)	Technologies that include smart phones and computer tablets that have Internet access and can be leveraged by companies to keep consumers connected.
marketing concept	The philosophy that an organization should try to satisfy customers' needs through a coordinated set of activities that also allows the organization to achieve its goals.
name equity	The value of the organization's name.

QSP	Categorization of customer value by quality, service, and/or price.
relationship marketing	A type of marketing that focuses on building long-lasting relationships with customers.
retail technology	Any tool that helps retailers succeed in carrying out strategy.
services retailing	A type of retailing in which the "product" being sold is a service; the customer derives value from the "service product" that is provided.
servicescape	All the variables of the service operation that are visible to consumers, including facilities, personnel, equipment, and the service's customers.
silo	A term used to describe how parts of an organization work separately from one another.
value	An amount, as of goods, services, or money, considered to be a fair and suitable equivalent for something else; monetary worth of something; relative worth, utility, or importance.
value proposition	A short, clear, simple statement containing the reasons that a customer would choose one brand over another.

Discussion Questions

1. What are some ways retailers can exceed customer expectations?

2. What is your definition of *customer value*? Compare your definition with a classmate's. How are the two definitions similar? How are they different?

3. Name a business that values you as a customer. How long have you patronized this business? What makes you continue to shop there?

4. Is it easier for a retailer that has a physical location to provide good customer service than it is for a retailer with a web-based location? Explain your answer.

5. What role does corporate social responsibility play in a company's reputation?

Exercises

1. Find three service retailing companies. Apply Lovelock's differentiation between physical goods and services in an analysis of these companies.

2. Go to the following websites:

> www.jcpenney.com (JCPenney)
>
> www.dell.com (Dell Computers)
>
> www.ikea.com (IKEA)
>
> www.tiffanys.com (Tiffany's)

Navigate through the sites to answer the following questions:

- What evidence can you find that shows the retailer values its customers?

- If you found evidence, explain how the retailer makes customers feel appreciated.

- If you found no evidence, explain how the retailer could implement the value concept online.

Case

Disney Faces Illness Aboard Cruise Ships

Many of the differences between goods and services as described by Christopher Lovelock became apparent when The Walt Disney Company experienced problems with its cruise ships. Disney, a global corporation, faced a service provider's nightmare when an outbreak of the norovirus sickened more than 200 passengers on the *Disney Magic* cruise ship in 2002. The virus causes nausea, vomiting, diarrhea, and abdominal pain. Disney offered to fly sick passengers home, but only one couple accepted. This was the second outbreak in a month on the *Disney Magic.* Although federal health officials declared the ship safe, Disney chose to cancel the following cruise so that the ship could be thoroughly disinfected. This marked the first time that Disney had had to cancel a voyage since the company began offering cruises in 1998.

The disinfection process included cleaning surfaces with bleach or other chemicals and steaming or discarding things that could not be disinfected. In this case, Disney discarded all mattresses and pillows. The sheets, towels, and pillowcases were washed in 160-degree water. Stuffed animals, available in gift shops, were washed, then stored in warehouses for thirty days before going back on shelves. In an effort to keep customer satisfaction high, Disney offered sick passengers a free future cruise. Those people affected by the cancellation received refunds and half-price offers for a future cruise.

In the case of a cruise, the customer takes part in developing the final product, so when a customer becomes sick during the experience, the satisfaction level can drop. In addition, the perishability of services and quality of the experience present control challenges for services retailers, whose "products" are more intangible than tangible.

In 2016 131 passengers and 14 crew members from the Disney Wonder cruise fell sick to the norovirus. Prior to 2016, there had been no serious Disney Cruise health incidents besides the 2002 Disney Magic outbreak. (*Disney Magic*).

Questions:

1. Where do cruises fall on the continuum of tangible and intangible elements in goods and services?

2. Check out Disney Cruise lines website (https://disneycruise.disney.go.com/) What do you like or dislike about the website?

3. Do you think that Disney management handled the crisis well? Why or why not?

4. Did the event affect the Disney reputation? Why or why not?

Sources: Denise Grady, "U.S. Health Officials Call Cruise Ships Safe, in Spite of Outbreaks," *New York Times*, November 28, 2002 (East Coast edition), p. 32; Jim Buynak, "Disney Ships' Illness Grows; 40 More Passengers, One Crewmember Report Sick," *Knight Ridder Tribune Business News*, November 29, 2002, p. 1; Sandra Pedicini, "Disney Magic Returns After More Passengers Become Ill," *Knight Ridder Tribune Business News*, November 30, 2002, p. 1.; Sandra Pedicini, (2016). CDC says norovirus caused recent illnesses on Disney Wonder. *The Orlando Sentinel* (May 13).

References

Aaker, D.A. (1991). *Managing Brand Equity: Capitalizing on the Value of a Brand Name.* New York: The Free Press, pp. 16-17.

Anthony, C. (2002). JC Penney Workers Still Follow Founding Philosophy. *Knight Ridder Tribune Business News,* May 12.

Baker, M. (2004). Corporate Social Responsibility – What Does It Mean? Retrieved from http://www.mallenbaker.net/csr/definition.php

Berry, L. L. (1980). Services Marketing is Different. *Business,* May-June.

Bitner, M. J. (1992). Servicescapes: The Impact of Physical Surroundings on Customers and Employees. *Journal of Marketing,* (April), pp. 57-71.

Chandler, K. and Hyatt, K. (2003). *Customer-Centered Design.* Hewlett-Packard Company, Upper Saddle River, NJ: Prentice Hall PTR.

Corporate Social Responsibility: The WBCSD's Journey. World Business Council for Sustainable Development, p. 23. Retrieved from www.wbcsd.org.

Dillard's homepage (2017). Retrieved from www.dillards.com.

Dorsch, M. J. and Carlson, L. (1996). A Transaction Approach to Understanding and Managing Customer Equity. *Journal of Business Research,* 35 (1996), pp. 253-264.

Geller, L. (1997). Customer Retention Begins with the Basics. *Direct Marketing,* (Sept), pp. 58-62.

Internet World Stats (2017). Access from http://www.internetworldstats.com/stats.htm

Kaufman, L. (2002). William T. Dillard, Founder of a Retail Chain, Dies at 87. *New York Times,* (Feb 9), p. A1 7.

L2 Inc (2016). Top 10 Specialty Retail Brands. https://www.l2inc.com/top-10-specialty-retail-brands-in-digital/2016/blog

Lovelock, C. H. (1996). *Services Marketing* 3d ed. Upper Saddle River, NJ: Prentice Hall.

Microsoft (2017). Website: Employee Giving. https://www.microsoft.com/en-us/philanthropies/our-employees/employee-giving/

Naumann, E. (1995a). *Creating Customer Value: The Path to Sustainable Competitive Advantage.* Cincinnati: Thompson Executive Press, pp. 17, 163.

Naumann, E. (1995b). *Customer Value Toolkit.* Cincinnati, Ohio: Thompson Executive Press, 1995.

Ogden, J. R. and Ogden, D. T. (2010). *Marketing Basics: Cutting Through the Clutter.* Dubuque, IA: Kendall Hunt Publishing Company, pp. 1-7.

Pine, J. and Gilmore, J. (1999) *The Experience Economy,* Harvard Business School Press, Boston, 1999.

Pride, W. M. and Ferrell, O.C. (2003). *Marketing* (12th ed.) Boston: Houghton Mifflin, p. 352.

Reichheld, F. R. (1996). Learning from Customer Defections. *Harvard Business Review,* March-April, p. 57.

Reputation Institute (2015). Reputation Institute Announces Top Companies for U.S. Public Perception of Corporate Social Responsibility. https://www.reputationinstitute.com/CMSPages/GetAzureFile.aspx?path=~%5Cmedia%5Cmedia%5Cimages%5Cpress-release-for-us-csr_final_3.pdf&hash=9509dcdfe5b2d245af53f59e3f1ad88e8ff2f77f50d4ac0d9c822d0a5d3c14db

Rosen, E. (2010, February 5), Smashing Silos. *Business Week.* Retrieved from http://www.businessweek.com/managing/content/feb2010/ca2010025_358633.htm

Sasser, E. W., Olsen, P.R. and Wyckoff, D.D. (1978). *Management of Service Operations: Text, Cases, and Readings.* Boston: Allyn and Bacon.

Shostack, G.L. (1977). Breaking Free from Product Marketing. *Journal of Marketing,* 41 (April), pp. 73-80.

Smith, J. (2012). The Companies with the Best CSR Reputations. *Forbes.* Retrieved from http://www.forbes.com/sites/jacquelynsmith/2012/12/10/the-companies-with-the-best-csr-reputations/

Swystun, Jeff (editor) (2007). *Interbrand: The Brand Glossary.* New York: Palgrave Macmillan, p. 122.

Tucker, R.B. (1995). *Win the Value Revolution.* Franklin Lakes, NJ: Career Press.

Turban, E. and King, D. (2003). *Introduction to Electronic Commerce.* New Jersey: Prentice Hall.

U.S. Department of Labor, Bureau of Labor Statistics (2017). Retrieved from https://www.bls.gov/iag/tgs/iag07.htm#workforce

Wright, N. D., Pearce, J. W. and Busbin, J. W, (1997). Linking Customer Service Orientation to Competitive Performance: Does the Marketing Concept Really Work? *Journal of Marketing Theory and Practice,* 5(4), pp. 23-34.

Part 2

Effective Retail Strategies

Source: g-stockstudio/Shutterstock.com

Chapter 3: *The Retail Planning and Management Process*
Chapter 4: *The Retail Environment: A Situational and Competitive Analysis*
Chapter 5: *Evaluation and Identification of Retail Customers*

Part 1 dealt with many important external, or macro, environments that affect retailers. Armed with a good understanding of these environments, retail managers can make better, more informed decisions. Part 2 takes a more micro approach, looking at the retail management functions.

Chapter 3 provides expanded coverage of the IRM flow chart. Each major step in the IRM is discussed in more detail. Chapters 4 and 5 look at the information necessary to build a solid situational analysis for the retail organization. Specifically, Chapter 4 addresses retail institutions involved in the situational analysis, and Chapter 5 focuses on identifying and evaluating potential retail customers.

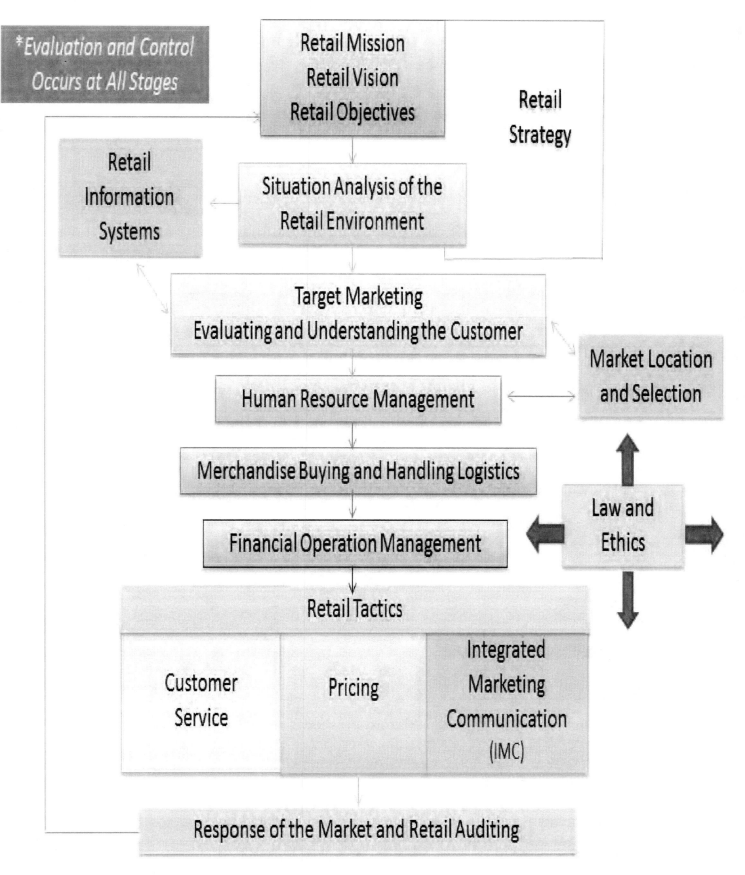

Chapter 3

The Retail Planning and Management Process

"Entrepreneurs have a great ability to create change, be flexible, build companies and cultivate the kind of work environment in which they want to work"
~ Tory Burch, American Businesswoman

Source: Monkey Business Images/Shutterstock.com

CHAPTER OBJECTIVES

After completing this chapter you will be able to:

- Discuss the importance of a retailer's mission and vision.
- Describe the activities that take place when conducting a situation analysis.
- Define strategy and describe how retailers develop strategic plans.
- Explain the importance of target marketing and understanding the behavior of a market segment.
- Describe how retailers determine markets and select retail locations.
- Discuss the following areas in relation to retail operations: financial operations management, merchandise buying and handling, human resource management, retail tactics, laws and ethics, and evaluation and control.

Neighborhood Markets

Walmart is the world's largest retailer, known for its discount stores and supercenters. One of the company's strengths is its strategic planning and innovative marketing. Because the discount store format was in the maturity phase of the retail life cycle, in 1998 Walmart moved into a new type of retail format. These new stores are called Walmart Neighborhood Market.

The neighborhood market concept focuses on convenience-oriented customers who want a smaller, easy-to-navigate store. These neighborhood markets provide a grocery store format in which typical Walmart shoppers can shop during the week. Each store is about 38,000 square feet which is about one-quarter the size of a typical Walmart store (www.walmart.com) The format complements the supercenter stores, which are frequented more often on weekends.

Each neighborhood market caters to the community in which it is located. For example, if the residents of a particular area are from a certain ethnic background, the neighborhood market carries more products targeted toward that demographic segment.

As of 2016, Walmart had 694 locations (Walmart Unit Counts by Country, 2016). Although estimated sales are lower than those of a typical Walmart supercenter, the lower revenues are offset by lower real estate costs because of the smaller locations (Howell, 2002).

Walmart is embracing the omni-channel experience. According to their 2016 annual report:

"We will reimagine Walmart by being the first and only to deliver a truly seamless shopping experience at scale, with great savings and massive selection. We want customers to:

- Trust us to save them money,
- Find it simple and easy to do business with us, whether digitally or physically,
- Know they can find whatever they're looking for, either in stores, on our e-commerce sites, or with our marketplace vendors, and
- Get items when and where they want them – in stores and clubs, through pickup on or off-site, or delivered to their door.

Ultimately, customers don't care about what channel they're shopping in, or about how we deliver them a product or service. They simply know they're shopping with Walmart" (p. 7).

Source: Walmart website: http://corporate.walmart.com/our-story/our-stores/united-states-stores

Introduction

This chapter centers on the processes involved in the development and execution of an integrated retail management plan. The chapter moves from a macro view of retailing to a more micro approach. It provides an overview of the retail planning process by utilizing an integrated retail management (IRM) flow chart. Some of these topics have entire chapters devoted to them later in the text; this chapter provides more concise coverage.

Planning is defined as the establishment of objectives, policies, and procedures to carry out goals. Planning is very important because it gives direction for capital and human resource expenditures. It allows for the development of logistical systems that are fully integrated into the retailer's way of doing business, as well as for the most effective methods of communicating with customers through integrated marketing communications. In addition, the plan provides data to be used by decision makers when developing effective plans for their specialized areas.

An integrated retail management plan is similar to a marketing plan, but it contains much more information. As such, IRM plans tend to be somewhat lengthy, but nonetheless, important tools for the success of a retail operation. *Integrated retail management planning* is defined as the establishment of objectives, policies, and procedures to carry out goals that are consistent within and across channels. A focus on integration provides direction for the retail firm and its employees. Integration is especially important as the number of channels increase. Effective communication among all units of the retail operation is essential so that customers are not confused by inconsistent practices. Macy's is an example of a company that integrates information very well across their stores, websites, mobile apps and social media. Imagine if a company's website announced a sale in their store and, when customers showed up, employees did not know there was a sale. Customers would be angry and there would be much confusion. Lack of integration occurs more often due to silos that have been built. A simple action, such as accepting merchandise that was purchased online for return in the physical store, helps to communicate that a customer is valued.

The information a retailer collects goes into the integrated retail management (IRM) plan and is used in the planning process. When planning, retailers develop one plan for the entire retail operation. Although the organization's IRM plan will offer direction for the retailer, many times divisions and branch locations also create plans. When the division creates plans there must be consistency with the overall IRM plan. Often functional areas such as human resources, marketing and marketing communication also coordinate their planning.

Source: CoraMax/Shutterstock.com

Many people believe that brick and mortar and online retailing are simple and only involve buying products and opening the doors (or website) to generate sales. Retailing is much more than this. Retailers engage in extensive business planning as they develop their Integrated Retail Management (IRM) plans. The IRM flow chart provides a tool for retailers to use when developing plans. These plans help to create measurement tools that tell a retailer how well they're performing and provide direction for future moves. Because many retailers use omni-channel retailing, the IRM plan is essential to create consistency and integration between the offerings and customer service across channels. While the areas were described briefly in an earlier chapter, here we provide more detail.

The Retailer's Mission and Vision

The heart of any plan is clear knowledge of exactly why the business or organization exists. The old saying, "If you don't know where you're going, you won't get there"---or better yet, "If you don't know where you're going, you're already there"---is humorous, but it exemplifies the need for careful planning. Retailers must answer to *stakeholders*, or groups that affect or are affected by the retailer. Stakeholders include employees and investors. The mission statement tells stakeholders about the business. The first question the successful retailer needs to ask is: Why are we in business? The intelligent retailer will spend a lot of time and resources to answer that question, because, without an answer retail executions will be ineffective. Thus, the first step in overall retail planning is to create a mission statement for the retail organization. All steps in the integrated retail management plan will then follow logically from that one guiding principle.

Although the steps illustrated in the IRM flow chart are sequential, in reality the successful retail manager may work at different levels within the flow chart simultaneously. While the mission statement is being updated, for example, the retailer also may be working on a strong merchandise buying and handling plan. The ultimate goal is to create sales and profits in the most efficient and cost-effective manner possible. Also note that although the arrows in the flow chart show a downward flow, in practice the flows can go in both directions. For example, if the situational analysis shows a change in consumers' needs, and as a result the retailer adds another line to its products, the mission statement may be updated to reflect the change in the operation.

Mission Statement

The first step in the flow chart is the retail mission. A *mission statement* describes what the organization wants to accomplish and what principles will guide the effort (Mondy, 2010). A mission statement should also be short, memorable and meaningful (Kotler & Keller, 2012). The mission statement answers the following questions about the retailer: Why are we in business? What do we do? What do we stand for? A good mission statement speaks of commitment to the customer, employees, shareholders, and society (Morin, 1995). A clear mission statement also helps employees distinguish what activities conform to organization goals and those that do not (Morphew, 2006, p. 457).

Think about questions you may encounter during your next job interview. The interviewer may ask you to tell "a little bit about you and your background." You need to summarize more than 20 years of your life in a few statements. You don't want to provide too much information, which would give the interviewer information overload; rather, you should give enough information to allow the interviewer to make a positive decision about your skills and background. The mission statement does the same thing for potential or current stakeholders of the retail organization.

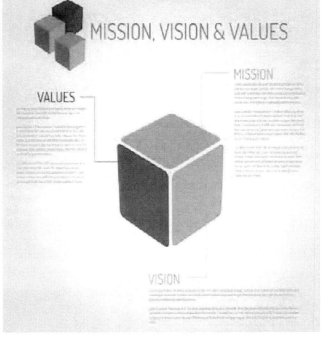

Source: Petr Vaclavek/Shutterstock.com

The key to a successful mission statement is to make sure it expresses values held by the organization. The mission statement, because it guides the retailer through good times and bad, should be the starting point for any retail business. All plans and processes emanate from the mission statement. Thus, an effective mission has employee and stakeholder buy-in.

Vision Statement

Closely related to the mission statement is the retailer's vision. While the mission statement deals with why the retailer is in business, it is grounded in the present. A *vision statement*, on the other hand, evolves from the mission but focuses on future goals. A good vision statement contains (1) a statement of a desired future for the retailer, (2) a reminder to the retailer of "why we do what we do," (3) values for the retailer to live by, and (4) enough information to serve as a touchstone for making the hard decisions on retail policy.

A vision provides many benefits for the retailer, including:

· Alignment of everyone on the team, so that they work for the same thing and move in the same direction

· Inspiration for employees

· An articulation of retailer values

· Motivation for all employees and stakeholders

When creating vision statements, retailers should answer the following questions:

· What are our values?

· What are we working toward?

· How should we set up our retail climate?

· What image do we want to present to our customers, employees and shareholders?

Vision statements should be updated regularly and should be distributed to everyone affected by them (Morin, 1995). Figure 3.1 provides an example of a mission, vision and values statement. When executed properly, vision and mission statements provide:

· An alignment of everyone on the retail team, so that they work toward the same goals and objectives and move in the same direction.

· An inspiration for employees and other stakeholders.

· An articulation of a retailer's values.

· Motivation for all employees and stakeholders to perform.

After the creation of the mission and vision statements, retailers then turn their attention to the creation of retailing objectives.

Figure 3.1 – Example Mission and Vision Statement

Patagonia

Mission Statement: Build the best product, cause no unnecessary harm, use business to inspire and implement solutions to the environmental crisis.

Our Reason for Being

Patagonia grew out of a small company that made tools for climbers. Alpinism remains at the heart of a worldwide business that still makes clothes for climbing – as well as for skiing, snowboarding, surfing, fly fishing, paddling and trail running. These are all silent sports. None require a motor; none deliver the cheers of a crowd. In each sport, reward comes in the form of hard-won grace and moments of connection between us and nature.

Our values reflect those of a business started by a band of climbers and surfers, and the minimalist style they promoted. The approach we take towards product design demonstrates a bias for simplicity and utility.

For us at Patagonia, a love of wild and beautiful places demands participation in the fight to save them, and to help reverse the steep decline in the overall environmental health of our planet. We donate our time, services and at least 1% of our sales to hundreds of grassroots environmental groups all over the world who work to help reverse the tide.

We know that our business activity – from lighting stores to dyeing shirts – creates pollution as a by-product. So we work steadily to reduce those harms. We use recycled polyester in many of our clothes and only organic, rather than pesticide-intensive, cotton.

Staying true to our core values during thirty-plus years in business has helped us create a company we're proud to run and work for. And our focus on making the best products possible has brought us success in the marketplace.

Source: Patagonia Website (2018) http://www.patagonia.com/company-info.html

Retail Objectives

Mission and vision statements usually are used to create a series of retail objectives (also known as corporate objectives). Retail objectives define actions that the retailer wants to achieve. The difference between goals and objectives is that goals are expressions of general desires where objectives are specific, measurable, and have a time frame. A retailer's goal may be to increase sales, but the objective would state specifically how much the sales increase should be and by when the sales objective will be achieved. Objectives are created to enable managers to measure the success of an integrated retail management plan. In addition, objectives motivate employees. Typically some type of compensation system is put into place for employees, managers and executives who achieve their objectives. This compensation may come in the form of time off, extra pay, trips, stock options, or other rewards for productive work and achieving results.

Retail objectives must be S.M.A.R.T.--specific, measureable, attainable, realistic and time-bound (Doran, 1981). In his book, *Attitude Is Everything*, Paul J. Meyer (2003) describes the characteristics of S.M.A.R.T. objectives:

Specific – A specific objective is clear and unambiguous. The retailer must state what is expected so that everyone in the company knows what's expected. For example, an objective to increase sales is vague. A specific objective would be "to increase sales from $250,000 to $300,000."

Measurable – A measurable objective has concrete criteria to measure progress toward attainment of the objective. An objective that states "obtain more customers" is not measureable because it is not known how many current customers there are and how many should be added. A measureable objective would be to increase the number of customer records in the company database from 75,000 to 125,000.

Source: g-stockstudio/Shutterstock.com

Attainable – An attainable objective is realistic. The objective should not be out of reach and should not be below standard performance. This criterion is more difficult to assess unless you are involved with a retail operation.

Relevant – A relevant objective is one that matters to the retailer. For example, a hair salon retailer manager's objective may be to buy 50 candy bars by 3 P.M. This objective is specific, measureable, and attainable but it is not relevant to the operation. Relevant objectives are determined by the mission or vision. Because the development of objectives may change depending on the environmental scan, often objectives are revised after the situation analysis. A relevant objective for a salon manager may be to decrease the number of dissatisfied customers from five a week to two a week.

Time-bound (sometimes referred to as tangible) – A time-bound objective stresses the important of adding a time frame to the objective so that the retailer focuses on achieving the objective on or before the due date. For example, a S.M.A.R.T. objective would be: To increase sales from $500,000 to $550,000 by December 2017. On January 1, 2018, the retailer can measure if the objective was achieved. In the development of objectives, keep in mind that "if you can't measure it, you can't manage it." Well-developed objectives are critical to the success of the business.

Retail Strategy

The mission, vision, objectives and situation analysis help to develop the retail strategy, depicted by lines that connect the first to boxes in the flow chart. While retail objectives are specific, the retail strategy is the "big picture" of how to achieve the objectives. Typically, the retail strategy covers all areas of the integrated retail management plan (IRM). Normally, when creating a strategy, retailers try and integrate their customers' behaviors, the market area, and technology strategy coupled with a supply chain strategy. Accordingly, the retail strategy is the "game plan" utilized by retailers to achieve their overall objectives and goals (Kotler and Keller, 2012). According to Michael Porter, there are three generic strategies that are excellent as a starting point for strategic thinking (Porter, 1980). These three generic strategies are:

1. Cost Leadership. The idea is to create the lowest possible costs associated with production and distribution. This allows a retailer to grow market share as they underprice the competition. The caveat is, "what will the competition do?" If the competition responds by lowering their prices, you may create a price war and be forced to compete on price. Walmart* has used this strategy effectively.

Source: Dragon Images/Shutterstock.com

2. Differentiation. The retailer must concentrate on creating and achieving superior market performance in areas where customers see benefits. The market must value the retailer's differentiation in order to capture additional market share using this strategy.

3. Focus. This strategy suggests focusing on narrow "targets" or target market segments (marketing segmentation analysis skills are needed). The idea is to create awareness, differentiation and cost leadership within a targeted segment. This eases the costs associated with executing strategies.

Strategies must be dynamic. In essence, "strategies can form as well be formulated" (Mintzberg, 1989). Thus, it is important for a retailer to develop a system of strategic thinking. Strategic thinking is "a way of thinking about customers, competitors, and competitive advantage: (Schnaars, 1991). The overall concept of *strategic thinking* is to utilize the retail mission statement, the vision statement, the environmental scanning analysis, and the situational analysis to understand the environmental forces that affect a retail business. The idea is to be able to create or control the future environment, not just react to it. According to Michael Porter, "Strategy is about making choices, trade-offs; it's about deliberately choosing to be different" (Hammonds, 2001).

In developing a retail strategy, the retail professional needs to keep in mind the customers, the competitors, the capital resources, and the human resources available to execute the strategy. Strategic plans tend to be about a year in length but often can be prepared for longer time periods, such as five or ten years. Long-term plans help the retailer get a better picture of the retail future. The plan may be extended, modified, or terminated depending on its perceived effectiveness.

Overall, a guiding retail strategy is generally made up of two types of variables: controllable and uncontrollable. *Controllable variables* are those areas of the retail operation that can be effectively controlled and changed by retail managers. These may include all management functions, logistics, store locations, product offerings, integrated marketing communication, and to some extent, price. *Uncontrollable variables* may include those environments mentioned in the section on environmental scanning, including the legal, technological, and competitive environments. Other uncontrollable variables include product or service seasonality, product or service obsolescence, and consumers' changing needs and wants.

Relationship between Objectives, Strategy and Tactics

As stated earlier, retailers create integrated retail management plans in order to provide direction to all retail personnel. As such, retailers must utilize the information from within the plan to create their overall strategies and objectives. In retail planning, students often get confused when they have to deal with objectives, strategies and tactics. Each of these areas is created for a specific purpose. Each element also has an important role to play in retail planning. For the purposes of retail planning, each of the following elements, objectives, strategies and planning need to be operationally defined. Thus far we have covered objectives and strategy. *Tactical executions*, or tactics for short, are the day-to-day, operational activities that help retailers achieve their strategy. This is "where the rubber hits the road" for retailers (Ogden and Rarick, 2010). All of the hard work done in planning show results through tactics which help a retailer achieve objectives and, ultimately sales.

Source: Robert Kneschke/Shutterstock.com

When engaged in business and retail planning, it's important to follow the pattern of developing objectives first, then create the strategy or "big picture" idea of how to achieve those objectives, and finally create the tactical executions defining who has the authority and responsibility for managing the executions. The following mnemonic is helpful to remember: *Link Objectives, Strategies and Tactics (LOST).*   Throughout the text, these topics are covered in detail. For now let's continue to build an integrated retail management plan.

The Situational Analysis

Once the mission, vision, and objectives are in place, the retail manager can begin an assessment of the overall retail environment. Because the only constant in the universe is change, retail professionals must prepare for change to occur. Chapter 4 explores situational analysis processes in depth. A *situational (or situation) analysis* examines the internal and external forces that impact an organization. It is conducted to get full understanding on the past and present situation. Included in a situational analysis are subjects such as the history of the company, the retailer's current position in the marketplace, product offerings and a competitive analysis.

Before and during the development of integrated retail management (IRM) plans, retailers must have a thorough knowledge of the environment in which they do business. This information is often incorporated into the situation analysis. Retail managers use a concept called environmental scanning to better understand how changes affect their business. *Environmental scanning* is the process by which businesses monitor the environment searching for changes in that environment that may affect their business operation. Managers use this information to assist in planning and determining future actions (Aguilar, 1967). A manager can respond to trends, customer problems, and opportunities more readily when the retail environment is understood. Ultimately it helps retailers increase customer retention. Additionally, the information allows the retailers to change strategies and new tactics developed for the IRM plans with a focus on the customer. The retailer needs to pay particular attention to any environment that could potentially affect operations. These environments may include social, legal, physical, economic, competitive, political, or technological environments, to name a few. Many retailers pay particular attention to the competitive environment, because competition is a driving force behind environmental change.

Figure 3.2 (next page) illustrates the environments that need to be considered in the process of environmental scanning. The forces affecting the environment come from within the organization (intraorganizational environment), the task being completed (task/mediating environment), and outside the organization (macro environment).

Figure 3.2 – Environmental Scanning

To scan these important environments, the retailer needs to develop a system. The following five-step process is useful in developing a system for environmental scanning:

1. Identify all relevant environments.

2. Look for relevant changes in these environments.

3. Understand and evaluate these changes in terms of their nature, direction, and magnitude.

4. Analyze and forecast the impact and timing of the changes; assess the potential consequences of the changes.

5. Create responses to the environmental changes through changes in strategy.

The retailer can look for environmental changes in newspapers, magazines, the business press, the trade press, trade associations, conferences, trade shows, the Internet, and other types of secondary sources.

The overall idea governing environmental scanning is to identify any environment that may affect the retailer and then forecast the impact of that environmental change. Armed with this information, the successful retail manager can integrate these changes into any plans being developed and create responses to the changes. Thus, the retailer takes a proactive approach to solving problems.

Think of the beverage industry as an example of the impact of the legal and political environments. Many years ago, in response to demands of environmentalists, some states adopted statutes that required a deposit on cans and bottles. To continue to do business in those states, beverage retailers set up systems that would allow for the most cost-efficient method of handling the returned bottles and cans. The retailers developed accounting systems for the cans and bottles. Suppliers and retailers developed physical logistical systems for handling the returned product. In addition, new price points were developed to take into account additional costs for the systems' development.

Now assume you're a beverage company and want to continue to sell in Michigan, Iowa, or any other state that enacted the deposit bill. You would lose competitiveness—sales and market share—if you didn't create and implement the systems prior to the bill's passage in the states' legislative bodies. If, however, you had an environmental scanning system in place, you could decide whether to do business in that state, and if the answer was yes, you would develop the systems necessary to manage all the additional problems. Finally, you might be able to stall the legislation (through lobbying or other methods) until you have your systems in place. As you can see, analyzing the situation is important.

The retail manager must continually look to the retailer's mission and vision statements to identify those environments that have the greatest potential impact on the overall retail operation. The environmental data must be accessible by all of the retailer's decision makers and must be integrated throughout the retail organization.

Bottle Bills and the Beverage Industry

Prior to World War II, the beverage industry required deposits on beverage containers so that glass bottles would be returned. The bottles were then washed, refilled, and resold. After World War II, cans replaced bottles, first in the beer industry. With the advent of the 1960s, the soft-drink industry followed with "no-deposit, no-return" bottles and cans. Because beverage companies were no longer reusing cans and bottles, a marked increase in litter resulted. Consequently, environmentalists proposed bottle bills in their state legislatures. Bottle bills placed a mandatory refundable deposit on beer and soft-drink containers.

In 1970, British Columbia enacted the first beverage container recovery system in North America. In 1971, Oregon was the first state in the United States to pass a bottle bill requiring deposits on beer and soft-drink containers. As of 2017, ten U.S. states/territories and all but one of the Canadian provinces have some type of bottle law.

Some benefits of bottle bills include reduced litter and conservation of natural resources by reducing the amount of solid waste that gets sent to landfills. Another benefit, according to the Container Recycling Institute, is the creation of jobs in the retail, distribution, and recycling sectors. Bottle bills also encourage producer and consumer responsibility.

Sources: Bottle Bill Resource Guide, retrieved from http://www.bottlebill.org/ The Ten Cent Incentive to Recycle," Container Recycling Institute, 1997, retrieved from www.container-recycling.org/publications/tencent/tencentintro.html.

Retail Information Systems

Data needed to develop an effective retail strategy can, in part, be generated from the situational analysis, mission statement, and vision statement. In addition, the integration of a *retail information system (RIS),* in which all data are gathered, stored, turned into useful information, and disseminated to employees and managers, can be a powerful tool in the development of the retail strategy. The RIS is a powerful tool for retailers because it is where all proprietary information is stored. The RIS can help a retailer define and redefine a target market as well as help a retailer to understand customer behavior by examining trends in the data.

Retail information systems are created and used to generate data and information for retail decision makers such as retail strategists and tactical specialists. For example, in 2013, Par Tech, Inc. announced the creation of a new point of sale (POS) terminal target to independent and small chain restaurants with limited budgets (Par Introduces..., 2013). The devices offer touch screen capabilities that speed the handling of orders and customer information.

Example of a point of sale terminal used to generate orders and accept payment information. Source: Par Tech, Inc.

Retrieved from http://mms.businesswire.com/bwapps/mediaserver/ViewMedia?mgid=356177&vid=5&download=1

In this information age, retail information is critical to survival for retailers. The RIS can be manual or electronic. Most large retailers prefer to generate and disseminate their data electronically, although manual systems are still in use, primarily by smaller retailers.

Source: Andrey_Popov/Shutterstock.com

A good RIS provides data based on marketing research undertaken by the retailer. The data can be primary or secondary. *Primary data* are generated specifically to solve some problem. *Secondary data* have already been collected and analyzed in another context and are *not* gathered to solve a particular problem. Consider television advertising. To create advertising prices, advertising agencies rely on secondary data collected by Nielsen Media Research, Inc. (www.nielsenmedia.com). Nielsen gathers viewership patterns and demographic data about viewers to help television stations and networks set a price for the air space they sell to agencies and ultimately to the retailer.

Target Marketing

Retailers do not have enough time or money to effectively sell to all customers in the world, and retailers cannot carry all products and services wanted or needed by consumers. To deal with these constraints, retailers must target their markets to match their products and services to consumers most likely to buy them. This is the idea behind developing a target market. There are four characteristics of a target market (Pride and Ferrell, 2003):

1. Consumers must have a need or desire for a particular product or service. If they do not, that consumer group (without a need or desire) is not part of the market.

2. Consumers must have the ability to purchase the product or service. Ability to purchase depends on the consumer's buying power. The consumer must also be physically able to make the purchase by having access to a bricks-and-mortar store or a credit card or PayPal account to use when shopping online.

3. Consumers must be willing to use their buying power to buy a retailer's products/services.

4. Consumers must have the authority to make the purchase of specific goods and services.

Target marketing is the process of identifying and attempting to reach people with a company's marketing efforts.

Customer Segmentation

To assess how large or small the market may be, the retail professional should count the number of potential end users. The best way to do this may be to count repeat customers. Utilizing superior marketing and retailing techniques, the retailer can usually get the consumer to try a product or service for the first time. Only after the consumer has used the product does the retailer know if she or he will continue to purchase or decide not to repurchase. Retailers often choose between segmentation and a mass marketing to reach their target market.

In *mass marketing* a retailer tries to reach the entire market with the same marketing strategy. The discount retailer, Target, uses a mass marketing strategy to reach their customers. *Customer segmentation* is the process of breaking down a retailer's entire target market into smaller subgroups or segments. The segments should be based upon a consumer's buying habits. Each segment should have buyers that are similar in buying behavior. There should be differences in buying behaviors between the segments. So the subgroups are homogenous (similar) within the segments and heterogeneous (different) between segments with regard to customer behaviors. When a retailer defines a segment, it then develops a marketing plan to reach that segment. A retailer can concentrate on one segment or multiple segments. Reaching multiple segments is more expensive because customers get their information in different ways. Thus a separate marketing plan and integrated communication plan is needed for each segment. Because of this, retailers only choose the number of segments that the budget allows. Segmentation allows retailers to align products and services with target customers and to take advantage of the customer response differences to a given retail plan or marketing mix. When creating market segments from the overall target market, retailers must be careful to create segments that are:

1. Profitable

2. Have a fairly large number of consumers within the segment

3. Sustainable over time which means that people in the segment won't change their response behaviors over a long period of time

4. Have identifiable characteristics that allow retailers to understand and reach the market segment

Source: Billion Photos/Shutterstock.com

Retailers typically use a segmentation strategy to customize products and solutions and better reach the segment with meaningful messages. Gap, Inc is a worldwide retailer with a family of retail brands that include Old Navy, Gap, Banana Republic, Athleta, and Intermix. Each store brand targets a particular segment of the overall target market. Old Navy targets families that want value-priced clothing. Gap targets the middle- to upper-class consumer, ages 17 – 25. Banana Republic positions itself as affordable luxury and targets a more affluent consumer. Athleta targets active women who want performance and sports apparel. Intermix is a boutique retailer that carries women's luxury clothing and accessories. Gap further segments the market through retail brands such as GapKids, GapBody and babyGap. Gap, Inc must customize the product offerings to best serve the needs of their segments.

When retailers are creating segments, they need to create bases or criteria that will allow them to identify the consumers in each segment. They can identify these consumers by constructing *typical customer profiles* for each target segment. The typical profile contains a few descriptive phrases of the typical customer for each segment and often a name of a fictional person is used to represent the entire segment. For example a typical customer profile for babyGap may be stated as: Kari is a first-time mother who is seeking comfortable, value-priced clothing that is stylish. She is a married, middle-income customer with a college education. In her spare time she enjoys reading, travel and spending time with her family. The retailer then takes the typical customer profile and uses it to create a marketing program for the segment of people that are similar to the typical customer profile. There are many tools that can be used to help segment the target market. These tools help retailers in plan their marketing executions.

Market and Location Selection

The next task in developing a good understanding of the market is to generate research for decisions about location of the retail business. The market and location selection information is generally found within the section on target markets in the retailer's integrated retail management plan. This decision is based on information from the situational analysis, the mission and vision statements, and the RIS. A retailer must decide how many stores or facilities are needed and whether or not the location will be brick-and-mortar only, on the Internet only, or a combination of both (bricks and clicks). These decisions are vital for the retailer in generating competitive advantage and in making sound investments when it comes to purchasing expensive physical property. Chapter 7 covers store location in greater depth.

Source: Monkey Business Images/Shutterstock.com

Financial Operations Management

Operations management refers to the ability of the retailer to efficiently manage all of the functions necessary in running a retail business. Financial operations management is difficult because the task of turning ideas and concepts into numbers and then turning numbers back into useful information is quite challenging. In reality, there is no significance in the number 6, for example. The vital information lies in what that number 6 represents and what it implies for the big picture. To effectively control financial operations, the retailer must understand both accounting and finance concepts.

Financial operations concepts range from asset management to budgeting. By thoroughly understanding and managing financial operations, the retail manager can then undertake resource allocation to make the integrated retail plan highly efficient and effective. Keep in mind that the financial operations plan *must* be integrated into all other areas of the retail plan. Because resources are often limited, the retailer must use every last resource effectively and efficiently.

Source: Andrey_Popov/Shutterstock.com

The financial operations plan includes many statements that are important to the retail business. The retailer may use these statements to show the major stakeholders how well the business is doing at any point in time. The retailer must at a minimum satisfy the wants and needs of its stakeholders (or the owners), including the retail management hierarchy, the employees, the Internal Revenue Service, and the customers. Financial operations management entails complex decision making. Based on these decisions, the retailer must implement an overall integrated retail management plan. Typical decision-making issues may pertain to the format of a retail outlet; the size and physical layout of a store; and the allocation of sales space, warehouse space, and office space. These important decisions are at least in some part based on the overall financial operations plan.

Inventories are managed through the use of inventory planning. Thus, the financial operations management plan is directly tied to the additional logistical decisions that retail managers must make. Through a logical and well-integrated flow, the retailer will be able to develop effective merchandise buying and handling strategies centered around the financial operation of the retail business.

Merchandise Buying and Handling/Logistics

Although merchandise management may include financial operations, because of its importance it is treated as a special topic within the textbook. *Merchandise buying and handling* includes the physical purchase of products and services and how those products and services are brought to the retail outlet, handled, and finally placed ready for sale. The price of a product or service has an impact on the retailer's ability to "move" its inventory and should be integrated into merchandise buying and selling.

Within the scope of merchandise buying and selling is the concept of logistics. *Logistics* is defined by the Council of Supply Chain Management Professionals (2013) as "The process of planning, implementing, and controlling procedures for the efficient and effective transportation and storage of goods including services, and related information from the point of origin to the point of consumption for the purpose of conforming to customer requirements. This definition includes inbound, outbound, internal, and external movements." Simply stated, logistics is every action taken to ensure that products and services get from the point of origin to the final consumer.

The Council of Supply Chain Management Professionals defines supply chain management as:

> "Supply Chain Management encompasses the planning and management of all activities involved in sourcing and procurement, conversion, and all logistics management activities. Importantly, it also includes coordination and collaboration with channel partners, which can be suppliers, intermediaries, third-party service providers, and customers. In essence, supply chain management integrates supply and demand management within and across companies. Supply Chain Management is an integrating function with primary responsibility for linking major business functions and business processes within and across companies into a cohesive and high-performing business model. It includes all of the logistics management activities noted above, as well as manufacturing operations, and it drives coordination of processes and activities with and across marketing, sales, product design, finance and information technology." (Supply Chain Management Terms and Glossary, 2013).

Many view supply chain management as a strategic process, whereas logistics is more of a tactical process. In conjunction with executing an excellent logistical plan and having an effective management system for the supply chain, the retailer needs to pay particular attention to inventory, order processing, and fulfillments. Finally, decisions about transportation, storage, and additional warehousing issues must be made in this section of the integrated retail management plan.

Merchandise buying and handling also refers to the decisions the retailer makes about the companies from which it will purchase. What kind of system would allow for purchasing products in the most convenient yet most economical manner? In addition, the retailer must determine where to buy inventory and how to evaluate the sources of supply for the retail outlet. Good negotiation skills are important when trying to get the best deal possible for products.

Think about the purchase of a car. How do you get the best deal for the car you want? Through up-front negotiation. In the majority of cases, by paying the least amount of money possible during the purchase

Source: Benjamin Haas/Shutterstock.com

phase, you save a lot of future money (i.e., less interest, lower fees, a shorter financing period). The result is the same when the retailer buys inventory: the less that is paid up front, the greater the savings that are realized. These savings can be passed on to the customer or reinvested into the retail operations.

As the supplies come in, the retailer has to make sure they are all accounted for and in good working condition. The retailer must also mark the products to verify how much product is on hand and must stock the products to make them available to customers.

Human Resource Management

After the logistical plan has been developed, the human resource element of the retail operation must be planned and managed. The overall job of the retail professional when it comes to human resource management is to make sure all employees are working toward the same goals, are working as a team, and are experiencing job satisfaction. The retailer must reward those employees who are contributing the most to the organization and eliminate or retrain employees who are performing below expectations. Because of the many tasks involved in retailing (see Table 3.1), human resource management is integrated throughout all operations. Additional coverage of human resource management appears in Chapter 10.

The key to human resource management is to ensure that the retailer's objectives are met. The best way to achieve objectives is by ensuring customer satisfaction (or, better yet, exceeding expectations), employee satisfaction, and stakeholder satisfaction. Human resource management is key to achieving the organization's goals in a timely, efficient, and effective manner.

Table 3.1 Selected Typical Retailing Tasks

• Selling Merchandise	• Inventory control
• Selling Services	• Theft control
• Demand analysis and forecasting	• Supplier contacts
• Research	• Negotiations
• Shipping	• Cash receipts
• Receiving and handling merchandise	• Customer service
• Delivery	• Merchandise marking
• Credit operations	• Integrated marketing communications management
• Reverse logistics (merchandise returns)	• Pricing
• Supply chain management	

Retail Tactics

Included in the final sections of an effective integrated retail management plan is the plan's execution, also known as tactics or tactical executions. The planning process moves systematically toward the overall execution of the IRM plan. In retailing, there are three main tactical areas: pricing, integrated marketing communications (IMC), and customer service.

The tactical executions must be integrated, or they will lose their effectiveness. Many of the tactical areas can also be used for retail differentiation, thus becoming a strategic element. For example, pricing tactics really are a reflection of the retailer's strategic decision regarding the level of retailing in which to become involved; that is, discount retailers offer low prices, and upscale retailers charge higher prices. Thus, the executions must be carefully planned and must follow the various retail strategies that have been developed. It is imperative that seamless integration be achieved during these executions. The following sections cover the three tactical areas in more detail.

Pricing

In each of the tactical execution phases, planning is undertaken just as in the overall IRM plan. Each tactical plan should include the same three areas used in the overall retail management plan: objectives, strategy, and tactics. Retail pricing includes the development of a pricing policy. A *pricing policy(ies)* refers to the method(s) used by a business to guide price setting for products and services that will be sold. Each decision about price must be integrated and synergistic with the rest of the retail plan and retail variables. Decisions regarding pricing objectives generally are based on sales, profits, return on investment (ROI), or cash flow. The objectives should be outlined and a price policy developed based on all of the objectives.

Source: bokmok/Shutterstock.com

Once the objectives and policies are in place, an overall pricing strategy can be developed. That strategy should give direction to all decisions made regarding the pricing variable. The strategy should help the retailer determine which types of tactics are appropriate.

The tactics are developed based on the objectives, policies, and strategy for the pricing variable. A section should be included in the IRM plan that covers any necessary price adjustments (markups, markdowns, discounts, and so on) that will be made periodically during the duration of the retail plan.

Integrated Marketing Communications (IMC)

Integrated marketing communications (IMC), often referred to as marketing communications or MARCOM, comprise all the tactics used to reach the retailer's targeted audience. The IMC mix is generally made up of any communication variables, including public relations, branding, publicity, direct marketing, Internet marketing, personal selling, sales promotion, and advertising. To ensure continuity, the IMC plan must be integrated within itself and with the other retail management variables. Objectives, strategy, and tactics are necessary to create the synergy and integration needed to carry out all of these functions.

Customer Service

Customer services are anything a retailer provides in addition to the core product or service that adds value (Pride and Ferrell, 2003). Customer service concepts will be discussed in detail in Chapter 13. For now, it is important to know that customer service tactics are crucial to the retailer's success. In e-tailing, customer service is essential to keep customers happy with their orders and to maintain a high level of customer response management (CRM).

As with the other tactical executions (IMC and price), the retailer must develop a plan for the execution of customer service, and this plan should follow the objectives, strategy, and tactics of the business.

Laws and Ethics

A *law* is "a rule established by authority, society, or custom" (The Free Dictionary, 2013). *Ethics* involves "systematizing, defending, and recommending concepts of right and wrong behavior" (Internet Encyclopedia of Philosophy, 2013). The laws and ethics governing the retailer's markets should guide all retail plans and actions. International retailing poses special issues; the retailer must be familiar with the laws, ethics, and customs of the places it does business. The retailer involved in e-tailing must be familiar with the numerous laws governing online business practices. Because the advent of e-tailing is relatively recent, laws relating to e-commerce are still being developed.

Any retailer conducting interstate commerce is bound not only by local and state laws but by many national laws as well. The federal government has restrictions on how firms may conduct business, as do regional, state, and local authorities. Retailers involved only in intrastate commerce are not subject to most federal regulations, but they must still operate under regional, local, and state laws.

Finally, many trade associations impose a code of ethics on their members. Members of these groups must follow the codes of ethics to maintain their memberships in good standing. Figure 3.4 shows a typical code of ethics for retailers. (In-depth coverage of laws and ethics as they pertain to retailing appears in Chapter 14.)

Figure 3.4: Typical Code of Ethics

Advance Auto Parts, Inc. Code of Ethics & Business Conduct

Honesty
We must be honest and truthful in all of our dealings and relationships with our customers, our vendors, our stockholders, our fellow Team Members and any other person or entity with whom we come into contact.

Fair Dealing
We must be fair and professional in all of our business dealings, including our dealings with our customers, our vendors and suppliers, our fellow Team Members and our competitors. We must never take advantage of anyone we do business with through manipulation, concealment, misuse of confidential information, giving or accepting bribes or kickbacks, antitrust violations, misrepresentation of material facts or any other unfair or dishonest business practice.

Respect and Teamwork
Working as a team, we must treat each of our Team Members, customers, vendors, suppliers and any other parties with whom we do business with dignity and respect. Team Members must be provided a work environment that is safe and free from discrimination or harassment of any type. Advance strictly prohibits discrimination on the basis of race, color, religion, sex, age, national origin, disability, sexual orientation, gender identity or any other legally protected status.

Compliance With Laws
We must comply with all federal, state and local laws and regulations that apply to our business, including insider trading laws. If there is any uncertainty about what is required by the law or our company policies, further guidance should be sought without delay.

Accurate Company Records and Public Disclosure
All company information and records, financial or otherwise, and all company disclosures and public communications must accurately reflect transactions and events, be consistently applied, and conform to both required accounting and reporting principles and Advance Auto Parts' systems of internal controls and policies.

Conflicts of Interest

Business decisions must be based on the best interests of Advance Auto Parts and its stockholders, and may not be motivated by personal considerations or relationships. Team Members are required to disclose to their supervisors any transaction or relationship that may create an actual or perceived conflict of interest. Officers and directors are required to disclose to the Chair of the Nominating and Corporate Governance Committee of the Board of Directors or our General Counsel any transaction or relationship that may create an actual or perceived conflict of interest.

Corporate Opportunities

Team Members, officers and directors are prohibited from (a) taking for themselves personally any business opportunities that are discovered through the use of company property, information or position, (b) inappropriate use of company property, information or position for personal gain, and/or (c) competing with Advance Auto Parts.

Confidential and Proprietary Information

We must properly use and protect the confidential and proprietary information of Advance Auto Parts, as well as that of our customers, our fellow Team Members, and our vendors and other business partners. Only those Team Members with a "need to know" should have access to confidential company information. Confidential information may only be disclosed to third parties as authorized or legally mandated.

Protection of Company Assets

We must protect the assets of the company from loss, theft, damage, carelessness and waste. Company assets and property may only be used for legitimate business purposes and with proper authorization and notice.

Source: Advance Auto Parts, Inc – Code of Ethics and Business Conduct (2017). Retrieved from
http://phx.corporate-ir.net/phoenix.zhtml?c=130560&p=irol-govConduct

Evaluation and Control

Perhaps the most important part of the integrated retail management plan is planning for effective evaluation and control. By continuous monitoring of the retail plan, retail managers can help to ensure the implementation of the plan is performing up to expectations. If the performance does not meet expectations, the company management can take steps to control the situation. Perhaps the easiest way to assess the plan's effectiveness is by examining the objectives. If the objectives were not achieved, something may be wrong with the plan. Perhaps the objectives were set too high, or perhaps the environment changed and wasn't effectively monitored.

As a student, you can measure your classroom objectives by looking at your grades throughout the semester. If you created an objective of getting an A in your retail management class, it would be wise to see if you are achieving that objective by referring to the grades you received on exams, papers, and presentations. Did you ace that all-important semester project? At the end of the semester, if you find that you didn't get an A, you need to evaluate why. Was it because you didn't study enough? Or did you study the wrong material? Maybe you didn't attend classes regularly. Whatever the reason, you need to evaluate the outcome.

After evaluating your success or failure and figuring out the reasons for any unmet objectives, you need to modify your plan to make sure you will succeed in the future. The control in the class situation would be either to increase your study time and attendance or to lower your objective to a more reasonable and achievable level---such as setting the goal of getting a B or C.

Retailers must do the same thing: They must evaluate whether their objectives were too high or whether they failed in the execution of their integrated retail management plan.

Another method of control for retailers is the development of a contingency plan. A contingency plan consists of alternative strategies or tactics to achieve the stated objectives. Contingency plans are used if the preferred strategies or tactics are hampered by uncontrollable environmental changes. The retailer must be able to respond to events such as power outages, changes in the economy, supplier bankruptcies, price wars, natural disasters, and so on.

It is essential to include all elements of the integrated retail management plan when assessing the performance of the business. For example, the forecasts should be rechecked. The IMC tactics should be scrutinized. The environmental scanning undertaken during the planning period should be examined in case any environmental changes have occurred.

Source: ImageFlow/Shutterstock.com

Many formal tools are available to help retailers evaluate and control. Many of the methods are quantitative techniques, but several qualitative techniques exist as well. For example, focus groups can be used to check for mistakes in execution and to gain valuable insights into how the retailer is perceived. Information gathered for the RIS is important, as are data generated from the execution of the customer service variable. Certainly the financial statements would be helpful in assessing the success of the retail establishment.

Because of the tremendous costs associated with the development of the integrated retail management plan, evaluation and control are not options---they are requirements. Proactive plans help keep the retailer competitive in today's retail environment.

Summary

Planning is crucial in today's retail environment. A comprehensive integrated retail management plan (IRM) is necessary to contain costs and generate the highest revenues possible.

The IRM plan starts with the mission and vision statements. The mission statement describes what the company does and the vision statement states future goals. The situational analysis provides a historical and current picture of the business, its competitors, and its potential growth. A retail strategy is developed based on the mission, vision, and situational analysis. The strategy provides guidance on how the objectives will be achieved. Retail information systems (RIS) are used to collect and disseminate data and information to employees and managers.

The customers to whom a retailer aims its marketing efforts are collectively called the *target market*. Along with determining the target market, a retailer must decide where to locate the business and whether to have an online presence. Merchandise buying and handling involve decisions related to the purchase of the products and how the products (or services) will be delivered to the final customer. Human resource management decisions establish who will run the day-to-day activities of the retailer. Retail tactics are comprised of three areas: pricing, the determination of the prices of products and services; integrated marketing communications (IMC), the coordination of all communication regarding the retailer and its products and services; and customer service, the decisions about which value-added services geared toward meeting and exceeding expectations are offered.

Decisions regarding laws and ethics occur at all phases of the IRM process. Local, state, national, and in some cases international regulations may dictate present and future action. To monitor the IRM plan, retailers need to set up an effective evaluation and control system. A good evaluation and control system, when applied to the plan step by step, will save the successful retailer additional costs in both time and money.

Key Terms

controllable variables	Those areas of the retail operation that can be effectively controlled and changed by retail managers.
customer services	Anything a retailer provides in addition to the core product or service that adds value.
environmental scanning	A systematic process whereby the retailer acquires and uses information to assist in the management and planning of future actions.
ethics	Concepts of right and wrong behavior.
Integrated retail management planning	The establishment of objectives, policies, and procedures to carry out goals set by retail managers.
law	A rule established by authority, society, or custom.
mass marketing approach	An approach in which the retailer utilizes one unique marketing mix to try to capture the market.
merchandise buying and han-dling	The physical purchase of products and services and how those products and services are brought to the retail outlet, handled, and finally placed ready for sale.
mission statement	A statement that explains why the firm is in business, what it does, and what it stands for.
operations management	The management of all of the functions necessary in running the retail business.
planning	The establishment of objectives, policies, and procedures to carry out goals.
pricing policy	Refers to the methods used by a business to guide price setting for products and ser-vices that will be sold.
primary data	Data that have been generated specifically to solve a problem.
retail (corporate) objectives	Define actions that the retailer wants to achieve.
retail information system (RIS)	A system in which data are gathered and stored, turned into useful information, and disseminated to employees and managers to assist in making retail decisions.
retail or corporate objectives	Goals that are for a medium-length term and provide measurable statements.
retail strategy	A plan that provides the retail decision maker with a framework for current and future actions and dictates how objectives will be achieved.
secondary data	Data that have already been collected and analyzed.
segmentation	The process of breaking up the target market into more controllable subgroups.
segmented approach	An approach in which the retailer breaks up the mass market into submarkets (called *segments*) and then develops a unique marketing mix for each segment.
strategic thinking	Utilization of the retail mission statement, the vision statement, the environmental scanning results, and the situational analysis to understand the environmental forces that affect a retail business.
supply chain management	The coordination of the functions and tactics across business functions within a com-pany and across businesses within the supply chain for the purposes of improving the long-term performance of the individual companies and the supply chain as a whole.
tactical executions	The day-to-day operational activities that implement the strategic plan.
target marketing	is the process of identifying and attempting to reach people with a company's market-ing efforts.
typical customer profile	A description of a retailer's most frequent customers.

uncontrollable variables	Those areas of the retail operation that cannot be controlled by retail managers.
vision statement	A statement that focuses on the firm's future goals.

Discussion Questions

1. Explain the purpose of a mission statement and a vision statement. Why it is important for a company to have a mission? Why must it have a vision?

2. What is the difference between strategy and tactics? Is one more important than the other?

3. When would a retailer engage in environmental scanning? What types of information might a retailer of women's accessories gather?

4. Why is it important for retailers to have an integrated retail management plan? What are characteristics of a good IRM plan?

5. What information is included in an effective definition of a retailer's target market?

6. Why is the evaluation and control function important in the implementation of a retail plan?

Exercises

1. Go to the Free People website at www.freepeople.com and navigate the site. Based on the contents of the site, how would you describe the target market?

2. Choose a retailer that has a website, and using the IRM flow chart as a guide, answer the following questions:

- How does the retailer approach each area in the IRM flow chart?
- How do you think the company performs evaluation and control of its strategy?
- In what areas could the company improve?

Case

Guilford Home Furnishings

Guilford Home Furnishings (GHF) was founded in 1961 as a manufacturer of upholstered furniture. Originally its business model was a traditional one: a manufacturer that sold to retailers through a group of self-employed manufacturers' representatives. In the late 1970s, when credit was very tight, the firm went through a cash flow crisis as retailers stretched payments out to 120 days and, in many instances, even longer. This was when Lisa and Scott Guilford's father, Karl, who was the primary stockholder and president at the time, made the momentous decision to open a factory outlet. Though very damaging to his trade relations—his largest retailer dropped the Guilford line--the gambit paid off with an immediate improvement in GHF's cash position.

At this time, Guilford also added private-label bedding to the line and several years later further complemented it with bedroom suites and kitchen sets manufactured in South Carolina. GHF's price points were set for the budget-conscious consumer and were considered the most competitive in the five-county area. Increasingly, customers came from out of state to buy GHF furniture.

Recently GHF had seen many large retailers move into the market. They built huge showrooms, carried multiple lines hitting several price points, and hired aggressive salespeople who derived most of their income from commissions rather than salary. Some of these operations had after-sale service that took care of repairs. Most of their advertising took the form of inserts in the Sunday newspapers as well as innovative, if not occasionally downright quirky, television spots.

Chapter 4

The Retail Environment:
A Situational and Competitive Analysis

"The one who adapts his policy to the times prospers, and likewise that the one whose policy clashes with the demands of the times does not."

~ Niccolo Machiavelli

Source: Syda Productions/Shutterstock.com

CHAPTER OBJECTIVES

After completing this chapter you will be able to:

- Describe the information that constitutes a situational analysis.
- Define the various types of retail establishments by ownership, merchandise type, and census classifications.
- Explain the purpose of methods such as NAICS and classification of retailers by ownership and merchandise type.
- Describe the elements that constitute a competitive analysis.

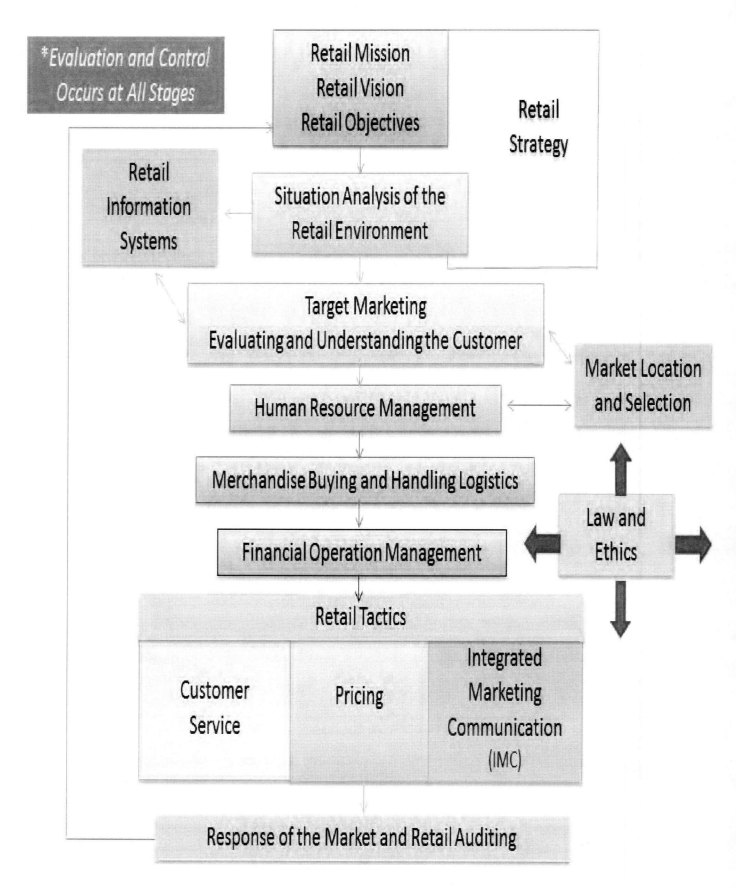

Burberry Reacts to Changing Environment

Source: Sorbis/Shutterstock.com

Burberry is a British luxury brand that manufacturers and retails clothing, fragrances, and fashions internationally. The company was started by Thomas Burberry in 1856. Over the years, the company has had to adapt to many changes occurring in the various environments that affected the firm. The company's name was originally Burberry but, after the public kept calling the company Burberry's, the name changed to reflect customer preferences. The original name was restored in 1999. Many of the actions taken by the company are a result of the changing environment. In 1914, the trench coat was created to help the War Department clothe soldiers. After the war the coat became popular with the public and today the trench coat is still popular (burberryplc.com). Starting with the 1970s the brand became more popular with sports and middle class segments, thus expanding the brand's reach (Day, 2004).

Burberry sold its brands to retailers until 2006 when the company launched a website for customers to purchase its products directly. In 2011, Burberry expanded its marketing channels and used social media to launch its fragrance called Body. The company used the marketing budget to promote the perfume on Facebook. Customers were encouraged to "like" the product on Facebook, in return for customer details. Based on the campaign, the company mailed samples to 250,000 customers. The brand also has a Twitter following of over 750,000 people. Microblogging sites such as Sina Weibo in China and music network Douban are used to promote Burberry products as well (Getting the measure..., 2012).

According to Duncan Taylor, director of product management for Epicor's Store Solutions, mobile devices likely will be a primary tool for shopping on retail websites in the next several years (Binns, 2010). Burberry is a global brand, so their social media efforts must expand beyond the U.S. to include China's WeChat and other international social media (Smilansky, 2017). Smartphone companies like Samsung and Apple will play a significant role in connecting consumers with retailers. If a retailer knows that e-commerce is the fastest growing retail channel, the retailer can take steps to create a strong presence.

Introduction

To effectively manage the retail business, the professional retailer must be aware of the environment in which the business operates. As stated in the previous chapter, it is essential that the retailer understand the current business situation as well as the environment that will affect that retail business. This chapter focuses on these issues. The chapter begins with an overview of a situational analysis, then discusses classification systems for retail businesses, and concludes with a look at some methods for undertaking a competitive analysis. Achieving a clear understanding of the overall retail operation enables the retailer to make better decisions regarding the executions of the integrated retail management (IRM) plan.

The Situational Analysis

The situational analysis of a retail organization provides the big picture: an overview of the company. Several things must be considered as inputs into the situational analysis. The analysis should include a product/service history and evaluation. It should analyze the competition and assess the geographical aspects of retail locations. Finally, the situational analysis should examine current consumers. A listing of the strengths and weaknesses of the retailer's product(s) or service(s) is often included to strengthen the analysis. Specifically, a SWOT (**s**trengths/**w**eaknesses/**o**pportunities/**t**hreats) helps to identify options.

Company Analysis

The *company analysis* should include as much of the following data as possible:

- Sales and profit figures
- Company mission and vision
- Risk position (risk oriented or more conservative)
- Corporate (or organizational) resources, including, but not limited to, financial, technological, and human
- Aggressiveness
- Market share
- Sales trends

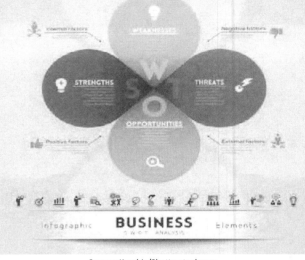

Source: Kraphix/Shutterstock.com

In addition, the following information is very useful in developing an effective retailing plan:

- What are the various environments (social, political, technological, cultural, economic, legal, natural, etc.) that may affect the company and the retailing plan execution?
- Within the industry, what have been the overall trends in sales?
- Within the industry, what have been the overall trends in market share?
- What business practices are used in the industry?
- Will major upcoming events influence the product or service?

This analysis should be in-depth but concise.

Source: Rawpixel.com/Shutterstock.com

Product History and Analysis

A product history and analysis records product successes and failures. Much of the necessary data may be found within the company itself. The retail manager or planner should understand how and why all the retailing mix variables fit together. Often these variables have been developed over time. No decisions should be made in a vacuum. Retail strategy and tactics (product, price, channels of distribution, and integrated marketing communications [IMC]) should be integrated and should match the firm's character. The following pieces of information are necessary to develop an effective product analysis:

- Product/service background
- Current problems facing the product, brand, or service
- Past retail successes or failures
- Past years' budgets and financial statements
- Past to present media spending

In addition, there should be a product evaluation that includes (but is not limited to) the following information:

- What is the quality of the product or service?
- How is the product or service differentiated?
- What aspects constitute the "total product"? (The total product concept includes the physical product or service, the benefits offered by the retailer, the needs/wants satisfiers that the company fulfills, and the retail brand and image.)
- What has been added or deleted from the product or service line over the past five years? What will be added or deleted in the future?
- How do intermediaries (wholesalers and other suppliers) feel about the retailer and its products?
- Is distribution effective? What type of distribution system is utilized? Is distribution intensive, selective, or exclusive?

Source: Irina Barilo/Shutterstock.com

- What problems have consumers experienced? How can these problems be addressed and/or corrected?
- What features and benefits of the retailer are unique? Are there features that differ sufficiently from the competitions to allow for adequate differentiation? Specifically, how is differentiation achieved (if at all)?
- How do consumers perceive the retailer (e.g., high tech, old fashioned, modern, trendy)?
- Are customers satisfied?
- What are the company's return policies?
- Are warranties or guarantees offered?
- How wide is the product selection?

Each individual situational analysis dictates a need for either more or less information. This information is found by conducting primary research; thus, a large amount of consumer testing is used to generate data necessary to answer certain questions. The goal is to develop a clear picture of the current retail environment using the data gathered in the situation analysis.

Selecting Channels for Today's Customers

Today's customers are knowledgeable about the products and services they want to purchase. In addition, there are more and more activities that consume their time. Savvy retailers understand consumer behavior and develop strategies and tactics that engage customers and make it easy to shop and buy products and services. Because of the changes in the retail marketplace, customer needs affect a retail organization in many ways, ranging from the company website (organization, design and navigational models) to the physical stores (ease of entry, correct product mix, etc.). These marketing changes blur the traditional channels of distribution for retailers. It has become both a science and an art to match the best sales channel with the right consumers. Traditional retail channels used to be simple to create, and the retailer's market was easy to identify. Retailers had distinct customer bases and used a simple value proposition to reach those customers. In this section, we describe the major channels of distribution, including brick and mortar, online and other channels which give retailers options to reach customers. Retailers can leverage one or many channels to reach their customers, but the trend is toward the integration of several channels thus giving the rise to omni-channel retailing.

Brick and Mortar Retailers

The brick-and-mortar channel offers many benefits to customers that they may not be able to get through the other channels. The biggest advantage of a brick-and-mortar store is the ability to create an experience for the consumer. For example, when one enters a Cabela's store, it is evident that the retailer is more than a place to sell products. Cabela's is laid out and merchandised as if it's a museum of natural history. The stores have a large aquarium that houses local fish. In addition, most stores have a Cabela's Mountain that showcases many different (stuffed) animals that can be found around the world and many near the Cabela's location. Cabela's also has a catalog presence; however, the focus of the catalog is the breadth and depth of the merchandise offerings, not the entertainment value offered in-store.

In addition to an experience, brick-and-mortar retailers offer instant gratification of purchases. The customer buys the merchandise and owns it instantaneously. He/she doesn't have to wait for the items to be shipped home or for a phone call telling the consumer the item is ready for pick-up.

Brick-and-mortar retailers have the ability to provide personal service, a very important tactic for retailers as it allows them to create relationships with their customer base. Retail clerks and other sales representatives can offer ideas to customers in terms of the latest fashions. They can tell a customer if the clothes the customer is looking to purchase match. They can offer advice on electronics and which cables work the best to transmit digital images. The sales associate is often seen as an expert. For new, high-end, or complicated purchases, sales associates can be especially helpful.

Touch me, *feel* me experiences are available in stores. Retailers have an opportunity to stimulate all their customers' senses by allowing customers to try on products, play with the new video games, make calls from a new phone, smell bakery items, try out a new camera, see actual colors and textures, and sit in a room with surround sound.

There are many customers who prefer to pay in cash instead of credit. Brick-and-mortar stores are the main channel that allows cash payments. In addition, brick-and-mortar stores have the advantage of reducing risk. Customers don't have to worry as much about orders being delayed, out-of-stock, or lost in the mail as they can go directly back to the store and exchange their item if it's defective or if it doesn't fit. Finally, when people come into a retail store they may only have a basic, general idea of what they want to purchase. Many items purchased at a physical retail store are impulse items, or items the consumer didn't plan on buying. Thus, customers come to a physical store to see what types of products are available to buy—that is, the customers browse the retailer's store in search of product and service ideas. Although there has been a trend toward virtual browsing and browsing through catalogs, consumers still prefer the ability to browse in a physical location.

The main disadvantage to a physical store is that only people who come to the store can buy products from the retailer, limiting the market in which the retailer can operate. Another disadvantage is the time it takes for a customer to get to the store. Many people don't have the time or desire to expend time traveling and shopping. Finally, although mobile technology makes price comparisons easier, it is more difficult to compare prices in a physical store.

e-Tailing

e-Tailing has helped retailers achieve multiple-channel retailing. In addition, there has been convergence between traditional and online retailers such that online and catalog retailers have acquired some brick-and-mortar properties (i.e., Amazon, Cabela's, and Victoria's Secret) and traditional brick-and-mortar retailers have adopted e-tailing. Some of the advantages of e-tailing are as follows:

1. Provides flexibility to the retailer because the retailer can more readily change the merchandise selection, prices and look of the site in comparison to a traditional retailer

2. Provides a way to track customers to conduct retail research that is quick and relatively inexpensive

3. Provides a way to open a business with less starting capital in comparison to a brick-and- mortar site

4. Provides an easy way to communicate with current and potential customers

5. Provides alternative methods to deliver products and services to customers (download, shipping, printing tickets, in-store pick up)

6. Offers a relatively easy way of bringing international buyers and sellers together into the same online marketplace, thus expanding a retailer's trading area

7. Less overhead costs such as rent, personnel and insurance

8. Convenience for the customer to shop anywhere there is Internet access

9. Provides an easy way for customers to compare product prices

10. Provides an international reach for both e-tailers to access customers and customers to access e-tailers

11. Consumers can find product ratings to help them make purchase decisions

Disadvantages of e-ailing include:

1. Concerns about fraud and security for both e-tailers and consumers

2. Consumer privacy concerns

3. It is difficult to determine the final cost of a product until check-out

4. Growth of e-tailing creates junk mail from e-tailers, which upsets customers and makes it difficult for an e-tailer to cut through the clutter

5. Customers often don't complete the transaction when online

6. Customers can't inspect the product physically before buying

7. Consumer must wait for many products to be shipped

8. It is often difficult to return a product bought online

9. Branding is more difficult for new e-tailers on the Internet

10. Consumers often use the Internet to search for the lowest prices, which places pressure on retailers

Although many retailers incorporate e-tailing into their IRM plans, they often neglect to use their online presence to push store traffic. In essence, retailers could use their online presence as a channel of distribution as well as a communication medium. Many in-store purchases are influenced by a retailer's web presence. Additionally, retailers can use social networking sites to create demand and to research customer feelings, attitudes, and perceptions about physical (as well as virtual) stores. Apps used on mobile technology might be used in-store to offer customers discounts or other promotional efforts. A recent trend is the use of chatbots such as Siri, Alexa or Allo to help consumers get answers to their questions (Pandey, 2017).

Source: Syda Productions/Shutterstock.com

Originally, online retailing included providing consumers with a lot of free products and services such as music and access to entertainment. Consumers became accustomed to receiving free products. Based upon that early tactic, much of the business conducted over the Internet was funded using sponsorships and advertising. With a reduction in advertising dollars for e-tailing, retailers have had to rethink their business model, many opting to charge for products and services that used to be free.

Rules for Effective e-Tailing

There are many ways that retailers can develop integrative systems that are convenient for customers and that create loyal customer bases. Some retailers allow customers to find and research products online that may not be available on the online site but are available in a physical location. Some retailers allow the online customer to pick the product in their brick-and-mortar store. Additionally, many retailers allow their customers the ability to return e-tail purchases to physical retail establishments, or they can return the product easily using self-addressed, stamped shipping labels. Using smartphones, retailers can attach quick response codes that allow customers to immediately connect with the retailer's website where they can gain more information or make a purchase. These channels allow the customer to put unwanted items into an envelope and mail them back to the retailer. Netflix ships DVDs to household customers, who, when they're finished viewing the movie, insert the DVD into an envelope, seal it and place it in the mailbox. Additionally, Netflix allows customers to stream video content to their home computers and television sets for a monthly fee.

Some rules that can aid in integration between online and brick-and-mortar stores are as follows (Chandler and Hyatt, 2003):

1. Develop the e-tail operation with the end in mind. Begin with an understanding of your customer base and consumer behaviors.

2. Make sure you bridge the gap between your physical store and your online store. Design the online store based upon your customers' expectations, not your web designers' desires. Start by considering how customers shop online and what they expect to find on your site.

3. Make sure you factor in the value of your product and service offerings, not just for the customer, but also for your business operation. Customers view value as more than price and may include customer services provided by the e-tailer. You must be sure to price products to consider quality of the products as well as the customer services provided. In addition to planned purchases, there are also numerous impulse purchases that occur online as well as in a physical store environment. You must make sure your value proposition meets the customer expectation.

4. Balance, and then integrate your knowledge of customers, your channels of distribution, and your product and service mix. This goes back to the idea of integration to make sure that there is consistency in the ways members of the channels of distribution approach the retail operation.

5. Integrate all your knowledge throughout the organization. This includes your marketing, IT, design, finance, accounting and purchasing departments to name a few. Your buyers should also be integrated into the overall system. All departments must be clear on the mission and vision of the e-tailer as well as objectives. Although there is a great deal of work at the beginning of your e-tail business development, this work will reduce the amount of time and effort needed to manage the operation.

Source: William Potter/Shutterstock.com

Approximately 69 percent of all e-tail customers will leave their shopping carts prior to check-out (Baynard Institute, 2017). This is called the *cart abandonment rate*. It's a type of customer back-out behavior. Because of abandonment, retailers should look at additional channels of distribution, besides brick and mortar and e-tailing, to reach customers when and where they're ready to purchase. In this section, other channels used by retailers are described. It's important to distinguish between channels of distribution and integrated marketing communication. The two are related but have very different purposes. It is confusing because many channels of distribution for products are also channels of communication for retailers. Catalogs can sell products, but they also communicate the value of the products. Mobile phones may advertise sales but products may also be ordered from the phones. Distribution channels deal with the flow of products and services while IMC conveys information about products and services.

Catalogs

Hard-copy catalogs offer consumers convenience in their shopping. Catalog customers can take their channel (the catalog) with them wherever they travel, and can place orders anytime during the day or night. Catalogs often provide more accurate colors of products than can be found online, provide entertainment value, and don't require a computer. The Sears department store "Wish Book," for example, was famous for inspiring the gift lists of customers since the late 1800s. The Sears "Big Book" catalog was hundreds of pages long and had everything from clothing to barber chairs. In 1993 the company stopped producing the general catalog. Instead, Sears offered specialty catalogs including the Christmas Wish Book, and catalogs for tools, auto accessories, home improvements, clothing, and even Barbie collectibles (History of the Sears Catalog, 2004).

People tend to keep catalogs, which helps to create an ongoing reminder of the retailer's brand. One form of a catalog that combines the look and feel of a magazine with a catalog is the *magalog*, a catalog developed in a magazine format. The magalog contains articles and information related to products for sale by a particular retailer. For example, a story might be created about the positive benefits of vinegar, and then the retailer's brand of vinegar appears in the story along with a method of buying the product such as a response card, 1-800 number or website. Magalogs were developed to entice consumers to buy by providing information within a catalog. Abercrombie and Fitch launched magalog, *A&F Quarterly,* in 1997. In 2003, the retailer came under fire by the National Coalition for the Protection of Children & Families who threatened to boycott the retailer because of its magalog, the "Christmas Field Guide" (Bhatnagar, 2003). Many felt that the nude models in suggestive poses and the sex-related articles in the magalog promoted sexual promiscuity. A&F discontinued the use of *A&F Quarterly* in 2003, two weeks after pulling the *Christmas Field Guide* from stores (Caggiano, 2003). Although A&F did not admit it, the discontinuance was probably due to the negative publicity. In July 2010, *A&F Quarterly* returned to the stores. Selling for $10, the 176-page publication had an 18 and older age restriction for purchase (Anderson, 2010). Many consumers prefer to shop from home but may not like Internet shopping. Catalogs provide a channel that considers safety and convenience.

Source: Hadrian/Shutterstock.com

According to the Data & Marketing Association (2016), the number of catalogs mailed per year has declined dramatically since 2007. More popular are online and e-commerce formats (catalog apps). In many cases catalogs help drive traffic to other channels.

Television

Although television primarily is a communications medium, it functions as an additional channel of distribution for retail products and services. In fact, television is a unique channel that is used with direct marketing. Television allows the retailer to provide product information, expose people to their brand and to increase sales. TV channels such as QVC or Home Shopping Club sell retail products to the mass markets, as well as provide product information that can't be found in a brick-and-mortar retail establishment. Retailers will attempt to stimulate immediate (or direct) sales by offering discounts on their merchandise. Often retailers place time limits on product purchases, again spurring immediate sales.

Ron Popeil and Billy Mays were well known for their use of television and direct-response marketing. Ron Popeil, "the grandfather of infomercials," was very successful pitching products on television. In the 1950s he sold the Chop-O-Matic, and in the 1960s he promoted the Veg-O-Matic. The Popeil Pocket Fisherman and the Showtime Rotisserie ("Set it, and forget it!") were sold in the

1980s and 1990s. Popeil convinced retailers to carry the product in their stores with the promise they could return anything that didn't sell (Popeil and Wehrum, 2009). Billy Mays, "the king of infomercials," followed Popeil's lead, pitching products such as OxiClean and "as seen on TV" products. He also starred in the Discovery Channel show, *Pitchmen*. Although he died June 28, 2009, his commercials ran posthumously, a tribute to his sales ability (Belcher, 2009).

Subscription video-on-demand services has been growing in recent years. The trend is toward content available on many devices such as television and mobile-connected devices. In the U.S., nearly every house has a television. There is an average of 5.6 screens (computer, television, mobile technology) per household. Each screen is a channel to deliver paid content (Dubravac, 2015).

Product Beginnings

It's always interesting to learn about the origins of products. Read below for some interesting ways in which these products were first marketed. Do you think these marketing plans would be effective today?

Corn Flakes. Originally this breakfast cereal staple was sold by mail order only.

Ragu. The famous spaghetti sauce was originally sold door to door.

Tea. Tea was originally sold wrapped in silk bags.

Perforated toilet paper. Can you imagine buying perforated toilet paper on the street, where it was first sold?

Tabasco Sauce. "This Tabasco sauce has a certain smell to it . . ." Perhaps this is what customers said when they first purchased Tabasco Sauce in used cologne bottles.

Source: "Chex in the Mail," *Morning Call* (Allentown, PA), September 18, 2002, p. E1.

M-Commerce

M-commerce is the newest channel of distribution (and communication) for retailers. M-commerce, short for mobile commerce, includes smart phones and computer tablets that have Internet access and can be leveraged by retailers to keep consumers connected and able to interact with the retailer twenty-four hours a day, seven days a week (Kotler and Keller, 2012). M-Commerce has created another channel of distribution for retailers. The link between the Internet and mobile devices illustrates how multiple channels work together to create new channels to reach customers and to deliver product information through integrated marketing communication (IMC).

An application of m-commerce is *point-of-sale systems (POS)*, which are systems used to complete sales transactions. POS systems are used in place of cash registers. Retailers are using m-commerce in conjunction with *mobile POS systems (m-POS)* which are hand-held devices used to complete a sales transaction. The m-POS came about because customers' least favorite shopping activity is waiting in line to check out. With an m-POS system, a person carrying the m-POS device comes to the customer to check them out, preventing customers from becoming frustrated and leaving the store. If customers are forced to wait too long to check out, the retailer loses sales and *share of wallet,* which is the percentage of a customer's total expenses that is spent at a specific retailer. Because customers get tired of waiting in line to check out, many times the retailer loses the entire *marketbasket,* which is everything a customer plans on purchasing. Apple has embraced m-POS. When entering an Apple store, the sales clerk stays with you during the entire transaction (if so desired) and completes the sale via his or her portable POS. The mobile POS systems are more applicable for retailers that sell higher-ticket items and would not be applicable for a retailer that sells thousands of products, such as a grocery retailer.

As the numbers of smartphones and cell phones increase, m-commerce retailers keep consumers connected. Retailers offer products and services in real time based upon current customer needs. Customers shop from anywhere in the world via their m-devices. Drug store giant CVS uses m-commerce to allow their customers to order and purchase prescription drugs (and other sundries) directly from their phones. Many travel companies target business people on the run. The drawback of m-commerce is privacy. Consumers hesitate to purchase from a retailer who they feel has too much information about them and who may share that information with others. Because many mobile electronics contain a global positioning system (GPS) a retailer can tell where a customer is located anywhere in the world.

Smartphone apps are often used in m-commerce. Launched in 2010, Shopkick is an app that gives users points (called kickbucks) for entering a store. Shopkick (www.shoptick.com) tells retailers when users are inside a store. If you pick up and examine a piece of merchandise, points are dropped into the app. Even customers entering dressing rooms get points through this application. The points are redeemable for gift cards at participating retailers, music downloads, or game credits on Facebook. Participants can even donate their points to a charity (Shopkick App..., 2010). It takes a lot of points to earn rewards. The app helps retailers to influence behavior with the expectation of increasing sales. Other apps allow customers to scan barcodes with their phones and get product prices and information.

Source: Georgejmclittle/Shutterstock.com

Email

Retailers use electronic marketing or email to send messages to customers over the Internet. The retailer can modify and personalize each message and select who should receive their messages. Too many messages sent to the same recipients increases clutter and the respondents begin to ignore the messages. Therefore, messages lose their effectiveness. It helps when the user opts to receive the emails instead of getting them unsolicited. Powell's Books claims to be the largest independent retailer of new and used books in the world. The company launched an email campaign that contained subject newsletters which recommended books in 10 areas. The personalized emails were successful and added 400 new email subscribers over the six-day promotion (ExactTarget, Inc, 2009).

Source: Leszek Glasner/Shutterstock.com

Consumers want to control what they see in their email. According to the Direct Marketing Association (2016), 59 percent of consumers stated that marketing emails influence their decisions especially when they contain some type of offer (coupon, savings).

Direct Marketing

The largest trade association for direct marketing is the Direct Marketing Association (DMA). The DMA defines *direct marketing* as "any direct communication to a consumer or business recipient that is designed to generate a response in the form of an order (direct order), a request for further information (lead generation), and/or a visit to a store or other place of business for purchase of a specific product(s) or service(s) (traffic generation)" (Direct Marketing Association, 2012). According to the DMA Statistical Fact Book (2016), marketers spent $153.2 billion on direct and digital marketing. Of that amount, $46.8 billion was spent on direct mail. The remainder was spent on email ($2.3 billion), display ($28.8 billion), search ($27.3 billion), teleservices ($42.6 billion) and other ($5.4 billion).

Direct marketing is closely linked with advertising, an IMC tactic because prospective consumers are exposed to a retailer's message through a medium such as newspapers, television, radio, magazines, catalogs, the Internet, or mail.

When used to sell products using direct marketing, companies are called direct marketers. There are retailers that solely use direct marketing to generate sales, but most use direct marketing in addition to other channels. There are general merchandise direct marketers, such as QVC, as well as food and specialty direct marketers such True2Life, a retailer of well personal care product (www.true2life.com). These retailers use direct marketing in addition to their other channels.

Direct retailing overlaps with other channels such as catalogs, telephone, magalogs, television, magazines, direct mail and radio. Anytime an immediate response is requested, direct marketing has occurred.

A subset of direct marketing is *direct selling.* If there is some type of personal contact in which an immediate response (sale, lead) is requested, direct selling has occurred. The personal contact can occur anywhere from a person's home or office (World Federation of Direct Selling Associations, 2012). Direct sellers also make extensive use of telephones. Examples of direct sellers include Mary Kay and Avon.

Source: Thinglass/Shutterstock.com

Vending Machines

Another channel of distribution for many retailers is the use of *vending machines,* a form of non-store retailing in which a consumer makes a purchase through a machine. The machine is built to complete the entire transaction, from attracting the consumer to providing the product and collecting the price of the product from the consumer. Vending machine merchandise ranges from soft drinks and candy to insurance, cameras, pizza, phone calls, movies, phone cards, books, paper and pens. In some areas, a person can buy bike parts, such as inner tubes and patch kits, from a vending machine.

Vending machines allow retailers to extend their service after business hours. For example, after the U.S. Post Office has closed its retail operations, customers can use vending machines to buy postage stamps. The major disadvantage of vending machines is that it is difficult to return defective or unwanted products (called reverse logistics). Also, machines tend to break. Consider a wasted trip to the bank to use the ATM, only to find it's being "serviced." Faulty vending machines can give customers a negative opinion of a retailer.

Vending machines enable retailers to locate near customers without the costs associated with the building of true brick-and-mortar retailing establishments. The key to successful vending is to locate the machine in high-traffic areas that are convenient to consumers. Public schools, universities, hospitals, and other large institutions typically have several vending machines. Red Box has used vending machines to rent newly released DVDs and Blu-ray Discs. According to its website, *Redbox* has rented more than five billion movies and is available at more than 35,000 locations nationwide (Redbox website: www.redbox.com).

Source: DeymosHR/Shutterstock.com

Vending machines as a marketing channel are not as popular as they once were. Cigarettes used to be the most common good sold in vending machines, but laws now prevent them from being sold this way. Sodas, candy, and other snack items are the main types of goods sold in vending machines. Today, some manufacturers have experimented with unconventional products in the vending machine channel. Products such as mp3 players, inkjet cartridges, printing paper, and even wine have been sold through more sophisticated vending units. However, vending machines are susceptible to vandalism and theft, so they are sometimes placed within a brick-and-mortar store. This placement defeats the advantage of accessibility at all hours.

Kiosks

Kiosks are small stand-alone structures that are often open on one side or more. They are used as a channel of distribution by many retailers. Many kiosks include a vending machine. A kiosk may be used to disseminate information such as the electronic directories of retailers seen at airports or malls. Other kiosks stand alone and sell various products and services such as books, massages and jewelry. To create effective kiosks, retailers should strive to get the consumer involved and engaged in the purchase of products. Large signs, colorful pictures, televisions playing product information, photographs, drawings and sound are tools that can be used in the creation of an effective kiosk.

Source: Sorbis/Shutterstock.com

Retailers who exhibit at trade and community shows often use kiosks, as do retailers at celebrations such as state fairs. Z-Coil (www.zcoil.com) uses a kiosk at the New Mexico Balloon Festival in Albuquerque each year. The company attempts to generate exposure to their unique products (shoes) with the kiosks, but it also generates large retail sales at the festival site.

Retail Classifications

Due to advances in technology there have been and will continue to be many dramatic changes in retailing. Many of these changes will affect the types and classifications of existing retail institutions. These institutions are generally based on some type of classification system that mirrors the retailer's business operations. For example, a retailer that specializes in getting the consumer a product or service in the most convenient way possible could be classified as a convenience retailer. Think of how many different retailers you know that specialize in convenience products. You have probably thought of 7-Eleven, Circle K, Wawa or perhaps even Sheetz or Loaf N Jug. What would you call retailers who specialize in the sale of food products? If you say "supermarkets," you are correct. There is some overlap among the types of retailers that exist and some differences in the way they are classified. For example, a convenience store and a supermarket may both be classified as food retailers. The classification systems discussed next will help you better understand the various types of retail institutions.

It is important to understand the types of retail institutions because they have a competitive impact on business. With this knowledge, managers are better prepared to develop comprehensive competitive analyses for use in their retail businesses. Retail professionals must strive to stay current with the numerous changes in their environments that may affect their businesses as well as their professional lives.

NAICS Method of Classification

The United States government developed a classification system called *NAICS (North American Industrial Classification System)*. NAICS allows businesses to compare economic data and statistics reported by North American Companies. NAICS was created with input and assistance from the governments of Mexico and Canada. According to the NAICS Association, the six-digit NAICS codes provide categories based on type of economic activity (North American Industry Classification System, 2012). The NAICS system makes it easier for North American companies to do business. It also forces the retailer to classify based upon the type of merchandise being carried by the retailer. Table 4.1 shows the NAICS hierarchical structure and the sectors identified by the codes.

Let's look at the NAICS code for one retailer. The NAICS code for the Autozone is 441310. The first 2 digits (44) identify the company as a retailer. Numbers 44 and 45 are reserved for retailers. The following numbers identify the industry subsector (Car parts and Suppliers) and products (automotive parts and accessories) sold by the company. Thus, the company must define its product or service offerings to get an accurate NAICS listing. The last number indicates that the company operates out of the U.S.

Table 4.1 – NAICS Hierarchy and Structure

Hierarchy Structure	
XX	Industry Sector (20 broad sectors up from 10 SIC)
XXX	Industry Subsector
XXXX	Industry Group
XXXXX	Industry
XXXXXX	U.S., Canadian, or Mexican National specific

NAICS Sectors	
Code	
11	Agriculture, Forestry, Fishing, and Hunting
21	Mining
22	Utilities
23	Construction
31–33	Manufacturing
42	Wholesale Trade
44–45	Retail Trade

Classification by Ownership

For some retail professionals, the NAICS method of classification does not provide enough information. Thus, other retail classifications are used to provide more information. As we discuss classification of retailing industries by ownership, keep in mind that most retailers are small and have only one or two locations. Most employment (and sales) comes from large retailers. Using these ownership differences, we can divide retailers into three main categories: 1.) Independents; 2.) Chain Stores, and 3.) Franchises. Two other classifications that are used less frequently are 4.) Leased Departments and 5.) Cooperatives.

Independents: *Independent retailers* operate one retail venue or location. Typically, these stores are family-owned and operated. This type of retailing offers ease of entry into the market. Thus, opening an independent retail outlet requires fewer capital resources. Most retailers in the U.S. are independent retailers, and nearly half of total retail sales in the U.S. come from independent retailers (Leinbach-Reyhle, 2014)

An advantage of independent retailers is their ability to respond quickly to changes in the retailing environment. If customers' needs and wants change, the independent can quickly provide merchandise that will meet those needs and wants. Independents typically live in their communities and thus have community contacts on which they can rely to generate sales. Rental costs for independents are typically lower than for the other categories in that independents usually locate their businesses in neighborhoods and more rural, stand-alone locations. The independents' smaller size and location allow the independent retailer a better opportunity to build and exploit customer relationships.

Because they are small, independent retailers are unable to achieve *economies of scale* and they have to charge higher prices for their goods and services than do larger chain retailers. Additionally, because independent retailers are often family-owned, they may lack retailing expertise, particularly in marketing communication, buying, management, accounting, and finance. There are also fewer resources for hiring and training.

In his book *Competing with the Retail Giants,* Kenneth Stone (1995) offers independent retailers the following suggestions for competing with large chain stores:

1. Improve your merchandising.
2. Revive your marketing practices.
3. Provide outstanding service to your customers.
4. Treat the customer right.
5. Improve the efficiency of your business.
6. Implement changes.
7. Build teams.

One way a smaller, independent retailer can improve its sales is through *strategic clarity*. Strategic clarity is the retailer's commitment to create and achieve an in-depth understanding of their strengths and weaknesses, including the strengths and weaknesses of the overall integrated retail management plan. A local hardware store, for example, may understand that they cannot compete with larger retailers on price, so they decide to create a strategic approach for their business that focuses on customer service as their customers have been bragging about the service for years. Another tactic undertaken by independent retailers is to band together with like retailers and form cooperatives to take advantage of economies of scale.

Chains: To be considered a *chain store,* retailers must operate at least more than one store. Although most chain retailers are small with only a few locations, the bulk of sales in retailing come from the larger chain stores such as Walmart, Target, Home Depot, and Macy's. Often chain stores are divisions of larger companies. For example, L Brands (Formerly known as Limited Brands) owns a few different chain stores such as Victoria's Secret and Bath and Body Works.

Chain stores benefit from economies of scale. Chain stores purchase in large volumes, which reduces the cost of the merchandise. By purchasing in large quantities, chain stores are better able to negotiate with their suppliers for lower costs, value-added incentives and marketing material. Larger chains usually use computer systems for inventory management and merchandise handling. They also have the ability to use large distribution centers equipped with the latest technology such as product picking machines. Finally, chains typically have better loss prevention systems that save on costs. Cost savings are often passed on to customers. This is why many times items found at chain stores are less expensive compared to an independent retailer.

Chains are able to find, select, and hire the best and brightest for their business. By hiring the best employees, the retailer is better able to keep up with trends and make decisions that benefit the organization. Chains can use specialists for each of their functional areas (i.e., buying, accounting, finance, merchandising, and research), again taking advantage of changes in the marketplace while driving down costs associated with running the stores.

The biggest disadvantage of chain stores is the cost associated with running large organizations. As a retailer's size increases, so do its costs and financial commitments, such as rent, lease, heating, air conditioning, labor, and increased merchandise purchasing. Additionally, because of their size, chains are typically slower to respond to changes in the retail environment than independents. Product assortment is also a challenge. In taking advantage of economies of scale, chains must purchase the same products and service, limiting the assortment of products to the customers or driving the costs associated with offering those products to higher levels. In terms of location, chains typically locate in higher-traffic areas to take advantage of larger groups of customers. This can be a disadvantage because it can be difficult to find parking. Chains also need a larger market to move their product offerings. Chains have unique types of advantages and disadvantages. The advantages can be exploited and the disadvantages minimized with good retail management.

Franchises: A *franchise* is a type of business based on a contractual agreement between a franchisor and franchisee. A *franchisor* is the owner of a franchise and has developed a successful business model. The *franchisee* is the buyer of the franchise. The agreement allows the franchisee to operate a retail business using the name and business model of the franchisor for a fee. The owner (franchisor) may be a wholesaler, retailer, manufacturer or a service provider. Burger King contracts with their individual restaurant owners, allowing the owners (franchisees) to use the Burger King name and operating system.

Although contracts for franchises vary, typically the franchisee pays the franchisor a fee plus royalties based upon sales. In return, the franchisee receives from the franchisor the rights to own and operate the business in a given geographic location. The franchisor also offers the franchisee assistance in site selection, building codes and requirements, marketing communication, managerial (or employee) training, merchandise selection, and inventory methods. The franchisee receives all the profits from the business after paying the royalty and other fees, giving the franchisee the motivation to increase sales. Another benefit for the franchisee is the ability to take advantage of the economies of scale of the franchisor when buying products and services for resale.

To be most effective, the franchisee should follow the guidelines set by the franchisor. Sometimes franchisees set different policies from the franchisor which confuses customers. For example, Subway conducted a national campaign, and a customer was confused when a local Subway did not honor the coupon released from the franchisor. Over the past twenty-five years, franchising has advanced and expanded. Franchising is now used for products, businesses and trademarks. Each of these types of franchising opportunities is unique. In *product/trademark franchising,* the franchisee agrees to sell a franchisor's products and services and/or operate under existing trade names or trademarks. Although there are a few rules for operating, the franchisee has much more autonomy in comparison with business franchising. Examples include gas stations such as Exxon and car dealerships such as a Ray's Chevrolet. With *business franchising,* the franchisee follows the Burger King model described above. The franchisor provides all the tools necessary for success (advertising, training, site selection, marketing, accounting, planning, legal, inventory issues, etc.). The franchisor provides a proven business model, which increases the chances of success. With this model, there are many rules and standards to follow to ensure consistency across different locations. Business franchising is common in the fast food and hotel industries.

Source: Susan Montgomery/Shutterstock.com

Franchising is popular because each franchisee is essentially the owner of the business. The franchisee can operate the business with a smaller capital outlay than would be possible if he or she were to operate on his or her own. Additionally, franchising reduces the barrier to entry into the retail industry by allowing the franchisee to sell established brand names and products.

Leased Departments: *Leased departments* are spaces in larger, already established retail stores that are rented (leased) to third parties or outside vendors. The organization or company that leases the space operates much like a small retail store within the larger retail store. The lessee is responsible for all activities within their store, including fixtures. Often large department stores such as Macy's or J.C. Penney's lease their jewelry or beauty departments to outside vendors. The advantage to the lessee is the ability to receive established customers and foot traffic to the store. Costs, such as security and parking, may also be reduced for the lessee.

Cooperatives: *Cooperatives* are groups of smaller retailers who have created a strategic alliance with one another to generate additional benefits from their alliance, such as lower costs per product through economies of scale. *Retailer-sponsored cooperatives* have the added benefit of centralized buying. In a cooperative, retail owners can increase their operating efficiency by sharing their retailing methods. Retailer-sponsored cooperatives are created and owned by the retailers involved. The National Automotive Parts Association (NAPA) distributes parts to both corporately and independently owned auto parts stores.

In *wholesaler-sponsored cooperatives,* the cooperative is owned and operated by a group of wholesalers. The wholesalers offer retail programs to retailers. Wholesalers may offer retail businesses many services such as transportation and warehousing, site selection, and store displays. The North American Wholesale Co-op Association (NAWCA) brings together wholesalers to assist small businesses.

Consumer cooperatives are owned and operated by retail consumers. Generally, these types of co-ops are created because a group of people feels it can offer products and services at lower prices than those currently in the market. People who run consumer cooperatives believe there is a need or want in the marketplace that isn't being met. Credit unions and food co-ops are examples of consumer cooperatives.

Classification by Merchandise Type

In addition to classifying retailers by ownership types, retailers are also often classified based upon the types of products carried by these retailers when selling their goods and services. Classifications provide retailers additional information about the competitive environment. There are two major classifications: 1.) General Merchandise Retailers and, 2.) Food Retailers.

General Merchandise Retailers

General merchandise retailers sell general, typically nonfood merchandise. Almost any nonfood item falls into this category. This section discusses the many types of general merchandise retailers. Tables 4.2 and 4.3 (next page) summarize general and food retail types.

Table 4.2 - General Merchandise Retailers

Type	Description
Department	Large retailers that carry a wide breadth and depth of products and services to offer to their customers
Discount Stores	The difference between a department store and discount store lies in the service, prices and merchandise assortments. In contrast to department stores, discount stores generally offer limited customer services, while pricing their merchandise offerings lower than would be found at a traditional department store
Specialty Stores	Carry a limited number of products or services within one (or a few) lines of goods and services. Specialty stores got their name because they "specialize" in just one type of prod-
Category Killers	Are also called power retailers or category specialists. Category killers are typically discount specialty stores that offer deep assortments of merchandise in a given category
Drug Stores	Although technically a specialty store, drug stores have been expanding rapidly over the past decade, morphing into larger stand-alone stores. Drug stores typically sell drugs, med-
Off-Price Retailers	Off-price retailers have grown in number and strength over the past five years, driven by many environmental factors, but the number one factor is the poor economy. Off-price retailers look like discounters in that they sell brand-name merchandise at every-day-low-prices (EDLP). Off-price retailers do not (or rarely) offer any additional customer services.

Department Stores: *Department stores* are large retailers that carry a wide variety and assortment of products and services to offer to their customers. Additionally, department stores tend to offer more customer service than do other general merchandise retailers. Most department stores belong to a large retail chain. Each department in a department store functions as a miniature store. The department is allocated sales space, managers, sales personnel, goals to meet and other areas that deal with retail management. Department stores often serve as anchors for major shopping centers. An *anchor* is the largest store in a shopping center and serves to draw customers to the center. Macy's, Nordstrom, Bloomingdale's, Saks Fifth Avenue, Neiman Marcus, and J.C. Penney are some popular anchors.

Table 4.3: Food Retailers

Type	Description
Conventional Supermarkets	Large department stores that specialize in food and food-related items. A conventional supermarket has traditionally been a large, self-service food store that generates at least $2 million in sales ("Language of the Food Industry…" 2003).
Superstores	Food-based retailers that are larger than a traditional supermarket. In addition to the offerings at a conventional supermarket, superstores carry expanded deli services as well as bakeries, seafood and nonfood products.
Combination Stores	Combine food items with nonfood items to create a one-stop shopping experience for their customers.
Supercenters and Hypermarkets	Supercenters are combinations of superstores and discount stores. Supercenters were developed based upon the European hypermarket concept. Hypermarkets are extremely large retailing facilities that offer many types and lines of products as well as food products.
Warehouse Clubs and Stores	Many food consumers look for shopping experiences that focus on low-prices and very little to no service. These customers are price sensitive and are willing to give up almost all service functions for lower prices. To satisfy the needs and wants of these customers, food retailers developed warehouse clubs and warehouse stores. Warehouse clubs and stores (also referred to as club stores) offer limited assortments of goods and services, both food and nonfood items (general merchandise). Warehouse stores sell to end users, but also have a significant portion of their sales coming from small and mid-sized businesses.
Convenience Stores	People around the world have developed very busy and complicated lives. Consumers have seen their time commitments expand extensively as they try to work, raise families, go to school, take their children to activities, socialize with friends and family and make time to take vacations. Because of these time demands, retailers responded by creating stores that focus on consumer convenience. These stores are called convenience stores (or in the industry c-stores). Convenience stores carry a very limited assortment of products and retail these products out of very small stores.
Limited Line Stores	Box stores, or limited-line stores, represent a small number of food retailers. Limited-line stores are essentially food discounters that offer a small selection of products at very low prices.

Department stores have more money to spend on marketing so they have high name recognition. The companies use marketing communication tactics such as advertising, point-of-purchase displays, m-commerce, couponing and newspaper advertising. In addition, Internet marketing, magazine advertising, radio, television and direct marketing are used to reach consumers. Department stores spend most of their marketing communication budget on sales promotions.

In recent years, department store growth and sales have slowed because consumers have favored specialty stores, warehouse clubs and discount stores, such as Sam's Club, Walmart, and Target. To compete against these types of retailers, department store retailers focus on customer service, sales training for front line sales personnel, marketing communication, and inventory management.

Because of the decline in their consumer bases, department stores are attempting to entice shoppers into the stores through innovation. Many department stores are in the process of reinventing their stores through store renovation. Renovations include new shopping carts, brighter signage, customer price-scanning stations, lounges, in-store entertainment, and coffee shops.

Discount Stores: *Discount stores* sell merchandise at lower prices compared to other retailers. Although discount stores are sometimes classified as department stores, there are differences between the two, most notably in service, quality, prices, and merchandise assortments. In contrast to department stores, discount stores generally offer limited customer services, while pricing their merchandise offerings lower than would be found at a traditional department store. Although discounters are attempting to change perceptions, discount stores tend to be more basic and offer less fashionable merchandise than do department stores. Some of the world's largest corporations are discount stores, such as Walmart and Target.

The main marketing strategy of discount stores is to create an image of high-volume, low-cost products and service offerings. Discount retail chains began in the United States in the late '60s. A key factor that spurs the growth of discounters is a poor economy, resulting in the growth of value-conscious consumers. Discount retailers have paid close attention to their core competencies such as merchandise buying and selection coupled with low prices. A result of this movement is that many of today's consumers no longer see a reason to pay higher prices at more fashionable or trendy retailers.

Specialty Stores: *Specialty stores* carry a limited number of products or services within one (or a few) lines of goods and services. These types of stores often specialize in just one type of product category, such as shoes, women's apparel, men's apparel, telephones, or electronics. These retailers cater to a smaller market segment and try to create a niche for their products. Although they don't carry many product lines, they offer many products within each line.

Customers will frequent a specialty store because of the extensive assortments of products and good customer service. Sales personnel at specialty stores tend to be more knowledgeable about the products and services offered for sale. Some of the larger specialty stores include Barnes and Noble Books, PetSmart, The Gap, Office Depot and Best Buy. Additionally, retailers such as Hallmark, the Body Shop, the Rocky Mountain Chocolate Factory and GNC nutritional stores are included in the specialty store classification.

In the last twenty-five years, specialty stores have seen the emergence of the category killer. *Category killers,* also called power retailers or category specialists, are typically discount specialty stores that offer deep assortments of merchandise in a given category such as electronics, baby clothes, shoes, toys, and sporting goods. These stores can be online, brick and mortar or both. Category killers also offer the consumer lower prices than the consumer may find at competing retailers. Best Buy, a leader in electronics retailing, is an example of a category killer. The company aims to be the source of technology services for consumers.

Many shoppers don't want to shop in large stores. Because of that, many retailers have created smaller stores stocked with select merchandise offerings. These stores give the customer a more intimate shopping experience. For example, in 2016 Kohl's opened six smaller-format stores. These stores allow Kohl's to open in smaller markets and to save on real estate costs (Lawder, 2016).

Drug Stores: Although technically a specialty store, *drug stores* (or pharmacies) are retailers that sell medicines and other items. They have been expanding rapidly over the past decade, changing into larger stand-alone stores. Drug stores had to reinvent themselves as supermarkets, and discount stores have added typical drug store products to their supermarket and discount store merchandise mixes, stealing valuable sales from drug stores.

Many drug stores have added larger assortments of merchandise, including food items, to keep their customers. Additionally, drug stores are focusing on customer services such as drivethrough windows for prescription pick-up and drop-off. Health care assistance is being offered at most of the drug stores to create a "value-added" feel for the customer base. Customers can now buy drugs online or through mail order from their drug store or other major prescription and drug distributors such as MEDCO. The largest drugstore chains include CVS, Walgreens and Rite Aid. In terms of sales, Walmart is the fourth-largest pharmacy operator in the United States.

Off-Price Retailers: *Off-Price retailers* sell merchandise at prices lower than usual. Retailers in the classification include stores that sell out-of-season products and distressed merchandise from other retailers, such as Big Lots (www.biglots.com) and Ollie's Bargain Outlet (www.ollies.us). Many times, when a retailer wants to get rid of merchandise (called closeouts), an off-price retailer will buy the excess merchandise at a reduced price. Also included are factory outlet stores, *flea markets,* and singular price stores, such as Dollar Stores.

During economic downturns, off-price retailers do well. *Everyday low pricing (EDLP)* is a strategy in which retailers offer the lowest price without having to use coupons or wait for a sale. Off-price retailers are similar to discounters in that they sell brand-name merchandise at EDLP, but off-price retailers seldom offer any additional customer services. Off-price retailers carry the same merchandise types as traditional department stores, but offer prices much lower (often 40-50 percent lower).

One sub-category of off-price retailing is known as *extreme-value retailers.* These retailers offer a very limited assortment of merchandise at very low prices. Examples of extreme-value retailers include Dollar Stores and Five Below.

Food Retailers

Food retailers sell food products to consumers as their primary function. Because there are many different types of food retailers, there may be some overlap between classifications. The world's largest food retailers include Walmart, Kroger, Royal Ahold, Albertson's, Inc., Safeway and Costco Wholesale Group. The main trade association for food retailing is the Food Marketing Institute (FMI) (www.fmi.org). The FMI conducts programs in research, education, industry relations and public affairs for its member companies in the food retailing industry. The last time you were in line at a supermarket or convenience store, were you tempted to add a package of gum or a candy bar to your purchase? Food retailers often employ tactics such as placing candy near the checkout, to get you to spend more.

Source: Pilon/Shutterstock.com

Food retailing is difficult because of foods and beverages have a limited shelf life. To remain competitive in the industry, many food retailers rely on carrying merchandise outside their traditional lines such as flowers and toys. So while general merchandise retailers are beginning to add food products to their lines, food retailers are beginning to add non-food items to their merchandise lines. Thus, food retailers may add merchandise such as greeting cards, in-store banking services, in-store pharmacies, classes in cooking, gas stations, and even child care.

Traditional Supermarkets

A *traditional supermarket* offers a full line of groceries, meat and produce with at least $2 million in annual sales and up to 15 percent of their sales in general merchandise/health and beauty care. The stores carry between 15,000 and 60,000 SKUs and may have a deli, bakery and/or pharmacy (Food Marketing Institute, 2017). A *stock keeping unit (SKU)* is a retailer-defined series of numbers or codes used to identify each unique product sold.

One of the biggest benefits generated from the development of traditional supermarkets has been when people buy items that are unplanned, called *impulse buying.* In their book, *America's Cheapest Family Gets You Right on the Money* (2007), Steve and Annette Economides describe the behavior of typical supermarket shoppers:

- Shoppers making a trip to the store to pick up a few items usually purchase 54 percent more than they planned.

- Forty-seven percent of shoppers go to the store three or four times each week.

- Consumers graze or look for things to buy at the grocery store, with impulse buys making up between 50.8 and 67.7 percent of total purchase.

To be successful in supermarket retailing, managers must create high-volume inventory turnover, which indicates how many times a retailer's products are sold and replaced in a given period. In recent years, supermarkets have faced increased competition from large retailers, convenience stores, warehouse stores and superstores, so the supermarket manager must develop effective strategies that keep driving people into the supermarket. For example, because Target and Walmart both now sell produce as well as other grocery items, supermarkets are facing increased competition from these well-known retail brands. Retailers often use integrated marketing communications (IMC) programs to combat the competitive efforts. Supermarket IMC programs generally use numerous promotional activities such as couponing, advertising, flyers, free samples and customer affinity cards (frequent buyer customer cards). The strategic use of coupons coupled with other promotions such as double or triple coupon values is called hi-lo pricing. In *hi-lo pricing* retailers set a higher price on less frequently purchased items and then discount the price of featured items through sales promotions and couponing. In this way consumers come in for the sale items but buy other higher-priced items as well.   Some supermarkets use very few promotional activities, but rather rely on an EDLP strategy.

Source: Andriy Blokhin/Shutterstock.com

Superstores: *Superstores* are food retailers that are larger than a traditional supermarket. Wegman's Food Markets is an example of a superstore, although the company refers to their stores as supermarkets. In addition to the offerings at a traditional supermarket, superstores carry expanded deli services as well as bakeries, seafood, and non-food products. Although superstores vary in size, they can be as large as 150,000 square feet. Typically, the superstore is no smaller than 20,000 square feet. Typical superstores run the gamut of size, but are usually between 80,000 to 120,000 square feet. Superstores carry an average of 60,000 products compared with a traditional supermarket which carries around 40,000 products on average (Wegman's Food Markets...2002). Often included in Wegman's stores are bakeries, ready-to-cook food items, international foods and photo labs.

Combination Stores: *Combination stores* combine food items with nonfood items to create a one-stop shopping location for their customers. Combination stores arose because consumers demanded more convenience. In a combination store, consumers can buy general merchandise along with their food products. Consumers take their products to a common check-out area. Combination stores emerged during the 1960s, but grew rapidly during the '70s and '80s. Combination stores are as large as 100,000 square feet.

In 1934, in Greenville, Michigan, Hendrik Meijer started what would be the first combination store in the United States (www.meijer.com). Meijer's Thrifty Acres (the original name of the store,) is a family-owned chain store with over 190 locations in Michigan, Indiana, Kentucky, Ohio and Illinois. Shoppers at a Meijer's store can pick up health and beauty suppliers, toys, furniture, a television, and a shotgun (as well as many other products) in the same shopping trip (Our Company, 2011).

 Supercenters and Hypermarkets: Supercenters are combinations of superstores and discount stores. Supercenters developed from European hypermarket (About Meijer, 2002). *Hypermarkets*, such as the retailer Carrefour, are very large retailing facilities that offer many types and lines of products as well as food products. In supercenters, over 40 percent of sales come from nonfood items. Supercenters were the fastest growing retail category during the past decade, and they encompass as much as 200,000 square feet of gross leasable area. Walmart is the supercenter category leader with an approximate 74 percent of the total market share of supercenter retail sales.

Supercenters sell food products at low prices, a strategy that stimulates demand and store traffic. By enticing customers to come in for low-priced food products, supercenter management can encourage the customers to buy nonfood items. The *market area* is the geographical area where consumers that have a demand for the product reside. The market area for supercenters and hypermarkets is much larger than the areas for other types of food retailers. Customers are willing to drive farther to patronize a supercenter than they would for the other types of food retailers. The major disadvantage of supercenters is that customers may not want to frequent these large centers for smaller purchases. Because of that, many of the supercenters are adopting strategies that will create smaller shopping venues for customers unwilling to make small purchases at the large stores. For example, in some Walmart supercenters there is a small section near the entrance that contains products such as milk, eggs and bread. Another disadvantage of supercenters is that customers have to search for many of the products they're looking for because the stores are vast.

Source: Cassiohabib/Shutterstock.com

Warehouse Clubs and Stores: Many food consumers are price sensitive and are willing to give up almost all retail services for lower prices. To satisfy the needs and wants of these customers, food retailers developed *warehouse clubs* and *warehouse stores.* Warehouse clubs and stores (also referred to as club stores) offer limited assortments of goods and services in a broad range of product categories selling both food and nonfood items (general merchandise). Warehouse stores sell to end users, but also attract small and mid-sized businesses by providing office supplies and furnishings. The larger warehouse clubs include Costco Wholesale, Sam's Club and BJ's Wholesale Club.

Warehouse clubs and stores are very large and typically, but not always, located in low rent areas of cities to keep their overhead as low as possible. Merchandise handling costs for warehouse clubs are reduced because these club stores transport merchandise directly from the truck to the floor using pallets and original product boxes. Barren steel shelving and concrete floors are the norm for warehouse clubs. No frills and self-service are the policies of most stores.

Warehouse clubs try and sell only fast-moving, high-turnover products and services. In addition to selling their own store brands, many warehouse clubs sell in large volumes, which allows them to generate sales before the bill to the manufacturer is due.

It is common for warehouse clubs and stores to charge their patrons an annual fee for membership in the clubs. These fees range from $30 - $80 per year. Free membership periods are offered to attract new customers. Warehouse clubs try and stay away from perishable products (or carry a very limited amount of these products).

Convenience Stores: *Convenience stores* (or c-stores) carry a very limited assortment of products and sell these products in a smaller store format. C-store location decisions are very important as c-store owners attempt to locate between their customers' homes and places of work. C-stores cater to people who don't have a lot of time. Customers can visit a convenience store, pick out the products they need. and check out quickly. There is little waiting in line, and the search for products is short. Most of the products purchased at a c-store are consumed within an hour of purchase. The best-selling products at convenience stores are cigarettes and nonalcoholic beverages. Other top selling items at c-stores include eggs, milk, and snack and prepared foods.

Convenience stores have high sales volumes and little space; thus, most receive supplies daily. Most of the products for sale in c-stores are impulse items which tend to have high markups and are therefore more expensive at a c-store in comparison to other types of retailers. Because of the amount of competition c-stores get from neighboring food retailers, they generate sales in unconventional ways. Some c-stores have added gasoline to their product lines. Those convenience stores that sell gas have found that gasoline accounts for a large portion of the store's sales

Limited-Line Stores: Box stores, or *limited-line stores* (also known as box stores), represent a small number of food retailers. Limited-line stores are food discounters that offer a small selection of products at very low prices. Limited-line stores have no frills and usually sell their merchandise out of boxes (called shippers). Typically, there are no refrigerated products and sales are cash and carry (no credit, credit cards, or checks). Limited-line customers do their own bagging, and often must bring their own bags as these stores often do not provide bags.

Aldi is an example of a successful limited-line retailer. There are 1,000 Aldi stores in 31 states (www.aldi.com). This no-frills retailer charges for bags and shopping cart usage; it accepts debit cards but no other forms of credit cards. Because 95 percent of the premium products sold are Aldi brands, the company does not accept manufacturer's coupons.

The overriding strategy in a limited-line store is to sell merchandise at least 20 percent below that of other competitors. Many limited-line stores focus on private label brands to further reduce costs.

Industry and Competitive Analysis

To better develop strategies and tactics, retailers conduct an industry and competitive analysis. *An industry analysis* requires a retailer to take an objective view of the attractiveness, and success factors, that determine the composition of an industry. According to strategy expert Michael Porter (1980), "These two questions are the fundamental questions in strategy. How can you understand your industry and your competitive environment, and how can you understand how to position your company within that environment?" A competitive analysis is the process of identifying the performance of brands or products within the retailer's market. The industry analysis is more general in scope compared to a competitive analysis, which is firm- or product- specific. Table 4.4 lists sources of information for creating and industry and competitive analysis.

Table 4.4 Industry and Competitive Analysis – Sources of Information

Source	Description
Company	Retail managers can find information about other companies through websites, annual reports, press releases, product catalogs, marketing material, patents and trademarks, suppliers and customers.
Industry	Industry analysis sources include trade journals, conference papers, industry websites and publications.
Publications and Websites	Shown are selected publications and websites that provide information to develop a competitive or industry analysis. **Thomson Research** - comprehensive collection of company information and analyst research. Includes reports from over 980 of the world's leading firms and covering more than 30,000 companies worldwide (http://research.thomsonib.com/tr_home1.asp) **Encyclopedia of Associations** - Provides information on associations and societies. **The Million Dollar Directory: Leading Public and Private Companies** - This directory includes brief summaries of more than 150,000 United States companies. The information is organized using NAICS. **Brands and Their Companies** and **Companies and Their Brands** These directories provide limited information and data about specific brands. **ThomasNet** – Searchable database providing information on manufacturers and sellers of industrial goods and services (www.thomasnet.com). **Edgar Online** – Searchable database of domestic and international company documents that are required by law, including Security and Exchange Commission (SEC) filings (www.sec.gov/edgar.shtml). **U.S. Census Bureau** – Provides information on industries and businesses. Studies published include county and business patterns, economic census and data by sector (retail, wholesale) (www.census.gov/)

Industry Analysis

An *industry analysis* helps retailers make smarter decisions because the analysis provides detailed information about the industry in which a retailer chooses to operate. Often businesses rely on an analysis of Porter's (1980) five forces to prepare an industry analysis. The five forces provide a framework for industry and competitive analysis. The forces are:

1. Rivalry among competing sellers in an industry

2. Competitive force of substitute products

3. Potential entry of new competitors in an industry

4. Bargaining power of suppliers

5. Bargaining power of buyers

For example, if Footlocker were conducting an industry analysis, company management would research the retail athletic footwear and apparel industry. They would look at Porter's five forces to help determine success factors needed to become a leader in the industry.

Competitive Analysis

Retailers perform a *competitive analysis* to gain knowledge of the other retailers competing in the market and determine how competitors will respond to a retailer's own strategy and tactics. The competitive analysis should include direct and indirect competitors. Once completed, the competitive analysis becomes part of the situational analysis portion of the integrated retail management plan.

If Footlocker were conducting a competitive analysis, they would analyze direct competitors such as The Finish Line and The Athlete's Foot. Indirect competitors analyzed might include department stores that carry athletic shoes and apparel such as Kohl's and JC Penney.

Because many products in the retailing industry have reached maturity in their life cycles, one of the only ways to increase business and sales is to take away market share from the competition. While a retailer is trying to increase market share, so are their competitors. So the retailer with the best information and the most knowledgeable personnel is set apart from others.

Types of Competition

There are three types of competitors to consider when conducting a competitive analysis: 1. Intratype competition, 2. Intertype competition, and 3. divertive competition. A competitive analysis should include all three types of competition.

Direct or Intratype Competition: *Intratype (or direct) competition* are those companies that compete for the same customer base and households. To be considered as an intratype competitor, the competing retailers must have the same NAICS classification. Thus, Walmart competes with Target for the same consumer dollars and both retailers have the same NAICS numbers.

Intertype Competition: *Intertype (or indirect) competitors* sell the same lines of products and compete for the same household dollars. To be considered an intertype competitor, retailers cannot have the same number in the NAICS classification. e-Tailing has created many intertype competitors. For example, an indirect competitor for Dunkin Donuts could be supermarkets, such as Wegman's, that have bakeries.

Divertive Competition: *Divertive competitors* sell the same type of merchandise or services, but they don't necessarily specialize in the merchandise or services that they sell. Divertive competition occurs when a customer is enticed away from a competitor. Divertive competition can be either inter- or intra-type. If you wanted to send some flowers to a sick friend to brighten his day, you would have many channels of distribution and retailers to select from. Before you go online to search for products and product information, you instead decide to stop at a local floral shop to see what the products look like. On your way to the florist shop, you pass a supermarket and decide to pick up a few grocery items to last over the weekend. While shopping inside, you note that the supermarket also sells floral arrangements and flowers. These flowers are less expensive than those you remember seeing in the flower shop or online, but the bouquets of flowers are nonetheless attractive. You decide to purchase the flowers at the supermarket thinking you won't have the hassle of going to the florist or searching online for flowers. The supermarket has just diverted you from purchasing from its competitors, and it has generated revenue in doing so.

Market Structures

Retailers need to understand the market structure of a particular industry as well as the competitive environment from both the supply and demand sides of retail management. In any market, there are a number of buyers and sellers and competitors that respond to changes in supply and demand. Retailers can choose suppliers to buy from and consumers choose retailers from which to purchase products and services. Thus, businesses and consumers can influence price. *Pure competition* arises when there are many different buyers and many different sellers in a given market. There are few barriers to entry in this type of market structure and consumers can choose from a number of available substitutes for products and services. A retailer raising prices in a purely competitive market will lose market share as customers choose another company selling the same products for a better price.

In some industries, there is no competition and no substitutes available for consumers. A *monopoly* has one seller of a specific good or service for a given market area. This seller, or retailer, can set any price it wants for its products and services, assuming there is enough demand in the marketplace. Consumers who wish to purchase the product must do so through the only seller available. There are costly barriers to entry into this type of market due to the prohibitive costs and the economic, social or political environment which places restrictions on entry. Many electricity providers and cable television services providers operate monopolies.

Monopolistic competition arises when there are a limited number of sellers in a given market. Thus, there is limited competition among the retailers for the consumer dollars available. Even if the retailers in the market are selling different products, consumers often perceive these products or services as substitutes. The consumers are often willing to purchase these substitute products to satisfy their needs and wants. Take professional sports for an example. Professional sports work in a monopolistic market situation. Customers are looking for entertainment. If the Philadelphia Phillies are playing, but so are the Philadelphia 76ers, a customer (except die-hard fans) may see no difference in either going to the basketball game or going to the baseball game, so they're willing to spend the ticket price on either option. In a monopolistically competitive market, retailers must realize they face competition from other retailers selling different products that satisfy the same needs or wants.

Source: CP DC Press/Shutterstock.com

An oligopoly exists when there are very few sellers who are selling similar products. In an oligopoly, one firm typically emerges as the market leader. When this market leader changes its retailing tactics, the other retailers generally fall in line and change theirs also. In an oligopoly, most of the prices for the same types of products are similar. Companies in this market structure do not compete on price because, due to the smaller number of competitors, they are interdependent, and changes in price have a drastic effect on all companies.

Most competitive market situations are monopolistic competition, but not all. Retailers must be sure they understand the competitive dynamics of the marketplace in which they compete. Without this understanding, many errors will be made in the development and execution of the integrated retail management plan.

Geographic Analysis

Geographic analysis is a topic in Chapter 7, but because it is part of the competitive analysis, we describe it briefly here. A geographic or market analysis is conducted to provide the retailer information about which geographic markets offer the most potential for the success of the retailing operation. Retailers need to ascertain which geographic areas are key areas, either because of the strong presence of the retailer in that market or because of problems associated with doing business in a geographic area. This analysis is essential for multinational retailers. The data gathered in a market analysis provide retailers with geographic information that guides decision-making, including budget and other monetary decisions.

Internet Analysis

Retailers involved in e-commerce or e-tailing require additional assessments of their markets. With a brick-and-mortar store, customer locations are identified as they relate to who shops at a given physical location. e-Tailers' customers can come from various parts of the world. From urban to suburban to rural physical locations, customers shop online from around the globe to find the most unique items, search for specific products, or save money. It is necessary for the retailer to find out where most of the shoppers and customers are located. Typically, there will be segments of customers that are located in the same region. Online retailers should have systems in place that capture information about where customers are located. This will help the e-tailer customize product solutions for different segments.

Differentiation

In the ever-changing competitive retail climate, one of the strategies that retailers use is differentiation. *Differentiation* distinguishes the retailer and their product from others. The concept is to create or highlight unique product or store offerings from those of the competition. Retailers use several types of differentiation strategies. Many use a price differentiation strategy that highlights differences in pricing between competitors like the Dollar Store does. Some retailers differentiate based upon creating a total shopping experience. Cabela's and Disney use this strategy. Other retailers use quality to differentiate their product offerings such as Saks Fifth Avenue and Tiffany's. Customer service can also be used to differentiate a retailer, such as the reputation of Zappos, the online shoe retailer (www.zappos.com). Because of the increased competition and the blurring of retail channels, retailers have been more aggressive in trying to differentiate themselves from the competition. Retailers typically choose one or two areas for a differentiation strategy. For example, Ritz-Carlton Hotels is known for quality and outstanding customer service. One of the problems in the creation of differentiation is how to maintain a brand's equity and the continuity created for the store brand, yet change to stay relevant. One solution to the problem of creating differentiation is the effective development of multiple channels of distribution while focusing on the customer's needs and wants.

The new retail reality is that consumers want to experiment in stores. They want to be entertained. They enjoy face-to-face interactions and demonstrations with store personnel. Retailing is becoming more active as opposed to passive. Both brick-and-mortar and online stores will continue to employ interactive technology and entertainment to differentiate their products from the competition. Retailers will step up their research programs to help them determine which technologies are useful to shoppers. Retailers will be able to match customer profiles with product and service offerings, creating a more personalized shopping experience and store atmosphere.

Summary

To fully comprehend and develop an IRM plan, retail professionals must have a good understanding of the environment in which they are operating. This chapter looked at the many competitive situations retailers can face. These concepts should be carried over to the many different areas of the overall retail plan.

An understanding of retail institutions is essential for building strategies and tactics that allow the retailer to gain competitive advantage over other retailers. Different classifications for retail institutions help retailers develop a synergistic plan that makes them successful.

A competitive analysis gives retailers a more thorough understanding of the competition they face in the marketplace. By understanding the competition, retailers can create IRM plans that respond to competitive threats. Armed with knowledge of competitors' products and services, retailers can differentiate their businesses from those of their competitors, giving consumers a reason to select their outlets.

Key Terms

anchor	The largest store in a shopping center and serves to draw customers to the center.
business franchising	A situation characterized by a great deal of interaction between franchisee and franchisor; the franchisor agrees to support all the business functions while listening to the needs and wants of its franchisees.
cart abandonment rate	Percentage of customers will leave their shopping carts (online or instore) prior to check-out.
category killer	Sometimes known as a *power retailer* or *category specialist*, a discount specialty store that offers a deep assortment of merchandise.
chain store	A retailer that operates multiple (more than one) retail stores.
combination store	A retail format in which food items are combined with nonfood items to create a one-stop shopping experience.
company analysis	An analysis that includes data on sales and profit figures, company mission/vision, company's risk or conservative orientation, corporate resources, level of aggressiveness, market share, sales trends, etc.
competitive analysis	Conducted to gain knowledge about the other retailers competing in the market and determine how competitors will respond to a retailer's own strategy and tactics.
consumer cooperative	A retail establishment owned and operated by a group of consumers.
convenience store	A retailer that caters to a neighborhood and carries a very limited assortment of products.
department store	A large retailer that carries a wide breadth and depth of product and is organized into departments.
differentiation	A strategy used to distinguish a company and their product from others.
direct marketing	An interactive system of marketing that uses one or more advertising media to generate a measurable response or transaction at any location.
direct selling	One-to-one selling directly to the consumer outside of a retail establishment, such as in-home and online.

discount store	A type of department store that offers limited customer services and has merchandise priced below that at department stores.
divertive competitors	Retailers that compete by selling the same type of merchandise or services; they do not necessarily specialize in that merchandise.
drug stores (aka pharmacy)	A retailer that sells medicines and other items.
economies of scale	Achieving lower costs per unit through higher-quantity purchases.
everyday low pricing (EDLP)	A retailing strategy that emphasizes consistently lower-priced merchandise.
extreme-value retailers	These retailers offer a very limited assortment of merchandise at very low prices.
flea market	A retail format in which many vendors sell used as well as new and distressed merchandise.
food retailers	Sell food products to consumers as its primary function.
franchise	A contractual agreement between a franchisor and a franchisee that allows the franchisee to operate a retail establishment using the name and (usually) the franchisor's operating methods.
franchisee	The owner of a retail establishment who has a contract with the franchisor to use the franchise's name and (usually) methods of operation.
franchisor	A business that grants the franchisee the privilege to use the franchisor's name and (usually) operating practices.
general merchandise retailer	A retailer involved in the sale of general, nonfood items.
hi-lo pricing	A pricing strategy in which retailers set a higher price on less frequently purchased items and then discount the price of featured items through sales promotions and couponing.
hypermarket	A large retailer that carries many types of products in addition to foods; originated in Europe.
impulse buying	The purchase of products and services by consumers that was not planned.
independent retailer	A type of retailer that operates a single establishment.
industry analysis	An analysis of the industry in which a retailer chooses to operate.
intertype competitors	Different types of retailers that compete by selling the same lines of products and compete for the same household dollars.
intratype competitors	Retailers that compete for the same customer bases or households.
kiosks	Small stand-alone structures that are often open on one side or more.
leased department	A department in a large retail store in which space is leased or rented to an outside vendor that in turn operates under the larger retailer store's policies.
limited-line store (box store)	No frills food and merchandise discounters that offer a small selection of products.
magalog	A catalog developed in a magazine format.
market area	The geographical area where consumers who have a demand for the product reside.
marketbasket	Everything a customer plans on purchasing.
mobile POS systems (m-POS)	Mobile systems, typically hand-held, that aid in the completion of a retail transaction.

monopolistic competition	A market in which there is a limited amount of competition from other retailers for consumer dollars.
monopoly	A market in which there is only one seller selling a specific good or service.
North American Industrial Classification System (NAICS)	A business coding system developed by the government that uses a coding system to identify types of businesses for better comparisons.
off-price retailer	A retailer that sells brand-name merchandise, which may include overruns or distressed merchandise, at 40 to 50 percent below traditional retailers.
oligopoly	A market characterized by similar products and very few sellers.
point-of-sale systems (POS)	Systems that aid in the completion of a retail transaction.
product franchising	A situation in which the franchisee agrees to sell the franchisor's products or services.
pure competition	A market in which there are many different buyers and sellers.
retail-sponsored cooperative	A type of retail organization in which several retailers have banded together to create an organization that helps to overcome many of the problems associated with running a small retail operation.
share of wallet	The percentage of a customer's total spending at a retailer.
specialty store	A store that carries a limited number of products within one or a few lines of goods and services.
stock keeping units (SKU)	Retailer-defined numbers or codes used to identify each unique product sold.
strategic clarity	The retailer's commitment to create and achieve an in-depth understanding of their strengths and weaknesses.
supercenter	A retailer that is a combination of a superstore and a discount store.
superstore	A food-based retailer that is larger than a traditional supermarket and carries expanded service deli, bakery, seafood, and nonfood sections.
traditional supermarket	A store that offers a full line of groceries, meat and produce with at least $2 million in annual sales and up to 15 percent of their sales in general merchandise/health and beauty care. The stores carry between 15,000 and 60,000 SKUs (stock keeping units) and may have a deli, bakery and/or pharmacy.
vending machine	A nonstore retailing format in which consumers purchase products through a machine.
warehouse club	A retailer that charges a membership fee to consumers or businesses who buy from the store.
warehouse store	A retailer that offers a limited assortment of goods and services, both food and merchandise, to both end users and small to midsize businesses at reduced prices.
wholesale-sponsored cooperative	An organization that is developed, owned, and run by a group of wholesalers.

Discussion Questions

1. Why is it important for retailers to analyze the retail environment?

2. What are the types of retailers by ownership?

3. What are advantages and disadvantages of the NAICS system?

4. What type of information do retailers collect to conduct a competitive analysis?

5. What challenges do you see in the future for department stores?

Exercises

1. Look up the website for Casual Male (www.casualmale.com). What makes this retailer a specialty retailer? What evidence can you find that illustrates multi-channel retailing?

2. Conduct an industry analysis of the retail discount market.

3. Conduct a competitive analysis for T.J. Maxx (www.tjmaxx.com).

4. Visit the Global Franchise website (www.globalfranchise.com). Choose three franchise opportunities that interest you and write a summary of the businesses, including costs to operate the franchise.

5. Go to the U.S. Small Business Administration website at *www.sba.gov* and do the following:

   • Browse through the website to get a good idea of the information available.

   • What information is offered that could prove valuable to a small-business owner?

   • What potentially useful information is *not* included on the website?

   • What are the most common types of information requested from this site by small-business owners?

6. Look up the following retailers and indicate how each of them would be classified:

   1. Barnes and Noble

   2. Sam's Club

   3. Dollar Tree

   4. Safeway

   5. Boscov's

   6. 7 Eleven

   7. IGA

   8. Dick's Sporting Goods

   9. Big Lots

   10. Pep Boys

Case

L Brands and Strategic Decisions

Many retailers adjust their strategy by capitalizing on their brand successes and adapting to the changing environment. The purpose is to broaden the retailers' customer bases by developing products and services that allow them to capture new markets or expand their current market base.

According to the website (www.lb.com), L Brands sells lingerie, personal care and beauty products and apparel and accessories. The company, then known as The Limited, was started in 1963 by Lex Wexner in the Kingsdale Shopping Center in Columbus, OH. The first day sales were $473. L Brands sold The Limited and Express chains in 2007 to focus on Victoria's Secret and Bath and Body Works. The name changed to L Brands in 2013. Today the company operates over 3,000 stores in the U.S., Canada, the United Kingdom and China. In 2015 L Brands recorded sales of $12.7 billion. In addition to Victoria's Secret and Bath and Body Works, L Brands owns Henri Bendel, La Senza, and Pink. As of June 2016, L Brands, Inc ranked #234 in the *Fortune 500* list.

In 2010, the company realized that the Victoria's Secret business was stagnant. Thus, the company started rolling out new styles and colors more frequently. The same strategy helped Bath and Body works. These changes have worked with young consumers who like the fashion and fresh merchandise. Consequently, revenue increased substantially.

The company announced plans to expand Victoria's Secret internationally. Initial plans included locations in the Middle East operated by M. H. Alshaya, a Kuwaiti company. The owner of the company, Mohammed Alshaya, also operates Payless and H&M stores (among others) in the Middle East. A franchise agreement was completed which allowed Victoria's Secret stores to open in Bahrain and Kuwait. The stores in the Middle East carry different clothing assortments than the U.S., based on the country culture.

L Brands discovered that the path to success in a very competitive environment is through product differentiation, developing partnerships with companies that have country-specific knowledge and appealing to a well-defined group of consumers. It's no wonder that they have been listed several times in *Fortune Magazine's Most Admired Companies*.

Sources: Alva, M. (2011, Aug 12). What market slump? Victoria's Secret shops are jammed. Limited Brands, Columbus, Ohio. *Investors Business Daily*, pp. A07; Jannarone, J. (2011, Oct 20). Victoria's overseas secret remains behind closed doors. *Wall Street Journal*, pp. C.14-C.14. D&B Hoovers (2017). L Brands website.

Questions

1. Based on your knowledge of the retailing environment, do you think introducing products more frequently is a successful strategy? Why or why not?

2. What challenges will Victoria's Secret face in the Middle East?

3. Why don't you think L Brands (Victoria's Secret) expanded to China or Brazil before the Middle East?

4. What suggestions would you give to L Brands to continue their success?

References

About Meijer (n.d). Retrieved from www.meijer.com.

Anderson, M. (2010). Abercrombie & Fitch Brings Back Racy Catalog. ABCnews.com, New York, June 25, (AP). Retrieved from http://abcnews.go.com/CleanPrint/cleanprintproxy.aspx?1289844522094

Baynard Institute (2017). 37 cart abandonment rate statistics. Retrieved from https://baymard.com/lists/cart-abandonment-rate

Belcher, W. (2009). Billy Mays' Death Leaves Infomercial Void, but Pitches Will Go On. McClatchy - Tribune Business News, June 30). Retrieved from ABI/INFORM (Document ID: 1769860921).

Bhatnagar, P. (2003, December 2). Abercrombie: What's the naked truth?
CNNMoney.com. Retrieved from http://money.cnn.com/2003/12/02/news/companies/abercrombie_catalog/

Binns, J. (2010). Survival of the Fittest: Retailers Grapple with Social Media, Technology. Apparel (Online) (Nov 3).
Retrieved from http://apparel.edgl.com/news/Survival-of-the-Fittest--Retailers-Grapple-with-Social-Media,-
Technology62745

Caggiano, J. (2003). Abercrombie & Fitch Drops Racy Publication; Consumer Groups Claim Victory. Knight Ridder
Tribune Business News, (Dec 11). Retrieved from ABI/INFORM (Document ID: 489289591).

Chandler, Kreta and Karen Hyatt (2003). *Customer-Centered Design*, Upper Saddle River, New Jersey: Prentice Hall
PTR.

Data & Marketing Association (2016). Direct mail statistics. Retrieved from https://thedma.org/marketing-insights/
marketing-statistics/direct-mail-statistics/

Day, J. (2004). Burberry Doffs its Cap to "Chavs" *Guardian*, (Nov 1). UK. Retrieved from http://www.guardian.co.uk/
media/2004/nov/01/marketingandpr.

Direct Marketing Association 2015 Statistical Fact Book (2016). Published by the Direct Marketing Association/
Winterberry Group.

Dubravac, S. G., C.F.A. (2015). Three shifts influencing the CE industry right now. *Dealerscope, 57*(9), 26-27. Retrieved
from Proquest Database.

Economides, S. and Economides, A. (2007) *America's Cheapest Family Gets You Right on the Money.* Three Rivers
Press: New York, NY.

ExactTarget, Inc. (2009). Retailer Boosts Online Sales with Specialty Emails, Social Media. *Marketing Business Weekly*,
411. Retrieved from http://search.proquest.com/docview/203240945?accountid=13158

Food Marketing Institute (20017). Retrieved from http://www.fmi.org/research-resources/supermarket-facts

Getting the Measure of Social Media Success. (2012). *Marketing Week,* (01419285), 12. Retrieved from http://
search.proquest.com/docview/921457998?accountid=13158

History of the Sears Catalog (2004). Sears Archives. Retrieved from http://www.searsarchives.com/catalogs/
history.htm

Kotler, Philip and Kevin Lane Keller (2012), *A Framework for Marketing Management,* 5th ed., Upper Saddle River, NJ:
Pearson Education, pp. 210.

Lawder, M. (2016). Kohl's to open smaller-format stores this fall, including some in Wisconsin. Milwaukee Business
Journal, Sep 23. Retrieved from http://www.bizjournals.com/milwaukee/news/2016/09/23/kohls-to-open-smaller-
format-stores-this-fall.html

Leinbach-Reyhl, N. (2014). Celebrating independent retailers: Their surprisingly strong future. Forbes. July 3, 2014.
Retrieved from https://www.forbes.com/sites/nicoleleinbachreyhle/2014/07/03/celebrating-independent-retailers-
their-strong-future/#578195f04334

North American Industry Classification System (2012). Retrieved from www.naics.com.

Our Company (n.d). Meijer Company website. Retrieved from www.meijer.com.

Pandey, A. (2017, Mar 09). Chatbots promising exponential growth for futuristic enterprises of today. Retrieved from
ProQuest database.

Popeil, R., & Wehrum, K. (2009). Ron Popeil Ronco: He Slices and Dices, and That's Not All! *Inc,* 31(1), 78-80. Retrieved
from ABI/INFORM Global. (Document ID: 1628929401

Porter, M. E. (1980). *Competitive strategy: Techniques for analyzing industries and competitors.* New York: The Free
Press.

Red Box website. Retrieved from www.redbox.com

Shopkick app now available on the app store: Just Walk in & Collect (2010) PR Newswire, (17 August). Retrieved from ABI/INFORM Dateline. (Document ID: 2112068721).

Smilansky, O. (2017). The case for unified commerce. *Customer Relationship Management, 21,* 14-15. Retrieved from Proquest Database.

Stone, K.E. (1995). *Competing with the Retail Giants.* New York: John Wiley & Sons.

Wegman's Food Markets, Inc.: An Overview (n.d). Retrieved from www.wegmans.com.

World Federation of Direct Selling Associations (2012). Retrieved from http://www.wfdsa.org/legal_reg/index.cfm?fa=directselling

Chapter 5

Evaluation and Identification of Retail Customers

"The secret is to know your customer. Segment your target as tightly as possible. Determine exactly who your customers are... Match your customer with your medium. Choose only those media that reach your potential customers, and no others. Reaching anyone else is waste."

~ Robert Grede, Naked Marketing: The Bare Essentials

Source: aodaodaodaod/Shutterstock.com

CHAPTER OBJECTIVES

After completing this chapter you will be able to:

- Discuss the importance to retailers of understanding customers.
- Discuss the four general means used to describe customers: demographics, psychographics, geographics, and behavioristics.
- Explain why it is important for retailers to study consumer decision processes.
- Describe the consumer decision process.
- Describe the models that attempt to explain consumer behavior.

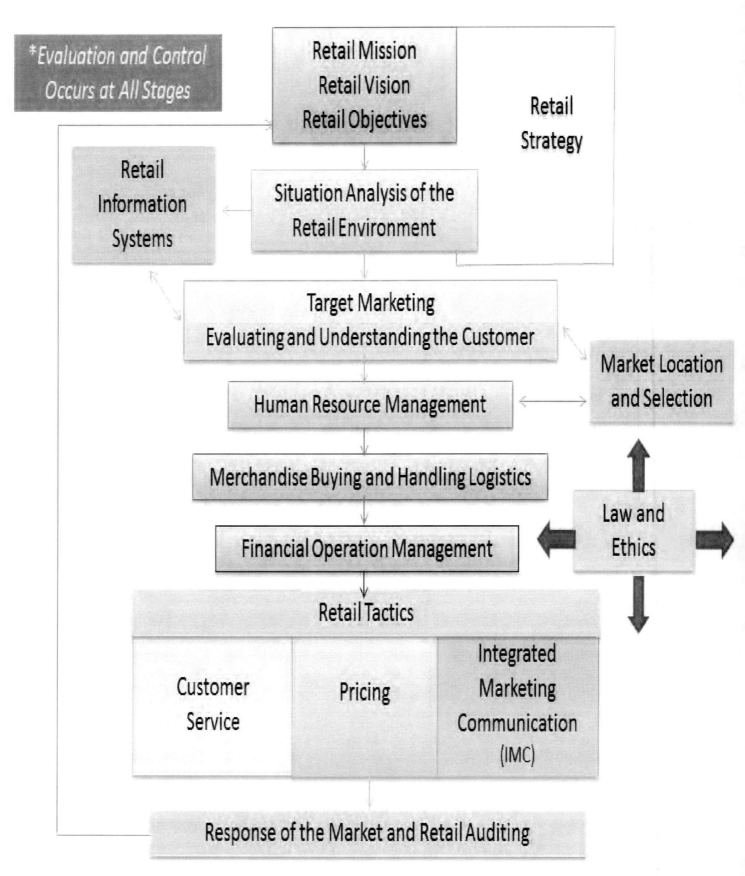

Dell Adapts to Changing Markets

In 2003 Dell Computer Corporation ranked number 2 in *Business Week*'s "Info Tech 100 list" (NeXtel communications…, 2003). Part of Dell's success was their ability to identify new market segments and to connect with their customer base. Prior to 1997, Dell did not target the final consumer because the company was concerned with the cost involved in after-sale support. Beginning in 1997, as more people were buying their second or third computers, the company began direct marketing to the final consumer.

When computer sales began to decline, an indication that the industry was in the maturity phase of the life cycle, Dell had to find new markets in order to continue to be profitable. Thus, in 2001, the company targeted a younger segment (Pletz, 2003) and hired a new media spokesperson, Ben Curtis (Lazare, 2002). The advertising campaign featured Curtis playing the role of Steven, the young surfer type who ended every commercial with the catchy phrase "Dude, you're getting a Dell!" This campaign was a big success for Dell, and sales of Dell computers skyrocketed (Rhey, 2002). However, the campaign got a bit tarnished with the arrest of Curtis in February 2003 on charges of purchasing marijuana from an undercover cop (Italiano, Schram and Hoffmann, 2003). Although the charges were dropped and the negative publicity did not affect sales, the company decided not to renew Ben's contract and instead turned to an inexperienced but eager cast of interns in their commercials (Howard, 2003).

Fast forward to 2015 when Dell personal computer sales lagged behind HP and Lenovo. Dell's PC sales dropped as the demand for desktop and laptop computers decreased. In 2015, a new campaign called "Future Ready" was launched. The campaign uses storytelling to show how technology can help people and businesses. The campaign was launched with an ad that featured a little girl waiting for a heart transplant (Maddox, 2016). The story was built around what happened to the girl after the transplant. The ads featured doctors interacting with computers, providing an image of how computers might be in the future.

Introduction

In retailing, the customer is the reason for existence. The people who enter a retailer's store (or visit its website) and make purchases are the ones who drive the business. In a service economy, the relationships the retailer builds with customers determine its success (Rust, Zeithaml and Lemon, 2000). Any successful retail establishment understands its customers, including how they think and behave, where they live, and their demographic characteristics. All retailing tactics should be directed toward those individuals who will inevitably purchase the products and services offered. Retailers who exhibit customer-focused activities are enacting the marketing concept.

Customers have a wide choice of businesses to patronize. The retailer that understands its customers' needs and wants is able to provide the products and services that will best satisfy those customers. In addition, the retailer is able to price the product at an appropriate level and at the same time generate a profit. The retailer can have an effective product mix available to customers when and where they want it if, and only if, there is effective communication with those customers.

This chapter discusses the many variables used to identify and understand the retail customer. The retailer that integrates this information into its retail plan is more likely to achieve profitable sales levels than those who are unaware of their customer base.

The retailer's target market should consist of consumers who have specific needs for its services or products. Consumers may wish to purchase the products as gifts, for daily family use, or for personal consumption. To be able to communicate with these consumers using integrated marketing communications tactics, the retailer must know precisely who they are.

There is an old saying in advertising, "We have met the consumer and he isn't us." In other words, retailers need to research *who* their customers are and how their customers make decisions. Retailers cannot rely only on intuition; they must employ outside research methods to gain insights into how and why consumers shop.

Retailers can use a number of methods to obtain a good picture of their customer base. The behaviors that consumers exhibit when shopping for goods and services, for instance, can teach the retailer a great deal. The information generated can be easily placed into the target marketing section of the integrated retail management plan, which deals with evaluating and understanding the customer. These data can then be used to help select the target market and are instrumental in the retailer's site selection activities. It is important to include all consumer data in the retail information system (RIS). This gives all retail decision makers access to the data at the push of a button and significantly reduces the work required to research these data manually.

Information about consumers usually falls into one of four categories (called the "four *ics*"): (1) demographics, (2) psychographics, (3) geographics, and (4) behavioristics. Often a clearer picture of the customer base emerges when these areas are combined. For example, when retailers analyze the demographics and geographics of a consumer base, the result is a consumer's geodemographics. It is important for retailers to understand the link between the four categories and consumers' responses to marketing efforts (Wind, 1978). We will consider the first three areas (demographics, psychographics, and geographics) first, followed by a look at behavioristics and the practice of combining the categories.

Demographics

Demographics are statistics about a given population. For retailers, demographics on their consumer base or potential consumer base are relevant. Demographic information helps the retailer better select target markets, or market segments, for its business. In addition, the retailer uses these data to help forecast product or service sales and to develop better communication with its customers. Useful demographics include age, gender, income level, education level, religious beliefs, and ethnicity. These demographics help to define the typical customer and are usually inserted into the typical customer profile. For example, a retailer of sports paraphernalia may describe their target market using demographics as males between the ages of 25 and 55 who earn $50,000 - $75,000 per year. Retailers can also use demographic data in selecting the appropriate market areas in which to operate. For a business selling an expensive, upscale product like a Rolls Royce automobile, the physical location should be close to those customers who have a need or want for that product and who can afford it.

Collection of demographic data is the most popular method of identifying customers, perhaps because these types of data are

Source: Monkey Business Images/Shutterstock.com

the easiest to obtain (Senguder, 2003). Demographic data can tell retailers what potential customers like to read, what television shows they watch, where they work, and many other statistics that may be used to increase the effectiveness of the retail plan. Demographic data alone may not provide a complete picture, but when tied to a product or buying situation, they provide useful information on consumer preferences (Winter, 1984). The three most common demographic variables are age, ethnicity, and income.

Age Groups

Generational marketing is the study of age groups and their relationship to the consumer market (Janoff, 1999). Marketers group the American population into generations, which are groups of people that were born and grew up in the same time span. Generational marketing is based on the premise that people in the same age range tend to behave similarly and respond to marketing in a like manner. Based on one particular age, once may exhibit certain behavior characteristics. Table 5.1 shows the different generations and summary information on each.

Table 5.1 – Generation Groups

Generation	Birth Date	Other Names	Age (in 2017)
Pre-Depression	Before 1930	G.I. Generation, Veteran Generation, and WWI Generation	88 and above
Depression	1930-1945	Silent Generation, Traditionalists, and Swing Generation	72-87
Baby Boom	1946-1964	Boomers, Me Generation, Love Generation, Woodstock Generation	53-71
Generation X	1965-1976	Baby Bust, Slackers, Why Me Generation, and the Latchkey Generation	41-52
Generation Y	1977-1994	Gen Y, Millennials, Echo Boomers, Why Generation, Net Generation, Gen Wired, We Generation	23-40
Generation Z	After 1994	Post-millennials iGeneration, Tweens, Baby Boomers, Generation 9/11, and Generation XD	Less than 23

Source: Adapted from Williams, K. C., & Page, R. A. (2011). Marketing to the generations. *Journal of Behavioral Studies in Business, 3*, 1-17.

There are numerous names for each generation and, depending on the source, the years used to define the generations may vary by a few years. Described below are six generations commonly used in marketing: Pre- Depression, Depression, Baby Boom, Generation X, Generation Y, and Generation Z (Williams and Page, 2011).

Source: Monkey Business Images/Shutterstock.com

Pre-Depression Generation – Most people in this generation experienced the Depression and suffered economically. They lived through two wars and have experienced social and technological change. Members of this generation prefer print media for information and tend to be conservative and altruistic. Concerns include health, aging and financial and personal security. Retailers selling vacations, products related to health, and prepared foods are popular with this group.

Depression Generation – People in this generation were children during the Depression or WWII. As a result, they value rationing, saving, and tend to be patriotic. Social tranquility and family togetherness are important to this generation. They don't like change and are slow to adopt new products. This generation is very active and many are wealthy. Retailers can reach this group by emphasizing traditional values and products, such as "Made in the USA." Although they do not use technology as much as younger groups, this group is the fastest growing group of Internet users. This group also prefers formality when communicating so retail employees should use Mr. or Mrs. when greeting members of this group.

Baby Boomers – People in this group were born in the period that occurred after World War II. Baby Boomers value individualization, self-expression and optimism. They are often described as self-centered and suspicious of authority. Many baby boomers define themselves by their careers and are workaholics. While some have retired, many plan to continue working in a different career. This generation is less price sensitive if they feel they are getting a good value. Retailers should give this cohort options and flexibility. While aging, this group does not want to be reminded of their age. Health and products designed to prolong youth are popular sellers. Many people in this generation have grandchildren and may even be caretakers for their parents and children. Since over 70 percent of Baby Boomers use the Internet, it is important to leverage the Internet for communicating with them.

Generation X – People in this generation have experienced tough economic times, thus success has been difficult. They value family first in part because of the rising divorce rates experienced during their lives. They are called latch-key children because they often returned home from school to an empty house due to both parents working. Consequently, this group has taken greater responsibility for raising themselves and tends to be less traditional than any other generation. This group tends to value multiculturalism and thinking globally. They are technologically savvy and tend to be highly educated. This group is seen as pessimistic and skeptical. They are not as career-oriented as Baby Boomers and seek a balance of family, work and fun time. This group tends to shop at retailers with a record of strong corporate social responsibility. Home improvement products are popular with this group. This group tends to be price conscious and will search to find the best price. Retailers should give Generation Xers access to information to educate them about a retailer's products, services and goals.

Generation Y - These are children of Baby Boomers and grew up with rapid technological and social change. This generation has a strong sense of independence and autonomy. They are results driven and care about image. Generation Y has a greater need for peer acceptance and connecting with their friends. Gen Y individuals are open-minded, optimistic and goal oriented. Mass marketing does not work with this generation. Retailers should focus on creating a positive shopping experience that provides entertainment. Social networking is an effective method to reach this group. Any Internet communication must be interactive. Because people in this group get bored easily, retailers should update their offerings to drive customer traffic.

Generation Z – This generation has experienced global terrorism, school violence, the aftermath of the attack on the World Trade Center and the recession. Their parents married later and are less likely to get divorced. Because they have always had access to the Internet and other technologies, they tend to have short attention spans, lack interpersonal skills, are not good listeners and are accustomed to instant gratification (Williams, Page, Petrosky and Hernandez, 2010). The Gen Z members are accustomed to using multiple media and are the first generation to use Chatspeak in real life (Example: *IHTWBSAP* – translation: I have trouble with basic spelling and punctuation) (Williams et al., 2010). This makes Generation Z the most technologically savvy generation of all (Walliker, 2008). They have grown up using the Internet and social media. Instead of talking on a telephone, they prefer to text. They are electronic multi-taskers and, as such, are easily distracted. In addition, they don't spend a lot of time outdoors unless it's through activities often organized by adults (Posnick-Goodwin, 2010). Generation Z is composed of a diverse group with wide experiences and ideas. Music, fashion, cosmetics and video games are popular products for Generation Z. Use technology in all forms to reach this generation.

Source: oneinchpunch/Shutterstock.com

The United States Census Bureau (www.census.gov) tracks changes in age groups to get a clear picture of social and economic change. Table 5.2 (on next page) shows the U.S. population by age in 2000 and 2013. According to the 2010 census, the population grew older with many states reaching a median age over 40 years old (Howden and Meyer, 2010).

To take advantages of the differences in generations, retailers can define their niche; adapt language to appeal to each segment and leverage technology. When defining a niche, it's important to realize that while Baby Boomers share characteristics, because the generation is defined by a long time span, there are differences within this generation. A retailer must decide if they are going to target more active Baby Boomers or those that have health problems, for example. The language used should be different depending on the generation that is targeted. Older generations react positively to messages that incorporate nostalgia which is not the case with younger generations. Older generations are also more likely to expect a company to reach out to them in comparison to younger generations who more often reach out to companies to communicate. A retailer can leverage technology with all generations, although the younger generations are more accustomed to using technology on a daily basis (Trese, 2011).

The overall concept for retailers in looking at these age categories is to gain insight into the market. Levi Strauss & Co. (LS&CO) saw a need in the 1980s for a line of clothing that could be worn anywhere. It introduced Dockers® Khakis in the United States in 1986. This product served as a link between jeans and dress slacks, and brought a shift to casual clothing in the workplace. In 1988, it launched Dockers® for Women, with a line of clothing designed to fit a variety of body types and

Table 5.2 - Population by Selected Age Groups: 2000 and 2013
Table 5.2 - Population by Selected Age Groups: 2000 and 2013

	2000		2013		Change, 2000 to 2013	
	Number	Percent	Number	Percent	Number	Percent
Total population.	281,421,906	100.0	311,116,000	100.0	27,323,632	9.7
Under 18 years	72,293,812	25.7	74,187,000	24.0	1,887,655	2.6
Under 5 years	19,175,798	6.8	19,917	6.5	1,025,564	5.3
5 to 17 years	53,118,014	18.9	53,980,105	17.5	862,091	1.6
18 to 44 years	112,183,705	39.9	112,806,642	36.5	622,937	0.6
18 to 24 years	27,143,454	9.6	30,672,088	9.9	3,528,634	13.0
25 to 44 years	85,040,251	30.2	82,134,554	26.6	−2,905,697	−3.4
45 to 64 years	61,952,636	22.0	81,489,445	26.4	19,536,809	31.5
65 years and over	34,991,753	12.4	40,267,984	13.0	5,276,231	15.1
16 years and over	217,149,127	77.2	243,275,505	78.8	26,126,378	12.0
18 years and over	209,128,094	74.3	234,564,071	76.0	25,435,977	12.2
21 years and over	196,899,193	70.0	220,958,853	71.6	24,059,660	12.2
62 years and over	41,256,029	14.7	49,972,181	16.2	8,716,152	21.1

Sources: U.S.Census Bureau, *Census 2000 Summary File 1* and *2010 Census Summary File 1.*

sizes, and today the brand has expanded to include a wide range of products for consumers in more than forty countries. Over the years, LS&CO has tried many different products, including the "leisure suit" of the 1970s. According to the company seven in ten men own a pair of Dockers (Hoover's... 2017). LS&CO developed a product that their retailers were willing to carry, their customers were willing to buy, and that returned sizable sales to the company.

Demographic data are so important that many for-profit research organizations, such as Research and Markets and Yankelovich, gather, analyze and report trends and consumer behavior statistics. Retailers and other marketers pay large sums for access to these reports. Many retail researchers have determined some new and emerging consumer groups to watch during the next several years. These include the youth market, and in particular children and teens and the aging market who are concerned with health (Kimmel, 2010). Although retailers have been following these markets for years, only recently have they been able to better quantify the data for each of these groups. Although generalizations are used to describe a particular group, individual members may vary considerably from the general descriptions.

The next time you go shopping or watch television commercials, observe how various retailers target their marketing toward the different generations. For instance, manufacturers and retailers appeal to the senior generation by using older models. Seniors understand that they are aging and generally appreciate that they cannot fight this natural process. The strategy in selling to seniors is to depict them as active and attractive. Think of all of the television commercials for new pharmaceuticals or fiber-enriched products that feature healthy, energetic seniors urging consumers to buy the products to enrich their lives.

Race and Ethnic Groups

As we continue into the 21st century, race and ethnicity are playing larger roles in American society. These changes are also occurring in American markets. Thus, retailers are relying, more and more, on race and ethnicity data to complete their typical customer profiles as well as to hone their marketing and marketing communications programs for their customers.

A **race** is a group of individuals sharing common genetic traits that determine physical characteristics. An *ethnic group* is "any group that is defined or set off by race, religion, national origin, or some combination of these categories" (Gordon, 1964). It is important for retailers to appreciate the differences and similarities of behavior within and among races and ethnic groups.

The U.S. Census Bureau uses five racial classes or categories to define race: White (Anglo), Black (African American), American Indian or Alaska Native, Asian and Pacific Islanders. A sixth category called "some other race," was added in 2000 to accommodate people who were from a race not listed. Ethnic groups are based upon origin or nationality. Hispanics may be correctly classified as any of the five races, which is why you often see survey results reported as "White (non-Hispanic)." This description tells you that the data do not include people of Hispanic or Latin American origin.

Almost three-quarters of the American population is White (72.4 percent); Blacks account for approximately 12.6 percent of the population; Asians 4.8 percent; American Indians and Alaska Native, 0.9 percent; and Native Hawaiian and other Pacific Islanders make up about 0.2 percent of the U.S. population. People who indicated "some other race" were 6.2 percent of the U.S. population (Humes, Jones and Ramirez, 2011).

In 2002, the Hispanic community became the largest minority group in the United States (with some 38.8 million members). In 2011, Hispanics/Latinos accounted for 16.3 percent of the population, a 43 percent increase from the 2000 census (Humes et al., 2011). In comparison, the non-Hispanic population grew at 5 percent between the 2000 and 2010. The U.S. Census Bureau also reports that the Asian population (non-Hispanic) grew faster than any other major race group between 2000 and 2010, increasing by 43 percent (2010 Census Shows…2011).

Buying power (also known as purchasing power) is the money people have to spend on products/services after paying taxes. Research shows that the combined buying power of racial minorities (African Americans, Asians and Native Americans) will rise from $1.6 trillion in 2010 to $2.1 trillion in 2015, accounting for 15% of the nation's total buying power. The buying power for Hispanics will increase from $1 trillion in 2010 to $1.5 trillion in 2015, which is almost 11% of the nation's buying power (Fahmy, 2010).

Income

Income levels determine ability for consumers to buy products and services. Retailers consider income levels of their target markets to determine the types of merchandise to stock and the types of marketing communications executions that would be required for various income levels. People in different income brackets demand different types of products and services. For example, many companies have developed unique stores to serve the upscale consumer.

Classifying income levels is difficult. What, for example, is middle class? Some marketers use income quintiles and consider the middle three quintiles to represent the middle class (60 percent of U.S. household income distribution). Others view middle class as a feeling. Yet others consider that being middle class depends on the number of people in the household and the state in which one lives (because geographical differences determine the cost of living). Some retailers think of income as one variable that makes up the middle class, but other variables, such as education and profession, also help to define middle class (Wellner, 2000). Despite the drawbacks and problems associated with income, retailers use income classifications to help them track their customer spending habits and identify consumer wants and needs. Lower-income consumers are more likely to eat at home than other groups. These consumers are also less likely to purchase luxury items, and they tend to be more practical in purchase decisions than other groups. Because they seek value, low-income consumers tend to shop at discount stores more frequently than do people in other income groups or levels.

The largest concentrations of individuals in the middle-income bracket live in the midwestern United States. People in this group tend to be college-educated and spend more on vacations. They eat meals outside of the home (at least more than lower-income people do). Middle-class consumers tend to search for higher-quality merchandise, but want it at lower prices, thus sales and couponing become important integrated marketing communications (IMC) tools for attacking this market. The middle class is often sub-divided into the upper middle class, consisting of college educated professionals and managers (white-collar workers), and the lower middle class, consisting of lower-level management and skilled craftsmen (blue-collar workers).

People in the upper-income category are often referred to as *affluent* (or rich). This group purchases luxury items, travels, and eats meals at restaurants (often upscale restaurants). Recently a new income category emerged: the *super-affluent* (or super rich). The top two percent of the U.S. population are the super-affluents (Shea, 2013).

Source: Fedor Selivanov/Shutterstock.com

The 2010 Census report indicated an increase in poverty. About 46 million people, or 15 percent of the U.S. population, lived in poverty in 2010. About 67 million people (23 percent of the population) lived in poverty areas, defined as census tracts with poverty rates of 20 percent or more. People living in high poverty areas are less likely to complete high school, work year round and own a home. They were also more likely to receive public aid and live in homes with one parent, typically a female (Bishaw, 2011). The rise in poverty has spurred growth in one-price stores, such as dollar stores, and discount retailers.

Retailers must convert demographic data into useful information. The better the data, the better the information. The better the information, the better the integrated retailing management plan. The better the plan, the more sales and profits retailers can expect. We now turn to psychographic analysis—the way in which the gathering of additional data makes the typical consumer profile more meaningful.

Psychographics

Psychographics is the study and analysis of consumer lifestyles. In generating psychographics, retailers find out what their customers do in their leisure or spare time. Do they like to fish? Do they enjoy Broadway musicals? Are they movie lovers? Any there sports fanatics out there? Do you enjoy spending time with family? Friends? Do customers have club memberships such as the Rotary Club, The Masonic Lodge or being a member of a book club? These are important psychographic variables. Psychographics are data that identify what consumers do over a period of time, ranging from a day or week to a year or more. These data typically include information on activities, interests and opinions (called *AIOs*). In addition, retailers generate information and data from consumers' VALS (**v**alues **a**nd **l**ifestyle**s**). Consumers' lifestyles provide retailers with more accurate and detailed information about their typical customers and the customers' purchasing patterns and behavior (Riche, 1989).

Psychographic studies are typically undertaken by firms that specialize in this type of study on behalf of specific clients. There are larger organizations and companies that collect general psychographic data that can be assessed by retailers and marketers. AIOs are a tool along with data from VALS. VALS data are generated by Strategic Business Insights (www.strategicbusinessinsights.com). The VALS framework is based on the premise that the combination of motivations and resources determines how a person will express himself as a consumer. The three primary motivations are: ideals, achievement, and self-expression. An individual's resources include income, education, energy, intellectual ability, leadership ability and innovativeness. The amount of resources enhances or inhibits a person's expression of his primary motivation. Based on primary motivations and resources, eight categories of lifestyles were developed: thinkers, believers, achievers, strivers, experiencers, makers, survivors and innovators (U.S. Framework and VALS Types, 2012). Figure 5.1 shows the VALS framework and Figure 5.2 describes each of the segments. A retailer can use this information to understand consumer motivations and resources to create the most effective customer profile.

Figure 5.1 – VALS Framework

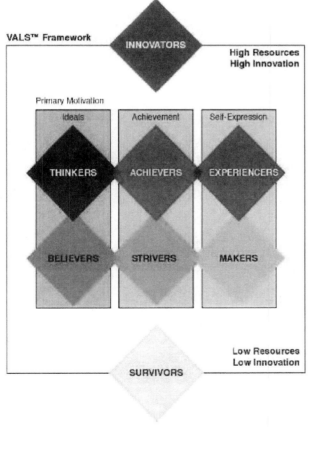

Source: Strategic Business Insights:
http://www.strategicbusinessinsights.com/vals/ustypes.shtml

Figure 5.2 – VALS Classification

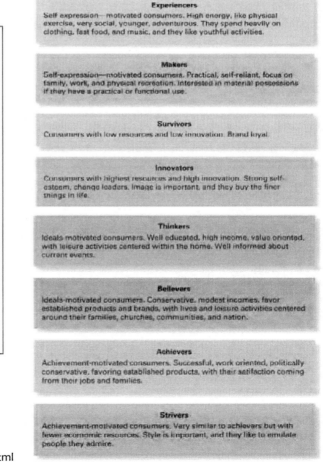

Psychographics are used in the integrated retail management plan, particularly in the identification of segments in the target market and the creation of the typical customer profile.

Geographics

Geographics describes the physical location of a retailer's customers, and it allows retailers to determine where the customer makes purchases. Information on where the customer lives is used in the integrated retail management (IRM) plan, particularly in planning advertising and other integrated marketing communications programs. Additionally, retailers use geographic information to help them execute corporate and social responsibility (CSR) initiatives, such as programs that help the community. Geographics can help retailers stock the most profitable products for their target markets. Adding sunglasses during the winter months to a product mix makes more sense for a retailer in Miami than in Seattle. In addition to being used to identify market segments, the data provide information that helps for retailers to communicate, identify and understand their customers.

Behavioristics

In addition to using geographics, demographics, geodemographics, and psychographics, retailers also are interested in how their customers behave when making purchases, called *behavioristics.* The idea underlying the use of *behavioristics* is to subdivide the retailer's current or potential markets based on buying responses, product usage patterns, product loyalty, or store loyalty. User profiles are developed to help explain who the customer is and how he or she responds to the various elements of the retail mix. Managers using behavioristics examine product benefits sought by consumers, how decisions are made, the occasion for the purchase, the time of purchase and place of purchase. Usage rate and whether a consumer is a light medium or heavy user of a retailer's products are also important. The more information a retailer can generate about consumers' buying behaviors, the better the retailer will be able to create appropriate products, services and shopping experiences.

One key finding of behavioristics is that a small number of customers may provide the majority of business for the retailer, a marketing concept called the 80/20 rule or the Pareto principle. The *80/20 rule* states that 80 percent of a retailer's sales are provided by 20 percent of a retailer's customers. This rule was established for industrial marketers, but many retailers are finding that it holds for retail products as well. In response to this rule, retailers have developed programs to treat this group of customers in a special way. CVS (drug store), for example, developed an affinity card

Source: Syda Productions/Shutterstock.com

called ExtraCare that rewards shoppers with points and rebates based on their purchase behaviors. Those shoppers who spend a lot of money at CVS stores are rewarded coupons. Similar programs are in effect at Hallmark, the major airlines, and a host of other retail businesses.

Geodemographics

In recent years, demographics and geographics have been combined to create a tool called geodemographics. *Geodemographics* uses geography and descriptive population statistics (demographics) to better understand the customer market. Demographics are added to geographical data (and maps) to create a better snapshot of the retailer's retailing landscape, or environment in which the retailer conducts business. Typically geodemographic data are placed into some type of geographic information system (GIS) to assist in the development and execution of IRM plans. Large real estate site specialists use GIS systems to create planned shopping centers by identifying the customers from alternative market areas.

The major providers of geodemographic data are Nielsen, CACI, and Experian Simmons. Nielsen offers a product called *PRIZM*, which stands for *P*otential *R*ating *I*ndex by *Z*ip *M*arkets. Nielsen PRIZM is one of the most widely used neighborhood target marketing software systems in the United States. CACI Limited (London) offers *ACORN*, which stands for *A C*lassification *O*f *R*esidential *N*eighborhoods. This software system helps the retailer analyze and profile customers based on demographic and geographic data. Experian Simmons Bureau collects and aggregates data used for demographic modeling. One of their products, Mosaic USA (Experian Marketing Services), is a consumer database of 126 million households segmented into lifestyles

Geodemographics allow retailers to identify differences among cities, suburbs, and rural areas and monitor the growth of distinctive regional marketplaces. Retailers are then able to tailor messages to reach their markets, rather than engage in the mass marketing.

Many other variables than those we discussed may influence a consumer's decision to buy. Family, culture, reference groups, and opinion of influential people will have an impact as does the marketing communication from a retailer.

Source: Daniel Jedzura/Shutterstock.com

Successfully Reaching Today's Customer

Targeted marketing communications drive customer visits and purchases. Numerous changes have been taking place in the retailing marketplace. Because market conditions are dynamic, marketing communications must also change to reach consumers. With an increase in omni-channel retailers, research-based IMC and IRM plans are developed to help retailers create operations that leverage changes. These plans are always developed with the customer's wants and needs in mind, which are tenants of the marketing and extended marketing concepts.

In addition to the increase in channels available to reach customers, there has been a movement from a mass marketing approach, to a segmented approach. Segmentation is useful because it exploits the differences in customers to provide a more targeted message for various groups. There has also been a movement toward mass customization, defined as "effectively postponing the task of differentiating a product for a specific customer until the latest possible point in the supply network" (Chase, Jacobs and Acquilano, 2006, p. 419). Thus customers wanting customization can be targeted. For example, a consumer can order a computer and choose the specification they desire in the product. These products are manufactured by automated systems and offered for sale at a lower, mass produced, price (Bearden, Ingram and LaForge, 2007).

Because of the rise of the Internet, many retailers can customize their product planning and development, distribution channels and systems and marketing communications (Bernhardt, Qihong, and Serfes, 2007). This is important because customers are playing a more active role in the customization process and this makes a retailer's job of reaching them much easier. Customers are helping to create retailer product offerings by providing feedback and ideas. Consumers use the Internet to gather and share information, connect to retailers, companies (manufacturers), friends and relatives. They are also using it to help define what e-commerce and m-commerce represent.

Retailers continue to undertake environmental scanning and are watching for new media technologies to appear (Kimmel, 2010).

The ability to identify brand community members is a new tool for retailers. *A brand community* is a group of consumers with product or brand attachments. Brand communities evolve, or exist, because a product's loyal customers desire some type of social interaction with each other. These communities almost always involve spontaneous evolution when starting. Retailers recognize that these communities have the potential to develop a close personal relationship with their companies and brands. Some brand communities include "Peeps" (Just Born Company), Apple, Inc., Harley Davidson, Barbie and Lego.

An offshoot of brand communities was the development of *web communities,* which are online websites that attract people with similar interests. Whether through blogs, Wikipedia, Facebook, or YouTube, many web communities are emerging that will have many differing implications for retailers who are trying to reach their markets in an effective and efficient manner.

Consumer Behavior

Consumer behavior is a classification of marketing that is applied to consumers. As it relates to retailing it is essentially the study of how customers buy products. Jacob Jacoby, Merchant Council professor of retail management and consumer behavior at New York University, provides a more in-depth definition of consumer behavior: "Consumer behavior reflects the totality of consumers' decisions with respect to the acquisition, consumption, and disposition of goods, services, time, and ideas. . . ." (Jacoby, 1976, p. 332).

Source: aodaodaodaod/Shutterstock.com

By getting a clear picture of their customers' behavior, retailers can increase product, brand, or product category sales significantly. Specifically, they can increase sales by studying the *hows*, *whys*, *whens*, and *wheres* of consumers' shopping behaviors.

To understand shopping behaviors, retailers need to know how consumers make purchase decisions. In retailing, purchase decisions are made at two stages of the shopping experience. First, the consumer selects a retailer with which to conduct business. Second, the consumer enters the store and goes through a second decision process related to selecting merchandise. The process used for both of these decisions is essentially the same.

Sometimes the consumer must first decide on a product or brand that she or he wants. After choosing the product or brand, the consumer selects a retail outlet based on store service, product price, or perhaps convenience. This scenario is common with potential customers who use the Internet to shop and obtain product information.

The Consumer Decision Process

Consumers typically follow a pattern of decision making when buying products. The five-step decision-making process is shown in figure 5.3 and is summarized as follows:

1.   Problem Awareness - the consumer becomes aware of a problem, an unsatisfied need, or desire

2.   Search for Information – the consumer conducts a search for information on the problem identified

3.   Evaluation of Alternatives - an evaluation of the available information and alternative solutions that will satisfy the needs and wants is undertaken

4.   Purchase - the purchase of the product or service is completed

5.   Post-purchase Evaluation – the consumer evaluates the total shopping experience

Knowledge of these stages helps retailers plan effective marketing communication plans to reach their targeted markets. For major purchases, consumers will go through each of the five steps. For routine or habitual purchases, consumers may skip the search and evaluation steps. Each step allows retailers an opportunity to help their consumers make purchases. Let's take a closer look at each stage.

Figure 5.3: The Five-Step Consumer Decision-Making Process

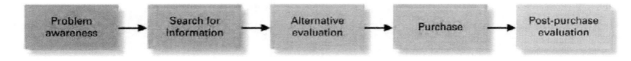

Problem awareness → Search for Information → Alternative evaluation → Purchase → Post-purchase evaluation

Problem Awareness: The first step, *problem awareness*, occurs only after a consumer realizes he or she has an unmet need or want. This can be in the form of a problem such as a broken smartphone; a need, such as hunger or a want for something, such as a new outfit. Consumers are only motivated by unmet needs and wants, thus it's important for retailers to know when consumers are ready to make a purchase. Need (or want) recognition can be either conscious or subconscious. Sometimes recreational shoppers (those that shop for fun) may realize they desire something when they see it online or in a window.

Figure 5.4: Maslow's Hierarchy of Needs

Self-actualization

Ego (Esteem Needs)

Social (Love, Belonging and Social Needs)

Safety and Security Needs

Physiological Needs

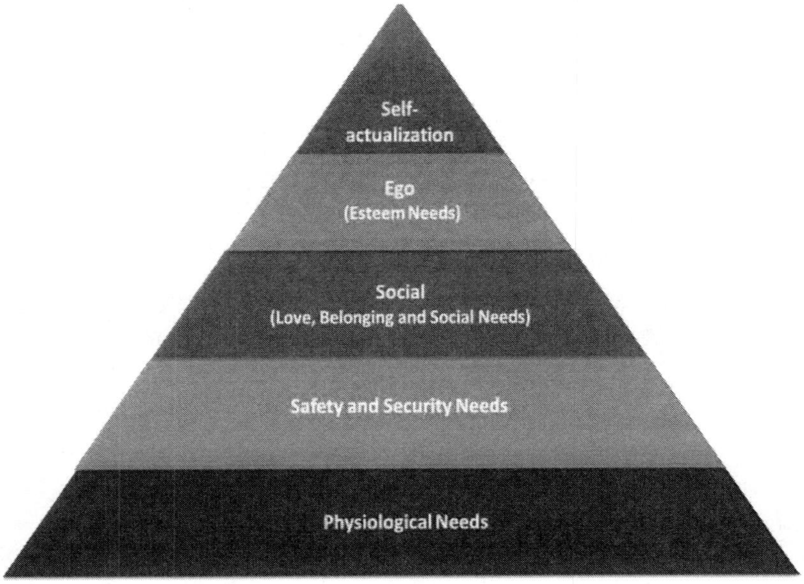

In assessing the consumer's problem awareness stage, retailers often refer to Maslow's Hierarchy of Needs, a theory developed by Abraham Maslow (Maslow, 1970), illustrated in Figure 5.4. Maslow suggested that there were five levels of needs that exist for each individual.

Maslow begins his hierarchy with lower level needs termed *physiological needs*. Physiological needs include the need for food, water, air, sleep and sex. Because these are lower level needs, they occur more frequently than the other needs do, and there is a stronger desire, among consumers, to satisfy these lower needs first. Because these are the strongest of the needs, and because consumers more frequently work to satisfy these needs, retailers use this level for most integrated marketing communication executions. Once the physiological needs are satisfied, consumers work to satisfy the next level of needs, or their *safety and security needs.*

Safety and security needs include the need for physical well-being, shelter and protection. When these needs are satisfied, consumers move to satisfy their *social needs* such as the desire to "fit in" or be part of a larger group, show affection and de-velop friendships. Then they satisfy their *ego or esteem needs,* which includes the need to be recognized for suc-cesses and accomplishments. Finally, they attempt to satis-fy their *self-actualization needs* which are usually defined as the needs related to self-fulfillment.

Only unsatisfied needs motivate consumers to shop. These unsatisfied needs create tension in shoppers, which in turn motivates them to shop. As an individual's needs are met at one level, such as the purchase of a Big Mac for hunger, the individual then seeks to fulfill the needs on the next level of Maslow's Hierarchy such as pur-chasing shoes that are in style. The Maslow model does

Source: Syda Productions/Shutterstock.com

have its critics who claim that the model isn't supported with sufficient evidence or research, how-ever, the model does provide retailers with a basic guide when assessing the consumer market.

A concept closely related to needs is that of wants. While a need is something a person has to have, a want is something a person would like to possess. We may have the *need* to be social and communicate, but we *want* an iPhone. Retailers and other marketers often attempt to turn con-sumer needs into wants or desires for their particular brand, company or product. Customers may need a lotion to treat their dry skin. L'Oreal may take that need, dry skin relief, and tell their cus-tomers that they should buy a better lotion because they are worth it. A retailer may carry adver-tisements that feature L'Oreal products. These efforts convert customers from buying a need, lo-tion, into the purchase of a want, a specific brand of lotion that provides the fulfillment of not only physiological needs, but may also satisfy higher level needs such as love and belongingness and self-esteem. The customer then thinks I'm worth a little pampering and their purchases are based upon want as opposed to a need. Sometimes people will turn wants into needs through rationaliza-tion. For example, upon seeing a new suit, Anne rationalized that the suit that she bought last month was already out of fashion. She convinces herself that she should buy the suit. The rationali-zation process gives a person permission to buy.

When looking at the awareness step of the consumer decision-making cycle, retail manag-ers attempt to determine *when* consumers are ready to make a purchase. This information will be useful to retailers when they assemble their IRM plans. Retailers can plan their tactics based upon when consumers are willing to buy.

Search for Information: Once the consumer has recognized that he or she has a problem, the consumer will begin to search for information to solve the problem. Depending on the time, effort, and cost associated with the problem, the information search may take a long time or have a short duration.

When you go to a vending machine to purchase a soda, you spend little time looking for a particular product that will quench your thirst. The products are all familiar to you, and you have made this purchase decision before. But what if you are planning to make a first-time purchase---say, a new car---and you know you will spend a lot of money for the purchase? In this instance, you most likely will spend considerable time and effort considering various purchase options. As a first step, you may get brochures and flyers from the many car dealers in your area, to compare options and costs.

When products and services are higher priced, have more importance to a consumer, or carry higher levels of risk, there is likely to be a higher level of consumer *purchase involvement.* The decision to buy a computer takes much longer than the decision to buy a beverage due to the cost and risk of making the wrong decision. Consequently, consumers will spend more time talking to other people about their experiences, checking consumer ratings of different brands and comparing price. The consumer may go to a store to try out the computer and while there may ask the salesperson many questions, thus furthering the information collection effort. Typically, when a consumer searches for information, he or she first searches internally. In an *internal search,* consumers rely on their experiences with the product or service and seek no other input in terms of their shopping behavior. The person may look through their smartphone for any archived information or perhaps they will attempt to remember what friends or family have said about the product. If the internal search offers no help, consumers search externally. The *external search* requires the consumer to gather information from a variety of sources including people, brochures, flyers, e-mail and m-commerce information. In their external search, consumers gather more information than they would in an internal search. Consumers use different methods in their searches. Younger consumers tend to use more technology in their searches than older consumers.

Alternative Evaluation; The evaluation process takes longer if the product is high priced, the consumer does not have experience in the product category or if there is a higher level of risk involved in the purchase. If it's a product that is purchased frequently or if the product has a low cost, the evaluation of alternative solutions will not take as long. To attract customers who are evaluating alternatives, retailers must show the consumer that their offerings are superior to those of their competitors. The retailer should provide product and service information to allow the consumer to make an educated purchase decision and to have the consumer choose their products or services. E-tailers often allow consumers to create a table that compares the features of various brands, which allows consumers to compare products by different attributes such as style and price.

Purchase: Having evaluated the alternative solutions to the problem, the consumer then purchases the product or service. Ideally, of course, the retailer wants the individual to make a purchase; but sometimes a person makes a decision not to purchase or to delay purchase. The purchase phase consists of something of value being traded for something else of value. In retailing, it is generally a trade of money from the consumer for a durable or nondurable good provided by the retailer. At this time, the

Source: Dusan Petkovic/Shutterstock.com

consumer becomes concerned with the place of business, the cost and terms of the transaction, and the availability of stock. Consumers always choose the most desirable place (for them) to shop. They want to feel welcome and comfortable in their surroundings.

Post-Purchase Evaluation: After the purchase, consumers go through a *post-purchase evaluation* step. If the consumer is happy with the overall shopping experience, he or she will likely think of the retailer when planning to purchase again. Customers may also tell several people about the positive experience. If the consumer had a bad experience, he may return the product, will be less likely to visit that retailer again, and may tell his friends about the bad experience. A post-purchase evaluation is more likely to occur with products and services that are not routinely bought.

In post-purchase evaluation, consumers may experience *cognitive dissonance* or buyer's remorse. This mental state refers to a consumer's doubt about a purchase, which creates discomfort in the consumer. For example, after purchasing a new pair of jeans, you may think that you

Source: Creativa Images/Shutterstock.com

paid too much or that you should have waited for a sale. Consumers attempt to alleviate or remove this negative feeling (Festinger, 1957). It is the retailer's job to help the consumer alleviate this negative state to feel good about their purchase. Although warranties and guarantees are effective tools to increase consumer satisfaction with a purchase, the human touch also helps. Retail personnel should tell the consumer that he or she made the right choice. Offering reasons why the purchase was a smart choice helps the consumer feel good about themselves and their decision to buy a specific product from a specific retailer.

Perhaps the best way to make sure that a customer doesn't experience cognitive dissonance is to make sure the dissonance doesn't occur in the first place. Retailers should ask for customer feedback and undertake consumer research to understand the channel choices consumers use.

Other Factors Influencing a Purchase

In addition to decision-making steps there are many other factors that will influence a retailer's customers. Retailers also need to pay attention to factors outside their control that influence how a buyer behaves. Four major outside influences on a consumer's spending are the family, culture, reference groups, and life cycles.

Family

The consumer's family consumes many products purchased over the consumer's lifetime. A buyer often thinks about other family members when shopping. Often the entire family participates in the decision-making process, as when family members weigh in on the choice of a restaurant when the family eats out. As the consumer goes through the decision-making process, the consumer's family may offer opinions about the purchase, particularly where to buy, what to buy, and when to shop. In addition, the family's size will dictate the quantity purchased for some goods.

Retailers must pay particular attention to the needs of children; it is estimated that children directly influence over $453 billion in family purchases (Mintel, 2010). According to Mintel's Kids as Influencers – US (2014):

- Nearly all parents agree that they ask for their kids' opinions before purchasing products

- The Disney Channel is the most popular TV network with nearly eight in 10 kids age 6-11 having watched it in the past week

- Moms are more likely than dads to seek their kids' input when making purchase decisions

- As household income increases, parents become more likely to buy their kids what they want at the grocery store

- Nine out of 10 parents agree that they ask their kids' opinions on purchases related to leisure activities

Reference Groups

In addition to their families, people turn to friends to get information about which products to purchase. When a consumer looks to others for assistance in making product choices, these people are the consumer's reference group. A *reference group* is those people to whom an individual compares him/herself to and whose attitudes and values guide the person's decisions. Individuals seek information from reference groups to help form beliefs, attitudes and many behaviors. The consumer's reference group will provide the consumer information about products and services during conversations or through the consumer's observations.

A reference group may include friends, family and colleagues; however, it may also include individuals that the consumer does not know, such as sports and entertainment celebrities. People belonging to clubs and trade associations often view the members as a reference group. Sometimes a person becomes an expert in a particular area due to her experience and knowledge. That person is sought out and becomes a strong influencer of decisions. Reference groups provide direction and information to consumers, so retailers need to be aware of reference groups and use them when possible to provide a positive image of the retailer's company. Many people followed Oprah Winfrey on her syndicated television program, The Oprah Winfrey Show. Oprah had an impact on her viewers in terms of products such as books. The viewers looked to Oprah for advice and information. When Oprah featured the product Spanx on her show it drove the product's sales to new highs and helped create a new industry based around the product. When Oprah launched the Oprah Winfrey Network (OWN) in 2011, many of the people that watched her television show started watching her network.

Source: Rawpixel.com/Shutterstock.com

Culture

Finally, a consumer's culture plays a role in influencing the purchase of products and services. *Culture* refers to a group's shared beliefs and values which affect their thinking and behavior. Individuals belonging to a specific culture may have differing shopping styles. Some cultures are price sensitive, while some are not. Many cultures like the U.S. stress individual accomplishments, while others, such as Japan and China focus more on group achievement. In addition to culture, researchers have found that subcultures also exist. A *subculture* is a group of individuals within a broader culture who share the same morals, beliefs and values, but are distinctive in some other ways. Subcultures may form on the basis of shared interests, religion, age or professions. Within a university culture there are subcultures such as athletes, business majors and members of the American Marketing Association.

Life Cycles

All buyers go through life cycles which affect their shopping behavior and purchase decisions. People who are going to college have different consumer needs compared to a retired person. Thus, it's important for retailers to understand there are various types of buying situations that follow a lifecycle. Buying life cycles follow consumer life stages. Life stages are changes in a person's life that correspond to a person's marital status, profession, and family status. In addition, retailers may seek other indicators to track life cycles, such as identifying whether the consumer is a teenager. Consumer purchasing behavior and the consumer's buying patterns change throughout their life as their needs change. Changes in family, education, income or health -- each is accompanied by varying needs and wants. If a retailer can track those needs and wants throughout a customer's buying lifecycle, it will be better able to create and carry products and services that are important for that customer. By monitoring customer lifecycle changes, retailers will be better able to create positive relationships that will last through their customers' buying lifecycles.

In-Store Decision Making

When the consumer begins the shopping process, it is essential that retailers understand the consumer's in-store or online shopping behaviors. Numerous researchers and retailers have studied consumer behavior at the point-of-purchase. Envirosell CEO and retailing guru Paco Underhill, who refers to himself as a retail anthropologist, researches consumer behavior at the point-of-sale by observing shoppers in retail stores (Underhill, 2009). Underhill suggests that there are biological constraints, such as physical and anatomical abilities and limitations, that are common to all people. By watching consumers shop, retailers can begin to understand those constraints. Retailers should pay particular attention to anything that obstructs a sale. For example, a customer may find it difficult to locate the price tag on a clothing item. The frustration may be so great that the customer abandons the product and moves on. Once a retailer realizes a problem exists, it can make changes to encourage instead of hinder sales. There are many things that a retailer can learn about consumers' shopping behaviors simply by understanding how consumers shop. One area that is important to understand is how the type of shopping trip influences the consumer.

Researchers J.J. Inman and R.S. Winer (1998) (Figure 5.5 on next page) suggest that the type of trip consumers take to shop has an impact on their behavior. Is the trip for a convenience product or a major purchase? By understanding the type of trip the shopper is making, retailers can react by executing tactics that please or excite the shopper. In addition to the type of trip being made, retailers should try to understand which aisles in the store are being shopped and the types of displays needed to interest the consumer in purchasing. Where should displays be located to excite consumers? Locations considered may include the end of the aisle, in the middle of the aisle, on a shelf or on the floor.

Inman and Winer continue by suggesting that a consumer's *deal proneness* will also have an impact on his shopping behavior. Deal proneness is a shopper's propensity to purchase products that are on sale or when they are offered some type of deal. Closely related to deal proneness is *feature proneness.* Consumers are feature prone when they use coupons, free-standing inserts (FSIs), or some other type of circular, e-coupon, physical coupon or other features to encourage them to make a purchase. Understanding which consumers are feature prone and which are not will help the retailer create more effective tactics, thus will create more success for the retailer.

As stressed in search and evaluation steps of the five-step decision-making process, the Inman and Winer model stresses that retailers need to be aware of the consumer's purchase involvement toward a particular product or service. Finally, retailers need to understand that a consumer's compulsiveness will also influence the buyer's behavior. *Compulsiveness* is the degree of openness shoppers have to impulse purchases. The more a consumer feels that impulse purchases are okay, the more compulsive he is toward purchasing. When you go grocery shopping do you come home with many unplanned items such as cookies, chips, soda, or granola bars? If so, you are high in compulsiveness.

Figure 5.5 – Model on In-Store Consumer Decision Making

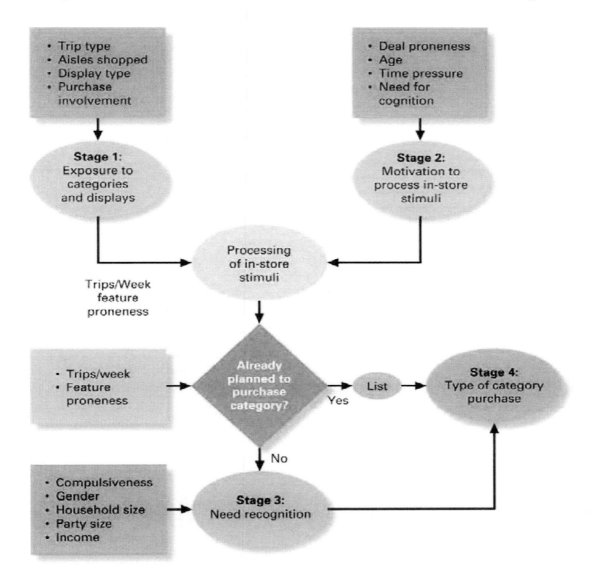

Source: Jeffrey Inman and Russell S. Winer, "Where the Rubber Meets the Road: A Model of In-Store Consumer Decision Making," working paper [report no. 98-122], Marketing Science Institute, October 1998, p. 6.

B2B Customer Buying Behavior

Business buyers behave differently than do final or ultimate consumers. Retailers found they could generate additional revenue by selling their products or services to other businesses. For some retailers B2B sales are a major source of revenue.

The B2B decision process is typically longer, involves more participants in the buying decision, is more formal, more complex, and often involves larger dollar amounts in comparison to sales to the final consumer. Just as with final consumers, building relationships with managers that make buying decisions is very important.

To take advantage of the B2B market, retailers will often participate in retail exchanges. *Retail exchanges* are organizations that help retailers sell to other businesses. Retail exchanges may operate on the Internet. These exchanges provide solutions and services to businesses such as software and other technology-based products and services. By using a retail exchange, retailers reduce the amount of time finding new business.

A retailer can create a business-to-business, online environment by following these steps (How to use..., 2007):

- Learn network members' interests and create a mix of white papers that focus on those interests

- Customize registration pages in order to collect lead qualification information and other member data

- Add leads to the customer relationship management system (CRM) that will help to facilitate sales and other marketing follow-ups

Summary

This chapter covered the evaluation and identification of retail customers. Although customers are diverse, they can be placed into similar categories where they have a propensity to respond in a like manner to the retailer's strategies and executions. In categorizing customers, retailers collect data using geographics, psychographics, demographics, and behavioristics, as well as geodemographics. Such information helps the retailer develop strategies that they then incorporate into the integrated retail management plan.

Consumers behave in different ways when deciding on where to shop and what to buy. The consumer decision process consists of (1) problem awareness, in which the need or want of a product is identified; (2) information search, in which the consumer searches for information on how to solve the problem identified in the awareness stage; (3) evaluation of the choices brought about by the information search; (4) purchase, in which the consumer decides whether or not to buy the product or service; (5) post-purchase evaluation, in which the consumer reflects on his or her decision. Knowledge of these stages helps retailers plan effective marketing communication plans to reach their targeted markets.

The models of the consumer decision process attempt to describe the consumer's decision-making process, both prior to deciding on a store and once in the store. These models give the retailer another tool to use in its quest to exceed customer wants and needs.

Terms

80/20 rule (aka Pareto principle)	A guideline stating that 20 percent of a retailer's customers make up 80 percent of its sales volume. Also known as the Pareto principle.
behavioristics	The subdivision of a retailer's current or potential markets based on buying responses, product usage patterns, product loyalty, or store loyalty.
brand community	A group of consumers with a product or brand attachments.
Buying power (also known as purchasing power)	The money people have to spend on products/services after paying taxes.
cognitive dissonance (aka buyer's remorse)	A consumer's doubt associated with a purchase.

compulsiveness	The degree of openness shoppers have to impulse purchases.
consumer behavior	The study of how customers buy products.
culture	A group's shared beliefs and values which affect their thinking and behavior.
deal proneness	The shopper's propensity to purchase products that are on sale or where some type of "deal" for the product is offered.
demographics	Statistics about any given population base.
ethnic group	Any group defined by race, religion, national origin, or some combination of these categories.
feature proneness	The tendency of shoppers to use or not to use coupons or other promotional items in their shopping decisions.
generational marketing	The study of age groups and how they behave in the consumer market.
geodemographics	The combination of geographics and demographics which is used to describe the customer more clearly.
geographics	Analysis that helps the retailer find out where customers are physically located.
psychographics	Lifestyle analysis data used to determine what consumers do over specified time periods.
purchase involvement	The consumer's involvement in the overall shopping experience.
race	A group of individuals sharing common genetic traits that determine physical characteristics.
reference group	Those people to whom an individual compares him/herself to and whose attitudes and values guide the person's decisions.
subculture	A group of individuals within a broader culture who share the same morals, beliefs and values, but are distinctive in other ways.
web community	Online websites that attract people with similar interests

Discussion Questions

1. Explain the consumer decision-making process. Why is this information important for a retailer to understand?

2. List the four primary segmentation variables. Briefly explain why each of these areas influences a consumer's behavior.

3. Why is it crucial to target your customers and have a thorough understanding of who those customers are?

4. What is B2B retailing? What makes it different from B2C retailing?

5. Use the Inman and Winer model to describe your in-store shopping behaviors.

Exercises

1. Examine your social networks and describe the reference groups that influence your consumer behavior.

2. Many retailers are combining their physical locations and Internet systems to better address their customers' needs. Two retailers that allow customers to order online and pick up the merchandise at a local branch location are Sears and Best Buy. Go to www.sears.com and www.bestbuy.com and

answer the following questions:

• Search for information on how to order online and pick up at a local store (sometimes called store pickup). How long did it take you (in seconds or minutes) to find this information?

• On which of the two sites was it easier to locate this information?

• Were the instructions for store pickup clear? Why or why not?

• What, if anything, would you change to make the site and its navigational capacities more user-friendly?

3. Jessie wants to purchase a smartphone. She values ease of use, customer service, brand visibility and has a limited budget.

• Using the consumer decision process steps, explain what happens in each step.

• In the search for information and evaluation of alternatives, list at least four smartphones that Jessie would consider and prepare a table that compares the smartphones on five features that may be important to Jessie.

• Research the customer service rankings of the companies that provide the smartphones you identified in step 2. Which company has the highest customer service rating? The lowest?

• Which smartphone would you recommend Jessie purchase and why?

Case

eCraft Furniture and the Internet Marketing Dilemma

"I think it's a totally insane idea!" exclaimed Lori Abrams, the marketing manager. "People buy our furniture because they know it holds up and we are flexible about putting any fabric on any style. We're price competitive, but people have to see the product and talk to us to appreciate it." Craig Julio, the information technology manager, leaned back in his chair and rolled his eyes. Lori just didn't seem to understand how technology was taking over business---as far as he was concerned, *all* business, even this one.

Background

eCraft Furniture was not yet an actual business; rather, it was a concept that the management of Craft Guild Furniture Corporation had been considering for the past six months. Craft Guild, with annual sales just shy of $10 million, was founded in the early 1950s by Lori's grandfather, Austin Trexler. For nearly fifty years the family-controlled company maintained an outstanding reputation throughout the Northeast for both a quality product and superior customer service. Craft Guild was not only a manufacturer but also a direct marketer that owned its own retail stores in several urban and larger suburban areas. The typical customer came from lower- and middle-income families who were interested in affordable but durable furniture. Most advertising was by word of mouth, and it wasn't uncommon to have a third generation of the same family as customers.

Austin Trexler had insisted that the company produce only six different product styles, each containing a chair, a loveseat, and a sofa. However, each piece could be upholstered in any of more than 750 different fabrics representing various patterns, colors, fibers (natural and synthetic), and protective treatments such as Scotchgard™.

Business had been profitable, but revenue growth was modest. Senior management had challenged everyone in the company to find ways to improve the situation. The ideas had run the gamut from increased television advertising to billboards to coupons, but the one truly innovative idea had been Craig Julio's. After considering the success of several companies who were supplying customization, Craig thought Craft Guild could do the same.

For starters, Craig designed an interactive website that would allow customers to try any fabric on any style and get immediate pricing, including shipping to their door. From a cash flow standpoint, customers would pay in full by credit card at the time of the order---a much better arrangement than the 20 percent down that the retail stores insisted on when taking a factory order. Moreover, there was no finished-goods inventory.

Craig was not alone in advocating that Craft Guild expand into e-commerce. With so many other industries making some attempt at it, most of the other managers were starting to accept the idea. Lori Abrams clearly was the most vocal opponent. There has to be some way to win her over, Craig thought. But what can that be?

The Next Management Meeting

At the next management meeting, the topic of eCraft came up again. Lori remained adamant about the importance of customer contact, and not only by the sales staff at the time of the initial sale. "Everyone at Craft Guild is a marketer," she explained. "Even the delivery personnel are always willing to do some of the little things, like getting a sofa into a third-story loft or rearranging existing furniture in an elderly customer's apartment." Craig again rolled his eyes, but she continued, "Everyone knows that our delivery people are so skilled that there have been times when they've removed doors from their hinges and window sashes from their frames to make a delivery! Who's going to do that when we're web based and having some unknown trucker delivering to an otherwise unknown customer thousands of miles away?"

"Lori, we've got to change with the times if the company is to survive. You just don't get it," Craig burst out, startling everyone in the room. "*I* don't get it? *You* don't get it!" Lori retorted. "You don't know why we have the customers we do. It's a good thing you want to call this new venture eCraft, because I'm not so sure that I want such a faceless concept contaminating the good name of Craft Guild!"

After a few more minutes of exchanging accusations about not understanding the business, the meeting moved to other agenda items without reaching any closure on the eCraft concept. The gridlock was nothing new, as the group had agreed to disagree many times previously in the hope that in the interim some new insight would generate a compelling argument one way or the other.

Questions

1. Make and support a detailed recommendation to management that endorses or rejects the long-debated eCraft concept. Answer the following questions in your analysis.

2. What is eCraft's target market?

3. How does this market differ from its traditional market?

4. What product attributes of upholstered furniture would suggest that it is or is not well suited for selling over the web?

5. Assuming management comes back with a decision to try the eCraft venture, what risks might there be for web customers who want the same services that in-store customers want?

6. How might the interactive website that Craig designed for eCraft help improve sales through the traditional channels?

7. If Craft Guild goes through with the concept, should it call itself by its own distinct name, eCraft? Explain your answer.

Source: This case was prepared by Richard R. Young, Ph.D., professor of supply chain management, Penn State Harrisburg, from actual business situations. It is intended to foster class discussion and not to suggest either good or inappropriate administrative behavior.

References

Humes, K. R., Jones, N.A., Ramirez, R. R. (2011). Overview of Race and Hispanic Origin 2010. Census Briefs (March). Retrieved from http://www.census.gov/prod/cen2010/briefs/c2010br-02.pdf

2010 Census Shows America's Diversity (2011). Press release from the U.S. Census, (Mar 24). Retrieved from http://www.census.gov/newsroom/releases/archives/2010_census/cb11-cn125.html

Bearden, W.O., Ingram, T.N. and LaForge R.W. (2007). *Marketing Principles and Perspectives*, Chicago, IL: McGraw-Hill/Irwin.

Bernhardt, D., Qihong, L. and Serfes, K. (2007). Product Customization. *European Economic Review*, 51, 1396-1422.

Bishaw, Alemayehu (2011). Areas with Concentrated Poverty: 2006-2010. American Community Survey Briefs. U.S. Census, Report # ACSBR/10-17.

Chase, R. B., Jacobs, R. F. and Aquilano, N. J. (2006). *Operations Management for Competitive Advantage (11th Ed.)*. New York: McGraw-Hill/Irwin.

Fahmy, S. (2010, November 4). Despite Recession, Hispanic and Asian Buying Power Expected to Surge in U.S. According to Annual UGA Selig Center Multicultural Economy Study, News Release dated Nov. 4 from the University of Georgia, Terry College of Business.

Family purchases: Kids as influencers-U.S. (2010). Mintel research company, June.

Family purchases: Kids as influencers-U.S. (2014). Mintel research company, April.

Festinger, L. (1957). *A theory of cognitive dissonance*, Evanston, Illinois: Row, Peterson.

Gordon, M. (1964). *Assimilation in American life*, New York: Oxford University Press.

Hoover's Company Records (2017). Levi Strauss & Co. Obtained from Proquest Database.

How to Use Social Networking Sites for Lead Generation (2007). *Marketing Sherpa*, (Sept 26)., Retrieved from http://www.marketingsherpa.com

Howard, T. (2003). Dude! You've Been Replaced; Dell Tries Interns to Pick Up Where Steven Left Off. *USA Today*, (March 10), p. B4.

Howden, L. and Meyer, A. (May 2011). Age and Sex Composition 2010. 2010 Census Briefs, Report # C2010BR-03.

Inman, J. J. and Winer, R. S. (1998) *Where the Rubber Meets the Road: A Model of In-store Consumer Decision Making*, working paper report (report no. 98-122), Marketing Science Institute.

Italiano, L., Schram, J., and Hoffmann, B. (2003). Dell Dude Nabbed in Lower East. Retrieved from www.nypost.com/news/ regionalnews/68896.htm.

Jacoby, J. (1976). Consumer Psychology: An Octennium. In *Annual Review of Psychology*, ed. Mussen, P. and Rosenweig, M. Palo Alto, CA: Annual Reviews, (27), p. 332.

Janoff, B. (1999). Targeting All Ages. Supplement 66th Annual Report of the Grocery Industry. *Progressive Grocer*, (April 1999), pp. 37-46.

Kimmel, A. J. (2010). *Connecting with Consumers: Marketing for New Marketplace Realities*, New York: Oxford University Press, Inc. pp. 59-93.

Lazare, L. (2002). Lew's Review—Latest Dell Ad a Dud Without the Dude. *Chicago Sun Times*, July 22, 2002, p. 51

Levi Strauss & Company (2003). Dockers. Retrieved January 2003 from www.levistrauss.com/brands/dockers.htm.

Maddox, K. (2016). Dell breaks three new tv spots using episodic storytelling. Advertising Age, Mar 21. Retrieved from http://adage.com/article/btob/dell-breaks-tv-spots-episodic-storytelling/303194/

Maslow, A. H. (1970), *Motivation and personality*, 2nd Edition, New York: Harper and Row.

NeXtel Communications Tops Business Week's 'Info Tech 100' List: Dell Computer, Samsung Electronics, Nokia, IBM and Hewlett-Packard Also Included (2003). *PR Newswire*, New York, June 12.

Pletz, J. (2003). Dell Takes over Top Spot. *American Demographics*, 25 (February), p. 14-15.

Posnick-Goodwin, S. (2010). Meet generation Z. (Feb) California Teachers Association. Retrieved from http://www.cta.org/Professional-Development/Publications/Educator-Feb-10/Meet-Generation-Z.aspx.

Rhey, E. (2002). Dell's Detour: 'Dude You're Getting a White Box' Doesn't Have the Same Ring as Dell's Well- Known Slogan, but the Company Has Announced that it Will Sell Unbranded PCs Known as 'White Boxes' Through Small-Business Dealers. *PC Magazine*, October 15.

Riche, M. F. (1989). Psychographics for the 1990s, American *Demographics*, (July), 24-31 and 53.

Rust, R. T., Zeithaml, V. A. and Lemon, K. N. (2000). *Driving Customer Equity: How Lifetime Customer Value Is Reshaping Corporate Strategy.* New York: The Free Press.

Senguder, T. (20003). An Evaluation of Consumer and Business Segmentation Approaches. *Journal of American Academy of Business*, (March), pp. 618-624.

Shea, E. (2013). Ultra-affluent Consumers Spent 14.1pc Less on Luxury 2009-2012: Unity Marketing. (April 16). In Featured, Industry sectors, Marketing, News, Research. Retrieved from http://www.luxurydaily.com/ultra-affluent-consumers-spent-14-1pc-less-on-luxury-2009-2012-unity-marketing/

Trese, H. (2011). Multigenerational marketing: The Ageless Approach to Reaching Prospects. *Agents Sales Journal*, Retrieved from http://search.proquest.com/docview/864489446?accountid=13158

U.S. framework and VALS types (2012). Strategic Business Insights. Retrieved from http://www.strategicbusinessinsights.com/vals/ustypes.shtml

U.S.Census Bureau, *Census 2000 Summary File 1* and *2010 Census Summary File 1.*

Underhill, P. (2009). Why We Buy: *The Science of Shopping: Updated and Revised for the Internet, The Global Consumer and Beyond*, Revised Edition, New York: Simon & Schuster.

Walliker, A. (2008, February 25). Generation Z Comes of Age. *Herald Sun*. Retrieved from http://www.news.com.au/heraldsun/story/0,21985,23269842-662,00.html.

Weeks, M. W. and Humphreys, J. M. (2017, Feb 28). UGA Report: Minority Groups Driving U.S. Economy, News Release University of Georgia, Terry College of Business. Obtained from http://www.terry.uga.edu/news/releases/uga-report-minority-groups-driving-u.s.-economy

Wellner, A. S. (2000). The Money in the Middle, *American Demographics*, 22 (April), pp. 56-64.

Williams, K. C., and Page, R. A. (2011). Marketing to the Generations. *Journal of Behavioral Studies in Business,* 3, 1-17.

Williams, K. C., Page, R. A., Petrosky, A. R., and Hernandez, E. H. (2010). Multi-generational Marketing: Descriptions, Characteristics, Lifestyles, and Attitudes. *The Journal of Applied Business and Economics,* 11(2), 21.

Wind, Y. (1978). Issues and Advances in Segmentation Research. *Journal of Marketing Research*, (August 1978), pp. 31 7 -337.

Winter, F. W. (1984). Market Segmentation: A Tactical Approach. *Business Horizons* (Jan/Feb), pp. 57-63.

Part 3

Internal Planning and Management

Source: Rawpixel.com/Shutterstock.com

Chapter 6: Research and Retail Information Systems

Chapter 7: Selecting the Appropriate Market and Location

Chapter 8: Operations Management: Financial

Chapter 9: Merchandise Buying and Handling

Chapter 10: Human Resource Management

Part 3 examines internal retail planning and management. Chapter 6 covers research activities and retail information systems (RIS). Market selection and location decisions that retailers face, are the focus of Chapter 7. Chapter 8 outlines the financial aspects of operations management including analysis of financial statements. Chapter 9 looks at the dynamic areas of merchandise buying and handling. Chapter 10 addresses human resource decisions that are made in the retailing environment.

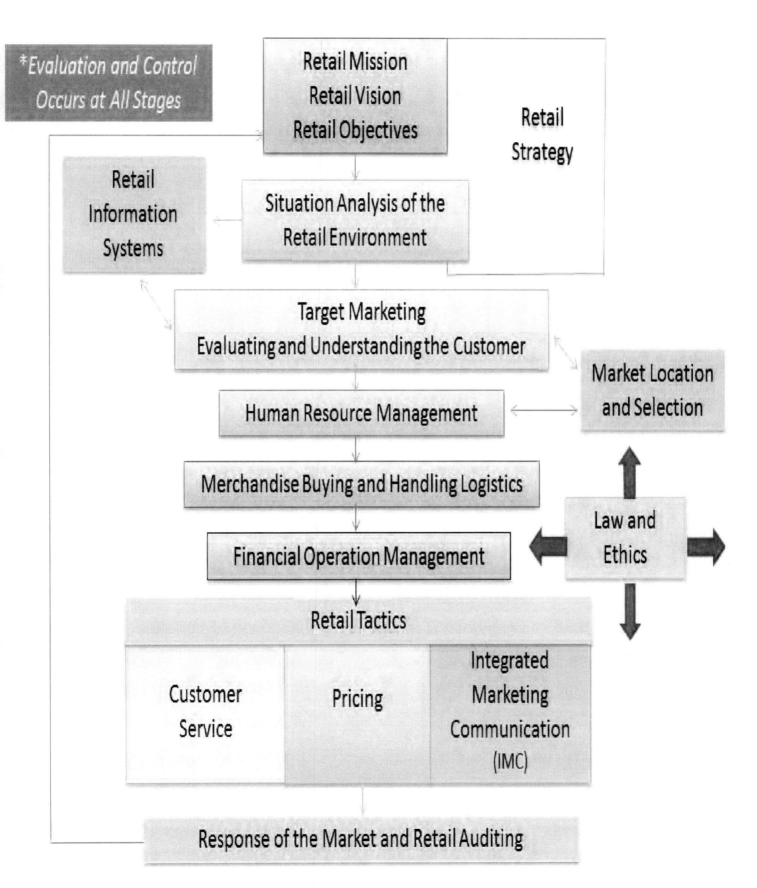

Chapter 6

Retailing Information Systems and Research

"The ability to "listen in" on conversations about you or your competitors may represent one of the best market-research values of the Internet, simply because it's unique to the medium. I'm talking, of course, about the newsgroups and discussion groups so prevalent in the Usenet section of the Internet." ~ Susan Greco, articles editor, Inc.

~ Susan Greco, Articles Editor, Inc.

Source: Jacob Lund/Shutterstock.com

CHAPTER OBJECTIVES

After completing this chapter you will be able to:

- Define and explain the purpose of a retail information system (RIS).
- Explain the steps in conducting marketing research.
- Describe the difference between secondary and primary data and identify some tools for collecting data.
- Discuss the role of technology in gathering data.

Dollar Shave Club Disrupts Industry

Mark Levine and Michael Dubin launched the Dollar Shave Club in 2012 by posting a funny YouTube video about how great their $1 razors are in comparison to the expensive ones bought at retail stores. Their first video had over four million views in a little over one month and had 12,000 subscribers in the first two days (Levick, 2012). Due to the popularity of the video, their website crashed and they ran out of inventory. The first orders were packed by hand. Today there are millions of subscribers.

The founders disrupted the razor blade industry by providing affordable razors in a direct-to-consumer model. The company now also sells other male grooming products, including its own line of shaving cream and butt wipes for men (One Wipe Charlies). As the company grew, reliance on technology, retail information systems and research also grew.

In 2016, Michael Dubin, CEO of Dollar Shave Club, sold the company to Unilever for $1 Billion. This is one of the largest sales ever of an e-commerce company (Isaac and de la Merced, 2016). As part of the deal, Dubin retained his position as CEO.

Source: Rawpixel.com/Shutterstock.com

Introduction

With advances in technology, more methods, processes and systems are created to help retailers understand the environments in which they operate. An overall understanding of the research theories, methods, processes and systems helps retailers create more effective and efficient integrated retail management plans that drive consumers into retail outlets and create profits for those retailers. Research is relevant to almost every area of the IRM including the development of a customer focus. Research efforts can help retailers make better decisions in all areas of the Integrated Retail Management Plan. Research helps retailers find better methods of operating and better meet the needs of the changing marketplace.

Our focus in this chapter is marketing research. In describing research methods, we examine the increasingly important role that research plays in marketing plans and the retail information systems (RIS) used by retailers

The Role of Research in the Integrated Retail Management Plan

When retailers begin their integrated retail management (IRM) plans, they must arm themselves with as much information as possible. The gathering and subsequent analysis and reporting of data helps retailers reduce their chances of error in decision making. Research allows retailers to better understand the retail environment in which they operate. Data on consumers, suppliers, personnel, the merchandise mix, prices, image, and integrated marketing communications management will help the retail manager create more effective plans. By conducting research, retailers are attempting to find solutions to everyday problems. Additionally, retailers conduct research to forecast their unit demand and sales. Research is used to help identify and define a retailer's target market; it helps the retailer to identify customers, segment customer groups, and make personnel decisions. Research may be particularly useful as retailers begin to execute their integrated retail management plans.

Before Walmart and Target came on to the scene, Kmart was leading the discount retail industry and was known as a cutting-edge retailer. Many experts believe that if Kmart had conducted more research to help the company management better understand the changes in customers' wants and needs, the company would not have filed for bankruptcy.

Conducting research can be expensive. To balance the benefits of research against the costs, retailers should assess the risk involved in making an incorrect decision. The research process must be an ongoing process that yields up-to-date, accurate information. Conducting research is helpful for all levels of a retailer's distribution channel; reports generated from research activities can be used by assistant department managers, department managers, suppliers and facilitators. In a channel of distribution, information flows in all directions among the three main groups of participants: suppliers, retailers, and

Source: Mooshny/Shutterstock.com

consumers. For research to be effective, it must be distributed to the correct individuals who will use the information to manage change. Important retail decisions must be based on research and not on a manager's intuition. It no longer works to say this is the way we've always done it and there is no need to change. There may be a reason for change, and that reason should be based on research or data.

Suppliers will rely on a retailer for information about inventory turnover, sales, product and service returns, different types and amounts of merchandise to order. Retailers require information from their suppliers and consumers for new product or service offerings, model closeouts, price increases, forecasts, employee training and other matters. A consumer may need information about product assembly, warranties and guarantees, instructions, price of products, discounts, where merchandise is located, payment methods, credit, and layaways. The role of retailers in the distribution channel is to generate and share research that makes the channel of distribution better.

Data and Information

There are a lot of data available to retail managers. But as the saying goes, data are cheap, information is expensive. Retail managers must be able to turn raw data into useful information. *Data* are "...news, facts, and figures that have not been organized in any manner. *Information* is a body of facts organized around some specific topic or subject" (Blankenship, Breen and Dutka, 1998). Thus, the research involves both the gathering and organizing of data. Retail managers must determine the best way to gather these data. Additionally, retail managers must decide what types of information are required.

To demonstrate how to convert raw data to usable information, consider the data shown in Table 6.1 (next page), which is from the U.S. Census Bureau. The raw data show estimated quarterly

U.S. retail sales for 2016 and the last quarter of 2015. Although it is organized by quarter and e-commerce sales, it is not in a format useful to a manager/retailer. The retailer must determine which numbers are relevant and how to use the data to forecast and develop strategies and make decisions for the business. Once data are used for specific and useful applications relevant to the retailer, it is information.

Table 6.1 - Estimated Quarterly U.S. Retail Sales: Total and E-commerce[1]

Quarter	Retail Sales (Millions of Dollars)		E-commerce as a % of Total	% Change from Prior Quarter		% Change from Same Quarter a Year Ago	
	Total	E-commerce		Total	E-commerce	Total	E-commerce
Adjusted[2]							
4th quarter 2016(p)	1,235,535	102,674	8.3	1.9	1.9	4.1	14.3
3rd quarter 2016(r)	1,212,677	100,742	8.3	0.9	3.4	2.3	15.1
2nd quarter 2016	1,201,330	97,392	8.1	1.5	4.7	2.2	16.0
1st quarter 2016	1,183,172	93,046	7.9	-0.3	3.6	2.1	15.5
4th quarter 2015(r)	1,186,513	89,792	7.6	0.1	2.6	1.4	15.5
Not Adjusted							
4th quarter 2016(p)	1,297,807	123,610	9.5	6.7	32.0	3.9	14.3
3rd quarter 2016(r)	1,216,071	93,609	7.7	0.1	2.5	2.3	15.5
2nd quarter 2016	1,215,431	91,290	7.5	8.8	5.7	2.2	15.9
1st quarter 2016	1,116,632	86,351	7.7	-10.6	-20.2	3.3	15.2
4th quarter 2015	1,249,081	108,175	8.7	5.1	33.5	1.7	14.8

[1] E-commerce sales are sales of goods and services where the buyer places an order, or the price and terms of the sale are negotiated, over an Internet, mobile device (M-commerce), extranet, Electronic Data Interchange (EDI) network, electronic mail, or other comparable online system. Payment may or may not be made online.

[2] Estimates are adjusted for seasonal variation, but not for price changes. Total sales estimates are also adjusted for trading-day differences and moving holidays.

Source: Retail Indicators Branch, U.S. Census Bureau, Last Revised: February 17, 2017

Screenshot

The Marketing Research Process

Many people confuse the terms marketing research and market research. *Marketing research* is "the function which links the consumer, customer, and public to the marketer through information – information to identify and define marketing opportunities and problems; generate, refine, and evaluate marketing actions; monitor marketing performance; and improve our understanding of marketing as a process" (Churchill and Iacobucci, 2002).

Marketing research encompasses all areas of research done by a marketer or retailer. *Market research*, on the other hand, is a subset of marketing research that focuses on the generation of information and data about a particular market, or group of markets. Thus, market research will help to identify customers, market areas, and other areas. It is also helpful in the creation of forecasting models for specific market areas.

In this section, we examine the systems used to collect and store retail data. The process begins during the retailer's environmental scanning. Retailers use environmental scanning to help identify future problems and issues. Then retailers create research-based problem statements that allow the retailer to develop research pertaining to market segmentation, pricing, logistics, financial operations, supply chain, customer service levels and more. After running an environmental scan, a decision is made on whether research is needed. An eight-step process is used by marketers when conducting research:

Step 1: Formulate the Research Problem

This is often the hardest step in executing the research program. The researcher looks for underlying causes of the problem. Often certain symptoms are incorrectly identified as the problem. Solving a symptom does not solve the underlying problem. For example, a retail manager of a gym finds that sales figures are a little low compared to those of the same time the previous year. The question she should ask is: "Are lower sales the primary problem?" The answer is most likely "no"; rather, the lower sales are probably a symptom of the primary problem. To uncover the primary problem, the appropriate question is: "What caused the sales decrease?"

When distinguishing symptoms from problems, the manager may find that sales are low for other retailers and that her gym's sales decrease is the smallest of all competitors'. This may be due to a slumping economic environment. Thus, there is no internal problem; instead the problem is industry-wide. Managers may need to develop response strategies to counter retail environmental issues.

Problem formulation is difficult for beginners because they are used to being given problems. Think about your last college examination. If it was a multiple-choice test, the professor gave you a series of problems or questions, along with a series of possible solutions. This is not the way it happens in the retail world, however. In professional retailing, you are not given the original problem to be solved (and far less a series of potential solutions from which to choose). Critical, analytical thinking must come into play.

In retailing, the research problem usually comes about because retail objectives are not being met. When this is the case, the first question to ask why?

To uncover the problem, the researcher must search for data in the specific area of interest to avoid collecting an excessive amount of useless data. A secondary data

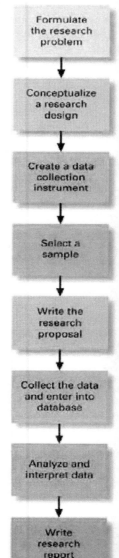

Figure 6.1 Marketing Research Steps

Formulate the research problem → Conceptualize a research design → Create a data collection instrument → Select a sample → Write the research proposal → Collect the data and enter into database → Analyze and interpret data → Write research report

Figure 6.1
Marketing
Research
Steps

search helps develop a better understanding of the retail environment under study. In addition, a comprehensive secondary data review may solve the problem and avoid the need to develop a more formalized approach to getting the necessary information. If the secondary data help solve the problem, the research process is complete. If it does not offer solutions to the problem, the research process must continue.

Once the research problem has been clearly defined---in other words, once the question "What needs to be accomplished or solved by undertaking the research process?" has been answered---the researcher is ready to continue. During this step, it is wise to identify variables that might alter the findings: What environmental issues and variables might have an impact on the final solution?

Step 2: Conceptualize a Research Design

In step 2, a choice needs to be made among the many available types of research designs (observation, survey, longitudinal study, and so on). The research design is used as a guide throughout the entire research process and is dependent on the type of data to be collected and how they are to be collected. Thus, a thorough understanding of the problem is needed to choose the research design that will be most effective in solving the problem.

Step 3: Create a Data Collection Instrument

Based on the identified problem, methods of data retrieval and collection are chosen. When creating a data collection instrument, options include a questionnaire, an observation feedback form, or a personal interview feedback sheet. For example, a retailer has ordered 100,000 pens to be used in the retail promotions department. When the shipment arrives, the retailer does not want to look at every single item to determine how many are defective. In this case, the retailer uses an observation feedback form to record defects. To save time, the retailer chooses a sample of pens and then extrapolates, or projects, the number of defective units from that sampling. In this case, a piece of paper, is the research instrument and, for this retailer, is sufficient to record the data pertaining to the problem.

Step 4: Select a Sample

To use statistics correctly, the selection of a sample must be somewhat scientific. One needs to understand the concept of sampling and to know whether a probability sample or a nonprobability sample is called for to complete the research project.

Step 5: Write the Research Proposal

It is not within the scope of this text to discuss the development of research proposals. Briefly, the proposal needs to cover the secondary data search, the problem, what is to be accomplished from the work, the hypothesis (es), the study design, and methodologies to be used in generating responses from the sample. The proposal should also include a section on how, and to whom, the findings will be communicated.

Step 6: Collect the Data and Enter into Database

In this step the data are collected and placed into some type of database to allow for analysis. The data collection process must be conducted in a sensitive and ethical manner. In most instances, subjects need to be briefed about the intent of the research.

Once the data are collected, the analyst codes the data. Coding involves assigning the data numbers and/or titles to help the computer read it. Not all researchers code data, but data coding helps organize and interpret the data, which is done in the next step. After coding, the data are then entered into the appropriate database.

Step 7: Analyze and Interpret Data

In this step, statistics are used to analyze the data. After statistics have been applied, an interpretation of the data is made.

Step 8: Write the Research Report

There are several things to keep in mind when writing the research report. Most important is to understand the audience that will read the report. Are they practitioners who have little time or use for every detail of the project? Are they researchers who will be very interested in the methods used to collect and present the data? Should the report include a "works cited" section, a reference section, or a bibliography section, or perhaps all three? Regardless of the audience, it is standard practice to include the conclusions and recommendations within the body of the report.

Often it is necessary to complete an executive summary at the beginning of the research report. An *executive summary* is essentially an abstract of the entire report. It should identify all the activities performed in the research process, including recommendations on how to solve the problem or issue, in a page or less.

Gathering Information

Because of capital resource and time constraints, it is not always possible to undertake a grand-scale research project in retailing. Retailers sometimes outsource the research function to consultants or other facilitators (such as advertising agencies). Research can be classified as

- primary or secondary
- qualitative or quantitative

Primary research is the gathering of data that have not been previously published. *Secondary research* is collecting data that has already been published. *Qualitative research* is "the collection, analysis, and interpretation of data that cannot be meaningfully quantified or summarized in the form of numbers" (Parasuraman, Grewal and Krishnan, 2007). *Quantitative research* is "research involving the use of structured questions in which the response options have been predetermined, and a large number of respondents are involved" (Burns and Bush, 2006).

Primary Research

Primary research is collected to solve a specific retail problem. Typically, primary research is gathered when secondary research failed to yield useful results. The major disadvantage of primary research collection is that the process can be time consuming, and the data are expensive to obtain. There are many advantages to primary research conducting that may outweigh the cost. These advantages include generating up-to-date, accurate information; the data are problem-specific and the data are confidential and private, meaning the data are *not* available to the public, including competitors. Often retailers leverage information collected through primary research to better understand customers and improve customer service.

Source: Rawpixel.com/Shutterstock.com

In the collection of primary research, retailers must enlist the assistance of research experts to help plan and execute the research program. When experts are not employed by the retailer, a third party may be hired to conduct the research. The systems used in research are complex and require some training and knowledge. During each step of the research process, researchers must assure that the data being collected are valid and reliable. This may lead to the outsourcing of many retail research projects to professional researchers. *Outsourcing* occurs when a company uses a third party supplier to perform activities instead of using internal company resources.

Source: Jacob Lund/Shutterstock.com

Secondary Research

Secondary research can be either internal or external. *Internal secondary research* is available from within a retailer's operation. These data might take the form of expense reports, profit-and-loss statements, comparative balance sheets, a company's annual report, newsletters, the prospectus for the retail operation, inventory records, purchasing records, or records on supply chain transactions. These data should be stored and available for retail employees.

External secondary research may be collected from all sources of data and information that are external to the firm. Secondary research can come from a library, various governments, trade associations, competitors or from any commercial information provider or seller.

Many research firms specialize in collecting industry research and selling these reports to retailers. For example, retailers can buy reports on the footwear industry, restaurant trends, and consumer behavior. Because of the amount of data available in a search for secondary research, retail managers and researchers often retrieve only secondary research relevant to the retailer's problem. The acquisition and storage of secondary research is easy and inexpensive when compared to the costs associated with the development and execution of primary research.

Trade associations, most notably in retailing the National Retail Federation (NRF), provide a wealth of data for retailers. Additionally, the NRF's research and education arm, the NRF Foundation, is actively involved in the acquisition and dissemination of data and information useful to retailers. Additionally, there are trade associations for almost all retail industry categories such as landscapers, electricians, food marketers, discounters, and footwear retailers.

The major advantage for conducting secondary research rather than primary research is that the research process can be completed more quickly and at a lower cost than larger primary research studies. Most libraries carry data needed by retailers for quick, efficient and accurate decision making. The second advantage of secondary research is its accuracy. Typically, secondary research is accurate, and large research companies stake their reputations on the accuracy of their data. Large government departments, such as the United State Census Bureau, develop and provide large amounts of highly accurate, valid and reliable data.

There are some drawbacks to the use of secondary research. When analyzing secondary research, retailers often find that it is incomplete or too general for their needs. In addition, secondary research may be outdated. Although older data are useful for some situations, they don't consider environmental changes. The newer the data, the more effective they are in terms of research findings and problem solving for retail managers.

To keep your research initiatives and findings confidential, researchers should begin with an internal secondary research prior to proceeding to a larger, external search. Often a department within an organization conducts research but does not share the results with the entire organization. The internal secondary search will help find any existing research, and further research may not be needed. The external search is only necessary if the internal search fails to provide enough data and information to solve a retailer's problem. When external sources of data are used, competitors may learn of a retailer's initiatives.

Secondary research is less costly to obtain than primary research. The data are available quickly, and their costs, compared with primary research costs, are very low. Table 6.2 summarizes the differences between primary and secondary research.

Table 6.2 - Differences between Primary and Secondary Research

	Primary	Secondary
Ease to gather	No	Yes
Cost	High	Low
Accuracy	High – depends on process	High – depends on source
Problem specific	Yes	No
Data Privacy	Yes	No
Currency of Information	Very current	Can be outdated

Reference guides provide an excellent starting place when assembling external secondary research. Reference guides are available and help researchers focus on those data applicable to their current retailing problems. The following reference guides are very useful:

1. The Wall Street Journal Index
2. The United States Census Bureau Census Catalogs and Guide
3. Books in Print
4. The Funk and Scott Index of Corporations and Industries
5. The Business Periodicals Index
6. The Encyclopedia of Associations
7. The Library of Congress Business Reference Services (https://www.loc.gov/rr/business/ondemand/subjectguides.html)

One of the cheapest and comprehensive sources for external secondary research is the United States Government's census data. The drawback is that the information may be dated and not as useful as more recent data. A couple of important reports are the Census of Manufacturing and the Census of Retailing. The Census data may be found at www.census.gov.

In addition to the United States Census data, the United States Government also produces additional publications that provide valuable information and data to retailers and retail researchers. These publications include *U.S. Retail Trade, American Fact Finder, Monthly Retail Sales and Inventory*, and *The Statistical Abstract of the United States*.

There are also some great sources of data for helping to identify a retailer's trading area. These sources include the United States Census Bureau's Topologically Integrated Geographic Encoding and Referencing (TIGER), a digital database that includes images of geographic features of the United States (www.census.gov/geo/www/tiger). It's a great tool to use while generating data on geographics or geodemographics. A link from the TIGER website goes to TIGERweb which allows users to view and query boundaries and attribute information for geographic entities that are stored in the TIGER database. Although TIGERweb does not include demographic data, it contains geographic entity codes that can be linked to the Census Bureau's demographic data, available at the American Fact Finder site (http://factfinder2.census.gov).

The Bureau of Labor Statistics has the Consumer Expenditure Surveys (CE) program (https://www.bls.gov/cex/) which provides data in various forms on expenditure, income and demographic characteristics of consumers in the United States.

There are many trade associations that offer their members varying types of data and information that are specific to the retailer's industry. The American Marketing Association (AMA) (www.ama.org) provides its members many differing research reports, white papers and other sources of information. The AMA provides this information to its many academic, practitioner and student memberships. The Point-of-Purchase Advertising, International (POPAI) creates, acquires and disseminates a lot of data on the impact of point-of-purchase (POP) or point-of-sale (POS) advertising on retail business (www.popai.com).

D & B's Hoover's Online (www.hoovers.com) allows a researcher access to general background information on companies and organizations that may have an impact on the retailer's operations. In addition to Hoovers, Standard and Poor's and Moody's provide extensive information on financials and competitors.

Source: ESB Professional/Shutterstock.com

There are numerous other organizations and companies that specialize in consumer data. The following sources are very useful: For consumer demographic data, the Simmons Market Research and Mediamark Research, Inc. (MRI) are exceptional. Both companies offer data online, hard copy or on CD-ROM (including flash drives). Both SMR and MRI offer products that provide data and information on consumer psychographics. *Standard Rate and Data Service* (SRDS) offers *The Lifestyle Market Analyst* as one of its products. This publication provides a great deal of information and data on consumer lifestyles. *The Sourcebook of ZIP Code Demographics* is a good source to identify markets.

It is the retail researcher's job to make sure they have acquired and analyzed all meaningful secondary research. Finally, the retail researcher may want to take some data gathered through secondary research to create a primary research project that is more relevant to a specific problem.

Qualitative Research

Qualitative research is often called "soft research" because it cannot be expressed in numbers. Nevertheless, qualitative research provides insight and a better understanding of problems and opportunities. Qualitative research normally employs small sample sizes and is often used to determine whether quantitative research should be completed. Because of the small sample size and the lack of probability sampling, the results of qualitative research can't be applied to the general population.

Qualitative research can be used to explore ideas, or to get opinions from people. Because it is exploratory, qualitative research is a type of *exploratory research*, which is conducted when there are no earlier studies from which to answer a question and the research problem has not been clearly defined. Typically, in conducting exploratory research one is not interested in creating specific findings from the data, but rather is looking for insight or to probe for more information to determine the cause of a problem, how a customer will react to a product, service or message, or other issues. Often qualitative research is more time consuming than quantitative research.

There are many different techniques and methods of conducting qualitative research studies. The most popular types of qualitative research, among retailers, are the in-depth interview, focus group interviews, observational research, and using experts. In-depth interviews use an open-ended method of questioning to discover the respondent's feelings and attitudes toward the company or existing and potential products. Responses are typically recorded, and often written notes are taken. It is important to document responses to gain a clear understanding of issues. *Focus group* interviews are conducted with small groups of current or potential customers on a topic. They are designed to collect information in a format that allows for discussion and group interaction. For maximum effectiveness, a trained facilitator or moderator should conduct focus group interviews. *Observational research* is a non-intrusive research tool that is used to evaluate consumer behavior, typically while they shop, either in a brick-and-mortar store or online. To be effective, the researcher must be not noticed. Often retailers will gather information from experts. The *Delphi technique* is used to generate information from a panel of experts. To use this tool experts answer questionnaires in two or more rounds. After each round, a moderator provides a summary of the experts' opinions. Based on the summary, experts are encouraged to revise their earlier answers. After a pre-defined number of rounds, a consensus is reached about how to solve a problem (Rowe and Wright, 1999).

Quantitative Research

Most research in retailing is quantitative. Quantitative research is a systematic process in which numerical data are collected to understand a research problem. Quantitative research is also referred to as causal research because the research studies attempt to link a cause with an effect. Questionnaires and other types of surveys are used heavily in quantitative research.

When using quantitative research techniques, researchers most often work with large samples that are representative of the population under study. Quantitative

Source:arka38/Shutterstock.com

research is more formal than qualitative research and relies on established rules throughout the research process. The research should follow a predetermined order as the researchers go through the quantitative research steps.

There has been a movement toward integrating quantitative and qualitative research. The result is *pluralistic research*, defined as "… the combination of qualitative and quantitative research methods in order to gain the advantages of both" (Burns and Bush, 2006). Thus, pluralistic researchers will begin their studies using qualitative research. The data from this research will then be used to formulate and develop additional quantitative research designs. As technology advances and retailing continues to migrate online, pluralistic research may become the research of choice as it will help identify and define online markets and key trends and issues that are occurring in cyberspace.

Sampling Concepts

In quantitative research, it is important to collect information that can be generalized to a larger population, such as a retailer's target market. Samples are subgroups of populations. The subgroups are drawn to represent the population during further analysis. Researchers take samples from populations to save time and money because they can't get responses from an entire population. Instead of sampling, researchers could take a census. A *census* is the process of asking *all* members of the population for their input. Imagine having to ask every single person in your target market what they thought about their last purchase. If you have a customer base in the millions, this could take a long time (and cost a lot of money). So rather than asking every person, researchers take a representative sample of their population, apply statistics to that sample, and base decisions about the entire population on what that subgroup, or sample, has to say.

The most accurate type of sampling is called *probability sampling*. In probability sampling, each and every member of the population under study has an equal and known chance of being selected for the sample. Although probability sampling is the most accurate and preferred choice of most researchers, in retailing timing limits its use. Decisions must be made regularly, and often researchers don't have enough time to select a probability sample. When time and money issues limit the research study, researchers often use *nonprobability sampling*. In nonprobability sampling, members of the population under study do not have an equal and known chance of being chosen as a unit of the sample. Nonprobability samples are often chosen based on convenience and are often used by novice researchers who don't have sufficient knowledge or budget required to conduct probability sampling.

In order to draw a sample of some known population, researchers use *sampling frames*. A sampling frame is a list of all potential and relevant members of a population. Let's say you are a student at a state university. You're working on a classroom paper dealing with the number of students who buy textbooks. You want to know if they buy textbooks, and if they don't buy them, you want to know why books aren't purchased. There are two ways you can generate these data. First, you can get a list of all students at the university. From that list, you can ask every student the questions. This may take a long time to accomplish; in fact, you find that the project is so time- consuming you won't finish collecting the data until after the project is due.

Source: Arthimedes/Shutterstock.com

So instead of asking every student the questions, you decide to sample the group. From your knowledge of sampling, you find a random number table in print or online. A random number table is a tool used by researchers to draw "items" from a chosen population under study. That list is your sampling frame. The list holds the names and contact information of everyone in your population. Thus, to get a random sample of the population, each person is given a number. Using the random number table, you choose the number of the student that matches the random number table. These people will make up your representative sample. The main reason to select participants at random is to lessen bias and minimize the chance that the people in the sample will differ too much from the target population which would increase the amount of error in the results.

Collecting Data from a Sample

After a sample has been established, retail researchers develop method of collecting data from the sample. Sometimes before data collection starts, a question will be asked to make sure the respondent is qualified to take part in the research. This question may be as simple as, "Have you bought a product from ABC Retailer in the last 6 months?" *Data collection instruments* are the devices used to collect data such as the paper that a survey is printed on or the computer used by researchers to record responses. The data collection instrument used will depend on the sample and resources available to a retailer. Researchers collect quantitative research using many methods including face-to-face, mail, online or over the telephone.

Any data collected are only as good as the data collection instrument. When structuring questions for the instrument, make sure they are clear of bias. To eliminate bias, researchers often resort to the use of *scaling techniques*. Scaling techniques are a series of methods or processes used to measure consumer knowledge, or opinions, preconceptions or even consumer attitudes. There are different types of scales, with the two most popular being the Likert-type scale and the semantic differential scale.

A Likert-type scale uses a rating system (or scale) to determine the degree to which an individual agrees or disagrees with a statement. With a Likert-type scale, the respondent chooses among several options such as Strongly Agree; Agree; Neither Agree or Disagree; Disagree; Strongly Disagree. A semantic differential scale also studies the choices for measuring agreement. Respondents of a semantic differential scale would select numbers that point to the strength of their agreement with issues, questions or situations. In addition, semantic differential scales employ two bipolar adjectives where subjects are asked to select their level of agreement or disagreement. The difference in the questions developed for the scales may look like these two examples:

Please place a check mark in the area that best represents or attitude or opinion toward the following questions:

Likert-type scale may read...

Circle your answer to indicate your agreement with the following statement.

The employees at ABC store are friendly.

Strongly Agree_   Agree_   Neither Agree nor Disagree_   Disagree   _ Strongly Disagree_

The semantic differential scale may read:

Please place a check in the area that best represents your opinion of this retailer's employees:

Unfriendly ----- ____ ---- _____ ---- _____ ---- _____ ---- _____ ----- Friendly

---

With both types of scaling, a series of statements is used to measure a characteristic by asking for a response that requires choosing from a series of predetermined responses.

After the researchers develop their data collection instruments, they turn their attention to data analysis. Typically, data are subjected to a series of statistical tests that determine the value of the data. The statistical tests will help reveal interesting facts about the sample. The statistics also yield population estimates, information that is useful in making decisions about the population. Finally, when all the data are collected and analyzed, a report must be generated that includes recommendations of how to use the analyzed data.

Applying the Research Process

The following example applies the eight-step research process. Imagine you own an upscale children's clothing store. Sales have been slipping and as a retail manager you want to know why. Step one is to identify the problem. You look back at your environmental scan and find that, although your sales are dropping, the industry sales for your area have been increasing. The gap between the performance of your company's sales and the industry sales indicates that there is a problem. Since your competitors have increasing sales, the problem may be your merchandise mix. After secondary research does not supply enough information, you recall that some customers

Source: Iakov Filimonov/Shutterstock.com

have lately been asking for different brands, colors and styles than you currently carry. Research is needed to determine if your hunch is correct. The problem statement you decide to research is whether the current merchandise is meeting the needs of customers. If so, why are sales falling? If not, what brands and styles should be carried?

After defining the research problem, the second step is to design the study. Options you may consider are qualitative or quantitative methods. A decision is made to conduct primary research in the form of a qualitative study. Focus group interviews will be used to collect data. The focus group sessions will be recorded so that you can analyze the sessions later. You hire a trained focus group moderator to conduct the sessions. Step four is to select your sample. Focus group participants will be recruited from existing customers. The sampling frame will be your company's customer database. Parents of children will be asked to participate. To be included the parent must have at least one child under the age of six. To make sure there is the money necessary to carry out the research you generate a research proposal that outlines the problem, budget, and approaches that will be used to determine whether the current merchandise carried is acceptable to customers.

Once the proposal is complete and a decision is made to move forward, you randomly select your customers from your customer database. The focus group sessions consist of six to eight customers and are conducted in the store after the store is closed. Six focus groups provide plenty of information. The videos of the sessions are analyzed and comments concerning brands or styles are recorded using a computer. Based on the findings of the research, a final report which includes recommendations is written. In this case, you discovered that customers thought the brands and styles carried by your store were outdated. Many current customers admitted to shopping a competitor. Several brands and styles were suggested by customers and you made changes to your merchandise mix to accommodate the changes in consumer taste.

Understanding Consumer Usage Behaviors

Retailers need to understand how products and services purchased by customers are being used. By understanding usage behaviors, retailers may be able to better bundle or customize consumer purchases and provide the proper product mix. For example, if a retailer knows that a customer buys two spare products in addition to the customer's regular order, the retailer may be able to bundle the regular order product with the spare order product to simplify the transaction, make the customer happy, and increase sales Additionally, if there is a customer segment that often buys more than one product at a time, a retailer could develop a promotion based on selling products on a BOGO (buy one, get one free) basis.

To understand the usage behavior of the target market, retailers may want to revisit historical purchase data to look for trends in the purchase line for specific customers or customer groups. Loyalty programs also help to identify usage data.

One of the best ways to fully understand the customers' usage behaviors is to spend time with the customers, with sales representatives, or in top performing stores. One can gather information about customers' usage behaviors by interviewing the store manager, the store checkout personnel, customer service personnel or any other people who may have some insight into how customers purchase products. Focus groups, personal interviews and qualitative research are useful as well. To get a good picture of customers' usage of products and services, all research should be longitudinal, which means the research should take place continuously over an extended period to obtain trend information that will help the retailer examine patterns of behavior. One-time research projects that deal with customers' usage don't provide information about the changing environments in which retailers operate.

Mystery Shopping

Because of the shift toward multiple and omni-channel retailing, shopping habits and other consumer behaviors are changing.   For the global retailer it is even more challenging because shopping and buyer behavior vary from country to country, calling for additional research into customers' shopping behaviors.

One of the tactics retailers use to get additional information on their shoppers' habits is the use of mystery shoppers. *Mystery shopping* is a form of observational research in which retailers hire shoppers to pose as customers to shop at various stores. The mystery shopper rates the retailer on pre-defined areas such as cleanliness of the store, customer service and quality of products.

Source:stegworkz/Shutterstock.com

All channels of the retailer's distribution network can be shopped including physical stores, catalog retailers, and Internet stores. The results of the research help managers make decisions about personnel and training. Additionally, the retailer may generate information about how the retailer's products and services are being used. Because of these benefits, mystery shopping is very popular among retailers. Retailers may hire individuals or firms that specialize in mystery shopping to assess how well their employees are trained, customer service levels, and store appearance among other data. Additionally, mystery shoppers are used to help generate data on how customers use recently purchased products and services. The data collected from mystery shopper programs can help determine whether a retailer is achieving its objectives developed in the formation of the IRM plan.

In-Store Observational Research

Another method of retail research is in-store observational research. The observational method of research involves human or mechanical observations of customer behavior during a shopping trip. Observations of in-store behaviors may include how customers use products, where they walk, the shopping differences by gender, the use of in-store promotions or even the time spent in the store shopping. Audio, video, and other electronic devices are available to assess and record in-store behaviors with tracking hidden from the view of consumers.

Although observational studies are considered qualitative, they provide important information that is critical to effective IRM planning. In using observational research, retailers avoid bias because customers are not directly involved in the data collection. In observational research, researchers don't need the cooperation of their sample since behavior is observed without the customer's knowledge.

There are many firms that specialize in retail observational research. Employees from these firms have the capability to watch and record store activity seven days a week, twenty-four hours a day. Data collected can help retailers set up their stores (both on- and offline); determine where to place merchandise, reduce shoplifting and determine where to place promotional material. The biggest disadvantage to observational research is the inability to gather attitude data.

Online Observational Research

Observational research is just as effective online as it is in-store. The same processes, concepts and activities that are used offline, are also used on-line. Often the executions of the research methods may vary, but offer the same types of data and information if executed correctly.

Online, word of mouth (WOM) is an area that deserves consideration because of its impact on consumer decision making. Researchers can assess word-of-mouth data by observing consumer-to-consumer (C2C) conversations and discussions as they occur over the various social media. *Netnography* is the analysis of online behavior (Kozinets, 1998). Netnography research is becoming more popular as researchers try to gain insight into social networking sites, blogs, online communities and other computer-based applications.

Source: weedezign/Shutterstock.com

Suppose a retail manager wants to find out perceptions about her brand. She plans to use social media and examine content generated by consumers in Internet forums and blogs. The company completed a quantitative analysis of the amount of discussion about its retail brand relative to other brands in their industry. The data were grouped into themes based on overall reasons consumers like or dislike the brand. By conducting the netnography, the retailer discovered a range of business opportunities including offering an activity space for children in their stores and providing an online assistant for consumers. They also discovered that the company needed to improve customer service.

Consumer Research Panels

Consumer research panels are composed of a group of customers who have agreed to participate for a period of time in marketing research. Many companies form an opinion research panel from existing customers who evaluate new product and provide opinions on products or events affecting a retailer. There are also many research companies such as Ipsos and e-Rewards that specialize in using consumer panels. Consumers are recruited and provided with incentives to participate in surveys, telephone interviews or polls. Demographic, psychographic, behavioristic and geographic data are collected on the panelists, which will help the company screen and select participants to meet the needs of the retailer. Incentives are often in the form of awards points for participation, and these points can be traded for merchandise.

One concern about using outside panels for research is a the panel is not a representative sample of the target market. Many consumers don't want to invest time and consider it a nuisance to participate. Another concern is respondent bias. Those that volunteer to participate in a consumer panel may respond differently than the general population. Nevertheless, consumer panels can be an important source of information for retailers.

Retail Information Systems (RIS)

As retailers increase the amounts of research needed to gain more insight, they need a central source for the storing and dissemination of this valuable information. A retailer's Retail Information System (RIS) is used to systematically gather, condense, analyze and store data gathered from marketing research. An RIS can be as technologically advanced as the retailer wishes, but it can also be as simple as a handwritten log used to record a retailer's inventory or sales. Most retailers in the United States use computerized systems for their RIS.

Source:leungchopan/Shutterstock.com

The RIS is used in almost all areas of a retailer's operations. Because of the demand for information and data contained in the RIS, the system must be general enough to be accessible and usable to all personnel, yet it must be specific enough to help create solutions to retail problems. The communication flow in an RIS must go in all directions: Any associate or member of the retailer's channel of distribution must have access to the system for either taking material out, or inputting into the system. The RIS must also have the ability to gather data. Thus, there's an inward flow to the system, as well as an outward flow of communications and information. Consequently, retailers need to set up their RIS systems in a way that releases the correct information to users. The system must also be able to prevent certain information and data from flowing to personnel who don't need or want the information. In particular, the retailer must make sure that confidential information doesn't flow from the RIS to competitors and others. Confidentiality of data and information is crucial to a well-developed RIS.

A properly developed RIS can be used in the management of a retailer's supply chain, or places where the retailer receives products, services and supplies; in the retailer's finance and accounting departments; for distribution and data warehousing. The information also will be used to help create and maintain competitive pricing, IMC, merchandising and product acquisition. The data could become part of the retailer's logistics programs and systems, including using the RIS for inventory planning and control. For example, merchandise optimization technology allows the retailer to identify the most profitable merchandising decisions and determine, in real time, approximately how many units remain in stock, when to order more inventory, how much inventory to order (called the *economic order quantity*) (What's So Groundbreaking, 2003).

As retailers expand their channels of distribution, they need to integrate their omni-channel operations. Good RIS systems provide for the integration of methods and processes and information exchanges between channels using electronic, and sometimes physical, transfer or exchange. The integration of concepts, processes, strategies and executions across channels is an important feature of the RIS. Having the ability to combine online data with catalog, brick-and-mortar, e-commerce and m-commerce channels allows for more efficient and effective IRM planning. Figure 6.2 shows the various elements to be included in an RIS.

Figure 6.2: Input and Output Elements for a Retail Information System

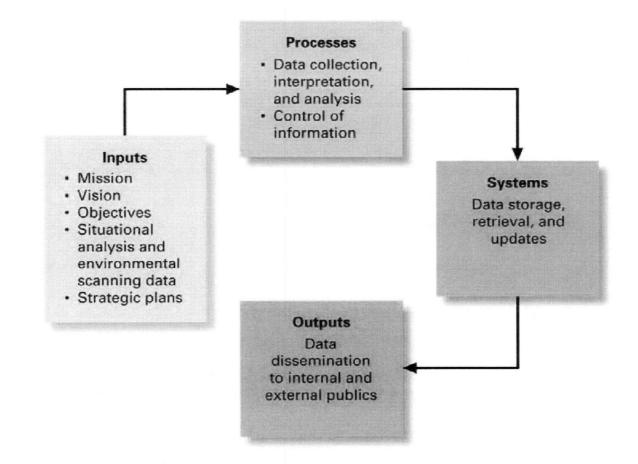

RIS Sources

With the advances in technology, retailers responded by creating systems that help drive efficiencies within the retail organization. As such, hardware and software has been developed that provide sources of data which is integrated into a retailer's RIS and IRM plan.

Universal Product Code: After a customer selects merchandise and is ready to pay, the clerk at the point-of-sale terminal (cash register) uses an optical scanner to read a barcode referred to as the *Universal Product Code* or simply the UPC. The product code holds pertinent information about the product and manufacturer and price. Started in 1973, UPCs originally stored data in printed parallel lines, but today they also come in patterns of dots and concentric circles; the code can even be hidden within images. UPC codes reduce the work related to inventory turnover and stocking because data is transferred to inventory management systems which automatically order products when inventory levels fall to a pre-defined level. The GS1 US (formerly known as The Uniform Code

Council, Inc. or UCC), is a not-for-profit organization that oversees implementation of UPC codes. (www.gs1us.org). GS1 US administers the UPC. and develops worldwide standards and solutions for identification numbers, data carriers, electronic commerce, and global data synchronization.

There are more than 200,000 GS1 US member companies. On a worldwide basis, the GS1 system (formerly called EAN International or the EAN.UCC system) is used by more than one million companies in 150 countries across more than 20 industries. GS1 oversees the UPC barcodes and works to establish and promote multi-industry standards for product identification and related electronic communications.

A typical UPC is a barcode with a company identifier built into it. The additional numbers are assigned by the retailer to identify specific SKUs (stock keeping units). SKUs are retailer-defined numbers or codes used to identify each unique product sold. The cost for retailers to get UPCs varies based upon the size of the retailing organization. In the United States as well as Canada, a 12-digit UPC is used. While there are many different types of barcodes, two common ones utilize an eight-digit (EAN-8) and a 13-digit (EAN-13) symbol for the code. All the numbers encoded in UPC and EAN barcodes are known as Global Trade Item Numbers (GTIN).

In the past, the difference in systems often created problems for retailers involved in international retailing. To improve the situation, GS1 created a process where U.S. and Canadian retailers must be capable of scanning EAN-8 and EAN-13 and 12-digit UPC symbols at the point of sale. This change has been positive in facilitating international retail trade (The Electronic Commerce Council…, 2005).

Radio Frequency Identification: To effectively integrate all the retailing information functions into a retailer's RIS, *radio frequency identification (RFID)* is often used. Akin to barcodes, RFID tags capture price and inventory data. Unlike barcodes, RFID tags (or smart tags) do *not* need to be in the line of sight of an optical scanner and RFID doesn't require human intervention to scan items (Teresko, 2003). RFID data can be read through clothing, the human body and non-metallic material. A basic RFID system requires an antenna, transceiver and RFID tag. The antenna on the RFID chips sends radio signals to activate the RFID tags. The data from these tags are then sent to the transceiver which reads the data and places those data into the retailer's computer, database or retail information system (What Is Radio Frequency Identification? 2003).

Enhancements to the RFID are being introduced, and the next level for standardization is called the Electronic Product Code (EPC), which was developed for global RFID. The developer of the EPC is EPCglobal, a joint venture between GS1 and GS1 US. The organization was set up to promote the worldwide adoption and standardization of EPC/ RFID technology. The goal of the organization is to create a worldwide standard for RFID. In addition, the organization wants to leverage the Internet to share data throughout the EPCglobal Network, the computer network used to share information between companies. This network will increase

Source: Jack_Talis/Shutterstock.com

the quality of information and efficiency throughout the supply chain (EPC Global site www.epcglobalus.org).

Quick Response Codes: Many retailers are using newer technologies that incorporate inventory planning, along with the ability to complete and process orders quickly at retail checkout. These systems utilize electronic data interchange (EDI) and *Quick Response (QR)* codes which are two-dimensional, square-shaped barcodes that allow people to retrieve information when scanned and are decoded by a scanner, mobile device or webcam (Beck, 2011). These systems work for retailers both for making inventory and merchandise purchases, and tracking sales at retail. A shopper with a smart phone loaded with a QR reader can point and click at the QR code on a product to get coupons, service agreements, features, and pricing information. The information is delivered to the smart phone. For consumers, scanning a QR code is a fast way to access information without typing in a URL.

Retailers using QR codes include Target, Home Depot, Best Buy, Walmart and Macy's. Macy's, as part of its Backstage Pass campaign, ran commercials that showed consumers how to use the codes and explained the information that is accessible when the QR code is scanned. After shoppers downloaded a free QR-code reader by scanning the code, the content appeared on their smart phone. The codes help the technology savvy Macy's consumers who want access to instant information. A Best Buy executive explained that QR codes are like having a personal shopping assistant (Zmuda, 2011).

Source:Bloomicon/Shutterstock.com

Seizing the opportunity to benefit from QR codes, the media, retailers and other businesses and organizations have placed QR tags in their marketing communication executions.

Efficient Customer Response: *Efficient Consumer Response* describes a process where all parties in a supply chain use technology to integrate information. ECR began because companies understood they could serve consumers better, faster and at less cost by working together with trading partners. To better serve the consumer, ECR set out to eliminate barriers by taking a holistic view of the supply chain and achieving integration to increase value to the consumer. Prior methods of inventory replenishment relied on retailers and wholesalers to predict demand. With ECR, systems for replenishing merchandise are based on consumer purchase activity. Benefits of ECR include reduced cycle times, less excess inventory and better planning. ECR also helps retailers develop their merchandise mix (ECR Community, http://ecr-community.org/).

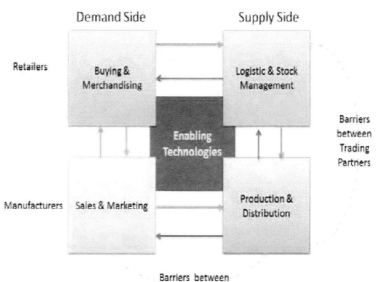

Figure 6.3 ECR: Working Together to Overcome Barriers

Summary

Thus far we have explored several aspects of the development of an integrated retail management plan. In this chapter, the marketing research process and retail information systems (RIS) and were covered.

Research processes help ensure the IRM process is successful in all aspects of retailing. This chapter looked at a research process used to generate data and to turn those data into useful, actionable information that allows managers to make better retail management decisions. There are many different approaches to marketing research. The goal is to provide useful, relevant, and current information to retail managers and other employees.

The chapter discussed the differences between market and marketing research. Market research is a subset of marketing research that aims to generate data from which retail managers can make intelligent choices to solve the organization's problems.

Retail research is used throughout the development of the integrated retail management plan. The research can be used to help develop strategies or tactical executions. In addition, it can help the retailer solve day-to-day retail management problems such as forecasting, inventory buying, selling, training, and market development and segmentation. Without good research, retail decisions will be inferior to those that are research based.

Secondary data are relatively easy and inexpensive to obtain. There are many sources of secondary data, including U.S. government sources, directories, and journals. In addition, internal secondary data such as balance sheets, sales records, and inventory information may be useful to retailers. Primary data, although more expensive, can provide more retailer-specific information than secondary sources of information.

RIS help retailers gather, store, and analyze data. Use of the Universal Product Code (UPC), point of sale technology, self-checkout, and radio frequency identification (RFID) aid in the RIS process. Some retailers choose to outsource data collection, verification, and analysis.

Terms

census	A count of *all* members of the population for input in a research study.
consumer research panels	A group of customers who have agreed to participate for a period of time in marketing research
data	News, facts, and figures that have not been organized in any manner.
data collection instruments	Devices used to collect data such as the paper that a survey is printed on or the computer used by researchers to record responses.
Delphi technique	A research method used to generate information from a panel of experts.
economic order quantity	A calculation of how much merchandise to reorder.
executive summary	A summary of an entire paper.
exploratory research	Research that is conducted when there are no earlier studies available to answer a question and a problem has not been clearly defined.
external secondary data	Sources of data and information that are external to the firm.
focus group	Interviews conducted with small groups of current or potential customers on a topic.

information	A meaningful body of facts organized around some specific topic.
internal secondary data	Sources of data and information that are internal to the firm.
market research	The process of data collection, organization, analysis, and dissemination of data relating to a particular area.
marketing research	Research conducted to identify and define marketing opportunities and problems; generate, refine, and evaluate marketing actions; monitor marketing performance;
mystery shopping	Form of observational research in which retailers hire shoppers to pose as customers
netnography	The analysis of online behavior.
nonprobability sampling	Sampling in which no member of the population has an equal and known chance of being selected for the research study.
observational research	A non-intrusive research tool that is used to evaluate consumer behaviors.
outsourcing	The practice of hiring an individual, a group, or an organization outside the company to perform certain work.
pluralistic research	The combination of qualitative and quantitative research methods when conducting
primary data	Data that are gathered for a specific purpose and have not yet been published.
probability sampling	Sampling in which each and every member of the population has an equal and known chance of being chosen for the sample.
qualitative research	Collection, analysis, and interpretation of data that cannot be quantified with numbers.
quantitative research	Research which uses structured questions in which the response options have been
radio frequency identification (RFID)	Wireless technology that uses radio waves to read product information.
retail information system (RIS)	A method for systematically gathering, analyzing, storing, and utilizing valuable retail information and data.
sampling	The process of choosing a subset of the population of interest to collect problem-specific data.
sampling frame	A list of all population members from which a sample will be drawn.
scaling technique	A method used to measure attitudes, knowledge, opinions, or perceptions on a given topic or issue.
secondary data	Published data that have already been collected for some other purpose.
stock keeping units (SKU)	Retailer-defined numbers or codes used to identify each unique product sold.
Universal Product Code (UPC)	A bar code found on many consumer packaged goods that stores all pertinent product information.

Discussion Questions

1. What are the distinctions between marketing research and market research?
2. Why is marketing research important to the retailer?

3. Explain the difference between primary and secondary data. Explain the difference between qualitative and quantitative research.

4. If you had to find out what your competitors are doing, what type of research would you undertake?

5. When is it appropriate to outsource retail research projects?

6. What sources of information do you use to decide which stores to patronize? Do you trust some stores more than others? If so, why?

7. What role does technology play in the gathering of data?

8. What are the benefits of utilizing an RIS? What are the disadvantages?

9. Identify some companies that you believe have a competitive advantage in the storage and collection of retail information.

Exercises

1. Using the steps in the retail research process, describe how a retailer would approach whether to open a new location.

2. Collect primary research on perceptions of a local retailer and write a summary of your findings.

3. Develop a score card that a mystery shopper might use for an online environment. Consider criteria such as customer service, easy of navigation, shipping and return policies and product selection (you can think of others).

4. Select three different online retailers and "mystery shop" them. Report your findings back to the class or your professor.

5. Visit a local supermarket and compare the behaviors of men shopping alone for groceries with those of women shopping alone. Write a summary of your observations.

6. Many retailers are combining their physical locations and Internet systems to better address their customers' needs. Two retailers that are recognized for this multichannel integration approach---allowing customers to order online and pick up the merchandise at a local branch location---are Sears and The Container Store. Go to *www.sears.com* and *www.containerstore.com* and answer the following questions:

   • Search for information on how to order online and pick up at a local store (sometimes called *store pickup*). How long did it take you (in seconds or minutes) to find this information?

   • On which of the two sites was it easier to locate this information?

   • Were the instructions for store pickup clear? Why or why not?

   • What, if anything, would you change to make the site and its navigational capacities more user friendly?

Case
Mystery Shopping Comes to India

Mystery shopping is well established in the United States and many other countries, but in many countries the concept is only recently being embraced. India is an example of a country where retail companies are beginning to realize the value of mystery shopping in helping to assess brands and improve customer satisfaction. In India, these "mystery shopping audits" are already used by the hospitality and aviation industries and a few retailers such as Axis Bank and Nirula's (a restaurant chain). As mystery audits reveal major areas for improvement, other Indian retailers are starting to use them. According to ChannelPlay Consulting Founder and CEO Sundeep Holani, most of the companies that are using mystery shopping services sell high-involvement products and require experiential selling.

The audits have revealed major failures in customer services such as salespeople telling customers incorrect information and in many cases even lying to customers. The audits have also shown that many salespeople only care about making the sale and not about the customer's needs.

Bare International, a company that offers mystery audits, helped a retailer realize that they needed improvement in suggestion selling. After the audit the store improved their training for salespeople to make recommendations for accessories when selling clothing to customers. Another audit revealed that a store was rated low on the grooming of their staff. The feedback helped the store improve their staff's appearance. If anything, the audits keep employees alert because they don't know when a mystery shopper will be evaluating them.

Unfortunately, many companies that started mystery shopping businesses in India are disappointed with the way the business has evolved. According to Charoo Aggarwal, managing director of Grass Roots India, a mystery shopping service provider, "Mystery Shopping as a service is very commoditized. Though there is an increasing awareness in India about mystery shopping, the market is still not mature as it is in (the) U.S. and Europe, where mystery shopping is a means to enhance their customer experience." It seems that retailers are only using mystery shopping when they face increased competition instead of on a regular basis.

Per Kumar Rajagopalan, chief executive of the Retailers Association of India, about 10 companies out of the group's 500 members would probably be using the services of mystery shopping companies. Many believe that retailing in India still has so many flaws and lack of standards that retailers need to focus on the basics before they can implement a mystery shopper program. Another reason for the lack of adoption of mystery shopping programs is that Indian retailers hire their own staff to investigate the quality of their services.

Although the mystery shopping industry is not as advanced in India compared to the U.S., the industry is gaining momentum as retailers use mystery shoppers to check on the integrity of their own staff.

Questions:

1. What are the advantages and disadvantages of mystery shopper programs?

2. Should companies use their own staff to mystery shop their offerings? Why or why not?

3. How can mystery shopping be incorporated into a company's marketing research process?

4. Why is the adoption of mystery shopping so slow in India?

Sources: Get Paid to Mystery Shop from RedQuanta [we mystery shopped them]. (2011, Mar 16). *PluGGd.in*, pp. n/a. Retrieved from http://search.proquest.com/docview/857155397?accountid=13158; Mystery Shopping Fails to Take off; Market Immature, say Firms. (2010, Sep 03). *Mint*, pp. n/a. Retrieved from http://search.proquest.com/docview/749272184?accountid=13158; RedQuanta Founder Pankaj Guglani on Mystery Shopping in India [interview]. (2011, Mar 21). *PluGGd.in*, pp. n/a. Retrieved from http://search.proquest.com/docview/857831888?accountid=13158; Dewan, N. (2011, Sep 01). Shoppers Stop, Kimaya, Nirulas, Samsung & Axis Bank Offer Mystery Shopping Audit to Improve Performance of Sales Staff [retailing]. *The Economic Times (Online)*, pp. n/a. Retrieved from http://search.proquest.com/docview/886450070?accountid=13158; Kumar, KPN (2014). Mystery Shoppers: The New Way to Check Service Standards and Employee Integrity, Economic Times (Online). Retrieved from http://economictimes.indiatimes.com/magazines/panache/mystery-shoppers-the-new-way-to-check-service-standards-and-employee-integrity/articleshow/44871090.cms

References

Beck, K. (2011). Barcodes Reach a New Dimension: CRM. *Customer Relationship Management*, 15(1), 14. Retrieved from http://search.proquest.com/docview/837430116?accountid=13158

Blankenship, A.B., Breen, G.E., Dutka, A. (1998). *The State of the Art Marketing Research*, 2d ed. (Lincolnwood, IL: NTC Business Books, p. 15.

Burns, A. C. and Bush, R.F. (2006). *Marketing Research*, 5th Edition, Upper Saddle River, NJ: Pearson Education, Inc., p. 202.

Churchill, G.A. and Iacobucci, D. (2002). *Marketing Research Methodological Foundations*, 8th ed. (Orlando: Harcourt College Publishers, 2002), p. 6.

ECR community website. Retrieved from http://ecr-all.org/about-ecr-europe/origins-of-ecr/

Isaac, M. and de la Merced, M. J. (2016). Dollar Shave Club Sells to Unilever for $1 Billion *The New York Times* (July 20). Retrieved from https://www.nytimes.com/2016/07/20/business/dealbook/unilever-dollar-shave-club.html?_r=0

Kozinets, R.V. (1998). On Netnography: Initial Reflections on Consumer Research investigations of Cyberculture. *Association for Consumer Research*, 25, 366-371.

Levick, R. S. (2012). 3 marketing takeaways from Dollar Shave Club's F***ing Great Ad. Fast Company, (Apr 23). Retrieved from https://www.fastcompany.com/1835082/three-marketing-takeaways-from-dollar-shave-clubs-youtube-ad

Parasuraman, A., Dhruv, G. and Krishnan, R. (2007). *Marketing research*, 2nd Edition, Boston, MA: Houghton Mifflin Company, p. 178.

Rowe, G. and Wright, G. (1999): The Delphi Technique as a Forecasting Tool: Issues and Analysis. *International Journal of Forecasting*, Volume 15, Issue 4, October 1999, p. 353-375.

Teresko, John (2003). Winning with Wireless. *Industry Week*, 252, 60-66.

The Electronic Commerce Council of Canada provides guidance to Canadian companies for international bar code compliance initiative 2005 Sunrise (2005). Press release dated Feb 1. Retrieved from GS1 Canada http://www.gs1ca.org/Page.asp?intNodeID=208&int PageID=407

What Is Radio Frequency Identification (RFID)? Webpage for the Association for Automatic Identification and Data Capture Technologies (n.d.). Retrieved from www.aimglobal.org.

What's So Groundbreaking About Merchandise Optimization? (2003). *PR Newswire*, (Jun 10).

Zmuda, N. (2011). QR Codes Gaining Prominence Thanks to Few Big Players: Macy's, Best Buy, Post Cereals Set Out to Attract Consumers with Educational Efforts, Campaigns. *Advertising Age*, 82(12), 8.

Chapter 7

Retail Site Location and Analysis

"Location, location, location."
~ William Dillard, founder, Dillard's department stores

Source: Roman Tiraspolsky/Shutterstock.com

CHAPTER OBJECTIVES

After completing this chapter you will be able to:

- Define terms related to location analysis.
- Describe the processes involved in selecting a retail market and site.
- Analyze a retail trading area.
- Discuss the various types of sites available to retailers.
- Explain the difference between a planned and an unplanned shopping district.
- Describe the various characteristics that influence a retailer's site selection.

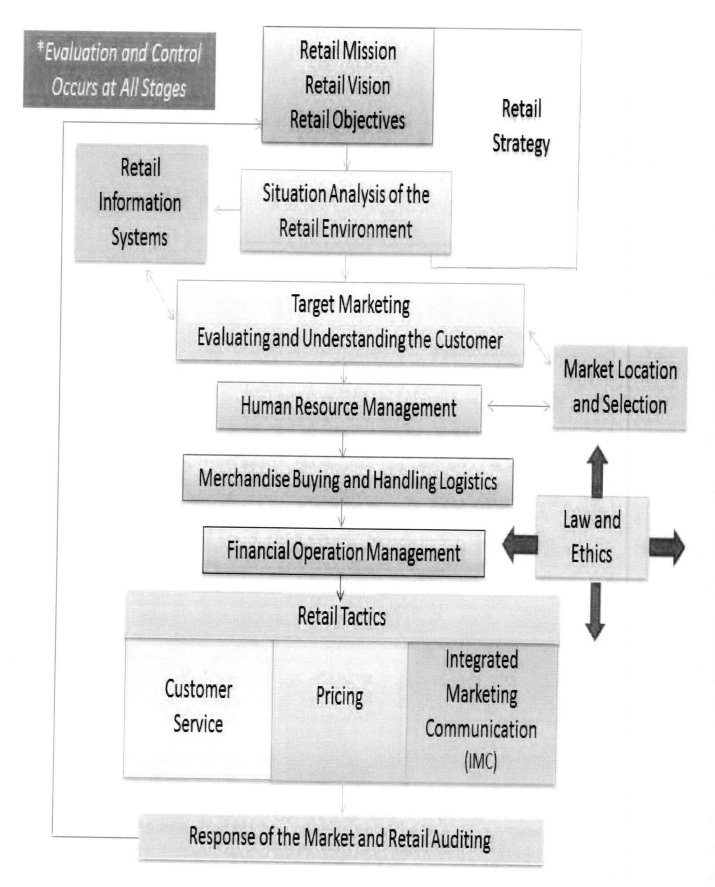

Cabela's Location Strategy

Cabela's tagline is the World's Foremost Outfitter. According to the website it is the "world's largest direct marketer, and a leading specialty retailer, of hunting, fishing, camping and related outdoor merchandise" (www.cabelas.com). This category killer has built a reputation for selection of products, customer service and value. Stores range in size from 35,000 to 247,000 square feet. They classify any store over 15,000 square feet as a "large-format destination store." In addition to targeting the tough-to-reach dad, Cabela's destination retail store appeals to families from a variety of backgrounds.

Source: B Brown/Shutterstock.com

Cabela's has a strong site location strategy and looks for certain criteria when deciding whether to open a store. When choosing a location, there must be a minimum of 22 acres of land, the store must have interstate access and visibility, and an existing or funded Interstate interchange. In addition, a community development incentive package is required. These subsidies are a part of the company's strategic growth plan and are often in the millions of dollars (LeRoy, 2006).

Cabela's management prefers a location with one million people within a 30-mile radius and to be within 20 miles of a metropolitan area. In addition to stand-alone stores, the company will consider a location in an existing retail development or an existing store with a minimum of 85,000 square feet. Cabela's often chooses rural, underdeveloped or underused sites which provide the promise of economic growth in a particular area (LeRoy, 2006). Another factor considered is the number of Cabela's catalog orders for an area and the number of fishing/hunting license holders in concentric mileage-based circles around a prospective location (Giddens, 2004). Bass Pro Shops, another major outdoor product retailer, acquired Cabela's for $5.5 billion in October 2016. The Federal Trade Commission approved the merger and the deal is expected to be complete by late 2017. It will be interesting to witness the change in location strategy with new ownership.

Introduction

One of the most important decisions a retailer makes is where to locate the retailing business. There are many benefits to understanding the retailer's physical market. Additionally, there are many pitfalls that may occur for retailers who don't understand their market. By making research-based market decisions, retailers can increase their customer base and use the physical location in marketing communication decisions, such as store signage. As the Cabela's example shows, a lot of thought and effort to into choosing a location.

The location decision is as important for single-unit, independent retailers as it is for the larger retailers such as the big-box stores. The location will drive customer traffic, which means more sales. The retailer's physical location impacts the retailer's inventory planning, their integrated marketing communications, and their pricing and customer service along with many other activities important to the retailer's success.

This chapter explores how to evaluate the external and internal variables inherent in the process of site selection. Topics covered include how the retailer assesses and analyzes the characteristics of the trading area from which it will operate. Also covered is how the retail specialist moves to the analysis and selection channels from which to operate.

What Is Market and Location Analysis?

The process of looking at various, potential markets, and a specific location within each of these markets, is called market and location analysis. Its purpose is to analyze, through market research, each potential market area, and a specific location within that market area.

Earlier in the text, the concept of creating a situational analysis was discussed. The retailer's situational analysis may be accessed via the retailer's retail information system (RIS). These data and information will assist the retailer in making good market and location analysis decisions. Of importance within the situational analysis is the undertaking and development of an environmental analysis. The environmental analysis will help the retailer understand the various retailing and marketing environments that impact their stores, as well as provide an overview, or landscape, of the environments in which the retailer will (or currently) operates. These data will also be useful in making decisions about the target area and the target customer groups (or target market segments).

As you know, a target market consists of all customers to whom the retailer decides to develop and aim their marketing efforts. Based upon how a retailer defines their target market and characteristics of their market, retailers develop a typical customer profile which provides a description of an "average customer". This typical customer profile will be used to understand a retailer's customer groups; it should provide an understanding of the customer's buying motives and buying behavior. By better understanding behavior, decisions regarding location can be made with the customer in mind.

Source: Roman Tiraspolsky/Shutterstock.com

Planning and Differentiation

The importance of planning and differentiation were discussed earlier in the text. These concepts are also important when considering location. Many think that choosing locations for a retailer only involves renting or leasing space. There is more involved and much of the activity takes place prior to the opening of a location or Internet site. The customer, competitors, and the retail environment in which one plans to operate and conduct business must be considered. The concept of differentiation relates to the retailer's competitive advantage. As such, retailers will typically differentiate utilizing tactics available to retailers such as price, merchandise/product mix, customer service, store layout and design, unique customer experiences at site and brand development. However, retailers also use market location as a differentiator. For example, early on, one of the tactics Walmart first used was to locate in mid-populated cities that did NOT have a K-Mart. Thus, Walmart could delay going into head-to-head competition with one their major competitors (K-Mart at the time), and select market areas that would have a good return on investment (ROI). Walmart also considers where distribution centers are located when making site selection decisions.

When retailers are looking to open new stores in new markets, the first thing they usually do is to check out the competition. They want to know how the market perceives the retailer. The retailer is attempting to differentiate their retail business in the consumer's mind; thus, every time the customer is exposed to the retailer's brand name, that customer already has an idea as to the type of retail operation. Using the above example, what concept comes to mind when you hear the word Walmart? Most people automatically think "large, global, discount operation!" Walmart continues to build its differentiation through its tag line, logo, advertising and store locations.

When planning, the omni--channel retailer must consider all channels in which they operate. Typically, the channels offer the same types of products and merchandise and use similar value propositions. The retailer's task is to make sure these channels don't cannibalize each other's sales. So, when developing the market area and physical site, retailers must make sure they create "synergy" between all their channels of distribution. When creating a differentiation strategy for market and site location selection, make sure the strategy complements, enhances or mirrors the overall retail value proposition.

The Role of the Physical Market in the Retail Plan

The store location is one of the most important decisions a retail market planner will make. The physical market, or the physical area in which the retailer operates, can signal success or failure for a retailer. The development of a physical location is a time-consuming, expensive task. Once the site is selected and developed, a retailer's flexibility is affected because the location cannot be easi-

ly changed. A strong location can positively affect a retailer's business even without outstanding marketing communications. For example, Wawa is a U.S.-based convenience store operating in the Mid-Atlantic states. Wawa does very little activity in integrated marketing communications because their stores are in high traffic areas where millions of people pass on their way to or from work.

As stated earlier, the location decision is typically based upon numerous criteria including area population size and population characteristics, the retailer's competitors, ease of entry for customers (there must be availability of parking and an ease of entering and exiting the retailer's store), costs of the site (i.e., taxes, rent, lease, buy, power costs, etc.) and legal and ethical constraints, among other issues.

Physical locations can impact a retailer's business in other ways. Once the retailer has expended monetary and human capital on the selection, they tend to be "locked" into that physical location for a sizable period. Additionally, store fixtures must be purchased and inserted into the store. There will be costs associated with operating the retail business such as electricity (and other forms of powering the store), advertising and store ambiance or environment. The development of a physical store within a given market area represents a long-term commitment to the area. When a retailer begins to analyze their options for market areas, they typically use a research-based process to ensure they are limiting incorrect decisions prior to opening the store. For example, when Five Below, the retailer selling goods ranging from $1 to $5, relocated their corporate headquarters to downtown Philadelphia in 2012, the company signed a 10-year lease (Daymark…, 2012).

Location analysis even comes into play when a retailer must close stores. For example, in 2010, Talbots, Inc. (women's clothing retailer), announced that it would shut 75 to 100 stores by 2013. To decide which stores to close, Talbot's analyzed sales and profits, lease expiration dates and whether to renew leases for a store (Nguyen, 2010).

Sometimes when the retailer leaves or goes out of business, it can be difficult to find another retailer to fill the void. In 2011, the Border's book store chain closed after 40 years in business.

Source: Susan Montgomery/Shutterstock.com

This left hundreds of 25,000 square foot stores vacant. Mall owners tried to get independent book stores to open in the vacant buildings, but the size was too big for independent retailers, which often use less than 10,000 square feet. The rent would also be an obstacle. Nevertheless, there are book retailers finding a new retail landscape in many of the locations once occupied by Borders. For example, Vanderbilt University in Nashville, TN is moving into a former Border's location that is close to campus. The location has ample parking and is located on a major thoroughfare. The Hudson Group (bookstores, newsstands, cafes) took over many of Borders' smaller airport locations (Stellen, 2011). Barnes and Noble acquired Borders' trademarks and customer list. The Borders website directed customers to the Barnes and Noble website to complete purchases.

There are many different venues where retailers can locate their physical retail outlets. Each of the venues offers unique environments. It is typical for retailers to begin their market area analysis by looking at the various physical store locations available to them. In this section, coverage is given to the various types of locations available to the retailer. This step in market analysis will provide the retailer the "big idea" as to what is available and in which areas their physical stores will succeed. After looking at the big picture, retailers continue to analyze the market area by searching for actual sites in which to place their stores. In addition, information is provided regarding international, national, regional and local physical locations. Finally, coverage of methods used to search for a retailer's trading area, and information on how to select the exact location for the retailer's physical store is provided. There are three general categories of shopping areas: planned, freestanding and uUnplanned.

Planned Shopping Sites

There are some shopping sites in which a developer puts a lot of time and effort determining which retailers would provide the best mix of products and services to customers. These are planned shopping sites. Other times there doesn't seem to be a reason for the mix of tenants in a particular area. For example, in some sites you may find a hardware store located next to an upscale restaurant. These sites emerge without much thought about what types of retailers go well together and are unplanned shopping sites. In the following section, we will examine each type.

Each planned business site or district is centrally managed and/or owned. The key to a successful planned business district is a balanced tenant mix, or tenancy, which allows the business district to offer complementary merchandise for the customer base. *Balanced tenancy* is the process of optimizing tenants with each other so that retailers provide greater relevancy to their customers. The success of one retailer should help other retailers in a tenancy mix. In a famous speech J.C. Nichols, a prominent real-estate developer, outlines mistakes made in developing shopping centers, such as don't place stores on hillsides. One of the tips he gives is related to developing balanced tenants: "Grouping of merchants whose clientele helps one another is desirable" (Mistakes we have made..., 1945). Although the speech was given in 1945, this tip is still relevant.

Retail tenancy is based on population data from the trading area. Planned business districts are shopping centers developed to attract customers from greater distances. Almost all planned districts have large parking areas and at least one anchor store (although many have more than one anchor). Let's look at some planned shopping sites.

Malls and Shopping Centers

One of the more popular categories for consumer goods retailing are malls and shopping centers. These planned centers of commerce tend to fall into one of three categories: regional shopping centers, community shopping centers and neighborhood shopping centers. Each of these centers offers retailers different advantages when planning a location.

Regional Shopping Centers

Regional shopping centers are large, planned facilities which appeal to a larger, geographically dispersed market. Each regional center has at least one department store (usually more), and at least 50 smaller retail businesses (usually more). Regional malls are typically enclosed with inward-facing stores connected by a common walkway (ICSC, 2017). Regional shopping centers tend to offer deep and broad assortments of shopping goods that appeal to their customer base.

Where do you shop for clothing, phones and jewelry? Most likely you're visiting a regional shopping center. These regional centers typically attract shoppers from longer distances -- at least 5 to 15 miles away. These enclosed structures protect customers from changes in weather. Parking is made easy for customers of regional malls, with parking lots surrounding the regional center.

Regional centers have at least one anchor store but typically have more. A typical anchor store is usually a large, full-sized department store such as Macy's, JCPenney or Nordstrom that attracts customers based upon their own merit, but coupled with additional tenants, generate mall traffic from greater distances. As a rule of thumb, a center should have at least 400,000 square feet of gross leasable area (GLA). Most regional centers are even larger than that (up to 800,000) square feet).

Regional centers were so popular that developers began to create even larger regional centers that are known as *megamalls* or *super-regional centers.* These centers typically have over 800,000 GLA and are located on 60 – 120 acres of land. The trade area is 5 – 25 miles. The top two megamalls in North America are the West Edmonton Mall, located in Edmonton, Alberta, Canada and the Mall of America in Minneapolis, Minnesota. There is always competition to claim the biggest mall in the world. For now, the largest mall in the world is the South China Mall, which is nearly three times the size of the Mall of America in Minnesota. The South China Mall is a $400 million fantasy land: 150 acres of palm-tree-lined shopping plazas, theme parks, hotels, water fountains, pyramids, bridges and giant windmills. There is a 1.3-mile artificial river circling the complex, which includes districts modeled on the world's seven "famous water cities," and an 85-foot replica of the Arc de Triomphe (Barboza, 2005). The site has about 7 million square feet of leasable area. Unfortunately, most of the mall does not have retailers to fill the vacant spaces but the theme park draws customers (World's largest shopping..., 2011). Perhaps a mistake of the mall was targeting an affluent market but locating in an area where the residents are poor.

Source: Plume Photography/Shutterstock.com

The West Edmonton Mall

Spanning the equivalent of forty-eight city blocks, West Edmonton Mall in Edmonton, Alberta (Canada), is the largest mall in North America. It has 5.3 million (yes, *million*) square feet. Besides shopping, the mall houses seven attractions: Galaxyland Indoor Amusement Park, World Waterpark (five acre indoor playland), Professor Wem's Adventure Golf, Ice Palace skating rink, Crystal Labyrinth (a maze-like hall of mirrors). Other diversions include a 3D IMAX theater, a live dinner theater, twenty-six movie theaters, a Las Vegas--style casino, more than 800 stores and services, and over 100 restaurants.

The complex was built in four phases opening in 1981, 1983, 1985 and 1998. Total cost to build the mall was $1.2 billion (Canadian). The planned site was developed to increase drawing power and trading area size. From the looks of it, the developers made a good choice of site. The West Edmonton Mall is an example of best practices in choosing a location and analyzing trading areas.

Prior to the presence of the West Edmonton Mall, the city was known to outsiders mainly for oil and hockey. Since the mall was built, tourists have numbered over 30 million annually. The primary visitors to the mall are families with school-aged children, followed by teens and seniors. The primary markets are women between the ages of 18 and 34 and teens.

Source: Ronnie Chua/Shutterstock.com

Sources: West Edmonton Mall website at (2017) www.westedmontonmall.com;
"'Eighth Wonder of the World' West Edmonton Mall has it All," retrieved June 2003 from www.wheredmonton.com;
Anna Elkins, "Did You Know?," *News Sentinel*, June 18, 2003, p. A11.

Community Shopping Centers

Community shopping centers are smaller than regional centers and substantially smaller than megamalls. A community shopping center will typically have between 125,000 to 400,000 square feet of GLA. They house smaller anchors, such as a supermarket, drug store or furniture store. Along with the anchor store, community shopping centers have smaller retailers, and often a convenience stores as tenants.

Much like the regional centers, community shopping centers have a diverse mix of tenants which may include several service businesses like banks, pharmacies and hair salons. Many specialty stores are housed in a community center, but these stores tend to be well suited for the physical market they are housed in. Tenant mix is very important for community shopping centers as they use heavy promotion to create a unique image.

Source: K2 images/Shutterstock.com

A type of community shopping center that has evolved based upon the success of the community shopping center is known as a *power center*. Power centers always have at least one category killer (i.e., Office Depot, Best Buy, Costco and the Sports Authority) with a mix of smaller tenants. Power centers have a larger market area than a typical community shopping center.

Neighborhood Shopping Centers

Neighborhood shopping centers are planned shopping areas with a small anchor store. In general, a neighborhood center has a supermarket or large drugstore, such as Walgreens, as its anchor.

Neighborhood centers tend to use convenience goods more than do regional or community centers (who typically carry shopping and specialty goods). Typical GLA is between 30,000 and 125,000 square feet.

In terms of market area, these centers draw consumers from limited distances (typically no more than three miles away). Most neighborhood centers are laid out in a "strip" and are usually outdoors in a straight, or somewhat curved line. One might find banks, dentists, dry cleaners and others offer consumer necessities as tenants of a neighborhood center. Because of their physical layout, neighborhood centers are often referred to as strip malls.

Source: Felix Mizioznikov/Shutterstock.com

Because of the types of products and services offered (necessities), these types of centers tend to do well in down economic times. Developers of neighborhood centers look for large populations.

Lifestyle centers have become another popular method of distribution for retailers of high-end merchandise and services. Lifestyle centers are basically neighborhood centers whose tenant mix includes stores that offer upscale products and services and who target upper-income consumers. The concept of a lifestyle center is to create a "main street" type of atmosphere or ambiance with tenants that sell nonessential items. Building and landscaping costs are typically higher than other retail developments. Parking is generally available for consumers to park right in front of the stores as well as a larger lot to take into account additional overflow traffic. The trade area is typically between 8 – 12 miles.

The term "lifestyle center" is attributed to Poag and McEwen Lifestyle Centers in Memphis, Tennessee. Poag and McEwen were among the first developers of these centers and they continue to operate today. Shown below are a few Lifestyle Centers in the U.S. (Poag and McEwen, 2011).

- Promenade Shops at Centerra (Loveland, CO),
- Promenade Shops at Orchard Valley (Manteca, CA)
- Promenade Shops at The Spectrum (Pearland, TX)
- Promenade Shops at Saucon Valley (Lehigh Valley, PA)
- Promenade Shops at Evergreen Walk (Hartford, CT)
- Promenade Shops at Briargate (Colorado Springs, CO)

Source: Felix Mizioznikov/Shutterstock.com

Typical tenants of a lifestyle center may include upscale retailers such as Ann Taylor, Restoration Hardware, L.L. Bean, the Apple Store, Williams-Sonoma, and Barnes and Noble as well as upscale restaurant retailers such as Shula's Steakhouse, Emeril's and others. Almost always included are smaller chains and independent retailers with special interest retailers such as needlework shops.

Outlet Centers, Internet Malls and Airport Malls

There are other types of planned shopping centers such as outlet centers, Internet malls and airport malls. Each of these types of planned shopping centers is explained below.

Outlet Centers: *Outlet centers* (also known as Factory Outlet Centers) are essentially community centers that offer off-price merchandise and have greater drawing power than do community centers. Outlet centers are popular, especially when the economy is down. The original outlet centers began in Reading, Pennsylvania. These centers originated as employee stores where manufacturers of goods and services would sell their flawed or overstocked merchandise to their own workers at deep discounts (Frankel, 2002).

Outlet centers evolved and began to welcome the public. Soon retailers, as well as manufacturers, began to operate outlet malls. Outlet centers have become destinations for tourists who want to do some shopping while on vacation. Some outlet centers are enclosed while others have been laid out in a strip configuration. Additionally, some outlet center developers have tried to create outlet lifestyle centers creating a small town atmosphere for their outlets. Primary customers of outlet centers are residents who live within a 25 mile radius of the center and who tend to visit the centers on a weekly basis. These centers also enjoy secondary customers who travel as far as 75+ miles to get to the centers.

Vanity Fair, now VF, was among the first manufacturers to convert old manufacturing facilities into outlets for their products and services. After seeing the success of the VF outlets, many retailers and manufacturers followed suit and opened their own outlet centers.

The Simon Property Group (Indianapolis, IN) is one of the bigger players in mall management. The company owns or has an interest in 229 retail estate properties (malls, outlets) (www.simonmalls.com). The company acquired The Mills Corporation in 2007 and now owns the shopping sites. Anyone who lives near a large city, or near large populations has probably visited one of the Mills centers such as Sawgrass Mills (near Fort Lauderdale, Florida), Opry Mills (Nashville, TN), or Gurnee Mills (near Chicago, Illinois) (Simon Property Group, 2017). Simon Property group also owns the Premium Outlets portfolio, where shoppers can expect a large collection of retailers selling designer brands. The sites are typically named after the city in which they are located, such as Cincinnati Premium Outlets.

Source: Ken Wolter/Shutterstock.com

Internet Malls: *Internet malls* (also known as virtual malls), are planned shopping centers located on the web. With advances in technologies, retailers have found additional institutions to create channels of distribution. Internet mall tenants are brought together online, or through some type of catalog or newspaper ad. These virtual malls also have a planned tenant mix and are created by Internet site developers. Popular internet malls include eCrater (www.ecrater.com) and Shopzilla (www.shopzilla.com).

SkyMall (1-800-SkyMall or www.skymall.com), which was developed for Delta Airlines, is an example of an Internet mall. Retail products and services are offered to consumers through its SkyMall catalog which is found on all Delta Airlines flights, or consumers may access the mall through the SkyMall website. SkyMall carries products from many different retailers and other vendors. In January 2015, SkyMall filed for Chapter 11 bankruptcy. The company was purchased at auction by C&A Marketing (Now C+A Global) for $1.9 million. C+A kept the brand name and expanded the offerings online. The company continues to offer novelty items as well as innovative and fun products that are used more in everyday life (Geuss, 2015).

Airport Malls: The airline industry also offers another type of planned shopping center called *airport malls*. Airport malls are effective because travelers are brought together at terminal points (airports), and after the consumer passes through airport security, they have little else to do and shopping provides a way to spend time until it is time to board a flight. In essence, airport malls are community shopping centers that are located in an airport. Whereas some of the earlier airports' retailers were brought together through evolution and were unplanned, airport developers have seen the value of planning their tenant mixes and have moved toward planned malls within the airports.

Source: Brendan Howard/Shutterstock.com

Today's airport travelers can spend time shopping in middle-to high-end shops and eateries. For example, Amsterdam's Schiphol Airport claims the first-ever airport library, a full-fledged casino, and a branch of the prestigious Rijksmuseum showcasing Dutch masterpieces. Stores include H&M, Nike and Crocs. In addition, Amsterdam-based Paolo Salatto supplies upscale dress shoes and heels, leather goods and accessories, and men's apparel. BLOEM! Sells fresh-cut flowers, seeds and bulbs (Shop 'Till You Takeoff, 2011).

There are two models used for the development of airport malls: the prime model and the developer model. In the *prime model*, the airport is responsible for the management of retail facilities. In the *developer model*, an outside company serves as the mall manager, and they use various marketing communications functions to draw successful retailers into the airport's mall. The shops in the developer model are typically owned and operated by individual retailers who do their own hiring, firing and other operational functions.

With the development of mobile commerce (or *m-commerce*), retailers are studying ways to create planned shopping centers on mobile devices. While not there yet, there is a strong growth in this area, and all retailers must keep an eye on these developments as they will offer additional planned channels of distribution for the retailers.

Freestanding Sites

Freestanding sites (also known as *isolated sites*), are generally planned sites, but do not fall into the category of planned business sites because they are stand-alone sites that are isolated from other businesses. These sites are not located within districts or groups of stores.

A retailer will move into a geographic area with no other retailers in the immediate vicinity. Generally the retail establishment is off of a main route, street or even a highway. Retailers often have a hard time attracting customers to a freestanding site because they are the only retailer there and the store is typically in an isolated area. Because of this, larger retailers and convenience store retailers are typically the type of businesses that occupy these types of sites. For example, Tahari and Walgreens are two retailers that often have freestanding locations.

A consumer may not be willing to drive 10 miles to buy a taco but may make the trip if a highly respected kidney doctor has a business there. An advantage to freestanding sites is there are no competitors (or limited numbers of competitors). The retailer can usually negotiate lower rents, leases or purchasing prices for these properties. Conversely, it is harder for the retailer to attract traffic. Costs associated with integrated marketing communications executions may be higher in a freestanding site as opposed to planned or unplanned sites. Finally, the retailer must know the laws and regulations that govern the site. Zoning laws, in particular, may keep retailers from opening businesses in isolated sites.

Source: Jonathan Weiss/Shutterstock.com

Unplanned Shopping Sites

Unplanned shopping sites result when two or more retailers decide to move into the same geographic area or are in close proximity to each other. The difference between unplanned sites and planned sites is the fact that unplanned sites develop based upon evolution, not planning. They are unplanned, but develop over time. There are numerous unplanned shopping sites, but most fall into one of four categories: central business districts, secondary business districts, neighborhood business districts and strip shopping districts. Each of these types is discussed below.

Central Business Districts

Central Business Districts (known as CBDs) are typically downtown areas of any city. Other terms for CBDs are downtown and city centre (international). Bigger cities may have more than one area considered a central business district. For example, London, England has three city centres, one in the city, another in Westminster and the third in the Docklands area. Some states, particularly those on the East Coast, refer to a CBD as center city. Finally, historic sections of a CBD are often referred to as "old town." Examples include Old Town Albuquerque (NM) and Old Town San Diego (CA).

Source: Pazut Wutigornsombatkul/Shutterstock.com

The CBD is often the hub of retailing for small and major metropolitan areas. Many of the city's public transportation systems have a link with the CBD. The growth of almost all of America's early department stores began in central business districts. Examples would include J.L. Hudson's (in Detroit, Michigan), Marshall Field's (Chicago, Illinois), Macy's (in New York City), The Denver Dry Goods (in Denver, Colorado), Eaton's (in Toronto, Ontario, Canada) and Neiman Marcus (in Dallas, Texas). In addition to department stores, CBDs typically have a fairly large number of specialty retailers doing business.

The growth of the CBD began when merchants decided they wanted a central location that was close to others selling goods and services. Little planning (usually none) was involved in the CBD's development. There are numerous advantages to locating in a CBD, such as those show below:

• Easy access to public transportation

- Wide assortments and a variety of products and services available to the consumer
- Varieties of price points for products and services
- Close proximity to other businesses and government offices (often including a retailer's suppliers)
- Proximity to social activities and facilities
- High levels of automobile, bus, subway and pedestrian traffic for the retail store

There are some disadvantages to selecting CBDs as a site possibility. These include:

- Expensive and inadequate parking for customers and employees
- High crime rates associated with the city (oftentimes this is a perceptual problem)
- Relatively high rents, leases or purchase prices for the physical store location
- No availability
- Older buildings, which mean older stores. This may cause the retailer additional capital in order to restore the building.
- Inner-city decay rates leading to area deterioration
- Consumer perceptions that the CBD lacks good shopping and new retail establishments
- High tax rates
- Congestion caused by inner-city traffic and deliveries
- Lack of balanced tenancies
- Long travel or commute times for employees and shoppers

Source: chuyuss/Shutterstock.com

Many CBDs are great trading area alternatives for retailers. The world's most visited tourist attraction, according to *Travel and Leisure* magazine (Matthews, 2011), is a destination in the United States is a CBD known as Times Square! The Eaton Center in Toronto, the Crowne Center in Kansas City and Peabody Place in Memphis are examples of great trading areas.

Revitalizing CBDs

CBDs began as the major trading areas for retailers, but they may have been their better days. Over the last few decades governments and private groups have been trying to revitalize downtown areas. A number of these cities are paying attention to what shoppers want in a trading area such as increased security, better and more parking, brighter colors, enhanced buildings and building facades, more walkways, more green space, lighting and pedestrian malls.

In many ways, healthy downtowns determine the success or failure for many retailers. With revitalization, downtowns can once again serve prominent and important roles within their communities. For example, the Borough of Newport, PA recognized the decline of their CBD. In 1990 a group of residents formed Newport Revitalization Inc. (NRI) to turn the city around. Today once boarded up buildings are now home to thriving retailers and the Perry County Arts Council. The formation of NRI, a non-profit organization, helped to obtain grants and other financial resources to help the process of renovating the downtown. NRI members developed a strategic plan which included a consumer survey and market analysis, a business owner survey and analysis, and a preliminary historic sites survey. This information was then used to guide the implementation of the plan (Shields and Farrigan, 2001).

According to a guide for small towns on how to improve their CBDs (Shields and Farrigan, 2001), communities should consider revitalizing their downtowns for the following reasons:

- *Improves the image of the town.* The first impression of a community is determined by the appearance of the CBD.

- *Makes use of existing buildings.* Reusing properties can help communities manage growth.

- *Develops community.* Because downtowns have been a traditional focal point in most communities, they are a source of identity to most local residents.

- *Provides residents with retail and services.* In many communities, the CBD is the main point for retailers, services, government offices and entertainment.

- *CBDs are employment centers.* Downtowns are still a major source of local employment.

- *Expands the tax base.* Successful downtowns generate local revenues to pay for community services.

- *Prevents blight and abandonment.* A strong CBD will have lower safety costs and concerns.

- *Keeps dollars in the community.* With services and goods available locally, residents will not need to shop outside the community as often.

Secondary Business Districts

In addition to CBDs, retailers may also opt to locate in secondary business districts, or SBDs. *Secondary business districts (SBD)* are generally smaller CBDs. These districts are typically located around major transportation networks of cities. A typical SBD would have at least one department store or variety store coupled with a number of smaller stores.

Although they're not as large as CBDs, the trading area of a SBD is still substantial. There are wide varieties of products and services available within the SBD but less product width and assortment compared to those of CBDs. A secondary business district will usually have a few convenience stores or larger stores that carry an assortment of consumer convenience goods. Often secondary business districts form next to a larger city.

Source: Konstantin L/Shutterstock.com

Advantages to selecting a SBD from which to retail include less congestion and better service offerings than a CBD and better parking (although sometimes this is still an issue). Disadvantages may include a smaller trading area, high rent, lease and own costs, and space for product deliveries. Many of the nation's SBDs are aging, which makes them less attractive to retailers. Finally, the tenant mix of a SBD is unplanned and weak.

Neighborhood Business Districts

Neighborhood business districts (or NBDs) are similar to the neighborhood shopping centers, but are unplanned. Like neighborhood shopping centers, NBDs rely on convenience products as the main product mix. The NBD provides shopping for a neighborhood as opposed to a larger trading area. Advantages of locating in a NBD include good neighborhood locations, expanded hours of operation for the retailer, adequate parking and less traffic congestion. Because of the limited number of products sold within a NBD, the prices of products and services for these districts tend to be higher than at other locations. The key to developing product and service offerings in a NBD is convenience.

Strip Shopping Districts

Another unplanned district is the *strip shopping district*, also known as strip or string districts. These districts have stores that are visible from the road and arranged in a long line. Strips are unplanned shopping districts containing retailers that sell comparable goods. Strip districts most likely began as freestanding sites. Competitors would then enter the sites as the popularity of the store increased. The stores in strips generally have the same types of products and services. Consumers often give these strips personal or special names based upon the type of merchandise retailed, such as the Auto Mile, Restaurant Row or Furniture Row, for example.

Strip districts will usually have lower rent, lease or own costs when compared with SBDs or CBDs. Store visibility is high and parking is above average. The overall cost of operating a retail outlet in a strip district is lower than most other options. Consumers seeking a wide variety of merchandise within a product line, such as cars, will come from longer distances because they know they will have a large choice of products in a fairly small area from which to choose.

Disadvantages include problems with zoning laws, higher advertising and marketing communications costs, limited availability of established locations (which may force a retailer to build rather than lease or rent), and a lack of flexibility in pricing due to the competition selling the same or similar types of merchandise.

Source: Philip Pilosian/Shutterstock.com

In addition to the many different types of freestanding, planned and unplanned sites, there are other types of sites in which a retailer may wish to locate. These include theme centers, festivals, specialty centers and fashion centers. Other sites may include kiosks, mixed-use developments (such as offices in retail outlet areas) and other nontraditional locations such as antique and craft markets and malls. Whichever site is pursued, the retailer must have a great knowledge and understanding of the nature and location of the site and its benefits or disadvantages.

Inshoppers and Outshoppers

Retailers location decisions and balanced tenancy may affect whether consumers stay in their local community to shop or go to another city for their shopping. People who tend to shop in their local communities are called *inshoppers*. Those more likely to shop outside their community are called *outshoppers*. Inshopping helps communities survive economic downturns. Location decisions by retailers can help keep people shopping within a particular community. A variety of retailers and offerings satisfies inshoppers, which leads to greater offerings and increased inshopping. Many people are unsatisfied with the selection of goods and services within their community and will seek retailers who will better fit their needs. These outshoppers will travel out of town for a better shopping experience.

Because people have different needs and wants at different times. Their desire to inshop or outshop depends on the amount of time available, convenience and variety seeking behaviors. Often, shoppers would prefer to do their shopping at a central location and prefer to spend time in one store, a collection of stores (mall) at one location or at an online site that offers different retailers in one website. Many times shoppers may have more time and prefer to have a variety of stores to select from and are willing to travel longer distances to see what products and services are offered. These situations affect inshopping and outshopping behaviors.

Consumers exhibit inshopping and outshopping behaviors depending on the buying situation. For example, the head of a household may prefer to do their grocery shopping locally rather than travel to different stores to find all of their daily or weekly needs. The same person may enjoy a weekend shopping trip to another city for apparel and entertainment needs.

Because of the differences in shopping types, retailers have responded by attempting to create one-stop shopping experiences. Superstores such as Target and Walmart, for example, added fresh produce to their merchandise mix in order to create additional sales of products and to offer consumers the convenience of product purchasing at one location. Planned shopping centers were developed based upon this concept. Mall planners are careful to create an overall atmosphere that allows shoppers to satisfy all of their shopping needs in one stop. Many retailers have developed multiple channels of distribution in order to satisfy shopping needs. Shoppers may be able to go online, to their phone (m-commerce), to a catalog or to a physical store where they will be able to shop in a centralized manner without leaving their home. Amazon.com offers an amazing width and breadth of merchandise in a centralized, one-stop format.

Source: Dragon Images/Shutterstock.com

Many people enjoy shopping. They may have a need or want to find "one-of-a-kind" merchandise. They may be looking for gifts for friends. During holiday seasons, many shoppers find outshopping makes them happier and creates a better shopping experience for them.

Store Types and Location

Consumers have desires, needs and wants for differing types of merchandise. Retailers have responded by creating specialty stores. When trying to identify the market, many retailers must make a decision as to which type of merchandise to carry. Additionally, the retailer must make a decision on the number of stores they want to develop. Location decisions are important to consider when determining number of stores.

Independent Retailers and Location Decisions

Independent retail operations offer ease of entry into the retailing industry. Because independent retailers typically operate in neighborhoods and more rural locations, rental expenses tend to be less for these stores as opposed to those operating in larger metropolitan areas or planned centers. Due to their smaller size and location, independent retailers have a greater opportunity to develop and maintain customer relationships than do chain retailers. In his book, *Retail Superstars: Inside the 25 Best Independent Stores in America*, author George Whalin (2009), profiles 25 successful independent retailers. Gallery Furniture (www.galleryfurniture.com) of Houston, TX is an independent retailer that is great at customer engagement. The management team talks to customers to determine their desires. This makes the customer feel important and gives the company insight when ordering inventory and designing the store. The furniture store displays only merchandise that is stocked in its warehouse, allowing local delivery on the same day the furniture is purchased.

When considering site locations, independent retailers cannot, typically, reach a large market base, because they only have one store. Thus, they must rely on their customer base to travel farther to shop. With the advancements in technology, independent retailers can overcome some of the issues related to location. Many independent retailers rely on technology to expand their market. Additionally, to increase their market presence, these retailers can develop apps that are appropriate for m-commerce. Applications that drive the customers to the e-tail store, or offer rewards, such as coupons, bogos (buy one, get one), special events, contests and other promotional activities are a must for the independent retailer because they provide access to additional customer markets.

An example of an independent specialty retailer is Bronner's Christmas Wonderland in Frankenmuth, Michigan. This retailer managed to stay afloat despite the recession. Although the company sells only Christmas merchandise, they manage to stay busy, attracting nearly two million customers throughout the year. Bronner's is successful because it sticks to its core offering and gives customers a reason to come to the store year round (Whalin, 2009). With a store the size of one and one-half football fields, it would be hard for the company to move their location!

Source: James R. Martin/Shutterstock.com

Chain Stores and Location Decisions

The advantages for retailers in creating a chain store is they are better able to locate near their customer base. For example with more than one location, retailers can be in more than one market with greater access to customers. Many chain stores are located in malls because there are more people available to pass by their location. Sprinkles cupcakes is an example of a specialty chain store that sells freshly baked treats. They top each item with the Sprinkles trademark, modern dots, rich chocolate sprinkles from France or seasonal sugar decorations. The treats have been featured on the Oprah Winfrey Show and The Food Network (www.sprinkles.com). They currently have 24 locations. The company is also known for their cupcake ATM (automatic cupcake dispenser).

The "Right" Place – Retail Site Location

The more information collected in regard to a retailer's market, the higher the probability the retailer will succeed. The "right" place is a difficult decision and should be research based. An incorrect location decision can result in lost customers and lost sales. Effective site location information will assist the retail site specialist in locating at the right spot(s). The first step prior to the identification of a site is to undertake an environmental analysis of the projected areas of operation. These data may be assessed from the retailer's RIS. Retailers should revisit the situational analysis and restate the retailer's target market group.

Based upon the information from the situational analysis, the environmental analysis and upon the target market, retailers will develop a typical customer profile. As stated previously, this profile is used to better understand the customer and their buying motives. Table 7.1 (next page) provides some suggestions on what to include in a typical customer profile.

Table 7.1 Selected Variables for Inclusion in a Typical Customer Profile

Variable	Example
Demographic consumer data	education, marital status, income, ethnicity, gender, age
Geographic data	consumer's location and physical boundaries that may keep a potential customer from shopping at the store
Psychographic data	customer lifestyles and the psychology of the customers
Behavioristic data	buyers' behaviors toward different products and different buying situations such as usage rates
Geodemographic data	population data coupled with demographics for a given market area
Type(s) of buyer(s)	consumer, industrial, business and not-for-profit

Retailers must understand their target groups prior to undertaking any type of process to evaluate and select locations. It makes no sense to sell surf boards in North Dakota because the local market probably doesn't have a need (or an ocean nearby to surf).

Advances in technology allow retailers to gather data and information more easily than in the past. The advent of omni-channel retailing also allows the retailer to reach consumers who may not be in their physical marketplace (through the use of e-commerce, m-commerce, catalogs and other electronic methods), thus the retailer must look at the entire marketplace prior to making location selection decisions. The site selection experts must identify the target market and then identify the geographic areas throughout the world where their market lives and works.

E-tailers, catalog retailers, m-commerce retailers as well as traditional brick-and-mortar retailers all need to undertake site selection. Because e-tailers have customer bases that may live all over the world, they pose a special problem for site selection personnel. The better the retailer's RIS, the better these experts will be able to identify their markets. Why does geographic location matter to those utilizing a single e-tail channel for distribution? There are two important reasons:

1. Because cost-effective product delivery options must be selected. It doesn't matter where the customer lives if the retailer cannot provide them with the product they purchased.

2. It is necessary to adapt websites to fit local market interests, needs, wants and concerns. Many retailers use different e-tail sites based upon country of sales and customer base. This holds true for the utilization of catalogs and m-commerce. Different customers respond differently to marketing communication based upon where they live.

Source: Africa Studio/Shutterstock.com

Armed with the above information, site selection personnel can begin the task of choosing the right location. Information is provided below based upon a funnel approach to site selection. First, nations are examined to see if there's a good fit for the retailer's prospective outlets. Once the country is chosen, retailers look at where in the nation to operate. Typically nations are regionalized, thus retailers look for the best part of the country in which to conduct retail business. Finally, the local areas within a region are assessed, and actual sites are selected for business operations. Let's take a quick look at each of these steps.

Country Decisions

The first decision a retailer will make in regard to site selection is the decision of "in which country do I operate?" The vast majority of retailers operate in one country because expanding to other counties is difficult. Many retailers operate internationally but don't have a physical presence. This can be accomplished with the utilization of omni-channel retailing. Using catalogs and e-tailing allows the retailer to offer products and services for sale internationally without locating in a different country.

U.S. retailers that operate internationally tend to be the larger retail chains. Many retailers from other countries pursue retailing opportunities within the United States. This is because an American family's buying power is much higher than most other countries and there are fewer tariffs in the U.S. This offers international retailers greater opportunity to pursue profits.

An example of a country that is experiencing growth from U.S. retailers is Russia. Despite poor protection of intellectual property rights, Russia is a magnet for many of the top fast-food companies. Consumers in Russia have increased disposable incomes and spend much of it on food. When McDonald's opened its first restaurant in Pushkin Square in 1990, there were long lines. Now McDonald's has over 500 restaurants in Russia. They are joined by Papa John's, Sbarro, Domino's, Burger King, Cinnabon, Subway, Carl's Jr, Wendy's, KFC, Pizza Hut, and Taco Bell to name a few. Russia's development of a modern infrastructure has helped the international expansion. In addition, Russian consumers are increasingly affluent and tend to have money to spend on food and entertainment. Consequently, fast-food chains can charge higher prices in Russia than in the U.S (Kramer, 2011).

Source: FotograFFF/Shutterstock.com

There are a few rules of thumb to follow when deciding to pursue international expansion. First, the retailer must make sure that their targeted international destinations have adequate spending power. If not, the nation will not be able to support the retailing operations. Second, the retailers must conduct exhaustive research studies in regard to the potential market. Retailers must cater to local tastes, needs and wants in order to be successful, so a thorough study of the consumer is necessary. Countries have unique customs, laws, rules, regulations and ethics within which the retailer must operate. The retailer falls under national and international laws which vary from U.S. operations.

Finally, retailers must gain country-specific or locally-specific expertise in order to succeed. The easiest and most effective way to do so is through the acquisition of local retailers, joint ventures, franchising or the creation of strategic alliances. One effective strategy of international retailers has been the creation of retail brands. Many retailers create brand positioning and take their retail operations international based upon this positioning.

The National Restaurant Association (2017) estimates that the restaurant industry generates about $799 billion a year. As a result, foreign companies are looking to the U.S. to expand. One example is YO!Sushi (www.yosushi.com), a UK restaurant company which opened in 1997. Their location strategy is to use the franchise system to gain market share in the U.S. The management team decided on this system because they felt it was important that people running the restaurants understand the local markets. The company established a minimum number of restaurants (five) that a franchisee must open to be approved. The first franchise agreement was for 10 restaurants in and throughout Washington, D. C. and Philadelphia. The company hired Baum Reality Group (Chicago) to help them find appropriate locations. YO!Sushi is not a destination retailer so it needs to be located near other retailers that drive traffic. Malls and regional shopping centers are good locations for the restaurant. YO!Sushi's target market is people aged 35-54 with annual household incomes of at least $70,000. Its restaurants take up anywhere from 900 sq. ft. to 3,500 sq. ft. of space (Misonzhnik, 2012).

KidZania Expands Internationally

Do you remember when you were young and pretended you were a doctor, firefighter, lawyer, or other great professional? Thanks to a Mexican business, many kids will get to engage in more realistic role-playing in a new theme park. Kidzania (www.kidzania.com), is a theme park, targeted toward children ages two through twelve, that allows kids to pretend they are adults. The theme park recreates a city complete with a town square, a hospital, and even an airport. Upon entering the park, kids are given a check for 50 "kidzos," the currency of the city. Their first stop is the bank, where they can cash the check for "money" that they will spend on food, merchandise, and "grown-up" activities. Kids can pretend to be doctors, dentists, television producers, car dealers, and much more. They can earn more kidzos to spend in the park. The theme park concept helps expand the customer base. It gives the target demographic customer groups (parents) an incentive to shop at this particular site.

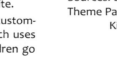

Source: S-F/Shutterstock.com

According to a company spokesperson, customers fall into four market segments, each of which uses the facility at different times: families with children go to the park on Friday nights and weekends; school trips occupy the park on weekday mornings; birthday parties are held on weekday afternoons; and corporations rent out the park on weeknights for their company celebrations.

The first park opened in Santa Fe (a suburb of Mexico City) in September 1999 and was originally called, *La Ciudad de Los Niños*, which means Kid's City. The first park had 52,000 square feet. After the first year there were over 800,000 visitors. Based on this success 12 more locations around the world were opened. A U.S. KidZania is planned for 2018. Location decisions are very important in developing a marketing strategy, especially in understanding markets located in countries other than the host company's headquarters.

Sources: Debra Hazel, "Export Child's Play for Mexican Theme Park," *Shopping Centers Today*, July 2002, p. 39; KidZania website: www.kidzania.com.

National

Once the retailer has selected the country or countries in which they decide to operate, they must assess that country's ability to support the retail operation. Research helps retailers decide if they want an international or national presence. National retailers operate in only one country. Because of this, the retailers can become familiar with the country's laws, culture, customers and typical buying behaviors. This also eliminates risks involved in international retailing such as changing economies, civil disturbances and other legal, technological, natural, ethical and societal concerns.

Regional

After selecting a country in which to operate, retailers will look at that country to try and define the differing regions within the country. Whether located in the United States or any other country, retailers must decide in which region(s) to operate. A region represents a large geographical area. It could be the part of a country, a state, or a city. In the U.S. designated market areas (DMA), core-based statistical areas (CBSA) and metropolitan statistical areas (or MSA) are often used to designate a particular region.

DMAs and CBSAs (or MSAs) reflect actual trading areas that traditional city and county (sometimes state) boundaries do not capture. These designations provide nationally consistent definitions for collecting, tabulating and reporting data and/or information. Typically these designations follow state, city and county boundaries, but not always. Because there are many different designations for assessing data, retail location specialists must be careful when looking at and analyzing data from different sources. Two of the most common designators are designated market areas (DMA) and core based statistical areas (CBSA).

A *designated market area (DMA)* is composed of counties (or oftentimes split counties depending on where the cities lie) assigned exclusively to a market area in which the home market television stations hold a dominance of total hours viewed (The Nielsen Company, 2017). For example, the Atlanta, Georgia DMA encompasses over forty-five counties including two that are in the state of Alabama. DMAs were developed by the Nielsen Media Research to help with measurement media reach. Their DMAs are defined according to a population's total television viewing hour percentages. This is helpful to retailers because it gives them an indication as to where their marketing communication and advertising dollars go. It also helps them in terms of identifying their regional market.

Core-based statistical area (CBSA), is a collective term for both metro and micro areas. A metro area contains an urban area of 50,000 or more people. A micro area contains an urban core of at least 10,000 but less than 50,000 people. They do not include college students who are not permanent residents. These designations are U.S. government assigned, specifically within the Department of Management and Budget. Each metro or micro area consists of one or more counties and includes the counties containing the core urban area and any nearby counties that rely on the core area for economic or social integration. These areas are reviewed every ten years prior to each decennial census.

When CBSAs are developed and reassigned, market areas change, thus retailers need to be aware of these changes. In 2002, for example, the Lehigh Valley of Pennsylvania was reassigned. The Lehigh Valley consisted, prior to the reassignment, of Allentown, Bethlehem and Easton, Pennsylvania (with numerous smaller cities located within this area as part of the MSA). In 2003, after the CBSA Warren County, New Jersey was assigned as part of the Lehigh Valley CBSA. Prior to the assignment, Warren County had been part of the Newark, New Jersey CBSA. With the change, the CBSA of the Lehigh Valley grew in population by sixteen percent. The demographics and geodemographics of the area changed significantly as well, showing a trend toward a younger, wealthier and better-educated core of consumers. This drew the attention of national retailers, who began to develop sites in this CBSA.

Local

After having chosen the nations they wish to do business in and after studying the nation and regions within that nation, retailers must begin a study of the local area in which they decide to locate. The local decision is usually undertaken through the use of trading area analysis. Based upon the retailer's situational analysis and location analysis, retailers find the correct local area that will provide advantage to the retailer.

The next section focuses on the development and understanding of the local trading area. From there, retailers will focus on characteristics of chosen sites. Information will be provided in regard to unplanned, planned and freestanding sites that are available for acquisition and location of retail establishments.

The Omni-Channel Markets

Because many retailers are involved in omni-channel retailing, site selection activities take on more importance. It is important to the business that all of the sites provide the consumers with the same perception. It is not good to have an upscale catalog and a trashy looking physical location. For example, the California Pizza Kitchen restaurant chain has food trucks, they call "mobile kitchens." The company must ensure that branding and quality are consistent with the company image. If the food quality is poor, it will also reflect on the overall brand.

In addition, there needs to be thorough integration of products, services and return policies. Consumers do not see multiple channels of distribution as being different retailers. The retailer's image is created by a combination of all of these channels. Thus an upscale catalog needs an upscale e-tail site along with upscale-looking physical facilities. Do not confuse the customer by creating differing images for each of the channels of distribution. The same goes for pricing, marketing communications and customer service. It is confusing to consumers to receive wonderful in-store service, yet when they get online, they find that the service isn't up to what it should be, creating cognitive dissonance in consumers' minds.

Trading Area Analysis

Trading area analysis is the analysis of the retailer's trading area which is the area from which the retailer will derive the majority of their customers. A *trading area,* is "a geographical area containing the customers of a particular firm or group of firms for specific goods or services" (Bennett 1995, p.287). A retailer's trading area should account for, minimally, fifty percent of total sales and customers. A trading area may be international (especially for those utilizing multiple channels of distribution such as catalogs and e-tailing) or national. Conversely, the trading area may be as small as a neighborhood block. The size of a retailer's trading area depends on the retailer's mission and vision as well as the firm's objectives. In defining the area, retailers typically look at how many customers will be needed to achieve profitability. In addition, the trading area should generate enough sales volume to establish a break-even point for the company. The objective or goal of the retailer involved in trading area definition is to select the most profitable area from the alternatives available to them.

When assessing the trading area, retailers need to note that there have been advances in technology that allow greater areas from within to trade. This technology has led to two types of retail outlets that are used to reach their markets. These two types are store-based retailers and non-store-based retailers. Store retailers have physical locations, whereas non-store retailers use many different channels for the distribution of their goods and services. They create a presence in the retail world through the utilization of the Internet, catalogs, m-commerce, vending machines, or other non-traditional places of business, including consumers' homes. As you know, retailers who have both store and non-store locations are called omni-channel retailers.

So how do retailers determine their trading areas? Armed with extensive knowledge about their customer markets and having a typical customer profile, retailers often look to break down their trading area by primary and secondary markets. In some cases, retailers examine tertiary or fringe areas, which would include all of the retailer's potential customers who don't fall into the primary or secondary markets. A *primary market* should account for at least 60 percent of the retailer's total business. The *secondary market* another fifteen to twenty percent of sales; and the *tertiary market or fringe market* should account for the remainder.

Note that even though a retailer has a physical geographic location, their business may come from outside of that geographic area (remember the discussion on outshopping). The main variable to look for in a trading area is a customer base that matches the retailer's target market, making the research used to determine the target market very important. In addition, retailers should also study the following variables to ascertain they have defined their trading area correctly:

- Area population (both size of the population and population characteristics) of the potential trading area.

- Availability of a labor force for clerical, managerial and sales clerks (as well as check-out personnel).

- Rules, regulations and laws that govern the given potential trading area.

- The state of the area's economy.

- The number and size of competitors.

- The communications or promotional networks available in the trading area.

- Types of transportation available to the retailer to facilitate shipping and receiving.

- Types of transportation networks available to assist shoppers in getting to the retail establishment.

- The proximity of suppliers for the retail store.

Geographic Information Systems

Typically, all of the information needed for the trading area analysis is available through the retailer's RIS, or through secondary and primary research. Secondary data may be purchased, downloaded or entered by hand into the retailer's RIS. An excellent tool for the analysis of trading areas and for use by the site selection personnel in helping to decide which trading area to use is a geographic information system. A *geographic information system* (or GIS) is a computer-based system for integrating various types of data and analyzing those data (which come from multiple sources) in terms of geographic area.

Retailers use geographic information systems to help determine their trading areas in addition to making specific location decisions. Because of that, a typical GIS used for retailing will include demographic and psychographic information in addition to the geographic information. These data include information on consumer purchase patterns, consumer purchase behaviors, competitors, numbers of consumers, effective buying incomes along with other information a retailer may deem important. Physical, geographic barriers, such as bridges, tunnels and rivers are typically also included in the GIS to help assess the natural retail environment, and to give the retailers a better snapshot of what their potential market areas look like geographically.

There are many different companies that develop and use GIS software. Some of the companies that provide software:

- ESRI, Inc. (www.esri.com)
- Mapquest (https://www.mapquest.com/)
- Simplymap (http://geographicresearch.com/simplymap/)
- MapInfo (http://www.pitneybowes.com/us/location-intelligence/geographic-information-systems/mapinfo-pro.html)
- Map Window GIS (http://www.mapwindow.org/)
- Mapping Analytics (www.mappinganalytics.com)
- Bing Maps (www.microsoft.com/maps/)
- PostGis (http://www.postgis.org/)
- Sites USA (www.sitesusa.com)
- Total Systems Inc. (www.totalsystemsinc.com)

The ESRI software, named ArcGIS, is a very popular program among retailers and is available for servers, desktop, online and even in a mobile app. Directions Magazine (http://www.directionsmag.com/) is one of the top industry resources which focuses on different ways the GIS systems can be used for the most effectiveness. GIS software is available in many countries, so it's useful for international retailers, or domestic retailers who are looking to expand internationally.

GIS systems contain data that allow retailers to visualize geographic shapes in order to get a physical picture of their market. Data are then linked to that geographic area allowing the retailer to make more accurate and informed trading area decisions. Thus GIS help retailers visualize the trading area as well as assist in the analysis of trading area data. Figure 7.1 shows a GIS software screen from ESRI. According to ESRI, a leader in the GIS category, GIS organizes geographic data so that a person reading a map can select data that is needed for a specific task, often site location analysis and selection. For example, an auto parts retailer might use the base map of Denver, Colorado and select datasets from the U.S. Census Bureau to add data layers to a map that shows residents' education levels, ages, and employment status. GIS enables retailers to visualize locations and physical barriers that will assist in predicting which sites will be most lucrative (GIS best practices, 2007). Many retailers including Petco, FedEx and Wendy's use GIS to reduce the risk involved in opening a new location.

Figure 7.1 Example of GIS Software

Source: Scott Prokop/Shutterstock.com

Geolocation Technology

The *Global Positioning System (GPS)* is a global navigation satellite system owned by the U.S. government and operated by the U.S. Air Force which provides users with positioning, navigation and timing services. GPS receivers get signals from GPS satellites and use the information to calculate the user's three-dimensional position and time. Because the GPS technology is free it has led to hundreds of applications in every industry (www.gps.gov).

E-tailers and other online retailers use GPS technology. *Geolocation* uses web geography technology to determine where an online buyer is located. Geolocation technology instantly identifies the originating Internet service provider's (ISP) address to provide data down to the city level. Consumers' personal data are not collected. For example, the office superstore Staples uses geolocation technology to send a coupon to a customer's smartphone when they are within a mile or so a Staples store (Hosford, 2012). Launched in 2009, Foursquare is a great example of the use of GIS and geolocation technology. Foursquare (www.foursquare.com) is a mobile social networking application with two apps. Four Square City Guide provides recommendations on restaurants and entertainment and Four Square Swarm, which allows users to "check-in" at venues and lists their locations where friends are checking in. Users are awarded points at check-in and may receive a coupon for the particular venue. Users can post their check-ins on other social networking sites such as Facebook and Twitter. A point system is in place that encourages people to check in to earn badges. According to their website, as of 2017, their two apps had over 50 million users a month, with over 10 billion total check-ins to date.

Another application of geolocation technology for retailers is *geofencing,* which is using a *geofence* (virtual geographic perimeter) to deliver marketing communications to a GPS enabled device. When a person enters a geofence an alert may be triggered on a person's smartphone with a text, email, coupon or other promotional material. The use of geofencing may create differentiation through the use of relevant special promotions which can help build and strengthen brand relationships. For example, Live Nation uses geofencing to determine the social media handles of people who are in a concert area. This enables them to deliver targeted brand messages. According to Live Nation their geolocation tools use the open APIs (application programming interface) of the social channels so permission is not required to collect this data (Kaye, 2016).

Defining the Trade Area

When analyzing a trading area, it is important to ensure that the trading area analysis data include all channels of distribution, not just physical store-based data. There must be an inclusion of the e-tailing function as well as other channels such as catalogs and television. The job of trading area definition and analysis may differ slightly from physical store data. For example, the trading area for non-store-based retailers may have a different shape, but data are still needed to develop, execute and exploit the various channels' distribution and communication links with the customer base. The analysis must include consideration of customers' attitudes about e-tailing and other channels.

For e-tailers, the following information in regard to trading area analysis will be helpful:

- Size of market - How many potential customers have a need/want for the products and services being offered by the e-tailer?

- Levels of product or service consumption and usage - The higher the level of product usage for a given market area, the better the value.

- Customer characteristics - This includes developing an accurate customer profile and analyzing behavior.

- Market area trends - What does the online customer look for? Remember needs and wants change, and retail environments change.

- Customers' e-travels - What websites do customers visit?

E-tailers and other non-store retailers develop market areas by cultivating market segments whose customers are similar in behaviors with others in the segment, but different from those customers in other segments. These data assist the retailer in developing a successful venture and integrated retail management plan for each of their chosen market areas and segments.

Characteristics such as populations, economic climates, competition, physical geography and lifestyles are important in site selection and trading area analysis. When assessing populations, retailers must include all necessary demographic data. Whether the retailer uses a GIS is not as important as the data and information about consumers within each area. There are numerous sources of high-quality data. Some of those sources are provided in table 7.2.

Table 7.2   Sources of Data for Consumer Analysis

- United States Census of the Population (https://www.census.gov/)

- Data.gov (https://www.data.gov/)

- Datahub (https://datahub.io/organization)

- Think With Google (https://www.thinkwithgoogle.com/tools/)

- Standard Rate and Data Service's (SRDS) (www.srds.com)

- GIS providers such as ESRI

- ArcGIS Open Data (http://opendata.arcgis.com/)

- ICPSR (https://www.icpsr.umich.edu/icpsrweb/)

- Yahoo Webscope (http://webscope.sandbox.yahoo.com/index.php)

- Pew Research Center (http://www.pewresearch.org)

- Commercial List providers such as D&B and ABI

In addition, there are numerous sources of competitive data available to help in assessing trading areas (Table 7.3 on next page). There are also sources of data and information available to e-tailers. Select sources are listed in Table 7.4 on next page.

Numerous quantitative and qualitative techniques can aid in the choice of a trading area. One easy technique is customer spotting, an observational technique in which the retailer utilizes various types of already acquired data to try to ascertain where customers are located. The technique is generally applied to existing retail locations; it can also be used with new locations, however-er.

In customer spotting, location information is gathered by looking at customer data such as credit card information, phone numbers or area codes. In addition, many retailers have customer relationship management (CRM) programs/software to store customer data. These programs offer a wealth of information to help retailers make more informed judgments on trading areas. Vendors such as PeopleSoft, SAP, and Oracle offer certified and effective CRM software.

The last step in the trading area analysis is to make an educated guess as to what the trading area physically looks like. To create synergy, this is a good time to employ a GIS, physically draw the trading area on a piece of paper, or outline the trading area on a map. It is important to pay attention to physical barriers such as rivers, highways, and train tracks. A number of theories and methods are available to help define the trading area. In the following sections, we discuss a few of the more popular approaches.

Table 7.3 Sources of Information for Selecting a Trading Area

Source	Where to find
U.S. Census of Retail Trade	www.census.gov/econ/www/index.html
U.S. Census of Wholesale Trade	http://www.census.gov/econ/wholesale.html
U.S. Chamber of Commerce	www.uschamber.org
International Council of Shopping Centers	www.icsc.org
Trade Associations	Use a search engine to find a particular trade association on the Internet
Redbooks (information on advertising and media companies)	http://www.redbooks.com/
Colleges and Universities	Seek out professors who are experts in particular areas
Local (and national/international) clubs and organizations	Organizations such as chamber of commerce, the Kiwanis club or Rotary club can help
The Small Business Administration	www.sba.gov

Table 7.4 Marketing Information for the E-tailer

Source	Website
USADATA	www.usadata.com
Claritas, Inc.	www.claritas.com
Forrester Research	www.forrester.com
Kantar TNS	www.tnsglobal.com/
Vision Critical	www.visioncritical.com/about-us
OdinText	www.odintext.com/
iTracks	www.itracks.com
GFK	www.gfk.com
ThomasNet	www.thomasnet.com/
Market Research	www.marketresearch.com/

Reilly's Law of Retail Gravitation

Developed by William J. Reilly, Reilly's law of retail gravitation is used to establish a "point of indifference" between two cities' locations that helps the retailer project the physical trading area. Reilly suggests that a consumer living between two cities will consider both trading areas for shopping based on the distance of each area from the consumer's home and the size of each area. Reilly suggests that inventory and selection may be more important to shoppers than distance; therefore, the consumer will travel a little farther to get to the bigger city. The travel distance being equal, Reilly posits that the consumer will choose the city with more population because she or he will assume more product assortment is available there.

Reilly's law was amended to include a point of indifference between cities. The *point of indifference* is the distance at which the consumer is indifferent about shopping at either location. In other words, if you live between Dallas and Fort Worth, how close to Dallas, in miles, would you have to live to have a propensity to shop in Dallas? Is there a distance beyond which you would decide to shop in Fort Worth instead? Where is the point at which you would become indifferent about which city to shop in? The algebraic expression of Reilly's law is as follows (Nelson, 1958):

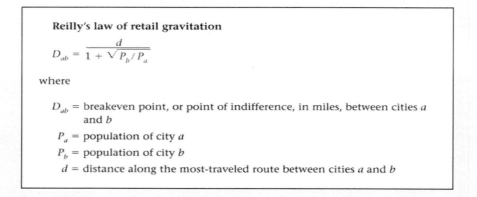

Reilly's law of retail gravitation

$$D_{ab} = \frac{d}{1 + \sqrt{P_b / P_a}}$$

where

D_{ab} = breakeven point, or point of indifference, in miles, between cities *a* and *b*

P_a = population of city *a*

P_b = population of city *b*

d = distance along the most-traveled route between cities *a* and *b*

Example:

You live between Fort Collins, Colorado, and Greeley, Colorado. The closest route between Greeley and Fort Collins is approximately 36 miles. The population of Greeley is approximately 61,000, and the population of Ft. Collins is around 90,000. Where would the point of indifference lie? Represent Ft. Collins as city a, so P_a equals 90,000. Let Greeley be city b, so P_b equals 61,000. The distance (d) between the cities equals 36. Thus, the point of indifference can be calculated as follows:

$$D_{ab} = 36 / (1 + \sqrt{61,000 / 90,000})$$
$$= 36/(1 + 246.98/300)$$
$$= 36/(1 + .823)$$
$$= 19.75 \text{ miles from Fort Collins}$$

and

$$D_{ab} = 36 / (1 + \sqrt{90,000 / 61,000})$$
$$= 36/(1 + 300/246.98)$$
$$= 36/(1 + 1.215)$$
$$= 16.25 \text{ miles from Greeley}$$

Reilly's law of retail gravitation assumes that both cities are accessible from a major thoroughfare and that population data represent differences in the amounts of goods and services available from each city (that is, the larger the population, the greater the amount of goods and services available to the consumer). Thus, consumers are attracted to the cities based on the amounts of goods and services available to them, including product lines, product assortment, and better facilities, and are not attracted simply by a larger population.

Huff's Gravity Model

Huff's gravity model, or Huff's law of shopper attraction, states that consumers will shop at a store or shopping center more often if the size of the store or center is increased and the distance to the shopping area is decreased. It is much like Reilly's law of retail gravitation; in fact, it is based in part on Reilly's early research. Huff's model can be used to help estimate sales for a particular trading area as follows (Huff, 1964):

Huff's gravity model (Huff's law of shopper attraction)

$$P_{ij} = \frac{\dfrac{S_j}{(T_{ij})^\lambda}}{\displaystyle\sum_{j=1}^{n} \dfrac{S_j}{(T_{ij})^\lambda}}$$

where

P_{ij} = probability of a consumer traveling from origin (i) to any given shopping center or store (j)

S_j = square footage of selling space in the shopping location, represented by j, that is expected to be devoted to the particular product or product category being sold

T_{ij} = travel time from the consumer's origin (i) to the shopping location (j)

λ = an exponent reflecting the effect of travel time on different kinds of shopping trips made by the consumer (*i.e.*, one may be willing to travel a greater distance for a heart transplant than for a soda)

n = number of different shopping locations available

In plain English, Huff says that the larger the shopping center relative to competing centers, the higher the probability that a consumer will patronize that center. The theory states that because the center is larger, it probably has a larger and wider assortment of goods and services. In addition, distance has the opposite effect on probability of patronage: the farther away the shopping center is from the consumer, the smaller is the probability that the consumer will shop there. All things being equal, the consumer wants a shopping area that is close to home.

Index of Retail Saturation Theory

Reilly's and Huff's models deal with the role of consumers' wants and needs in their decisions to patronize a given shopping location. What about the competition? It is strategically sound to assess how deeply competitors are entrenched in a given market area. The index of retail saturation (IRS) theory was developed to help the retailer assess the levels of supply and demand in various trading areas.

A trading area in which supply and demand are in equilibrium exhibits a condition referred to as retail saturation. *Retail saturation* means consumers' needs are just being met with the existing retail facilities. When that trading area has too few stores (or selling space), the area is said to be *understored*. If too many stores or too much selling space are devoted to a product or product line, the area is said to be *overstored*. Thus, when assessing trading areas, the retail site specialist looks for areas that are minimally saturated, but a better scenario would be areas that are understored. Following is a formula to assess the saturation levels of various trading areas. This ratio is called the *index of retail saturation (IRS)* (LaLonde, 1961).

Index of retail saturation

$$IRS = (H \times RE)/RF$$

where

IRS – index of retail saturation for any given trading area

H = number of households in the given trading area

RE = annual retail expenditures for the retailer's line of products per household in the trading area

RF = retail square footage of a particular product or product line for the trading area (including the proposed square footage)

Thus, the IRS is simply the sales per square foot of retail space for a trading area for a given product or product line. If the IRS is high, the area is understored; if it is low, the area is overstored. Experienced retail site selection personnel also assess trading area saturation in terms of the number of employees per retail establishment, average sales per store (both overall and by department), average sales per employee, and average sales per retail store category.

Numerous other methods have been used to assess trading areas for the retail location. We looked at the most popular models. Other models include *Sales and Marketing Management*'s buying power index (BPI), the analog approach (Drummey, 1984) and multiple regression analysis (for use only in chains with more than twenty stores).

Which of these methods is the best one to use? It depends. It is a good idea to try more than one, or all, of the methods and utilize the ones that work best. As stated in Chapter 6, the more data and information available to make a sound, research-based decision on the trading area, the better the decision. Only through academic and professional training, as well as pragmatic experience, can one decide which method will yield the best results.

Selecting the Most Appropriate Sites and Locations

Armed with useful information and data sources, retailers must now select those sites where they want to locate. Early in the chapter, the concepts of planned and unplanned locations were discussed. Below is a discussion of additional categories of types of sites available to the retailer.

Site Characteristics

It is always essential to make sure the potential site best suits the retailer's needs, generates competitive advantage, yet, at the same time, keeps overall costs as low as possible. To make the best decision, retailers must look at their potential physical location and the characteristics of alternative sites. Many variables are important in the selection of a site; among the most important is the traffic to and from the potential site.

Traffic

There are two types of traffic of concern to retailers: vehicle and pedestrian. By studying these patterns, the retailer can make an educated guess as to the value of the site for potential retail sales. The retailer must make a decision regarding the type of customers the site may generate. Although higher-volume traffic is generally preferred, this traffic may not be of the kind the retailer prefers or wants. Let's consider a convenience retailer for example. In evaluating a site in a CBD, the retailer will find that there is a higher volume of traffic than at a SBD or NBD, but the traffic at the CBD may be consumers who are looking for specialty goods and services, not convenience goods, which makes the site inappropriate for this retailer.

Source: Igor Stepovik/Shutterstock.com

Vehicle Traffic

To gauge the vehicular traffic patterns, retailers should not only look at the number of vehicles that pass by, but also the types of vehicles. The vehicles should have ready access to the potential retail site. Some key areas to look for may include: "Is the site located on a one-way street?" If so, will this impede accessibility for the cars and trucks? Is the potential site accessible to and from all major highways in the area? The easier the site is to get to, the more business the site will generate.

Another important area is the quality of the infrastructure surrounding the site. What is the quality of the roads and streets that abut the site? If traffic backs up, is this a good thing or bad thing for the retailer? Will a traffic light allow the retailer's customers easy turns into and out of the site? Parking is a major consideration. The retailer must assess the parking situation on and around the potential site's property. Are there adequate parking spaces for the number of customers contemplated? Is there enough parking for employees as well as customers? The retailer will address these questions by looking at the size of the potential retail establishment, the types of products and services to be sold, the frequency of consumer visits to the store, the length of time a customer might spend in the store and the proximity to public transportation to the store's entrance.

When evaluating parking at a large retail center, there should be about ten parking spaces for each 1,000 square feet of selling area within the center. Customers tend to stay longer at regional centers than at the other types of retail districts. In a SBD or community shopping area, a retailer may need only five parking spaces per 1,000 square feet of selling area. Parking requirements may also be determined by local zoning codes.

The grocery store chain Trader Joe's requires 88 parking spaces for most of their stores. This limits the number of customers who want to shop at the store, but gives the customers inside the store a more relaxed or laid back shopping experience because crowds are controlled. Additionally, it allows Trader Joe's to create sales that will drive profits into the company.

Finally, physical barriers to store entry must be evaluated. Are there any bridges that limit the trading area in terms of traffic flow? Are there one-way streets that may defer potential traffic from stopping and shopping?

Source: Photomika-com/Shutterstock.com

Pedestrian Traffic

Retailers must consider the types of people that will pass by their stores in addition to the sheer numbers that will pass by. Sites with heavy pedestrian traffic make excellent choices for a retail location. However, the retailer must determine if the people passing the store are actual consumers of the retailer's product and service offerings, or are they just passing by on their way somewhere else? It is a very good idea to segment pedestrian traffic patterns for each of the alternative locations.

It is a good idea to look at other variables in pedestrian traffic such as gender, age, and the number of shopping bags each person is carrying. What are they wearing? Are they walking alone or with others? Much of these data should be "matched" against the typical customer profile or target market data found in the integrated retail management plan. Oftentimes retailers develop research methodologies that allow them to interview pedestrians so they may learn more about them and the way they shop. Retailers may research which shops pedestrians enter and the amount of time they spend in those outlets. Information may also be generated in regard to whether the consumer purchased or did not purchase products from a store. In some cases the retailer may simply check whether the consumer leaves the store with a shopping bag.

When checking for pedestrian patterns, one needs to ensure there is good accessibility to the site. Customers must be able to get in and out of the shopping district in the least restricted way possible.

Transportation Considerations

Another major consideration is the availability of transportation. For example it is important to know if trucks can deliver merchandise to the retailer with some ease. The transportation into the site (and around the site for that matter) should allow for the smooth delivery of the retailer's products. Many roads prohibit trucks because of the damage they cause to roads. Additionally, turns are often too sharp to allow trucks access to the delivery docks.

Availability of mass transportation is also important. The retailer needs to know if public transportation is available to their customers. This is especially important in CBDs. Many people who live in downtown areas don't own cars and rely on other means of transportation to get them around. Make sure the site is visible from major thoroughfares that surround it, if possible.

Site Availability

The final major variable to consider would be the one of site availability. Retailers must not only establish that the site is a perfect location for them physically, but they must also research the conditions required to acquire the site. The terms of the rental agreement, lease or purchase agreement must be studied.

If the retailer does not want to purchase, is the site available for lease or rent? What will the basic lease payment be? When is the rent due? What length of time is the owner asking for in the duration of the lease? How much does the current owner pay to maintain the property? What are the operating costs? How much are the taxes? Are there requirements such as memberships in various merchants' associations? If a retailer moves into a CBD, does the business have to become a member of the downtown revitalization committee? Are there dues required? What happens if a breach of contract occurs?

Finally, what do the retail location's neighbors look like? Are they desirable or undesirable? Do they offer complementary products or are they direct competitors? Do they keep their properties looking well groomed? Is there new construction? Is this new construction blocking the retailer's visibility?

Site Location Specialists - Cushman & Wakefield

One of the United States' top developers, Cushman & Wakefield has developed a six-step methodology for taking consumer profiles and data, converting them to information and providing site location specialists with potential retail sites. Below is the six-step process (How Data Become a Store: Case Study, Cushman and Wakefield Retail Services, 2009).

The Process:

1. Gather Data

2. Connect data to rooftops

3. Learn which rooftops to count

4. Count the right rooftops

5. Find Space

6. Profit

In step one, gather data. Cushman & Wakefield suggest gathering data starting with sales data. According to them, sales data provide an empirical window into the customers you've been attracting. Use point-of-sale data (household, transaction level and Zip Code summary level). Add loyalty program data (voluntary, address-based, track purchase habits) and credit card transactions.

For step two, the retailer would connect the sales data to household and attached psycho/demographic data and information. Consumers make choices where to live based upon affordable advantages to the living site, compatible lifestyles, backgrounds and perspectives and access to infrastructure. Look at physical characteristics that help to define neighborhoods. Combine the place with household demographics and behaviors to segment consumers at both the geographic and household levels. This will provide a report defining how far potential and current consumers are willing to drive. It also provides tourist sales and the places the tourists come from.

Step three involves aggregating household data, and then isolating which rooftops to count. This step provides a typical customer profile. It provides reports about customers' information such as habits, spending styles and marketing insights.

With this information in hand, a GIS-based map is created that helps the retailer count the right rooftops to locate clusters (segments) and targets. This step provides a target market(s) heat map. It provides regional maps that show revenue-generating hot spots.

Once the hot spots are identified, step five is to locate and evaluate available sites within the targeted markets. Thus, this step provides a site evaluation. This site evaluation is based on customized criteria including individual store performance forecasts.

Finally, in step six, all of the data are amassed and placed into a report and the site selection process is executed, resulting in profit. This process involves integrating state-of-the-art technologies as well as statistical methodology. Is it effective? Many clients have come to Cushman & Wakefield because of their success in the site location and trading area analysis. Cushman & Wakefield have numerous clients such as *Crate & Barrel, Sonic Drive-ins, Lowes, North Face and Citibank* among others.

Source: (How Data Become a Store: Case Study, Cushman and Wakefield Retail Services, 2009.)

Summary

This chapter dealt with the difficult issue of finding a retail market and assessing that market for potential site location. The chapter covered issues involved in site location, trading area analysis and processes used to help find the best market area for a retail location. A lot of information was provided to help the retail student understand the importance of making correct location decisions.

Types of different levels for assessment were covered. In particular, this chapter provided information on developing channels of distribution in the physical as well as non-physical environments. An in-depth look at the usage of GIS systems was also provided. Issues involved with omni-channel retailers were covered.

It is very important for retailers to gain competitive advantage when it comes to site location. Once a site is found and developed, it's very expensive to change locations. There are many different categories of location sites including planned, unplanned and freestanding sites. This chapter provided information in regard to those sites.

Armed with the information necessary to create a great site, retailers can move to the next steps of management.

Terms

airport mall	A community shopping center located in an airport.
balanced tenancy	The process of optimizing tenants with each other so that retailers provide greater relevancy to their customers.
central business district (CBD)	An unplanned shopping site in the downtown area of any city.
community shopping center	A retail center typically between 100,000 and 400,000 square feet in size. Tenants often include smaller stores, branch department stores, and a large discount store.
core-based statistical areas (CBSA), also known as **metropolitan statistical areas** (MSA)	A government designation of an area within the United States that has a minimum of 50,000 permanent residents.
customer spotting	An observational technique in which the retailer utilizes various types of already-acquired data to try to ascertain where customers are located.
designated market area (DMA)	A designation developed by A.C. Nielson to describe a particular geographic area that serves a specific market.
freestanding sites	Retailers located in a site with no immediate retailers in close proximity.
geographic information system (GIS)	A computer-based tool for integrating and analyzing spatial data from multiple sources.
geofence	Virtual geographic perimeter around a real-word physical area.
geofencing	Using a geofence to deliver marketing communications (text, email, coupon, other promotional material)
geolocation	Technology that uses Web geography to determine where an online buyer is located.
Global Positioning System GPS	A global navigation satellite system owned by the U.S. government and operated by the U.S. Air Force which provides users with positioning, navigation and timing services.

index of retail saturation (IRS)	A formula used to assess the saturation levels of various trading areas.
inshoppers	People who tend to shop in their local communities.
Internet malls	Shopping centers located on the World Wide Web.
lifestyle center	A planned shopping center targeted to upper-income shoppers. Typically outdoors with a "Main Street" ambience, tenants that sell nonessential items, higher building and landscaping costs than those of other retail developments, and parking in front of the stores.
megamall	A mall that is often several times larger than a regional center; also known as a *superregional center.*
neighborhood business district (NBD)	An unplanned shopping site that provides shopping for a neighborhood rather than a larger trading area.
neighborhood shopping centers	Planned shopping areas with a small anchor store.
non-store retailer	A retailer that has no physical location but sells via cyberspace, catalogs, vending machines, or other nontraditional places of business, such as a home.
outlet center	A type of community center that brings together retail establishments for manufacturers and retailers of consumer goods. These centers increase drawing power by providing deep discounts on brand-name products.
outshoppers	People who are more likely to shop outside their community.
overstored	A situation in which too many stores (or too much selling space) are devoted to a product or product line.
planned shopping site	Retail site typically planned by a developer. Upfront planning is done to determine which retailers would provide the best mix of products and services to customers.
point of indifference	The distance at which the choice between two shopping destinations is equal.
power center	A type of community center that includes at least one category killer with a mix of smaller stores.
primary market	The group of people that account for at least 60 percent of the retailer's total business.
regional center	A retail site that provides general merchandise and is typically enclosed with parking surrounding the center.
regional shopping centers	Large, planned facilities which appeal to a larger, geographically dispersed market. Each regional center has at least one department store (usually more), and at least 50 smaller retail businesses (usually more).
retail saturation	The point at which consumers' needs are just being met with the existing retail facilities.
secondary business district (SBD)	An unplanned shopping site (smaller than a CBD) that is located around the major transportation intersections of cities. A typical SBD has at least one department store or variety store, coupled with a number of smaller stores.
secondary market	The group of people subordinate to the primary market that accounts for the fifteen to twenty percent of sales.
store-based retailer	A retailer that has one or more permanent, fixed physical location(s).
strip (or string) shopping district	An unplanned shopping site with stores that are visible from the road and arranged in a strip.
tertiary market or fringe market	The group of people subordinate to the primary and secondary markets that account for the remaining sales not represented by these two groups.

trading area	A geographical area containing the customers of a particular firm or group of firms for specific goods or services.
understored	A situation in which a trading area has too few stores (or too little selling space).
unplanned shopping site	A site that develops when two or more retailers move into the same area or in close proximity to each other. These sites are a function of evolution; they are not planned but develop over time.

Discussion Questions

1. Define the market analysis and site analysis.

2. Why do retailers undertake research-based studies to find where their customers are?

3. Do you think college students prefer to shop at independent retailers or chain retailers? Explain your answer.

4. What are the advantages to creating chain stores? Disadvantages?

5. Why is it important to integrate all of the retailer's channels of distribution?

6. What is omni-channel retailing? Why do you think it has come about?

7. Why are traffic patterns so important for retail locations?

8. Why are power centers important to retailers?

Exercises

1. Research the city you live in, or the largest city near your home. In which statistical area does it lie? Provide demographic data in regard to the closest CBSA to your house.

2. Go online and access the United States Census Bureau (www.census.gov). On the census page, find the population of your hometown. What is the medium income for your area? What is the typical household size?

3. Pretend you're a site location specialist. Select the best location for a Starbucks Coffee shop within the city you live. Provide rationale for why the location was selected.

4. Visit your closest regional shopping center (in person or online). Who are their clientele? What types of products and services are offered?

Case

Retailer on the Go: Homier Mobile Merchant

Homier sells thousands of brand-name tools, general merchandise, furniture, and collectibles at prices the company says are 30 percent below the competition. The concept behind the company is to eliminate the middleman and pass the savings directly to the customer. The company targets the "average Joe," people looking for discounted merchandise.

Homier began as a small auction business in Andrews, Indiana, in 1958. Much of Homier's success was due to its ability to recognize trends and capitalize on them. In the winter of 1978, a blizzard caused the roof of the Homier warehouse to collapse. The entire inventory, at the time worth $500,000, was destroyed. Because the company had no insurance coverage for natural disasters, it had to start over.

Shortly after that incident, the founder, Charles Homier, Sr., became disabled due to an automobile accident. His son, Chuck Homier, had just completed his college degree and began to explore some new opportunities within the family business. The competition was fierce due to the advent of department stores and category killers. In addition, consumers' wants and needs were changing.

In 1979, a man who attended the Homier auctions asked Chuck Homier if he could sell some of Homier's excess inventory at fairs and flea markets throughout the area. That winter, to pare down the inventory, Homier decided to rent a banquet room at a hotel for three days in Warsaw, Indiana. To advertise the event, he took out a full-page ad in the local paper. On opening day there was a line to get into the sale, and by the end of the day Homier was sold out. This success was too good to pass up, and the family gave up the auction business and started Homier Mobile Merchants.

The company grew at an average rate of 25 to 30 percent per year. As it grew, so did inventory storage needs. Currently the company has a site in Huntington, Indiana with over 200,000 square feet of space. Although the primary product is tools, Homier also sells products from leather jackets to dining room sets. The company holds sales in all forty-eight contiguous states. Typically it rents a convention center or places tents in a parking lot to sell its products. Homier is in a town for only one to four days before moving on to the next location. The company manufactures their own products and brands including Blue Max, Speedway Series and Professional Woodworker.

The mobile retail concept is not new---most people are familiar with more traditional mobile merchandising such as hot dog and beverage vendors who sell from carts. They are much less accustomed to tractor-trailer trucks loaded with merchandise coming to town for a few days, however. It's like a merchandise carnival. Homier Mobile Merchants maintains a fleet of trucks and sales and service crews. Nationwide, Homier conducts sixty sales per week, fifty weeks per year, on average. Customers who are dissatisfied with merchandise after purchase can call a toll-free customer service line. Homier's refund policy is "no questions asked." In addition, customers can buy from the online catalog at www.homier.com. The company also has a wholesale distribution network.

Questions

1. Why is Homier so successful?

2. How would you describe Homier's location strategy?

3. Would Homier be able to sell products to people who are in upper-income brackets? Why or why not?

4. What disadvantages does Homier's strategy have?

5. How can Homier use geographic information systems?

6. What is the advantage or disadvantage of a "no questions asked" return policy?

7. What are the advantages/disadvantages of Homier manufacturing their own products?

Sources: "Innovation at Work: The History of Homier," retrieved September, 2002 from www.homier.com; Natalie Morris, "Under the Big Top: Homier Offers Everything from Drill Presses to Oil Paintings at Its Tent," *State Journal Register* (Springfield, IL), July 22, 2000, p. 17; Howard Riell, "Boldly Going Where Customers Are," *Foodservice Equipment & Supplies,* May 1999, pp. 77--78; Don Nelson, "Homier Mobile Merchants," *Knight Ridder Tribune Business News*, April 16, 2002, p. 1; "Business Briefs," *Knight Ridder Tribune Business News*, March 31, 2002, p. 1; Homier website: www.homier.com.

References

Barboza, D. (2005). China, New Land of Shoppers, Builds Malls on Gigantic Scale. *New York Times,* (May 25). Retrieved from http://www.nytimes.com/2005/05/25/business/worldbusiness/25mall.html

Bennett, P. D., ed., (1995) *Dictionary of Marketing Terms,* 2nd Edition, Chicago: American Marketing Association, p.287.

Daymark Signs Long Term Lease With Retailer Five Below at 1818 Market Street in Philadelphia (2012). Press release from Daymark Realty Advisors, (Jan 26).   Retrieved from http://retail.ocregister.com/2010/10/16/clothing-retailer-to-close-up-to-100-stores/36232/

Drummey, G. L. (1984). Traditional Methods of Sales Forecasting. In *Store Location and Store Assessment Research.* Ed. Davies, R. L. and Rogers, D. S. New York: John Wiley and Sons, pp. 279-299.

Foursquare website (2012). Retrieved from www.foursquare.com/about

Frankel, M. S. (2002). Outlet Centers Come of Age Overseas (2002). Sept/Oct. Retrieved from www.nareit.com

Geuss, M. (2015). Company Buys SkyMall for $1.9 Million, Will Make "Dramatic Changes". *Ars Technica,* (May 30). Retrieved from http://arstechnica.com/gaming/2015/05/company-buys-skymall-for-1-9-million-will-make-dramatic-changes/

Giddens, D. (2004). Hunting for Business. *Dallas Business Journal,* 27(52), 33.

GIS best practices: GIS for retail business (2007). ESRI, Redlands, CA. Retrieved from http://www.esri.com/library/bestpractices/retail-business.pdf

Hosford, C. (2012). Staples Mobile Strategy Based on Customer Convenience, Loyalty. *B to B,* 97(3), 14. Retrieved from http://search.proquest.com/docview/928077011?accountid=13158

GPS.gov. Global Positioning System. Accessed from http://www.gps.gov/

Huff, D. L. (1964). Defining and Estimating a Trade Area. *Journal of Marketing* 28, pp. 34-38.

ICSC (2017). The International Council of Shopping Centers (ICSC). Retrieved from http://www.icsc.org/

Kaye, K. (2016). Smart Concerts. *Advertising Age,* 87(21), 22-n/a. Retrieved from Proquest Database.

Kramer, A. E. (2011). Russia Becomes a Magnet for U.S. Fast-Food Chains. *New York Times, (Aug 3). Retrieved from* http://www.nytimes.com/2011/08/04/business/global/russia-becomes-a-magnet-for-american-fast-food-chains.html?ref=fastfoodindustry

LaLonde, B. (1961). The Logistics of Retail Location. In *American Marketing Proceedings,* ed. Stevens, W. D. Chicago: American Marketing Association.

LeRoy, G. (2006). Not Very Sporting: Outdoor Sporting Good Retail Subsidy Scam. *Multinational Monitor,* Sep/Oct; 27(5), 15-18.

Matthews, L. (2011). World's Most-Visited Tourist. Attractions. *Travel and Leisure* magazine (October). Retrieved from http://www.travelandleisure.com/articles/worlds-most-visited-tourist-attractions

Misonzhnik, E. (2012). British Chain Prepares for U.S. Invasion. *Retail Traffic,* (15444236). Retrieved from http://search.proquest.com/docview/929073633?accountid=13158

Mistakes we have made in developing shopping centers (1945). Planning for permanence: the speeches of J.C. Nichols, Western historical manuscript collection – Kansas City. Retrieved from http://www.umkc.edu/whmckc/PUBLICATIONS/JCN/JCNPDF/JCN078.pdf

National Restaurant Association (2017). Retrieved from http://www.restaurant.org/News-Research/Research/Facts-at-a-Glance

Nelson, R. L. (1958). *The Selection of Retail Locations.* New York: F. W. Dodge.

Nguyen, H. (2010). Clothing Retailer to Close Up to 100 Stores. (Oct 16). Retrieved from http://retail.ocregister.com/2010/10/16/clothing-retailer-to-close-up-to-100-stores/36232/

Poag and McEwin Lifestyle Centers Website (2011). Retrieved from http://www.pm-lifestyle.com/lifestyle_center/managed.html.

Shields, M. and Farrigan, T. (2001). A Manual for Small Downtowns. The Pennsylvania State University, (Apr 9). Retrieved from http://retailmarkets.aers.psu.edu/images/manual.pdf

Shop 'till You Takeoff: Top Airports for Shopping (2011). By Sherman's Editorial Staff – February 2, Today Travel. Retrieved from http://today.msnbc.msn.com/id/41629241

Simon Malls Website (2017). Retrieved from http://www.simon.com/

Simon Property Group, Inc. Website (2017). Retrieved from http://www.simon.com/about_simon/index.aspx

Skymall Website (2011). Retrieved from http://www.skymall.com/shopping/homepage.htm?pnr=ING

Sprinkles Cupcakes Website (2011). Retrieved from www.sprinkles.com

Stellen, S. (2011). Filling the Void Left by Borders, *New York Times*, (Sept. 27). Retrieved from http://www.nytimes.com/2011/09/28/realestate/commercial/independent-booksellers-scramble-to-fill-borders-void.html?_r=1

The Nielsen Company (2017). Retrieved from http://www.nielsen.com/intl-campaigns/us/dma-maps.html

Whalin, G. (2009). *Retail superstars: Inside the 25 best independent stores in America*, Penguin Group, New York, NY.

World's Largest Shopping Centers (2011). Shopping Center Studies at Eastern Connecticut State University. Retrieved from http://nutmeg.easternct.edu/~pocock/MallsWorld.htm

Chapter 8

Financial Issues in Retailing

"Your income is directly related to your philosophy, NOT the economy.
~Jim Rohn

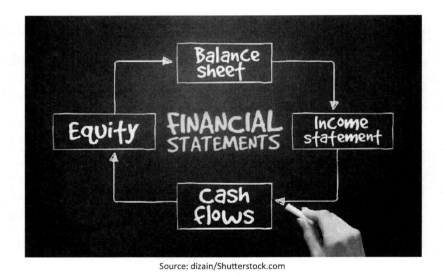

Source: dizain/Shutterstock.com

CHAPTER OBJECTIVES

After completing this chapter you will be able to:

- Explain why it is important for retailers to plan for profit and to develop a financial plan.
- Describe the main types of reports found in a retail accounting system.
- Describe the main categories in a balance sheet and income statement.
- Explain the types of financial statement fraud.
- Describe cost behavior and cost-volume profit analysis.

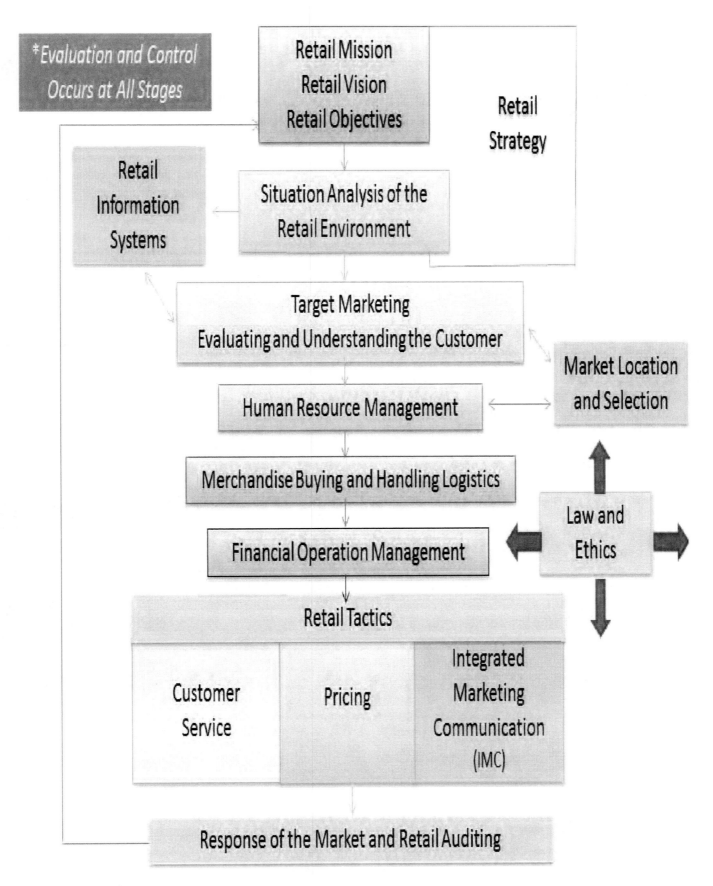

Retailers and Financial Difficulties

Financial difficulties can happen to even the largest retailers. Just look at Circuit City. Once the second largest U.S. consumer electronics retailer, the firm filed for bankruptcy in November, 2008 and closed its last remaining 567 U.S. stores in March, 2009, laying off almost 34,000 employees (Kane, 2008; Ogg, 2008).

Blockbuster, Inc., once the dominant leader in DVD rental chains, filed for Chapter 11 bankruptcy protection in September, 2010, and in April, 2011 was sold to Dish Network in liquidation. At the highest point, Blockbuster had 9,000 locations. Dish Network created an online streaming product branded Blockbuster@Home (Pankratz and Vuong, 2013). Over time Blockbuster @Home became Dish Movie Pack, an add-on package which allows subscribers to stream movies to a TV, PC or mobile device.

Another large retailer that fell is Borders Group, Inc. This second-largest bookstore chain filed for bankruptcy in February, 2011. The 40-year-old chain listed debt of $1.29 billion and assets of $1.28 billion as of Dec. 25, 2011 in its Chapter 11 petition.   In September 2011, Borders closed its last remaining 399 stores, resulting in the layoff of over 11,000 employees (Fulham, 2011; Spector et al, 2011).

Even though many analysts attempt to explain these bankruptcies as merely casualties of the Internet, poor strategic vision or the Internet's impact on consumers, it is not only one of these management faux pas that resulted in the collapse of these retailing giants. Overexpansion, shrinking profit margins, crushing debt and the resulting lack of adequate cash flow to meet their obligations are elements common to all of these bankruptcies. A very similar case is the landmark bankruptcy of W. T. Grant in 1975. The Grant bankruptcy was instrumental in the development and integration of the statement of cash flows as one of the four major required components of a set of financial statements. The other three components are the balance sheet, income statement, and notes to the financial statements. Prior to 1975, an evaluation of a company's cash flow position was not considered a necessary element in evaluating a company's financial stability. Since then, the importance of a company's cash position, particularly for retailers, has continued to grow. In fact, many introductory financial management courses stress that "cash is king."

Source: JLRphotography/Shutterstock.com

As the Circuit City, Blockbuster and Borders situations illustrate, a company's cash position can have a significant impact on the firm's stability and even its viability. A company can have millions of dollars in revenues and assets, yet still not have enough cash to pay current bills. Just like their predecessor, W. T. Grant, Circuit City, Blockbuster and Borders shuttered their doors forever.

Introduction

This chapter focuses on the financial aspects of operations management. Essentially, *operations management* (also known as *ops management*) deals with the implementation of store policies, tactics, and procedures. Resources must be allocated and monitored to accomplish every function. The plan should be directed by the marketing concept of satisfying customer wants and needs while earning a profit. Operations managers generally have the responsibility of overseeing the human resource functions of the retail establishment; purchasing, accounting, and inventory systems; supply chain management and logistics; and various areas of marketing, such as sales and service.

Operations specialists develop plans that enable the integrated operation of the entire retail business. This operation must be seamless and create synergies wherever possible. Accounting

systems, budgets, and inventory management are all part of the overall operations management plan. In addition, monies for the development of the retailer's tactics are allocated based on the information contained in the operations management plan. This plan is then integrated into the overall integrated retail management plan to give retail managers and owners the big picture of what is going on within their stores. This chapter provides an overview of the main financial documents used in retailing as well as ways that retailers analyze this information. Keep in mind that the concepts in this chapter and the next chapter (Merchandise Buying and Handling) overlap.

Source: El Nariz/Shutterstock.com

Developing a Financial Plan

Understanding the concepts involved in developing an integrated retail management plan is the basis for the development of the financial plans. Financial plans encompass three major objectives:

- Profitability - To generate profits for the retailer
- Liquidity - To manage cash such that obligations can be satisfied as they come due
- Manage Growth – Manage company growth so that it does not outpace the company's ability to obtain the cash necessary to maintain current operations

Financial reporting, which includes the preparation of the company's financial statements, allows management and third parties, such as investors and creditors, to evaluate whether these objectives have been met. Most of the information needed to develop a financial plan and monitor the company's financial performance can be gathered by constructing budgeted financial statements (financial plans) and comparing those statements to actual results (financial statements). The financial statements allow the retailer to monitor the organization's financial performance and to evaluate and control those activities that are not producing the desired results. The past performance of a retailer can provide a basis for future planning. It is wise, therefore, to refer to the financial statements when developing retail objectives. Communication and exchange of information is critical in the financial reporting process. Conflicting department goals often interfere with the data collection and can create silos.

Retail Accounting Systems

The *retail accounting system (RAS)* is a subset of the Retail Information System (RIS). Retail accounting systems systematically gather, store and analyze financial data and information to help retailers make better decisions. An understanding of the financial condition of the business is necessary to effectively control the overall business functions. Primary reports found in most retail accounting systems are the balance sheet, income statement, and statement of cash flows. Information from these documents aids in the analysis of ratios and asset management. Retail accounting systems are computer based, paper based, or a combination of both. Integration of the RAS with the primary RIS provides a competitive advantage when it comes to developing strategy and tactics.

The Income Statement

The first step in understanding and evaluating a retailer's performance is the construction of financial statements. The first and most often discussed financial statement is the income statement. An income statement has nine main categories:

1. net sales
2. cost of goods sold (COGS)
3. gross profit
4. operating expenses
5. net income from operations
6. other income (expenses)
7. net income before taxes
8. income taxes
9. net income after taxes.

Let's take a look at each area.

Net sales represent all gross sales the retailer earns during a period of time (usually monthly, quarterly, seasonally, or yearly) minus sales discounts given to customers to promote sales and minus returns and allowances given to customers for returned items or defective products. In other words, net sales is the gross sale price of the products the retailer sold for cash, or on account, to customers during a specified period of time, subtracting out returns, discounts, and any markdowns taken during that specified period.

Cost of goods sold (COGS), or *cost of sales*, represents just what it says: the cost the retailer pays for the merchandise it sells. This includes the actual purchase price of the goods and services plus the freight-in costs associated with getting the products to the retail warehouse or outlets. Purchase discounts are subtracted from the merchandise cost and freight-in costs are added to come up with the actual COGS. *Purchase discounts* are reductions in the payment amounts vendors are willing to accept to satisfy the amount due if the payments are made earlier. Purchase Returns and Allowances are also subtracted for returned items or defective purchases.

Gross profit, or *gross margin*, is the difference between the retailer's net sales and the cost of goods sold. In other words, this is the amount the retailer has left to cover expenses related to the operation of the retail business.

Operating expenses are the normal costs associated with doing business, not including the cost of the merchandise for sale. They may include personnel costs (wages), insurance costs, and utilities expenses. Retailers often break up the costs into selling expenses, general expenses, and administrative expenses. By doing so, the retailer gets a much better idea of where the costs of running the business actually come from.

Net income from operations is the gross profit minus the operating expenses; it represents the extent to which the retailer is generating profits from its major business operations. Net income from operations is the major performance indicator that retailing management use.

Other income (expenses) includes income and expense items such as interest income, dividend income, interest expense, and gains or losses on disposal of assets such as fixtures or a store location. These types of income and expense are not considered part of the business operations and are therefore separated from the sales and expenses directly related to operations.

Net income before taxes (NIBT) (also called *net income before income taxes*) is the difference between net income from operations and the net effect of other income (expenses). Even though retailing management usually concentrates on net income from operations, outside stakeholders such as financial institutes and investors will often consider NIBT as the overall measure of a company's performance.

Income taxes are federal and state taxes on the net income before taxes. Often overlooked is that income taxes are a cost of doing business. The top corporate income tax rates can exceed 30 percent of income before income taxes (NIBT). Also often neglected is that income taxes can be managed through the use of "tax planning." Income tax regulations are complex. Therefore, retailers should consult with tax professionals when considering how to minimize the effect of taxes on the organization.

Net income after taxes is the difference between net income before taxes and income taxes. Figure 8.1 shows the 2015 and 2016 income statements for our hypothetical retailer, The University Bookstore (TUB). As you can see, the bookstore had a very profitable year in 2015. It started out with sales of $1.5 million and subtracted the cost of the merchandise, or $1.0 million (freight costs are high for many of its products). The University Bookstore showed a gross profit of $500,000. From the $500,000, the bookstore

Figure 8.1 Income Statement for a Fictional Company

The University Bookstore (TUB) - Income Statements for the Years Ended December 31, 2016 and 2015

	2016 Amount	2015 Amount
Net Sales	$1,250,000	$1,500,000
Cost of goods sold	950,000	1,000,000
Gross Profit	$300,000	$500,000
Operating Expenses:		
Sales commissions	$125,000	$150,000
Salaries expense	22,000	45,000
Payroll tax expense	5,350	6,750
Fringe benefits expense	10,400	13,200
Rent expense	32,000	48,000
Insurance expense	6,000	5,000
IMC expense	27,000	46,000
Maintenance expense	3,200	4,500
Utilities expense	9,200	9,000
Advertising expense	20,000	16,000
Depreciation expense	10,000	6,000
Total Operating Expenses	$270,150	$349,450
Total Operating Income	$29,850	$150,550
Other Income (Expenses):		
Interest income	$500	$1,000
Interest expense	(30,000)	(25,000)
Total Other Income (Expenses)	($29,500)	($24,000)
Net Income Before Income Taxes	$350	$126,550
Income Taxes (assume 35%)	123	44,293
Net Income After Taxes	$228	$82,258

subtracted the operating expenses of the business. Because TUB has a small operation, it had only $349,450 in operating expenses. After subtracting the $349,450 from the gross profit, the bookstore had a net income from operations of $150,550. After other income and expenses of $24,000 and $44,293 in income taxes, TUB was left with a net income after taxes of $82,258.

The same cannot be said about 2016. TUB had lower net sales than in 2015, and its cost of goods sold was close to the previous years, leaving the company with a gross profit of $300,000 instead of the $500,000 in 2015. With operating expenses of $270,150, the company was left with an operating profit of only $29,850. Subtracting other income and expenses of $29,500 and income taxes of $123, TUB's net income after taxes was only $228 for the year ended December 31, 2015.

The Balance Sheet

A *balance sheet* itemizes the retailer's assets, liabilities, and net worth at a specific point in time. Thus, a retailer can develop a balance sheet for any day of the year. Typically, balance sheets are prepared for the end of a month, quarter, or year. The basic concept underlying the balance sheet is:

Assets = Liabilities + Net worth

Assets are anything of value (a resource) that the retailer owns. Some commentators feel that assets can be best explained as cash, claims to others' cash, and things that can be sold for cash. Generally assets are broken down into two distinct groups: current and long-term assets.

Current assets are cash and other resources that can be converted to cash or are used within the year, such as inventory, accounts receivable and supplies. *Long-term assets* (also known as fixed assets) are property, equipment, and other assets that are used to operate the business. These assets will not be converted to cash within the year and will be used for an extended period of time.

The management of a retail business is similar to an individual's financial management, only on a much larger scale. For example, any cash you have in the bank right now – say $500 – is a current asset. This cash is considered to be liquid because you can access it whenever you need to. Now suppose your friend Steve owes you $45 that he borrowed last week to purchase a textbook. This $45 is also a current asset and is referred to as an *account receivable – money that is owed to you*. Thus, you have a total of $545 in current assets.

To continue, suppose your generous parents have bought you a car to use for college. The price of the car was $14,000. Since you do not intend to sell the car anytime soon for its $14,000 value, the car is a long-term, or noncurrent, asset.

Your total assets, therefore, are $14,545: $545 in current assets and $14,000 in fixed assets. Unfortunately, you also have financial obligations, amounts you owe, referred to as *liabilities*. Like assets, liabilities are divided into two distinct groups: current and long-term liabilities. *Current liabilities* include any debt that must be paid back within the upcoming year. Long-term liabilities include debt that needs to be satisfied in more than a year's time. Added together, current and long-term liabilities equal total liabilities.

Suppose you borrowed $34 from Sylvia last week. She expects you to pay her back on payday (next Friday). You have incurred a short-term debt, or current liability, of $34. In addition, you recently took out a student loan for $10,000 to cover your mounting college costs. You have 25 years to repay the loan; thus, this debt is a long-term liability. Combined, these two figures amount to total liabilities of $10,034.

Net worth is the third major component of the balance sheet. *Net worth*, often referred to as *owner's equity*, is simply assets minus liabilities. Net worth represents the net value of a retail business on a cost basis. Using the preceding example, your net worth is $4,511: your assets of $14,545 minus your liabilities of $10,034.

Figure 8.2 depicts balance sheets for The University Bookstore.

Figure 8.2 Balance Sheets for a Fictional Company

**The University Bookstore (TUB) Balance Sheets
as of December 31, 2016 and 2015**

	2016 Amount	2015 Amount
Assets		
Current Assets:		
Cash	$45,320	$35,000
Accounts receivable	12,900	22,000
Inventory	197,633	100,000
Total Current Assets:	$255,853	$157,000
Property Plant & Equipment:		
Land	$250,000	$250,000
Furniture	60,300	60,300
Shelving	51,000	51,000
Accumulated depreciation	(25,000)	(15,000)
Property Plant & Equipment Net	$336,300	$346,300
Total Assets	$592,153	$503,300
Liabilities:		
Current Liabilities:		
Accounts payable	$96,500	$65,000
Salaries payable	6,000	10,000
Interest payable	7,000	3,500
Payroll taxes payable	2,000	1,400
Other payables	19,450	12,200
Line of credit payable	130,275	3,000
Current portion mortgage payable	2,500	2,500
Total Current Liabilities	$263,725	$97,600
Long-Term Liabilities		
Mortgage payable	$197,500	$200,000
Long-term debt	100,000	100,000
Total Long-Term Liabilities	$297,500	$300,000
Total Liabilities	$561,225	$397,600
Net Worth	$30,928	$105,700
Total Liabilities and Net Worth	$592,153	$503,300

The Statement of Cash Flows

One of the most important statements for retailers, and yet the least understood, is the Statement of Cash Flows. The collapses of retailing giants such as Circuit City, Blockbuster and Borders are only the most recent examples of the importance of cash flow to retailers. The primary purpose of the statement of cash flows is to provide information about a retailer's cash receipts and disbursements for a period of time. A second objective is to provide information about the company's cash flows from (1) operating activities, (2) investing activities, and (3) financing activities.

Cash flow from operating activities includes the cash received or disbursed from all of the activities involved in the company's operations. All activities that are a component in determining net income are included in the cash flow from operating activities. Therefore, any cash receipts from sales of goods and services are considered cash inflows from operations. At the same time, any cash disbursements resulting from those transactions are included as cash outflows. Finally, interest and dividend income received and interest expenses paid are included in cash flow from operations.

The difference between cash inflows and cash outflows is considered the net cash inflow or outflow from operations. For example, a department store's sales from merchandise are cash inflows and monies owed on the merchandise, as well as amounts paid for supplies, are cash outflows. Companies obviously prefer to have more cash inflows than outflows from operating activities.

Cash flow from investing activities is the cash received or disbursed from extending or collecting loans and acquiring or disposing of investments or long-term assets. For example, if a company owns the building in which it operates but rents out a portion to another business, those proceeds are cash inflows. As stated previously, interest or dividends received are not considered investing activities; rather, they are included in operating activities.

Cash flow from financing activities includes activities that deal with the company's own debt and capital instruments. In other words, cash receipts from a company issuing its own debt or capital instruments are included as financing activities. Cash disbursements would include the reacquisition of a company's stock or repayment of its own bonds or debt instruments. In addition, dividends paid to stockholders are included as a financing activity cash disbursement.

The statement of cash flows is particularly important to the retailer because it identifies which activities are generating cash and which are using cash.

Some rules of thumb apply in evaluating a statement of cash flows. For example, there should be at least enough positive cash flow from operations to cover cash outflows from investing and financing activities. There should be cash outflows from investing activities for property, plant, and equipment and from financing activities for repayment of debt and dividend disbursements to stockholders. These are only guidelines and could differ depending on the retailer's organizational objectives. For example, if a retailer is utilizing a high-growth strategy, the net cash inflows from operating activities may not be sufficient to finance the investing activities necessary for property, plant, and equipment. Therefore, cash inflows will be required from financing activities to cover the difference in cost.

Figure 8.3 (next page) shows the statement of cash flows for TUB for the years ended December 31, 2015 and 2016.

Figure 8.3   The University Bookstore Statement of Cash Flows

The University Bookstore (TUB)
Statement of Cash Flows
for the Years Ended December 31, 2016 and 2015

	2016	2015
Cash Flow from Operating Activities:		
Cash Receipts:		
Cash Receipts from customers	$1,259,100	$1,550,000
Cash Receipts from interest income	500	1,000
Total Cash Inflows (Outflows) from Operating Activities	$1,259,600	$1,551,000
Cash Payments:		
To suppliers of merchandise	$1,016,133	$956,000
To employees	151,000	185,000
For payroll taxes	4,750	7,000
For fringe benefits	10,400	13,600
For rent	29,334	45,333
For insurance	6,000	13,600
For IMC	21,532	46,000
For maintenance	3,200	4,500
For utilities	9,200	85,000
For interest	26,500	15,000
For income taxes	123	51,993
For advertising	20,883	15,000
Total Cash Payments	$1,299,055	$1,438,026
Net Cash Inflows (Outflows) from Operating Activities	(39,455)	112,974
Cash Flow from Investing Activities:		
Purchase of furniture and shelving	0	(26,700)
Total Cash Inflows (Outflows) from Investing Activities	0	(26,700)
Cash Flow from Financing Activities:		
Proceeds from increase in long-term debt		19,000
Payments to owners	(75,000)	(142,000)
Contributions by new owners	0	20,000
Decrease in long-term debt	(2,500)	0
Increase in line of credit	127,275	0
Total Cash Inflows (Outflows) from Financial Activities	49,775	(103,300)
Net Increase (Decrease) in Cash	10,320	(16,726)

Notes to the Financial Statements

The *notes to the financial statements* provide supplemental information about the financial statements. If there is anything significant not presented in the main body of the financial statements, the information should be found in these notes. The main purpose of the notes to the financial statements is to provide readers with the information necessary to fully understand and interpret the financial statements. Reviewing financial statements without also reviewing the notes could lead to misinterpretations.

Financial Statement Analysis

Financial statements report the historical results for a company. The objective of financial statement analysis is to use historical information and data to predict the company's future. Investors and prospective employees can also use these statements to evaluate the firm's financial health. In addition, financial statement analysis can be used for asset and liability management.

Types of financial statement analysis include (1) horizontal analysis, (2) vertical analysis, and (3) ratio analysis. No matter which type of analysis is performed, no single measure means much when analyzed alone. Each measure must be compared to some other measure. For example, company measures can be compared to prior years' company results, industry averages, or industry leaders' measurements. To illustrate financial statement analysis, we will use a set of financial statements for TUB.

Horizontal Analysis

Horizontal analysis uses *comparative financial statements* for two consecutive years, allowing managers to compare the changes in dollar amounts and percentages in each item measured over the two-year period. The objective of horizontal analysis is to determine the year-to-year change in each financial statement item, why it changed, and whether the change is favorable or unfavorable. Figures 8.4 and 8.5 depict (next pages) comparative balance sheets and income statements, respectively, for TUB for the years ended December 31, 2015 and 2016.

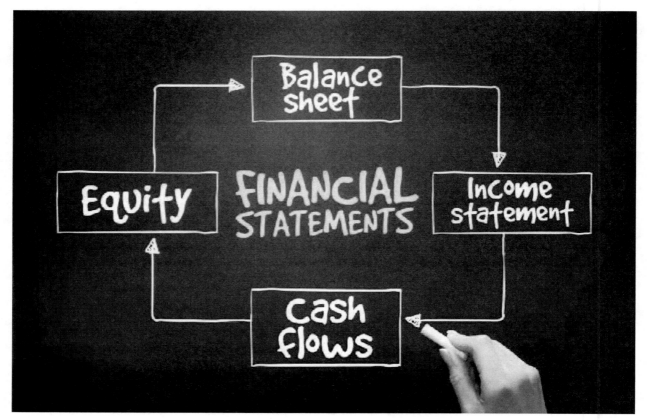

Source: dizain/Shutterstock.com

Figure 8.4 The University Bookstore Comparative Balance Sheet

The University Bookstore
Comparative Size Balance Sheet
As of December 31, 2016 and 2015

	2016 Amount	2015 Amount	Increase or (Decrease) Amount	Percent
Assets				
Current Assets:				
Cash	$45,320	$35,000	$10,320	29.49
Accounts receivable	12,900	22,000	(9,100)	-41.36
Inventory	197,633	100,000	97,633	97.63
Total Current Assets:	$255,853	$157,000	$98,853	62.96
Property Plant & Equipment:				
Land	$250,000	$250,000	$0	0.00
Furniture	60,300	60,300	0	0.00
Shelving	51,000	51,000	0	0.00
Accumulated depreciation	(25,000)	(15000)	(10,000)	66.67
Property Plant & Equipment Net	$336,300	$346,300	(10,000)	(2.89)
Total Assets	$592,153	$503,300	$88,853	17.65
Liabilities:				
Current Liabilities:				
Accounts payable	$96,500	$65,000	$31,500	48.46
Salaries payable	6,000	10,000	($4,000)	(40.00)
Interest payable	7,000	3,500	3,500	100.00
Payroll taxes payable	2,000	1,400	600	42.86
Other payables	19,450	12,200	7,250	59.43
Line of credit payable	130,275	3,000	127,275	4242.5
Current portion Mortgage payable	2,500	2,500	0	0.00
Total Current Liabilities	$263,725	$97,600	$166,125	170.21
Long-Term Liabilities				
Mortgage payable	$197,500	$200,000	($2,500)	(1.25)
Long-term debt	100,000	100,000	0	0.00
Total Long-Term Liabilities	$297,500	$300,000	($2,500)	(0.83)
Total Liabilities	$561,225	$397,600	$163,625	41.15
Net Worth	$30,928	$105,700	($74,773)	(70.74)
Total Liabilities and Net Worth	$592,153	$503,300	$88,853	17.65

Figure 8.5   The University Bookstore Comparative Income Statement

The University Bookstore
Comparative Size Income Statement
For the Years Ended December 31, 2016 and 2015

	2016	2015	Increase or (Decrease)	
	Amount	Amount	Amount	Percent
Net Sales	$1,250,000	$1,500,000	(250,000)	(16.67)
Cost of goods sold	950,000	1,000,000	(50,000)	(5.00)
Gross Profit	$300,000	$500,000	(200,000)	(40.00)
Operating Expenses:				
Sales commissions	$125,000	$150,000	($25,000)	(16.67)
Salaries expense	22,000	45,000	(23,000)	(51.11)
Payroll tax expense	5,350	6,750	(1,400)	(20.74)
Fringe benefits expense	10,400	13,200	(2,800)	(21.21)
Rent expense	32,000	48,000	(16,000)	(33.33)
Insurance expense	6,000	5,000	1,000	20.00
IMC expense	27,000	46,000	(19,000)	(41.30)
Maintenance expense	3,200	4,500	(1,300)	(28.89)
Utilities expense	9,200	9,000	200	2.22
Advertising expense	20,000	16,000	4,000	25.00
Depreciation expense	10,000	6,000	4,000	66.67
Total Operating Expenses	$270,150	$349,450	($79,300)	(22.67)
Total Operating Income	$29,850	$150,550	($120,700)	(80.17)
Other Income (Expenses):				
Interest income	$500	$1,000	($500)	(50.00)
Interest expense	(30,000)	(25,000)	(5,000)	20.00
Total Other Income (Expenses)	($29,500)	($24,000)	($5,500)	22.92
Net Income Before Income Taxes	$350	$126,550	($126,200)	(99.72)
Income Taxes (assume 35%)	123	44,293	(44,170)	(99.72)
Net Income After Taxes	$228	$82,258	($82,030)	(99.72)

Vertical Analysis

Vertical analysis concentrates on the relationships among items within the same set of financial statements. Often managers evaluate the dollar relationships; however, in many cases the percentage relationships are more revealing. On the balance sheet, individual dollar amounts are often converted to percentages of total asset dollars. On the income statement, individual dollar amounts are often converted to a percentage of sales. These converted statements are called *common size financial statements*. Vertical analysis allows managers to identify the magnitude of different items on the balance sheet and income statement. Figures 8.6 and 8.7 (next pages) present common size financial statements (balance sheets and income statements) for TUB.

Figure 8.6 - The University Bookstore Common Size Balance Sheet

**The University Bookstore
Common Size Balance Sheet
As of December 31, 2016 and 2015**

	2016		2015	
	Amount	**Percent**	**Amount**	**Percent**
Assets				
Current Assets:				
Cash	$45,320	7.65	$35,000	6.95
Accounts receivable	12,900	2.18	22,000	4.37
Inventory	197,633	33.38	100,000	19.87
Total Current Assets:	$255,853	43.21	$157,000	31.19
Property Plant & Equipment:				
Land	$250,000	42.22	$250,000	49.67
Furniture	60,300	10.18	60,300	11.98
Shelving	51,000	8.61	51,000	10.13
Accumulated depreciation	(25,000)	(4.22)	(15,000)	(2.98)
Property Plant & Equipment Net	$336,300	56.79	$346,300	68.81
Total Assets	$592,153	100.00	$503,300	100.00
Liabilities:				
Current Liabilities:				
Accounts payable	$96,500	16.30	$65,000	12.91
Salaries payable	6,000	1.01	10,000	1.99
Interest payable	7,000	1.18	3,500	0.70
Payroll taxes payable	2,000	0.34	1,400	0.28
Other payables	19,450	3.28	12,200	2.42
Line of credit payable	130,275	22.00	3,000	0.60
Current portion Mortgage payable	2,500	0.42	2,500	0.50
Total Current Liabilities	$263,725	22.54	$97,600	19.39
Long-Term Liabilities				
Mortgage payable	$197,500	33.35	$200,000	39.74
Long-term debt	100,000	16.89	100,000	19.87
Total Long-Term Liabilities	$297,500	50.24	$300,000	59.61
Total Liabilities	$561,225	94.78	$397,600	79.00
Net Worth	$30,928	5.22	$105,700	21.00
Total Liabilities and Net Worth	$592,153	100.00	$503,300	100.00

Figure 8.7 - The University Bookstore Common Size Income Statement

The University Bookstore
Common-Size Income Statement
For the Years Ended December 31, 2016 and 2015

	2016		2015	
	Amount	Percent of Sales	Amount	Percent of Sales
Net Sales	$1,250,000	100.00	$1,500,000	100.00
Cost of goods sold	950,000	76.00	1,000,000	66.67
Gross Profit	$300,000	24.00	$500,000	33.33
Operating Expenses:				
Sales commissions	$125,000	10.00	$150,000	10.00
Salaries expense	22,000	1.76	45,000	3.00
Payroll tax expense	5,350	0.43	6,750	0.45
Fringe benefits expense	10,400	0.83	13,200	0.88
Rent expense	32,000	2.56	48,000	3.20
Insurance expense	6,000	0.48	5,000	0.33
IMC expense	27,000	2.16	46,000	3.07
Maintenance expense	3,200	0.26	4,500	0.30
Utilities expense	9,200	0.74	9,000	0.60
Advertising expense	20,000	1.60	16,000	1.07
Depreciation expense	10,000	0.80	6,000	0.40
Total Operating Expenses	$270,150	21.61	$349,450	23.30
Total Operating Income	$29,850	2.39	$150,550	10.04
Other Income (Expenses):				
Interest income	$500	0.04	$1,000	0.07
Interest expense	(30,000)	(2.40)	(25000)	(1.67)
Total Other Income (Expenses)	($29,500)	(2.36)	($24,000)	(1.60)
Net Income Before Income Taxes	$350	0.03	$126,550	8.44
Income Taxes (assume 35%)	123	0.01	44,293	2.95
Net Income After Taxes	$228	0.02	$82,258	5.48

Ratio Analysis

Ratio analysis involves the computation of one or more financial ratios that are derived from the financial statements. Ratio analysis can provide extensive insights into the company's financial position that would not be detected in any other manner. To illustrate ratio analysis, we will use Figures 8.3 and 8.4 for the calculations. At the same time, we will use Perfect Bookstore, a major competitor of TUB's, to generate competitive ratios for comparative purposes.

Liquidity Ratios

The first group of ratios, called *liquidity ratios*, reflects management's control of current assets and current liabilities. Generally, current assets are considered to be those assets that are expected to turn into cash within the year. Current liabilities can be defined as debts that are to be paid back within the year.

The first liquidity ratio is the *current ratio*, the ratio of current assets to current liabilities. TUB's current ratios for 2015 and 2016 are computed as follows:

2015

Current ratio = $157,000/$97,600 = 1.61 to 1

2016

Current ratio = $255,853/$263,725 = 0.97 to 1

As you can see, TUB's current ratio declined over the one-year period. If this trend continues, TUB may have trouble paying current liabilities as they come due.

A common rule of thumb is that the current ratio should be 2 to 1, meaning a company should have twice as many current assets as it does current liabilities. This is a general guideline; in reality, appropriate current ratios can vary widely among industries and companies.

The current ratio has a limitation. A company whose current assets consist mainly of cash and accounts receivable might be considered much more liquid than a company with small amounts of cash and accounts receivable and a large amount of inventory. Of all current assets, inventory normally takes the longest to convert into cash. Also, market changes can lower inventory value in unforeseen ways.

The second liquidity ratio is the *acid test ratio*, or *quick ratio*. The acid test ratio is a better indicator of a retailer's ability to meet short-term obligations as they come due. Due to sales and markdowns, inventories sometimes are not worth what they are listed for on the balance sheet. Therefore, many analysts use the acid test ratio as an indication of a company's ability to meet short-term needs.

The acid test ratio is calculated as follows:

Acid test ratio = Quick assets/Current liabilities

Or

Acid test ratio = (Current assets – Inventory)/Current liabilities

Quick assets include cash, accounts receivable, and current notes receivable. These assets can usually be converted quickly into cash. Inventory and prepaid expenses are not included because they require a longer time to convert into cash.

The computations of TUB's acid test ratios for 2015 and 2016 are as follows:

2015

Acid-test ratio = $57,000/$97,600 = 0.58 to 1

2016

Acid-test ratio = $58,220/$263,725 = 0.22 to 1

By using the acid test ratio instead of the current ratio, TUB shows a considerable decline in its ability to meet current obligations as they become due. A general rule of thumb for this ratio is 1 to 1. Managers may need to consider cash-generating tactics such as sales and/or loans.

Activity Ratios

A second set of ratios, *activity ratios*, are used in cash management.

The first activity ratio, *accounts receivable (A/R) turnover in days*, measures the number of days, on average, it takes for accounts receivable to turn into cash. In retailing, A/R turnover should be calculated using two different methods. The first is to determine the number of days required, on average, for credit sales to turn into cash. Using this method, A/R turnover in days is calculated as follows:

$$\text{Accounts receivable turnover in days} = \frac{365}{\text{Sales on account/Average accounts receivable balance}}$$

To compute TUB's A/R turnover in days for 2015 and 2016, we must include certain assumptions not available in Figures 8.3 and 8.4. First, credit sales are $80,000 in 2015 and $100,000 in 2016 Second, 2015's beginning accounts receivable equals $15,000. Based on these assumptions, the calculations for TUB's A/R turnover in days for 2015 and 2016 are as follows:

2015

$$\text{A/R turnover in days} = \frac{365}{\$80,000/(\$15,000 + \$22,000)/2)]} = 84 \text{ days}$$

2016

$$\text{A/R turnover in days} = \frac{365}{\$100,000/(\$22,000 + \$12,900)/2)]} = 64 \text{ days}$$

Based on these calculations, TUB appears to have reduced the number of days needed for its credit sales to turn into cash by 20 days. This calculation is important for two reasons. First, the longer accounts receivable are outstanding, the greater the chance that they may not be collected. Second, the faster the cash is collected, the more cash is available to pay current liabilities.

The second method of calculating A/R turnover in days is used to help determine the overall cash collection cycle from the time inventory is received until it is converted into cash (the cash conversion cycle). This cycle is an important part of cash management. The major difference in the two approaches is that instead of using credit sales in the denominator, total sales are used. This difference is important for retailers if the vast majority of their sales are cash. In other words, the conversion of sales into cash is immediate. Following are examples of the ratio using this method:

2015

$$\text{A/R turnover in days} = \frac{365}{\$1,500,000/(\$15,000 + \$22,000)/2)]} = 4.5 \text{ days}$$

2016

$$\text{A/R turnover in days} = \frac{365}{\$1,250,000/(\$22,000 + \$12,900)/2)]} = 5.1 \text{ days}$$

By including cash and credit sales, these ratios indicate that, on average, it took 4.5 days in 2015 and 5.1 days to convert sales into cash. These calculations, added to inventory turnover in days, are an estimate of the total cash cycle.

The second and probably most important activity ratio for retailers, *inventory (I/V) turnover in days*, measures the amount of days, on average, from the time the retailer receives inventory until the time the inventory is sold to the customer. Inventory turnover in days is computed as follows:

$$\text{Inventory turnover in days} = \frac{365}{\text{Cost of goods sold/Average inventory balance}}$$

To determine TUB's I/V turnover in days, the only assumption is that $110,000 is the beginning inventory for 2015. By adding this assumption, we can calculate the I/V turnover in days as follows:

2015

$$\text{I/V turnover in days} = \frac{365}{\$1,000,000/(\$110,000+\$100,000)/2)]} = 38.3 \text{ days}$$

2016

$$\text{I/V turnover in days} = \frac{365}{\$950,000/(\$100,000 + \$197,633)/2)]} = 57.2 \text{ days}$$

A comparison of these ratios for 2015 and 2016 indicates that TUB's conversion of inventory into sales, on average, has increased significantly, which further restricts the availability of cash for paying obligations as they become due. The cash cycle is the total number of days from the time a company receives goods until the goods are converted into cash. In TUB's case, in 2015, the total cash cycle is 4.5 days plus 38.3 days, equaling 42.8 days. In 2016, the total cash cycle is A/R turnover in days of 5.1 plus I/V turnover in days of 57.2, or 62.3 days.

Efficiency Ratios

Efficiency ratios comprise the third set of ratios. *Efficiency ratios* provide evidence of how effectively management is running the retail business.

The first efficiency ratio is the *return-on-assets ratio*. The higher the return-on-assets ratio, the better management appears to be using the retailer's assets efficiently to generate net income. Return on assets can be calculated as follows:

$$\text{Return on assets} = \frac{\text{Net income} + (\text{Interest expense, net of tax effect})]}{\text{Average total assets}}$$

Interest expense net of tax effect is added because management of assets should be separated from the means by which those assets are financed, which is a financial management decision. If retail financial managers decide to finance some assets by incurring debt rather than con-

Source: Fh Photo/Shutterstock.com

tributing capital, interest income will be incurred, which in turn will reduce net income. The interest expense is added back to net income net of tax effect because the total interest expense reduces net income before taxes, which is used to calculate income taxes. Thus, if total interest expense were subtracted from net income before taxes, income taxes would be higher and net income after taxes would not increase by the total of the interest expense.

To determine TUB's return on assets, the only assumption needed is that the beginning total assets for 2015 are $387,000:

2015

Return on assets=

$$\frac{(\$82,258 + \$25,000) \times (1 - 0.35)}{(\$387,000 + \$503,300)/2)} = 22.13\%$$

2016

Return on assets =

$$\frac{(\$228 + \$30,000) \times (1 - 0.35)}{(\$503,300 + \$592,153)/2)} = 3.60\%$$

The second efficiency ratio is the *return-on-equity ratio*. This ratio views the efficiency of management from the common stockholder's position. The ratio indicates how well management is using owner's equity to generate net income that could be available to owners. It is calculated as follows:

Return on equity = Net income available to owners/Average owner's equity (net worth)

To determine TUB's return on equity, the only data not available in the financial statements is the beginning net worth for 2015, which we will assume to be $120,000:

2015

Return on equity = $82,259/($105,700 + $120,000)/2)] = 72.89%

2016

Return on equity = $228/($105,700 + $30,928)/2)] = 0.33%

The third efficiency ratio is the *return-on-sales ratio*. This ratio indicates how well the retailer is converting sales dollars into net income. It is computed as follows:

Return on sales= Net income/Sales

TUB's return on sales is calculated as follows:

2015

Return on sales = $82,258/$1,500,000 = 5.48%

2016

Return on sales = $228/$1,250,000 = 0.02%

The final and important ratio, the *debt-to-equity ratio*, is a capitalization ratio because it indicates whether financial managers have financed the retailer's assets with debt or with owner's net worth. Often retailers find themselves in financial difficulties as a result of relying too heavily on debt to fund the company's assets. The reason debt can be troublesome is because debt requires financing (interest) payments, as well as, the eventual repayment of the amount borrowed. The same is not true with equity or owners' contributions since payments to owners, although favorable, are not required and are therefore less risky to the financial health of the company. The debt-to-equity ratio is calculated as follows:

Debt-to-equity ratio = Total liabilities/Total owner's equity (net worth)

The debt-to-equity ratio for TUB is computed as follows:

2015

Debt to equity = $397,600/$105,700 = 3.76 to 1

2016

Debt to equity = $561,225/$30,928 = 18.15 to 1

The 2016 debt-to-equity ratio is probably the most troublesome of all the ratios for TUB. As a rule of thumb, the debt-to-equity ratio should be around 1 to 1. At 18.15 to 1.00, TUB could shortly find itself in a situation where it will be unable to obtain additional financing from lenders or investors. Table 8.1 summarizes all the ratios discussed in this section.

Table 8.1   Summary of Common Ratios

Ratio Equations	
Liquidity Ratios	
Current Ratio	Current assets/Current liabilities
Acid Test (Quick Ratio)	Quick assets/Current liabilities Or (Current assets – Inventory)/Current liabilities
Activity Ratios	
Accounts Receivable Turnover in Days	365/(Sales on Account/Average Accounts Receivable Balance) 365/(Total Sales/Average Accounts Receivable Balance)
Inventory Turnover in Days	365/(COGS/Average Inventory Balance)
Efficiency Ratios	
Return on Assets Ratio	([Net Income + Interest Income), net of its tax effect]/Average Total Assets.
Return on Equity Ratio	Net Income available to owners/average owner's equity (Net Worth).
Return on Sales Ratio	Net Income/Sales.
Debt to Equity Ratio (Net Worth)	Total Liabilities/Total Owner's Equity (Net Worth)

Asset Management: Inventory

Source: XiXinXing/Shutterstock.com

To ensure that the retail business is using its assets to their fullest potential and to implement control systems for revenues generated, the retailer must engage in asset management. A prime example of asset management is management of inventory. Inventory is usually one of the retailer's most important assets because it typically represents the largest dollar value on the balance sheet.

To illustrate the importance of inventory management, consider apparel retailers. Because of such factors as changing fashion trends and seasonality, apparel retailers need to be concerned about their inventory becoming obsolete. A second concern is *carrying costs*, the costs of storing and maintaining inventory. Carrying costs can include the rent or depreciation on the warehouse, warehouse utilities, and insurance, as well as personnel costs for safeguarding the inventory. Some estimates of the carrying costs of inventory are as high as 20 to 30 percent of the cost of the average inventory on hand. The following example illustrates the impact of carrying costs and obsolescence of inventory.

A clothing retailer has a winter dress that costs $70 and has a list price of $120. The retailer is unable to sell the dress, so it decides to warehouse the product until next year. The following year, the dress has gone out of style and the retailer is again unable to sell it. This time the retailer decides to dispose of the dress. The impact on the retailer is as follows:

Cost of Dress	$70.00
Carrying cost of dress for one year (assume 30%)	21.00
Total loss	(**$91.00**)

If the retailer had sold the dress in the first year at a 30 percent discount off the list price of $120, the result would have been as follows:

Sale Price of Dress	$84.00
Cost of dress	70.00
Total gross profit	$14.00

Financial Statement Fraud

Clearly, many formulas are available for organizing and maintaining a retailer's financial environment. Though laws bind retailers to maintain lawful and truthful records, some retailers choose to ignore them. The unfortunate result is financial statement fraud. Determining the impact of financial statement fraud is difficult because many fraudulent practices go undetected. Most companies, when given the choice, will hide incidences of fraud by quietly dismissing those involved. According to Joseph T. Wells (2000), CPA and CFE, five types of financial statement fraud schemes exist:

1. *Fictitious revenues.* This is the most common way to make up sales figures that place the company in a positive light.

2. *Fraudulent asset valuations.* The most frequent instances of fraudulent asset violation occur in inventory valuations. Companies inflate the value of inventory, double-count inventory, or create inventory on the books that does not exist in reality.

3. *Timing differences.* Companies may overstate assets and income by taking advantage of the accounting cutoff period to boost sales and/or reduce liabilities and expenses.

4. *Concealed liabilities and expenses.* To pull off this type of fraud, companies hide their bills or other paperwork that show liabilities. The rationale for this fraud is: If the accountants don't see the liabilities, they don't exist.

5. *Improper disclosures.* Generally accepted accounting principles (GAAP) require companies to disclose all changes in accounting procedures in the financial statements or accompanying footnotes. Businesses commit fraud when they knowingly omit information that would affect the analysis of financial reports.

The lesson to be learned from the fall of Arthur Andersen, one of the world's largest financial auditing firms, is that unethical business practices, no matter how small, can have a devastating effect on a business.

Forecasting Sales Volumes and Profits

One of the most difficult aspects of financial management is forecasting sales volumes and profits. A small mistake can be costly over time. The forecasts made impact a significant asset, which is inventory. A retailer who makes mistakes may end up with a warehouse of unsold products. In many cases retailers forecast for too little inventory and the retailer ends up losing sales due to stockouts (running out of products). When a retailer makes mistakes in forecasting demand, profits are also impacted. In this section cost behavior and cost-volume profit analysis is examined.

Cost Behavior

Cost behavior relates the changes in total costs when sales volume increases or decreases. Changes in sales volume can be determined based on any fluctuation in activity. In most cases, retailers usually evaluate fluctuations in sales activity as either being fluctuations in total units sold or fluctuations in total sales dollars. Fluctuations in sales volume are common in retailing, especially during the winter holiday season.

Cost behavior accumulates costs into two categories:

1. Fixed costs are total costs that do not change with changes in sales volume (activity). For example, the total rental cost of the retail outlet space will probably not change when total sales activity increases or decreases.

2. Variable costs are total costs that increase when sales volume increases and decrease when sales volume decreases. For example, the total cost of merchandise sold increases (decreases) as the total sales volume increases (decreases).

Once total fixed and variable costs are separated, many different methods can be used to develop a cost equation relating total costs with fluctuations in sales volume. The cost equation most often used with cost behavior is:

Total cost = Total fixed cost + (Unit variable cost per unit of sales activity x Total sales activity).

A fast way to determine this cost equation is the use of the high-low method. Simply put, the high-low method compares the fluctuations in total cost at the highest and lowest levels to the highest and lowest levels of sales volume activity. For example:

Month	Units Sold	Total Sales $	Total Cost
January	26,000	850,000	**175,000**
February	**23,750**	**900,000**	245,000
March	32,000	**475,000**	**250,000**
April	**45,000**	520,000	240,000

The first step is to select the highest and lowest cost - $250,000 and $175,000, respectively. Then the highest and lowest activity to be used is selected. In this example units sold is the activity, therefore the highest level of units sold is 45,000 and the lowest level is 23,750.

The second step is to determine the variable cost per unit sold. This is accomplished by first determining the change in total cost ($250,000 - $175,000 = $75,000) and the change in total units sold (45,000 – 23,750 = 21,250). Second, the change in total cost is divided by the change in total units sold to determine the unit variable cost-per-unit sold ($75,000/21,250 = $3.53).

The third step is to determine the total fixed cost by using either the high or low actual total cost selected in Step #1 and the corresponding high or low units sold selected in Step #1 (If actual high cost is selected then select the actual high activity). In this example, the highest total cost of $250,000 and the highest total units sold of 45,000 are used. The total cost, total units sold and the unit variable cost determined in Step #2 are entered into the cost equation and the total fixed cost is derived.

Source: pattarawat/Shutterstock.com

Total cost = Total fixed cost + (Unit variable cost x # of units sold)

$250,000 = Total fixed cost + ($3.53 x 45,000)

Total fixed cost = $91,176.

The result is a cost equation that can be used to estimate total costs at any given level of units sold. When selecting an activity level for estimating total cost, care must be taken that the activity level is not outside the relevant range. The relevant range is usually the range of activity that does not exceed facility capacity or the range of activity when variable unit costs do not change. For example the cost per unit of merchandise may be subject to different volume discounts at different levels of quantity purchased, which results in a different unit variable cost. This equation is often termed the company's cost structure.

Total cost = $91,176 + ($3.53 x # of units sold).

In the next example, the only difference is that the sales activity selected is sales dollars instead of units sold.

Step # 1: The highest and lowest total costs selected = $250,000 and $175,000. Highest and lowest total sales dollars = $900,000 and $475,000.

Step # 2: The change in total cost is $75,000 ($250,000 - $175,000) and the change in total sales dollars is $425,000 ($900,000 - $475,000). Dividing the change in total cost ($75,000) by the change in total sales dollars ($425,000), unit variable cost per sales dollar is determined to be $0.18 ($75,000/$425,000). The unit variable cost of $0.18 means that for every $1.00 in sales, $0.18 in variable cost is incurred.

Step # 3: Total fixed cost is determined by selecting the highest or lowest total cost. In this example, the highest total cost ($250,000) was selected. Then the total cost selected, the corresponding highest or lowest sales dollars from Step #1 and the unit variable cost determined in Step #2, are entered into the cost equation and total fixed cost is derived.

$$\text{Total cost} = \text{Total fixed cost} + (\text{Unit variable cost} \times \text{Total Sales dollars})$$

$$\$250,000 = \text{Total fixed cost} + (\$0.18 \times \$900,000)$$

$$\text{Total fixed cost} = \$175,000$$

As in Example #1, the result is a cost equation that can be used to estimate total costs at any given level of units sold. This equation is often termed the company's cost structure.

$$\text{Total cost} = \$175,000 + (\$0.18 \times \text{Total sales \$}).$$

Two important cautions that need to be emphasized when estimating unit variable cost and total fixed cost are as follows:

1. As in example #1 and #2 above using different activities (# of units sold and total sales $) will often result in different estimated total fixed cost (Example #1 = $91,176 and Example #2 = $175,000). This is due to the match or fit of the fluctuation in the activity and the fluctuation in total costs. The most accurate estimation is achieved when the fluctuation in the activity closely matches the fluctuation in the total costs. Although the high-low method is the simplest means of estimation, it does not provide any indication of the fit of the activity to total cost. The comparison of the coefficients of determination ($R2$) derived when simple linear regression is used to determine total fixed cost and unit variable cost can provide guidance as to which activity best matches the changes in total cost.

2. Since most retailers sell multiple products, changes in the proportion of each product sold or *sales mix* can affect the accuracy of the estimated unit variable cost. It is important to monitor changes in the sales mix over time as these will necessarily change the unit variable cost. Advertising, promotions and sales discounts on specific products may influence the sales mix. Evaluating current and future marketing activities can indicate changes in the sales mix. With the widespread use by retailers of perpetual inventory systems and the recording of inventory at retail prices, monitoring changes in sales mix can be accomplished. A more detailed discussion of sales mix and the impact of changes in sales mix on profits are addressed in the next section on cost-volume-profit analysis.

Cost-Volume-Profit Analysis

Cost-volume-profit (CVP) analysis is the integration of cost behavior and changes in sales volume into a forecasted income statement termed a contribution margin formatted income statement. A contribution margin income statement is an income statement that accumulates costs based on fixed and variable cost behavior rather than the traditional accumulation of cost by cost of goods sold and selling and administrative expenses.

Table 8.2   Calculating Contribution Margin

+	Sales
-	Variable costs
=	Contribution Margin
-	Fixed Costs
=	Net Profit (Loss)

The best way to understand the use of the contribution margin income statement and CVP analysis is through examples of a retailing operation where a single product is sold.

Example #1:

Cole Leather Coat Company is a retailer who sells a single product, a high-end leather coat largely sold to famous rock stars. Cole has one retail outlet in London, England. Shaun Michael, Cole's store manager, has accumulated some basic information on Cole's business as follows:

Sales price per coat	15,000
Cost to purchase one coat from manufacturer	6,000
Other variable store costs (sales commissions, electric, etc.) per coat	4,000
Total fixed costs (store rent, store insurance, store manager's salary etc.) per month	300,000

Required:

1. What is Cole's contribution margin in dollars per coat?

2. How many leather coats must Cole sell each month to breakeven (profit/net income = 0)?

3. What is Cole's contribution margin percent?

Cole Leather Coat Company - Breakeven Income Statement for one month

	Total $ =	$ Per Coat x	# of Coats Sold	% of Sales
Sales	900,000	15,000	60	100% = ($900,000/$900,000)
Less Variable Costs	600,000	10,000	60	67% = ($600,000/$900,000)
Equals Contribution Margin	300,000	5,000	60	33% = ($300,000/$900,000)
Less Fixed Costs	300,000			
Equals Profit	0			

When using the contribution margin formatted income statement demonstrated above, the best way to complete the income statement is to start by entering the desired profit (in this example, profit is equal to $0) and proceeding from there up the statement entering total fixed costs and then adding desired net income to total fixed cost to determine total contribution margin in dollars ($300,000).

The second step would be to enter the unit sales price per coat less the unit variable cost per unit to derive the contribution margin per unit ($15,000 - $10,000 = $5,000 – Solution to Requirement #1). At this point, divide the total contribution margin by the unit contribution margin to find the number of coats that must be sold that will result in the desired profit ($300,000/$5,000 = 60 coats – Solution to Requirement #2).

To determine total sales $, multiple units required to be sold by unit sales price (60 x $15,000 = $900,000). Finally, to determine % of sales following the division equation illustration under percent of Sales above. The % of sales for total contribution margin (33% - Solution to Requirement # 3) is called the contribution margin ratio.

The contribution margin ratio is important in that it can be interpreted as the dollar amount of each sales dollar that remains after variable costs are incurred to cover fixed costs and profits. (For every $1 in sales - $0.33 remains to cover total fixed costs – in this example total fixed costs = $300,000). Once total sales equals breakeven sales (in this example, breakeven sales = $900,000), every dollar in sales contributes $0.33 to profit. If total sales equal $900,001 then the $1 over breakeven sales equals $0.33 in profit/net income. If total sales equal $1,000,000, total profit would be $33,000 (1,000,000 - $900,000) x $0.33].

The next example demonstrates how CVP analysis can be used to determine the number of units that must be sold and total sales required to obtain any desired profit.

Example # 2:

Cole's store manager, Shaun Michael, has a second question. How many coats would Cole Leather Company need to sell to generate a profit of $100,000?

Required:

1. How many leather coats must Cole sell each month to obtain a profit/net income of $100,000?

2. What is Cole's contribution margin in dollars per coat?

3. What is Cole's contribution margin percent?

Solution:

Cole Leather Coat Company - Breakeven Income Statement for one month

	Total $ =	$ Per Coat x	# of Coats Sold	% of Sales
				100% =
Sales	1,200,000	**15,000**	80	($1,200,000/$1,200,000)
Less Variable Costs	800,000	**10,000**	80	67% = ($800,000/$1,200,000)
Equals Contribution Margin	400,000	5,000	**80**	33% = ($400,000/$1,200,000)
Less Fixed Costs	**300,000**			
Equals Net Income	**100,000**			

As discussed in Example #1, by first entering the desired profit and adding it to total fixed costs, total contribution margin required can be determined ($100,000 + $300,000 = $400,000). From this point the steps to determine required sales in units, total sales $ and the percent of sales amounts can be obtained by following the same steps as discussed in Example #1. The result is that Cole must sell 80 coats to obtain a profit of $100,000).

Again, an important contribution that cost-volume-profit concept provides for retailers is the relationship of the total contribution margin in dollars, the contribution margin percent and total sales dollars. This relationship is illustrated in Example #3. Please note that in Example #1 and Example #2 the contribution margin percent is the same (33%). This percent should be the same in all cases except if unit sales price and/or cost behavior changes. A further discussion of this issue is presented at the end of Example #3.

Example # 3

Shaun Michael has one last question. What would Cole's total sales in dollars need to be to obtain a profit of $150,000?

Required:

1. Using only total contribution margin in dollars and the contribution margin percent, determine what Cole Leather Coat Company's total sales in dollars needs to be to generate a profit of $150,000.

	Total $	% of Sales
Required Sales	1,350,000	
Less Variable Costs		
Equals Contribution Margin	**450,000**	33%
Less Fixed Costs	300,000	
Equals Desired Profit	150,000	

This example demonstrates that if total fixed costs and the contribution margin percent are known, total sales dollars can be determined without completing the entire income statement. Any desired profit plus total fixed costs will equal total contribution margin ($150,000 + $300,000 = $450,000). Dividing total contribution margin by the contribution margin percent will equal total sales dollars ($450,000/33% = $1,350,000).

Important Note:

It needs to be stated again that care must be taken when using the total contribution in dollars and the contribution margin percent to determine total sales in dollars for three reasons:

1. In order to increase sales, unit sales price may have to be decreased, which would reduce the contribution margin percent.

2. Extreme increases in sales may change the assumed cost behavior relationships. Extreme increases in sales may increase total fixed costs. For example, additional floor space and storage space may be needed. Second, extreme increases in sales may reduce the cost of purchasing the coats due to volume discounts which would increase the contribution percent.

3. Most importantly for retailers who sell multiple products is that changes in the *Sales Mix* (percent of total sales of each product) of highly profitable products versus low profit products would change the contribution margin percent. Increases in unit sales of highly profitable products would increase the contribution margin percent and increases in low profit products would decrease the contribution margin percent.

Example #4 is an illustration of the issue of changes in sales mix and the results on these changes on profits.

Example # 4:

During 2017, Cole is considering selling a second leather coat. This coat is a low-end coat that will be largely sold to rock star fans. The following information relates to Cole's two coats.

	High-end Coat	Low-end Coat
Sales price per coat	15,000	1,000
Cost to purchase one coat from manufacturer	6,000	800
Other variable store costs (sales commissions, electric, etc.) per coat	4,000	100
Total fixed costs (store rent, store insurance, store manager's salary etc.) per month	300,000	

In 2017, Cole expects to sell 100 high-end coats and 20 low-end coats. Using Cole's estimated 2016 sales mix and calculating the *average contribution margin*, a forecast of Cole's profit can be determined.

Step #1 one is to determine the contribution margin per coat.

	High-end Coat	Low-end Coat
Sales price per coat	15,000	1,000
Less variable cost per coat	10,000	900
Equals contribution margin per coat	5,000	100

Step #2 is to determine the sales mix ratio percent. Since Cole believes he will sell 100 high-end coats and 25 low-end coats, his sales mix ratio percent would be 80% high-end coats (100/125) and 20% low-end coats (25/125)

Step # 3 is to calculate the average contribution margin per coat sold. By multiplying the contribution margin for each coat by the coat's sales mix ratio percent and adding the two results together the average contribution margin is determined.

The average contribution margin is equal to the sum of the contribution margin for each coat times the coat's contribution margin ratio percent: ($5,000 x 80%) + ($100 x 20%) = $4,000 + $20 = $4,020.

Step # 4 is to determine Cole's estimated profit using the contribution margin income statements.

	Total $ =	$ Per Coat x	# of Coats Sold
Sales			
Less Variable Costs			
Equals Contribution Margin	482,400	4,020	120
Less Fixed Costs	300,000		
Equals Net Income	182,400		

In 2018, Cole's believes that it will sell 90 high-end coats and 810 low-end coats. Following the same steps as for 2017, the contribution margin ratio % would be 10% for high-end coats (90/900) and 90% for low-end coats. As in Step # 3 above, the average contribution margin is equal to the sum of the contribution margin for each coat times the coat's contribution margin ratio percent: ($5,000 x 10%) + ($100 x 90%) = $500 + $90 = $590.

Cole's estimated profit using the contribution margin income statements would be:

	Total $ =	$ Per Coat x	# of Coats Sold
Sales			
Less Variable Costs			
Equals Contribution Margin	531,000	590	900
Less Fixed Costs	300,000		
Equals Net Income	231,000		

Cole's results for 2017 and 2018 illustrate the impact that changes in sales mix can have on the estimated average contribution margin per unit sold and profits. Even though Cole's believes it will sell 900 coats in 2018 versus only 120 coats in 2017, Cole's profits only increase by $48,600. This small increase in profits is because the sales mix ratio percent changed from 80% high-end (high contribution margin) coats and 20% low-end (low contribution margin) coats in 2017 to 10% high-end coats and 90% low-end coats in 2018.

From these sections on cost behavior and cost-volume-profit analysis it is apparent how important these concepts are to retailers in managing their operations.

Summary

This chapter explored issues and processes in financial planning for a retailer's operation. The data gathered during financial planning allow the retail manager to make more effective decisions. The financial operations management function is particularly important when designing the integrated retail management plan because cash management and financial statement analysis allow retailers to evaluate various aspects of the organization's performance.

Because one of the main goals of retailing is to turn a profit, the retail manager devotes a great deal of time to planning. All activities need to be integrated so that everyone knows why and where the retail dollars are going. In addition, because a finite number of dollars are available to the retailer, the allocation of those dollars is crucial in retail decision making.

Important financial statements were discussed and illustrated, including the balance sheet, the income statement, and the statement of cash flows. The chapter then discussed financial fraud.

Inventory valuation is an important step in financial planning. The next chapter focuses on issues involved with inventory valuation and methods involved in managing the inventory function.

Finally, the financial concepts of cost behavior and cost-volume-profit were discussed. The usefulness of these concepts in planning was emphasized, as well as the interrelationship these concepts can have with advertising and promotion and ultimately profits.

Terms

accounts receivable (A/R) turnover in days	A measurement of the number of days, on average, it takes to convert accounts receivable into cash.
acid test ratio (quick ratio)	Quick assets divided by current liabilities.
activity ratios	Ratios used to determine how well a firm manages current assets, pays off current liabilities, and uses assets to generate sales.
assets	Anything of value that a retailer owns.
balance sheet	A financial statement that itemizes the retailer's assets, liabilities, and net worth as of a specific point in time.
carrying costs	The costs of storing and maintaining inventory.
cash flow from financing activities	Cash received or disbursed from activities dealing with a company's own debt and capital instruments.
cash flow from investing activities	Cash received or disbursed from extending or collecting loans and acquiring or disposing of investments or long-term assets.
cash flow from operating activities	Cash received or disbursed from all of the activities involved in a company's operations.
common size financial statement	A financial statement in which common size ratios are used to compare financial statements of different size companies. For balance sheet items, ratios are typically expressed as a percentage of total assets. For income statement items, ratios are expressed as a percentage of total revenue.
comparative financial statement	A financial statement that reflects more than one year of financial information, to show changes over time. The information is typically presented in a side-by-side columnar format.
cost of goods sold (COGS)	The amount a retailer pays for its merchandise.
current assets	Cash and other items that can be converted to cash quickly.
current liabilities	Financial obligations that must be paid back within the upcoming year.
current ratio	Current assets divided by current liabilities.
debt-to-equity ratio	Total liabilities divided by total owner's equity.
efficiency ratios	Ratios that provide evidence of how effectively management is running the business.
gross profit	The difference between the retailer's net sales and the cost of goods sold.

horizontal analysis	An analysis that uses comparative financial statements for two consecutive years.
inventory (I/V) turnover in days	A measurement of the number of days, on average, from the time a retailer receives inventory to the time the inventory is sold to the customer.
liabilities	Financial obligations owed by a retailer.
liquidity ratios	Ratios that reflect management's control of current assets and current liabilities.
long-term assets	Property, equipment, and other fixed assets used to operate a business.
net income after taxes	The difference between net income before taxes and income taxes.
net income before taxes (NIBT)	The difference between net income from operations and the net effect of other income (expenses).
net income from operations	Gross profit minus operating expenses.
net sales	All gross sales a retailer earns during a specified period of time, minus sales discounts given to customers to promote sales and minus returns and allowances given to customers for returned items or defective products.
net worth (owner's equity)	Assets minus liabilities; represents the net value of a retail business on a cost basis.
notes to the financial statements	A financial statement that provides supplemental information about the balance sheet, income statement, and statement of cash flows.
operating expenses	The normal costs associated with doing business, not including the cost of the merchandise for sale.
operations management	A planning function dealing with the implementation of store policies, tactics, and procedures.
purchase discount	Reduction in the payment amount a vendor is willing to accept to satisfy the amount due if the payment is made earlier.
quick assets	Assets that can usually be converted quickly into cash (includes cash, accounts receivable, and current notes receivable).
ratio analysis	The computation of several financial ratios derived from the financial statements.
retail accounting system (RAS)	A method for systematically gathering, analyzing, storing, and utilizing financial information and data.
return-on-assets ratio	Net income plus interest income, net of its tax effect, divided by average total assets.
return-on-equity ratio	Net income available to owners divided by average owner's equity (net worth).
return-on-sales ratio	Net income divided by sales.
statement of cash flows	A financial statement showing cash receipts and cash payments during a given period.
vertical analysis	An analysis that concentrates on the relationships among items within the same set of financial statements.

Discussion Questions

1. Why is it important for retailers to understand financial statements?

2. Why is cash management so important to retailers?

3. What is the difference between current assets and long-term assets? Between current liabilities and long-term liabilities? What other information is needed to interpret these ratios?

4. What type of financial information should be available to investors?

5. What are the consequences for companies that cheat when reporting their financial status?

Exercises

1. Public companies are required by United States law to file required paperwork, go to the Securities and Exchange Commission's (SEC) EDGAR (Economic Data Gathering and Retrieval) website (www.sec.gov). On the website, select the *fillings and forms* section and do the following:

a. Complete the tutorial on EDGAR (https://www.sec.gov/edgar/quickedgar.htm)

b. Use EDGAR to find recent filings for two retailers of your choice.

c. From the list of filings, choose a report for each of the retailers chosen in step b.

d. In written form, summarize the data found for each retailer. Analyze and report on the implications of the data you found.

2. Select two retailers. Get their latest annual report. Look at their net profit margin. Are there any significant changes in the retailers' financial performance? Write down your results. Look at the key financial ratios for these retailers. Are they different or the same? Why are they different? Why are they alike?

3. Find a retailer who has committed financial fraud. Why do you think the retailer decided to defraud their customers? What would you do differently? Why?

4. Select three retailers in the same industry. Calculate their quick ratio and then compare the three ratios. Are they different? Why? Why not? What do these ratios tell you about the retailers' operations?

Case

Land's Bend - Merchandising Mix and Profitability

Land's Bend Company is a retail women's apparel company that specializes in high-end women's shoes, handbags and jewelry. The president of Land's Bend has come to you and is concerned about the profitability of the company. Some of the important changes occurring at Land's Bend from 2015 to 2016 were:

1. Land's Bend increased their sales prices on all their merchandise by 20% from 2015 to 2016.

2. Total units of merchandise sold increased by 30%.

3. The company's gross sales in dollars increased by almost 10%.

4. The unit costs to purchase the merchandise and total fixed costs remained relatively the same from 2015 to 2016

5. The company's profits dropped by 38% in 2016

The president has provided you with the following information concerning the last two years of operations. The president would like you to evaluate this information and see if you can determine a reason for this drop in profitability.

Land's Bend Financial Data

	2015				2016			
	Total	**Shoes**	**Handbags**	**Jewelry**	**Total**	**Shoes**	**Handbags**	**Jewelry**
Total Sales in Dollars	1,200,000	60,000	900,000	240,000	1,314,000	234,000	360,000	720,000
Total Units Sold	1,500	200	900	400	1,950	650	300	1,000
Average Sales Price per Unit		300	1,000	600		360	1,200	**720**
Average Variable Cost per Unit		200	280	500		200	280	500
Total Fixed Costs	4,000,000				4,010,000			
Total Net Income (Profit) -	308,000				190,000			

Questions:

1. What are the contribution margins for each of the product lines Land's Bend sells?

2. Were there changes in the number of units sold of each product line from 2015 to 2016? Explain.

3. Determine Land's Bend's sales mixes for 2015 and 2016? Did the Sales Mix change from 2015 to 2016? Explain.

4. Based on the 2015 and 2016 sales mixes, what are Land's Bend's average contribution margins per product line for 2015 and 2016? How did the average contribution margin change from 2015 to 2016?

5. Using the average contribution margins for 2015 and 2016; determine Land's Bend's profits for 2015 and 2016? Check your calculated profit with the profit dollar amount listed in Land's Bend Financial Data section above.

6. How did the changes in the sales mix affect the profitability of the company?

7. What suggestions might you have to improve the profitability of Land's Bend?

Source: This case was developed by Craig Latshaw, Ph.D., CPA and Sylvia D. Clark, Ph.D. Associate Business Professors at St. John's University (300 Howard Avenue, Staten Island, NY 10301).

References

Fulham, P. (2011). Borders to Close for Good, *The Slatest Online*, July 18. Retrieved from: http://slatest.slate.com/posts/2011/07/18/borders_faces_liquidation_as_it_heads_into_bankruptcy_auction_.html

Kane, M. (2008). Circuit City Files for Bankruptcy, November 10. *CNET Online*. Retrieved from: http://news.cnet.com/

Ogg, E. (2008). For Circuit City, Holidays Not Looking Happy, *CNET Online*. November 3. Retrieved from: http://news.cnet.com/8301-1001_3-10081736-92.html

Pankratz, H. and Vuong, A. (2013). Dish to Close 300 Blockbuster Stores. *The Denver Post* (Jan 21). Retrieved from http://www.denverpost.com/ci_22419439/dish-close-300-blockbuster-stores

Spector, M. and Trachtenberg, J.A. (2011). Borders Forced to Liquidate, Close All Stores. *The Wall Street Journal Online*, (Jul 19). Retrieved from: http://online.wsj.com/article/

Wells, J.T. (2000). So That's Why It's Called a Pyramid Scheme. *Journal of Accountancy Online*. Retrieved from http://www.journalofaccountancy.com/Issues/2000/Oct/SoThatSWhyItSCalledAPyramidScheme

The authors wish to thank Craig Latshaw, Ph.D., CPA, Sylvia D. Clark, Ph.D. and David Wagaman, CPA for their expertise in helping to write and edit this chapter. Dr. Latshaw and Dr. Clark are Associate Business Professors at St. John's University (300 Howard Avenue, Staten Island, NY 10301). Mr. Wagaman is an Associate Professor at Kutztown University of Pennsylvania (Department of Business Administration, College of Business, Kutztown University of Pennsylvania, Kutztown, PA 19530).

Chapter 9

Merchandise Management

"Different is what sells. Our customers want to go into a place of business that's different. They want to shop at stores that stock diverse merchandise and have diverse promotions. It's the key to not only staying ahead, but staying in business."

~ Rick Segel, retail consultant and founder of Rick Segel Associates

Source: Creative Lab/Shutterstock.com

CHAPTER OBJECTIVES

After completing this chapter you will be able to:

- Define merchandise and merchandise planning.
- Define the components of a merchandise mix.
- Understand the concept of category management.
- Calculate inventory values at cost and retail price.
- Understand the relationship between suppliers/vendors and retailers.

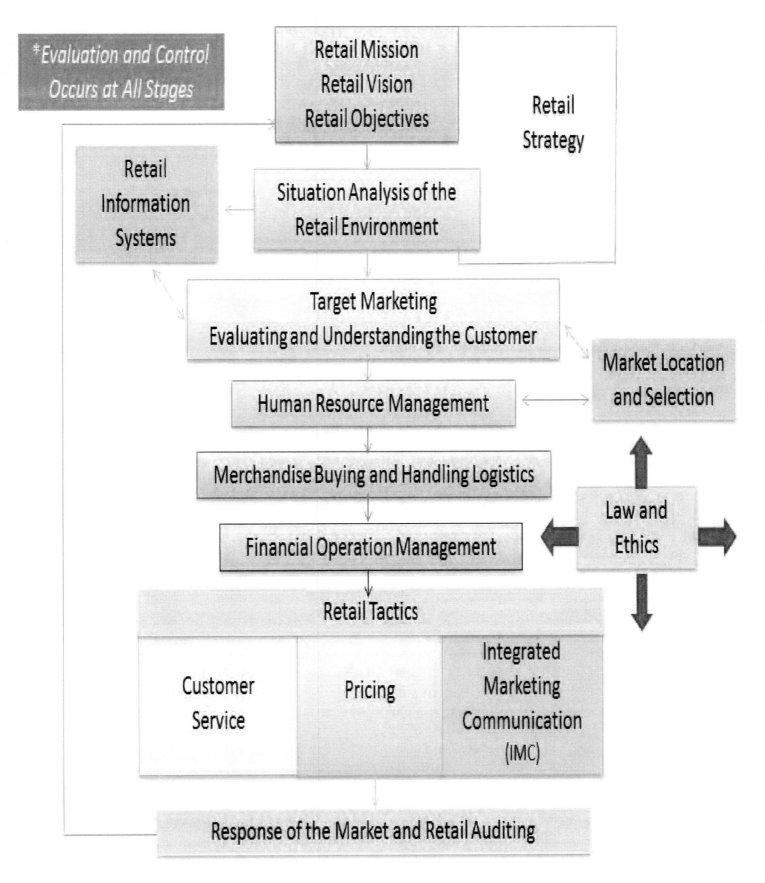

Retailers Monitor Merchandise Trends

Because inventory is typically the largest investment a retailer makes with their financial resources, retailers are very concerned about changes in the environment that will impact their product lines. *Fortune 500* retailers such as Walmart and Carrefour assess the environment for data that will help them plan their merchandise mix for upcoming periods. Vend (2017) released a report on retail trends and predictions. The report contains information on the retail landscape and discusses trends in retailing. According to the report:

Source: Zapp2Photo/Shutterstock.com

· Stores that provide unique in-store experiences are more likely to survive.

· Omni-channel shopping experiences will increasingly be integrated with in-store experiences.

· Mobile payments solutions will become the norm.

· Personalization will become more important.

· Retailers will turn to apps, services and third parties to fulfill shopping needs.

Based on reports such as this, many retailers reassessed, or are currently reassessing, their financial and merchandise plans to create more room for product categories that look like they will increase; and deleting or reducing product lines in those categories that look like they will have no, or negative, gains in the market. The in-store and online experiences are becoming more important to merchandise decisions. Central to these decisions are customers' wants and needs.

Environmental scanning and retail research help a retailer develop financial and merchandise plans as well as helping to generate store looks, customer service plans and other retail executions. Great merchandise planning is essential to the financial health of a retailer, and great plans can only be developed based upon great environmental scanning and great retail research.

Introduction

Once retailers have established their financial plans, they have an idea of how much money is available to spend and where the monetary resources should be spent. As stated previously the financial management concepts are directly related to merchandise management due to the overlap in both areas. In this chapter we look at the development of merchandising systems that allow retailers to fill their shelves with merchandise customers are looking for. In particular, retailers are concerned about generating revenue from each product they carry. In that regard retailers must

know which products to carry. Retailers must know the value of their inventory and which products or services have the greatest profit potential.

In order to understand their inventory, retailers begin by developing merchandising systems. Once the systems are in place the retailer will concentrate on valuing the inventory, finding sources of supply and creating relationships with the various vendors that carry the needed supplies. Let's begin by looking at the merchandising systems.

Source: 06photo/Shutterstock.com

Developing Merchandising Plans

Merchandise consists of the products or services the retailer currently offers, or plans to offer, for sale to customers. *Commercial merchandise* is defined as articles for sale, samples used for soliciting orders, or goods that are not considered personal effects. The *merchandise plan* is a dollar projection of the products needed for a retailer for a given period of time, usually six months. Based on this projection, the retail buyer can determine what to buy within the budget. *Merchandising* refers to activities involved in organizing the display of products or services (Ivanovic and Collin, 1996). In a buying sense, *merchandising* refers to the process of buying and selling goods and services to generate profits from the consumer and business markets. To plan for current and future products and services, the retailer needs a good understanding of the costs involved in merchandising and an idea of what consumers will want in the future. These requirements are key to establishing effective merchandise budgets.

The beginning point for establishing a merchandise plan budget is to set responsibility: Who, specifically, will be responsible for the process? Many retailers use budgeting committees or ask for input from several departments. Some retailers use a *top-down approach*, wherein upper management personnel prepare a budget and then pass it down to their various departments. The budgets are often based upon a department's past performance. The departments are then instructed to try to stay within budget when making merchandise-buying decisions. Other firms elect a *bottom-up approach* to budgeting. In this method, each retail department manager supplies data for the budget; these budgets are then scrutinized and passed on to the next level, until the budgets for all departments get aggregated to form the store's overall or master budget. It is possible to combine the bottom-up and top-down approaches to ensure adequate input from the retailer's employees, yet leaving the final decision making to the financial merchandise expert. Figure 9.1 illustrates the differences between the two approaches. Components of merchandise plans include forecasting sales and stock planning. A strong merchandise plan will help the retailer maximize profits and increase turnover of merchandise by delivering customers products they want, when they want them.

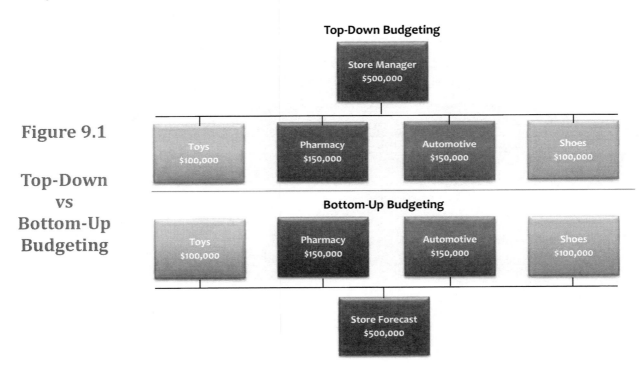

Figure 9.1

Top-Down vs Bottom-Up Budgeting

Merchandise Buying and Handling

Merchandise buying and handling includes the physical purchase of products and services and how those products and services are brought to the retail outlet, handled, and finally placed ready for sale. The merchandise buying and handling process is vital and must complement the strategic focus of the firm. When merchandising decisions are inconsistent with strategy, it can damage the retailer's image and confuse customers. The decisions made in buying are significant because they help determine the consumer's perception of the retailer. Consequently, many retailers employ specialists who purchase products and services for the retail organization.

The *buyer* for a retailer organization is charged with purchasing merchandise for the company. The buyer will attempt to get the best products at the lowest cost. Although this description sounds simple, the job is very demanding and complex. While there is the excitement of travelling to many places to find the newest styles, much of the buyer's job is spent on the financial calculations involved in merchandise forecasting and planning.

Advances in technology, rapid changes in consumers' wants, needs, and desires, and new retail channels have made the buying process far more sophisticated than it was even ten years ago. Integration and consistency of merchandise across locations are also paramount. Therefore the buyer's job can be fun but very stressful. Imagine being responsible for a budget of several million dollars and making a mistake! A buyer's specific responsibilities will depend of the type of retailer, but in general the job entails understanding customers, competition, and attempting to forecast trends to determine what type of merchandise decisions to make. According to the Occupational Outlook Handbook (2016), the average median pay in 2015 was $59,620/year ($28.66/hour). There were 443,200 jobs in 2014 for buyers and purchasing agents, and employment is expected to increase two percent through the year 2024. Table 9.1 shows employment projections.

Developing a winning merchandise mix is exciting. It's very satisfying to guess the next fad---and be right. Unfortunately, retail buyers sometimes make wrong guesses, resulting in excess, slow-moving stock. To ensure greater accuracy in retail merchandise planning, the astute retail buyer develops a good understanding of the concepts and methods necessary to create "great buys," as well as knowledge of customers' current and future wants and needs.

Table 9.1
Employment Projections Data for Buyers and Purchasing Agents, 2014-24

Occupational Title	SOC Code	Employment, 2014	Projected Employment, 2024	Change, 2014-24	
				Percent	Numeric
Buyers and purchasing agents	13-1020	443,200	450,300	2	7,200
Buyers and purchasing agents, farm products	13-1021	12,900	13,500	5	600
Wholesale and retail buyers, except farm products	13-1022	129,500	137,500	6	8,100
Purchasing agents, except wholesale, retail, and farm products	13-1023	300,800	299,300	0	-1,500
Bureau of Labor Statistics, U.S. Department of Labor, *Occupational Outlook Handbook, 2016-17 Edition,* Buyers and Purchasing Agents, on the Internet at https://www.bls.gov/ooh/business-and-financial/buyers-and-purchasing-agents.htm					

It is essential that the buyer understand the type of retailer for which he or she is buying. For example, buying for a consumer electronics chain such as Best Buy involves different buying decision criteria from those for an independent, one-store retailer. In addition, the buyer needs to understand the industry in which the retailer competes. For example, a department store and a food retailer require different merchandise mixes. Similarly, buying for a brick and mortar retailer differs considerably from buying for a non-site retailer such as an e-tailer, a catalog retailer, or a home shopping network. Finally, the buyer must be familiar with the dollar volumes for a particular market. Most buyers have at least some duties and responsibilities in common, but the types of merchandise being purchased will influence the buying methods used.

A buyer will usually report to a merchandise manager. These managers plan and coordinate activities involving merchandise buying and handling. They oversee the overall budget and allocate resources to buyers. Merchandise planning and forecasting merges quantitative analysis with qualitative assessment, making the process a science as well as an art. The marriage of quantitative assessment and intuition has been coined "rocket science retailing" (Fisher et al., 2000). The merchandise manager is responsible for decisions concerning the merchandise assortment. Assortment decisions can include styles, price points, quantity, quality, variety, and sizes.

Inventory Planning

It is important to plan for various levels of inventory that will need to be stocked during any given sales period. Too much stock costs the retailer valuable space and ties up capital. Too little stock may cause the retailer to run out of products that customers want, resulting in lost sales and

Source: Pixza Studio/Shutterstock.com

unhappy customers. The buying function should be performed by individuals with a good knowledge of the retail outlet. For small retailers, the function may be performed by the owner or manager, who might also make pricing decisions. Large firms often have buying centers or purchasing agents.

Most retailers utilize beginning-of-month (BOM) and end-of-month (EOM) inventory figures to evaluate their stock conditions. These numbers provide a method to effectively assess inventory turnover rates. The most commonly used techniques in planning inventory levels are the basic stock method, the percentage variation method, the stock-to-sales method, and the weeks' supply method. To help with inventory planning, the open-to-buy is calculated. The *open-to-buy* is the amount the buyer has left to spend for a given time period, typically a month. Each time a purchase is made, the open-to-buy amount decreases.

Basic Stock Method

The *basic stock method* is used to help estimate required inventory levels. It is very useful to the retail merchandise planner. The basic stock method involves calculating inventory levels *after* the retailer has developed a viable sales forecast. The inventory levels must match the sales forecast, allowing for potential changes in the environment that might create inaccuracies in the forecast.

Remember, the only constant in the universe is change; in other words, no sales forecast will be 100 percent accurate. The astute retail buyer understands this and builds a "fudge factor," or a small amount of additional inventory, into orders for merchandise. The basic stock method was developed to allow the retailer to include a few more items (called *basic stock*) than were forecasted in the order for a given period of time. This method provides a cushion should the merchandise shipments be delayed for any reason (labor strikes, weather conditions, lost orders, etc.).

The basic stock method is best for retailers who have a somewhat low inventory turnover or who experience erratic sales over the specified sales periods.

Using the basic stock method, stock levels are estimated as follows:

Basic stock (at retail) =

Average monthly stock for the sales period (at retail) - Average monthly sales for the sales period

Average monthly sales for the sales period are calculated as follows:

Average monthly sales for the sales period =
Total planned sales for the sales period/Number of months in the sales period

Average monthly stock for the sales period is computed as follows:

Average monthly stock for the sales period =
Total planned sales for the sales period/Inventory turnover for the sales period (estimated)

From this result, the amount of beginning-of-month (BOM) stock is calculated using the following formula:

BOM stock (at retail) = Planned sales (monthly) + Basic stock

Thus, the BOM stock is simply the planned, or forecasted, sales for the month added to the basic stock amount.

As an example, assume Weston Wire Service has forecasted its sales to be $95,000 per month. Owner Jim Weston would like to have at least 5 percent more stock on hand because of historical fluctuations in sales. Weston's largest sales usually occur during the month of July, and he is projecting sales of $108,000 for July of this year. How much stock should he plan to have for the beginning of the month of July? Here is the calculation:

Weston's basic stock (at retail) = ($95,000 x 1.05) - $95,000 = $4,750

Weston multiplies $95,000 by 1.05 because he wants an extra 5 percent of stock on hand. Thus, Weston wants the total amount (or 1), plus the additional "fudge factor" stock (.05). Using the result from the basic stock formula, Weston calculates the BOM stock level for July as follows:

Weston's beginning-of-July level = $108,000 + 4,750 = $112,750

Note that these are dollar amounts that should be spent on inventory, not units that are needed in the store.

Percentage Variation Method (PVM)

Perhaps the retailer has stable inventory turnover rather than erratic turnover. Or maybe the retailer has a somewhat high inventory turnover rate---as a rule of thumb, more than six times per year. The *percentage variation method* reduces the BOM stock for retailers with annual inventory turns greater than 6. If the turnover rate is 6 or less, the basic stock and percentage variation methods will yield approximately the same results. The percentage variation method also assumes that stock percentage fluctuations each month will be no greater than one-half of the average stock on hand. The percentage variation method (PVM) uses the following formula:

BOM stock (at retail) =

Average stock for the sales period (at retail) x 1/2 [1 + (Planned monthly sales/Average monthly sales)]

Remember that the planned monthly sales and the average monthly sales are estimates of the population parameters. Therefore, these methods should only be used as guidelines in inventory planning.

Suppose Weston Wire Service wants to have at least $95,000 worth of stock per month, on average. Jim Weston estimates his sales for the month of July to be about 2 percent under the average of $91,000 per month. What would Weston's planned inventory level be for July?

BOM July inventory level (at retail) = $95,000 x 1/2 [1 + ($89,180/91,000)] = $94,050

Because planned monthly sales were expected to be 2 percent less than usual for the month of July, the planned monthly sales would be 1 - .02 = .98, and .98 x 91,000 = $89,180.

Stock-to-Sales Method

The *stock-to-sales method* helps retailers establish costs for their inventories; it is a good tool for retailers who want to maintain a level of inventory that correlates directly to sales. The investment in inventory is measured at cost rather than at retail. To assess the return on the investment in inventory, the retailer can use the *stock-to-sales ratio*, calculated as follows:

Stock-to-sales ratio = Value of stock/Actual sales

For example, if a retailer had inventory stock valued at $50,000 at the beginning of the month and sales were $44,000, the stock-to-sales ratio would be (50,000/44,000), or 1.136. This 1.136 value suggests that for each dollar of product sold, there should be approximately $1.136 worth of products in stock. Thus, an inventory investment of $1.136 for every dollar of sales is needed.

This ratio gives the retailer an idea of how much inventory is needed at the beginning of the month to support the month's sales. A retailer that knows what the stock-to-sales ratio is for the store, or even for a given department, can multiply planned sales by the stock-to-sales ratio and calculate the BOM stock budget. The formula for calculating the BOM stock figure is as follows:

BOM stock = Stock-to-sales ratio x Planned sales

If a retailer knows the stock-to-sales ratio is 1.136 and plans for $50,000 in sales, BOM stock will equal 1.136 x 50,000, or $56,800. Thus, the retailer needs $56,800 in beginning-of-month merchandise.

Utilizing this calculation, the stock-to-sales ratio allows the retailer to maintain a required ratio of goods or services on hand to sales. The ratio is used in the stock-to-sales method to tell the retailer how much product is needed at the beginning of the month to achieve that month's sales forecast. For example, a stock-to-sales ratio of 1.5 indicates that the beginning of month inventory should be one and one-half times that month's expected sales. The retailer should be able to retrieve the data for the ratio from the retail information system (RIS). If a good RIS is unavailable, the retailer can get average ratio data from external sources, such as trade associations, or may want to use a different ratio for comparison. Sources of external information are suggested at the end of this section.

Suppose Weston Wire Service has developed a stock-to-sales ratio of 1.15. This means Weston must have $109,250 worth of inventory for the month of July to have planned sales (at retail) of $95,000 (1.15 x 95,000). A stock-to-sales ratio of 1.5 would require $142,500 in inventory (1.5 x 95,000).

The major problem with the stock-to-sales ratio is that it attempts to adjust the retailer's inventory to a greater extent than the retailer's sales may require. This may cause too much fluctuation in inventory levels. In other words, in the months in which sales increase, inventory levels also increase, but at a slower rate than sales, and the stock-to-sales ratio decreases. In months with large sales decreases, inventory levels also decrease, but at a slower rate than sales, causing the stock-to-sales ratio to increase. This disadvantage can be overcome if the retailer uses subjective judgments during times of large sales increases or decreases. In addition, the retailer should make the adjustments when major, unforecasted changes occur in the retail environment. For example, after the debut of "Finding Nemo," the Disney/Pixar Studios animated movie about fish, aquariums throughout the country were inundated with requests for clown fish. Sales of clown fish were as high as 10 to 15 percent over average. Sales of other aquarium fish also increased significantly. Although some aquarium retailers anticipated the fad, many were caught off-guard and experienced inventory shortages (Salisbury, 2003).

The advantage of the stock-to-sales ratio is that the retailer can generate comparison data from external sources, such as the publication from the National Retail Federation, *Merchandising and Operating Results of Retail Stores.*

Weeks' Supply Method

Many supermarkets and other food marketers utilize the *weeks' supply method* of inventory planning because these businesses have a relatively fast turnaround on their inventory and consequently plan inventory levels more frequently than other types of retailers. Many supermarket managers, such as the produce manager, plan sales on a weekly basis rather than monthly, quarterly, or yearly. In addition, sales levels at a supermarket do not fluctuate nearly as much as

Source: Sorbis/Shutterstock.com

they do at other retail outlets. Thus, with the weeks' supply method, the retail merchandise planner needs to estimate how many weeks' supply of merchandise is needed. The inventory level is then set to equal that amount. The weeks' supply is directly correlated with the inventory turnover. The method assumes the retailer's inventory is in direct proportion to sales. The sales estimates are usually generated from previous months' sales. The weeks' supply of inventory is calculated as follows:

BOM (at retail) planned inventory =
Average weekly sales (estimated) x Number of weeks to be stocked

Assume Weston Wire Service has forecasted weekly sales to average $25,000 for the last quarter of the year (October 1 to December 31, for a total of 13 weeks). How much inventory does Weston need to have on hand at the beginning of this period?

BOM stock = $25,000 x 13 = $325,000 (at retail)

Thus, Weston needs to have $325,000 (at retail) in beginning inventory for the quarter.

If the retail buyer is looking for additional information on the number of weeks to be stocked and the average weekly sales, the following calculations can be used:

Number of weeks to be stocked =
Number of weeks in sales period/Stock turnover rate (for sales period)

Average weekly sales estimate =
Estimated total sales (for sales period)/Number of weeks in sales period

By performing these calculations prior to calculating the BOM stock for the weeks' supply method, the retailer can keep track of where the numbers are coming from and use them for other ratio calculations.

Open-to-Buy

As explained earlier in this chapter, open-to-buy is the amount the buyer has left to spend for a given time period, typically a month. Open-to-buy planning helps the retailer keep track of how much money has been expended on inventory for any given period, plus the amount of inventory on hand. In some instances unplanned purchases may come up and the buyer must check open-to-buy records to make sure there is money left in the budget for those purchases. Reasons for unplanned purchases include the introduction of new products into the market and opportunities to buy at substantial discounts, such as when a supplier is trying to move merchandise to clear its warehouses for new shipments.

The retailer must have resources left in the budget to take advantage of sales and markdowns by suppliers. To calculate open-to-buy, the retailer simply takes the planned purchases and subtracts out any commitments to purchase products (already committed orders):

Open-to-buy (at retail) = Planned purchases - Purchase commitments

Weston Wire Service has the following situation:

Inventory needed for July:	
EOM inventory	$20,000
Estimated sales	5,000
Markdowns (planned)	500
Needed merchandise	**$25,500**
Available inventory:	
BOM	$10,000
Purchase commitments	5,000
Available merchandise	**$15,000**
Open-to-buy	**$10,500**

Weston has an additional $10,500 in the budget to allow him to take advantage of new styles, new products, supplier sales, and so on.

A retailer can determine its open-to-buy on any day of any year by accessing the RIS, whether computerized or manual (assuming the open-to-buy system has been placed in the RIS). Numerous software packages are available to help both small and large retailers calculate open-to-buy.

The inventory planning methods presented so far cover the retail plan from a cost perspective (because that basis really defines the amount of investment in inventory). Keep in mind, however, that the retailer puts units, not costs, on the shelves. At some point, the retailer needs to convert those all-important dollar values into units to get a bigger picture of what is and is not moving. Products, not dollars, are stocked and sold.

Most staple merchandise that retailers stock does not immediately lose its value. However, for products such as apparel, sporting goods, and fad items, the season will end and the fad will dissipate, and markdowns on this merchandise will be necessary to clear them from the selling floor. Methods of discounting merchandise to ensure it is cleared prior to acquiring new supplies of inventory are discussed later in the chapter.

Inventory must match the needs of the retailer's target market. Thus, the retailer needs to consider several factors when developing the merchandise mix, the subject of the next section.

The Merchandise Mix

The merchandise manager looks for a number of things when purchasing inventory for the store. Merchandise *assortment* is the collection of products a retailer carries.   These include the variety and quality of merchandise and the merchandise price points, which in combination are referred to as the *merchandise mix.* The overall key to effective merchandise planning is to ensure

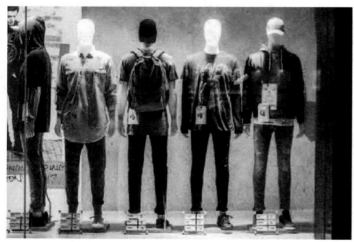

that the merchandise mix meets or exceeds the needs and wants of the retailer's market. Once again, the retailer should access the situation analysis and target market data to verify that the merchandise is indeed a good fit for the targeted customers.

Merchandise mix decisions are important because of the costs involved. When a retailer carries many categories and SKUs, carrying costs increase because the retailer must have enough stock on hand as well as back-up stock for each SKU.   The target market's needs must also be a consideration when determining the merchandise mix.

Source: Creative Lab/Shutterstock.com

Breadth

The number of *product lines* (or categories) the retailer offers is referred to as the *breadth.* For example, shoe retailers need to decide whether to carry just athletic shoes, work shoes, and boots or to offer a wider variety of products including dress shoes. Breadth can also refer to the number of brands carried within a product line. An athletic shoe retailer may decide to carry Asics, New Balance, Z-Coil, Saucony, Brooks, Adidas and Mizuno.

Breadth is often described along a continuum of narrow or broad. A store that offers twenty categories of shoes may be said to have broad assortment (breadth). In contrast, a store that offers only one category may be said to offer a narrow assortment (breadth).

The merchandise variety must be consistent with the retailer's mission and vision, and should be developed with the retailer's objectives in mind. The customer will make a number of decisions about the retailer based on the merchandise mix.

Depth

Depth consists of the stock keeping units (SKUs) or variety within a category (this could include colors, styles and sizes that the retailer stocks within each line it carries). Depth is often described along a continuum of shallow to deep. They also must decide whether to carry a limited assortment of shoe accessories or a full line of shoe accessories

Merchandise depth is directly related to quality, assortment, and variety of merchandise offered. To monitor merchandise depth, retailers use stock keeping units, or SKUs, to determine the average quantity of merchandise carried for each of the various brands sold in their stores. SKU (pronounced a letter at a time or as one word) is the smallest unit of measure used to inventory products. SKUs are established by the retailer and are typically an alpha-numeric combination. For example, a shirt of a particular style and color could have an SKU of 091766-B, meaning "style number 091766, in blue". An SKU tells the retailer exactly what product is in inventory. The SKU may or may not be visible to the customer.

The retailer must let the buyer know the assortment policy so that the buyer can develop a merchandise mix that is in line with the retailer's mission, vision, and objectives.

Figure 9.2 shows the relationship between breadth and depth. By cross-classifying breadth (narrow or broad) by the depth (shallow or deep), a two-by-two dimensional matrix is formed, as depicted in the figure. The four cells in the matrix may be described as follows:

1. Deep and narrow: many types of goods in one or a few product lines. Examples: category killers (*e.g.*, Office Depot, PetSmart).

2. Shallow and narrow: few types of goods in one or few product lines. Examples: specialty stores (*e.g.*, Rocky Mountain Chocolate Factory, Kaufman's Tall and Big Men's Shop).

3. Deep and broad: many types of goods in each of many different product lines. Examples: department stores (*e.g.*, JC Penney, Macy's).

4. Shallow and broad: few types of goods in each of several different product lines. Example: discount stores (*e.g.*, Wal-Mart, Target).

Figure 9.2   The Merchandise Mix: Variety and Assortment

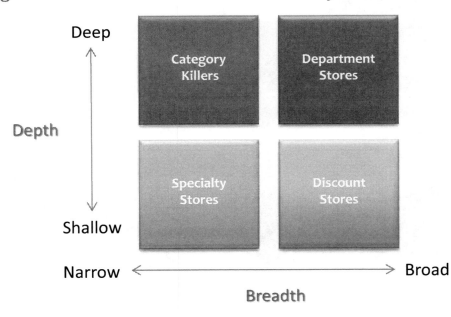

Each individual brand can have its own level of depth. For example, consider a shoe retailer that carries Z-Coil pain relief footwear (www.zcoilcom). For each brand of Z-Coil (such as Freedom 2000, the Cloudwalker, and the Desert Hiker), the retailer must decide which sizes, or depth of offering, to include. Many retailers carry only the most popular sizes and colors of Z-Coils so they can have faster inventory turnover (shallow assortment). Other retailers that focus on customer service may carry the whole depth (deep assortment) of sizes and colors so that all customers will be able to find a particular brand of Z-Coil shoe in their size and preferred color. Figure 9.3 shows how stores vary in terms of breadth and depth.

Figure 9.3   Example of Breadth and Depth

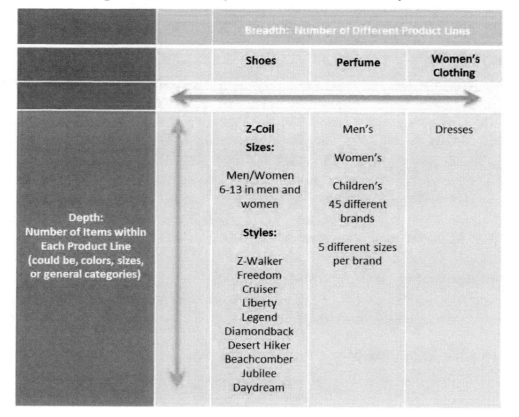

All retailers face trade-off decisions regarding assortment and variety. Some like specialty online retailer, Z-Coil (www.z.coil.com) will decide to carry one brand with much depth within the brand. Others like Macy's will carry a number of different categories with a broad assortment within each category.

Private vs. National Brands

One problem retailers face when developing their merchandise assortment is achieving an appropriate balance between their brands (private labels) and the national assortment of products (national brands). This balance is important because the retailer has to allocate shelf space for each of these products. National brands generally have a smaller profit margin for the retailer but are supported with national advertising and IMC from the supplier. Thus, there is consumer demand for these products. In contrast, private labels provide higher margins---an advantage to the retailer---but carrying them also requires associated additional costs and tasks, such as communicating the brands to consumers and developing consumer brand loyalty to the private labels.

According to the Private Label Manufacturers Association (PLMA, 2017), store brands, account for over $150 billion in sales/year. JCPenney is an example of a retailer that carries both private brands and national brands. Its private brands include Arizona Jeans, Hunt Club, Stafford, and St. John's Bay. National brands include Levi Strauss's Dockers, Adidas, Lee, and Ocean Pacific.

One of the ways to control retail price is to carry private label brands. The trendy small grocery chain Trader Joe's has done just that. Trader Joe's is based in Monrovia, California and they opened their first retail store in 1967. Since that time, Trader Joe's has grown to a chain of more than 461 stores. Trader Joe's has relatively small stores with a small width of product lines. Although a typical grocery store will carry at least 50,000 SKUs (stock-keeping units), Trader Joe's has about 4,000. The vast majority of the SKUs are private brands (usually about eighty percent of the SKUs). This gives Trader Joe's an advantage when it comes to setting price. Since they don't carry a lot of national brands, there are limited price comparisons going on in a Trader Joe's store. Trader Joe's can maintain a trendy image, while at the same time providing their customer base with lower than market prices for items the consumer's want and need (Kowitt, 2010).

Source: Roman Tiraspolsky/Shutterstock.com

Quality

Suppliers of merchandise provide varying levels of quality in their merchandise assortments. Therefore, retailers must decide what level of quality they want when purchasing inventory. A consumer shopping at an electronics store, for example, may find television sets priced hundreds or even thousands of dollars apart, based on product quality.

Consumers have developed firm attitudes and opinions regarding the quality of products. Thus, the retailer needs to be clear about what its consumers want from a product (long life, low price, and so on) and to offer the appropriate merchandise mix of high-quality and/or lower-quality products.

Once again the retailer should look to the retail mission and vision to determine what to offer the consumer in terms of quality. The merchandise quality should be consistent with all other messages communicated to the consumer about the retail operation. A retailer that is located in an upscale area, uses high-quality communication vehicles, and offers an elegant shopping atmosphere complete with top-notch customer service should carry only high-quality merchandise. Conversely, a discount retailer's customers look primarily for value for their dollars. Therefore, the discount retailer should concentrate on merchandise that can be offered at a lower price. As a result, the overall merchandise mix should contain lower-quality products.

Price Points

Price points are another consideration when selecting merchandise assortments. (Pricing is covered in detail in Chapter 11.) *Price points* are the range of prices for a particular merchandise line. Price points help attract the retailer's target market into the store. Retailers must decide if they want to have market-average, above-average, or below-average price points for the products they offer. Price points generally have a fairly wide range. For example, the price points for the various types of Z-Coils may run from $199 to $359. The benefit of establishing price points early in the merchandise mix development process is that it helps the retailer select the market for the product. Consumers who are not interested in expensive, high-quality shoes will probably not be attracted to a shoe store that markets Z-Coils.

Other Variables That Affect the Merchandise Mix

In creating the merchandise mix, a number of other variables have an impact on merchandise purchases. These variables can hinder the retailer's ability to achieve merchandise mix goals and objectives. The main variables are budget constraints, space limitations, product turnover, and stock replenishment.

Budget Constraints: One problem encountered by many firms is that the retail buyer is constrained by the amount of money available to make purchases. In an ideal world, buyers are able to purchase anything and everything they desire, provided a customer need for those products exists. In the real world, the retailer's budget may not be large enough to generate the price points, variety, assortment, quality, and depth of product the buyer would desire. The retail buyer must make the best decisions possible given a limited budget.

Space Limitations: Another problem is that the retailer's selling venue (store, catalog, etc.) has inherent space limitations. Thus, the retailer has to decide which products will most appeal to consumers and at the same time return a good investment to the owners of the retail outlet.

In an e-tailing environment, there is also limited space to display products. Therefore, the e-tailer has to determine which types of merchandise to feature given the limited amount of web store selling space. In addition, e-tailers, like traditional retailers, cannot inventory all the products available for sale. However, the e-tailer has the advantage of being able to quickly place their customers' orders with its suppliers, thus avoiding the need to stock all the items offered for sale.

Product Turnover Rates: Closely related to the problems of budget and storage limitations are product turnover rates. In general, the more variety of merchandise (greater breadth) and the deeper the assortment (greater depth), the lower the inventory turnover rates. Although some products turn over faster than others, many retailers need to carry a lot of depth to ensure customer satisfaction. In addition, carrying too few units of a product may lead to a stockout situation. Substitution is the willingness of a customer to buy another similar product within a category if the one wanted is not available. If customers are more likely to substitute in a product category then providing depth is not as important. On the other hand if a customer is product or brand insistent then it is important to provide more SKUs so the customer does not go to a different retailer (Kök, Fisher, and Vaidyanathan, 2006).

Department stores typically buy only a few units of an item in XS (extra small) and XXL (extra, extra large) sizes and buy the bulk in the most popular sizes (medium and large). Because of this, department stores may experience stockouts on the less popular sizes. The lack of variety in these sizes creates a niche position for retailers specializing in small sizes as well as those specializing in larger sizes. The Petite Shop (www.thepetiteshop.com) caters to women requiring smaller clothing whereas Lane Bryant (www.lanebryant.com) and Avenue (www.avenue.com) focus on women who need larger size clothing.

Stock Replenishment: Finally, the retailer needs to know when the various levels of stock for the stores must be replenished. By establishing these stock levels, the retailer will know when to reorder the various products. Reorder points are calculated using software specifically developed for that purpose. The POS system scans the product data and, when it detects that inventory levels are becoming depleted, triggers the main database to ship more merchandise. However, the retailer has to input these levels into the computer. To get accurate information on the reorder point, the retailer needs to know the order lead time, the product usage rate, and the amount of safety stock required within the retail unit.

Source: Kheng Guan Toh/Shutterstock.com

When a retailer places an order for merchandise, a certain span of time is required for the order to be fulfilled. The order has to be sent to the supplier. The supplier then develops a payment plan and fills the order through its warehouse. In addition, the supplier has to transport the load to the retailer. This time span between placement and fulfillment of the order is the *order lead time.*

The product's *usage rate* is the average sales per day of the specific product in units, *not* in dollars. To avoid an out-of-stock situation, the retailer needs to build in some additional stock in case the merchandise shipment is damaged or lost or some other emergency occurs. This additional stock is known as *safety stock.* The retailer should establish a customer service level that will help determine how much safety stock to keep on hand. If the retailer is customer focused and aims to have merchandise available for sale at all times, the service level will be high. However, as mentioned earlier, the cost of carrying merchandise can be high, and carrying high levels of safety stock can be even more costly. Apple Computer builds in safety stock when forecasting inventory levels. It is important to reassess optimal stock levels on a frequent basis. Calculating safety stock once a year instead of several times a year is a common mistake. More frequent calculations help maintain more efficient stock levels.

The following formula shows how to calculate the required reorder time, or point, for merchandise:

Reorder point = (Usage rate x Lead time) + Safety stock

Economic Order Quantity

Equally important is the determination of how much merchandise to reorder. This concept is called the *economic order quantity (EOQ).* Deciding on the amount of merchandise to reorder will influence the decision on when to reorder. Remember that the larger the order, the lower the unit costs for the merchandise. Also, the cost of stocking the products---inventory costs---will be higher with larger shipments of merchandise.

The retailer wants to minimize the costs of ordering and carrying inventory. The EOQ is derived by finding the lowest point on the total inventory cost curve. A retailer's economic order quantity is determined by four variables: demand for the product, the costs associated with order placement, the percentage of carrying costs to unit costs, and the unit cost of an individual item. The formula to determine EOQ is as follows:

$$EOQ = \sqrt{\dfrac{2DS}{IC}}$$

where

D = Annual demand for the products (in units)

S = costs to place the order (not including the merchandise cost)

I = percentage of carrying costs to unit costs (annually)

C = unit cost of an item

Suppose Weston Wire Service needs to order watches for sale in its stores. Jim Weston has estimated that the company will sell 1,000 watches per year, and the per-unit cost of the watches is $100. Weston has accessed the RIS and found that the cost of carrying the watches (including insurance, warehousing, sales space, and shoplifting) is 35 percent. Every time Weston places an order, it costs the company $2, mostly for time. Thus, Weston wants to estimate the EOQ and calculates it as follows:

$$EOQ = \sqrt{\dfrac{2(1,000)(\$2)}{(.35)(\$100)}} = \sqrt{\$4,000 / \$35} = \sqrt{\$114.28} = 10.69$$

Weston Wire Service needs to order 10.69 units every time it places an order for the watches. Because watches are not fractional---that is, you cannot order 1/69 of a watch---Weston would use an EOQ of 11 watches. By ordering 11 watches at a time, Weston will order 91 times per year (1,000/11), or approximately every four days (365/91).

Merchandise Forecasting

Armed with an understanding of accounting systems and legal and ethical issues, retailers are prepared for the ambitious task of merchandise allocation. This section discusses the various methods used in budgeting for merchandise and forecasting the right amounts to purchase. The process of visual merchandising is one of integrated marketing communication and is covered more fully in Chapter 10.

To effectively utilize the budgeting process, the retailer needs a comprehensive financial merchandise plan that includes a section on performance objectives for finance personnel. In addition, the retailer needs to know which products are to be purchased and in what quantities (forecasting). Many retailers establish plans that allow them to see both the physical product purchases and the dollars spent on those purchases. Although these concepts are covered briefly in the next chapter, the data generated at this point can ease the process of merchan-

Source; ZullU InFocus/Shutterstock.com

dise buying. Inventory valuation, discussed in the next section, should be integrated into the merchandise budgeting process.

Budgets

Budgets can be prepared for any length of time. For short-term planning budgets are typically prepared for six months to one year. Many retailers, however, generate budgets on a monthly, quarterly, seasonal, or every-four-week basis. Some retailers prepare budgets on a rolling basis, meaning that if a retailer is budgeting on a four-week basis, another week is added to the budget as one week of the budget period expires. In this way, the budget always includes four weeks.

Although not common, budgets can be prepared for four-month and six-month periods. The time period is left to the discretion of the retailer and the company's financial analysts. Retailers often have to purchase inventory six to twelve months in advance, so an inventory plan may be completed well in advance of receipt and stocking of the inventory merchandise.

The retailer needs to determine a timeline for putting the budget into effect. Unfortunately, many retailers must order merchandise three to six months, or even a year, before the goods are received and ready for sale. Therefore, a six-month or one-year budget may be necessary. Even if the budget is for six months or a year, the retailer may want to break it into monthly or even weekly components due to the constantly changing retail environment. In this way, the accuracy of the budget can be determined by comparing the weekly or monthly budgeted amounts to the actual amounts. This approach allows the retailer to either change the product mix, purchase more products that are moving quickly, drop products that are not moving, reduce the price of slow-moving merchandise, or increase the price of fast-selling merchandise, to name but a few strategies. Whatever the reaction to the budget, developing a budget gives the retailer a method of control and evaluation on an ongoing basis. Therefore, a key to effective budgeting is flexibility.

Numerous methods have been developed for merchandise budgeting. Most of the methods have common inputs, or variables, that are essential to the retailer and financial planner. The following elements are generally included in the budgeting process:

- Planned monthly sales
- Planned beginning-of-month (BOM) stock
- Monthly retail reductions
- Planned end-of-month (EOM) stock
- Planned purchases for the month at retail price
- Planned purchases for the month at cost
- Initial markup for the month
- Planned gross margin for the month

Forecasting

To develop a budget, the retailer must forecast planned sales. Sales should be estimated for the entire budget period, but also on a weekly or monthly basis. There are numerous methods for inventory forecasting. The easiest is to look at the past year's performance. Another method is to examine the average of the last two years, the last five years, and so on. This is a good method as long as ad-

Source: Blend Images/Shutterstock.com

justments are made for changes in the environment that could affect the purchases and forecasts, such as inflation, marketing changes, and the economy.

A forecast should include as many external variables as possible. These variables might include changes in the population mix for a particular retail market, changes in the economy of that market, and changes in any of the environments identified in the situational analysis. Larger firms use computer models (programs) that combine environmental inputs with past sales data. Small firms use a more informal approach, but still take new industries, population changes, and similar factors into account when deciding how much to purchase.

The next step is to assess planned beginning- and end-of-month stock. Because of changes in demand for products, retailers generally carry safety stock. An excellent method of determining beginning-of-month (BOM) and end-of-month (EOM) stock balances is to calculate a stock-to-sales ratio. A *stock-to-sales ratio* allows a comparison of stock levels to levels of sales. In other words, the ratio indicates how much stock is needed during a given sales period – say, one month – to prevent a stock shortage. This ratio supports the retailer's forecast. A good way to assess BOM and EOM inventory levels is through the use of point-of-sale (POS) databases. In addition, training and practice helps in the execution of this task.

Source: pathdoc/Shutterstock.com

You may recall that carrying inventory costs the retailer in two ways. First, the inventory takes up valuable selling space and capital (carrying cost of inventory). Second, slow-moving or non-selling merchandise occupies space that could be given to more current or faster-moving products. Walgreens is an example of a company that used technology to decrease inventory costs. The drugstore chain improved its strategic inventory management system and thereby cut safety stock and cycle times in its warehouses and stores from 53 days in 2002 to 44 days in 2003. As a result, inventory carrying costs were reduced by $1.5 billion over three years (2003–2006). The retailer needs to plan for any retail reductions that may occur during the budget period. As stated earlier, retail reductions are any stock shortages, markdowns, or employee discounts that accrued during the budget forecast period. Next, purchases must be planned at the selling price and at cost amounts. Finally, the gross margin needs to be added, allowing the retailer to generate profits.

To acquire the data necessary to create a budget, the retailer needs to understand the system of inventory valuation used by the company's accountants. The next section takes a close look at methods used to determine inventory value and the advantages and disadvantages of each of the methods.

Return on Inventory Investment and Stock Turnover

Inventory represents a large investment for retailers. Therefore, retailers want to know what kind of return they are getting from their merchandise. To do this, retailing professionals have developed a method to assess the return on investment (ROI) from inventory investment. This method is called the *gross margin return on inventory (GMROI).* The GMROI is particularly helpful to retailers because it brings together the concepts of other performance measures such as return on assets, asset turnover, profits, and sales. The formula used to calculate GMROI (see Table 9.2) shows how these performance measures are incorporated into the calculation.

Table 9.2 Gross Margin Return on Inventory Calculation

GMROI = Gross margin percentage × Stock-to-sales ratio

    Gross margin percentage = Gross margin (in dollars)/Net sales

    Stock-to-sales ratio = Net sales/Average inventory (at cost)

Thus,

GMROI = Gross margin/Average inventory (at cost)

The gross margin percentage provides an idea of how much investment is being returned for each type of merchandise purchased. The retailer can compare and contrast the figures with those of competitors, the retailer's historic margins, and the industry averages. A GMROI of $3.25 means that $1 investment in inventory generated a return of $3.25. To see how effectively their investments in inventory are performing, retailers utilize inventory turnover formulas.

Inventory Turnover

Inventory is typically a retailer's largest asset. To measure the productivity of the merchandise being purchased, retailers use a concept known as *inventory turnover,* a measure of how many times a store sells its average investment in inventory during a year. The faster the merchandise turns over---that is, is bought, marked, stocked, and sold---the more money is generated for the retail outlet. It is important to know how to measure inventory turnover, because this shows how quickly each product is moving. For example, an inventory turnover ratio of 8 means that a retailer sells and replaces its inventory 8 times in a given period, typically a year.

There are two basic ways to calculate inventory turnover:

Inventory turnover = Net sales (at retail)/Average inventory (at retail)

and

Inventory turnover = Cost of goods sold (COGS) (at cost)/Average inventory (at cost)

These computations allow the retailer to measure stock productivity. In addition to dollar amounts, the retailer may want to know the inventory turnover in units. This calculation is as follows:

Inventory turnover (in units) = Number of units sold for the year/Average inventory (in units)

Using these formulas the retailer can track, analyze, and compare the turnover rates for its store to competitors' rates. It is also important to know the average amount of inventory being carried. The average inventory is used in numerous formulas to determine merchandise performance. To calculate the average inventory, the retailer first determines the number of months to use for the average inventory period. For example, a music store calculating average inventory for the year's first quarter would use the first three months of inventory. (Note that any number of months up to twelve can be used to calculate the average inventory for a year.) The calculation for the music store example is as follows:

Average inventory = (Month 1 + month 2 + month 3)/3

Thus, if the music store had $25,000 in inventory in month 1, $15,000 in month 2, and $50,000 in month 3, the average inventory would be $30,000.

Smaller retailers use the preceding formula more often than larger ones do. Large retailers can calculate their inventory data point-of-sale terminals.   Advanced POS systems scan and input daily sales figures into a database that the retail manager can access at any time to get an average inventory (on-hand) figure. Thus, the retailer can know its levels of turnover at any point in time. POS systems are excellent tools for developing product assortments and determining amounts of shelf space for products. In addition, POS systems can help retailers track sales and measure the effectiveness of integrated marketing communication (IMC) tactics such as coupons, contests, point-of-purchase promotions, and other in-store activities. They can also help retailers decide which products to feature within stores and flag those products that are underperforming (Shor, 2003). (POS terminals can be linked to other databases to generate interconnected information on demographics, geographics, and psychographics. The generated data are valuable to retail buyers for decisions on order size and customer types. The effective use of a POS system relies on the analytical skills of the retail manager.)

A well-developed POS system can be tied in to many inventory management programs, such as vendor-managed inventory (VMI), quick response (QR), effective customer response (ECR), just-in-time (JIT), and other forms of electronic data interchange.

Cash Conversion Cycle

Financial managers often assert that "cash is king." This is true for all internal business operations and certainly true for retailers. In fact, outside analysts evaluate retailers based on the effectiveness of the retailer's cash management. One method used to evaluate cash management is the cash conversion cycle. The *cash conversion cycle (CCC)* indicates how many days it takes to turn purchases of inventory into cash (see Figure 9.4). Retailing success is tied to a company's ability to manage this cycle (Richards and Laughlin, 1980).   If a retailer does not effectively manage the cash conversion cycle, the firm may find it necessary to borrow money to maintain operations, thus increasing debt and limiting the range of opportunities available to the retailer (Cote and Latham, 1999).

Figure 9.4   The Cash Conversion Cycle

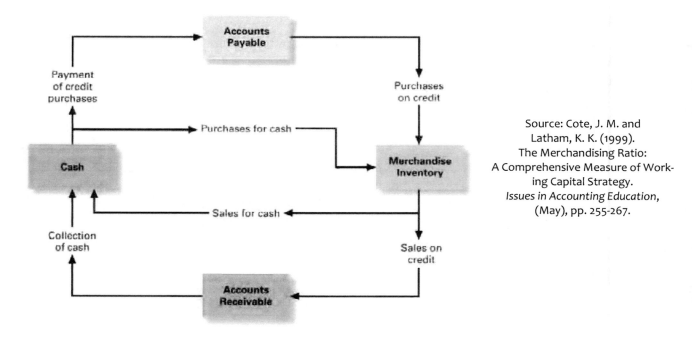

Source: Cote, J. M. and Latham, K. K. (1999). The Merchandising Ratio: A Comprehensive Measure of Working Capital Strategy. *Issues in Accounting Education*, (May), pp. 255-267.

The CCC incorporates accounts receivable, inventories, and accounts payable into a single figure. The smaller this figure, the better the cash management situation. The CCC is calculated by adding days sales outstanding (DSO) to days inventory outstanding (DIO) and subtracting days payables outstanding (DPO):

CCC = DSO + DIO - DPO

where

DSO = Accounts receivable/(Sales/Number of days in cycle)
DIO = Inventory/(Cost of sales/Number of days in cycle)
DPO = Accounts payable /(Cost of sales/Number of days in cycle)

The DSO and DIO should be as low as possible, indicating a fast collection of receivables (the DSO calculation) and a fast inventory turnover (the DIO calculation). The DPO should be as high as possible without damaging the company's credit rating. A high DPO indicates that the retailer is taking advantage of the interest-free loans (*i.e.,* payables) from its suppliers (Weiss, 1999).

The cash conversion cycle is important for merchandise managers because to effectively manage cash, the retailer must turn over inventory as quickly as possible, avoid stockouts that may lead to lost sales, collect accounts receivable quickly, take advantage of cash discounts, and pay accounts payable as late as possible without damaging its credit rating (The Entrepreneur's Guidebook Series, 2011). The last factor requires careful timing: The retailer wants to take advantage of cash discounts usually given for prompt payment, yet make the payments at the latest possible moment.

Table 9.3 shows the CCC for a few retailers (GuruFocus, 2016). Amazon.com has the best cash conversion cycle with -37 days. How does Amazon accomplish a negative cash conversion cycle? Management holds inventory for a period of days. It takes the company a longer time in days to pay their bills to their suppliers resulting in a negative cash conversion cycle. Thus, Amazon collects money from customers before it has to pay its suppliers for inventory. While this is great for the company and stockholders, it's not as great for their suppliers who have to wait for payment from Amazon.com.

Table 9.3   Cash Conversion Cycles for Selected Retailers

Walmart	11 days
Target Corp	11 days
Amazon	-37
Home Depot	38 days

Source GuruFocus (www.gurufocus.com).
Calculations based on Jan 2016, except for Amazon which is Dec 2016

According to John Cravenho (2002), managing director of Excel Consulting, one of the best ways to improve the cash conversion rate is to focus on faster collections of receivables. Some areas to concentrate on are as follows.

· Train team members on the entire cash conversion cycle so they understand how cash flow is maximized and how they play a role in improving the cycle.

· Prioritize the largest receivables outstanding and problem accounts on a daily basis. Be pro-active in contacting these accounts before they fall behind on payments.

· Implement a system to capture communication and track reports that summarize statistics on how quickly receivables are being collected.

· Make sure all parties involved in the cash conversion cycle have shared goals and incentives to improve the conversion rate.

· Eliminate any non-value-added activities.

Inventory Valuation

Retailers use two methods to place a value on their merchandise: inventory valuation based on merchandise costs (the cost method) or inventory valuation based on the merchandise's retail price (the retail method). This section looks at each method in detail.

The Cost Method of Inventory Valuation

Although most large retailers have moved toward the retail method of inventory valuation because of advances in technology, especially off-the-shelf POS systems, many smaller retailers still use the *cost method of inventory valuation.* This method consists of recording the value of the merchandise at cost and adding in the cost of shipping (in-bound freight). The retailer must value each item in the inventory as it is purchased, when it is sold, and whenever the retailer undertakes a physical inventory.

A key to successful cost accounting is to assign a code to each product or product line. The easiest and most common coding method is simply to turn the letters of the alphabet into numbers so that the numbers can be entered into the RIS and accessed when needed. Because the letters are arbitrary, it does not matter which letters are used, as long as there are ten letters representing numbers 0 through 10. For example, if letters A through J are used, A becomes 1, B becomes 2, C becomes 3, and so forth, until J becomes 10. Thus, a product coded DADE would have an associated cost of $41.45. Many firms use ten-letter words such as *Charleston* for coding prices, because the ABC code may be too easy for customers to decipher.

A cost accounting system of valuation works well with both physical and book inventories. Slightly different methods of cost accounting are used, such as periodic or perpetual inventory systems, which are dependent on the retailer's specific needs.

Periodic Inventory System

In a *periodic inventory system,* sales are recorded as they occur, but the inventory is not updated. Therefore, a complete inventory must be taken periodically. Retailers using a periodic inventory system need to calculate sales receipts for the period under study. The merchandise costs are recorded, at cost, for the required time period. Let's assume a skateboard retailer is costing on a monthly basis, so the merchandise, at cost, is recorded monthly. The retailer then calculates all purchase invoices (those purchases that have already been made and billed). The retailer then counts up the merchandise value at the end of the month (EOM) and enters that value. The gross profit can then be calculated, at cost:

Gross profits =
Sales - (BOM merchandise value [at cost] + Purchase invoices)
- EOM merchandise value [at cost]

Keep in mind that with this type of system, the actual gross profits cannot be calculated until after a physical inventory has been performed. Again, many retailers have opted for inventory systems that allow for more frequent, electronic inventories to keep track of their merchandise. Physical inventories are generally undertaken infrequently – such as once or twice a year. Thus, the retailer may be unable to uncover any theft or other shortages until the physical inventory is finished.

Source: Montri Nipitvittaya/Shutterstock.com

Perpetual Inventory System

A perpetual inventory system can give the retailer a fairly accurate idea of the merchandise value on a constant basis. With a *perpetual inventory system* (or *book inventory system*), calculations for shortages can be made without a physical inventory; purchases are added to the books when they are made, and sales are subtracted as soon as they occur. This gives the retailer an idea of the current value of the inventory at cost. When developing a perpetual inventory system, it is important to recognize that there are several ways to account for sales of merchandise, depending on the sophistication of the retailer's accounting system. Because of the affordability of sophisticated POS hardware and software, most large retailers use specific identification in determining the items sold and their inventory value by using a perpetual inventory system. Each time an item is scanned for sale, the information system subtracts it from inventory.

FIFO and LIFO

Less sophisticated retailers might use the FIFO or LIFO method of accounting. The *FIFO* (first in, first out) method assumes that older stock is sold before newer stock; in other words, the first products the retailer receives are the first products to be sold. "First come, first served" is a FIFO method of valuation. For example, when you buy a new gallon of milk and store it in your refrigerator, you place the new gallon behind the already opened gallon (or so you should) so that the older milk is consumed first.

The *LIFO* (last in, first out) method assumes that newer merchandise is sold first; older merchandise stays in inventory or on the shelves until the newer merchandise is gone. Under the LIFO method, current sales are matched with current rather than noncurrent costs. FIFO does the opposite, matching inventory values with costs. If the inventory values are rising, using LIFO can generate tax advantages.

The cost method may be difficult without automated and POS inventory systems. In the case of manual accounting systems, the cost method may favor retailers who have low inventory turnover and high-priced products. These types of retailers have limited merchandise assortments and do not change prices on a daily, or frequent, basis. In addition, a cost system does not allow the retailer to adjust inventory values. The retail value of the inventory may increase or decrease during any given time period, but with a cost system the retailer cannot account for such fluctuations in price. The bottom line is that the retailer may get an inaccurate assessment of what the merchandise is worth. For example, suppose the inventory increases in value, but the retailer has not received an updated estimate of its worth and fails to obtain additional insurance coverage. In the event of a disaster, the retailer may stand to lose a great deal due to being underinsured. What if the inventory value decreases? In this case, the retailer may be paying too much for the merchandise, space, and insurance. To alleviate some of these disadvantages, retailers often use the retail method of inventory valuation.

The Retail Method of Inventory Valuation

Retailers, who wish to value merchandise at current retail values, or prices, use the *retail method of inventory valuation.* This method virtually eliminates the disadvantages associated with the cost system. The retail method of inventory valuation requires a number of interrelated steps because the retailer has to convert from cost to retail price and then convert back again. The steps are as follows.

1. **Calculate the cost complement** (the total value at cost divided by the total value at retail). In retail costing, the values of all merchandise are recorded at both cost and retail value, allowing the retailer to calculate the relationship between the two values. The beginning-of-period (BOP) inventory is shown at cost and at retail. Net purchases (the total purchases the retailer makes, plus freight-in, less purchase discounts, returns, and allowances) equal the total net cost of purchases. The purchases are also valued at the retail sales price. The formula for the cost complement is as follows:

Cost complement = Total value at cost/Total value at retail

For example, assume the beginning inventory is worth $25,000 at cost and $40,000 at retail. Now assume purchases of $56,000 at cost and $188,000 at retail. Freight-in costs are $6,990. The additional markups to merchandise (usually due to an increase in demand for the product or to cover inflation), at retail, are $7,000. Here is the computation:

	At Cost	At Retail
Beginning inventory	$25,000	$40,000
Purchases (net)	56,000	188,000
Additional markups	---	7,000
Freight costs (in-bound)	6,690	---
Total inventory for sale	$87,690	$235,000

The cost complement is equal to the total cost value of $87,690 divided by the total retail value of $235,000. Thus, the cost complement equals $87,690/$235,000, or .373.

2. **Record any reductions made in the physical inventory levels.** Reductions to inventory come from the sales of products, but they also come from other areas that have reduced the level of inventory, such as markdowns on damaged, seasonal merchandise. The retailer may have reductions due to discounts given to students, senior citizens, or employees (and any other discounts allowed during the given time period). A good chance exists that there is lost inventory due to theft by employees or store customers. Finally, more reductions to inventory may be needed because of damage to the goods (or, in the case of a food retailer such as a supermarket, spoilage).

Although the retailer has a grasp of how much inventory has been marked down and discounted, there is no such knowledge of stock shortages, such as those due to theft. The only way to get an accurate financial picture of stock shortages is to take a physical inventory, which involves actually counting the merchandise. This is an expensive and time-consuming process, usually done only once or twice a year. For this reason, the retailer needs to estimate the stock shortages, typically by using historical data from the RIS. Because of the estimation process, the retailer must correct the estimates by inserting the actual stock shortage values *after* taking each physical inventory. The following calculation shows what the input would look like for step 2:

Available merchandise at retail		$235,000
Less Reductions:		
Sales	$208,000	
Markdowns	6,700	
Discounts	1,300	
Total reductions		216,000
Ending (book) retail value of inventory		$19,000

3. Convert the ending retail (book) value of inventory to the cost value. This allows the calculation of the closing inventory value at cost. This step is fairly simple: multiply the cost complement by the ending adjusted retail inventory value to get the cost value. Remember, the ending retail book value of inventory must be adjusted after a physical inventory to allow for an accurate costing of stock shortages. Thus, the books may look something like the following:

	Cost	Retail
Ending retail book value of inventory	---	$19,000
Physical inventory	---	18,500
Stock shortages		500
Adjusted ending retail book value of inventory	---	$18,500

The closing inventory at cost is equal to the adjusted retail book value of inventory (in the example, $18,500) multiplied by the cost complement (in the example, .373):

$$\$18,500 \times .373 = \$6,900.50$$

This calculation is not exact, so the retailer must use a cost complement that represents an average. The actual number calculated for the ending cost inventory value is an approximation, not the actual closing inventory at cost.

Although the retail method of inventory valuation overcomes most of the problems associated with the cost method, it has some shortcomings. The biggest disadvantage involves the use of averages. Indeed, accounting statements can be generated for any point in time; however, these statements are based on approximations, not on definite numbers. In addition, as discussed earlier, closing inventory is valued on the cost complement, which is an average of the relationship between costs and retail values. If there are many different lines of products, a cost complement will be needed for each individual product line (or department). In addition, a great deal of bookkeeping is required to keep the figures up to date. Each time a retailer purchases and sells merchandise, it must record the retail price and cost information associated with these purchases. These and many other disadvantages can be overcome with POS computer systems and computerized inventory systems.

Remember, inventory value is a dollar amount. It is also important to understand the numbers of units of products processed through the retail outlet.

Resource Allocation

Once the retail manager has a firm grasp of the organization's financial operations, she or he uses the information to make allocations for the firm's various resources. These resources consist of both capital resources and human resources. Although human resource management is discussed in subsequent chapters, the wise manager uses the information presented in this chapter to help make allocation decisions. The overlap between the elements comprising the integrated retail management plan means that many decisions link to other areas, and sometimes simultaneous decisions must be made to ensure consistency.

In terms of generating information for financial decisions in operations management, the retail manager makes a number of decisions regarding resource allocation. Depending on the size of the organization, the retail manager must work with other people in the organization such as buyers to decide how the various retail forecasts needed for effective financial management will be organized. For example, a decision must be made as to how many different forecasts should be undertaken. Are data needed for the store as a whole, or is it better to create forecasts for product lines, departments, or retail divisions? Sales forecasts help ensure that the retailer will have enough of the right stock to satisfy consumers' needs, wants, and desires.

The retail manager and/or buyer must determine the levels of stock needed on hand. To achieve this goal, the manager must be informed about the turnover rates for the various departments, divisions, and product lines and for the store as a whole. Department managers are likely to want increased resources. Thus, allocation receives close attention and concern in every department.

To meet sales objectives, the retail manager needs to preplan for reductions from the retail price of merchandise. Many things happen throughout the year that may make merchandise obsolete. Food retailers have the additional problem of spoilage; food products often need to have their prices reduced to move them off the shelves in a timely manner. The retail manager can look at the accounting systems, particularly previous years' income statements and balance sheets, to estimate how much in retail reductions will be necessary to move merchandise and meet sales objectives. Remember, these estimates are forecasts, or guesses, as to how the product inventories will perform. In the case of fast-moving merchandise, the retailer may have to plan for additional purchases to ensure an adequate supply of the "hot" products. For example, whenever a new video game system comes on the market, many electronics stores make extra efforts to have enough inventory to satisfy demand. Some stores allow customers to order ahead when a new product launch has been announced.

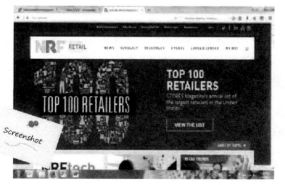

Screenshot

It is important to establish cost categories for the retail business. Many retailers use standard categories such as fixed costs or direct costs. Some retailers set up the categories as capital costs versus operating costs. Others use costs associated with departments. The National Retail Federation (NRF: www.nrf.com) has developed standardized categories that are used by many retailers to set cost categories. One advantage of using the NRF's categories is that it allows for direct comparisons between the retailer's products and those of competitors and the industry averages.

In regard to a retailer's need for resource allocation and financial management, two more financial concepts that can aid retailers are the concepts of cost behavior and cost-volume-profit analysis. The application, interpretation and relevance to retailers will be explored in the next two sections.

Vendor Interactions

Vendor interactions are a very important part of the merchandise buying and handling process. Effective partnerships can help both parties and serve as a competitive advantage. Three important areas of focus are (1) the identification of vendors, (2) technology used by vendors, and (3) vendor negotiations and discounting.

Vendor Identification

Once a merchandise order has been planned, the retailer must identify potential vendors to supply merchandise to the retail operation. Many variables need to be assessed during the vendor identification process. The retail buyer should compare the types of merchandise offered by various vendors with the types of products the retail outlet carries. Does the vendor's merchandise align with the retailer's mission statement? Does the merchandise fit with the overall image that will be communicated to customers? The buyer then compares the retailer's current products with potential products offered by vendors, in terms of price points, brand names, styles, and depth and width of the product lines. The buyer also looks for discounts available for buying larger quantities.

A second variable to look at is the vendor's distribution policies. Does the supplier offer the same merchandise to geographically close competitors? For an e-tailer, does the vendor offer competitors the same products? At what price points? For retailers selling merchandise that has intensive distribution (that is, products that are sold everywhere they can be placed, such as convenience goods), the vendor's distribution policies may not matter. If exclusive or even selective distribution is important to the retailer, however, it may want to go with a vendor that limits sales of products to given geographic areas.

A third consideration is the vendor's IMC. In particular, the retailer should look for vendors who provide promotional assistance such as advertising allowances. Many vendors have product lines that are overruns or are distressed (such as "seconds"). Depending on the retailer's strategy, the retailer may wish to take these vendors into consideration when selecting suppliers. Closeouts, overruns, and distressed merchandise allow the retailer to offer its customers product sales throughout the year. Sales attract a wide range of customers, and suppliers that give the retailer the opportunity to take advantage of these types of products offer the retailer a better margin when sales times roll around.

The retail buyer also needs to be aware of the shipping arrangements the supplier uses. Many suppliers ship only large quantities of product to their retailers, whereas others are willing to ship in smaller quantities. Merchandise buyers decide which of the suppliers provide the best fit for their particular organizations.

An imperative for retail buyers is to compare various vendors' product prices. Generally, numerous suppliers offer the same products. Product price may end up being the deciding factor in the choice of vendors.

Following are some questions the retailer considers when identifying potential vendors:

· Is the vendor reliable?

· If the vendor has promised products or services to the retailer, has it fulfilled its promise?

· Can the supplier expedite orders when needed?

· Can the supplier handle special orders?

· What is the vendor's order-processing record?

· Can the vendor get the products to the store in the shortest time possible?

· How much risk is the retailer to assume as the buyer? (This is particularly important in food retailing.)

· What are the rights of the buyer? (Is the retailer being offered exclusive rights to the products?)

· Will the vendor customize orders and products?

· How does the vendor provide product and company information to its retailers?

· Do warrantees or guarantees accompany the products' purchase?

· Does the supplier offer credit? If so, what are the terms?

· Does the vendor have a reputation for running an ethical business?

· What is the vendor's return policy?

The answers to these questions will help the retailer acquire the best merchandise fit at the least cost. In addition, by asking and answering these questions up front, retailers can save themselves a great deal of time and trouble and create a mutually rewarding relationship with their suppliers.

Retailers have many resources available to assist them in identifying potential vendors. Following is a list of some of these resources:

· Trade shows

· Chambers of commerce

· Resident buying offices

· Trade organizations

· Vendor's place of business

· Wholesale market centers

· Manufacturers

· Raw producers (In the case of food marketers, the store can often buy products directly from the producers, such as chicken farms, dairy farms, and so on.)

· Internet buying services

· Directories (such as the *Thomas Register*)

Sometimes vendors seek out retailers and set up appointments to show their products and services.

Technology

An important consideration in vendor interactions is the use of technology. Vendors that have a good electronic inventory system may get products into to the retailer's hands in a more timely fashion. If it is decided to use an inventory system such as *just-in-time (JIT)*, the retailer should select a vendor that has the capabilities for vendor-managed inventory (VMI) or electronic data interchange (EDI).

What do JCPenney, Kmart, and Walmart have in common? They all use a software/hardware technology called *vendor-managed inventory (VMI)*. VMI is technology that allows vendors to track sales of their products through their various retail outlets using scanner data. With VMI, the responsibility for inventory management is shifted to the suppliers. E-tailers, direct retailers (especially catalog retailers), and brick-and-mortar retailers can rely on this technology to replenish their inventories and create additional data for the RIS and communications within the channel of distribution.

With VMI, it is common for vendors and retailers to share pertinent data. This data sharing helps create and solidify a mutually beneficial vendor-retailer relationship. Companies adopting VMI have achieved significant benefits in scheduling and inventory control (Buyers Launch…, 2003).

In addition, the use of electronic data interchange (EDI) enables retailers to conduct business with vendors electronically. Often the retailer uses EDI to access information about various vendors and their products. Whenever possible, the retailer should select vendors that have an EDI or VMI system, so that long-term goals and objectives for merchandising buying and planning can be met.

Vendor Negotiations and Discounting

The final step in the merchandise buying and planning process is the negotiation process between the retailer and its suppliers. Vendor negotiation revolves around the cost of merchandise. Suppliers offer products and services to retailers at different price levels. Of course, the supplier wants to make a return on its investment, just as the retailer does. To facilitate the buying process, the negotiations generally begin with the products' list prices. A *list price* is the price given in the vendor's price list. Before the advent of computerized databases, vendors carried lists of their products and entered a corresponding price for each inventoried item.

Vendors adjust their list prices based on what the retailer negotiates in return for a reduced price. Vendors can also adjust their prices upward if there is nothing of value in the deal for them. A vendor can create discounts for its products or even create add-ons, which involves a price increase. Several types of discounts exist.

Trade Discounts: Probably the most common discount is the trade discount. A *trade discount* is an offer by the vendor to reduce the price of the merchandise if the retailer provides the vendor a service in return for the discount. For example, a vendor may offer a retailer a 10 percent discount if the retailer takes responsibility for picking up the product from a distribution center.

Quantity Discounts: *Quantity discounts* are given to retailers who purchase inventory in large quantities. Quantity discounts can be one-time, or noncumulative, discounts, or they can run for the entire purchase period (a cumulative discount.) A *cumulative discount* allows the retailer to order several times until the amount of the total of all orders equals some figure predetermined by agreement between the retail buyer and the vendor. The more products a retailer purchases cumulatively, the greater the discount it receives for the purchases.

To illustrate, suppose Great Toys, Inc., a toy vendor, offers its retailer customers a 2 percent discount if they purchase at least $100,000 of product a year. A 4 percent discount is given for orders of $150,000 to $200,000 per year. One of Great Toys' customers is Fun Toys, a small, independent retailer. Fun Toys used to purchase products four times a year in lots of $20,000. To take advantage of the cumulative discount, Fun Toys has decided to purchase $150,000 in products per year.

If a retailer decides to carry a certain brand of paint, but the retail store has a small (but steady) volume of customers, the retailer can ask the supplier to add or accumulate the amount of products that are purchased over time. When the retailer gets to that predetermined number---say, $10,000 worth of product, or 500 units---the vendor reduces the cost by a certain percentage or dollar amount. Vendors often use this type of discount to encourage additional retailer purchases and to create a relationship between themselves and the retailers. In addition, a vendor may offer retailers "free" merchandise after they purchase a minimum quantity of goods or services.

Seasonal Discounts: *Seasonal discounts* are given to retailers for making purchases out of season. If the retailer is willing to store and pay for off-season merchandise, the vendor may reduce the cost of the products to the retailer. The benefits to the vendor are that it has a sure order for those products, and it does not have to store all the products it is manufacturing until the appropriate sales season. The vendor saves money on storage and overrun costs; the retailer, for its part, performs the storage function for the vendor but gets a reduced price for the merchandise it will sell in season. For example, if a sporting goods retailer purchases baseball bats during the off-season, the manufacturer may provide the sporting goods store with a discount.

Cash Discounts: *Cash discounts* are sometimes given to retailers to encourage them to pay early or pay with cash. Thus, the terms of a vendor-retailer contract may read "2/10, net 30," indicating that a 2 percent discount will be provided to the retailer if the merchandise is paid for within a ten-day period. If the retailer does not pay within the specified limit, there is no discount. In any case, the total amount due is payable in 30 days. Many retailers take advantage of this type of discount to save money. Even good investments do not return that much money to investors (2 percent for 10 days).

Allowances: Often suppliers provide retailers with discounts called *allowances* for retailer cooperation during IMC executions. For example, if a retailer advertises the vendor's products in its retail ads, the vendor may provide the retailer with an advertising allowance. Or the vendor may give the retailer a discount for preferred product placement within the retail store. Vendors give retailers *slotting allowances* to get their products and/or services on the retailer's shelves or in choice locations in its retailer's stores. In addition, many vendors provide the retailer with display materials for certain products or with other types of promotional materials. Slotting allowances can be extremely expensive for vendors, making it difficult for small vendors to introduce their products in larger chains. Slotting allowances have generated some controversy because some view this practice as a bribe paid by suppliers to retailers to get the best shelf position. Retailers support slotting fees as insurance for taking the risk of carrying new products, most of which fail. Vendors sometimes provide retailers with free merchandise in exchange for the performance of some channel function such as advertising or sales promotion.

In addition to the various types of discounts and allowances, the vendor-retailer negotiation process includes coming to agreement about the transportation of merchandise. Who pays for the freight charges---the retailer or the vendor? In addition, the retailer and vendor need to negotiate where the title to the merchandise changes hands, who must file claims on lost or damaged merchandise, and who is responsible for obsolete or damaged merchandise.

Source: Monkey Business Images/Shutterstock.com

The overarching theme in the vendor-buyer relationship is that almost everything is negotiable. Good retail negotiators can save their organizations a great deal of money, time, and responsibility if they are practiced at the art of negotiation.

Finally, the retail buyer must establish a method for buying the products and for the receiving and handling of all merchandise. This function is often referred to as merchandise logistics. The following section deals with the logistics necessary to get merchandise into the store and out to the customers.

Logistics Management

Logistics management includes all aspects of a company's logistical systems. Some of the main functions included in logistics planning include selecting modes of transportation; receiving, checking, and storing merchandise; and supply chain management.

Retailers have the additional burden of the development of a *reverse logistics* process, wherein policies and procedures for the return of merchandise by customers are developed. The reverse logistics process also includes steps to return products back to the vendor or manufacturer of the product. Reasons to send products in reverse through the chain include attempting to recapture value or properly disposing of returned or damaged goods (Beltran, 2002).

Many retailers once defined the functions of getting the product to the retail store and then to the end user as *materials management (MM)* or *purchasing.* These terms are often used interchangeably. As defined by the Council of Supply Chain Management Professionals (CSCMP) (2013):

> "*Logistics management* is that part of supply chain management that plans, implements, and controls the efficient, effective forward and reverse flow and storage of goods, services, and related information between the point of origin and the point of consumption in order to meet customers' requirements. Logistics management activities typically include inbound and outbound transportation management, fleet management, warehousing, materials handling, order fulfillment, logistics network design, inventory management, supply/demand planning, and management of third party logistics services providers. To varying degrees, the logistics function also includes sourcing and procurement, production planning and scheduling, packaging and assembly, and customer service. It is involved in all levels of planning and execution---strategic, operational, and tactical. Logistics management is an integrating function which coordinates and optimizes all logistics activities, as well as integrates logistics activities with other functions, including marketing, sales, manufacturing, finance, and information technology."

The success or failure of a business can depend on the efficiency of its logistics methods. One company that has used logistics as a competitive advantage is the Raymour and Flanigan Furniture chain (www.ramourflanigan.com). The furniture industry historically has been slower than others in their product delivery. Typical delivery times can take weeks. Raymour and Flanigan guarantees a three-day delivery for items displayed in its stores. They use Demand Solutions Requirements Planning Software which helps the company manage nearly 2,700 SKUs carried. In addition to two distribution centers, the company has an additional 15 customer service centers which allow them to meet the three-day delivery service (Furniture Delivered..., 2007).

Source: l i g h t p o e t/Shutterstock.com

Modes of Transportation

There are many facets to creating an effective logistical system. A major advantage of a well-planned logistical system is increased profitability. Vendors and retailers, by working in collaboration, can help satisfy each other's needs and wants, which increases all the companies' bottom lines. Effective integrated and coordinated logistical systems reduce the time and costs associated with the delivery of products. Suppliers work to physically move products to a retailer's venue in a timely matter. The movement of these goods is achieved through one of four basic modes of transportation: trucks, railway, water carriers, and air transportation. Each of these modes has advantages and disadvantages (see Table 9.4).

Table 9.4   Advantages and Disadvantages of Transportation Modes

Transportation Mode	Advantages	Disadvantages
Trucking	• Door-to-door delivery • Fast delivery speed • High frequency of deliveries	High costs
Rail	• Lower to average costs • Good for hauling extremely heavy materials	• Services to small retailers not as good as for large retailers • No access to cities without rail • Low shipment frequency
Water	Very low costs	• Services not available in cities without access to waterways • No door-to-door delivery • Slow delivery speed • Low frequency of deliveries
Air	Fast delivery speed	• High costs • No door-to-door delivery

Receiving Merchandise

The receipt of merchandise, including order processing and fulfillment, has recently become more automated. Larger retailers have attempted to create positive vendor-retailer relationships and have eased the process of receiving and checking products through the use of EDI, QR, and VMI programs. Smaller retailers use these systems less often. Whether small or large, all retailers must receive and check merchandise. The process is generally handled by centralized receiving departments, decentralized (district or regional) receiving centers, or a single store.

Centralized receiving departments receive, check, and mark merchandise at one central location. They offer greater physical merchandise control compared with decentralized systems. Centralization helps ensure consistency among many branch sites. Central receiving also offers better financial control than decentralized receiving, because the company can record inventory more efficiently when it is handled in one location instead of several. District or regional receiving centers perform the same functions but place the merchandise closer to the stores where the merchandise will be sold. Decentralization has the advantage of having more flexibility in tailoring merchandise to local tastes.

Single-store receiving also involves the same functions, but these are handled at the store where the merchandise will be sold. Of the three methods, single-store receiving has the greatest flexibility in catering to the tastes of the local market. Independent retailers generally use single-store receiving, whereas larger retailers and chains may use any of the three methods.

Specialized equipment, including many different types of conveyors, is needed for merchandise receiving. In addition, records must be kept indicating the vendor, shipper, date and time of arrival, total units in the shipment, cost, and other invoice information. The quality and actual quantities of merchandise must also be checked.

Once received, the merchandise must be marked either by hand or through an automated system. Today most marking is computerized. POS terminals coupled with the use of uniform product codes (UPCs) and radio frequency identification (RFID) have provided for efficient merchandise marking. By using POS systems, individual merchandise information can be placed in a database that might include department names, vendor information, product information, and price. Most of the information is coded by the retailer; customers do not have access.

The retailer stores the physical merchandise on the floor, in a small in-store warehouse, or at a regional or central location, depending on the distribution method. Larger chains often use central locations and handle their own distribution. Many retailers still have merchandise delivered and stored at the store where it will be sold.

As merchandise is sold, the retailer needs to track it. Tracking involves recording which products were sold, how often, how many units, and at what price. Tracking allows for more efficient product replacement.

Supply Chain Management

Supply chain management is much broader than logistics management and includes attempts to coordinate the whole supply chain so that all members of the chain benefit. According to the Council of Supply Chain Management Professionals (CSCMP) (2013), supply chain management includes "all activities involved in sourcing and procurement, conversion, and all logistics management activities. Importantly, it also includes coordination and collaboration with channel partners, which can be suppliers, intermediaries, third-party service providers, and customers. In essence, supply chain management integrates supply and demand management within and across companies." To fully understand the supply chain process, it is important to know all the key parties in the chain, from the raw material producers to the end user. By understanding each party's goals, constraints, and environmental issues, a retailer can identify which issues are likely to affect product availability. Customers are an important part of the process because their wants and needs dictate product assortments. As stated earlier in the discussion of reverse logistics, the customer plays a role when returning unwanted products. Figure 9.5 depicts an example of a supply chain.

Figure 9.5 Example of a Supply Chain

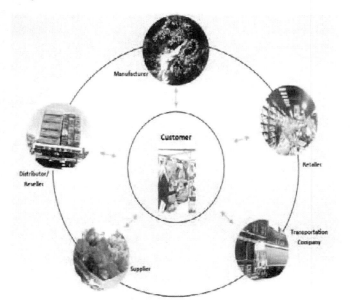

Supply chain management specialists and academicians have developed systems to create a "seamless" supply chain that satisfies all members of the chain, in particular the customers. Techniques such as JIT and QR are very popular with retailers (and others involved in the movement of goods and services). It is common to include the supply chain management functions, as well as the logistical systems, in the RIS to allow retail decision makers instant access to important data and information.

Category Management

Related to supply chain and logistics management is category management, a disciplined method of managing categories instead of individual products. A category is a group of similar or related products. Examples of product categories are soup, coffee, tools, paint, and jewelry.

The Category Management Association (2013) defines category management as "A Retailer-Supplier Process of managing categories as strategic business units, producing enhanced business results by focusing on delivering consumer value." Originally supermarkets were the only type of retailer using category management, but once the benefits became clear other types of retailers started using the method as well.

Retailers use scanner data and loyalty programs to keep track of consumer purchases. This allows the retailer to use the data for better category management. Effective category management helps a retailer better plan promotions. Often complementary products are promoted to increase sales.

The Partnering Group (1996), a consulting company, developed an eight-step process for category management, which is as follows:

1. Define Category – Based on how customers shop, a retailer will define the category. Customer actions considered are whether consumers shop based on brand, packaging, quality or product groupings (such as buying toothpaste and dental floss together).

2. Category Role – How important is the category to the retailer? What role does the retailer want the category to play in the store? This should be based on the target market's needs and wants.

3. Category Appraisal– In this step the category management team determines how well the category is performing for the retailer and in the industry. A competitive analysis of the category is also conducted.

4. Category Scorecard – In this step the manufacturer and retailer jointly decide what needs to be done to reach goals and objectives for the category.

5. Category Strategies – The manufacturer and retailer determine the best strategies that will be used to reach objectives.

6. Category Tactics – In this step the category management team explains specific actions that will be taken to meet objectives. For example, implementing BOGO promotions six times a year for a specific category may be considered.

7. Plan Implementation – In this step the plan is acted upon.

8. Category Review – Measurement and evaluation of the results is ongoing but is also done once the time frame for the objectives has passed.

Figure 9.6   Steps Involved in Category Management

Source: arka38/Shutterstock.com

Figure 9.6 illustrates these steps. Closely related to category management is *efficient customer response (ECR)*. ECR is defined as "a cooperative value-creation strategy whereby retailers and suppliers jointly implement collaborative business practices with the ultimate objective of fulfilling consumer wishes together, better, faster and at less cost" (Corsten and Kumar, 2005). ECR encourages manufacturers and retailers to work together to implement joint marketing programs, optimize supply chain activities, and improve information technology used for category management (Ibid, 2005).

Channel and Category Captains

Because the supply chain is made up of many individuals and organizations, it becomes a task to delineate which member is in charge of the supply chain. Though the process can be formalized, in practice leadership often falls to the most dominant power in the chain. The company or person that plays the biggest role in the supply chain is deemed the *channel captain*. The channel captain can be a wholesaler, manufacturer, or retailer. The captain organizes and controls the chain. For example, suppliers of Walmart understand that the large discount giant is the channel captain and dominates supply chain processes. Consequently, Walmart systems should (and often must) be used to develop an effective supply chain.

The retailer, being on the front line between the business organizations and the buyers, is in a unique position to generate relationships with consumers. Hence the retailer can gather important data and information from consumers that can be used by all members of the supply chain. This situation gives the retailer somewhat more leverage in its buying and selling of goods and services and in negotiations with vendors and other members of the supply chain.

Early on retailers realized that it was difficult to coordinate efforts in category management. Eventually a trusted manufacturer who committed to grow the category was selected as a *category captain*. While not always the case, the largest manufacturer is often the category captain. The category captain coordinates efforts and makes recommendations. Larger manufacturers have teams of people assigned to a retailer to offer category support (A.C. Nielson, 2006).

The person that coordinates the efforts of the businesses involved in category management is the *category manager*. According to Ian Walters (2011), a commercial development manager for IGD, successful category managers work on the following principles:

· Ensuring the shopper is at the core of the strategy

· The strategies of both retailers and suppliers are aligned

· They understand and consider the entire category, including brands and private labels

· They engage in true collaboration with partners

Managing Shrinkage

Shrinkage is the loss of product or inventory that occurs from theft, fraud, or errors in receiving, accounting, or tracking. It is calculated by looking at the difference between reported and actual inventory. As a multi-billion dollar problem, retailers know they must seek solutions that don't hinder normal consumer shopping while still protecting their profits.

Shrinkage concerns are typically managed by loss-prevention departments. However, because the issue broadly affects entire organizations, many areas within a company are involved in stopping these losses. It's important that everyone in the retail organization is thoroughly familiar with understanding how shrinkage occurs, the potential solutions, and the impact it has on revenue.

In 2015 retailers lost about $45 billion due to retail shrinkage, representing 1.38 percent of retail sales. This amount was up by $1.2 billion compared to 2014. In previous years, employee theft had been the greatest cause of shrinkage but in 2015, shoplifting was the major cause in 2015 (2016 National Retail Security Survey). The average loss to shoplifting is $377 per incident. Robberies were also up in

Source: Fotosenmeer/Shutterstock.com

2015 due to high average losses reported by jewelry stores. The average loss due to robberies was $8,180 per incident (National Retail Federation, 2017). Other reasons for shrinkage include organized crime and administrative error. Retail shrinkage affects everyone and results in higher prices for consumers to cover escalating losses.

Types of Theft

Shrinkage can occur out the front door of a retail establishment (shoplifting), out the back door (vendor theft) or from employees. It can also be the result from administrative errors such as inventory tracking errors, ineffective merchandise return systems, or damage. The combination of employee theft and administrative errors makes up over half of shrinkage losses.   Other forms of theft include burglary such as "smash and grab" (breaking store windows and removing products – usually valuables such as jewelry) theft, and forms of fraud, such as check fraud or credit card fraud.

Source: Mega Pixel/Shutterstock.com

Below are some of the primary ways shrinkage takes place:

Shoplifting: Shoplifting involves stealing products from a store's shelves by an individual or a group. Shoplifters might steal one item or walk out of a store with boxes full of inventory – most often, but not always, concealed. The most devastating loss to a retailer usually happens when organized crime rings strike a store. Typically, these professional thieves will target particular product categories that are easy to steal and have a high resale value. They will often focus on a regional area, city, or store chain, execute their plan, and move on to another area quickly.

Employee Theft: Employee theft can occur at the register or through employee shoplifting – taking merchandise from the front of the store, or by stealing products from the back of the store. Employees can also cause shrinkage if they under-ring a product at the register in order to give a friend or a relative an unauthorized discount or free product. This form of employee theft, "sweethearting," may also involve an accomplice in order to split the proceeds from the theft. When employees steal products from stock rooms or loading docks, the volume of loss may be significant and may occur over a period of time. In 2015, employee theft was responsible for about 36% of inventory losses. The average loss was $1,233 per incident (2016 National Retail Security Survey).

Vendor Theft: Because delivery or pick up involves trucks and pallets of product, vendors and delivery services can steal truckloads at a time. Detection is more difficult because, at this point in the logistics flow, the material may not yet be captured in a retail inventory system. In the absence of good inventory receiving systems, vendors can also intentionally or inadvertently short merchandise.

Accounting and Tracking Errors, Shrinkage Solutions

It's easy for an employee to take a product off a shelf for store use and forget to account for it. When employees do this, the product loss shows up as shrinkage. Poor inventory tracking and receiving discrepancies can also be responsible for accounting disparities and may add to shrinkage. Shrinkage figures may also rise if damaged products or perishable goods are not accounted for in tracking systems. Charge backs, misplaced merchandise, fitting room recovery, UPC errors, retail price errors, and housekeeping problems all contribute to shrinkage. Inventory errors can include product overages as well as product shortages.

Over the years, retailers have become more sophisticated in dealing with shrinkage and theft. However, there is no single remedy, and the most effective way to counter the problem is to incorporate a combination of solutions. Technical and mechanical products are useful when combined with employee training, diligent observation and surveillance, asset tracking, secure packaging, and merchandise placement.

Summary

This chapter provided a lot of information in regard to the development of a merchandise plan focusing on finances. To begin with we looked at the development of merchandising systems and budget development. Additionally, types of systems were assessed, and important financial ratios were discussed. These ratios offer metrics to the retailers so that the retailers may assess how their businesses are doing compared to the competition. The chapter continued with coverage of sales volumes and profits based upon a retailer's forecast. As the budget was built, retailers were able to begin looking to stock their shelves with merchandise. Methods of assessing and managing the merchandise were then discussed.

Then the chapter examined issues involving vendor interactions, including vendor identification and the negotiation process. The chapter concluded with a discussion of the concepts of logistics, supply chain management and category management as they apply to retailing

Shrinkage impacts how products are merchandised. Customer access to products and entire categories can be compromised due to high shrinkage levels. Overall profitability is affected by shrinkage, and some of the solutions currently available to curtail this problem were addressed. With the financial structure in place, the remainder of the text focuses on the management and execution of the integrated retail management plan.

Terms

allowance	A discount offered to retailers that agree to participate in the vendor's marketing efforts.
assortment	The collection of products a retailer carries.
basic stock method	Inventory planning tool that allows the retailer to include a few more items (*basic stock*) than were forecasted in an order for a given period of time. BOM stock (at retail) = Planned sales (monthly) + Basic stock.
bottom-up approach	A method of budgeting in which each retail department supplies data. The budgets are passed up to the next levels of management until all budgets reach an individual who is responsible for the budgeting process.
breadth	The number of product lines (or categories) the retailer offers. Breadth is often described along a continuum of narrow or broad.
buyer	The employee whose basic responsibility is to make purchases.
cash conversion cycle (CCC)	A measure of how many days it takes to turn purchases of inventory into cash.
cash discount	A discount offered to retailers to encourage them to pay early or pay with cash.
category captain	A trusted manufacturer that coordinates efforts and makes recommendations for category management.
category manager	The person that coordinates the efforts of the businesses involved in category management.
channel captain	The company or person that plays the biggest role in the supply chain.
commercial merchandise	Articles for sale, samples used for soliciting orders, or goods that are not considered personal effects.
cost complement	Total value at cost divided by total value at retail.

cumulative discount	A discount that runs for an entire purchase period and allows the retailer to order several times until the agreed-on discount level is reached.
depth	Consists of the stock keeping units (SKUs) or variety within a category (this could include colors, styles and sizes that the retailer stocks within each line it carries). Depth is often described along a continuum of shallow to deep.
economic order quantity (EOQ)	A calculation of how much merchandise to reorder.
efficient customer response (ECR)	Category management strategy devised through joint efforts of retailers and suppliers with the objectives to increase sales and better fulfill customer wants and needs.
electronic data interchange (EDI)	A technology that allows retailers to conduct business with vendors electronically.
FIFO (first in, first out)	An inventory costing method that assumes older merchandise is sold before newer stock is sold.
gross margin return on inventory (GMROI)	A calculation of how much investment is being returned for each type of merchandise purchased.
inventory turnover	A measure of how many times a store sells its average investment in inventory during a year.
just-in-time (JIT) inventory	A process in which a supplier delivers products to a retailer right before they are needed, thus saving the retailer storage costs.
LIFO (last in, first out)	An inventory costing method that assumes newer merchandise is sold before older stock is sold.
list price	The price given in the vendor's price list.
logistics management	Every action taken to ensure that products and services get from the point of origin to the final customer.
merchandise	The products or services the retailer currently offers, or plans to offer, for sale to customers.
merchandise buying and handling	The physical purchase of products and services and how those products and services are brought to the retail outlet, handled, and finally placed ready for sale.
merchandise mix	The combination of merchandise variety, assortment, depth, quality, and price points.
merchandising	Activities involved in organizing the display of products and services.
open-to-buy	The amount the buyer has left to spend for a given time period, typically a month. Each time a purchase is made, the open-to-buy amount decreases.
order lead time	The span of time required to fulfill an order.
percentage variation method	Inventory planning tool in which the beginning-of-month planned inventory during any period (typically a month) differs from planned average monthly stock by half of that month's variation from average monthly sales. BOM stock (at retail) = Average stock for the sales period (at retail) x 1/2 [1 + (Planned monthly sales/Average monthly sales)].
periodic inventory system	A cost accounting system in which sales are recorded as they occur but inventory is not updated.
perpetual inventory system	A cost accounting system that shows the level of inventory on hand at all times.
price points	The range of prices for a particular merchandise line.
product line	A category of products with similar characteristics.
quantity discount	A discount offered to retailers that purchase in large quantities.

reverse logistics	The development of policies and procedures for the return of merchandise purchased by customers to a store or to a vendor or manufacturer.
safety stock	Extra merchandise carried to keep a retailer from running out of a product.
seasonal discount	A discount given to retailers for making purchases out of season.
slotting allowance	An allowance given to retailers to get the vendor's products and/or services on the shelves or in choice locations in the retailer's stores.
stock-to-sales ratio	A measurement that compares a retailer's stock levels to levels of sales.
top-down approach	A method of budgeting in which members of upper management prepare budgets and pass them down to departments to follow.
trade discount	An offer by a vendor to reduce the price of merchandise if the retailer provides the vendor with a service in return for the discount.
usage rate	Average sales per day of a specific product in units.
vendor-managed inventory (VMI)	A technology that allows a vendor to track sales of its products through its various retail outlets using scanner data.
weeks' supply method	Inventory planning tool in which beginning of the month inventory equals several weeks' expected sales. BOM (at retail) planned inventory = Average weekly sales (estimated) x Number of weeks to be stocked.

Discussion Questions

1. Identify three companies that you think do an excellent job of merchandising. What makes their merchandise appealing? What about stores whose merchandise you don't like? Why doesn't the merchandise appeal to you?

2. What are the responsibilities of a retail buyer? Does the position of retail buyer appeal to you? Why or why not?

3. Explain the techniques for determining inventory planning. Under what circumstances should one method be chosen over another?

4. What are the components of the merchandise mix?

5. What is the advantage to the retailer of calculating the GMROI?

6. Explain the differences in the following inventory planning methods: basic stock, percentage variation, and weeks' supply.

7. What is the difference between logistics management and supply chain management?

8. Do you think Wal-Mart is primarily concerned with its depth of product assortment? Why or why not? Would Bloomingdale's have the same concern? Why or why not?

9. What types of data are collected from category management systems? How are they used?

10. How would you manage shrinkage in an office supplies store?

11. Which system of budgeting would work better for a small retailer, bottom-up or top-down budgeting?

Exercises

1. Go to a retailer's website. Browse the site and answer the following questions:

a. Define the merchandise mix

b. Define the price points for the merchandise. Why do you think that these price points are being used? Who do you think the customer may be (demographically)?

c. List items in the merchandise mix that you would eliminate. What would you add?

d. Why do you think this retailer has placed the specific products on the site? Which products don't belong?

2. The Hot Chica Clothing Chain wants to have extra stock on hand at the end of the month that is equal to five percent (5%) of its average monthly stock which is $55,000. Sales for next month are estimated to be $47,000. Would is the BOM stock level for next month?

3. Billy's Buddies is a pet retailer. Billy just found out about a great sale on neon tetra fish. Billy has planned to purchase $10,000 worth of merchandise and has made purchase commitments of $7,000 for the month. What is Billy's open-to-buy? Can he purchase the neon tetras? If so, how many?

4. Go to a local retailer. Inside the store, see if you can identify each of the categories the retailer is carrying. Do these products occupy shelf space near each other? Why? Why Not?

Case

Macy's Adapts to Changes

Because the Millennial market offers retailers a large market for development, clothing retailers focus on this market segment. This market segment is often indecisive in their product choices and they follow fads and fashions more than other market segments. Because of this, buyers at fashion retailers must assess the market and create a merchandise mix that is acceptable. In 2012 Macy's announced and outlined a plan to select and stock clothing lines much faster than previously done. The system targeted purchases made by the Millennial Generation. In addition to creating a faster system for ordering and stocking, Macy's also deepened their brand assortments. The new policies were in line with the My Macy's initiative that was started to entice and hold millennial shoppers. This system allows regional stores a better ability to cater to local tastes. Over time, My Macy's evolved from localization to personalization.

2015 and 2016 were tough years for Macy's. There was a labor slowdown in West Coast ports, the 2015 winter was warmer than expected which impacted sales of cold-weather clothing, and international tourist traffic was down. The company closed 41 underperforming stores in 2015 and 69 in 2016. Part of their plan is to reduce expenses and tighten spending so the company can focus on growth initiatives. As of January 2017, there were 731 stores.

In 2016, Macy's announced it was opening Macy's Backstage, an outlet store located within some Macy's stores. To stay relevant the company hosts special events such as the Macy's Thanksgiving Day Parade, flower shows, fashion extravaganzas and celebrity appearances. The company continues to evolve the way it interacts with customers. Their websites and mobile apps have improved their functionality and merchandise offerings. In addition, Macy's is a leader in developing private brands which include Alfani, American Rag, Bar III, Charter Club, Club Room, First Impressions, Giani Bernini, Hotel Collection, Ideology, I.N.C International Concepts, JM Collection, Maison Jules, Martha Stewart Collection, Material Girl, Style&CO, Tasso Elba and Thalía Sodi.

Questions

1. Do you think that this move by Macy's helped bring Millennials into Macy's stores?

2. Why would Macy's want to focus on Millennials?

3. Provide ideas of how inventory would be different if Macy's were targeting the Baby Boomer generation instead of the Millennial Generation?

4. What are the downsides to carrying private labels?

Sources: 2015 Annual Report http://investors.macysinc.com/phoenix.zhtml?c=84477&p=irol-irhome; www.macys.com; Wahba, Phil (March 21, 2012), *Macy's Has a New Mindset on Millennials*, Reuters, accessed March 25, 2012 from http://today.msnbc.msn.com/id/46810098

References

2016 *National Retail Security Survey* (2015). University of Florida.

A.C. Nielsen (2006). *Consumer-Centric Category Management: How to Increase Profits by Managing Categories Based on Consumer Needs.* Hoboken, NJ: John Wiley & Sons.

Beltran, L. S. (2002). Reverse Logistics: Current Trends and Practices in the Commercial World. *Logistics Spectrum*, 36 (Jul - Sept), pp. 4-8.

Buyers Launch 7 Major Initiatives to Reduce Inventory (2003). *Supplier Selection and Management Report*, 3 (April 2003), p. 1.

Category Management Association (2013). What Is Category Management. Retrieved from http://www.cpgcatnet.org/page/whatisCatMan/

Corsten, D. and Kumar, N. (2005). Do Suppliers Benefit from Collaborative Relationships with Large Retailers? An Empirical Investigation of Efficient Consumer Response Adoption. *Journal of Marketing*, (69: July), pp. 80-94.

Cote, J. M. and Latham, K. K. (1999). The Merchandising Ratio: A Comprehensive Measure of Working Capital Strategy. *Issues in Accounting Education*, (May), pp. 255-267.

Council of Supply Chain Management Professionals (2013). Retrieved from http://cscmp.org/sites/default/files/user_uploads/resources/downloads/glossary-2013.pdf

Cravenho, J. (2002). Revenue Chain Excellence: Using Speed as the Best Practice. *Business Credit* (Sept) pp. 20-21.

Fisher, M. L., Raman, A., and McClelland, A.S. (2000). Rocket Science Retailing Is Almost Here: Are You Ready? *Harvard Business Review*, (Jul-Aug), pp. 115-124.

Furniture Delivered in 3 Days or Less (2007). Retrieved from www. ds_magazine_2007_03_19_ramour.pdf

GuruFocus (2016). Retrieved from www.gurufocus.com

Ivanovic, A. and Collin, P.H. (1996). *Dictionary of Marketing*, 2d ed. Middlesex, England: Peter Collin Publishing, p. 132.

Kök, G., Fisher, M. L. and Vaidyanathan, R. (2006). Assortment Planning: Review of Literature and Industry Practice. Retrieved from http://qbox.wharton.upenn.edu/documents/opim/research/APchapter.pdf

Kowitt, B. (2010). Inside Trader Joe's. *Fortune*, (Sept 6), pp. 86-96.

National Retail Federation (2016). Retail inventory shrinkage increased to $45.2 billion in 2015.

Occupational Outlook Handbook (2016). Buyers and Purchasing Agents. Retrieved from https://www.bls.gov/ooh/business-and-financial/buyers-and-purchasing-agents.htm

PLMA: Private Label Manufacturers Association (2017). Store brands sales climbed in the mass channel in 2016; dollar and unit volume grew four times the rate of national brands. Retrieved from http://plma.com/storeBrands/marketprofile2017.html

Richards, V. D. and Laughlin, E. J. (1980). A Cash Conversion Cycle Approach to Liquidity Analysis (1980). *Financial Management*, 9 (Spring 1980),pp. 32-38.

Salisbury, S. (2003). Nemo Spawns Clown Fish Craze. *Palm Beach Post*, West Palm Beach, Florida, (Jun 11), 1A.

Shor, R. (2003). Control Inventory to Control Costs. National Jeweler, 97 (Mar 16), p. 18.

The Entrepreneurs Guidebook Series (2001). Retrieved from www.smallbusinesstown.com.

The Partnering Group, Nordic (1996), Category Management: Increased customer value. Best Practices Report.

Vend's 2017 Retail Trends and Predictions Report. Retrieved from https://www.vendhq.com/university/retail-trends-and-predictions-2017

Walters, I. (2011). Category Management Skills: The Next Level (Dec 13). IGD. Retrieved from http://www.igd.com/our-expertise/building-trading-relationships/Category-management-and-shopper-marketing/4817/Category-management-skills-the-next-level/

Weiss, P. (1999). Warner-Lambert vs. Pfizer, Plus an Explanation of the Cash Conversion Cycle. (Nov 2). Retrieved from The Motley Fool at www.fool.com. http://www.fool.com/portfolios/rulemaker/1999/rulemaker991102.htm

Chapter 10

Human Resource Management

"Appreciate everything your associates do for the business. Nothing else can quite substitute for a few well-chosen, well-timed, sincere words of praise. They're absolutely free and worth a fortune."

~ Sam Walton, founder, Wal-Mart Stores, Inc.

Source: Daniel Krason/Shutterstock.com

CHAPTER OBJECTIVES

After completing this chapter you will be able to:

- Describe the types of information to include in a human resource management plan.
- Explain the differences between short-term and long-term human resource planning.
- Explain how tasks and positions within a retail organization are developed.
- Describe the major types of organizational charts and discuss the purpose of each type.
- Explain the processes involved in hiring and firing employees.
- Give examples of effective training and human resource management techniques for retailers.
- Explain concepts related to diversity management and the business case for diversity.

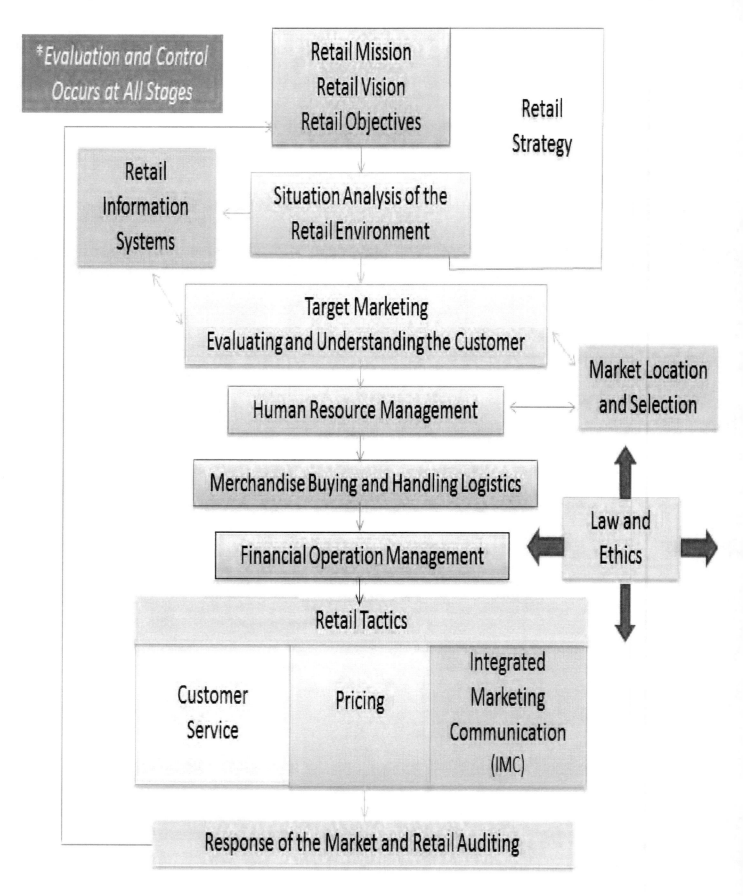

Wegmans' Competitive Advantage: Human Resource Management

In 1916, John Wegman opened the Rochester Fruit & Vegetable Company. His brother Walter joined him a year later. This was the beginning of Wegmans Food Market. In 1921 the bothers purchased the Seel Grocery Co. and expanded operations to include general groceries and a bakery. In 1931 Wegmans stores were incorporated and in 1953 Wegmans implemented an employee benefits program.

Today Wegmans Food Markets, Inc. is one of the largest private companies in the U.S. with 92 stores in six states. The company has been named one of the "100 Best Companies to Work For" by Fortune Magazine for 20 consecutive years, becoming one of 12 companies to reach this milestone. In 2017, Wegmans was #2 on the list. According to the company website (www.wegmans.com), in 2016, the company received over 7,800 requests from people asking the company to open a store in their community. Another 8,000 customers wrote to express their appreciation for the products/services and the friendly employees. Their employee benefit program is strong and has an employee scholarship component which provides about $4.5 million in tuition assistance to employees each year. Since the scholarship program started in 1984, Wegmans has awarded $105 million in scholarships to more than 33,000 employees. Says CEO Danny Wegman, "Our employees are the number one reason our customers shop at Wegmans. I'm convinced there is only one path to great customer service, and that is through employees who feel they are cared about and empowered" (Wegmans Makes It..., 2013).

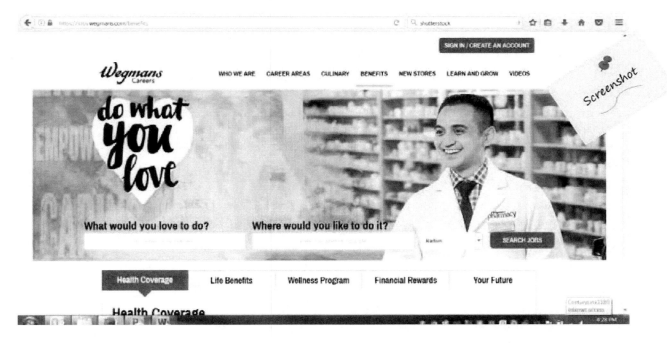

Introduction

Up to this point, we have dealt with the development of managerial tools for all functions in retailing except the management of personnel. Management of personnel is one of the most important functions a retailer performs. According to Sandy Kennedy (2003), president of the International Mass Retail Association, one of the greatest challenges retailers face is attracting and developing employees. The retailer's employees have direct contact with customers. Sales and customer relations employees are generally the first and last individuals with whom customers interact.

The process of managing the retailer's employees is called *human resource management*. *Human resource management (HRM)* is the "policies, practices, and systems that influence employees' behavior, attitudes, and performance" (Noe, Hollenbeck, Gerhart and Wright, 2003, p. 5). This chapter discusses the various policies, practices, and systems retailers use to run their operations efficiently.

Retailers, and especially individuals involved in HRM, need to be knowledgeable about the legal and ethical issues associated with this function. Laws and ethics are discussed in Chapter 14; for now, note that HRM personnel face ethical decisions in many areas, such as employee health and safety, drug and alcohol use, discipline, dismissal, discrimination, privacy, working conditions, and pay.

Planning for Human Resources

According to the National Retail Federation (2016), about two-thirds of the U.S. Gross Domestic Product (GDP) comes from retailing. The retailing industry supports one in four jobs and benefits over 13 million non-retail jobs. (National Retail Federation, 2013). Employment of retail salespersons is expected to grow seven percent from 2014 to 2024 (Bureau of Labor Statistics, 2017). Because of the global nature of the industry, the planning for human resources can be complex. One of the many roles retail managers fill involves the development and implementation of a comprehensive human resource management (HRM) plan. The plan should attempt to take advantage of the various skill sets and abilities of the retailer's employees. The HRM plan---whether for large or small retailers---follows the same pattern as the integrated retail management (IRM) plan: the retailer needs to create an overall mission and vision for human resources, followed by a series of objectives to guide human resource personnel in their day-to-day operations.

The HRM plan needs to specify the *tasks* to be performed, the jobs that will fulfill those tasks, an organizational chart showing reporting relationships, hiring guidelines for the retailer, and possible causes for employee dismissal. In addition, HR is responsible for personnel compensation and benefits packages. If unions operate within the organization, the HR department may also be responsible for ensuring that the retailer complies with union contract(s).

In a small, independent retail firm, the owner of the firm performs most of the HR duties or assigns the tasks to an employee within the organization. In larger chains, the general practice is to develop a separate department that handles all the HR functions. In either scenario, the HR functions must be carefully defined and efficiently managed. Table 10.1 lists the functions performed by most HR departments.

Table 10-1 Human Resource Functions

- Job analysis and job design
- Recruitment and selection of retail employees
- Training and development
- Performance management
- Compensation and benefits
- Labor relations
- Managerial relations

Source: Adapted from Fisher, C., Schoenfeldt, L. and Shaw, B. (2003). *Human Resource Management*, 5th ed. Boston: Houghton Mifflin, pp. 14-27.

Source: Pressmaster/Shutterstock.com

The key point when developing a human resource management plan is to include all tasks that will help the retailer satisfy or impress customers. HR's job is to make sure retail personnel have a good understanding of the retailer's customers. The HR manager should access the retail information system (RIS) databases to become familiar with the target consumers' behaviors, lifestyles, demographics, and geographics prior to the development of the HR plan.

The HR manager should begin the planning phase by creating a list of tasks that need to be undertaken within the retail environment. In addition, HR personnel should talk to the managers and employees of other functional areas to confirm the list and allow them to add additional tasks to it.

To assist with the collection and dissemination of HR-related information, HR managers utilize *human resource information systems (HRIS)*. HRIS is software or an online method for systematically gathering, analyzing, storing, and utilizing information and data related to personnel management.

Advances in information technology have changed the human resource function. Today HRIS helps professionals manage the recruitment function, store and maintain employee information and assist with schedules and workflows. HRIS can help HR professionals with short- and long-term planning. The implementation of HRIS has also allowed HR professionals to spend more time on strategic planning. The top concerns of HRIS are security of information and privacy (Zafar, 2012). Additional concerns are as follows (Top HRIS Challenges, 2002):

- Integration of various HR applications
- Making information available electronically to employees
- Developing and improving intranets
- Self-service implementation
- Accomplishing HRIS goals with limited or reduced resources

Short- and Long-Term Analysis and Planning

One of the HR manager's responsibilities is to identify all the tasks to be performed by the retailer and members of the channel of distribution. These tasks are divided into long-term and short-term plans. Long-term generally refers to a plan with a scope of more than one year, whereas short-term refers to a plan that is in effect one year or less.

Long-Term Analysis and Planning: To pursue a long-term approach to HR planning, the retailer should focus on the overall growth of the organization. In other words, the retailer needs to be knowledgeable about the organization's growth patterns and then project future growth. Generally growth is documented by sales volume.

Company growth affects all areas of the business, especially HR. If the projected growth for the retailer is high, the organization may want to expand by increasing the number of stores or pursuing other retail formats such as e-tailing, catalog retailing, or direct retailing. Based on the retailer's projected growth, the HR staff needs to ensure that adequate numbers of employees are available to staff the expansion. Also, it needs to train the new (and possibly current) employees in their new positions.

Often a retailer is unable to expand due to an insufficient number of employees or a lack of employee skill sets. The retailer must monitor where company growth will occur—to develop an understanding of the customers within that geographic market and, in turn, to train the employees who will service those customers.

Short-Term Analysis and Planning: Although long-term planning is important, in this age of "we want it now," larger retailers are emphasizing short-term analysis. As stated earlier, short-term analysis refers to plans that are less than one year in duration. Generally, it is a good idea to break the short-term plan into smaller units that are aligned with merchandise seasons, quarters, or months. During the Christmas season, for example, the need for different functional areas, and especially for additional employees, is usually high.

Part-Time Employees: A final issue the retail HR specialist must plan for is the number and type of part-time employees. Retailers use many part-time employees to accommodate heavier customer traffic during peak buying periods.

Restaurant retailing has day-parts (different times of the day) that are more popular than others. Most people prefer to eat during their "regular" at-home dining hours. Thus, the most popular customer times are the day-parts of breakfast, lunch, and dinner. In some instances employees are needed for late-night meals, such as at a bar and grill or a diner. These patterns vary from country to country and even region to region. For example, in Boca Raton, Florida, where the seasonal elderly population is high, most restaurants commonly have a surge of dinner patrons from 4 to 5 P.M. In contrast, in Spain dinner is usually served no earlier than 9 P.M. It is the job of HR professionals to make sure enough full-time and part-time employees are "on the clock" to meet or exceed customers' expectations.

Increased Skill Sets for E-tail Employees

E-tailing poses some additional challenges for retailers. The human resource department needs to be aware of the different skill sets needed for employees of an e-tail firm. In addition to having basic business skills, e-tailing personnel need a background in technology. Skills in computing and networking are important. E-tail employees should also have training in applicable hardware and software management, maintenance, and development. Table 10.2 (next page) lists some potential career areas for people interested in the e-tail field.

Although many specialized positions exist, e-tailers follow the same processes in hiring employees that brick-and-mortar retailers do. The special challenge is to find individuals qualified to staff these positions. The e-tailer also needs human resource personnel with a background in both e-tailing and technology to be able to manage employees effectively.

After dealing with the planning process, the retail HR manager can move on to other areas to be included in the HR plan, such as task development, job creation, development of organizational charts, hiring and firing processes, and employee compensation.

Source: thodonal88/Shutterstock.com

Table 10.2 Positions in an E-tail Environment

- Business intelligence and analytics
- Distribution center and supply chain management
- Loss prevention specialists
- Mobile technology specialists
- Network technicians
- Network administrators
- Network designers
- Systems administrators and technicians
- Programmers
- Systems analysts
- Web programmers
- Database managers, administrators, analysts and programmers
- Management, marketing and sales
- Customer service
- Web designers, writers and editors
- Social media manager
- Search engine optimization technician

Source: racorn/Shutterstock.com

Developing Tasks

Task development is an essential part of the overall HR plan. Figure 10.1 provides a list of general tasks. Some tasks are specific to a particular retailer, such as insurance negotiations for delivery businesses. Delivery firms, such as UPS and Federal Express, hire numerous employees to take retailers' products directly to customers' homes or businesses. For these types of retailers, it is the task of the HR manager to make sure that insurance coverage is in place.

Figure 10.1 General Tasks in the Development of the HR Plan

The Retail Site	Marketing	Merchandising	Administration	Customer Service
Who will:	Who will:	Who will:	Who will:	Who will:
Determine site locations	Develop IMC components	Handle shipping and receiving	Develop store and credit policies	Handle customer contact
Handle security	Sell	Handle pricing	Handle budgeting	Develop customer service
Manage store appearance		Mark merchandise	Purchase supplies and equipment	Handle complaints
		Handle inventory warehouse and storage	Manage people	Evaluate customer service
		Handle damaged/ returned merchandise		

Frequently, other members of the channel of distribution, such as a vendor, can perform a number of the tasks associated with running a retail business. This is important to a retailer involved in negotiations with merchandise vendors. For example, the retailer may be able to negotiate a liberal advertising allowance with a manufacturer. An *advertising allowance* is a price concession given by a manufacturer of a product to a retailer to defray the retailer's costs associated with advertising the product. Depending on the agreement, in some cases, the manufacturer performs many of the advertising activities that would typically fall on the retailer. The amount of the allowance is negotiated between the buyer and seller. When another channel member performs activities for the retailer, the amount of capital and human resources the retailer would need to perform that function is reduced.

Often tasks can be outsourced. Many retailers, such as Home Depot, have in-house advertising and integrated marketing communication (IMC) professionals that work on tasks associated with those areas. However, some retailers may want to outsource those tasks---not only to reduce expenses, but also to take advantage of various areas of expertise that are unavailable in-house. For example, an advertising agency may be better equipped than the retailer to achieve large media purchases at a reduced cost.

Task Analysis

Whether the retailer chooses to outsource tasks or not, the retailer still needs to develop a complete list of the tasks required to efficiently run the retail operation. Task analysis is one method of facilitating the listing of tasks.

Figure 10.2 illustrates the steps involved in task analysis. To perform a task analysis, the retailer (or HR manager) first identifies the tasks believed to be essential to the smooth, integrated operation of the retail business. The HR manager then determines which employee positions will be responsible for the tasks. Finally, performance standards for each position are developed.

Identify Tasks: In this step, the retail manager lists all the tasks needed to run the business. Additionally, decisions are made about whether any tasks can be assigned to other members of the channel of distribution. If so, the tasks are assigned to those members. For example, the advertising task may be assigned to an internal employee who has the responsibility of working with the retailer's advertising agency (another member in the channel) in the development of the necessary functions of integrated marketing communication.

Retailers should not overlook customers as potential sources of task performance. If one retail task is home delivery of products, the retailer may be able to negotiate with a customer to have the customer assume the task of home delivery. To assign this task to the customer, the retailer may need to offer the customer a concession, such as a percentage off the product's price or a discount on future purchases. Many retailers find that customers like this idea and are willing to perform the delivery task if given some incentive. The incentive should be in line with the amount of money the retailer would save by not having to perform the task itself. This practice is fairly common in the do-it-yourself (DIY) industry, factory outlets, and home improvement retailers.

Figure 10.2
Stages in Task Analysis

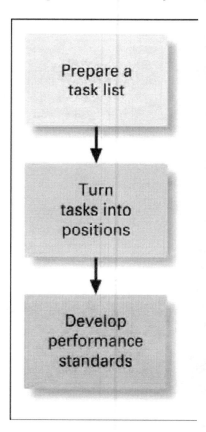

Retailers need to keep in mind that the customer is the reason they are in business. This means that if a customer refuses to perform a task, the retailer should respect the customer's feelings and perform the task itself. The retailer must use critical-thinking skills to determine who can best perform the task to meet the customer's expectations.

A final consideration is that the more the retailer outsources tasks, the more control the retailer gives up. Because no one provides a service for free, the retailer needs to understand channel members' wants, needs, and reasons for task performance. When a task is critical to a retailer's operation, performing it in-house may be the only way to ensure reliable, efficient results at a reasonable price.

Turning Tasks into Positions: In this step of the task-development process, the retailer groups the tasks into jobs or positions. *Jobs* (or positions) are general categories managers use to assign responsibility of task performance to members of the retail organization.

In this step, tasks developed in the first step are classified into positions within the organization. Each task can be broken down into subtasks, or steps taken to accomplish a particular task. Similar tasks/subtasks are assigned to one person or group of people. The key in turning tasks into positions is to make sure that both the tasks and the positions are clearly defined. Employees need to know exactly what they are doing and why they are doing it.

One method for clarifying tasks is to create *job descriptions*, also known as job classifications, job specifications, or position descriptions. The chief characteristic of job descriptions is that they tell employees exactly what needs to be accomplished. A good job description includes the job's title, the employee's immediate supervisor, the overall objective of the job, and the specific duties and responsibilities. This communicates to the employee, as well as other retail personnel, who is accountable for the completion of various tasks and who reports to whom.

A potential negative aspect of job descriptions is that they can limit employee performance. Most people have experienced the "it's not part of my job description" attitude from an employee at one time or another. If an employee finishes his or her work before other employees, that employee, due to the limitations of the job description, may have down time---nonproductive time that could be better spent helping other employees accomplish their tasks. Thus, the specificity of a job description can hinder maximum productivity.

Many retailers agree that job descriptions can be restrictive for their employees. Others ar-

Source: Dragon Images/Shutterstock.com

gue that the only good job description is one that states, "Your job is to make sure the customer is happy while at the same time providing a return on investment to all of our stakeholders." The way to achieve appropriate specificity may be to include in the job description a statement that the employee has primary responsibility for a given area but is also expected to perform other tasks as assigned by her or his manager.

Keep in mind that one retail institution may have many tasks another does not. Therefore, the tasks and jobs developed must be specific to the particular retailer. Also, small "mom and pop" retailers may not have written job descriptions simply because they do not need them. This is especially true with family-run businesses in which every family member grew up working in the store and takes on tasks as needed. The bigger the organization, the more likely it is to have written human resource policies and job descriptions.

Developing job descriptions is an iterative process; it is necessary to analyze tasks periodically to incorporate changes into the design. The task analysis process can be time-consuming and involve many hours of research. An online source available from the Bureau of Labor Statistics can aid in this task. The Occupational Outlook Handbook (2016-2017, http://www.bls.gov/ooh/) is a nationally recognized source of career information that is revised every two years. The searchable handbook describes the tasks performed for specific jobs, working conditions, necessary training and education, earnings, and trends. It offers guidelines for preparing job descriptions and for determining salary and training requirements. In addition, individuals seeking employment can use the website's resources to find information related to their career search.

Develop Performance Standards: The third step in the task-analysis process is to develop performance standards for the tasks listed in the job description. These standards document the level of proficiency required to meet quality and quantity expectations. The performance standards can be used to identify training needs as well as to provide feedback to employees.

Based on the short-term and long-term human resource plans and, in particular, the tasks and positions created, the retailer creates an organizational chart, the subject of the next section. The organizational chart presents the hierarchy of the company in a graphical form.

Organizational Charts

Organizational charts delineate who is responsible for the various areas of the retail firm. The chart provides a visual display of what the retail organization looks like. Software programs such as PowerPoint make it easy to produce organizational charts.

Small, independent retailers may have a simple organizational chart or, for that matter, no chart at all. It may be understood that the owner is "the boss" and responsible for the entire operation. If the organization does have a hierarchy, it may grow out of previous family arrangements. Figure 10.3 (next page) depicts a typical organizational chart for a small, independent retailer.

Figure 10.3 Organizational Chart for Small Retailer

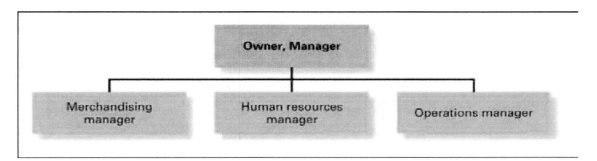

Larger retailers, particularly the big chains, need organizational charts to inform employees about who has responsibility and authority for the various retail departments or product lines. Organizational charts usually fall into functional, regional, divisional, or product/brand structures. Each retailer determines the type of chart that best meets the organization's needs. Figure 10.4 depicts the four types of organizational charts generally used by larger retailers.

Figure 10.4 Types of Organizational Charts

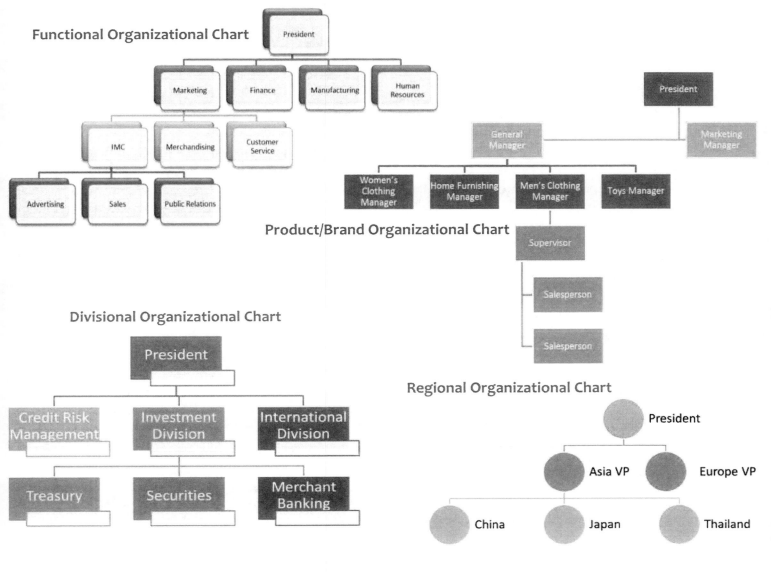

Types of Organizational Charts

The *functional chart* is based on the retailer's functional activities, including marketing, human resources, and customer service. *Regional charts* are based on geographic designations. These charts contain titles such as Manager---East Coast Division or Vice President of Asian Operations. *Divisional charts* are based on particular divisions or business units within the organization. *Product/ brand charts* are based on the products or brands the organization carries. These charts contain designations such as Apparel Manager, Automotive Manager, or Sporting Goods Associate. Retailers may combine these chart structures. For instance, one may find titles such as Eastern Division Manager---Men's Apparel or Vice President of Customer Relations---U.S. Division.

Each type of retailer finds that a specific type of chart best fits the organization. Hospitals set up their organizations differently than food retailers. In addition, an organization may have a number of different structures, including for instance, one for its corporate offices and one for its franchise divisions.

Organizational Design

Although tasks and jobs often vary among different retailers, some organizational design issues are universal to all retail organizations. Every retailer should strive to match its organizational structure to its mission, vision, and overall strategic direction.

Another universal consideration is that employees within the hierarchical structure need to have a clear understanding of where

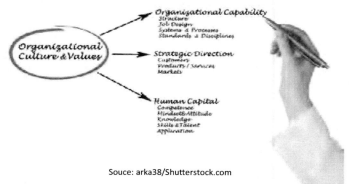

Souce: arka38/Shutterstock.com

responsibility and authority lie within the organization. The organizational chart illustrates the chain of command. Additionally, by attaching authority and responsibility to the job description, the retail store manager or firm CEO knows who is or is not performing as expected.

Finally, appropriate reporting structures are essential to any type of organizational structure. There needs to be an effective mix of employees who directly report to any given manager. Too many direct reports result in lost productivity because a manager cannot devote enough time to the individuals who report to him. Too few direct reports will also result in lost productivity because the manager may have too much time on her hands. Thus, achieving balance in this area is important.

The organizational design should take into account the type of work being performed. Is the work specialized or general in nature? One may argue that store managers should be retail generalists. Retail generalists have an understanding of all functions within the retail organization but may be unable to perform all of them equally well. Retail specialists, on the other hand, focus on a specific type of task or job. Researchers, for example, are generally specialists. The store manager may understand the researcher's output but not have a good grasp of what is required to initiate and execute a research project. The store manager may not know how to calculate the various statistics or even which statistics to use to get the information required, whereas the research specialist is trained in that specific task.

Organizational Design for Retailers' Specific Needs

Different types of retailers use different organizational designs. Department stores tend to use a functional organizational structure. Retail researcher and author Paul Mazur (1927) developed an organizational design in the form of a chart in the 1920s that is still utilized by many retailers today, especially department store chains. Mazur's chart has been updated to reflect current operations. The basic structure is depicted in Figure 10.5.

Figure 10.5   Sample Organizational Chart for a Department Store

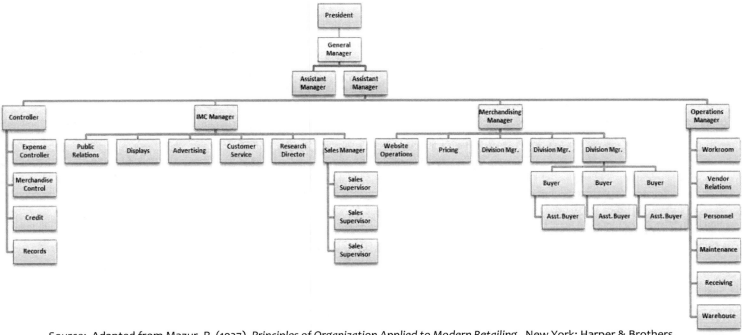

Source: Adapted from Mazur, P. (1927). *Principles of Organization Applied to Modern Retailing.* New York: Harper & Brothers.

When designing the organization, the retailer should address structural issues that affect the retail group. For example, is the retailer centralized in terms of decision making? In a *centralized organizational structure*, decisions are made from one central location, often termed headquarters or the home office. The primary advantage of a centralized organizational structure is that it makes integration and coordination easier to achieve when compared to a decentralized organizational structure.

In a *decentralized organizational structure*, decisions are made at the local level instead of from a central location. In a chain store operation structured in this way, for example, each store makes decisions regarding its own operation with little or no coordination among other branches. The primary advantage of decentralization is that it allows retailers to cater to the needs of the local market. Decentralization is preferred by firms that are very diverse in their business offerings. Whether centralized or decentralized, the key is to choose a structure that best fits the company's overall design.

Source: Rawpixel.com/Shutterstock.com

After the organizational design and charts have been developed, the retailer needs to determine who is best qualified to fill the positions within the organization. The next section focuses on how human resource personnel recruit and hire qualified job applicants.

The Hiring Process

Recruitment is an often-overlooked yet critical function of human resource personnel. Potential employees must be a good fit for the organization. Sometimes the criteria for "good fit" can be surprising, as shown in the following example.

A graduating senior went for an interview for an entry-level position at a large retail firm. When the student returned from the interview, her professor asked her for the details. She explained that she thought she had done her homework by studying the retailer and the types of people the retailer was seeking for its work force. She had also given a lot of attention to her personal appearance. She purchased an "interview suit," appropriate shoes, and understated jewelry. The morning of the interview, she took particular care that her hair and makeup looked appropriate. When she entered the interview, she felt confident. At the end of the interview, however, the interviewer politely told her that she would not be asked back for a second interview.

The professor, who could vouch for the student's extensive retail and marketing knowledge, wondered what had gone wrong in the interview. Curiosity got the best of him, so he decided to call the personnel manager (who, coincidentally, was a former colleague). When he asked why the student had not been invited back, he got a surprising answer. The interviewer assured him that the student had done a wonderful job preparing for the interview and that he was impressed with her company and industry knowledge. However, the one defining feature of the interviewee was that she didn't smile enough. The personnel manager explained that this particular retailer was extremely customer-focused and that each employee was expected to communicate this fact to customers through the simple act of smiling. He went on to explain that the appearance of being happy was the number one attribute they were looking for and this student just wouldn't fit with the overall organizational culture. When the professor relayed this conversation to the student, the importance of studying the corporate culture prior to applying for a position was clearly driven home.

Many retailers have specific wants in terms of their employees. It may be that some positions within the retail organization require different types of people than others do. Doing homework on the retail firm's organizational culture may be the most advantageous step for the retail job applicant. Frequently information about a firm's culture is not found in published reports. A good way to find out about a firm is to talk to current or former employees. When visiting a retail site, one employee was asked if she liked her job. She smiled and enthusiastically replied, "I love my job!" This is the type of employee retailers want.

In hiring, HR personnel look for the best match between the employee and the organization. Numerous techniques can be used to determine which potential employees are best suited to the job. When performing the hiring function, the main task is to recruit the best possible employees. Effective recruitment saves

Source: Rawpixel.com/Shutterstock.com

valuable time and effort in training and can even avoid the need to fire an employee who does not fit well with the organization.

Human Resource Recruitment

Hiring retail employees can be a challenging task. The field of retailing is known to have lower starting wages than many other industries. In addition, there are many more part-time employees in retailing than in other industries. Consequently, benefit packages may be less attractive for part-timers. Long and varied hours of work are not unusual, especially in the hospitality and tourism segments.

Human resource recruitment is the process of identifying and attracting the best potential employees (Barber, 1998). To ensure effective management, recruitment activities can be broken down into the following tasks: (1) determine the number of potential employees who will be attracted to the position, (2) clarify the type of potential employees desired, and (3) identify those potential employees who will accept the job offer (Chowdhury, Endres and Lanis, 2002).

The first task is to recruit as many applicants as possible, provided they are qualified. Having a large number of applications is not helpful if the applicants are not qualified to do the job. Therefore, it is important to generate a large pool of qualified applicants.

The second task is to clarify the type of employee that is desired. The student in the preceding example would have been better prepared for her job interview had the hiring firm communicated clearly that the organization was looking for enthusiastic, upbeat people. Finally, the retailer needs to identify the candidates most likely to accept the job offer. The HR professional should consider what potential employees may want prior to searching for qualified individuals. It is pointless to recruit potential employees who will turn down the offer. People look for certain things in a career. Certainly compensation is a key factor. An applicant whose objective is to receive a starting salary of at least $55,000 upon graduation may not want to interview with a retailer for a position offering only $45,000. Other things many applicants look for include excellent benefits, a satisfying quality of life, and working in a given geographical location. All of these factors can influence a candidate's decision to accept or reject an employment offer.

Company Policies and Practices

Company policies and practices provide guidance to managers on how to recruit. For example, company policy may require HR professionals to recruit employees from particular sources. Many retailers have policies that call for internal recruitment prior to taking the recruitment process out of house. Internal recruitment refers to the act of promoting people from within the company. An internal recruitment policy might state that 80 percent of open positions should be filled through internal promotion. In other words, the policy would be that internal employees (those already working for the retailer) are given preference over external (outside) candidates for eight out of ten open positions.

Some retailers have more general policies. For example, Enterprise Holdings (rental cars) stores have a policy of promoting from within for managerial positions. They do hire new college graduates as manager-trainees, but once employed these trainees are given the first shot at any new openings (Burkhart, 2013).

A company's pay policies and practices can also play a role in recruiting personnel. How does the retailer's pay structure compare to that of the industry? Does the retailer have better benefits than its competitors do? Do desirable employees prefer straight salaries or salaries with commissions? Are bonuses given? How rapidly are raises earned? The retailer should strive to create competitive advantage when recruiting potential personnel.

Another practice with regard to recruitment is to use *image advertising*. Image advertising is a type of advertising that attempts to enhance the retailer's overall standing in the eyes of the consumer (or in this case, the potential employee). Instead of, or in conjunction with, a detailed position vacancy ad, the retailer may advertise the advantages of working for the company. This practice helps recruitment efforts because it portrays the retail operation as a great place to work with a superior work environment.

Other common practices in recruiting employees are requiring potential employees to submit an application form and/or résumé, requiring references from the applicant, conducting interviews for the most preferred candidates, and administering various types of tests to ensure the applicant is a good fit. These areas are discussed in greater detail below.

The Application Form/Résumé: The application form and/or résumé helps ensure that the applicant has at least the minimal required qualifications. Through the application form, the firm can gather information for use during the recruitment process or later during the employee's tenure with the retailer. The application or résumé becomes a permanent record if the applicant is hired. Many firms use the application or résumé to screen out unsuitable candidates. This is an advantage if the retail organization has openings for popular jobs or if the job pays above the market average, resulting in a large influx of applications and résumés. For example, if an application or résumé contains spelling or grammatical mistakes, or if the candidate has obviously lied about something in the document, the retailer can immediately weed out that candidate.

References: For those applicants that will be called in for an interview, the HR professional should check the applicant's background through the references the candidate has supplied. This can be done before or after the interview, depending on time constraints and past practices. It is suggested that written recommendations be required, because they provide documentation and can be distributed more easily to those involved in the hiring process. Through the candidate's references, the retailer can obtain information helpful to the recruitment and hiring processes. Information about work habits and motivation level are often uncovered from references, for example. In addition, a reference check allows the retailer to verify the honesty and accuracy of the employment application and résumé.

Interviews: Interviews may be face-to-face or online (using Skype or other meeting technology). For the HR professional, the interview is the best opportunity to get to know the applicant prior to his or her employment. Often a phone interview or online interview is done to determine the top candidates to invite in for a face-to-face interview. A recent trend is to use a software program to screen applicants. HireVue (www.hirevue.com) is one example. After software and algorithms scan a resume for keywords, the best applicants receive an email invitation for a video interview. An online robot asks the applicant questions. Another robot scans the video to determine if

a person makes it to the next step. If the video does not match the template the employer uses to choose finalists, the applicant is not hired. This process does have critics. Many people believe interviews should be conducted by a person (Miller, 2015). Regardless, it's important for people to be prepared for robo-recruiting

An interview can be formal or informal. Formal interviews place the candidate "on guard." Because they can anticipate typical questions, candidates can prepare for the

Source: Monkey Business Images/Shutterstock.com

interview ahead of time. In a more informal setting (such as dinner, lunch, or after the formal interview), the candidate may speak a little more freely, allowing the interviewer to further assess the applicant's abilities. There may be several interviews before a person is chosen for a position.

Testing: Many retailers utilize various testing methods to get a better picture of potential employees. Often hard decisions must be made regarding whom to hire. If the field has been narrowed down to two equally qualified candidates, a test may help the HR manager break the tie. Employment tests vary in their applications and uses, but personality tests, psychological tests, and achievement tests are common in the retail industry.

Tests should be performed only on those applicants the retailer intends to hire. Tests are often set up to identify leadership skills and ability, intelligence level, or critical-thinking skills. Other tests help assess the applicant's physical strength. Many retail jobs require some degree of physical strength and endurance, especially jobs in the loading zones or on the docks.

Many retailers require drug tests for certain employees. A drug test should be considered if the job is such that the use of drugs or alcohol makes it dangerous not only to the potential employee but also to other employees and the public at large. In administering a drug test, the retailer must take care not to infringe on the applicant's basic rights. The courts generally hold that a drug test is permissible if the use of drugs or alcohol would impair the employee's job performance and/or endanger other people. A job involving delivery is an example of a position that would call for drug and/or alcohol testing.

Sources of Job Applicants

Once the recruitment policies and strategies have been established, HR personnel need to find sources of potential employees. The search may be limited by the retailer's hiring policies. Internal searches are somewhat easier than external searches. Generally, with an internal search, job announcements can be posted in common areas around the retail outlet. In addition, HR personnel can insert job postings in the retailer's internal correspondence, such as the company newsletter or intranet.

In the search for employees from external sources, the HR manager may want to employ one of the following methods:

1. Local, regional, or national newspapers' help-wanted listings

2. Trade association publications, such as Supermarket News

3. Direct applications (job seekers often send in unsolicited application letters and résumés)

4. Referrals (either internal or external)

5. Contracts with private employment agencies (sometimes called headhunters) for high-level internal positions

6. Recruitment at colleges and universities, especially those with majors or courses in retailing, marketing, or related areas

7. Postings on electronic bulletin boards or websites (see table 10.3)

One source for recruiting in LinkedIn. Launched in 2003, LinkedIn (www.linkedin.com) is a social networking site for business professionals. According to their website, the site has over 225 million members in over 200 countries (LinkedIn – About us, 2013). LinkedIn allows members to grow their professional networks within an environment that is free of games and has limited advertisements. Individual profiles are used to share both personal and professional information. In addition to individual LinkedIn profiles, LinkedIn groups can be created or joined. Linkedin allows users to join up to 50 groups. These groups allow interaction with people that are not in a user's network. Company web pages on LinkedIn often have information on open positions. Other job search websites where employers post are listed in table 10.3.

Table 10.3 Popular Job Post/Search Websites

Beyond	www.beyond.com
CareerBuilder	www.careerbuilder.com
Employment Crossing	www.employmentcrossing.com
Find the Right Job	www.findtherightjob.com
Indeed	www.indeed.com
Job	www.job.com
Monster	www.monster.com
SimplyHired	www.simplyhired.com/
Snag a Job	www.snagajob.com
StepStone	www.stepstone.com/
The Ladders	www.theladders.com

Once the best candidates have been identified and have passed all of the necessary screenings, they can be hired for employment. One word of caution concerns the numerous laws governing the hiring of employees, particularly laws that pertain to discrimination in the hiring process. These include the Vocational Rehabilitation Act (1973) and the Americans with Disabilities Act (1991), which extends the Vocational Rehabilitation Act. In addition, the Age Discrimination in Employment Act (1967), the Civil Rights Act (1964), and the Civil Rights Act (1991) provide guidance to HR professionals in hiring decisions.

Finally, a number of excellent candidates have been hired to work in the retail firm. Now that they are on board, they need training and management, topics to which we turn next.

Training and Management

At this point, the retailer's task is to attempt to retain its best employees. This can be achieved by developing an outstanding training program. Frequently, especially during down sales periods, retailers cut their training programs as a quick, short-term financial fix. This action, however, can set up employees and the entire organization for future failure. Training is crucial. It provides new employees with valuable information about the organization's culture, as well as information about the company's products, services, and policies. Training also helps make new hires feel at home in the organization. Training for current employees provides retail personnel with new information and innovative ways to get tasks performed faster, more accurately, and with less stress.

Training

It is preferable to break down training information into two areas. First, the retailer provides to current and new employees information about the organization as a whole so that employees will understand

Source: Robert Kneschke/Shutterstock.com

how what they do affects the larger organization. Employees should have information about the organizational structure and the retailer's policies and procedures, rules, objectives, and expectations. In addition, it is helpful to give employees (especially new employees) historical information about the retailer.

A second area of training is functional training. The retailer needs to generate training for each of the company's functional areas. Employees need to have training in basic skills such as customer relations, selling techniques, inventory control methods, reorder methods, and POS operation, among others, to ensure that they perform their jobs successfully.

The two main venues for conducting training are on-the-job training and off-the-job training.

On-the-Job-Training: *On-the-job training (OJT)* occurs at the location where the employee works, such as on the sales floor, in the office, or at the delivery docks. The employee is under direct supervision from his or her manager or supervisor, and the manager provides positive reinforcement as well as helpful hints on areas of needed improvement.

Off-the-Job Training: *Off-the-job training* occurs in conference rooms or classrooms specifically set up to provide intensive training for employees. Off-the-job training is more formal than on-the-job training. The trainers use various methods to dispense the necessary information to employees, including PowerPoint presentations, flip charts, cases, simulations, role playing, and any other technique that allows the employees to learn about the retailer's products, services, and brands, as well as areas such as inventory management or new and other applications for the retail operation.

Training Information: Training information can be provided in many formats. Generally the formats are referred to as individual, programmed, group, and mentor training. With *individual training,* employees take the responsibility to train themselves. This approach resembles a trial-and-error system. Employees are allowed to ask questions and are encouraged to observe other successful employees and managers. Most retailing experts do not recommend this method because the feedback loop is not formalized and new employees may model themselves after a system or method that is unproductive. In addition, because existing employees have other functions to perform, the new employee may be forced to "fly solo."

Methods of programmed learning can be very effective. *Programmed learning* is a structured, formal process that allows employees to study important material pertaining to the retailer's operation and then respond to questions about the material. It is much like taking a course and then having an examination covering the material of study. Employees can check their answers to questions from a "teacher's manual" or answer key. If they respond incorrectly to most of the questions, they can repeat the first two steps in the training process, study and examination, and take the test again. If they still have not mastered the material, they repeat the process until they get it right.

Source: Rawpixel.com/Shutterstock.com

Group training involves more than one employee. Employees are placed in groups that have similar training needs. Thus, cashiers may be included in one group, managers in another group, soft-line clerks in another group, and so forth. In group training, lectures and demonstrations, role playing, and case studies may be used to effectively convey information to employees. Group training also allows employees to get to know one another and share questions and information. It instills the value of teamwork and the need for integration within the retail organization.

Mentoring is another method of training employees. The retailer identifies employees who are ambitious, hard workers who exemplify the retailer's corporate culture. These employees are then assigned a new hire for whom they serve as role models. The difference between individual training and mentoring is that in mentoring, an existing employee takes responsibility for the development of a new employee. With individual training, the new employee is responsible for training himself or herself. Because hard-working role models have been identified as mentors, the mentor training method is very effective. Each of the skill sets needed for effective selling, buying, and customer relations can be taught and role-modeled for the new employee. This method also helps the new employees feel like they are part of a family.

Retailing executives and managers may require additional training not provided to other employees. Large department stores and chain stores in particular utilize a training method for upper-level employees labeled *executive training programs (ETP).* ETP may also be used for ambitious employees who are working their way up the corporate ladder.

ETP training is sometimes outsourced. Sometimes retailers provide funding for executives and managers to take coursework at various colleges and universities. In addition, retail trade associations frequently offer seminars or courses that award continuing educational units (CEUs) upon completion. The educational value of these programs includes the opportunity for employees to interact with others in the industry.

Whichever training method is chosen, the goal is to offer employees additional education about basic skills and functional skills areas. Training in reading, mathematical ability, and cognitive abilities is not uncommon. The training needs to focus on the teaching of transferable skills (skills that can be used in almost every area of the retail operation). Feedback is an important component of training programs. If employees do not know what they are doing right or wrong, the training will be useless.

Assessing the Outcome of Training: At some point, the outcomes from the training sessions need to be assessed. What were the cognitive outcomes? Were the skills learned effectively? What benefits did the employee gain from the training?

A final application of training is to assess on-the-job results. It would be beneficial to develop a method of tracking employees to see if the training paid off. A tracking system can provide management with a return-on-training investment and allow for changes in areas that need them.

The training process involves certain legal issues. The trainer needs to be up to date on issues dealing with injury, confidentiality, copyrights for training materials, and other potential problems. Legal training for the trainer is generally an expense that pays off in the long run.

Management

Retail management can be broken down into three areas: supervision and evaluation, motivation, and compensation. Another area of interest is diversity management.

Supervision and Evaluation: *Supervision* involves the retail manager directing employees as they perform their tasks to ensure the tasks are completed. In addition to overall direction of employees, the manager must ensure that employees are performing at a productive level.

Evaluation of employees is generally tied to minimum performance levels or objectives designed for each

Source: SFIO CRACHO/Shutterstock.com

position in the firm. It is the role of a supervisor to determine the objectives for a given position. The objectives, or goals, should be based on the overall retail objectives, divisional objectives, and departmental objectives. Having established objectives helps the retailer ensure that everyone in the organization is working toward the same goals and that employees' tasks have been coordinated to minimize duplication.

As a rule of thumb, performance appraisals should be fair, systematic, and formal, and should contain quantifiable criteria. Even though performance appraisals are done on an individual basis, all employees performing the same tasks should be evaluated using the same criteria.

One way to appraise individual employee performance is to provide ongoing informal evaluations plus formal evaluations that become part of the employee's record. Time periods for formal evaluations should be based on the retailer's schedule. Usually formal evaluations occur yearly; some retailers evaluate more often, but rarely more than quarterly.

The formal evaluation should enlighten the employee regarding his or her job performance. The employee should leave the formal evaluation with a firm understanding of what she or he did right and where there is room for improvement. The criteria used to evaluate employees should be provided to them prior to their evaluations. It is a good idea to give employees a detailed list of the tasks they are expected to perform and the level at which they are expected to perform them. The various levels of performance should also be included in the performance evaluation.

To illustrate, consider a retail sales clerk who is scheduled for an evaluation. The criteria or objectives that are developed should include how the clerk will be assessed. For example, the retailer may have developed an overall corporate culture of consumer service and friendliness. This objective needs to be quantified. What is meant by "friendliness"? How can this employee know whether she is performing as she is expected to? For example, a retail manager may use mystery shoppers as part of the evaluation process, to help quantify performance. In this scenario, one part of the evaluation would read, "number of mystery shoppers who complained about employee X," or "number of mystery shoppers who complimented the work of employee X." The principle is that the evaluation of employee X should be as specific as possible.

Let's say the number of complaints for an "average" rating on the appraisal is between 3 and 5; for an "above average" rating, complaints fall between 1 and 2; and an "outstanding performance" rating is zero complaints. An employee with more than five complaints would know that his or her job performance is below average. Some quantitative measure must be tied to the employee's performance evaluation.

Often formal evaluations are directly tied to employee compensation. Employees may receive bonuses or even pay raises based on their overall performance in meeting or exceeding the retailer's objectives.

Motivation: *Motivation* is a basic drive of all humans. The motivational drive is usually associated with unsatisfied needs or the desire to create personal or job satisfaction. Individual employees have different levels and types of motivation. For this reason, the motivational process is sometimes difficult for managers. The key to successful motivation is to develop an overall organizational culture for the retailer. The *organizational culture* is "the pattern of shared values and beliefs that help individuals understand organizational functioning and thus provide them norms for behavior in the organization" (Deshpande and Webster, 1989). Many believe that culture is the most important factor accounting for the success or failure of a company (Deal and Kennedy, 1982).

The organizational culture should evolve from the retailer's vision statement and should include the organization's values, traditions that have developed over time, and customs or practices. The organization's culture is *not* written, other than the information contained in the vision statement. It is generally passed verbally or by example from employee to employee within the organization. The members of the retailer's channel of distribution usually understand the organization's culture, as well, by having worked with its employees.

Two types of motivation exist: intrinsic and extrinsic. *Intrinsic motivation* comes from an employee's internal feelings. Someone who says "I work because it makes me happy" is indicating that he or she is intrinsically motivated. In other words, intrinsic motivation is an internal reward the employee receives for doing a good job. External rewards such as awards, trips, and a pat on the back help develop intrinsic motivation. In fact, intrinsic motivation often can be tied to extrinsic motivational processes, such as bonuses. The retail manager must motivate employees to want to perform.

Source: Phovoir/Shutterstock .com

Extrinsic motivation comes from outside the individual. The most common types of extrinsic motivators are monetarily based incentives: the employee is rewarded for good work with cash or other prizes. Commissions and bonuses are the main types of incentives used in retailing. Commissions are tied to productivity and typically represent the amount of money an employee will earn for each individual sale---a fixed amount developed by formula. For example, a retail furniture salesperson may receive an additional 10 percent of the selling price for each piece of furniture he sells over $500.

A bonus is compensation, in addition to base salary and commissions, given to the employee for reaching additional levels of performance. For example, the furniture salesperson might be rewarded with additional amounts of money if he reaches certain objectives in terms of customer service and product sales. Bonuses are generally given for a specified period of time. They may be tied to the employee's job appraisal or evaluation, to a department's overall sales performance, to the store's performance, or to the retailer's overall performance.

It is wise to use both extrinsic and intrinsic motivational tools to encourage employees to work to their fullest potential. The retail manager needs to be a cheerleader, a frenzied fan, or a coach, as appropriate, when it comes to employee motivation. Above all, the manager must be fair and impartial in attempting to generate high levels of employee motivation.

Compensation: One key factor in attracting and retaining employees is the method used to compensate and otherwise reward them. Employee compensation refers to both the payment of money for services performed (commissions, salaries, hourly rates, bonuses) and any benefits the employee is to receive from the retailer, such as health insurance, life insurance, paid personal days, paid vacation days, retirement benefits, and perhaps a car allowance for out-of-store retail salespeople. Whatever the method chosen to reward employees for their work, the compensation plan should be fair to all employees as well as to the retail organization.

Traditional compensation structures work for any type of retail organization from brick-and-mortar to brick-and-click to click-only retailers. Following are descriptions of the various compensation plans.

Hourly Wage. Under an hourly wage compensation system, the retailer and employee agree on an amount of money the employee is to be paid for each hour of work. The retailer may predetermine the wage, or it may be negotiable with input from the employee.

Straight Salary. Straight salary is an agreed-on, fixed amount paid to the employee for a specified period of time at work. A salary can be stated in quarterly, weekly, or monthly periods, but is almost always yearly.

Straight Commissions. A straight commission is compensation for the amount of sales an employee generates, in either units or dollars. Employees who are individualists and hard workers often prefer the commission structure because it rewards them with payments based on their own performance. It is a good fit for those employees who are highly extrinsically motivated.

Salary Plus Commission. In a salary-plus-commission arrangement, the employee gets a fixed salary but also receives commissions for sales of products (either units or dollars) above what is expected during normal performance of his or her duties. The salary-plus-commission system allows the retailer some control over employees, but it also generates a strong level of employee motivation.

Salary Plus Bonus. Many executives and upper-level managers prefer a system that gives them a salary but also provides a bonus for extraordinary work. Under this system, the employee receives a straight salary but also gets periodic bonuses (weekly, monthly, quarterly, or yearly) for extraordinary sales or behavioral performance. This system allows the employee to earn a good living while also having the opportunity to work harder and earn more money. Bonuses are not given to employees who fail to meet their basic retail objectives. Job appraisal and evaluation decisions should be separate from whether or not an employee receives a bonus, however.

In addition to the above plans, retailers often provide employees with fringe benefits. These benefits allow employees to have a satisfying lifestyle without additional out-of-pocket costs for necessities such as health and life insurance. Table 10.4 (next page) lists the major types of benefits.

In some instances, benefits are paid for directly by the retailer. Recently, however, it has become more common for employee and retailer to share the cost of fringe benefits. For example, the employee may pay the first $250 to $300 of health insurance, with the employer paying 100 percent of the remainder.

Many retailers use a "smorgasbord" or "cafeteria plan" approach to benefits. A cafeteria plan allows employees a certain amount of money for benefits; then, from a prepared list, employees select those benefits that are most beneficial to them, up to the paid amount. They are then allowed to purchase additional benefits for themselves or their family members out of their own pockets. The out-of-pocket costs are usually affordable because the health care provider has given the retailer a quantity discount that is passed on to employees. Thus, the retailer incurs no expenses from the employees' additional benefits. Generally the retailer deducts these payments directly from the employees' paychecks.

Involuntary Employee Turnover

The two main reasons for involuntary employee turnover are termination and downsizing. Termination most often occurs due to unsatisfactory performance. Because of the costs associated with employee turnover, the retail manager should strive to retain good employees and at the same time help poor to average employees boost their performance. There are varying reasons that an employee may underperform. Reasons such as poor training or an unsatisfactory employee-task fit can be corrected. When it becomes evident that an employee is not a good fit for the organization, however, it is to the benefit of both retailer and employee to sever the relationship.

Table 10.4 Major Fringe Benefits

1. Insurance: Both health insurance and life insurance. The insurance may be for the employee only, or may be designed for the employee's immediate family.

2. Sick Leave: This is paid time off given to the employee because of illness. Many times the retailer allows the employee to take "sick time" for members of their immediate family as well as for themselves.

3. Personal Time Off: In many instances, the retailer will allow their employees to take time off, with pay, to take care of family or household problems and issues. Thus an employee can take a "personal day" for almost any reason, without having to report that reason to the employer.

4. Recreational facilities: Many employers offer the employee facilities to relax or workout. This may come in the form of health club memberships for the employees. It may be a small weight room that can be used by the employees for working out.

5. Employee Discounts: Employees are often awarded discounts at the retail outlet for products that they purchase from the retailer. This discount is good for both the employee and the employer. It shows the customer that the employee is also a patron of the store because they are wearing clothing from the retail outlet. In service retailing, it is common to let the employee take advantage of the service or the services facilities as part of the benefit of working for the retailer. An example would be the airline industry, where employees can fly "for free" if they follow many of the restrictions for this program.

6. Pension or Retirement Plans: Often the retailer will contribute to the employee's retirement program.

7. Profit Sharing: In order to create a "family" culture, or to motivate employees to work harder, many retailers have come up with profit-sharing programs. These programs allow the employees to share in the overall profit of the retailer to some level. E-tailers, when they were first starting out, utilized profit sharing and stock options as a method of recruiting good employees. Because they couldn't afford to pay new employees the amounts of money they were making in the brick-and-mortar stores, the e-tailers developed this plan that allowed them to pay the employees less, but at the same time allowed the employees to buy back into the organization through the use of stock options, or to get additional monies at the end of the period through the use of profit sharing.

8. Holiday Paid Leave: Many retailers offer their employees certain days of the year off as a result of national holidays. In most cases these employees are paid for their time.

9. Paid Vacations: Paid vacations are not uncommon in retailing. This is an incentive and reward to the employee. The retailer designates the number of days off, per year generally, that the employee can take with pay. As a general rule, the longer the employee has been with the retailer, the more days off with pay he or she receives.

The step of terminating an employee should not be taken unless the employee cannot be "turned around" into a positive, contributing member of the retail organization. Employee termination, or firing, is one of the hardest tasks a retail manager faces. After all, the terminated employee may have a family to support or other pressing financial obligations.

The employee should have been given numerous warnings about the possibility of termination; it should not come as a surprise. Many laws deal with employee firing or termination. The key is to develop and implement a system that is in line with all laws and regulations applied to human resource management. Terminated employees often blame the system that was developed to assess their performance, claiming it was discriminatory or unjust. The wise manager has a tried-and-true system in place prior to firing any employee. Unjust dismissal and discrimination dominate legal cases against retailers.

Downsizing is another form of involuntary employee turnover. Downsizing (also called rightsizing, reduction in force, layoff and reengineering) occurs when a company eliminates large numbers of employees, typically to boost financial performance (Lewison, 2002). *Downsizing* often occurs after a company merges with or gets acquired by another company. In an unstable economy, employees lose jobs more to downsizing than to termination (Holstein, 2002).

Downsizing poses challenges to human resource managers, who must decide who to let go and whether or not to offer severance packages. After the downsizing, the managers must attend to the motivation of those who remain with the company. In an effort to assist downsized employees with the process of finding other employment, many retailers turn to outplacement services.

Outplacement is a process in which a business hires experts to offer support, personal assessments, and job-search skills training to employees that are being downsized (Lewison, 2002). Outplacement firms offer services that range from resume writing to providing phones and computers for job seekers (Oh, 2003). Outplacement has many benefits to the organization, including lessening the likelihood of litigation and creating a caring reputation. On the downside, outplacement services can be very expensive.

Voluntary Employee Turnover

In addition to involuntary employee turnover, most retailers experience numerous situations of voluntary employee turnover. Employees leave their companies because they wish to retire, want to change careers, have personal issues, have found other job opportunities outside the organization, or are simply unhappy with the retail organization. If possible, the retailer should set up exit interviews with departing employees to find out why they are leaving.

Information gained in exit interviews should be used to help the retailer develop managerial processes and systems that will better retain good employees. The cost associated with attracting and retaining employees is high; thus, retention directly affects the firm's profitability. Many firms, such as Chick-fil-A, offer college scholarships to employees who stay with the company for a minimum period of time. The costs associated with this practice are offset by the low employee turnover.

Target is an upscale discounter with over 1,800 stores located in the U.S. DiversityInc lists Target as #22 on their 2017 "Top 50 Companies for Diversity" list. According to their website (www.target.com):

> "We believe diversity and inclusivity make teams and Target better. And we'll live that belief as champions of a more inclusive society by creating *a diverse and inclusive work environment*, cultivating *an inclusive guest experience*, and fostering *equality in society*."

According to Brian Cornel, CEO of Target (On Women Taking the Lead..., 2016), "What I've seen throughout my career is the power that individuals and trusted brands can bring to the quest for greater opportunity and equality. By better understanding and serving our guests, by striving to create a more diverse and inclusive career environment and workforce, and by being smart and purposeful about the range of products and experiences we bring to market, we help create a better Target for our team and guests—and a better society for all."

To recruit employees (called team members), the company sponsors conferences and career fairs hosted by organizations that promote diversity and inclusion. Their goal is to recruit team members that represent the communities that the company serves. The company uses internal business councils to further diversity and inclusion efforts. More than 10,000 team members participate in these councils, which serve as sounding boards and for business issues, recruitment, professional development and mentoring. The members share their perspectives, experience and expertise to support the business. For example Target tapped the Hispanic Business Council to choose movie assortments that would appeal to the Hispanic market. The council's selections helped grow sales (Spotlight on Target's Hispanic Business Council, 2013).   The councils represent six groups: African American; Asian American; Lesbian, Gay, Bisexual, Transgender and Ally; Hispanic; Military; and Women. All team members volunteer personal time to serve on the councils.

Diversity and Inclusion in Retailing

Diversity is defined as differences among people. These differences include but are not limited to age, gender, ethnicity, race, and ability. According to diversity consultants Miller and Katz (2002), "Inclusion is a sense of belonging: feeling respected, valued for who you are; feeling a level of supportive energy and commitment from others so than you can do your best work." According to DiversityInc (2013), diversity management is the method of implementing diversity and inclusion strategies to maximize benefits of corporate diversity in the workplace.

The challenge for many businesses is to leverage diversity. Leveraging diversity occurs when different voices are sought out and viewed as opportunities for added value. Different perspectives and frames of reference have been proven to offer competitive advantages in teamwork, product quality, and work output (Kaleel-Jamison, 2008). People feel valued when they can apply individual and identity group perspectives to help and organization grow, as in the Target example.

Source: Rawpixel.com/Shutterstock.com

Numerous laws have been passed to foster diversity in the workplace. Equal employment opportunity (EEO) laws collectively prohibit discrimination on the basis of color, race, sex, religion, national origin, age, or physical disability. Affirmative action (AA) addresses conditions that systematically disadvantage individuals based on group identities such as gender or race.

Race and Ethnicity

Given the changing American ethnicity demographic, retailers need to pay increasing attention to the issue of diversity in the U.S. and well as in the retail work force. Table 10.5 (next page) gives a view of the projected growth of the four largest ethnic groups in the United States.

Based on United States 2010 counts, the following is the demographic breakdown of the United States: of the 308.7 million people, about 223.6 million (72.4.2%) were white (non-Hispanic); 39 million (12.6%) were black or African American (non-Hispanic); 15 million (4.8%) were Asian (non-Hispanic); 3 million (.9%) were American Indian or Alaska Native (non-Hispanic); and 540,013 (.2%) were Native Hawaiian and other Pacific Islander (non-Hispanic) (U.S. Census Bureau, 2013). As of 2010 there were 50 million (16.4%) Hispanics. Because Hispanics can be of any race, the breakdown includes the term non-Hispanic, to show that Hispanics have been taken out of the count for that category. As the United States moves toward a population with lower percentages of whites and higher percentages of Hispanics, African Americans, and Asians, it becomes essential for businesses to manage diversity well.

Table 10.5 Projected Growth of Four Largest Ethnic Groups

	2020	% of Pop	2030	% of Pop	2040	% of Pop	2050	% of Pop
White (NH)	255,346	76	267,604	75	276,438	72	282,959	71
Black (NH)	44,810	13	49,246	14	53,412	14	57,553	14
Asian (NH)	18,884	6	22,833	6	26,838	7	30,726	8
Hispanic	63784	19	78,655	22	94,876	25	111,732	28

Note: NH = Not Hispanic
Hispanics can be of any race
Source: U.S. Census Bureau (2012). Population Division. Percent Distribution of the Projected Population by Sex, Race and Hispanic Origin for the United States: 2015 to 2060 (NP2012-T5). Released Dec 2012.

These changes in demographics are also reflected in the workforce. Figure 10.6 shows the percentage distribution of employed people by occupation, race and Hispanic ethnicity.

Figure 10.6   Projected Growth of Four Largest Ethnic Groups

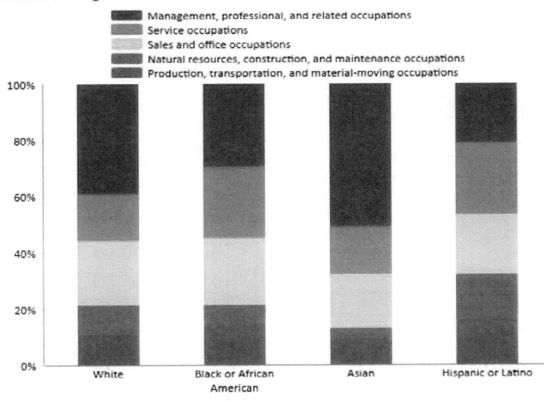

Employed people by occupation, race, and Hispanic or Latino ethnicity, 2014 annual averages

- Management, professional, and related occupations
- Service occupations
- Sales and office occupations
- Natural resources, construction, and maintenance occupations
- Production, transportation, and material-moving occupations

Note: People whose ethnicity is identified as Hispanic or Latino may be of any race
Data may not sum to 100 percent due to rounding.

Source: U.S. Bureau of Labor Statistics.

As the charts show, there are higher percentages of Asians and white people in management, business, and financial operations occupations compared to blacks or Hispanics, who are represented in higher percentages in service occupations. Employed black and Hispanic people also were more likely than white or Asians to work in production, transportation, and material moving occupations.

Although the workforce is more diverse, there is still a lack of diversity on the boards of Fortune 500 companies, but the situation is improving. According to Deloitte and Alliance for Board Diversity, women and minorities held about 31% of board seats in 2016. This is an increase from 25.5% in 2010 and 26.7% in 2012. About 80% of boards were male in 2016 compared to 83% in 2012 (Farber, 2017).

Graying of America

In addition to ethnic and racial changes, the growth of the 50-plus age group is a trend that will change the retail landscape. The Administration on Aging provides the following facts about older Americans (2015):

Source: Rawpixel.com/Shutterstock.com

- The older population (65+) numbered 46.2 million in 2014
- About one in every seven, or 14.5% of the population, is an older American.
- The number of Americans over age 65 is expected to grow to be 21.7% of the population by 2040
- Between 2004 and 2014, the number of Americans aged 45-64 (who will reach age 65 over the next two decades) increased by 17.8% and the number of Americans age 60 and over increased by 32.5% from 48.9 million to 64.8 million.
- In 2014, there were 25.9 million older women and 20.4 million older men, or a sex ratio of 127.2 women for every 100 men. At age 85 and over, this ratio increases to 192.2 women for every 100 men.
- Since 1900, the percentage of Americans 65+ has more than tripled (from 4.1% in 1900 to 14.5% in 2014), and the number has increased over fourteen times (from 3.1 million to 46.2 million).
- In 2014, persons reaching age 65 had an average life expectancy of an additional 19.3 years (20.5 years for females and 18 years for males).
- A child born in 2014 could expect to live 78.8 years, about 30 years longer than a child born in 1900.
- In 2014, 22% of persons 65+ were members of racial or ethnic minority populations—9% were African-Americans (not Hispanic), 4% were Asian or Pacific Islander (not Hispanic), 0.5% were Native American (not Hispanic), 0.1% were Native Hawaiian/Pacific Islander, (not Hispanic), and 0.7% of persons 65+ identified themselves as being of two or more races. Persons of Hispanic origin (who may be of any race) represented 8% of the older population. Almost half of older women (47%) age 75+ live alone.

- In 2014, about 554,579 grandparents aged 65 or more had the primary responsibility for their grandchildren who lived with them.

The population 65 and over has increased is projected to increase to 98 million in 2060. By 2040 there will be about 82.3 million older people, over twice their number in 2000. The 85+ population is projected to triple from 6.2 million to 14.6 million in 2040. Minority populations have increased from 6.5 million in 2004 (18% of the elderly population) to 10 million (22% of the elderly) in 2014 and are projected to increase to 21.3 million in 2030 (28% of the elderly) (Administration on Aging, 2013). Figure 10.7 shows the growth of people 65+ from 1900 – 2060.

Figure 10.7   Number of People 65+: 1900 – 2060
(numbers in millions)

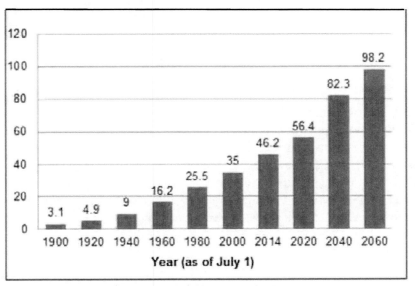

Note: Increments in years are uneven.
Source: U.S. Census Bureau, Population Estimates and Projections.

Retailers will have to pay attention to this group---because of its size, but also because it is wealthier than younger populations. Retailers must adapt to the environmental changes regarding diversity. Focus on inclusion and leveraging diversity and keep abreast of changes in the U.S. demographic profile to determine how these changes will alter their strategy.

Affirmative Action

Although there were early economic incentives for a diverse work force, many companies chose not to have one. Consequently, the federal government passed the Civil Rights Act of 1964, which prohibited employment discrimination by companies with more than fifteen employees and established the Equal Employment Opportunity Commission (EEOC). In 1965, President Lyndon B. Johnson signed an executive order requesting all government contractors and subcontractors to take "affirmative action" to expand job opportunities for minorities (Klingbeil, 2002). Women were also included in a 1967 order. Under affirmative action, among equally qualified candidates, those from underrepresented groups may be favored over those from overrepresented groups.

Source: iQoncept/Shutterstock.com

Affirmative action has sparked much controversy over the years, with numerous lawsuits related to discrimination as well as reverse discrimination. The University of Michigan (U of M) has been in the spotlight for several years because of its affirmative action policies. In 1997, three white students sued U of M, claiming that the university's racial preference programs resulted in reverse discrimination (Supreme Court Upholds, 2003). The case went to the U.S. Supreme Court (Gratz et al. v. Bollinger et al., and Grutter v. Bollinger), and in July, 2003 the court rendered two decisions. In the first decision, the court struck down the use of a point system that awarded minority undergraduate applicants an automatic 20 points on a 150-point scale. The second decision upheld the practice of the university's law school of considering race as one of the many factors in its applicant review process (Wilkie, 2003). In essence, the ruling allowed affirmative action programs to continue as long as universities are careful in their application and head toward race-neutral alternatives. In 2006, voters in Michigan voted to ban affirmative action in public colleges and universities. Arizona, California, Florida, Nebraska, New Hampshire, Oklahoma and Washington have also banned affirmative action (Hartocollis, 2016).

The court received seventy briefs in support of affirmative action and sixteen against. One brief in support came from sixty-five Fortune 500 corporations, which argued that diverse student enrollments aid businesses in achieving a diverse workforce---a requirement to compete globally (Walsh, 2003).

The most recent case to come to the Supreme Court was Fisher v. University of Texas. In 2008 Abigail Fisher sued the University and asked the court to rule that the University's admissions practice that considered race was inconsistent with the Grutter ruling. On June 24, 2013, the case was vacated by the Supreme Court in a 7-1 ruling and sent back to the 5th Circuit Court of Appeals for reconsideration (Psencik, 2013). In 2016, the Supreme Court rejected a challenge to Fisher v. University of Texas.

Acceptance of the programs related to affirmative action depends on how the particular business presents the programs. A recent trend in the recruitment of members of underrepresented groups is to focus on the business case for diversity instead of the underrepresentation argument.

The Business Case for Diversity

The business case for diversity centers on the premise that a company will be more profitable if it has a workforce that mirrors the demographics of the environment. The U.S. Census Bureau estimates that 90 percent of total population growth through 2050 will be among blacks, Hispanics, Asians and Pacific Islanders, and Native Americans (Alterio, 2002). The implications of increased diversity in the work force and in the customer base will position retailers to better meet the needs of target markets.

Customers prefer to purchase products from people to whom they can relate. As an example, the impetus for change in a then Fortune Service 500 company resulted from listening to its customers' request for a more diverse personnel base. The company had sent out a team of salespeople to try to create a relationship with a potentially large client. When the team came back to the corporate office, one of the vice presidents got a call from the client, who asked why the office had not sent out a team of salespeople who "looked" like the client, or at least people to whom the client could relate. The vice president realized that the group he had sent was representative of the company rather than of the client and that the company lacked a broad, diverse personnel base from which to select its sales teams. This incident made the company realize that without a diverse work force it would lose sales; that realization led to a major thrust toward diversity management and inclusion.

In addition to improving a retailer's bottom line, diversity initiatives help the company avoid future corporate complications. Benefits of diversity initiatives include decreases in complaints and litigation and improved image as some of the benefits of diversity programs (Alterio, 2002). Some retailers learned this lesson the hard way. For example, in the early 1990s, the Denny's restaurant chain was sued by a group of black customers for racial discrimination. The company eventually settled the lawsuit for about $54 million. The lawsuit forced Denny's Corporation (formerly Advantica Restaurant Group) to examine its treatment of customers and its hiring practices. Since then, Denny's has become a model for its diversity initiatives. Other companies, such as Texaco and Coca-Cola, have also settled lawsuits and have changed their hiring practices for the better (Jacobs, 2002).

Organizations, generally serving companies within particular industries, have formed to promote diversity and deal with diversity issues. One such organization is the Multicultural Foodservice and Hospitality Alliance (MFHA; www.mfha.net). Its goal is to be an educator, facilitator, and source of information on multiculturalism in its industry.

Recruitment

Retailers should develop a personnel base that mirrors their current and potential target markets. Thus, for an international retailer, employees should mirror the populations of the countries where the retailer does business. A retailer conducting business in Asia, for example, will improve its chances for success if it employs Asians. For domestic companies, the retailer's personnel should mirror the basic U.S. or regional population base. For example, for a retailer located in a city with a large population of Hispanics, hiring employees with Hispanic backgrounds can be a competitive advantage (Thiederman, 2003).

A common misunderstanding about diversity programs is that they are designed to benefit only women and "minorities." Diversity encompasses not only differences in gender, skin color, and ethnicity but also differences in religion, age, sexual orientation, and varying physical and mental abilities. The goal of diversity programs should be to offer a work environment that fosters growth and encourages each individual to thrive. Mary Jane Sinclair of Sinclair Consulting Inc. suggests that instead of just talking about "minorities," companies focus on an inclusive culture. An inclusive culture "welcomes what everyone can contribute" (Alcorn, 2003). The more acceptable term instead of minority is person of color (people of color or persons of color), which is used to describe a person (people) that are not white.

According to Sandy Kennedy, president of the International Mass Retail Association, "retail, in its simplest form, is about relationships. For retailers, the most important are the relationships with their customers and employees. Indeed, one of the most significant challenges faced by retail today may not be the drive for market share, but how to retain, attract, and develop human capital" (Kennedy, 2003). Retailers must examine their recruitment methods and benefits. A workplace offering benefits that appeal to a diverse group of people will attract more diverse employees. For example, a trend among companies is to offer domestic-partner and other family-friendly benefits. Family-friendly policies include such programs as child care and elder care. In 2013, Walmart changed its benefits to cover domestic partners including same-sex partners. Walmart management believes extending benefits to same-sex partners makes the company more competitive and appeals to a contemporary workforce (O'Connor, 2013). As of 2015, 66% of Fortune 500 companies offer domestic partner benefits (LGBTQ Equality…, 2015).

The U.S. Equal Employment Opportunity Commission (2017) interprets and enforces Title VII's prohibition of sex discrimination as forbidding any employment discrimination based on gender identity or sexual orientation. These protections apply regardless of any contrary state or local laws. While there are state laws that offer protection, according to the Human Rights Campaign (2017, www.hrc.org), it is still legal, in more than half of the states, to discriminate on the basis of sexual orientation. In a landmark ruling, in 2013 the U.S. Department of the Treasury and the Internal Revenue Service (IRS) announced that all legally-married same-sex couples will be recognized for federal tax purposes regardless of where they live.

In summary, all employees and customers have different needs and wants. Retail employees want to feel valued and contribute to an organization's success. The goal of inclusion and leveraging diversity should be based on these principles. Retailers need to refine and develop methods of inclusion and diversity management for future success. Retailers must create a corporate culture that includes the development of a broad and diverse employee base. Diversity management should include programs that allow for continuous training of employees, support groups or mentoring programs that facilitate diversity, career development programs that focus on inclusion, and promotional programs that include diverse ideas and populations (Dass, 1999).

Summary

This chapter focused on the human resource function of retailing. The chapter covered processes used in planning the overall human resource functions. These functions, and the overall plan, must be tied into the comprehensive IRM plan.

The chapter looked at two methods of analyzing the human resource function: short-term analysis and long-term analysis. Then it discussed the development of retailing tasks and managers' responsibility for turning these tasks into retail positions.

Next, the chapter discussed the development and types of organizational charts. It examined the creation of authority and responsibility within the retail organization.

The chapter then turned to recruitment and evaluation of employees. Problems associated with attracting qualified employees and creating job readjustments for employees who are performing poorly were examined. Some methods used to assess employee performance, such as job evaluations and ratings, were also provided.

Next, the chapter looked at various methods of compensation for retail staff, including hourly wage, straight salary, straight commission, salary plus commission, and salary plus bonus plans. It then discussed employee benefits such as insurance, sick leave, profit sharing, and paid time off.

One of the most difficult aspects of human resource management is termination. The chapter covered the two main types of termination: involuntary (such as termination through firing or downsizing) and voluntary. Finally the importance of diversity management, inclusion and leveraging diversity was discussed.

Terms

advertising allowance	A price concession given by a manufacturer of a product to a retailer to defray the retailer's costs associated with advertising the product.
affirmative action	Programs that address conditions that systematically disadvantage individuals based on group identities such as gender or race.
centralized organizational structure	An organizational structure in which decisions are made from one central location, often termed "headquarters" or the "home office."
decentralized organizational structure	An organizational structure in which decisions are made at the local level, such as at individual stores.
diversity	Differences among people, including but not limited to age, gender, ethnicity, race, and ability.
diversity management	The method of implementing diversity and inclusion strategies to maximize benefits of corporate diversity in the workplace.
divisional chart	An organizational chart based on the divisions or business units within an organization.
downsizing	The planned elimination of a group of employees to increase organizational performance.
Equal Employment Opportunity (EEO) laws	Laws that collectively prohibit discrimination on the basis of color, race, sex, religion, national origin, age, or physical disability.
evaluation	An area of management that involves assessing an employee's performance in relation to goals and objectives designated for that employee's position.
executive training programs (ETP)	Training available to the company's managers or executives.

exit interview	An interview conducted when an employee leaves an organization, for the purpose of determining the reasons behind the departure.
extrinsic motivation	The desire to achieve something that comes from outside the individual (money, acknowledgment, etc.).
functional chart	An organizational chart based on the company's functional activities.
group training	A type of training offered to groups of employees with similar training needs.
human resource information system (HRIS)	Software or online method for systematically gathering, analyzing, storing, and utilizing information and data related to personnel management.
human resource management (HRM)	Policies, practices, and systems that influence employees' behavior, attitudes, and performance.
human resource recruitment	The process of identifying and attracting the best potential employees to an organization.
image advertising	A type of advertising that attempts to enhance the retailer's image.
individual training	A trial-and-error approach to training in which employees take responsibility for training themselves.
intrinsic motivation	The desire to achieve something that comes from within the individual (happiness, satisfaction, etc.).
job (position)	A general category used by managers to assign responsibility of task performance to members of a retail organization.
job description	An explanation of the tasks involved in the performance of a given position in an organization.
leveraging diversity	The practice of seeking out different voices and viewing them as opportunities for added value.
mentoring	A type of training in which an experienced employee is assigned to train and act as a role model for a new employee.
motivation	A basic drive of all humans; in business, it is usually associated with the need to create personal or job satisfaction.
organizational chart	A graphical display that delineates who is responsible for the various areas of the firm.
organizational culture	The pattern of shared values and beliefs that helps employees understand how their organization functions and provides guidelines for behavior on the job.
outplacement	A process in which a business hires experts to offer support, personal assessments, and job-search skills training to employees that are being downsized.
product/brand chart	An organizational chart based on the products or brands an organization carries.
programmed learning	A structured, formal training process that allows the employee to study material pertaining to the retailer's operation and then respond to questions about the material studied.
regional chart	An organizational chart based on geographic designations.
supervision	An area of management in which managers direct employees in various tasks and monitor employees' productivity.
task	A duty to be performed in a given job.
task analysis	A technique used to facilitate the listing of tasks.
termination	The legal dismissal of an employee.

Discussion Questions

1.   What are the qualities of a good human resource manager? What are the potential consequences of ineffective HR management?

2.   Name some methods retailers use to recruit employees. Are there other methods that could be used to recruit more effectively?

3.   Do you think e-tailers need to use nontraditional approaches to finding employees to staff their organizations? If so, what approaches would you recommend?

4.   What are the differences between the HR functions performed by an e-tailer and those performed by a typical brick-and-mortar retailer?

5.   What do you believe is the most important aspect of retail training?

6.   What rewards motivate you to work harder? Are intrinsic rewards more important to you than extrinsic rewards? Why or why not?

7.   What methods of compensation can be used to motivate an employee who prefers to work in groups? An employee who prefers to work alone?

8.   What role do you believe diversity/inclusion will play in the next five years? Ten years?

9.   Does having online information about diversity programs increase the success of recruitment efforts? Why or why not?

Exercises

1. Go to the *Occupational Outlook Handbook* at www.bls.gov/ooh/home.htm and answer the following questions:

   a. What are the ways to find information on a particular occupation?

   b. Look up the following occupations on the website and write a paragraph that describes each position, include salary information.

   - Purchasing manager
   - Retail manager
   - Retail salesperson

2. Create a job description for a Complaint Manager for a retail supercenter. Identify the skills required for success.

3. Find the diversity and inclusion sections of three retailers and compare/contrast them.

Case

The Container Store: Consistently One of the Best Places to Work

In 2017, The Container Store was number 49 on *Fortune* magazine's list of "Best Companies to Work For." Over the last 18 years, the company has consistently appeared on the list. The company was founded in 1978 by Kip Tindell (CEO and president) and Garrett Boone (chairman), who shared a vision of selling multifunctional products that would save customers space and, ultimately, time. Headquartered in Dallas, the company has more over 4,000 employees in 86 stores, located mostly in big cities in 23 states. Each store carries more than 10,000 items. Major competitors are Bed Bath & Beyond and Walmart. Worldwide revenues were over $794.6 million in 2016.

In terms of diversity, 65% of employees are women, 68% are white, 11% African American, 13% Hispanic/Latino and 5% Asian.

Kip Tindell believes that if the company hires one great person, that person can do the work of three good people. Its strategy of attracting outstanding employees works well and fits its goal of "fewer, better people." Most employees are college educated, and most were first customers of the company.

According to their website (www.thecontainerstore.com) following are some of the benefits employees receive:

- Medical, dental and vision plans
- Paid time off
- 401(k) plans
- Discounts
- Pet insurance
- 24-hour employee assistance program
- A leadership development program
- Celebrations like We Love Our Employees Day

Many retail companies experience turnover rates as high as 100 percent. The Container Store's turnover rate for full-time employees is lower than industry average (less than 10%/year). Pay is 50 – 100% higher than the industry average. New full-time employees get 263 hours of formal training compared to the industry average of 8 hours. The company's "Golden Rule" is a quote by Andrew Carnegie: "Fill the other guy's basket to the brim. Making money then becomes an easy proposition." The Container Store serves as a role model to other retailers on how profitability increases when employees are treated respectfully and compensated fairly.

Questions

1. What qualities of The Container Store would a potential employee find appealing?

2. What is The Container Store's primary human resource strategy?

3. If the strategy implemented by The Container Store is so successful, why aren't other retailers copying it?

4. What effect do you think the HR strategy has on other areas of the company?

5. How does a happier work force give a retailer a competitive advantage?

Sources: The Container Store homepage at www.containerstore.com; Fortune – 100 Best Companies to Work For (2017), Retrieved from *Fortune* http://beta.fortune.com/best-companies/the-container-store-49; Harnish, V. (2002). The Right People---Why One Great Hire Is Better Than Three Good Ones. *Fortune Small Business*, (Apr 12); A Principled Approach to Retention and Service (2001), *HR Focus*, (Oct), pp. 6-7; Our Employee First Culture (2017). Retrieved from http://standfor.containerstore.com/putting-our-employees-first/

References

Administration on Aging (2013). Department of Health and Human Services. Retrieved from http://www.aoa.gov/AoAroot/Aging_Statistics/Profile/2011/2.aspx

Alcorn, E. (2003). Good-Bye M Word. Retrieved from www.monster.com.

Alterio, J. M. (2003). Does Diversity = Dollars? *The Journal News*, (Mar 29). Retrieved from www.thejournalnews.com.

Barber, A.E. (1998). *Recruiting Employees.* Thousand Oaks, CA: Sage Publishing.

Bureau of Labor and Statistics (2012). *Occupational Employment Statistics,* 2012 Retail Sales Workers Retrieved from http://www.bls.gov/ooh/sales/retail-sales-workers.htm

Bureau of Labor Statistics, U.S. Department of Labor, *Occupational Outlook Handbook, 2016-17 Edition,* Retail Sales Workers. Retrieved from https://www.bls.gov/ooh/sales/retail-sales-workers.htm

Burkhart, B., (2013). Why Some Companies Promote from Within. *New York Times,* (June 27). Retrieved from http://boss.blogs.nytimes.com/2013/06/27/why-some-companies-promote-from-within/?_r=0

Chowdhury, S., Endres, M. and Lanis, T. W. (2002). Preparing Students for Success in Team Work Environments: The Importance of Building Confidence. *Journal of Managerial Issues 14* (Fall), pp. 346--359.

Dass, P. (1999). Strategies for Managing Human Resource Diversity: From Resistance to Learning. *Academy of Management Executive,* (May), pp. 68-69.

Deal, T. and Kennedy, A. (1982). *Corporate Cultures---The Rites and Rituals of Corporate Life.* New York: Addison-Wesley.
Deshpande, R. and Webster, F. E. (1989). Organizational Culture and Marketing: Defining the Research Agenda. *Journal of Marketing* (Jan), pp. 3--15.

DiversityInc (2013). Diversity Management 101: This Definition of Diversity Management Can Help You Make a Business Case. Retrieved from http://www.diversityinc.com/diversity-management/diversity-management-101/

Farber, M. (2017). Board diversity at Fortune 500 companies has reached an all-time high. Fortune (Feb 6). Retrieved from http://fortune.com/2017/02/06/board-diversity-fortune-500/

Fisher, C., Schoenfeldt, L. and Shaw, B. (2003). *Human Resource Management,* 5th ed. Boston: Houghton Mifflin, pp. 14-27.

Hartocollis, A (2016). As Justices Weigh Affirmative Action, Michigan Offers an Alternative. *New York Times* (Jan 4). Retrieved from https://www.nytimes.com/2016/01/05/us/affirmative-action-supreme-court-michigan.html

Holstein, W. J. (2002). Making a Career Leap, Sore Muscles and All. *New York Times* (East Coast, late edition). (Dec 22), section 3, p. 5.

Human Rights Campaign (2017). Website. Retrieved from www.hrc.org

Huppke, R. W. (2013). Diversity Fades Up the Corporate Ladder. *Morning Call* (Sept 1), p. 39.

Jacobs, K. (2002). More Companies Seek Diversity as Internal Bias Suits Increase. *Houston Chronicle,* (Feb 10), p. 2.

Kaleel Jamison Consulting Group, Inc. (2008). Compliance, Leveraging Diversity, Inclusion: They're Not All the Same! Retrieved from http://outandequal.org/documents/theyarenotallthesame.pdf

Kennedy, S. (2003). The Three R's. *Chain Store Age,* 79 (Feb 2003), p. 24.

Klingbeil, A. (2002). History of Diversity in Business Tied to Economics, Laws. *The Journal News,* (Mar 22). Retrieved from www.thejournalnews.com.

Lewison, J. (2002). From Fired to Hired. *Journal of Accountancy,* 193 (Jun), pp. 43-50.

LGBTQ Equality at the Fortune 500 (2015). Human Rights Campaign. Retrieved from http://www.hrc.org/resources/lgbt-equality-at-the-fortune-500

LinkedIn about us (2013). Website retrieved from http://www.linkedin.com/about-us

Mazur, P. (1927). *Principles of Organization Applied to Modern Retailing.* New York: Harper & Brothers.

Miller, C. C. (2015). Can an Algorithm Hire Better than a Human? *The New York Times,* (June 25). Retrieved from https://www.nytimes.com/2015/06/26/upshot/can-an-algorithm-hire-better-than-a-human.html?_r=0

Miller, F. A. and Katz, J. H. (2002). *The Inclusion Breakthrough: Unleashing the Real Power of Diversity.* San Francisco: Berrett-Koehler Publishers

National Retail Federation (2013, 2016). Retail means jobs. Retrieved from http://www.retailmeansjobs.com/data-home

Noe, R. A., Hollenbeck, J.R., Gerhart, B. and Wright, P. M. (2003). *Human Resource Management: Gaining a Competitive Advantage.* New York: McGraw-Hill Higher Education, p. 5.

O'Connor, C. (2013). Walmart Extends Benefits to LGBT Employees' Same-Sex Domestic Partners. *Forbes* (Aug 28). Retrieved from http://www.forbes.com/sites/clareoconnor/2013/08/28/walmart-extends-benefits-to-lgbt-employees-same-sex-domestic-partners/

O'Donnell, J. (2013). Walmart to Offer Same-Sex Domestic Benefits. *USA Today* (Aug 27). Retrieved from http://www.usatoday.com/story/money/personalfinance/2013/08/27/walmart-same-sex-domestic-partner-benefits/2710675/

On Women Taking the Lead: Target CEO Brian Cornwell Joins Catalyst's Board of Directors (2016). Retrieved from https://corporate.target.com/article/2016/03/brian-cornell-catalyst

Psencik (2013). Both Sides Claim Victory in Fisher v. UT. *USA Today* (Jun 25). Retrieved from http://www.usatoday.com/story/news/nation/2013/06/25/fisher-ut-supreme-court/2457939/

Supreme Court Upholds University of Michigan Affirmative Action (2003). *Jet*, 104 (Jul 7), pp. 4--5.

Thiederman, S. (2003). Why Diversity Counts: The Business Case. Retrieved from www.monster.com.

Top HRIS Challenges (2002). *HR Focus,* (Oct), pp. S1, S3.

U.S. Census Bureau (2012). Population Division. Percent Distribution of the Projected Population by Sex, Race and Hispanic Origin for the United States: 2015 to 2060 (NP2012-T5). Released Dec 1012.

U.S. Census Bureau (2013). Website. Retrieved from www.census.gov

Walsh, M. (2003). Court Deluged with Advice on Michigan Case. *Education Week,* (Apr 2), p. 31.

Wegmans Makes it 16 Straight Years on FORTUNE '100 Best Companies to Work For' List, Ranking #5 (2013). Press release (Jan 16) obtain from http://www.wegmans.com/webapp/wcs/stores/servlet/PressReleaseDetailView?productId=754400&storeId=10052&catalogId=10002&langId=-1

Wilkie, D. (2003). Racial Preferences Upheld. *The San Diego Union-Tribune,* (Jun 24), p. A1.

Zafar, H. (2012). Exploring Organizational Human Resource Information System Security. *AMCIS 2012 Proceedings.* Paper 26. (Jul 29. Retrieved from http://aisel.aisnet.org/amcis2012/proceedings/ISSecurity/26

Part 4

Retail Tactics, Laws, and Ethics

Source: Zapp2Photo/Shutterstock.com

Chapter 11: Pricing in Retailing

Chapter 12: Developing an Effective Integrated Marketing Communications (IMC) Mix

Chapter 13: Customer Service in Retailing

Chapter 14: Laws and Ethics

Chapter 15: Diversity and Trends in Retailing

Part 4 deals with the retail tactics necessary to execute the integrated retail management plan; the laws and ethics that help guide these decisions; and some of the trends the retail environment is facing and will face in the future. Chapter 11 covers the development of pricing tactics. Specific focus is on the need for price integration as well as the development of pricing objectives and policies and the actual establishment of retail price. Chapter 12 focuses on the development of an effective integrated marketing communication mix for retailers. Chapter 13 centers on the development and execution of customer service in retailing. The chapter stresses the importance of customer service throughout the retail firm and describes some methods for creating effective customer service. Chapter 14 discusses the legal and ethical environments that affect retail decision making. Chapter 15 focuses on diversity in the retail environment and explores current trends and issues in retailing.

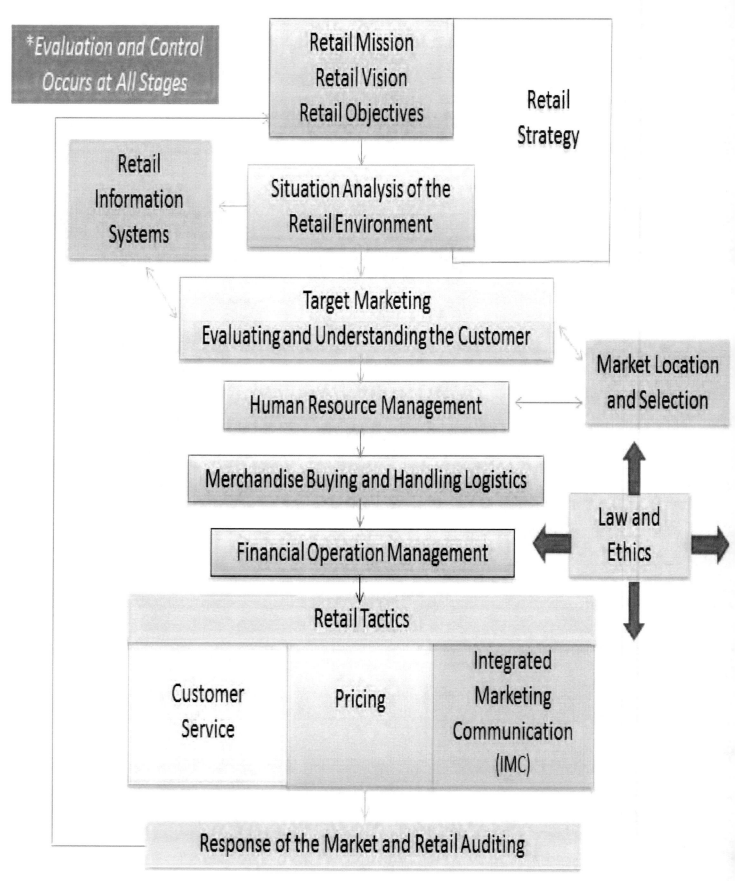

Chapter 11

Pricing in Retailing

"People want economy and they'll pay almost any price to get it."
~ Lee Iacocca

Source: astephan/Shutterstock.com

CHAPTER OBJECTIVES

After completing this chapter you will be able to:

- Explain and create pricing objectives for retailers.
- Outline the main types of pricing policies.
- Develop retail prices for products and services.
- Explain why and how prices are adjusted.

Adjusting Container Size Instead of Price

Ice cream is often touted as a favorite dessert. Standard container sizes for ice cream are a pint, half-gallon, and gallon. Most people are accustomed to buying a "brick," or half-gallon container. In 2001, Breyers, a leading ice cream manufacturer, boosted its half-gallon price by 30 cents. Breyers claimed that prices of butterfat and other ingredients had skyrocketed. Costs also increased because consumers were demanding more assortments in flavor and the extra ingredients were often more expensive. This led the way for other manufacturers to increase their prices or try other methods of adjusting to the environment. According to John T. Gourvill, Harvard Business School, "Consumers are generally more sensitive to changes in prices than to changes in quantity," (Clifford and Rampell, 2011).

Source: Keith Homan/Shutterstock.com

Other ice cream manufacturers grappled with higher costs (and, as a result, lower profits) as well. Some responded by making their ice cream packages smaller but keeping the same price (called *weight out*). This strategy is frequently employed when customers are especially concerned about price increases for products (Song, 2003). According to Turkey Hill management, the ice cream manufacturer was faced with three choices: use cheaper, lower quality ingredients, keep the containers the same size and increase price, or reduce the package size and keep price the same (The Truth Behind, 2011). Some manufacturers, like Breyers, also changed many of their flavors from "ice cream" to "frozen dairy dessert" because the ingredients do not fit the FDA's definition of ice cream.

The downsizing of ice cream containers initially went down from half gallon (the brick, 64 ounces) to 1.75 quarts (56 ounces) to the newest standard of 1.5 quarts (48 ounces) (The Truth Behind, 2011). Downsizing has occurred in hundreds of products including coffee, toilet paper, toothpaste, soap, yogurt, candy, condiments and chips. Sometimes the package gets smaller and other times manufacturers fill space with air to give the illusion that there is more product in the package (called *slack fill*). Consumerist.com calls the phenomenon, "grocery shrink ray" (Rathe, 2014). Often customers initially don't notice the smaller package size, but when they realize they are getting less product for the same amount of money, they may feel cheated, and retailers carrying the merchandise may receive complaints (Smith, 2003). Even so, this doesn't stop many consumers from buying ice cream. One reason is that consumers see ice cream as a luxury and will "splurge" for their favorite flavors. These consumers are less concerned when prices go up or package size decreases.

Introduction

Up until now, we have concentrated on the functions of setting up and organizing the retail establishment. In the next few chapters, we focus on how to execute and coordinate the functions of the IRM plan, particularly on the pricing, integrated marketing communication (IMC), and customer service tactics necessary to generate a comprehensive retail program. Many variables impact pricing. There are numerous internal variables that will have an impact on how much a retailer can charge for a product as well as external variables that also limit the amount that can be charged for a given product or service. The other tactical areas, such as which customer services to provide and IMC, also impact pricing. For example, a retailer providing a full line of customer services may have products priced higher than one providing fewer customer services. Similarly, a retailer that spends heavily on IMC must consider the impact on price. Many times the economy dictates pricing decisions. In 2012, Wegmans announced a freeze on prices from January 8 through April 28 for a list of more than 50 products families use most (Wegmans announces…, 2012). The list was almost exclusively made up of Wegman's own brand of products because the company could be more aggressive with the pricing for their own branded products. Wegmans is an example of a company that considers customer needs when making pricing decision. In the 2017 Harris Poll Reputation Quotient, Wegmans was ranked #2 in a study of the 100 most visible companies.

Determining a final price for a product is complicated and is based on a number of differing variables that impact the company. Figure 11.1 depicts selected determinants of the final price of a product.

Figure 11.1 Determinants of Product/Service Prices

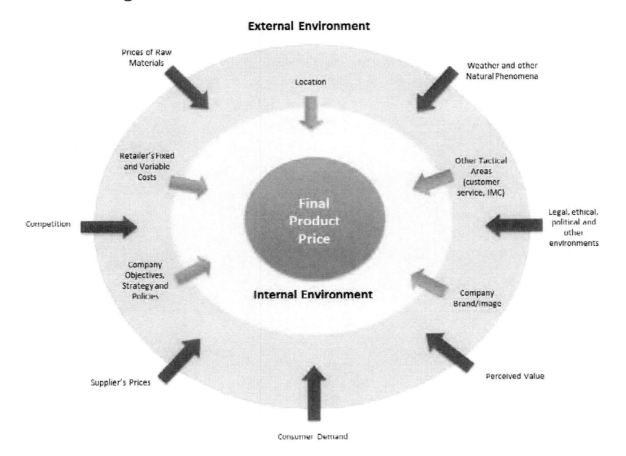

This chapter examines the pricing decisions retailers make to satisfy customer wants and needs at a profit. As with the overall IRM plan, pricing follows some clearly established steps, including the development of objectives and strategies, and tactical executions. Figure 11.2 (next page) depicts major pricing decisions that will be covered in this chapter.

The following internal and external variables influence pricing and are discussed throughout the chapter:

- *Pricing objectives:* Goals for pricing products and services
- *Price flexibility:* The range of prices consumers are willing to pay for a particular product or service

· *Pricing policies:* Overall retail guidelines for price setting

· *Competition:* The retailer's competitive environment

· *Demand:* How much of a product consumers want

· *Price adjustments:* Changes to price based on sales results

Determining Pricing Objectives

The retailer must develop a pricing strategy in a systematic manner, starting with the identification of overall pricing objectives. Objectives are necessary to achieve effective price points (or *price levels*). In pricing, the objectives should follow the same rules that apply to other areas, that is, they must be measurable and realistic.

Categories of Potential Pricing Objectives

Although there are many different ways to develop pricing objectives, some primary types of pricing objectives are most often used. These include objectives based on the following:

- Product quality
- Skimming
- Market penetration
- Market share
- Survival
- Return on investment
- Profit
- Status quo
- Cash flow
- Brand/Image

Figure 11.2 A Typical Pricing Decision Flow Chart

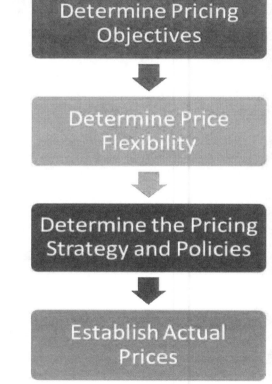

Product quality objectives center on recouping costs associated with retail research and development. In addition, product quality objectives can be used in conjunction with IMC tactics to create the perception of high product quality, and thus high retail store quality, in the consumer's mind. This objective is often used together with a skimming objective by high-end retailers.

Example: A retailer prices items at 300 percent above cost to ensure that its prestigious image is firmly established in the consumer's mind.

With *skimming objectives* (also called *skimming strategies*), the retailer sets an initial relatively high price for a product. A skimming strategy is often used to recoup costs incurred when selling a new product---costs associated with research, development, and marketing, for instance.

The term *skimming* comes from dairy farms, where personnel skim the high-quality cream from the top of the milk. The cream is more valuable than the milk and can be sold at higher prices. Likewise, the product marketer skims the market with an initial high price to sell to customers who are relatively unconcerned about price. The price may be lowered later to attract additional customers who are more price conscious. With this strategy, the customer must be somewhat price insensitive and view the product or service as premium quality.

Example: A retailer initially prices 4D TVs at $5,000. After a period of six months, the cost will be lowered to $4,000. Once competitors enter the market, the price will be set to remain competitive.

Market penetration objectives are the opposite of skimming objectives. Prices are initially set lower to attract large numbers of customers. Market penetration objectives are effective when the retailer's customers are price sensitive. The key to an effective market penetration strategy is to increase sales volumes to offset the low product price. As a general rule, after a certain point, retail costs do not increase very much when sales volume increases. Market penetration objectives have

the added benefit of allowing the retailer to discourage competition from entering the trading area because of the lower prices the retailer has already established for the market. In addition, market penetration may help establish a new product as a popular alternative for the consumer, thus creating social pressure to own the product as well as an economic benefit.

Source: Zapp2Photo/Shutterstock.com

Example: A retailer sets prices at lower levels for the first two months of operation to increase market share and discourage competition.

Market share objectives allow the retailer to adjust price levels based on competitors' changes in price, enabling the retailer to create additional *market share* or reduce market share in relation to the competition. This can be done for the entire retail operation (that is, all stores), for a division, or for a specific store. The retailer can also set a market share objective for each department, product line, or product and brand.

Example: To stand by its "we will not be undersold" policy, a retailer sets its average prices below those of its three main competitors.

Survival objectives allow the retailer to increase price levels to meet sales expenses. This type of objective is generally used to match sales volumes to overall store (or company) expenses.

Example: A retailer sets pricing to cover expenses and increase store profitability over last year's by five percent.

Return-on-investment (ROI) objectives are created to help the retailer meet or exceed stated return on investment figures. Management creates a target return figure it thinks will be satisfactory to stakeholders (primarily stockholders). Then the price is set to reach that targeted return level.

Example: A retailer sets prices to deliver a 15 percent return on investment within one year.

Profit objectives are like ROI objectives, except that target profit levels rather than ROI levels are the goal. If management uses a profit maximization approach to retailing, there is a good chance that profit objectives will be set.

Example: A retailer sets prices to increase profits by 15 percent within one year.

Status quo objectives don't change from year to year. Retailers using these types of objectives embody the attitude that "everything is going well---let's not rock the boat." A retailer that wants to stabilize sales will probably utilize a status quo objective.

Example: In the upcoming year, a retailer will price items to match last year's sales.

Cash flow objectives allow the retailer to generate money quickly. These objectives are designed to encourage additional sales volumes. Generally they are short-term objectives.

Example: During any given month(s), a retailer sets prices lower to encourage sales volume and increase cash flow.

A retailer must establish a clear idea of their brand personality and positioning. This is done through the use of *brand or image objectives*. Price plays a big role in establishing the brand and image of a company, so often brand and image objectives are considered in developing pricing objectives. For example, the Dollar Store, Dollar General and Five Below are retailers that use price to establish awareness of their brand and create a price-associated image.

Market share and product quality have a major impact on the retailer's profitability and are therefore often used to help set pricing objectives. For example, when management at Quaker Oats Company received complaints from food retailers that its line of cereal products was overpriced compared to the competition, the company decided to reduce their prices to appease the retailers and hopefully generate additional market share. To offset the lower price, Quaker Oats changed the product's packaging: instead of using the traditional box, Quaker Oats placed cereal into bags, thus allowing the company to reduce the cost of the product to food retailers. The change increased Quaker Oats' market share while meeting pricing objectives (Leonhardt, 1998). In this example, both manufacturer and retailers achieved their pricing objectives. As a result, Quaker Oats increased its market share by two percent.

As can be seen, pricing objectives are set for many reasons. Additional factors that are often considered when developing pricing objectives include development of customer traffic for movement of slow-selling products, an attempt to desensitize consumers to price, and avoidance of legal and ethical problems associated with price, and an attempt to dissuade other competitors from cutting or reducing their prices. Retailers can use multiple pricing strategies simultaneously while keeping all of these concerns in mind.

Competition and Customer Demand $

Maximum price

↑↓

Minimum price

The Retailer's Variable and Fixed Costs $

Figure 11.3 Pricing Ranges Based on Demand and Cost

Determining Price Flexibility

Although the step of determining pricing flexibility comes after that of setting price objectives in Figure 11.3, in practice pricing flexibility for goods and services helps the retailer establish its pricing objectives. *Pricing flexibility* refers to the "best" range of prices that the retailer can set. Two factors retailers consider when determining pricing flexibility are the costs associated with running the business and selling the products (both fixed and variable costs) and the demand by the store's existing or potential customers. These factors help the retailer develop the range over which to set its final retail prices. The costs help set the floor, or lower limits, of this range, whereas the competitors and consumers (product demand) set the upper pricing limits. Figure 11.3 illustrates this relationship.

There are three steps in determining pricing flexibility. The first is to determine the costs associated with the retailing operation. Data that will help the retailer determine costs are located in the retailer's financial documents and in the retail information system (RIS). The second step is to estimate the demand for the products and services, taking the competition into account. The demand estimate helps set the upper price limits for the products. The greater the difference between the upper and lower limits, the more flexible the price is said to be. Finally, in the third step, the retailer estimates the elasticity of price for its products and product lines.

Price Elasticity

Price elasticity of demand (also called *elasticity*) is a measure of the consumer's sensitivity to price. It is important to understand the relationship between price and consumer purchasing habits. Consumers make many decisions based on price; thus, the elasticity of price may change during the course of a given sales period. In addition, there is a high correlation between price and consumer perceptions and, thereby, purchases (Kim, Srinivasan and Wilcox, 1999).

Source: Michal Chmurski/Shutterstock.com

Price elasticity of demand measures the responsiveness of quantity demanded to a change in price, with all other factors held constant. In some cases, a decrease in price results in an increase in demand or, conversely, an increase in price results in a decrease in demand. In each case, consumers are price sensitive; put another way, demand is relatively *price elastic.* When a price reduction or a price increase occurs and demand remains relatively the same, consumers are less sensitive to price changes, and demand is said to be *price inelastic.* When assessing price elasticity of demand, one of three situations can occur: price elasticity, price inelasticity, or unitary elasticity of price.

1. *Price Elasticity.* In this situation, when the retailer raises price, a relative decrease in total revenue occurs. Conversely, when the retailer lowers price, a relative increase in total revenue results. The elasticity of price and demand coefficient (E_p) would be greater than 1 ($E_p >$ 1). This situation most often occurs when there is low urgency to purchase products or services and when substitutes for the products or services are available. An example is a shirt that one can buy at several other retailers at a competitive price.

2. *Price Inelasticity.* In this situation, when the retailer increases price, a relative increase in total revenue occurs. Conversely, when the retailer decreases price, a relative decrease in total revenue results. Thus, the elasticity of price and demand coefficient is less than 1 ($E_p <$ 1). In this situation, consumers are not sensitive to a change in price; they are willing to pay the current price and possibly a higher future price. This situation typically occurs when purchase urgency is high and no acceptable substitutes exist. A life-saving drug is an example of a product that would exhibit price inelasticity.

3. *Unitary Elasticity.* In a situation of *unitary elasticity,* the percentage change in price equals the percentage change in quantity demanded. This rarely occurs, because the marketplace is extremely dynamic. The retailer can use unitary elasticity to create a midpoint, or mean, for the inelastic and elastic pricing situations. In unitary elastic situations, a price change has no impact on total revenue; thus, E_p is equal to 1 ($E_p =$ 1).

When comparing elasticity of price quotients (*i.e.,* E_p), the quotients should be compared only for a given store, product, or product line. In other words, there are no benchmarks defining a "good" or "bad" elasticity of price quotient. Thus, in the example that follows, the E_p is calculated as 4.0. Is this high or low? On the surface it appears low; however, when compared to the quotient in the second example ($E_p =$ 1.5), it is actually high.

The formulas used to calculate the elasticity of price are as follows:

Elasticity of price = E_p

$$E_p = \text{Percentage change in quantity demanded/Percentage change in price}$$

or

$$E_p = \underline{\text{Absolute change in demand at new price/Demand at old price}}$$
$$\text{Absolute change in price/Old price}$$

or

$$E_p = \frac{\underline{\Delta Q/Q}}{\Delta P/P}$$

Where: Q = quantity sold and P = relative price

For example, suppose a retailer wants to check on its price elasticity because it is considering a drop in price. The price of the product may be dropped from $20 to $15 (a 25 percent reduction). Research reveals, however, that if the price is dropped from $20 to $15, demand will increase from 100,000 units to 200,000 units (a 100 percent increase). Is this situation price elastic, price inelastic, or unitarily elastic? If you answered *price elastic,* you are correct. To see this, let's plug in the numbers given in the following formula:

$$E_p = \frac{\underline{(200,000 - 100,000)/100,000}}{(20 - 15)/20}$$

$$E_p = \frac{\underline{100,000/100,000}}{\$5/\$20} = 4.0 \text{ or } 100\%/25\% = 4.0$$

This is a highly elastic situation.

Let's take another example using some of the same numbers. Suppose the price increases from $15 to $20, thus reducing demand from 200,000 units to 100,000 units. Though the numbers being used are the same, the situation is quite different. Let's see how elastic this situation may be:

$$E_p = \frac{\underline{100,000/200,000}}{\$5/\$15} = 1.5 \text{ or } .5/.333333 = 1.5$$

In this example, the price is still elastic, but not quite as elastic as in the prior situation. The coefficient of elasticity of price and demand is 1.5 compared to the coefficient of 4.0 calculated earlier. In this example, the elasticity of price is closer to unitary elasticity and is less elastic than in the previous situation, where the calculation was 4.0.

When assessing elasticity of price, it is important to monitor the competition and the legal and ethical constraints placed on retailers in the United States (or other countries, if the retailer does business there). Numerous laws and regulations---international, national, regional, or local---govern price levels. It is essential that the retailer understand the rules, laws, and regulations affecting price. Important laws in the United States are the Sherman Act (1890), the Clayton Act (1914), and the Federal Trade Commission Act (1914). These laws are covered in more detail in Chapter 14.

Determining Price Elasticity

In real-world problem solving, the elasticity of price coefficient needed to determine price is usually known and used in decision making about raising or lowering price. Based on the formula used to generate the coefficient of elasticity of price and demand (E_p), it is necessary to know the elasticity coefficient. This can be obtained in two ways. The first is to use the retailer's historical sales and pricing data to forecast the level of price elasticity. The second, and probably more accurate, method is to undertake research by sampling a group of consumers from the targeted market segment with regard to various price/quantity relationships. Both methods produce fairly crude estimates, but those estimates are useful when calculating the value of E_p. An example using a hypothetical retail firm follows.

The owner of Computers, Inc., has estimated overall price elasticity to be 1.5 (E_p = 1.5). The owner wants to know if a price reduction of $100 for each fully loaded computer system would be profitable. Currently the average price for a computer system is $2,500 per unit, with a forecasted sales volume of approximately one million units. A price reduction of $100 would generate a reduction of four percent ($2,500 - $100 = $2,400; $100/$2,500 = 4%).

The price elasticity of 1.5 would thus generate an increase in sales of six percent. This is because an increase of four percent times the elasticity figure equals a six percent increase in unit sales (1.5 X 4% = 6%). Because the price is elastic, reductions in price increase total revenues. The owner of Computers, Inc. wants to know the amount by which revenues will increase. Based on these data, the new sales volume would increase from 1.00 million units to 1.06 million units.

Here is how that number was derived:

$$1,000,000 \times 1.06 = 1,060,000$$

At the old price of $2,500 per unit, revenues would be $2.5 billion (1 million units x $2,500 per unit = $2.5 billion). At the new price of $2,400, anticipated sales revenues would increase to $2.544 billion ($2,400 x 1.06 million units = $2.544 billion). Thus, revenues would increase by $44 million by lowering the price from $2,500 to $2,400.

The above scenario does not take into account other costs associated with the sale of additional computer models, such as transporting, storing, shipping, increased sales staffs, and so on. It assumes that everything stays the same. In real life, however, additional costs associated with the acquisition and sale of so many additional computers would exist. In addition, government regulations could limit some of the activity, or rivals might respond with price reductions and other competitive tactics.

After implementing pricing flexibility, the retailer needs to develop pricing policies that will guide the actual price determination. The pricing strategy is derived from the pricing objectives, pricing flexibility, and pricing policy phases of the overall pricing plan.

Determining Pricing Strategies and Policies

Pricing policies help create the overall pricing strategy. Therefore, the retailer must establish general guidelines for price development. Because prices are influential in consumers' perceptions of the quality of the retailer's products (Fisk and Grove, 1996) and stores, retailers must pay special attention to pricing tactics and the integration of these tactics into the overall IRM plan. Because product quality and pricing are so interrelated, it is vital that the retailer be consistent when developing and implementing pricing policies. It would be inconsistent for a high-end retailer to offer products and services at a discounted price. Neiman Marcus would not sell a no-name or off-brand perfume at $3 a bottle. Conversely, if a low-end retailer such as Wal-Mart offered expensive, prestigious products such as Rolex watches, consumers might become confused about the retailer's image.

Source: zhu difeng/Shutterstock.com

Common factors involved in establishing pricing policies include the need for short-term profits, competitors' prices, product and supply-chain costs, and historical actions (Price Doesn't Count…, 2002). Several pricing policies are particularly widespread in the retailing industry, including price variability, promotional pricing, price leveling, life cycle pricing, price lining, price stability, and psychological pricing.

Price Variability

In setting a *price variability* policy (also known as *differential pricing*), the retailer asks, "Do we want to charge the same price for our product(s) to all our customers, or do we want to charge different prices to different customers?" Although there are some legal restrictions on price variability, retailers have the option to offer the same product to customers at different prices. Sometimes this policy can anger or confuse consumers; thus, an understanding of consumer perceptions is paramount. Price variability used to be referred to as *price discrimination,* but due to the negative connotation of the term *discrimination,* it is rarely used today. Many online retailers, such as Staples.com, ask shoppers to enter their zip code first before they can see products and prices. This is due to different pricing of same items in different geographical areas, primarily states.

Federal, state, and local laws impose limitations on price variability. These regulations discourage retailers from varying their prices for "classes" of buyers. The laws relating to price discrimination are not clear-cut and are often open to interpretation.

In general, it is legal to develop different prices for the same product as long as there is no discrimination against a class of buyer (Hispanics, African Americans, men, women, people with disabilities, and so on). Because most of the pricing antidiscrimination laws are mandated by state or local governments, challenges often arise in state or local courts. Typically, if no one is injured by the differences in price, a formal complaint is not registered.

Source: ESB Professional/Shutterstock.com

There are many examples of price variability policies. Car dealers utilize price variability in selling cars. Most people don't pay the same price for a "like" model of automobile; rather, the price is determined based on many factors, such as credit, down payments, trade-in allowances, discounts, the consumer's ability to negotiate, and so on. Airlines also offer variable pricing to customers. Most passengers on a given flight have paid different prices for their seats. Those who travel in the first-class or business-class section have paid premium prices for the extra service and legroom. Also, travelers can expect to pay more during the holiday season, when demand is relatively high, than during "off-peak" times. Similarly, the price of a ticket to a major concert varies based on the location of the seat. Senior citizen discounts have become more common as more retailers offer discounts to this group. For example, Kohl's and Bon-Ton offer discounts as high as 15 percent to senior citizens.

It is important for retailers to educate customers on their pricing policies. When consumers understand the basis for price variability, they are usually more accepting of these policies. If they perceive the variability to be valid and equitable, they are less likely to harbor negative feelings toward the product, service, or retailer. For example in 2011, Adidas manufactured and sold rugby shirts for the *All Blacks,* New Zealand's national rugby team, at different prices depending on the country in which the shirt was sold. When sports fans discovered the shirts were being sold online in the U.S. for one-half the local price (220 New Zealand dollars or about $182), and in Britain for slightly more than the U.S. price, New Zealanders felt like they were being cheated. A public outcry

Source: zao4nik/Shutterstock.com

broke out and some disgruntled fans covered the Adidas logo on the shirts (Hutchison, 2011). Adidas admitted that they poorly handled fans' concerns about price and that they would have to win back the trust of their customers.

Promotional Pricing

In *promotional pricing,* a retailer coordinates pricing with the promotion variable of IMC. Because the two areas are interrelated, many times the pricing policy becomes tied to promotions. Two main types of promotional pricing are leader pricing (often called *loss leaders*) and special-event pricing. *Leader pricing* occurs when products are priced at less than the usual markup, near cost, or below cost. Leader pricing is used to increase traffic and attract customers to a store with the promise of a bargain, and it wards off competition. In the process of buying the sale item, the customer typically picks up items at regular prices, thus offsetting the lower revenues from the price leaders. With *special-event pricing,* advertised sales are used to generate store traffic. Typically, sales coincide with a major holiday or event, such as Valentine's Day or an inventory clearance.

Price Leveling

Under a *price leveling* policy, the retailer attempts to maintain price levels for the long term. Also called *customary pricing*, this type of policy is typically implemented prior to the actual opening of a retail facility. Retailers use price leveling to communicate to their publics the type of business they are operating. A discount retailer such as Wal-Mart might choose to set lower prices for all of its products (everyday low pricing, or EDLP), thus supporting its image of a low-price retailer. Many stores are using digital signage to educate their customers on price comparisons and sales.

When using price leveling, retailers take into account many variables, including the organization's vision and mission statements, corporate culture, and product line objectives; competitors' strengths, weaknesses, and prices; and the state of the economy. The retailer should refer to the situational analysis before setting a price-leveling policy.

It is difficult to change a price strategy once it's been established in the minds of consumers. For example, in 2012, department store JCPenney announced a change in its pricing strategy from promotional pricing, which emphasized sales and specials, to everyday low pricing they called "Fair and Square" pricing. Their customers were confused with the change, in part because there were three pricing tiers (Every day, Month Long Values, and Best Day Fridays) and felt like the company took something away from them when they stopped issuing coupons. The strategy did not improve profits. Customers left JCPenney for other department stores even though the prices were cheaper in comparison (Ofek and Avery, 2013). By 2013, JC Penney had abandoned the EDLP strategy and returned to promotional pricing.

Most retail stores have a level at which they set prices. This level may be based on an overall skimming strategy or on a market penetration strategy. The thing to remember is that overall prices can be set at market, below market, or above market prices.

Life Cycle Pricing

Pricing might be planned based on the product or store life cycle. Under *life cycle pricing*, price points are set based on the stage of the product life cycle (introduction, growth, maturity, and decline) that the product (or store) has reached. For example, a retailer might use a penetration strategy to enter the market with low prices when it first opens the store. As consumers demand more products (during the growth phase), the retailer raises the prices slightly. As the product reaches maturity, the retailer levels off the price to current market prices. Finally, during the decline phase, the retailer either raises or lowers the price because demand and sales have decreased significantly.

When a new product, such as an MP3 player, is introduced, the initial price may be very high. One reason may be that the manufacturer is trying to recoup research and development costs. Another possible reason is that the manufacturer wants to capitalize on retailers' desire to carry the new, hot product and therefore sells the product at a higher price. After more competitors start building MP3 players and more people start buying the product, the price typically decreases. In the decline phase of the product life cycle, retailers offer products at substantial discounts. The DVD has entered this stage; in the late 2000s, one could buy a VCR for less than $50.

In other situations, new products are introduced at a lower price to gain market share or acceptance; this is especially true when a similar product already exists in the marketplace. As the product moves through the life cycle, the price is usually adjusted.

Life cycle pricing is uncommon in retailing because of the time and costs associated with preparing and planning prices for each individual product or product line. A retailer would need to know in advance when discounts or sales would occur; therefore, prices would need to be pre-planned throughout the cycle. The retailer would need to know at what moment the product would be entering another stage of the life cycle and then would need to decide whether to raise or lower prices in response. Life cycle pricing is contingent on the pricing strategy and the type of product.

Price Lining

A retailer using a *price lining* policy offers various products in a limited range of price points with each point representing a different level of quality. Price lining is also referred to as the *development of price points*. Therefore, each line of products receives special pricing. This allows the retailer to compete at different levels within a given product line. The goal in a price lining strategy is to maximize profits for the whole line versus focusing on only one product's profitability.

The Chevrolet division of General Motors (GM) is a good example of a retailer supplier that utilizes a price lining strategy. GM offers luxury, full-size, mid-size, compact, subcompact, and sport-utility vehicles, as well as other products, to appeal to each type of consumer who has a need or want for an automobile. Chevy's Trailblazer, for example, allows Chevrolet to compete in the SUV market. In addition, price lining helps avoid *cannibalization* of each product; that is, GM can achieve different levels of competition by attracting additional buyers from the market rather than moving current GM customers from product to product. The price of each product type is often a signal of the quality of the merchandise.

Source: Asia Images/Shutterstock.com

The cosmetics industry also utilizes price lining, allowing retailers to have many different types of cosmetics at different prices to appeal to different consumers. For example, Procter & Gamble offers the Olay line, which is priced highest; Covergirl, which is average priced; and Max Factor, which is the least expensive line. Thus, a consumer looking to purchase cosmetics can choose among three differently priced lines.

Price lining helps position products as good, better, and best (Koprowski, 1995). The consumer is willing to pay more for the perceived "better" product and less for the perceived "generic," or low-cost, product.

Source: Ken Wolter/Shutterstock.com

Price Stability

At times, retailers try to create a stable price, or a "one-price policy," for certain products, to avoid price wars with the competition. The popular dollar store formats (Dollar General, Five Below, and Dollar Store) operate under this *price stability policy*. These stores do not have to run frequent sales because their customers know prices will remain stable.

A good way to create a stable price is to negotiate with suppliers for exclusive product rights for a given geographic territory. Because of the costs associated with exclusivity, retailers often negotiate selective distribution clauses that allow them to be among a handful of retailers that carry the product or service for each territory. If a company is an upscale retailer, management will not want to charge a lot of money for a product that can be purchased a block away from a retailer that charges 20 percent less. Pottery Barn, a home decoration retailer, is an example of a company that pursues price stability.

Although by law retailers cannot be required to adhere to minimum retail prices set by manufacturers, many suppliers maintain price stability by dealing only with retailers that traditionally adhere to the manufacturers' suggested retail prices.

In some cases, in exchange for retailers agreeing to minimum retail prices, manufacturers provide promotion money to assist the retailer. Such was the case in the music industry in the mid-1990s. In an effort to avoid price wars, record manufacturers instituted a minimum advertised price policy, known as MAP. Under the policy, record labels gave retailers millions of dollars to be spent on promoting new releases. Retailers who took the money agreed to adhere to minimum advertised prices set by the major record labels. This meant that retailers could not sell new releases and other popular music below a specified price. In 2000, the Federal Trade Commission issued a cease and desist order because the MAP policies were a form of price-fixing. To avoid a federal lawsuit, the record labels dropped MAP policies (Segal, 2000). Additionally, in 2010, the U.S. District Court in Southern California consolidated over 30 class action suits that dealt with MAP. These alleged that between 2004 and 2009, the National Association of Music Merchants (NAMM) conspired with Gibson, Fender, Yamaha and Guitar Center, among others to force supplies into adopting restrictive "Minimum Advertised Price" policies that artificially inflated prices. In response to the suit, the defendants asserted that the MAP is a legal business practice that doesn't restrict what retailers actually charge (Defendants say, 2010).

Another way to establish price stability is to sell by consignment. In *consignment selling,* a retailer sells goods for the supplier and receives a commission on sales instead of taking title to the merchandise. Under this method, the retailer bears less risk in terms of product sales. If the products fail to move, they are simply returned to the supplier. If they do sell, the retailer gets a percentage of the sales price and the supplier keeps the rest. Many suppliers sell only to retailers with a reputation for good customer service because the products' prices tend to remain stable with these retailers.

Psychological Pricing

Because consumers make a correlation between the price of a product and the product's quality, many retailers set prices using psychological pricing. *Psychological pricing* takes into account a consumer's perceptions and beliefs. The three main types of psychological pricing are odd/even pricing, reference pricing, and prestige pricing.

Source: astephan/Shutterstock.com

The retailer using *odd/even pricing* places prices on individual products that end in either an odd or even number. Consumers often perceive the price to be lower if it falls below an expected threshold. For example, a product that is priced at $39.99 is perceived as less expensive than one priced at $40.00. In many cases, consumers expect prices to end in an even number. For example, for products sold from a vending machine, an even price such as $1.00 is more practical than an odd price such as $0.49.

Odd/even pricing allegedly began in grocery retail outlets. Before the development of effective point-of-sales instruments such as POS terminals and cash registers, grocery retailers hired employees to work as cashiers. Retailers had to put their trust in the cashiers, but sometimes employee theft occurred. Theft was easy because many products had an even price on them (this was prior to the taxing of food products in many states). Because an even price was associated with the products, cashiers didn't have to make change. They didn't even have to open the cash register to show that a transaction had taken place. The cashier could just set the money on the cash register, wait until the customer left, and then pocket the money. To combat this practice, food retailers changed the pricing structure of their products to odd numbers, forcing cashiers to make change. Making change required opening the cash register and recording the transaction into the retailer's records.

Odd/even pricing continues to be used today, despite the advent of POS systems. Why do food retailers still offer most food products with odd-numbered prices? They do so because consumers expect them to. Consumers may see a food product with an even price as being too expensive.

Gasoline is also priced using an odd-number pricing strategy. The price for a gallon of gas nearly always ends with 9/10 of a cent. Therefore, an advertised price of $4.67 per gallon is really $4.67 and 9/10 of a cent, or closer to $4.68 per gallon. In retailing (and marketing), the consumer's perception is reality. If the consumer thinks a price that ends in an odd (or even) number is more affordable, retailers most often price the product accordingly.

Reference pricing uses a consumer's frame of reference to help set price. A frame of reference is established through information searches or previous experience purchasing other like products (Rajendran and Tellis, 1994). To uncover customers' expectations, it is important that the retailer survey customers to determine the *just noticeable difference (JND)*. This is the price at which consumers believe they are paying more or less than the norm or reference price. The key is to find out the magnitude of change necessary for a change in price to be noticed by the consumer Monroe, 1973).   For example, in 2011, as the cost of cotton and other materials got more expensive, retailers slowly raised the prices of clothing because they ran out of ways to avoid passing on higher expenses to the consumer. American Eagle Outfitter quietly raised the price of polo shirts from $29.50 to $34.50. Brooks Brothers raised the price of a shirt from $79.50 to $88. Aéropostale experimented with price on different clothes to see how much of an increase the customer would accept. Some retailers hide higher prices in complicated promotions that confuse the customer (Clifford, 2011).   These retailers are trying to find the point where customers won't notice price increases.

A retailer would not want to raise the price of a product above the JND because the customer may perceive the price as unfair. For example, let's say a consumer's experience tells her that popcorn should be priced at $1.50 for a medium-size bag and she complains about paying $4.50 for a similar-sized bag in a movie theatre. In this case, the JND was surpassed. Many times retailers raise prices gradually, thinking that consumers are less likely to notice gradual price changes than drastic price increases.

Selling products at high prices to establish a reputation of quality is called *prestige pricing.* This pricing strategy aims to create "snob appeal" (Koprowski, 1995). Manufacturers that spend a great deal of time and money developing their brands often sell high-end products that are associated with prestige to retailers. The products demanded by these retailers' customers generally carry a higher, or prestige, price. Think about the last time you shopped for clothes. What stores did you visit? Did you shop at True Religion (truereligionbrandjeans.com) to buy a $300 pair of jeans, or did you go to Kohl's for less expensive jeans? Your decision to shop at either one of those stores shows that you are brand or price sensitive. Car manufacturers and retailers often use prestige pricing for their top-of-the-line models. BMW and Mercedes are good examples of companies that utilize prestige pricing. Other examples are the makers of Rolex watches, Mountblanc pens, Tiffany's fine jewelry, and Vermont Teddy Bears.

Source: Gustavo Frazao/Shutterstock.com

Once pricing policies have been established, specific product prices must be determined. Retailers can use many methods to create a final price for products. The next section discusses the most popular of these methods.

Understanding Competitive Pricing

One of the key components in establishing price, as discussed above, is the competition. Retailers must make sure they understand how their competitors price and how their competitors react to changes in pricing. If a retailer is assessing the elasticity of their price, they must take into account competitive changes. If McDonalds decides to lower their prices, they can be pretty sure that other members of the fast food industry will follow suit and drop their prices also. This occurred when Taco Bell developed their "value menu," with other fast food retailers soon creating their own versions of a value menu.

Because price is one of the few environmentally controllable variables a retailer can use to generate business, they must be sure price is integrated into the entire marketing mix, and that price helps in creating desire in consumers.   Retailers typically don't want to compete on price alone.   Price competition drops profit margins for retailers.   Thus, it is often a strategy to reduce price competition.   Retailers can reduce price competition by creating effective brand strategies for their products and outlets.   One branding technique is to offer unique merchandise.   By offering and carrying merchandise that isn't carried by competitors, retailers can create a unique price for that merchandise.   Additionally retailers can create private-label brands or merchandise that is "exclusive" to their stores.   Many of the discounters have begun to carry exclusive, designer-based clothing in order to attract customers to those brands and to have the ability to create higher prices for those products.   For example, the following retailers have exclusive merchandise linked to celebrities):

· Macy's – Madonna's Material Girl and Diddy's Sean Jean Line

· Kohl's – LC (Lauren Conrad); Jennifer Lopez Collection; Marc Anthony Collection

· Urban Outfitters – Tupac Merchandise

The key: carry some merchandise where customers can't make price comparisons easily.

One last issue in regard to competitive pricing focuses on the usage of competitive data or intelligence.   It is usually to the retailer's advantage to shop at their competitors' stores.   By doing this, retailers can collect price information in order to see if they need to make any adjustments to their own lines and prices.   IRi (Information Resources, Inc.) and A.C. Nielsen also collect these types of data, making it easier for the retailer to generate this information.

Gray and Black Markets

An area that impacts companies' pricing efforts are gray and black markets. A *gray market* (aka grey market or parallel market) is the selling of goods outside of their authorized channels of trade (What is the parallel market, 2007). These channels, while legal (unlike a black market, which is illegal), are unauthorized or unintended by the original manufacturer.

Gray Markets

In retailing the most common type of gray markets are imported goods that would be more expensive in another country. The retailer sells the products at lower (or higher) prices. While this practice introduces brand names to consumers who may not be able to afford them, the quality and distribution are no longer in control of the intended company. Electronics, clothing, cigarettes, fragrances, cosmetics and even wine are common gray goods. In 2016, Fujifilm filed lawsuits against several gray market retailers because cameras sold were not authorized for sale by the company. In many countries, the gray market is significant. For example, in Argentina the gray market in digital cameras accounts for as much as 30 percent of sales.

The gray market is hard to track because manufacturers do not track the sale of goods to the final consumer. For example many people buy items on sale and then turn around and sell them on eBay for a higher price. How many times have you seen college clubs selling water that they bought at a discount retailer for a higher price to raise money? These are examples of gray markets and what makes them so difficult to track.

Black Markets

Unlike the gray market, black market goods are illegal. According to the International Chamber of Commerce, the total of counterfeit and pirated goods globally was between about $923 billion – 1.13 trillion in 2013. Counterfeiting and piracy costs are expected to rise to $1.9 – $2.8 trillion by 2022 (Frontier, 2016). Items sold in the black market include clothing, electronics, movies,

Source: G.Evgenij/Shutterstock.com

music, software, cigarettes and drugs. Even human organs, such as kidneys, are sold on the black market. The cigarette black market is a major problem. Smugglers of cigarettes in low tax or no tax areas sell the cigarettes in high tax areas such as New York. All the profit represents tax fraud.

In China, where a widespread black market exists, there are indications that the black market is declining. A survey by China Market Research found that 95 percent of Chinese women between 28 and 35 said they would be embarrassed to carry counterfeit handbags. Because the demand for fake goods has declined, retailers such as Nike, Columbia Sportswear and North Face are expanding their presence in China. North Face, whose products were widely counterfeited in the late 1990s and early 2000s, has over 500 stores in China (Burkitt, 2012).

An increased presence in China is not without problems. Columbia Sportswear has to monitor the Internet for counterfeit versions of their products. There can be 100,000 listings on a daily basis on websites for pirated versions of their products. Despite improvements, China is the leading source of counterfeit and pirated goods seized in the U.S., accounting for 62 percent of the $124.7 million goods seized in 2011 (Burkitt, 2012).

The Internet has given rise to new areas for black markets to operate. There are imitation websites, fake branded retail outlets and the use of social media to sell illegal goods. People who engage in the online black market are harder to catch because they are anonymous. Deborah Reeves, general counsel for luxury jeans brand True Religion, says the company has seen an increase in online black market activity for their brand. She says that people running these websites have sophisticated marketing techniques such as claiming they are authorized factory outlets and lifting content from the True Religion website. The company uses security tools and works with search engines and credit card companies to suspend fake merchant's accounts (Costa, 2011).

Countries lose out on tax revenue when a significant gray or black market exists. Large gray/black markets also make it difficult for retailers to compete with lower prices on similar goods.

Establishing Price

The three major categories of methods used to establish product prices are cost-oriented pricing, competition-oriented pricing, and demand-oriented pricing. A retailer might use one or a combination of the methods. The most common is cost-oriented pricing.

Cost-Oriented Pricing

To generate a profit, product costs *must* be covered. *Cost-oriented pricing* (also called *cost-plus pricing*) has two approaches: markup pricing (the more common) and breakeven pricing. The retailer needs to determine its markup percentage; one way to do this is to look at traditional product markups within the industry and at the manufacturer's suggested retail price. The retailer must also consider the product's average turnover, the amount of competition for the product, the levels of service required, and the amount of sales time and effort involved in selling the product. All these factors, along with the inclusion of the expected or targeted profit margin, determine the *markup.*

Markup Pricing: In markup pricing, two options exist for determining the markup percentage: markup based on the retail, or selling price of the product, and markup based on the product's cost. The chosen method is generally selected based on the accounting systems the retailer employs.

The vast majority of retailers use *markup based on selling price,* because expenses and profits for the product's sales are calculated as a percentage of sales. In addition, this method keeps the markup percentage from exceeding 100 percent. Manufacturers and other suppliers most often quote discounts and price reductions from the retail selling prices they provide to the retailer. Finally, retail sales information is easier to acquire than cost information is; thus, it is easier to compare sales to those of competitors (and other stores) than it is to compare costs. The general formula for developing a markup based on the retail price of the product is as follows:

Amount of markup = Selling price (retail price) - Cost

If a product's selling price is $100 and the cost is $40, the markup is calculated as $100 - $40 = $60. To calculate the markup percentage, use this formula:

Markup percentage = Amount of markup/Selling price

Using the example above, the percentage markup at retail would be $60/$100, or 60 percent.

To calculate the selling price rather than the cost, use the following formula:

SP = C + M

or

Selling price = Cost/(1 - % of SP)

where SP = selling price, C = cost, and M = markup.

Assume the cost associated with the product is $100 and a markup percentage, based on the selling/retail price, of 40 percent is desired. Then:

SP = C + M;   SP = $100 + .40(SP); SP -.40(SP) = $100 + .40(SP) - .40(SP)

.60(SP)/.60 = $100/.60 = $166.67, or $100/(1 - .40) = $100/.60 = $166.67

Thus, the selling price (or retail price) = $166.67.

In addition, the cost of the product can be calculated given the selling price and markup percentage based on selling price using the following formula:

SP = C + M, so C = SP - M

Assume the product has a cost of $1,000 and a markup percentage based on selling price of 60 percent. Then:

$1,000 = C + .60(1,000); $1,000 = C + $600; therefore, C = $400

Finally, both the cost and the selling price of the product can be calculated using the following formula:

Markup percentage based on retail (selling) price x Retail price (selling price)
= Amount of markup

Suppose the desired markup percentage on the retail/selling price is 55 percent and the amount of markup is $200. The cost and retail price are calculated as follows:

.55 x SP = $200.00; .55(SP) = $200.00;   SP = $200/.55 = $363.64

Now we have the retail price of $363.64, so SP = C + M, or $363.64 = C + $200.00. Therefore, cost = $163.64 ($363.64 -$200.00).

Another markup method is based on the *cost of the product.* The following formulas will guide you through the steps to calculate markup based on product cost:

Retail price = Cost + Markup

If the retail price is $1,000 and the cost for the product is $600, the markup based on cost is $400, or $1,000 - $600. The percentage markup based on the product's cost can be calculated by taking the amount of the markup and dividing it by the cost, as follows:

$400/$600 = 66.67 percent.

To calculate the selling price for a product using a cost basis, see the following example (remember, SP = C + M, or cost/(1 - % of selling price).

If a product costs $25 and a markup percentage on cost of 30 percent is desired, what will be the selling price? The calculation is as follows:

SP = $25 + .30 ($25); SP = $25 + $7.5; thus, SP = $32.50 or 1.30 x $25 = $32.50

The retail price for the product would be $32.50.

The product's cost can also be calculated. Consider the following example.

A product's selling price is $50 and the markup percentage, based on cost, is 65 percent. If SP = C + M, then SP/(1 + markup) will give the cost. Let's calculate this problem using both methods:

SP = $50.00; M = 65 percent of the cost

SP = C + M; thus $50.00 = C + (.65)C (keep in mind that the cost is equal to 1 x C)

$50.00 = 1.65C; thus, $50/1.65 = Cost (again) = $30.30

Finally, let's calculate both the retail price and the cost for a product.

Assume a markup percentage of 20 percent on cost (C = .20). Also assume that the amount of markup for the product has to be $32 (M = $32). The calculation is as follows:

Markup percentage on cost x Cost = Amount of markup

If the markup percentage is 20 and the amount of markup is $32, then:

.20 x Cost = $32; Cost = .20C/.20 = $32/.20 = $160

SP = C + M; thus, SP = $160 + .20(160) = $160 + $32 = $192

Keep in mind that the cost of goods equals the cost, per unit, of the merchandise (invoice price) plus the inbound freight costs associated with getting the merchandise. In addition, any discounts received from the trade as part of a purchase (including quantity discounts) are also taken out.

Breakeven Pricing: *Breakeven pricing* is the other method used in the creation of a cost-oriented pricing system. With breakeven pricing, the retailer determines the *breakeven point (BEP),* or the level of sales needed to cover all the costs associated with selling the product. The breakeven point is calculated using the following formula:

BEP (in quantity)= Fixed cost/Unit price - Unit variable cost

This formula can be modified to calculate the BEP in dollars by multiplying the BEP (in quantity) by the selling price of the item.

Competition-Oriented Pricing

In *competition-oriented pricing,* the retailer identifies the industry leader and then replicates the leader's prices. In using this method, the retailer assumes that the industry leader is best equipped to select appropriate price levels for its products.

Retailers often "shop" the competition to ascertain competitors' price structures. A representative from the retailer's organization visits a competitor's store to see what prices are set for the product mix. Shopping the competition is not always welcomed by retailing competitors, especially when done in person. It is understood that environmental scanning should be an ongoing, not sporadic, process, however many retailers see these actions as not necessary. Particularly in service retailing, the same information often can be obtained from phone calls to competitors. For example, a large hotel chain in southern Colorado regularly has disguised "shoppers" call competing hotels and ask for a list of prices for the various rooms. Different rates, such as state rates, government rates, AAA rates, and frequent-traveler rates, are checked. The chain then adjusts its prices based on the competitor's rates.

If competitors raise or lower their prices, the retailer follows suit with price increases or decreases. Competition-oriented pricing assumes that costs, demand, competition, and other factors external to the retail firm remain fairly constant. Therefore, it is safe to follow the leader or follow the general trends within the industry.

Demand-Oriented Pricing

Under the *demand-oriented pricing* method, prices are set based on consumer demand. In this approach, retailers often raise prices based on unusual environmental changes. These changes might include unusually high customer demand (*e.g.,* for fad products), events such as natural disasters, or conflicts in other countries that affect supplies of various products such as gas or oil. For example, in 2011, designers had to re-think their offerings when the price of cotton, silk, wool and leather reached all-time highs. Retailers braced for an increase in prices as designers attempted more innovative designs and making use of every scrap of material. Designers risk skimping too much and alienating customers who love upscale designs (Holmes and Dodes, 2011).

In some instances, retailers raise their prices to exorbitantly high levels, a tactic called *price gouging.* Although this tactic may appear to be a sound business practice, it is an ethical gray area. Customers might pay the demanded price initially, but they may harbor negative feelings toward the retailer, thus decreasing long-term business and goodwill. For example, Marathon Petroleum Company LLC was accused of price gouging during a state of emergency brought about by massive flooding. The attorney general of Kentucky alleged that the company illegally raised the wholesale price of gasoline and other motor fuels in markets across Kentucky during a time of emergency.

This action made gas prices jump about 30 cents overnight. Customers complained about the drastic increase (Attorney General Conway, 2011).

The three major types of demand-oriented pricing are modified breakeven, consumer market, and industrial market pricing.

Modified Breakeven Pricing: *Modified breakeven pricing* assumes the retailer estimates the market demand for the product and then applies it to the breakeven point. In so doing, the retailer can estimate, or forecast, sales at different price points or levels.

Consumer Market Pricing: When using a *consumer market approach* to pricing, the retailer generates data about prices based on controlled store experimentation. Many techniques can be applied here, but the general idea is that consumers enter the store and are allowed to make product purchases. The prices on the various products are changed, and the retail researcher tracks the price points that are most popular with the consumers. The retailer then implements these price points throughout its locations. Auction websites (eBay, Ubid, etc.) use market-based pricing models.

Industrial Market Pricing: A technique much like the consumer market approach is the *industrial market approach.* With this approach, the retailer sells its products to other businesses in addition to the final consumer. The retailer performs a wholesaling function aimed toward other businesses. If the retailer is reselling products to intermediaries or industries (such as Home Depot, Office Depot, or Office Max may do), the retailer identifies the benefits of its products compared to competitors' products and sets prices accordingly. The assumption is that industrial buyers do not buy as much on emotion as ultimate consumers do. Rather, industrial buyers, or intermediary buyers, purchase more on a need basis. Consequently, by identifying the benefits these buyers are seeking, the retailer is better able to set price. This technique is also used when responding to government bids; in this situation, the government agency purchasing products is treated like another business.

Once prices for products and services have been set, retailers need to prepare for the possibility that they will not sell all the products at the established prices. Retailers must develop *initial markups, maintained markups,* and gross profit margin projections for the store inventory. In addition, retailers must consider creating markdowns for products to move slower-selling items off the shelves. We will next look at how an initial markup percentage is developed.

Initial Markup Percentage

The *initial markup percentage* is a starting point for setting individual product prices. After calculating an initial markup percentage, the retailer can calculate the impact of markups, markdowns, and discounts. Initial markup percentages are usually calculated based on the retail selling price. Initial markups are calculated by taking the estimated retail expenses, adding them to the planned retail profit, and adding that figure to the planned reductions. This figure is then divided by the planned net sales plus the retail reductions:

Initial markup percentage =

Planned expenses + Planned profit + Reductions

Net sales + Reductions

The markup is based on the original retail values placed on the merchandise after subtracting out the costs associated with the merchandise. By looking at the actual prices the retailer paid for the merchandise and again subtracting out the costs associated with that merchandise, the retailer can calculate its *maintained markup percentage:*

Maintained markup percentage =

Retail operations expenses (actual) + Actual profit

Actual net sales

Another method is to take the average retail prices of products and then subtract out the costs associated with the merchandise and divide by the average retail price:

Maintained markup percentage =

Average retail price – Product costs

Average retail price

Finally, the retailer may want to know what its gross margin will look like. The *gross margin* is the total cost of goods sold (COGS) for the retailer subtracted from the retailer's net sales:

Gross margin in dollars = Net sales - COGS

Gross margin allows the retailer to adjust for cash discounts and other expenses associated with sales of goods and services. The retailer may still have to adjust the prices on some merchandise. The process of changing prices is called *price adjustment.*

Variables in the Initial Markup Percentage: Variables in the initial markup percentage can affect the initial price. One variable is the influence members of the retailer's channel of distribution can have on the organization. In distributor relationships, members of the channel of distribution have expectations of the other channel members. One expectation may be that the retailer adheres to the manufacturer's suggested retail price. The amount of influence a given channel member has is based on the type of supply chain used and the dominance of the channel member. For example, because Wal-Mart purchases in very large quantities, its suppliers give the discounter a smaller markup than they would give other retailers that purchase less. Wal-Mart then passes on those savings to its customers, thus creating a competitive advantage.

Source: vvoe/Shutterstock.com

Related to the influence of channel members are the variables of quantity discounts and shipping arrangements. These variables are negotiated with suppliers and consequently have an impact on the price the retailer sets. In their infancy, e-tailers got into trouble by failing to factor in the shipping and handling costs associated with retailing products to end users. This was one of the significant factors that contributed to the failure of a number of dot-com companies.

Pricing for Internet sales can be a difficult task. Although e-tailers have an advantage over brick-and-mortar businesses in that they have lower physical location expenses and a less labor-intensive environment, in other ways they are at a disadvantage: customers can access the prices of competitors with the click of a button (Freedman, 2009). Thus, e-tailers should avoid using price as a main tactic in attracting customers. They should also stay away from price wars with well-established retail outlets that have deeper pockets than they do.

Price Adjustments

No matter how thoroughly the retailer plans for the execution of pricing, some change in the retail environment is bound to alter the product's value to the consumer. These value changes can take two forms. In one case, an environmental change increases the value of the product. More frequently, however, changes in the environment decrease the product's value.

To respond to these changes, retailers make two major types of product adjustments: additional markups and markdowns. If the retail environment changes or the economy weakens, prices may have to come down (markdowns). In some situations, additional markups may be warranted. During the holiday season, for example, if demand for a particular item is high, retailers often raise the price on that item because its demand exceeds its supply.

As seasons change, so do consumers' desires for certain types of products. Price adjustments allow the retailer some flexibility in its day-to-day business operations. It is important for retail managers to understand the concepts of additional markups and markdowns.

Additional Markups

At times retailers will see an increase, or a spike, in the sales of a particular product. When this occurs, the retailer may be able to increase its profits and margins by adding additional dollar amounts to the product's retail price. These additions are called *additional markups* (or, sometimes, *markons*).

Trendy or fad products often lend themselves to additional markups. Remember, an additional markup is an increase in the retail price of a product in addition to what was already added as a markup. Popular toys may be subject to increases in selling price during the holidays. Popular car models may also carry additional markups to increase the retailer's bottom line. When creating additional markups, the retailer should pay particular attention to the demand functions of economics, particularly the law of supply and demand.

Sometimes during pricing periods, unexpected rises occur in the costs of merchandise purchased from suppliers. When costs rise, the retailer needs to pass the increases on to the consumer. The retailer may utilize an additional markup for this purpose. For example, when suppliers' prices for gas increase, the retailer can no longer generate the required markup percentage, so it adds an additional markup to help make up for the added costs associated with carrying the product.

Markdowns

Retailers can rarely sell all the merchandise they carry at the established original prices. Frequently the retailer needs to encourage consumers to purchase products so the retailer can move the products out of the store to make way for newer products or products and services that will yield a higher return. In these cases, the retailer initiates *markdowns,* or decreases in the overall markup percentage (or dollar amounts).

Markdowns are regular practice for many types of retailers. For example, in promotional apparel retailing, most clothing in department stores is sold at lower-than-retail price through the use of markdowns (Adams, 2016). Markdowns can be calculated in much the same way as markups. To calculate the dollar markdown amount, subtract the new product retail price from the original or regular retail selling price:

Markdown (in dollars) = Retail selling price - New selling price

Consider an owner and operator of a small retail business. He wants to know what his markdown is on a product he was selling for $50. His new selling price is $30. His markdown is $50 minus

$30, or $20. In addition, he wants to know what his markdown percentage was. To calculate the markdown percentage, he needs to take the dollar amount of the markdown and divide it by the new selling price. He can calculate the markdown percentage using either the new retail price or the old retail price. Each calculation yields a slightly different percentage:

Amount of markdown (new retail price) = Percentage of markdown on new retail price

Amount of markdown (old retail price) = Percentage of markdown on old selling price

Using the numbers given in the example, if the new retail price is $30 and the old retail price is $50, the markdowns are as follows:

Amount of markdown = $20, so $20/$30 = .66666, or approximately 67% of the new retail price

Amount of markdown = $20, so $20/$50 = .40, or 40% of the old retail price

Which method is better? It depends on the retail mission, vision, and philosophy. It also may depend on which accounting method the retailer uses. Either calculation is correct. A consumer, however, obviously would prefer a 67 percent markdown over a 40 percent markdown. Thus, consumer perception may have an impact on which method is chosen for creating markdowns. Next time you go shopping, pay attention to the fine print under the sales signs; your savings may not be as much as you think they are!

The pricing tactic is very useful for retailers, but pricing policies and strategies often do not receive attention by managers. Pricing is the marketing mix variable that has the most direct impact on revenues and therefore can substantially influence the bottom line for all retailers.

As we have seen, many variables affect price, and the approaches used to set prices vary depending on the type of retailer and the other tactical areas. Retailers must not overlook the importance of pricing in retail management. In the words of Mark Bergen, marketing professor at the University of Minnesota, "It's easy to set a price. It's hard to set a good price" (Saitz, 2003).

Pricing and the Customer

It should be noted that customers must be at the center of the pricing equation. When making pricing decisions, retailers must always keep an eye on their customer profiles. Keep in mind that different customer groups or segments may have differing pricing needs and wants. Additionally, there may be some adjustment required in price depending upon the retailer's customers. It will ultimately be the customer who purchases the product, so the customer is always right when it comes to price.

Source: pixfly/Shutterstock.com

Customers' perceptions of price and retailers' perceptions of price can be quite different. Retailers view price in terms of strategy, odd/even pricing, EDLP and other pricing tactics. Consumers view price in terms of benefits and value. Both are correct, but both perceptions need to be addressed. Often when times are tough, retailers must be creative with pricing strategy. Jos. A. Bank Clothiers, Inc. (www.josbank.com) used unique promotions to keep sales and profits coming. For example, the retailer used to have "buy one, get-three-free" sales. Customers who bought one product could get three of equal or lesser value. These price promotions keep customers loyal. In 2015, the retailer stopped these promotions because they were no longer sustainable. Instead the company started offering new clothing and shoes designed to reach a younger target market (Peterson, 2015). The company continues to offer sales on merchandise, just not sales with massive discounts.

Because of differences in the customer base, retailers might wish to charge different prices for their different market segments. For example hotels and motels may give discounts to loyal members of their affinity clubs. There might be discounts for senior citizens (AARP members), AAA members or students.

Retailers sometimes utilize different prices for different geographic zones. Because of this, consumers may see different prices for the same products depending on where they are shopping geographically. Often, omni-channel retailers will ask consumers for certain information such as a zip code or area code. They are doing this in order to assess which price is appropriate for that geographic area. Additionally, many times retailers create pricing based upon zones within a given city. Each zone might have a different price for the same product. Although there are numerous strategies and tactics involved in setting price, retailers must keep in mind that the customer is the base for price setting.

Summary

In the IRM planning process, there are many issues that relate to pricing of products and services. In addition to integrated marketing communication (IMC) and customer service, price is one of the three main tactics retailers use to help them communicate with their target market. This chapter covered the development of overall pricing objectives and how those objectives can help create specific pricing objectives, including product quality, market share, survival, ROI, profit, status quo, cash flow, penetration, and skimming. Next, the chapter focused on the pricing policies of price variability, price leveling, life cycle pricing, price lining, price stability, and psychological pricing. When establishing pricing objectives, integration with the other tactical areas in the IRM structure is important.

The chapter provided a number of formulas to determine retail prices for products. It provided a discussion on how to mark up a product at both selling price and product cost, along with various methods used to adjust price after the initial price has been set. Finally, the chapter examined the concepts of initial markup and maintained markup and provided formulas to calculate these important numbers and percentages. Although retailers tend to favor one method over others, they often use more than one approach, depending on their accounting methods.

Terms

additional markup	An increase in the retail price of a product in addition to what has already been added as a markup.
black market	The illegal selling of goods outside of their authorized channels of trade.
brand or image objectives	Objectives used to establish a clear idea of brand personality and positioning.
breakeven point (BEP)	The level of activity at which income from sales (total revenue) equals total costs.
breakeven pricing	A pricing method in which pricing is based on the breakeven point for a given product.
cannibalization	A situation in which a company introduces a product that takes away sales from an existing product.

cash flow objective	A type of pricing objective in which the retailer attempts to generate money quickly.
competition-oriented pricing	Pricing of products based on the industry leader's prices.
consignment selling	A method in which the retailer sells goods for the supplier and receives a commission on sales instead of taking title to the merchandise.
consumer market approach	A method in which a retailer generates data about prices based on controlled store experimentation.
cost-oriented pricing	A pricing method in which a fixed percentage is added to the cost of products; also called *cost-plus pricing*.
demand-oriented pricing	Pricing of products based on consumer demand.
gray market	The selling of goods outside of their authorized channels of trade. While legal, these sales are unauthorized or unintended by the original manufacturer.
gross margin	The total cost of goods sold subtracted from net sales.
industrial market approach	An approach in which the retailer sells its products to other businesses in addition to the final consumer. Prices for products or services may be different for business customers than for nonbusiness customers.
initial markup	The price set on a product less the cost of the merchandise.
initial markup percentage	The initial markup expressed in percentage form.
just noticeable difference (JND)	The price at which consumers believe they are paying more or less than the norm or reference price.
leader pricing	A type of promotional pricing in which products are priced below the usual markup, near cost, or below cost. Also called *loss leader pricing*.
Life-cycle pricing	Price planning based on the stage of the product (or store) life cycle that the product (or store) has reached.
maintained markup	The amount of markup the retailer attempts to sustain for a particular product or product grouping. Calculation: Net sales – COGS.
maintained markup percentage	The maintained markup expressed in percentage form.
markdown	A decrease in the initial retail price, typically expressed as dollar amounts or a percentage.
market penetration objective	A type of pricing objective in which product prices are initially set low to attract large numbers of buyers. The resulting increase in sales volume offsets the lower introductory price.
market share	The proportion of sales of a particular product (or brand) to the total sales of that product (or brand) in a given area.
market share objective	A type of pricing objective in which the retailer adjusts price levels based on competitors' changes in price, with the goal of gaining market share.
markup	The dollar amount added to the cost of a product to determine its final price.
modified breakeven pricing	A method wherein the retailer estimates the market demand for a product and then applies it to the breakeven point.
odd/even pricing	The practice of using prices that end in either an odd or even number.
prestige pricing	The practice of selling products at high prices to build a reputation for quality.
price elasticity	A term referring to changes in price that consumers will tolerate.
price elasticity of demand	A measurement of the responsiveness of quantity demanded to a change in price, with all other factors held constant; also called *price elasticity*.

price gouging	A tactic wherein a retailer takes advantage of high demand and limited supply to raise the price of a good or service beyond customary amounts.
price inelastic	A term referring to consumers who are relatively insensitive to price changes.
price leveling	The practice of setting prices on products and services so that prices remain stable for a defined period of time. Also called *customary pricing*, products are generally priced above, below, or at market prices.
price stability policy	A practice in which the retailer attempts to create a one-price policy for individual products.
price variability	The practice of varying price of merchandise or services based on established criteria.
pricing flexibility	The range of prices consumers are willing to pay for a particular product or service.
pricing policies	General rules or guidelines for price development based on company strategies.
product quality objective	A type of pricing objective that focuses on recouping costs associated with retail research and development or to develop a desired product image.
profit objective	A type of pricing objective in which the retailer attempts to meet or exceed projected profit levels.
promotional pricing	The practice of coordinating pricing with the promotion variable of IMC.
psychological pricing	A method of pricing in which the retailer takes into account consumers' perceptions and beliefs.
reference pricing	A concept of what the price of a product should be based on consumers' frame of reference.
return on investment (ROI) objective	A type of pricing objective in which the retailer attempts to meet or exceed stated return on investment figures.
skimming objective	A type of pricing objective in which the price for a newly introduced product is set high. After competitors enter the market, the price is adjusted down.
special-event pricing	A type of promotional pricing in which advertised sales, typically coinciding with a major holiday or event, are used to generate store traffic.
status quo objective	A type of pricing objective in which the retailer attempts to maintain the current situation.
survival objective	A type of pricing objective in which the retailer increases price levels to meet sales expenses.
unitary elasticity	A situation in which the percentage change in price equals the percentage change in quantity demanded.

Discussion Questions

1. What do you think are the most difficult aspects of determining prices for products?

2. What are some reasons a retailer might choose a particular pricing strategy?

3. Assume you have been given the responsibility of setting prices for Macy's department stores. Which of the following policies would you choose to implement, and why?

a. Price variability

b. Price leveling

c. Life cycle pricing

d. Price lining

e. Price stability

f. Psychological pricing

4. Is it fair to consumers when a retailer manipulates prices? Why or why not?

5. What types of retailers attract price-sensitive customers? What types of retailers have customers who are not as price sensitive?

6. Which types of retailers make frequent price adjustments?

Exercises

1. Use your local town newspaper to find advertisements for three or four items. Use the Internet to comparison-price shop for the items selected. Compare the online prices to the prices found in the print advertisements. Answer the following questions:

· What were the differences in price for each item?

· Are there factors other than price that would make you choose one retailer over another? If so, what are they?

· When shipping and handling were added to the online price, how much did the total price increase?

2. If the price of a product drops from $50 to $25, resulting in an increase of demand from 1,000 units to 1,500 units, what is the elasticity of price?

3. If the retail price of a new cell phone is $150 and the cost of each phone is $90, what is the dollar amount of markup? What is the percentage markup on the phones?

4. A new watch costs a retailer $25. If the retailer wants to generate a 50 percent markup on the watch, at what selling, or retail, price should the retailer set the watch?

5. An e-tailer wants to generate a markup percentage, on retail, for a new DVD set. If the amount of markup is $100, what is the cost for the product, and for how much should the DVD sell retail?

6. A video game retailer wants to generate a markup percentage of 35 percent on a new video game *at cost*. The amount of this markup is $64 (at cost). At what price should the merchant sell the new game? What is the cost of the game to the retailer?

Case

Kohl's Pricing Policies Under Fire

Kohl's pricing strategy is to position itself as a budget department store (instead of a discounter) and use promotions to stress the chain's value. Kohl's appeals to its target market by offering quality national-brand merchandise at affordable prices in easily accessible and convenient retail outlets.

In 2012, Sacramento, California shoppers complained that Kohl's was inflating prices so that items on sale looked like a better deal than they were. Kurtis Ming, a CBS consumer investigative reporter from Sacramento, found a few instances where a price tag showed a higher price than other price tags under the visible one. For example, a consumer bought sheets for $105 which was

50 percent off the $210 price tag. The customer discovered a price underneath the $210 one that said $170, and that price had been marked up three times before reaching the $210 price. What she thought was a great deal didn't look so good after finding the tags with the lower prices.

CBS sent producers with a hidden camera crew to several of Kohl's stores to investigate. One producer found 15 items marked up, some as much as $100. Some of the products had higher price tags than the ones stuck below them. Other items had different price tags on different areas of the product. A sheet set was listed as 50 percent off of $89.99, but inside the plastic packaging there was an earlier price tag showing $49.99. Customers expect to find cheaper prices when there are multiple tags stuck together, not more expensive ones.

According to a Kohl's store spokesperson, "As is common in the retail industry, from time-to-time, product prices are increased due to production and raw material costs. When these types of price increases are implemented, our stores are instructed to re-ticket all items currently in our inventory to match the price tags for all in-coming merchandise... Price increases at Kohl's are not common. However, the unprecedented increases in the cost of certain commodities such as cotton over the past 24 months have caused us to take these actions." The manager in the above example honored the lower price when approached by the CBS producer.

This isn't the first time that Kohl's has been under fire for their pricing policies. Due to a four month inquiry into Kohl's pricing policies by the Boston Globe in 2002, the Massachusetts attorney general investigated Kohl's Department Stores' pricing policies. In October 2002, Kohl's was in-formed by the state that its pricing policies appeared to be in violation of state law and asked Kohl's management to bring the company's Massachusetts stores into compliance. Kohl's aggres-sive sales pricing is at the heart of the state's complaint. According to the complaint, Kohl's appears to offer some items "on sale" throughout most of the year. This means these items never have a "regular" price to which consumers can compare other retailers' prices. This practice creates ficti-tious "regular prices," percentage discounts that do not reveal the original prices and sales tags that do nothing to clarify the item price. According to Kohl's management, the chain is in compli-ance in Massachusetts.

Kohl's pricing strategy also created problems for the company in Kansas during 2000 and 2002. Although Kohl's did not admit to guilt, the company paid $500,000 in fines. Most recently in 2015, two consumers filed suit against Kohl's for deceptive pricing practices. The suit alleges Kohl's misled customers through "false reference pricing" such that consumers thought they were get-ting big deals when they were not. Although Kohl's did not admit to wrongdoing, in May of 2017, Kohl's agreed to pay $6.15 million to California shoppers to settle the class action suit. Kohl's also agreed to change its price-comparison advertising policies.

As this example illustrates, retailers must be very careful in developing and implementing a pricing strategy.

Sources: Morran, C. (2012). Is Kohl's Marking Up Items Before it Puts Items on Sale? (Online) *The Consumerist*, (Feb 7). Retrieved from http://consumerist.com/2012/02/is-kohls-marking-up-prices-before-it-puts-items-on-sale.html; Felgner, B. (2002). Kohl's Under Fire in MA. *Home Textiles Today*, (Nov 11), pp. 1, 23; Mohl, B. (2002). Kohl's Told to Act on Pricing Policies: AG Asks Chain to Comply with State Law on Sale Advertising. *Boston Globe*, (Oct 22), p. C1; Kimberlin, J. (2003). Area Retailers Beware: Kohl's to Be a Major Player: Incoming Chain Will Challenge Discounters and Department Stores. *Virginian--Pilot* (Norfolk, Virginia), (Jan 12), 2003, p. D1. Popken (2016). JCPenney, Sears, Macy's and Kohl's Sued for Fake Sale Pricing. NBC News (Dec 9). Retrieved from http://www.nbcnews.com/business/consumer/jcpenney-sears-macy-s-kohl-s-sued-fake-sale-pricing-n694101

Questions:

1. How could Kohl's eliminate the customer complaints about pricing?

2. What advice would you give to Kohl's in establishing pricing policies?

3. How are ethics and laws involved in setting price?

4. Apply the terms "reference pricing" and "just noticeable difference" to the Kohl's case

5. Using terms from this chapter, analyze Kohl's pricing strategy.

References

Adams, E. Can American Retailers Kick Their Discounts Addiction? (2016). BOF, (Apr 28). Retrieved from https://www.businessoffashion.com/articles/intelligence/can-american-retailers-department-stores-jcrew-gap-quit-the-discounting-promotions-drug

Attorney General Conway Accuses Marathon Oil of Price Gouging - Asks Court to Require Company to Lower Wholesale Prices (2011). US Fed News Service, Including US State News, (May 16). Retrieved from http://search.proquest.com/docview/866511255?accountid=13158

Burkitt, L. (2012). Chinese Shoppers Lose Taste for Fakes. *Wall Street Journal* (Online) (Feb 13). Retrieved from http://search.proquest.com/docview/921231698?accountid=13158

Clifford, S. (2011). Camouflaging Price Creep. *New York Times*, (April 22). Retrieved October 10 from http://www.nytimes.com/2011/04/23/business/23prices.html?nl=todaysheadlines

Clifford, S. and Rampell, C. (2011). Food Inflation Kept Hidden in Tinier Bags. *The New York Times*, (Mar 28). Retrieved from http://www.nytimes.com/2011/03/29/business/29shrink.html?pagewanted=all&_r=0

Defendants Say MAP Isn't Price-Fixing (2010). *Musical Merchandise Review*, 169(10), 10-10.

Fisk, R. P. and Grove, S. J. (1996). Applications of Impression Management and the Drama Metaphor in Marketing: An Introduction. *European Journal of Marketing*, 30, pp. 6--12.

Freedman, L. (2009). Comparison Shopping is a Way of Life. The e-tailing group (Sept). Retrieved from http://www.e-tailing.com/content/wp-content/uploads/2009/12/winbuyer_102209_brief.pdf

Frontier Economics (2016) The Economic Impacts of Counterfeiting and Piracy – Report prepared for BASCAP and INTA. Retrieved from https://cdn.iccwbo.org/content/uploads/sites/3/2017/02/ICC-BASCAP-Frontier-report-2016.pdf

Holmes, E. and Dodes, R. (2011). New York Fashion Week: Materials Girls: Designers Trim Hemlines, Costs ---Runway Fashions Get Revamped as Cotton, Wool, Leather and Silk Prices Rise. *Wall Street Journal*, (Feb 17) pp. D.1.

Hutchison, J. (2011). The Price of a Jersey Sets Rugby Fans Against Adidas. *New York Times*, (Aug 24). Retrieved October 14 from http://www.nytimes.com/2011/08/25/sports/rugby/adidas-angers-all-blacks-fans-with-price-policy.html?_r=1&ref=adidasag&pagewanted=print

Kim, B-D., Srinivasan, K. and Wilcox, R. T. (1999). Identifying Price Sensitive Consumers: The Relative Merits of Demographic vs. Purchase Pattern Information, *Journal of Retailing*, 75 (Summer), pp. 173--193.

Koprowski, G. (1995). The Price is Right. *American Demographics*, (Sept), pp. 56--61.

Leonhardt, D. (1998). Cereal-Box Killers Are on the Loose. *Business Week*, (Oct 12), pp.72--77.

Monroe, K. B. (1973). Buyers' Subjective Perceptions of Price. *Journal of Marketing Research*, 10 (Feb), pp. 70--80.

Ofek, E and Avery, J. (2013). J.C. Penney's "Fair and Square" pricing strategy. Harvard Business School, (Jan 4). Retrieved from https://services.hbsp.harvard.edu/services/proxy/content/26533289/27082010/de352b490f2276266456baf05402f9c1

Peterson, H. (2015). The End of an Era – Jos. A Bank is Holding One Final Buy 1, Get 3 Free Sale. *Business Insider* (Oct 22). http://www.businessinsider.com/jos-a-bank-holds-final-sale-2015-10

Price Doesn't Count for Everything in Retail (2002). *Home Textiles Today*, 23 (May 27), p. 6.

Rajendran, K. N. and Tellis, G. J. (1994). Contextual and Temporal Components of Reference Price. *Journal of Marketing*, 58 (Jan), pp. 22--34.

Rathe (2014). Increasing Food Prices Spark Trend of Package Downsizing. *Boston Globe*. Retrieved from: https://www.bostonglobe.com/lifestyle/food-dining/2014/02/11/the-incredible-shrinking-package/Ti6VwQCCcgowhLdr8bHnyJ/story.html

Saitz, G. (2003). Why We Pay What We Pay. *Newhouse News Service*, (Jun 10), p. 1.

Segal, D. (2000). Overcharged Music Buyers Stuck with the Bill. *Washington Post*, (May 13), p. C1.

Smith, L. (2003). The Incredible Shrinking Products: Consumers Cry Foul at 'Weight Out' Pricing. *Times Union* (Albany, NY), (Jul 21), p. C1.

Song, S. (2003). The Shrink Rap. *Time*, New York, 161 (Jun 2), p. 81.

The Truth Behind the Incredible Shrinking Ice Cream Package (2008). Ice Cream Journal: The Inside Scoop on Ice Cream and Turkey Hill Dairy, (Aug 15). Retrieved from http://icecreamjournal.turkeyhill.com/index.php/2008/08/15/shrinking-ice-cream-package/

Wegmans Announces No Price Increases on Winter List of Products Families Buy Most. Company news release dated 1/05/2012. Retrieved from http://www.wegmans.com/webapp/wcs/stores/servlet/PressReleaseDetailView?langId=-1&storeId=10052&catalogId=10002&productId=733558

What is the Parallel Market? (n.d) The Gray Blog. Retrieved from http://espinosaiplaw.com/wordpress/?page_id=5

Chapter 12

Developing an Effective Integrated Marketing Communications (IMC) Mix

"Make the customer the hero of your story."
~ Ann Hendley, Chief Content Officer, MarketingProfs

Source: I AM NIKOM/Shutterstock.com

CHAPTER OBJECTIVES

After completing this chapter you will be able to:

- Define the concept of integrated marketing communications (IMC).
- Explain the differences among all tactical elements of the IMC mix, including advertising, sales promotion, direct marketing, Internet, personal selling, public relations, and publicity.
- Describe the importance of effective customer communications.
- Explain how a store's layout can be an effective tool in communicating with customers.

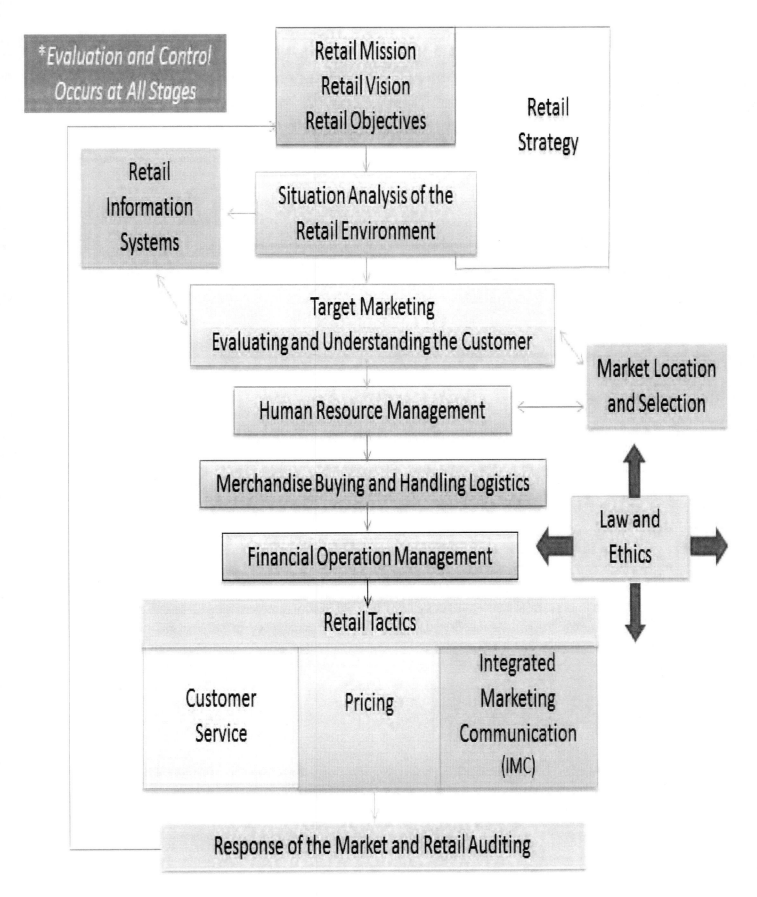

Whole Foods Market Believes in Real Food

Whole Foods Market (www.wholefoodsmarket.com), a U.S. supermarket chain based in Austin, Texas was started in 1980. The company employs 87,000 employees (called team members) and has over 350 retail and non-retail locations in the U.S., Canada and United Kingdom. The chain emphasizes organic foods and high quality. Their motto, "Whole Foods, Whole People, Whole Planet" illustrates their commitment to sustainable agriculture.

The company uses social media to connect with customers and has a presence on Twitter, Pinterest, Google+, Instagram, YouTube and Facebook. In 2015, Whole Foods launched their first national advertising campaign in television, print and digital. The campaign touted the company as "America's Healthiest Grocery Store" with the tagline, "Values Matter." In 2017, the "Eat Real Food" national campaign was launched. The tagline of the campaign was "We Believe in Real Food." Both campaigns underscore the values of the company. Two of Whole Foods' priorities for 2017 that related to marketing com-

Source: Roman Tiraspolsky/Shutterstock.com

munication were to progress to an "always on" unified marketing and media plan and to intensify personalization efforts through the roll out of a rewards program (Whole Foods 2016 Annual Report). In June 2017 Amazon acquired Whole Foods Market. It will be interesting to see how the company evolves under the Amazon brand.

Introduction

The process of communicating with various publics is known as *integrated marketing communications (IMC).* Although relatively new, the concept of IMC is catching on with many retailers. Individuals involved in the communications process have seen a need to integrate all the communications functions to create a synergistic, seamless incorporation of all of these activities into the IMC process. According to faculty at the Medill School at Northwestern University, ". . . the IMC process starts with the customer . . . and then works back to determine and define the forms and methods through which persuasive communications programs should be developed" (Schultz, 2001).

Consumers do not see all the various functions that businesses provide; rather, they see only the resulting product and/or brand and the physical retail store or e-tail site. They do not care about any of the functional areas required to bring them products or services; they care only about how those products or services satisfy their needs and wants. The satisfaction of these needs and wants generates sales for the retailer.

To effectively reach customers with a consistent message, everyone involved with internal and external customer communications must tell the consumer the same thing. Often the biggest challenge in IMC is executing the plans to meet marketplace demands while at the same time meeting company goals (Schultz, 1993). How many times have you seen an advertisement for a product you want only to find out that the store does not carry the product, the salesperson has never heard about the sale, or the price of the product is higher than in the advertisement? These inconsistencies could have been reduced or eliminated had the retailer used some type of system to integrate all its communications functions.

This chapter discusses the various methods and issues involved in the creation of an effective IMC mix for the retailer. In addition, the chapter examines the use of the store itself as an effective tool in customer communications.

Developing an Integrated Marketing Communication Program

The primary purpose for developing a retail IMC program is to generate consumer traffic--- that is, to draw consumers to the retail site, whether a physical or an e-tail site. To attract consumers to the site, the retailer must inform them about items on sale, the location of the site, the reasons the consumer should shop there, and so on. The communications program should also inform consumers about the product and service offerings and any other areas that differentiate the retailer from competitors. In addition, the IMC program can develop customer loyalty that will yield repeat business for the firm.

Large retailers sometimes develop different communication plans for specific geographic markets to take advantage of geographic differences. Plans might also be developed to take advantage of differences among the retailer's target market segments. For example, in 2003, Office Depot launched the company's first Hispanic-focused IMC campaign (Office Depot Launches..., 2003). The back-to-school campaign integrated retail, direct marketing, catalog, e-commerce, public relations, and advertising efforts. To create consistency in the program, several advertising agencies had to work together. Today many retailers are targeting the Hispanic market; most recently Target is using bilingual signs in markets with large Latino populations (Moylan, 2013).

Source: Monkey Business Images/Shutterstock.com

Several tactics are used to communicate with the retailer's internal and external publics. Together these tactics are known as the *IMC mix*. Components of the mix are advertising, sales promotions, direct marketing, electronic/Internet, personal selling, public relations, and publicity. An argument can also be made to include the brand or product itself in the overall mix.

What makes you want to shop at a particular retailer? Are you searching for hard-to-find products or brands? Are you trying to find a particular brand? How did you hear about the brand? How did you hear about the retailer? IMC can help determine the answer to all of these questions. Many communications variables can influence the decision to shop at a particular retailer. Given the thousands of product offerings and the thousands of retailers offering them, retail marketers must ensure that their communications with their customers are "clear, concise, and integrated" (Ogden, 1998).

Retailers invest a lot of time and money developing a positive image of their business and stores. This image carries a certain value, called equity. *Equity* is the marketing and financial value resulting from a firm's marketing investments. Marketers also attempt to develop *name equity,* which is the value of the organization's name. *Brand equity* refers to the consumer's perceived level of quality for the company's product lines. If the consumer has a positive perception of the brand, they are more likely to have a positive perception of the company. *Customer equity* is the value of the resources that customers invest in a firm (Dorsch and Carlson, 1996).

An effective communications plan builds and enhances equity for the retailer. IMC is essential for the continued operations of the retail organization. One example of a company that used its established image and brand equity to break into retailing is the General Motors Corporation (GM). In 2016, the GM Company Store opened at the global headquarters in the Renaissance Center in Detroit. The store sells a variety of merchandise such as clothing and die-cast toys, all featuring GM brands like Chevrolet, Buick, GMC and Cadillac. The products are also available online (www.gmcompanystore.com). GM is embracing the omni-channel approach to make sure consumers can stay connected with the brand both in and outside of the car. For example, there is the On-Star At Your Service mobile app which provides customers with retail offers tied to points of interest, locations and destinations. In addition, there are many apps that help customers experience the brands, such as myChevrolet, myGMC, and myCadillac.

In developing an IMC plan, communications specialists (i.e., marketing communications managers) conceive of a plan and then execute it so that the consumer is exposed to the end result of this planning process. Essentially the same steps are taken in developing an IMC program as in developing the integrated retail management (IRM) plan: creating objectives, then strategies, and then tactical executions.

Costs associated with IMC (also called *marketing communications* or *marcom* for short) are often high. Therefore, the IMC plan includes a budget that allows management to see where money is being spent and determine whether the budget allocations are effective. A typical plan includes the following elements:

• The IMC mission or vision

• A situational analysis, including profiles of current users, a competitive analysis, and the geographic locations of the retail outlets and their customers

• Overall objectives

• The budget

• The overall strategy

• The tactical executions---including personal selling, direct marketing, sales promotions (which include point-of-purchase advertising), Internet, public relations and publicity, advertising, and in some instances, the packaging and branding of the products sold in the store

Source: Rawpixel.com/Shutterstock.com

• Resource allocations (including human and capital resources)

• Methods of evaluation

IMC Mission or Vision

The IMC mission or vision is written in exactly the same manner as the overall retail mission and vision statements, except that it focuses on marcom only. The mission explains why the retailer is using IMC to communicate with customers. Specifically, it explains where the marcom function fits into the overall IRM plan.

Situational Analysis

Most of the information for the situational analysis (also known as situation analysis) can be generated from the retailer's general situational analysis. With marcom, however, there should be a comprehensive analysis of the company, including the level of retailer "aggressiveness" in the marketplace, sales and profits from the past few years, the corporate culture, the mission and vision, market share for each product line and for the retailer as a whole, and sales trends. The analysis should also include corporate resources, such as technology and human resources that are available for use in integrated marketing communications.

In addition, the situational analysis should include the environments within which the retailer operates, product and service histories, a competitive analysis, a current user analysis, and geographic data. Data for the situational analysis come from the same sources provided in our discussions of the retail information system (RIS) and site selection (see Chapters 6 and 7). The more information and data available to facilitate IMC executions, the more effective the executions will be.

A SWOT analysis (Strengths, Weaknesses, Opportunities and Threats) on the existing marketing communications is also typically part of the situational analysis. The SWOT will identify key internal (strengths and weaknesses) and external factors (opportunities and threats) relevant to marcom objectives.

Developing Objectives

General IMC objectives are developed to provide a basis for determining the extent of the IMC program's success. Like the objectives for other parts of the IRM plan, IMC objectives should be measurable and realistic. In creating marcom objectives, the retailer needs to have a good understanding of who the target audience is, when the objectives should be met, and specifically what the retailer wants to accomplish by undertaking the executions. The objectives can be either long term, short term, or both. The idea is to provide motivation and direction for the entire campaign. The SMART acronym helps students remember how to develop a good objective which must be Specific, Measurable, Attainable, Realistic and Time-bound (see figure 12.1).

Figure 12.1 Developing SMART Objectives

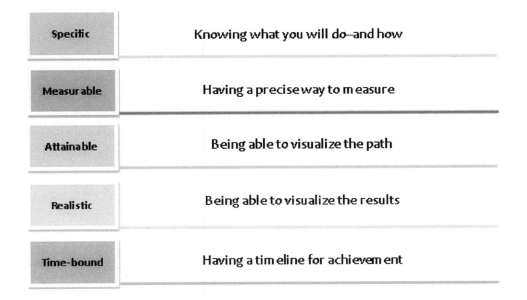

Specific	Knowing what you will do—and how
Measurable	Having a precise way to measure
Attainable	Being able to visualize the path
Realistic	Being able to visualize the results
Time-bound	Having a timeline for achievement

Typical categories of retail IMC objectives are described next.

Positioning Objectives: The purpose of positioning objectives is to create an image in consumers' minds about the retailer, typically in relation to the competition. Positioning objectives help build the retailer's brand name. This is also called *brand building* (Aaker, 1995). Retailers can also position by attributes, price, or quality (Myron and Truax, 1996).

Example: "Our objective is to become the number one retailer in the children's shoe category, as measured by market share, within the greater Los Angeles, CA, area by the year 2023."

Increased Sales: The purpose of increased-sales objectives is to stimulate the sales of certain products (or all products) during a given time period.

Example: "Our objective with this advertising campaign is to increase sales of women's apparel by 10 percent in one year."

Communications Objectives: Communications objectives usually deal with the influence of the retailer's communications on consumers over a period of time. Communications objectives tend to be both long and short term, to try to persuade consumers to do something (continue buying products from the retailer, learn that the retailer is open twenty-four hours a day, and so on).

Example: "To create awareness of the company's website such that at the end of three months, 40 percent or more of a random sample of 100 surveyed customers indicate knowledge of our website and 25 percent or more have accessed the website at least once during the three-month measurement period."

Source: Icatnews/Shutterstock.com

Traffic Objectives: Traffic objectives aim to draw increasing numbers of customers to the retailer's store over time. These objectives may be particularly useful in an e-tailing environment.

Example: "The objective is to increase store traffic by 10 percent over a one-year period and to increase website traffic by 30 percent over the same period."

Image: Image objectives focus on developing the overall image of the retailer (as opposed to product or sales revenue objectives).

Example: "The long-term objective is to, within the next five years, change our image from the 'lousy customer service retailer' to the 'we respond quickly to customers' needs retailer,' as measured by customer image surveys."

Objectives are usually specific to each type of retailer. Although there is no one "right" IMC plan for each and every retailer, some elements are common to all plans and must be included in the retailer's IMC mix. The following sections discuss budgeting for IMC and the tactical areas of the IMC mix.

The IMC Budget

Once the objectives are developed, the budget for the marcom executions should be determined. A number of techniques can be used for marcom budgeting, but our discussion focuses on the most popular methods. Dollar amounts for any type of IMC campaign must be included in the budget. Often retailers are given advertising allowances or are encouraged to create cooperative advertising or IMC with their suppliers. These additional incentives must be included in the overall IMC budget.

Developing a budget can be a difficult process because decision makers often deal with competing pressures such as long-term objectives versus short-term needs, personal success versus company success, and risks versus rewards (Low and Mohr, 1999).

Although there are many different ways to calculate a budget, most retailers and IMC professionals choose among the percentage-of-sales method, the percentage-of-profit method, the objective-and-task method, follow-the–leader budgeting, the all-you-can-afford method, and the best-guess method.

Percentage-of-Sales Method: With the *percentage-of-sales method* of budgeting, the retailer or IMC specialist allots a basic percentage amount for the store and, in some cases, for each of the store's brands or products (or product lines). This basic percentage is usually based on a past trend or a researched forecast for the retailer's sales. Thus, the retailer decides on a basic percentage amount---say, three percent of total sales---and that amount of money is placed in the marcom budget. This is the easiest budgeting method and thus is fairly popular. However, the percentage-of-sales method does have some drawbacks.

The first problem occurs when sales are decreasing. In a period of declining sales, one potentially effective communication tactic is to expand rather than reduce the amount of communication or advertising. With the percentage-of-sales method, however, the retailer would budget *less* money for IMC when sales decreased.

Another problem occurs when competitors increase their advertising and promotional budgets to achieve a stated objective or to follow a planned strategy. When the competition increases their budgets, a retailer following the percentage-of-sales method may not follow suit. Consequently, this retailer may face a loss of market share. For example, if the retailer planned a special event to introduce some new products or services, the percentage-of-sales method would restrict the retailer's ability to implement these events. Because of these shortcomings, the percentage-of-sales method is usually used in conjunction with one or two of the other budgeting methods discussed next.

Percentage-of-Profit Method: The *percentage-of-profit method* of budgeting is very similar to the percentage-of-sales method. With the percentage-of-profit method, the basic percentage amount to be used for IMC is created based on the retailer's overall profits, rather than sales. This can be done division by division, for specific product lines, or for the retail operation as a whole. The percentage-of-profit method of budgeting has the same disadvantages as the percentage-of-sales method, so it too is usually coupled with one or two other budgeting methods.

Objective-and-Task Method: The *objective-and-task method* of budgeting for IMC is probably the best method of those described here because it requires a more thorough analysis of the role of the IMC components in achieving objectives. The retailer specifies the exact role the IMC program is to play in the overall retail operation. In addition, the retailer clearly defines the desired outcomes of the IMC plan. The retailer's budget is then based on the stated outcomes.

The objective-and-task method of budgeting consists of five steps:

1. The retailer specifies the retailing objectives to be achieved (profit increases, heightened consumer awareness, increased sales, increased market share, and so on).

2. The retailer specifies which variables are required to achieve the stated objectives.

3. The retailer defines the role each IMC variable is to play in achieving the objectives (e.g., the retailer decides whether point-of-purchase advertising, print advertising, or more salespeople would be required).

4. The retailer specifies the levels of response required to achieve the overall goals.

5. The retailer assigns budgeted dollar amounts based on the first four steps and by taking into account the time and costs associated with meeting the objectives.

Follow-the-Leader Budgeting: In *follow-the-leader budgeting* (also known as the *competitive match*), the retailer generates estimates of competitors' budgets and adjusts the budget (possible sources of information are the *Standard Directory of Advertising Agencies,* the *Standard*

Directory of Advertisers, LNA [Leading National Advertisers] listings, or some of the sources discussed in Chapter 6). Because most IMC data are proprietary, the retailer may have to make an educated guess as to the amount budgeted for IMC functions by competing retailers. The retailer can then match the industry leader's IMC budget or budget higher or lower amounts, depending on the organization's overall needs.

In addition to the problem of trying to generate accurate budget data for competitors, follow-the-leader budgeting takes a reactive rather than proactive stance in customer communications. This method also assumes all competitors have the same communications needs when in fact each retailer's needs are unique. Retailers differ in size, have different target markets, and generate different types of communications. Thus, follow-the-leader budgeting may be ineffective for many types of retailers.

All-You-Can-Afford Method: The *all-you-can-afford method* is exactly what the name implies: the retailer allots all the money it can afford to IMC functions. Although it is not recommended, with the all-you-can-afford method the retailer develops the other retailing budgets and allots the leftover amounts to the IMC budget. This is not an effective budgeting method because it assumes IMC is the least relevant function in running a business when in fact IMC is critical to the success or failure of the organization. IMC activities should receive a great deal of emphasis, but this budgeting method precludes that. In times of decreasing sales, it is important to increase rather than decrease customer communications. All-you-can-afford budgeting is common in small to mid-size retailers that are conservative in their attempts to increase market share and company sales.

Best-Guess Method: The *best-guess method* is most often used by retailers that have very little experience or training in budgeting. In essence, the retailer has no idea of how much to allocate and therefore develops a subjective estimate ("guesstimate") as the budget figure. Because this method is largely subjective, it is inefficient.

The Overall IMC Strategy

The IMC strategy should emanate from the first few phases of the IMC and IRM plans. The mission and vision provide direction in determining the strategy for achieving the overall goals. In addition, the situational analysis should provide information about competitors and customers. These data help frame the IMC strategy.

Two steps should be completed before undertaking the development of an IMC strategy. The first is to identify the main consumer or store problem (or opportunity) for which the IMC plan can provide a solution. This key fact may explain why consumers prefer a particular retailer over its competitors. It may deal with product offerings, customer service, responsiveness to the customer, and so forth. The key fact should be stated in the consumer's language, not in the language of retailing or marketing. For example, instead of saying, "We offer the largest number of stock keeping units related to spices in our geographic trading area," it would be better to say, "We offer a greater variety of spices than any other retailer in the world."

Source: Rawpixel.com/Shutterstock.com

Figure 12.2 Developing an Effective Retail IMC Strategy

The second step is to identify and list the key marketing problems (or opportunities). This problem or opportunity should be based on prior research and approached from the point of view of the retail IMC specialist. For example, an opportunity may be stated as, "According to a survey taken last month, brand recall is up 10 percent within our primary target market compared to the same period last year, but down 30 percent within our secondary target market and 50 percent within our tertiary target market. An opportunity exists to increase brand awareness in our secondary and tertiary target markets."

Once these two steps are completed, the retailer is ready to identify the key IMC objectives from which the desired outcomes of the IMC executions are developed. If the objective-and-task method of budgeting is being used, this information already exists. Then the retailer should develop and document the *creative platform* (or creative strategy). The creative platform includes the target market, major competitors, reasons that consumers should purchase from the retailer, and a promise to consumers (i.e., a solution to the problem or opportunity identified in step 2).

Finally, the retailer is ready to establish the essential components of the creative strategy, including both creative and non-creative information (legal requirements, tag lines, logos, etc.). The strategy represents the "big picture" for IMC personnel, guiding them as they develop IMC campaigns for the retail outlet(s). It is also used to plan the tactical executions. Figure 12.2 outlines the process for developing the IMC strategy.

IMC Tactics

Once the retail IMC strategy is in place, the retailer concentrates on executions. The following sections describe the variables in the tactical executions.

Advertising

Advertising is "a form of either mass communication or direct-to-consumer communication that is non-personal and is paid for by various business firms, nonprofit organizations, and individuals who are in some way identified in the advertising message and who hope to inform or persuade members of a particular audience" (Shimp, 2000). The retailer generally uses advertising to remind, inform, or persuade the targeted market to act. A retailer also might use advertising to create an overall retail image (information and persuasion for the consumer).

Whatever the reason for using advertising, the key to effective advertising is ensuring that a lot of people are reached in a relatively short period of time. Per-product advertising is relatively inexpensive;

Figure 12.3 Developing and Advertising Plan

in contrast, the cost for an overall advertising program can be quite high. Advertising allows a business to communicate with a large audience through various media such as television, radio, newspapers, billboards, magazines, the Internet and so on.

Author Lisa Fortini-Campbell (2001) compares successful advertising to hitting the "sweet spot." In sports, the sweet spot is the special place on a baseball, tennis racket, or other piece of equipment that makes the ball travel faster with less effort. Advertising's sweet spot is the place in the consumer's mind where a connection is made between consumer insight and brand insight.

When assessing what type of advertising to undertake, the retailer creates an advertising plan. This plan should give direction to IMC employees and should be integrated into all other functions as well, so that everyone understands the purpose of the advertising.

Establishing an advertising plan includes six major steps (Ogden, 1998) as depicted in figure 12.3.

1. Review the IRM plan to get a clear picture of what needs to be accomplished.

2. Restate the target market, taking care to include information that will help develop the best advertising plan. Data that are irrelevant should be ignored.

3. Develop and list the advertising communications objectives. Included within this step should be the key fact, the marketing problem, and the communications objectives. Like all objectives, the advertising objectives must be realistic, measurable, specific, cost effective, and timely. Each objective should be worded to allow for a specific outcome (and only one outcome).

4. State the advertising strategy. The strategy should contain information about the target markets and audiences, the principal competition, the consumer promise, and the reason that the consumer should purchase from the retailer. In other words, the advertising presents the rationale for shopping at a particular retail outlet. Advertising agencies usually create *copy platforms,* or creative strategies, that speak to all of these issues.

5. Develop samples of creative executions that will be pursued. These examples may be in the form of sample print layouts, television storyboards, radio scripts, or other samples of the creative work.

6. List all media recommendations. In this step, all the available media should be assessed to choose the best methods for communicating to targeted audiences. The media recommendations should include the key media problem and the objectives to be achieved.

Media objectives are usually expressed in terms of reach, frequency, continuity, geographic weighting, costs per thousand exposures (CPM), and gross rating points (GRPs). *Reach* is the number of different people (or households) exposed to a message at least once. *Frequency* is the average number of times an individual is exposed to a message. If a retailer runs a commercial on television, the reach is the number of households who watched the commercial. So if there are one million households that were exposed to the commercial, the reach is one million. If the company decides to run the commercial 15 more times, the frequency is 15. Because company's want to drive both reach and frequency at the lowest cost possible, retailers desire all components of the IMC mix to be understood and integrated. *Gross Rating Points (GRPs)* (pronounced as grips) combine reach with frequency to develop a metric or summary measurement that provides a weight for a given media schedule. To calculate the GRPs you multiply reach times frequency (r x f). In the previous example the GRPs would be 15 million (1 million x 15).

Continuity is created by addressing the timing of the advertising campaign. The retailer must determine when the advertising should run. Should the advertising run throughout the entire campaign, or spend heavily upfront when the campaign is launched and then reduce expenditures? The decision is based upon the type of product or service being advertised, budget, objectives and views of managers. *Cost per thousand (or CPM)* will help the advertiser compare across media. The CPM refers to the cost of reaching 1,000 people through an identified medium.

Each time an advertising choice is recommended, management or the readers of the advertising plan should be given a rationale for that choice. This makes it easier for managers to see at a glance why various methods, objectives, platforms, and so on were developed.

All advertising should be dynamic, strategic, based on consumer needs and wants, creative, integrated, persuasive, and informative. There are short-term and long-term results from advertising. Short-term results include increased sales, brand awareness, and traffic. Long-term results include increases in market share, customer loyalty, and brand equity (Birritteri, 2002).

Each retailer has specific advertising needs. In addition, each retailer has certain times or periods that are more effective for its advertising programs. For example, Wednesdays and Thursdays are good times for supermarkets to advertise their products. Shoppers look at the ads on those days and begin writing shopping lists for the weekend trip to the supermarket. They also clip coupons and note any special sales occurring over the advertised period. Large department stores usually begin advertising back-to-school products during the end of July and early August rather than spending the bulk of advertising dollars on weekly ads. Because advertising budgets are fixed, retailers must make sure they get the most reach and frequency out of their budgets

Sales Promotions

Tactical executions can also take the form of sales promotions. *Sales promotions* are used to complement the other IMC tactical areas. The overriding purpose of a sales promotion is to stimulate customer purchases with various nonrecurring sales efforts.

Although initially used to stimulate short-term sales, sales promotions today play a much bigger role in the IMC process. They can be used to tie in a branding strategy with a product in the retail store. They can be used to generate customer databases for use with site location planning or with direct-marketing campaigns.

Consumers can benefit from sales promotions, as well. These benefits include contributing to shopping enjoyment, increased satisfaction with the retail experience, and monetary savings (Four-year Research…, 2002).

An example of a successful sales promotion was done by Pepsi. In an attempt to drive customers to Facebook, Pepsi created vending machines that provide free samples of Pepsi products. In order to get your free sample, consumers have to go to Facebook and give Pepsi a "like" on their Facebook site (Kooser, 2013). As of press time the company had over 17 million likes on their site but it is unclear how many resulted from the promotion. When planned properly, sales promotions can stimulate

Source: Monkey Business Images/Shutterstock.com

both short-term sales and long-term demand. Table 12.2 lists the most common types of sales promotions.

Table 12.1 Common Types of Sales Promotion

Consumer	Trade
• Price deals	• Push money
• Premiums	• Trade allowances
• Samples	• Trade contests
• Contests and sweepstakes	• Point of purchase (POP) displays
• In-pack coupons	• Trade shows
• BOGO (buy one, get one free)	• Business cards
• Warranties and guarantees	• Vendor support programs
• Tie-in promotions	• Training programs
• Loyalty rewards programs	• Specialty advertising (pens, pencils, caps, jackets, etc.)
• Coupons	• Cooperative advertising
• On-shelf couponing	
• Online and mobile couponing	
• Point of sale coupon dispensers	
• Rebates	

One of the most popular form of sales promotion among retailers is *point-of-purchase (POP) communications* (also called *point-of-purchase advertising*) which are marketing communication tools such as displays, signs, audio and visual used in a store to encourage sales and impulse buying. Point-Of-Purchase Advertising International (POPAI) (www.popai.com) is a trade association devoted to the execution of POP communications. POPAI created a trade publication called *Marketing's Powerful Weapon: Point-Of-Purchase Advertising* as a guide for the retailer in the development of effective POP communications (Liljenwall and Maskulka, 2001).

Direct Marketing

Many types of retailers, including e-tailers, use direct marketing to reach customers. Through *direct marketing*, retailers use one or more advertising media to generate immediate action from consumers (i.e., the purchase of products and services). The idea behind direct marketing is to solicit from customers an order or a request for additional information about the store or products being sold, or to increase traffic to the retailer's place of business (including online sites). Referred to as "customized persuasion," direct marketing attempts to create immediate sales (Stone, 1989). Frequently, direct marketing is integrated into the other IMC tactical executions, especially advertising.

Direct-response advertising, direct-mail advertising, membership programs, and telemarketing are examples of direct marketing. Direct marketing can be used to reward frequent customers through loyalty programs that provide incentives for shopping at a particular retailer. Colloquy Research Group reports that in 2017, U.S. consumer held 3.8 billion memberships in customer loyalty programs. Restaurants and drugstore memberships experience the highest rate of growth in loyalty membership.

Source: ShevalierArt/Shutterstock.com

The use of direct mail is growing due to recent limitations imposed on telemarketing. Tie-ins with sales promotion activities, such as coupons, have increased the effectiveness of direct mail. Consumers are often more willing to open direct-mail pieces that provide additional value, such as coupons, than those that don't. In addition, many brick-and-mortar retailers have non-store divisions that specialize in direct mail, such as catalog retailers. These divisions focus on the use of mail to get their product offerings into consumers' hands.

Like the other tactical areas, direct marketing requires a plan. Because of the nature of direct marketing, the plan must show how it integrates with the other IMC variables. For the most part, the objectives behind direct marketing include customer retention, product trial, brand switching, increased sales, or sales through direct response (as in catalog sales). Database marketing is a form of direct marketing, although it is also used to create non-direct sales.

Source: T. L. Furrer/Shutterstock.com

Electronic and Internet Marketing

Electronic marketing (also called digital marketing) is the use of digital technologies to sell goods and services. Electronic marketing includes e-tailing, CD-ROMs, e-mail, blog development and execution and electronic data interchange (EDI). Electronic marketing applies traditional marketing in the online channel. Although electronic and Internet marketing terms are often used interchangeably, Internet marketing is more specific and involves using the Internet to sell products and services. Social media marketing is even more specific and uses social media sites to connect with customers and generate website traffic. Electronic marketing has increased consumer-generated marketing, which is when a consumer gets directly involved with the marketing activities of a company.

The use of electronic and Internet marketing is increasing in marketing plans, replacing some dollars that were spent on traditional media like radio, TV or print advertising.

Some advantages to electronic/Internet marketing are the lower cost, timeliness, availability, exposure, easy to personalize and the global reach. Disadvantages include loss of control of messages, must be kept current, requires coordination and integration, and the potential for bad news to spread quickly.

For retailers and e-tailers, an online presence is not enough to ensure a company's success. How well marketing is executed will send a message to customers about the quality of products and how much value and attention is paid to the target market. Electronic and Internet marketing are tools that retailers have to reinforce messages, drive awareness of the company, support the brand and achieve the objectives of the overall campaign. While many think these tools are free, they are not. It takes significant time and money to achieve sustained success with electronic and Internet marketing. One area that is getting increased attention is search engine optimization (SEO). *Search engine optimization* are actions taken to increase the visibility of a website or page in the results of a search using a search engine.

There is some overlap between electronic and Internet marketing and the other areas of IMC. Certainly advertising and sales promotions and sales can be executed online. Like the other areas of IMC, Internet marketing requires developing a comprehensive plan. The plan should integrate this format with the retailer's other channels and methods of communication.

Social Media

Social media allows people to shares ideas and content. People exposed to social content are more likely to increase their spending (Ogilvy-ChatThreads, 2011). The term "word of web" (as opposed to "word of mouth") is used to describe communication occurring on the Internet. Known as "The Big 5" in social media, Facebook, Google+, Twitter, YouTube and LinkedIn are the most widely used social media websites around the world. Other popular sites are Pinterest, Snapchat, Tumblr and Instagram. Retailers consider these sites first when developing electronic marketing/social media plans. The

Source:Twin Design/Shutterstock.com

key for retailers is to determine which sites their target market use and establish a presence on these sites. For example, millennials have strong ties to utilizing Snapchat. Marketing research can help determine which segments of the target market are on which sites. This will help determine where to spend time and money.

Issues in the Use of Technology

As we have seen, electronic technology can be used for a number of retailing functions. Therefore, it is best to deal with the use of these technologies from a functional rather than a general perspective. Certainly the Internet can be used as a channel of distribution, but that function is entirely different from using the Internet as a marketing communications tool. Thus, if the Internet is used as both a channel of distribution and a means of communication, the purpose for each function should be made clear in planning documents. Uses of electronic technologies are expanding rapidly; new applications of these powerful tools are found every day. IMC specialists focus on technology's power to communicate.

Personal Selling

Personal selling is the oldest form of communicating with customers. It is the salesperson at the retail level who can most effectively close sales. The importance of this function is often underestimated. In IMC, it is one of the most effective tools for creating retail sales. *Personal selling* involves face-to-face, or person-to-person, communication. The seller attempts to persuade customers to buy the retailer's products. The primary advantage of personal selling is its one-on-one nature, which allows the salesperson to be flexible when finding products or services to satisfy or exceed the customer's needs and wants.

Source: nullplus/Shutterstock.com

Often salespeople are the only contact a customer has with a retail store. The customer may then look upon the salesperson as the retailer. Customers come to retail salespeople with specific needs and wants, and a well-trained salesperson makes sure that those needs and wants are met or exceeded. The downside to personal selling as a communications vehicle is that it is very expensive when looked at on a per-customer-contact basis.

To increase the chances of success, a sales plan is needed for the sales function. Salespeople should receive ongoing training to ensure they have the answers to customers' questions, or at least know where to go to get those answers.

Personal selling entails a great deal of integration among the retailing functions. Human resource personnel train salespeople, customer service depends on personal customer contact, managers supervise salespeople, and all IMC functions rely on salespeople to close many sales. It can be argued that personal selling is the most important aspect of retailing.

Retailers often have different hiring criteria for the sales staff than for employees in many of the other areas. Demographic characteristics, prior work experience, and personality are important considerations when selecting sales personnel.

Examples of using demographics in the hiring of salespeople are found at Nordstrom department stores. If you have shopped at a Nordstrom store, you may have noticed that the salespeople in each department mirror the department in which they work. For example, the

Source: XiXinXing/Shutterstock.com

salesperson working in the women's petite clothing department is usually a petite person. This approach allows the salesperson to better understand customers' needs.

On a recent trip to Nordstrom, two retail consultants were looking around in each department. One thing that caught their attention was the age demographic of the salespeople. In the junior department, salespeople were younger. In the women's departments, salespeople were older than those in juniors, and all the sales clerks were women. Similarly, male sales personnel staffed the men's departments. This pattern held throughout the store. Consumers are likely to feel more confident about their purchases when they relate to salespeople who "look" like them. Other retailers can learn from the Nordstrom example by hiring and training salespeople who understand customers' concerns. The salesperson wearing a suit is probably more effective in his job---selling men's suits---than he would be if he worked in the athletic apparel section.

Training for sales personnel takes a slightly different approach than that for employees in other IMC areas. Selling techniques and product knowledge are the main issues in sales training. Many retailers rely heavily on role playing to enforce the processes being taught to sales staff.

Once again, it is the retail managers' job to ensure that personal selling is integrated with the other IMC variables. No customer likes to be confused by a retailer's communications process. If advertisers tell consumers that the retailer is "friendly," consumers expect to see friendly employees. To them, "friendly" may mean being greeted by smiling employees who thank them for their business. If shoppers do not experience friendliness, they may get confused and the IMC message will get lost in the execution. Sales employees should be trained to follow the "golden rule": "Treat customers as you would want to be treated were you to shop at the store." Chapter 13 addresses customer relations in greater depth.

Public Relations

Public relations (PR) is an organization's efforts to win the cooperation of various publics (Lesly, 1981). The basic task of the PR department is to generate goodwill toward the retail organization, creating long-term, profitable relationships with the retailer's community. In particular, the PR department needs to create and maintain positive relationships with the various media, including newspapers, radio and television stations, and regional or local magazines. The task of internal employee communications also generally falls on the shoulders of the PR office.

Although the Internet has improved the speed of communication with various publics, there is also a risk in doing so, due to increasing expectations of accuracy (Weiner, 2002). PR professionals must learn to balance the time pressure to get information out on the Internet with the need to check facts before posting content on the retailer's website (Brandt, 1997) or social media site.

The area of public relations requires a plan, so that it will be integrated with the other IMC functions. It is very important that the PR department be connected to the RIS. The PR manager has the added responsibility of monitoring the publicity that the retailer seeks to generate.

Thomas L. Harris (1998), management consultant and author of a book about public relations, calls PR the secret weapon of IMC because PR can make the other IMC components (e.g., advertising, Internet, and sales promotion) more credible. For retailers, credibility in the eyes of the customer translates into increased sales and loyalty.

Publicity

Source: Radu Razvan/Shutterstock.com

Publicity is a sub-function of public relations in which the organization attempts to attract attention through various media without paying for the time or space to do so. The attention can be controlled or uncontrolled and can be positive or negative. Publicity might be about a retailer's employees, its customers (a very good idea), or the retailer as a whole (perhaps, for instance, about the retailer being the largest contributor to a town beautification project).

In general, publicity is seen as more credible than advertising. The reason for this is that in many instances publicity comes from an objective source as opposed to from an advertisement paid for by the retailer (Harris, 1998).

Publicity is referred to as being "free" because media time and space are not purchased. There are many costs associated with PR, however, such as those for hiring people to write press releases, purchasing supplies, and so on. One example of the costs associated with publicity involves the Harry Potter book craze. Due to publicity surrounding the release of a new book, retailers had to adopt increased security measures to guard against theft of the book before its release (Fasig, 2003).

Retailers must attempt to control and plan publicity, and it must be integrated with all the other areas of the IMC mix. Unplanned publicity must be limited or eliminated completely. All communications vehicles should provide customers with the same ongoing message, to achieve continuity and thereby more communications power for the retailer.

There are two types of publicity: good and bad. Obviously, no retailer wants to generate any bad publicity for its operations. Unfortunately, due to the number of media outlets, complaints and misinformation about a retailer can spread rapidly and affect an organization's IMC efforts (Weiner, 2002). For example, in 2017 The clothing brand LuLaRoe faced criticism when customers started complaining about leggings that begin to tear after a few hours of wear. A Facebook group was started for people to share their stories. The group quickly had over 10,000 members. The company responded by sharing tips on how to avoid getting holes and releasing a statement that they are working to correct the problem. LuLaRoe products are sold through a network of "fashion consultants," mostly women, who buy the clothes at wholesale and then sell the products to friends using websites and living room parties, similar to how Avon and The Pampered Chef sell products (Peterson, 2017).

When planning for publicity, one or more of the following objectives is generally pursued:

- Reputation management
- Publications (annual reports, brochures, manuals, other house organ--type publications)
- Speech writing (for the CEO or other members of the executive staff who do not have the time to write their own speeches)
- Special-events management (sports marketing, sponsorships, etc.)
- Lobbying (also known as *public affairs management*)

Some methods of generating publicity, in conjunction with the PR department, would be through news releases, photographs, event marketing, posters, exhibits, free sampling, and fact sheets or media kits.

Resource Allocation

The biggest challenge for those involved in IMC tactical executions is to fully integrate them with one another; the overall IRM plan; and the retail mission, vision, and objectives. Once the tactics have been integrated, resources for executing the tactics need to be allocated.

The IMC manager is responsible for allocating both dollars and human resources to each tactical area. Effective plans facilitate the allocation process; those with the best rationales for their tactical executions generally get the lion's share of the resources.

Evaluation

The final step in the overall IMC plan is the development of methods to assess the effectiveness of the company's communications. Although deemed the "final step," in practice the evaluation process should occur on an ongoing basis. Many methods can be used to assess communication effectiveness, but the most popular is simply to track sales. If outstanding advertising and promotions are created, sales should increase. However, evaluating the effectiveness of an IMC program is not always that easy.

Many variables affecting customer communications are beyond the control of the retailer and IMC planner (the economy is a major example). Therefore, in evaluating IMC, estimates are used to assess how well the programs are working. Because there are objectives for each tactical area, the first step in evaluation is to ascertain whether the objectives have been met. If they have not been met, the next step is to try to figure out why not.

Advertisers and IMC specialists use many techniques to test IMC effectiveness, such as pretest/posttest research, concept tests, copy tests, and tracking studies, among others. Different methods are used to measure the effectiveness of each of the IMC variables. Generally, direct marketing tends to be the easiest to monitor because there is an immediate response to the marketing effort.

When putting the IMC program together and evaluating the outcomes, it is wise to keep in mind the words of the first large department store owner, John Wanamaker: "I know that half of my advertising is wasted; I just don't know which half." He was referring to the difficulties encountered when attempting to evaluate the effectiveness of IMC programs.

Using Store Layout and Design to Increase IMC Effectiveness

In addition to the concepts discussed earlier, the store itself can be used as an effective method of customer communications. The store's design should evolve through planning and integration, not through a haphazard approach. Ideally, the store layout and design is planned prior to leasing or building a physical location. If e-tailing is a component of the business, the e-tail outlet must also have a creative layout and design that is integrated with the other communications tactics

Source: Sorbis/Shutterstock.com

The store layout and design can help the retailer create differentiation for its products and services. Think about a restaurant that you visit frequently. What makes that particular restaurant attractive to you? The answer may be that you enjoy the atmosphere, the restaurant is close by, the customer service is excellent, and you enjoy the food. To attract consumers to a particular retail venue, the retailer needs to ensure that the overall store design is appealing to its target market groups.

In a physical store, the retailer has the means to make patrons comfortable. For example, when women shop for clothes with a male companion, chances are that he will want to take frequent breaks. An aware retailer can create a comfortable area for people who are waiting while their shopping partners try on clothes. A simple couch may be just what is needed to appeal to customers. Customers will return to a retailer that has treated them well.

Design and Layout Objectives

To ensure that the store's layout and design are communicating the same message as other IMC variables, a plan is required. Within that plan are objectives, strategies, and tactics. The three main objectives in design and layout development are related to (1) creating an appropriate overall atmosphere, (2) designing the store to allow easy shopping, and (3) creating a design and layout that allots retail space so as to maximize the store's productivity.

Each time selling space is used to provide customers with added amenities, valuable selling space is lost. Thus, the question to ask is: How much do the design and layout add to overall sales? Another question is: Do the layout and design generate repeat business by bringing consumers back to the store?

Source: BBA Photography/Shutterstock.com

Atmosphere: The first objective is to create an overall positive atmosphere in the retail outlet; retailers refer to this as *atmospherics.* The retail store's physical characteristics affect the overall communications that are sent to the target market. They also contribute to the overall store image. When you hear the words "Hard Rock Café," you can picture in your mind the atmosphere of that restaurant. You may even be able to "hear" the music played there or recall the smells of a Hard Rock Café you have visited. These elements help define a retailer and create continuity in all

IMC attempts.

If you have ever been to a mall that had a Cinnabon store, you can probably recall the fragrance of the fresh cinnamon rolls baking. Similarly, people who have shopped at a Victoria's Secret store tend to remember the smell of perfume that permeates the store. The smells associated with Cinnabon and Victoria's Secret help create an overall image for these retailers.

E-tailers and other types of non-store retailers also rely on consumers' senses as they develop images for their companies and products. For example, many websites use audio or pop-up banners that make them memorable to visitors. A music e-tailer may include sounds on its websites to create not only an image but also the continuity needed when communicating to customers. Many catalog direct marketers use smells to help create an overall retail image by inserting "scratch and sniff" products or free product samples within their catalogs.

To develop an overall store image, retailers use lighting, fixtures, point-of-purchase displays, music, smells, and other tools to enhance the customer's buying experience. This technique is often referred to as *visual merchandising*. The objective is to inspire the customer to purchase through the use of design techniques that enhance the overall buying experience. A *planogram* is used to help employees arrange a store (see Figure 12.4). A planogram is a visual map of a store's layout and shows where products and displayed should be placed to maximize sales. The store's windows are also important communications vehicles that add to the store's ambiance. The image can convey or reinforce the retailer's product mix.

Figure 12.4 A Planogram of a Hypothetical Clothing Store

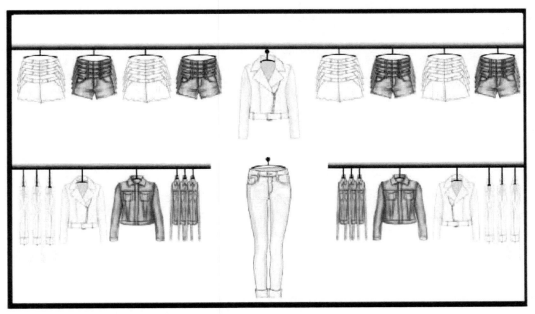

Source: Ggillustrations/Shutterstock.com

Some elements used to create an overall store atmosphere involve the use of the store's exterior. The storefront must make the store look like an attractive place to shop. A marquee can also help the retailer create an overall store atmosphere. *Marquees* are generally large signs that include the retailer's name. They can be manufactured or purchased as stock pieces. Marquees come in many different styles and can be flashy (especially when used in conjunction with neon lights or other decorative lighting) or subdued.

The key to an effective marquee is that it generate interest and traffic. The use of the AIDA model (*attention*, *interest*, *desire*, and *action*) fits in well with the selection of a marquee. A sign that attracts attention and creates interest in the retail store should be selected. Once the store has captured potential customers' attention and instilled interest in the store, the marquee can help develop customers' desire to visit the store. Finally, the marquee causes action when customers enter the store.

Ease of Shopping: A store's interior should allow customers to shop with ease. It is important to understand how the customer shops and then to plan a store design that facilitates the shopping process. Many supermarkets and smaller grocery stores use a "ring of perishables" design, in which perishables are placed in a semi-ring around the back part of the store's interior. When customers enter the store, they turn to the right and find themselves in the bakery. After the bakery, they may find themselves in produce. As they proceed around the far walls of the store, they may find dairy, deli, flowers, fresh meats, poultry, and other product types that are perishable. Customers have been "trained" to shop this way at a grocery store; thus, they feel comfortable knowing where various products are located.

Source: Pavel L Photo and Video/Shutterstock.com

Productivity: In terms of the third objective, the retailer needs to assess which of the many design options to choose for displaying merchandise. The productivity of the store's selling space is called *efficiency*. The retailer should select displays that create the most efficiencies. For example, clothing retailers may want to display clothes on waterfall fixtures. A *waterfall fixture* is usually a standalone fixture (although many can be attached to walls) that holds the same product at different eye levels. Thus, the customer can see each item easily, from first to last.

The question, then, is: Does this display generate enough sales to be placed at this particular location? Compare the standalone waterfall display to one that connects to the wall. Which one provides more efficiencies? A retailer may find that the wall display uses less selling space, yet is equally appealing to customers.

The earlier ring-of-perishables example shows how the design and layout objectives can be integrated with each other. Although the ring of perishables can be used to influence the customer to shop and buy, it has a secondary function in terms of efficiency. Because most perishables require refrigeration, special fixtures are needed that not only refrigerate the products but also display them. With this display comes an added cost for electricity. Because of the internal refrigeration, the displays emit a great deal of heat. Thus, if displays are kept in the middle of the store, the retailer has to utilize additional air conditioning to offset the heat. With a ring-of-perishables technique, however, the additional energy costs can be reduced. In fact, the displays may actually help heat the areas to the back of them (including stockrooms), resulting in additional efficiency for the retailer.

When designing its store layout, the retailer needs to assess the outlet's floor space and plan for space allocation for merchandise storage, merchandise selling, store employees, and customers. It is also important to assess customer traffic patterns within the store. In creating traffic space, the retailer can have customers flowing in a straight line, a curved line, or a combination of the two.

Home Depot stores favor straight lines, as do most food retailers. This format allows customers to locate products easily and makes it easy for the retailer to stock. Department stores and boutiques prefer a curved format, because it encourages customers to browse and spend more time in the store. A downside to a curved pattern is that customers can get confused or be unable to find a product. When developing the store design, the retailer should begin with the traffic flow. Within the store, unique areas dedicated to certain types of product lines should be created. This approach enables a store manager or owner to create smaller store patterns within the overall design. This is effective if the retailer decides to create product groupings for its merchandise.

As an example, consider a situation in which a new Disney movie is playing at a local theater. A clothing retailer or a department store may want to bundle all the Disney merchandise into a single location, thereby giving customers a choice among the various licensed products.

Another possible store layout is to group products together based on their function. This can be accomplished using a functional grouping display (as an example, all over-the-counter drugs might be placed together within the store).

Design with the Customer in Mind

Effective designs allow customers to make purchases easily. Store design must be set up based on what the customer expects. To facilitate sales, many of the IMC tactics, such as POP displays and store signage, can be utilized. In addition, the interior of the store can be changed through the use of freestanding fixtures. Finally, efficiencies can be created by using the walls of the store, end caps (displays at the end of an aisle), and exterior store areas (such as sidewalk sales).

Source: I AM NIKOM/Shutterstock.com

Non-store retailers must also create a layout and design for their venues. Like brick–and–mortar retailers, non-store retailers must also give attention to their storefronts (i.e., webpages), their stores' exteriors and interiors (including displays), and their checkout areas. An advantage for non-store retailers, especially e-tailers, is that they can change their displays much more quickly and inexpensively than can their brick-and-mortar counterparts.

Customers' judgments about a store can have a powerful effect on the store's image. Thus, the retailer must ensure that the layout and design of all the store's spaces are effective and regularly maintained. This includes the design and cleaning of customer restrooms. In addition, customers may begin to get bored with the store layout; thus, interior and exterior changes should be scheduled on a periodic basis. Signage and display fixtures should be updated. The retailer must strive to keep customers excited about their shopping experiences.

An important tool for the retailer is an evaluation program to assess the effectiveness of the overall store design and layout. Any time customer communications occur, both the IMC and the store layout and design must be integrated to send consistent messages and, in the long run, increase store sales and profitability.

Summary

This chapter covered the overall communications process and its vital role in the integrated retail management plan. It discussed the different methods of communicating with customers and examined IMC objectives, budget creation, and strategy.

Next, the chapter looked at each element of IMC tactics, including advertising, sales promotions, direct marketing, electronic and Internet, personal selling, public relations, and publicity. Each of these areas is extremely important to communications, and the messages conveyed by all areas must be consistent.

Finally, the chapter focused on some issues involved in store layout and design. The objectives of layout and design were discussed, along with the need to keep these important functions integrated with the IMC variables.

Terms

advertising	A form of either mass communication or direct-to-consumer communication that is non-personal and is paid for by an identifiable sponsor to inform or persuade members of a particular audience.
all-you-can-afford method	A method of budgeting in which the retailer allots all the money it can manage to bear toward the IMC functions.
atmospherics	The attempt to create an overall positive atmosphere in a retail outlet.
best-guess method	A method of budgeting in which the retailer makes a subjective guess at how much to allocate to IMC.
consumer-generated marketing	When a consumer gets directly involved with the marketing activities of a company.
continuity	One of the attributes of media objectives, indicating a stable level of IMC activity.
cost per thousand (or CPM)	Refers to the cost of reaching 1,000 people through an identified medium.
creative platform	The creative strategy of a selected IMC tactic; includes the promise, creative objectives, and reasons the customer should buy. Also called *copy platform* or *creative strategy*.
efficiency	The productivity of a store's selling space.
Electronic marketing	The use of digital technologies to sell goods and services. Also called digital marketing.
follow-the-leader budgeting	A method of budgeting in which the retailer generates estimates of competitors' IMC budgets from outside sources and attempts to match the industry leader's budget.
frequency	The number of times a target audience is exposed to an advertising message over a particular time period.
gross rating points (GRPs)	An advertising measurement taken by multiplying reach by frequency.
Integrated Marketing Communications (IMC) mix	All the communications activities undertaken in an integrated marketing communications approach, including personal selling, advertising, public relations, direct marketing, sales promotions, and electronic/Internet marketing.

Internet marketing	Using the Internet to sell products and services.
marquee	A large exterior sign that includes the retailer's name.
objective-and-task method	A method of budgeting in which the retailer specifies the role IMC will play and the outcomes desired in the overall operation.
percentage-of-profit method	A method of budgeting in which the retailer determines a basic percentage amount to be used for IMC based on overall profits.
percentage-of-sales method	A method of budgeting in which the retailer allots a basic percentage amount for the store and, in some cases, for each of the store's brands or products (or product lines).
personal selling	Using face-to-face communication to sell products and services.
planogram	A visual map of a store's layout and shows where products and displayed should be placed to maximize sales.
point-of-purchase (POP) communications	A type of sales promotion that includes in-store materials such as posters and displays designed to influence consumer purchases. Also called point-of-purchase advertising.
public relations (PR)	The efforts of an organization to win the cooperation of various publics.
publicity	A sub function of public relations in which the organization attempts to attract attention through various media.
reach	The percentage of a target audience that is exposed to an advertising message at least one time during an advertising campaign.
sales promotion	A short-term activity that enhances or supports other IMC variables.
social media marketing	The use of social media sites to connect with customers and generate traffic.
visual merchandising	An attempt to inspire customers to purchase through the use of design techniques that enhance the overall buying experience.

Discussion Questions

1. Why is it necessary to create integration and synergy in communicating with current and potential customers? With internal employees?

2. What types of budgets do you think are used by market leaders such as Macy's and Wal-Mart? Why?

3. Why is it important to develop an overall mission and vision for the IMC functional area?

4. Do you feel that there is some overlap in each of the tactical IMC variables? Explain and cite examples.

5. What type of store layout do you feel would be best for clothing boutiques such as Old Navy, Abercrombie and Fitch, and Go Jane? Why do you feel this layout would be effective?

6. Develop a store layout and design for a new retailer of phones and related products. Provide the rationale for your layout.

Exercises

1. Visit the following websites (alternatively, choose three retailing sites that interest you), and answer the questions below.

- www.HM.com
- www.UrbanOutfitters.com
- www.Pier1.com

a. How is the website used to promote the retailer? How effective is the site in promoting the retailer?

b. Is the IMC message clear?

c. What changes, if any, would you recommend to enhance communications?

2. A non-profit organization with a small marketing communication budget seeks your advice on how to allocate resources. Which of the IMC mix components would you recommend and why?

3. In June 2017, Amazon announced an acquisition of Whole Foods Market. How do you think this will change the philosophy of Whole Food Market?

Case

L.L. Bean's IMC Success

L.L. Bean is a privately held retailer headquartered out of Freeport, Maine. The company started in 1912 by Leon Leonwood Bean, who developed a waterproof boot and began selling it through mail order out of his brother's basement. The company is known for high quality products and customer service. Today the company is an international retailer that sells outdoor equipment and clothing. Sales for 2015 were in excess of $1.6 billion. The company operates 27 retail stores outside of Maine as well as 10 outlet stores.

The company website, llbean.com, was launched in 1995. According to the website, in addition to buying merchandise from the site, customers can search for information on state, national and international parks, contact customer service, watch product videos, find out about Outdoor Discovery Schools® programs, get directions to the stores and share personal comments related to products through Ratings and Reviews and the newly launched Share Your Story feature on both llbean.com and L.L.Bean's Facebook page.

In 2016, L.L.Bean produced over 50 separate catalog titles that were distributed to customers in all 50 US states and over 170 countries. In 2011, L.L. Bean re-introduced everyday free shipping to the U.S. and Canada with no minimum purchase. The founder started this practice in 1912, offering products in his catalog "postpaid." As of 2017, the company continues the free shipping policy. In 2015, the company launched a mobile app which has become one of their fastest growing channels. Their website serves over 200 countries and territories. This involved price conversions into 60 currencies as well as the applicable tax and duty charges.

The company is active on social media sites including Facebook, Twitter, YouTube, Instagram, Pinterest and Google. In 2012 L.L. Bean launched a campaign to commemorate their 100th anniversary. The year-long celebration began with an unveiling of a "Bootmobile," a 13-foot-high, 20 foot long vehicle that generates no CO_2 emissions. Another Bootmobile was added in 2013. The Bootmobiles tour major cities in the U.S. with the goal of inspiring people to go outside and be active.

Questions:

1. Go to the L.L. Bean website (llbean.com) and evaluate the company's website. What do they do well? Where could they improve?

2. Evaluate L.L. Beans social media efforts.

3. Look up the company's 100th anniversary celebration events. How did the company use IMC to communicate this benchmark?

4. How does free shipping help or hurt L.L. Bean? Do you think they will continue this practice forever? What has been the competitive response to this practice?

Sources: Stranahan, S. Q. (2011). Keeping up with posts and tweets down east. *New York Times* (Dec 7). Online. Retrieved from http://www.nytimes.com/2011/12/08/fashion/l-l-bean-creates-a-new-team-to-keep-up-on-facebook-and-twitter.html?_r=1&adxnnl=1&adxnnlx=1327083516-c2QLIz32RMbxoCCMJyvbrg; LLBean Website (llbean.com); L.L. Bean 2012 Company Fact Sheet. Retrieved from http://www.llbean.com/customerService/aboutLLBean/images/120518_fact-sheet2012.pdf; L.L. Bean at a Glance (2016). Retrieved from https://www.llbean.com/customerService/aboutLLBean/images/160428_company_fact_sheet.pdf

References

Aaker, D. (1995). *Building Strong Brands.* New York: The Free Press.

Colloquy (2017). U.S. Customer Loyalty Program Memberships Reach Double Digit Growth at 3.8 Billion, 2017 Colloquy Census Reports, (June 29). Retrieved from http://www.businesswire.com/news/home/20170629005694/en/U.S.-Customer-Loyalty-Program-Memberships-Reach-Double

Birritteri, A. (2002). Monitoring the Success of Advertising. *New Jersey Business*, 48 (Nov 1), p. 20.

Brandt, R. L. (1997). Internet Kamikazes: Interview with CNET's Halsey Minor. From *Perspectives: Marketing on the Internet*, Ekin, A.C. ed. St. Paul: Coursewise Publishing, Inc., pp. 16-21.

Dorsch, M. and Carlson, L. (1996). A transaction approach to understanding and managing customer equity, *Journal of Business Research*, 35. pp. 253–264.

Fasig, L. B. (2003). Harry Carries---The Magic of Marketing Has Lots to Do with Harry Potter's Success. *Providence Journal* (Rhode Island), (Jun 21), p. A1.

Fortini-Campbell, L. (2001). *Hitting the Sweet Spot.* Chicago: The Copy Workshop, p. 15.

Four-Year Research Study Concludes: Sales Promotion Benefit to Consumers and Businesses. *PR Newswire*, (Jun 11).

Harris, T. L. (1998). *Value-Added Public Relations.* Chicago: NTC Business Books, p. 10.

Kooser, A. (2013). Pepsi Vending Machine Takes Facebook Love, Not Money. (June 4). Retrieved from www.cnet.com.

Lesly, P. (1981). "Report and Recommendations: Task Force on Stature and Role of Public Relations. *Public Relations Journal*, (Mar), p. 32.

Liljenwall, R. and Maskulka, J. (2001). Eds., *Marketing's Powerful Weapon: Point-Of-Purchase Advertising.* Washington DC: Point-Of-Purchase Advertising International.

Low, G. S. and Mohr, J. J. (1999). Setting Advertising and Promotion Budgets in Multi-Brand Companies. *Journal of Advertising Research*, 39 (Jan/Feb), pp. 67-79.

Moylan, M. (2013). Target Works to Win Loyalty of Hispanics. MPR News, (May 29). Retrieved from http://minnesota.publicradio.org/display/web/2013/05/29/business/target-hispanic-loyalty

Myron, M. R. and Truax, P.L. (1996). Product's Positioning Vital to Getting Noticed. *Denver Business Journal*, (Nov 11). Retrieved from www.bizjournals.com.

Office Depot Launches First Hispanic Television and Radio Campaign in Support of 'Back to School' Initiatives (2003). *Business Wire*, (Jul 14).

Ogden, J. R. (1998). *Developing a Creative and Innovative Integrated Marketing Communication Plan: A Working Model.* Upper Saddle River, NJ: Prentice Hall.

Ogilvy-ChatThreads (2011). New Study: Social Media Has Outsized Impact on Sales and Brand Perception. Retrieved from http://www.ogilvypr.com/en/press/new-study-social-media-has-outsized-impact-sales-and-brand-perception

Peterson, H. (2017). This Clothing Company Is Facing Claims that Its "Pants Rip Like Wet Toilet Paper". *Business Insider*, (Feb 22). Retrieved from http://www.businessinsider.com/lularoe-customers-complain-popular-leggings-are-tearing-2017-2

Schultz, D. E. (1993). Integrated Marketing Communications: Maybe Definition is in the Point of View. *Marketing News*, 27 (Jan 18), p. 17.

Schultz, D. E. (2001). Foreign Countries Getting IMC Concept Right. *Marketing News*, 35 (Aug 27), p. 9.

Shimp, T. A. (2000). *Advertising Promotion: Supplemental Aspects of Integrated Marketing Communication*, 5th ed. Fort Worth, TX: Dryden Press.

Stone, B. (1989). *Successful Direct Marketing Methods*, 4th ed. Lincolnwood, IL: NTC Business Books, p. 2.

Weiner, M. (2002). A Forward Look at Public Relations. *Public Relations Strategist*, 8 (Spring), pp. 32-35.

Whole Foods Annual Report (2016). Retrieved from http://s21.q4cdn.com/118642233/files/doc_financials/2016/Annual/2016-WFM-Annual-Report.pdf

Chapter 13

Customer Service in Retailing

"Being on par in terms of price and quality only gets you into the game. Service wins the game.

~ Tony Alessandra, Professional Speaker on Customer Service

Source: Rawpixel.com/Shutterstock.com

CHAPTER OBJECTIVES

After completing this chapter you will be able to:

- Explain why the targeted customer is always right.
- Define customer service and explain the rater system.
- List and explain the key customer service activities for retailers and e-tailers.
- Explain customer response marketing and why it is important in retailing.
- Identify and describe various customer service levels.

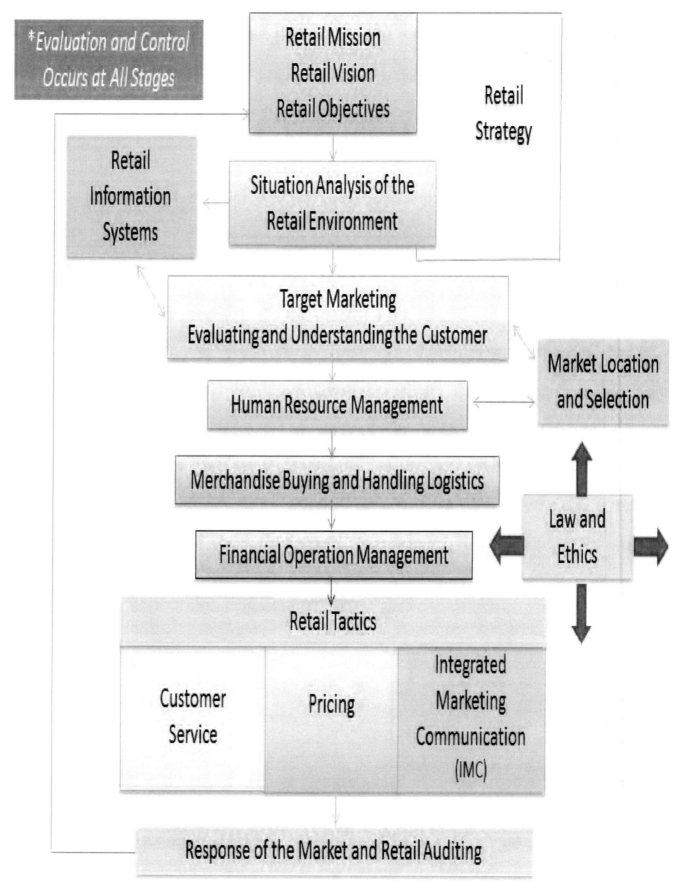

Men's Wearhouse Utilizes Consultative Approach

In past years, the men's clothing industry has experienced several changes. Many retailers specializing in men's clothing went out of business. One company that survived is Men's Wearhouse. According to their website (www.menswearhouse.com), "Our purpose is to help people love how they look and we accomplish this by providing a personal, convenient, one-of-a-kind shopping experience with compelling products and world-class service." The company's core values are live the Golden Rule, practice teamwork, have respect, be trustworthy and keep an open mind and heart.

The Men's Wearhouse brand is part of the Tailored Brands, Inc holding company. Other brands under the Tailored Brand umbrella include Jos. A. Bank, Moores Clothing for Men; designer brand Joseph Abboud; family retailer K&G Fashion Superstore; dry-cleaners MW Cleaners; and corporate apparel leaders Twin Hill, Alexandra, Dimensions and Yaffy.

According to the annual report (Tailored Brands, 2017), Men's Wearhouse targets 25 – 55 year-old men. The merchandise mix allows men to purchase all wardrobe needs, including shoes, from the store. Currently there are over 700 Men's Wearhouse locations in 50 states, the District of Columbia and Puerto Rico. They are in regional strip and specialty retail centers or in freestanding buildings to make it easy for customers to park in front of the store. These types of stores are primarily located in regional malls and lifestyle centers. In addition, there are 58 rental stores in 24 states under the Men's Wearhouse and Tux brands. Customer satisfaction is a priority. The company offers free lifetime pressing on all suits, sport coats, slacks and tuxedos purchased at their stores. Upon request, there is 24-hour tailoring availability, which comes in handy for tuxedo fittings.

Employees take the consultative approach, which focuses on building long-term relationships with customers, rather than the salesperson approach. The company's "wardrobe consultants" strive to exceed customer expectations.

Introduction

At this point in the IRM flowchart, we find ourselves at the third important tactical area: customer service. Recall that customer services are the additional benefits, both tangible and intangible, that an organization provides in addition to its core product or service. Many retail firms live or die by their customer service. Everyone wants to be treated fairly and with respect. On the whole, customers are willing to pay a bit more for excellent customer service and will return to the retailer's venue if they receive it. It is also true that customers tell horror stories about bad customer service. These anecdotes are passed from person to person and can threaten the retailer's business.

Retailers need to be aware of the equity they have in their image and name. Most of this equity results from the way the retailer handles customers. In this chapter, we focus on the applications of customer service to both store-based and non-store-based retailing.

The Targeted Customer is Always Right

By definition, a customer is an individual who buys goods or services from a retailer. This definition can be expanded to say that there are two types of customers: good and bad. For our discussion, we will differentiate between good and bad customers, and conclude that the only "true" retail customers are the "good" customers. The astute retailer is able to generate classifications for its customers. Of course, not all people who visit a retail store are customers. In fact, the retailer has the opportunity to select customers; in other words, who, specifically, does the retailer prefer as its customers? Will this group generate enough revenue to sustain the retail business? These are the questions this chapter addresses.

Source: Diego Cervo/Shutterstock.com

Customer Profiles

Although it is a common belief among retailers that they have to satisfy the wants and needs of everyone who walks into their store, the retailer actually is in the position to choose the customers who appear to be a good fit for the store. This is done through the process of target marketing. Retailers look for those groups of people toward whom they wish to aim their marketing efforts. Unfortunately, not all people can be satisfied. A good method of identifying and understanding customers is to develop customer profiles. This approach is similar to that used in market segmentation, where a company chooses a target market and divides that market into segments that respond differently to the product, store, or brand.

In segmenting the market, the retailer creates some basis for dividing the various customer groups (psychographics, geographics, geodemographics, demographics, and/or behavioristics) (Dickson, 1982). From each segmented group, the retailer then develops a "typical" customer profile.

Customers enter a store with different needs and wants as well as varying levels of needs or wants. The retailer's job is to identify those needs and wants and to develop different types and levels of customer service that will make these groups of customers happy. This approach may cost a little more up front, but it pays off in the long run. According to a Consumer Reports survey, 90 percent of Americans have dealt with customer service representative within a year. Half of the survey respondents stated they left a store without a purchase because of poor service. Seventy-five percent of people surveyed were annoyed by rude salespeople and 64 percent of people reported being ignored by sales personnel. In addition, 75 percent survey respondents got irritated when they could not reach a human when calling a company (*Consumer Reports*, 2015).

Providing excellent customer service has become increasingly difficult. American shoppers have become more vocal and insistent on having their way. As one author puts it, America has turned into a "nation of whiners" (Glen, 1990). In the words of famous jazz musician Fats Waller, the retailer's job is to "find out what they [customers] like, and how they like it, and let 'em have it, just that way" (Find Out What…, 1935). Once a retailer chooses a target market, "the customer is king" (or queen), and the old adage "the customer is always right" should become a top retail policy. As Jack Smith, former CEO of General Motors, once said, "Focus everything---all assets, all decisions---on your customers. They are the ultimate arbiters of success or failure." Smith was a successful CEO because he recognized the importance of the "customer is always right" credo.

Undesirable Customers

Equally important to determining the target market is defining those customers that are not in the target market. Some people are simply undesirable customers. Many retailers tell stories of individuals who come into a store and make a purchase, only to return the goods to the store after using them. Consider a shoe retailer. Each year, just before the local high school proms, a number of teens flock to stores looking for shoes to complement their dresses or tuxedos. Although the vast majority of these customers are honest, some are not; they wear the shoes for just the one night and then return them with some complaint so they can receive a refund. Often the same people are actually good customers during the rest of the year. In this case, the retailer may want to keep them as customers. How does the retailer know which of these customers to retain? The retailer can use a database that includes the top customers in terms of their returns and purchases (by number of units and by dollar expenditures).

Source: pathdoc/Shutterstock.com

An example of a retailer that banned customers from its store comes from the now-defunct Filene's Basement. The retailer's parent company, Value City, sent a letter to two sisters from Newton, Massachusetts, banning them from all Filene's Basement stores. The letter stated, "Given your history of excessive returns and chronic unhappiness with our services, we have decided that this is the best way to avoid any future problems with you and your sister" (Sisters Face…, 2003). According to James McGrady, chief financial officer at Value City, customer bans are extremely rare. In this case, the company decided it didn't want customers who commanded a disproportionate amount of their employees' time and labor in handling the complaints (Many Unhappy..., 2003). In a more recent occurrence a 37-year old man was banned from a Starbucks store in Washington for asking a 16-year-old barista (Starbucks employee) on a date (CBS News, 2017). Because stores are considered private property, retailers can ban customers.

Another type of bad customer behavior is entering a store with the intent to shoplift. Although shoplifters may purchase some products, they actually steal more than they purchase (if they buy at all). According to the National Association for Shoplifting Prevention (2017), shoplifting is the most prevalent crime in the U.S. More than $13 billion worth of goods are stolen from retailers each year, amounting to more than $35 million per day.

In some instances, retailers refuse customers based on state or federal laws, such as laws prohibiting the sales of liquor and cigarettes to people under twenty-one years of age. Lowes, the home improvement retailer, had good intentions when it banned minors from buying products that might be abused as chemical inhalants. The stringent policy blocked minors from buying 2,000 products. Although other home improvement retailers, such as Home Depot, had similar policies, the other retailers applied them only in the seventeen states that regulate the sale of potential inhalants to minors. As a result of customer complaints, Lowe's was forced to cut back the list of banned products from 2,000 to 1,200 items (Carlo, 2003).

Finally, some individuals become verbally or physically abusive to a retailer's employees. At Dorney Theme Park in Allentown, Pennsylvania, a "guest" was physically abusive toward one of the ride operators. The abusive guest was waiting in line to get on a popular rollercoaster when the ride attendant noticed that the guest allowed some individuals to "line jump," or cut into the line, in front of some other guests who had been waiting for more than twenty minutes. The attendant explained that the park did not allow line jumping and that the guests would not be permitted to enter the ride unless they went to the back of the line. The party ignored the attendant and held their place in the line. When it was their turn to get on the ride, the attendant did not let them enter and reminded them of his warning. Then the original guest physically assaulted the ride operator. Dorney Park prosecuted the guest and barred him and his party from ever entering the park again. The guest was also barred from all parks owned by the parent company, Cedar Fair. The former guest was placed on an "unwanted" list, which was circulated to all the other properties (Man

Source: Robert Kneschke/Shutterstock.com

Charged.., 2002). In 2016 50 people were arrested for drug activity within the park (Heinze, 2016).

According the Dorney Park website, "... guests must behave in a manner that will not cause or contribute to safety risks, have negative impact on another guest's family-fun experience, or disrupt the peace and tranquility of the Park. Failure to comply may be cause for dismissal from the Park with no refund given." With the advances in technology, it is easier to put a person's name on a banned list. The amusement retailer decided that individuals who don't abide by the rules are not worth having as customers.

Identifying and Segmenting Customers

When developing strategies to provide excellent customer service, the place to start is with the customers themselves. Creating and accessing information about the customer base is greatly facilitated using the retail information system (RIS). The retailer first attempts to pull a typical customer profile from the RIS, which contains important data such as customers' purchases and product usage. If no profiles of customers are available, the retailer should build an information collection system to house these data. As stated earlier, a customer profile consists of data about various groups of consumers. From those data, the retailer creates an overall average customer profile.

Customer profiles can be created by segmenting. In terms of segmenting for customer service, customer usage rates are among the most useful data. The segmentation process can be simple (for example, categorizing customers as heavy versus medium versus light users of the store or its products or brands), or it can be far more complex. The reason a retailer would want to segment by usage is that heavy users generally supply the highest percentage of sales.

Retailers often base customer service levels on the Pareto principle or the 80/20 rule. If you recall from a previous chapter, this principle says 80 percent of a retailer's sales come from 20 percent of a retailer's customers. Developed by Joseph Juran, the Pareto principle is based on the work of Vilfredo Pareto. Pareto's research uncovered an interesting pattern in the dispersion of wealth: 85 percent of the wealth in Milan, Italy was owned by 15 percent of the citizens (Hartman, 2001). Although a general rule of thumb, the 80/20 mix is accurate for many industries as well as individual companies within the industry. The Pareto principle percentage mix varies among retailers depending on the type of retailer, the levels of customer services provided, and the customer mix.

In the airline industry, for example, 65 percent of all airline revenues are generated by 15 percent of the passengers. In the U.S. brewing industry, 20 percent of all beer drinkers consume approximately 70 percent of all beer. One can see the importance of segmenting customer groups to create outstanding customer service. By knowing their customer base, retailers can customize additional retail tactics to reach their most important customers. Likewise, they can greatly enhance customer service based on these customer groups and the typical customer profiles within each group.

Although many retailers believe all customers should be treated alike, it makes good business sense to treat the most important customers with higher levels of service. This is not to say that the smaller customer segments should be ignored; rather, it means the retailer should invest more heavily in the loyal user groups. It is important to manage customer expectations so that customers understand why certain customers are receiving value-added services. Retailers can do this by communicating policies to current and potential customers and by applying services consistently based on the customer group. Loyalty programs, such as frequent flyer programs, can help solidify customer relationships.

For over a decade Mattersight (www.mattersight.com) analyzed customer conversations to develop a system that would help businesses improve customer interactions and reduce costs associated with customer service. The company believed that if a customer service representative understands a customer's personality, he/she can be better equipped to respond in a way that is favorable to the customer. Thus, for consumers calling into customer service centers around the world, the system identifies the caller's personality which, after training, gives retailers an indication of how to deal with the customer that's calling. Based upon this personality, callers are sent to customer service reps who are best trained to handle that type of customer. The system is based on the premise that personality is audible (can be determined by spoken language) and actionable (organizations can take steps to address personality types to include improved outcomes). The system can classify personality type within the first 30 seconds of analyzing speech, making a better guess than random. After five minutes of speaking the confidence level of a correct personality profile is 90 percent (Traba and Moore, 2016).

Ideally, clients will experience lower call center operating expenses based upon a shorter duration of phone calls. Based on their analysis the company identified six major types of personalities (Traba and Moore, 2016):

1. The Organizer – process oriented; logical responsible, organized. Some common phrases and organizer uses are: "That's a good plan," "That's logical," "If it's going to be done right, I have to do it myself"

2. The Connector – relationship-focused; compassionate, sensitive, warm. Some common phrases a connector uses are: "I'm so relieved. You seem to really care," "Why does it have to be so confusing," I'm so happy…sad…excited…scared"

3. The Advisor – commitment-driven; dedicated, observant, conscientious. Some common phrases an advisors uses are: "In my opinion," "We should….You should…We must…We ought to…"

4. The Original – contact-seeking; spontaneous, creative, playful. Some common phrases an original uses are: "This is great," "Brilliant…Horrible…Cool."

5. The Doer – action-oriented; adaptable, persuasive, charming. Some common phrases a doer uses are: "I was born ready," Bottom-line it for me," "Come on…all ya gotta do is just look it up and take it off my bill."

6. The Dreamer – solitude-seeking; calm, imaginative, reflective. Some common phrases a dreamer uses are: "There are so many possibilities," "I imagine…," I've been going over that in my mind."

Source: Rawpixel.com/Shutterstock.com

Customer Perceptions

Customers have different opinions and perceptions about what good service is. Much has been written about the various types of services and levels of service that customers want. Retail customers are becoming more and more demanding in terms of the levels of service they expect from retailers. Research has found that these services can be classified into a finite number of categories of customer service wants and needs.

Keep in mind that there is a difference between offering services to customers and offering service to customers. Services deal with additions to the total product, whereas service is integrated into every aspect of the retailer's operations. Consider a services retailer that sells hairstyling services. Whereas cutting and styling hair is a service, the provision of a "no wait" policy for customers with reservations is a form of customer service. It adds value to the core product or service offered to the consumer.

Perceptions of Quality

In 1988 three researchers developed a technique, called *SERVQUAL,* to measure service quality (Parasuraman, Zeithaml and Berry, 1988). Although the initial research was developed for the service industry (e.g., banking, long-distance telephone services, securities, credit cards, and product repair and maintenance), it has been generalized to include service-quality assessment for other industries. The researchers found that the majority of consumers' perceptions of quality fall into five main areas: reliability, assurance, tangibility, empathy, and responsiveness.

Reliability: From the customer's point of view, *reliability* means dependability: Does the retailer perform the promised service dependably and accurately? Because of the importance of reliability, retailers must take care not to promise anything they cannot deliver. This caveat applies not only to management but to the entire retail staff. Have you ever been promised something by a businessperson only to find out that he or she could not deliver on the promise? This incident probably made you angry with the service provider and perhaps led you to shop at a competitor.

Source: Dmitry Kalinovsky/Shutterstock.com

Assurance: *Assurance* means customers must be confident that they made the right choice in buying the retailer's products and services. The entire retail staff needs to be courteous and have a thorough knowledge of the products and services available.

Tangibility: *Tangibility* refers to the physical characteristics of the retail outlet. What will the customer's first impression of the store be? Are the physical facilities and equipment up to date, clean, and well maintained? How is the space utilized? Are restrooms clean and attractive? (Cleanliness of restrooms is a major issue in the tourism industry.) Are employees well groomed? If they wear uniforms, are the uniforms clean? Are backroom areas that are visible to customers also clean and organized?

Empathy: To convey *empathy*, the retailer needs to provide caring and individual attention for customers. Customers want to know that the retailer understands them and has had the same type of experiences they have. One good way for a retailer to express empathy is to use a customer's name. This makes the customer feel welcome and "closer" to the retailer.

Because of the vast numbers of customers who enter the stores, this tactic may be difficult to execute. However, if a retailer has done a thorough job of developing customer segments, a database of top customers (heavy users) will be available so that the retailer can concentrate on those individuals. If there is not a database, a simple way to create this relationship relates to customers who make purchases with a credit card. When a salesperson rings up an order for someone charging a purchase, the salesperson should look at the name on the credit card and simply call the customer by that name. Some airlines do this with their first-class travelers. To execute this superior customer service, they provide a list of the first-class passengers to their flight attendants, who call each first-class traveler by his or her title (Dr., Mrs., Mr., Rev., Ms., etc.) and name.

Responsiveness: The retail staff must be *responsive* to customer needs. They must be willing to provide a high level of prompt customer service and assistance. For example, a salesperson at Meijer Thrifty Acres is trained not only to tell a customer where a product is but also to walk the customer to the area where the product is located and make sure the product is indeed the correct one.

To facilitate the above tactics, a programmed approach to meeting and helping customers should be developed. The first step in successful response is to greet the customer and make him or her feel welcome. The next step is to develop an understanding of the customer by asking questions. The retailer needs to help the customer find the desired product and ensure that she or he is satisfied with the "find." Finally, the retailer should confirm the customer's satisfaction in an effort to ensure a return visit. To make customers feel valued and appreciated, retailers should develop a philosophy of truly wanting to help customers.

Researchers think that consumers' perceptions of quality service are influenced by a number of "gaps" (Parasuraman, Zeithaml and Berry, 1985). The gaps are important because they give retailers a hint as to tactics and strategies that can help ensure a good service relationship (see Table 13.1) (Zeithaml, Parasuraman, and Berry, 1990).

Table 13.1 Service Quality Gaps

1. Not knowing customers' expectations
2. Providing the wrong service-quality standards
3. Expected versus actual service
4. Promises do not match performance
Source: Zeithaml, V., Parasuraman, A. and Berry, L. L. (1990). *Delivering Quality Service: Balancing Customer Perceptions and Expectations.* New York: The Free Press, pp. 15 - 33.

Gap 1: Not Knowing Customers' Expectations: To address this gap, the retailer needs to learn what customers value most in terms of service offerings. Once the retailer has segmented its market, it should develop a profile that shows the customers' value for each segment. It has been suggested that benchmarking and best practices are good tools for this research process. In addition, a competitive analysis such as a SWOT (strengths, weaknesses, opportunities, and threats) analysis helps identify the retailer's strengths and weaknesses, as well as those of its competitors.

Gap 2: Providing the Wrong Service-Quality Standards: To address this gap, the retailer should create a system for the planning and design functions. To ensure that the "correct" standards are set for service quality, it is important to capture standards in an easily accessible format. The information should be incorporated into the existing RIS, but in many instances it exists as a standalone document or computer file.

Gap 3: Expected versus Actual Service: The third gap deals with the difference between the quality standards promised to customers and the actual quality of service delivery and performance. The retailer must take care to avoid discrepancies between the service specifications and the performance of the service. This is a communications gap that centers on the retailer's standards for its product offerings.

Gap 4: Ensuring That Delivery of Service Matches Promises Made by the Retailer: The basic principle here is that retailers must be honest with their customers in regard to service guarantees. Thus, information should be provided to customers about the actual level and type of service a retailer provides. The retailer must then ensure that all promises are fulfilled (Weinstein and Johnson, 1999).

Retail/E-tail Customer Service

Although there may be some differences in the delivery of e-tail customer service versus bricks-only service, the goal is the same: to make the customer happy. The key to offering customers high levels of service is a total organizational commitment. Lillian Vernon, founder and CEO of Lillian Vernon Corp., a specialty and online retailer, believes the building blocks of happiness center around three things: selecting the right products, being honest with customers, and welcoming communications between the company and its customers (Vernon, 2003).

Retailers that provide superior service can use the service as a differentiation tool. High-quality service translates into repeat buyers. As stated earlier, services must be tailored to the identified customer profiles, and the levels of service must be applied by all employees. The level of customer service the retailer will provide should be included in the mission and vision statements. This section provides an overview of the many services a retailer can offer.

For e-tailers, some of the key customer service activities are (1) effective handling of complaints, (2) electronic confirmations of orders, and (3) developing relationships with customers. Because of the nature of e-tailing, customers and salespeople do not participate in face-to-face communications; therefore, the task of providing customer service is somewhat more difficult.

The latest technology for e-tailers is live chat. Live chat is a way to provide customer service in the online environment. Typically a customer will receive a message or other way to begin live chat. The customer can type a question and receive an answer from a company representative in an instant message box that appears on the screen. Many customers prefer live chat to the telephone or email (Enright, 2011).

From 2015 to 2016 demand for live chat grew by 43.4 percent and the average amount of time it took to help a customer over live chat was 12 minutes and 24 seconds (LiveChat Customer Service Report, 2017). According to Shep Hyken (Hyken.com), a customer service expert, chatbots and artificial intelligence are also being used to answer customer concerns. A chatbot can recognize when a customer is confused and can transition over to a human to continue the conversation. Hyken believes that one day most customer service questions will be answered by robots.

Technology allows companies to monitor millions of messages posted on social media sites in real time. According to Jay Baer, customer service consultant, "Customers are no longer whispering their complaints to their neighbors at dinner tables. They're making the world aware of their experiences. Social media can help make one disappointed customer's complaint go viral in hours and your brand needs to be paying attention because everyone else already is" (Gaab, 2015).

According to Ron Burley (2012), consumer advocate and entrepreneur, complaints via social media are different from complaints issued at a brick and mortar store. He lists five rules to use when handling customer complaints:

1. Respond – Retailers must respond to all customers, especially when complaints are issued. In the world of social media, companies can't afford to ignore complaints.

2.   Acknowledge – When the company is right, make the case professionally. When the company is in the wrong, admit the error and take steps to improve.

3.   Elevate – Managers must behave in a professional manner at all times. No matter how personal complaints become, gloating or blaming a customer are losing strategies.

4.   Apologize – When wrong, company management should apologize, fix the problem and promise to never do it again.

5.   Downsize – When a complaint is issued, downsize the discussion by being informative, casual and interactive. Treat the complainer as an individual.

Customer Service Activities

Numerous types of services can be offered to retail customers. Some work well for e-tailers; others work better for brick-and-mortar and brick-and-click retailers. Service offerings can range from basic to quite complex and luxurious.

Basic Service Offerings

Although this can vary on an individual basis and by the type of retailer, basic services expected from any retailer include a convenient retail location, convenient hours of operation, clean facilities, and product availability. Security is also a consideration, especially for online retailing.

Customers must be able to easily access a physical or cyber retail location. The customer's time is a vital consideration. It is also good business practice to be open when the customer wants to shop. Many retailers understand this concept and have expanded the basic premise by keeping many of their stores open twenty-four hours a day. This practice not only provides shoppers with a service but also positions these retailers in consumers' minds as "a store that never closes." Thus, a customer who needs to go to a store at an odd hour knows that Walgreens will be open. In these cases, the benefits associated with continuous operation must be greater than costs.

Have you ever been to a bank on a weekend? Were you able to interact with the tellers? The answer is probably no, since banks generally are open only until 5 P.M. on weekdays and for limited hours on Saturdays. This can be quite frustrating for a bank's customers. Not surprisingly, when a large retailer that stays open twenty-four hours a day was asked about business traffic during that period, the busiest time reported was between 10:00 A.M. and 7:00 P.M. So why does this retailer operate twenty-four hours a day? Why not open from, say, 9:00 A.M. to 8:00 P.M.? The retailer's response would make any customer grin: The store is open to let the customer know that it is always open and available. This service actually increases business throughout the day. Although keeping the operation open at night may not be very cost effective, the increase in the customer base during other hours makes up for the costs.

Facility cleanliness is another basic service offering. Nothing turns off customers more than a dirty store. Researchers have found that cleanliness is one of the most important factors in choosing a restaurant (What Seniors Want…, 2003).

In addition, customers expect product availability. Outstanding retailers try to keep at least a 95 percent stock level. When customers come into the store, they know there is a high chance the product will be in stock. Have you ever gone into a store looking for a particular item only to find it was out of stock? Did you leave the store to shop at a competitor that was more likely to have the product in stock? This situation translates into lost sales for the first retailer and in fact may result in lost future customers and revenues. For very popular items, the retailer should have a stock level of higher than 95 percent.

Finally, security is another important basic customer service. Security for the store retailer could mean providing security guards, cameras, and computer systems to protect safety and privacy. For the online retailer, privacy and security are major concerns.

Additional/Luxury Services

What about additional and luxury-type services? For any retailer, the most important service provider is the sales team. To the customer, the salesperson *is* the retail store. Poor service from a salesperson translates into unfavorable customer perceptions of the store. An

Source: jassada watt_ /Shutterstock.com

adequately staffed service desk or toll-free service number should be available whenever the retail operation is open. There is nothing more frustrating than buying a defective product or service and having to wait in a long line to replace it or, worse yet, being unable to find someone who can help resolve the problem. All types of retailers need to decide which types of services to offer. Many retailers offer special services such as gift wrapping, product packaging and shipping, personalized orders, special orders, or personal shoppers.

Buckle (www.buckle.com), the Kearney, Nebraska–based chain store, has a philosophy of providing the best selection and best service to their young, fashion-conscious customers. Some of the services they offer include free alterations, layaways, and a frequent shopper reward program (About Buckle, 2017). These services differentiate the retailer and keep customers coming back for more.

Most retailers offer delivery services as well as credit services. In addition, many retailers offer their customers product information. The key is for the retailer to consider its vision and mission, as well as its target market and market segments, to develop the desired level of customer service.

Source: Miami2you/Shutterstock.com

Different types of retailers need different types of services and service levels. For example, the Ritz-Carlton is known for providing outstanding customer service. Their motto, "We are Ladies and Gentlemen Serving Ladies and Gentlemen," illustrates their dedication to customer service. In 2016, the hotel chain ranked highest in the luxury brand segment by the J.D. Power and Associates North America Hotel Guest Satisfaction Index Study. The chain received 896 points out of 1,000, the maximum ever recorded (The Ritz-Carlton..., 2016).

Figure 13.1 (next page) illustrates the development of policies for a retail outlet while taking into account the types of products and their prices.

Figure 13.1 Development of Service Policies

Complexity of Product

High ◄──────────────────────────────────────► Low

High

Price of Product

High

Highest Level of Sales Support	**Full Service**
Expect: • Highest number of customer questions • Highest level of expectation for support Examples: cars, computers	Expect: • Customer to seek advice and information from salespeople • To provide some support services (i.e., gift wrapping, delivery) Examples: jewelry, some appliances
Low Service Expect: • Some product-related questions Examples: builder's tools, car parts, some clothing	**Complete Self-Service** Expect: • Few or no customer questions Examples: grocery store items

Low

As Figure 13.1 illustrates, the choice of what types of services to offer depends on the type of retailer, the complexity of the product, and the product's price. In addition to the aforementioned services, many retailers offer the following: layaway, Christmas or holiday clubs, kiosks or touch-screens for bridal registry, a baby registry or other gift suggestions, automated teller machines (ATMs), shoppers' service (such as a concierge), coat and hat checking, package checking, valet parking, children's carts, multilingual salespeople and/or customer service personnel, complimentary beverages (sometimes including wine, champagne, and other hard and soft drinks), tourist maps, brochures or coupons, furniture for resting, guarantees, support salespeople (especially for do-it-yourself retailers such as Home Depot), parking shuttles, music, drinking fountains, classes, and workshops for customers (especially for technological products such as computer software and hardware), a store directory (both manual and computerized), a post office, bill-paying services, customer service reps for help with packages (especially at food retailers), drive-through services, special orders, restroom attendants, attached restaurants or coffee shops (such as in Barnes and Noble), child-care or child-play areas, free delivery, and delivery and shipping services (especially where the customer does not live near the retail site, such as tourism retailers).

Customer Focus

Types of services offered vary based on customers' wants and needs and the type of retail operation. The key to developing excellent service is to keep the customer as the focal point. The retailer must find out what the customer wants. Even simple actions, such as displaying the retailer's phone number and website address on all company-related information, sends a message that the retailer cares about customers' concerns (Neuborne, 2000).

In an effort to get all employees focused on the customer, Bruce Leval, a former senior vice president at Disney, coined the term "guestology" (Ford, Heaton and Brown, 2001). In practice, guestology means systematically uncovering key factors that determine quality and value from the customer's perspective. The ultimate goal is to keep customers coming back.

Some of the following tools can be used to generate more information about customers and the types of services they think should be offered to satisfy their wants and needs:

- Primary retailing research through surveys

- Bill-stuffer questionnaires

- Questionnaires accompanying warranty or registration cards

- Shopper-intercept studies (in which customers are asked in person what types of services they would like to see in the store)

- Focus groups

- A shopper's panel of six to twelve loyal customers who agree to serve as panelists for a longitudinal (long-term) study

- Trade associations

- Competitors' offerings

- Employee contact via suggestion boxes, continuous improvement initiatives, or other methods

Domino's Pizza conducts online surveys of customers. Questions are asked about response time, friendliness of employees and overall satisfaction. In 2009 when Domino's changed their Pizza recipe, the company encouraged feedback from customers using social media. The company welcomed both positive and negative feedback and rented an electronic billboard in New York City's Time Square that displayed the feedback (Alfs, 2013). Customers respected the honesty and the company's sales went up. Remember that loyal customers are very valuable to retailers. The idea is to create equity in the retail operation by making customers want to come back.

Source: Kvitka Fabian/Shutterstock.com

Increasing sales and customer satisfaction are overall objectives of customer service programs. When retail executives cut back on customer services, the retailer's profits may increase in the short run. In the long run, however, the retailer runs the risk of losing a significant number of previously loyal customers, resulting in potential losses of sales and profits.

Developing the Customer Service Level

It can become a challenge for retailers to offer the right levels of customer service. There are costs associated with creating and maintaining high customer service levels. A number of factors should be addressed when developing customer service tactics. These five variables help retailers develop their customer service level:

1. Customer Service Costs. In determining customer service costs, retailers need to access their financial records and create a breakeven analysis based upon the cost of the services and the expected return on service investment.

2. Competitive Analysis. Retailers need to look toward their competition in order to assess competitive service offerings and levels. Customers may begin to ask why a retailer's competitors provide certain services not offered by the retailer. This may translate to lost sales (or customers).

3. Store or Channel Characteristics. Is the retailer an off-price retailer? A high-end retailer? As a general rule, the higher the retailer's prices, the higher the level of customer service. Other characteristics or factors that influence service levels based upon the store's characteristics include the store's location, size and type of retail institution. In addition, the type of merchandise sold will also help a retailer determine service levels. The mission and vision of the retailer (philosophy) dictate customer service levels as well.

4. Income Level of the Targeted Segments. The income of the retailer's target market will have an impact on service levels. As a general rule, the higher the income levels, the more customer service is expected.

5. Customers' Wants and Needs. It all boils down to providing service levels that the customers expect. Above all, the customer should be the focus when determining and setting service levels.

The decision as to what customer service level to provide is a difficult one. Costs must be calculated and the retailer's overall image, the pricing structure, types of merchandise offered, the target market's income, and the competition must all be taken into account when determining a customer service level.

Source: Kritsana Maimeetook/Shutterstock.com

Supplier Customer Service Levels

In addition to determining the "right" customer service levels for its customers, the retailer needs to assess what kind of customer service it wants from its supply channel. In evaluating suppliers, many businesses use a supplier rating system that allows them to rate each supplier choice. Variables of high importance to retailers are quality, delivery time, performance history, production facilities, price and reputation (Thiruchelvan and Tookey, 2011).

In a supply chain relationship, the retailer is dependent on the supplier to deliver products and services when they are promised. Thus, the supply chain becomes an important part of the overall customer service process for the retailer, and to build the retailer-supplier relationship, retailers must also practice good customer service. A Sam's Club executive vice president of merchandising was concerned that the warehouse club was losing out on obtaining new items because suppliers complained that store buyers were inaccessible. Sam's Club management starting tracking when their employees were late for appointments, and everyone worked to improve. The company realized that treating suppliers with respect causes the retailer-supplier relationship to improve (Focus on the Core Customer, 2003).

Customer Relationship Management

Customer service focuses on developing relationships with the retailer's customers. Ideally these relationships would be personal; however, given the large customer bases most retailers have, this is difficult to achieve. Many retailers utilize systems known as customer relationship management (CRM) (also called *customer response management* or *customer-responsive management*) to help them develop customer relationships that enhance customer service. *Customer relationship management* refers to a systematic process for managing customer relationships. Companies implementing CRM are better able to identify, acquire, retain and nurture profitable customers by focusing on relationship building (Sin, Tse and Yim, 2005).

Database marketing is often an integral part of a CRM strategy. *Database marketing* is a form of direct marketing that uses databases with consumer information to create more relevant marketing materials. Some database marketing systems are very sophisticated and are used to predict customer behavior. A retailer can use database marketing to develop programs designed to increase brand loyalty, align sales and marketing departments and leverage big data (Shah, 2017). To be successful, CRM must be integrated throughout the entire retailing process.

In addition, CRM processes allow retailers to communicate with millions of consumers and at the same time make the communications appear personalized. This personalization of products and services is called 1:1 marketing (Peppers and Rogers, 1993).

1:1 Marketing

1:1 marketing (pronounced "one-to-one marketing") focuses on generating increased business from current customers (Greco, 1995) With 1:1 marketing, the CRM database is used to make products and services more personalized. For example, many retailers identify the top customers by lifetime value in terms of how much these customers spend and how recent their last purchase was. The best customers get special perks not available to others such as preferred mailings, and sneak previews on the newest merchandise and gifts during holidays. 1:1 marketing has become successful not only in the United States but internationally as well.

Customer Retention Strategies

Because customers are valuable and have many choices available to them, retailers need to work hard to retain them. It is important to ensure that all customer-service programs are integrated with the overall strategy. In addition, customer service levels must be planned. In this planning process, there must be a top-down and bottom-up commitment to the customer service process.

The retailer must be willing to develop ongoing, intensive customer service training for all employees. A system must be developed to generate customer service ideas from retail stakeholders and customers themselves. In addition, the retailer must use selective hiring and reward outstanding employees to help reduce employee turnover. Investment in front-line employees pays off. For example, many of the companies on the *Fortune's* Human Capital 30 list, have lower employee turnover rates because they focus on training, paying employees higher than industry averages and making employees feel valued. Standards must be established to allow for evaluation and control of the customer service program.

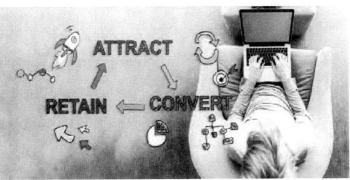

Source: Melpomene/Shutterstock.com

Employees who are not committed to providing customer service must be allowed "career readjustment" (or termination). Electronic systems for service support should be developed and integrated into the overall RIS. Finally, and perhaps most important, customer service personnel, especially salespeople, must be empowered to deal with customer problems.

Salesperson training requires a large amount of up-front and continuous investment in both capital and human resources. Like ROI (return on investment), this program is long term. The rewards for excellent customer service include increased sales and profitability and improved shareholder value (Badgett, Connor and McKinley, 2002).

Although the same general concepts apply to both e-tailing and retailing, in e-tailing eight factors that help to create customer loyalty have been identified. These factors have been labeled the 8Cs: customization, contact interactivity, cultivation, care, community, choice, convenience, and character (Srinivasan, 2002).

Customization is "the ability of an e-tailer to tailor products, services, and the transactional environment to individual customers."

Contact interactivity is "the dynamic nature of the engagement that occurs between an e-tailer and its customers through its website." Factors here might include easy navigability of the website, high levels of product or store information, and zero delays in responding to customers via e-mail, social media, live chat or phone. A key to high interactivity is the creation of two-way customer communication.

Cultivation is "the extent to which an e-tailer provides relevant information and incentives to its customers in order to extend the breadth and depth of their purchases over time." This factor includes suggestion selling as well as cross-selling initiatives.

Care is "the attention that the e-tailer pays to all the pre- and postpurchase customer interface activities designed to facilitate both immediate transactions and long-term customer relationships." The customer should be provided with delivery information, tracking information, and notice of the availability of products (especially those the customer prefers). The e-tailer needs to take carevto minimize any service interruptions to its customers.

Community is a system developed by the e-tailer to "facilitate the exchange of opinions and information regarding offered products and services." An example of community would be the ability of consumers to review books online; other consumers who are interested in these books can then access the reviews.

Source: Tyler Olson/Shutterstock.com

Choice refers to the range of products offered for sale. This includes offering not only a wider choice of product categories but also a wider range of products within product categories. Choice is a big competitive advantage for the e-tailer compared to the brick-and-mortar retailer.

Convenience refers to "the extent to which a customer feels that the website is simple, intuitive, and user friendly."

Character is "an overall image or personality that the e-tailer projects to consumers through the use of inputs such as text, style, graphics, colors, logos, and slogans or themes on the website."

Figure 13.2 (next page) summarizes the 8Cs.

Figure 13.2   The 8 Cs of Customer Loyalty in e-Commerce.

Whether a brick-and-mortar, click-only, or brick-and-click retailer, customer service is extremely important. The retailer must maintain a two-way, satisfying relationship with its customers to generate customer loyalty and, in turn, increased sales.

Summary

This chapter focused on customer service in retailing. Customer service is an extremely important part of the integrated retail management process and should be consistent with the other strategic and tactical areas in design and implementation.

The chapter began with a discussion of who the retailer's customers are and how they are defined. Once targeted customers have been segmented, a profile for each group is developed. This process enables the retailer to assess who its best customers are and provides insights into how to better serve them.

Next, the chapter discussed different types of customer service programs for retailers and e-tailers. Discussed were customer characteristics. Those people that abuse a retailer's policies are undesirable as customers. One of the difficulties encountered by retailers is that each person has their own perception of good quality service. A retailer must find gaps in service and work to improve service levels by addressing the gaps.

Customer service offerings range from basic to additional/luxury services. Basic offerings may include a convenient location, clean facilities, security, and product availability. Additional and luxury services include anything over and above the services in the basic category.

It is important to discover whether customers are satisfied with service levels by conducting surveys. Excellent customer service translates into happy customers, increased sales and profits, and higher stakeholder satisfaction.

Terms

1:1 marketing	Using customer response management techniques to personalize products and services.
assurance	A component of quality that addresses a customer's satisfaction with the retailer or its products and services.
customer response management (CRM)	The management of databases that assist retail managers in identifying trends and responding to customer characteristics.
database marketing	A form of direct marketing that uses databases with consumer information to create more relevant marketing materials.
empathy	A component of quality that promotes understanding of the customer's needs.
reliability	A component of quality that addresses the dependability of the retailer or its products and services.
responsiveness	A component of quality that tells the customer the retailer is willing to provide high levels of prompt customer service.
tangibility	A component of quality that involves the physical characteristics of the retail store.

Discussion Questions

1. Why should retailers focus on ensuring customers are happy with their shopping experience?

2. Why is it important to understand customers before developing customer profiles?

3. How is target marketing used in customer service?

4. What are the main differences between retail and e-tail customer services? What aspects are similar?

5. What are some uses for customer relationship management? What additional applications might become important during the next five years?

6. What service level do you believe discounters such as Target should offer? What about upscale retailers such as Neiman Marcus or Bloomingdale's?

Exercises

1. Visit the following online retailers. What indications are there of customer service provided by each retailer?

- Asos (www.us.asos.com)
- American Eagle (www.ae.com)
- Topshop (www.us.topshop.com)

2. Visit a retailer and write about your customer service experience.

3. Find an example of a consumer who got results from a company by complaining on social media. Write about the incident and how the company responded.

4. Many retailers are using chatbots for customer service.

- Find two retailers that use online chatbots for customer service.

- On which of the two sites was it easier to locate this information?

- What, if anything, would you change to make the chatbot more appealing on the site?

- Would you prefer a robot chatbot or a chatbot with human interaction? Explain.

Case

Customer Service at AutoZone Stores

AutoZone, the number one auto parts chain in the United States, sells auto and light-truck parts, chemicals, and accessories through more than 5,000 AutoZone Stores in the U.S., Puerto Rico, Mexico and Brazil. Founded in 1979 in Forrest City, Arkansas, AutoZone is a $10+ billion company (as of 2017). Founder J. R. "Pitt" Hyde III retired in 1997, but his philosophies still drive the company. One of the company's top priorities in 2016 and beyond is, "Great People Providing Great Service." According to a 2016 letter to shareholders the initiative, "… has been and will continue to be a constant as it is imperative we have great people providing great service. This initiative is focused on hiring, retaining, training and developing the best people in the industry." Meetings conducted throughout the year are filled with enthusiasm and a customer focus that has differentiated the company from its competitors.

Many of the strategies AutoZone employs are variations of Wal-Mart's strategies and tactics. From the company cheer to inventing its own acronyms, AutoZone has incorporated the practices that have made Wal-Mart successful. In addition to generating enthusiasm, AutoZone has adapted Wal-Mart's everyday low prices (EDLP) strategy, an inventory system that leverages technology, lower-cost ad strategies, international expansion, and emphasis on the customer.

According to the company, "We have always understood there are choices our customers can make on where they shop, and we don't take that for granted. Every customer interaction is an opportunity for us to 'surprise and delight,' leading our customers to say 'WOW!' or conversely, an opportunity for us to disappoint a customer – an unacceptable outcome."

The company also provides specialty tools through their Loan-A-Tool program where customer borrow tools that are only required for a single job. As another example of their dedication to customer concerns, AutoZone was the first in its segment to create a quality control program for parts. The company is regularly recognized for outstanding customer service. Although the competition is strong---Advance Auto Parts, Pep Boys, and O'Reilly automotive, among others---AutoZone is confident that it will continue to beat the competition.

Questions

1. What elements have made AutoZone so successful?

2. What can competitors do to overtake AutoZone? Do you believe AutoZone will eventually be outdone by one of its competitors? Explain your answer.

3. How can AutoZone leverage its reputation for outstanding customer service?

4. At what point does a company such as AutoZone overdo its customer service efforts?

Sources: AutoZone annual report 2016. Shareholder letter 2016
(http://media.corporate-ir.net/media_files/IROL/76/76792/AZO_Shareholder_Letter_2016.pdf).
About Us," AutoZone homepage, retrieved August 2017 from www.autozone.com

References

About Buckle (2017). Buckle Website. Retrieved from http://corporate.buckle.com/about

Alfs, L. (2013). Patrick Doyle: How Domino's Pizza Used Social Media to Change Its Reputation. Retreved from AnnArbor.com at http://www.annarbor.com/business-review/patrick-doyle-how-dominos-pizza-used-social-media-to-change-its-reputation/

Badgett, M., Connor, W. and McKinley, J. (2002). Customer Satisfaction, Do You Know the Score? Report #G510-1675-00, IBM Institute for Business Value, IBM Corporation.

Burley, R. (2012). Customer Service: 5 Rules for Handling Complaints. *Inc.* (Apr 25). Retrieved from http://www.inc.com/ron-burley/customer-service-5-rules-for-handling-complaints.html

Carlo, A. M. (2003). Lowe's Dilutes Inhalants Policy. *Home Channel News*, (June 2), p. 3.

CBS News (2017). Man Alleges Ageism After Getting Banned from Starbucks for Asking Teen Barista on Date (Jan 1). Retrieved from http://www.cbsnews.com/news/spokane-man-banned-from-starbucks-after-asking-teen-barista-on-date/

Consumer Reports (2015). Driving Them Crazy: Americans' Top Customer Service Complaints (Nov 2). Retrieved from http://www.consumerreports.org/cro/news/2015/11/top-customer-service-complaints/index.htm

Dickson, P.R. (1982). Person-Situation: Segmentation's Missing Link. *Journal of Marketing*, (Fall), p. 59.

Dorney Park (2013). Park Policies. Retrieved from https://www.dorneypark.com/guest-services/park-policies

Enright, A. (2011). Live Chat Use Is on the Rise, Survey Says. *Internet Retailer* (May 10). Retrieved from http://www.internetretailer.com/2011/05/10/live-chat-use-rise-survey-says

Find Out What They Like and How They Like It (1935). Words by Andy Razaf, music by "Fats" Waller.

Focus on the Core Customer (2003). *Chain Store Age*, 79 (May), pp. 52-56.

Ford, R. C., Heaton, C. P. and Brown, S. W. (2001). Delivering Excellent Service: Lessons from the Best Firms. *California Management Review*, 44 (Fall), pp. 39-56.

Gaab, K., (2015). Listen, Then Speak: 10 Quotes on Social Media Listening. Cision. Retrieved from http://www.cision.com/us/2015/10/listen-then-speak-10-quotes-on-social-media-listening/

Glen, P. (1990). *It's Not My Department! How to Get the Service You Want, Exactly the Way You Want It*. New York: William Morrow and Company, pp. 11-19.

Greco, S. (1995). The Road to One to One Marketing. *Inc.*, 17(14), p. 56.

Hartman, M. G. (2001). Separate the Vital Few from the Trivial Many. *Quality Progress*, (Sept), p. 120.

Heinze, J. (2016). Police Arrest 50 People in Dorney Park Drug Crackdown, Reports Say. *Pottstown Patch* (Aug 18). Retrieved from https://patch.com/pennsylvania/pottstown/police-arrest-50-people-dorney-park-july-drug-crackdown-reports

Hyken, S. (2017). Guest Blog: How Companies are using Bots to Enhance Customer Experience. Retrieved from https://hyken.com/customer-care/companies-using-bots-enhance-customer-experience/

LiveChat (2017). LiveChat Customer Service Report 2017. Retrieved from https://www.livechatinc.com/livechat-resources/customer-service-report-2017/

Man Charged with Attack on Ride Attendant (2002). *Morning Call* (Allentown, PA), (July 12), p. B3.

Many Unhappy Returns: Sisters Banned in Boston (2003). *Chicago Tribune*, (July 15), p. 36.

Men's Wearhouse (2017). Website. Retrieved from www. menswearhouse.com

National Association for Shoplifting Prevention (2017). Website: www.shopliftingprevention.org." Retrieved from http://www.saynotoshoplifting.org/

Neuborne, E. (2000). It's the Service, Stupid: E-tailers May Be Missing Their Biggest Chance to Snare - and Keep - Customers. *Business Week*, April 3, p. EB18.

Parasuraman, A.; Zeithaml, V. and Berry, L. L. (1985). A Conceptual Model of Service Quality and Its Implications for Future Research. *Journal of Marketing*, 49 (Fall), pp. 41--50.

Peppers, D. and Rogers, M. (1993). *The One to One Future: Building Relationships One Customer at a Time*. New York: Doubleday, p. 15.

Shah, S. (2017). 5 Reasons a CRM is Essential for Retailers. *Customer Think* (Jan 14). Retrieved from http://customerthink.com/5-reasons-a-crm-is-essential-for-retailers/

Sin, L., Tse, A. and Yim, F. (2005). CRM: Conceptualisation and Scale Development. *European Journal of Marketing*, (39:11/12), 1264-1290.

Sisters Face Ban at Filene's Basement Because of Too Many Returns, Complaints (2003). *St. Louis Post–Dispatch*, July 20, p. E8.

Srinivasan, S. S., Anderson, R. and Ponnavolu, K. (2002). Customer Loyalty in E-commerce: An Exploration of Its Antecedents and Consequences. *Journal of Retailing*, 78 (Spring), pp. 41--50.

Tailored Brands Annual Report (2017). Retrieved from http://ir.tailoredbrands.com/annual-reports#

The Ritz-Carlton Wins Top Honors in Luxury Category for J.D. Power and Associates 2016 North America Hotel Guest Satisfaction Index Study (2016). Retrieved from http://news.ritzcarlton.com/2016/07/the-ritz-carlton-wins-top-honors-in-luxury-category-for-j-d-power-and-associates-2016-north-america-hotel-guest-satisfaction-index-study/

Thiruchelvan, S. and Tookey, J. E. (2011). Evolving Trends of Supplier Selection Criteria and Methods. *International Journal of Automotive and Mechanical Engineering*, 4 (Jul-Dec), pp. 437-454.

Traba, A. and Moore, M. (2016). Here's What Personality Sounds Like. Mattersight Personality Labs. Retrieved from http://www.mattersight.com/wp-content/uploads/2016/09/Heres-What-Personality-Sounds-Like.pdf

Vernon, L. (2003). Make Someone Happy --Your Customer. *Inc.*, (July). Retrieved from Inc.com.

Weinstein, A, and Johnson, W.C. (1999). *Designing and Delivering Superior Customer Value: Concepts, Cases and Applications*. Boca Raton, FL: St. Lucie Press, pp. 70-77.

What Seniors Want in Restaurant Dining (2003). *USA Today*, (May), p. 7.

Zeithaml, V., Parasuraman, A. and Berry, L. L. (1990). *Delivering Quality Service: Balancing Customer Perceptions and Expectations*. New York: The Free Press, pp. 15 - 33.

Chapter 14

Laws and Ethics

"The reputation of a thousand years may be determined by the conduct of one hour."

~ Japanese Proverb

Source: David Evison/Shutterstock.com

CHAPTER OBJECTIVES

After completing this chapter you will be able to:

- Explain the difference between laws and ethics.
- Describe the different fields of ethics.
- Explain how a company can incorporate ethics into its business operations.
- Discuss specific laws governing the retail and e-tail industry.

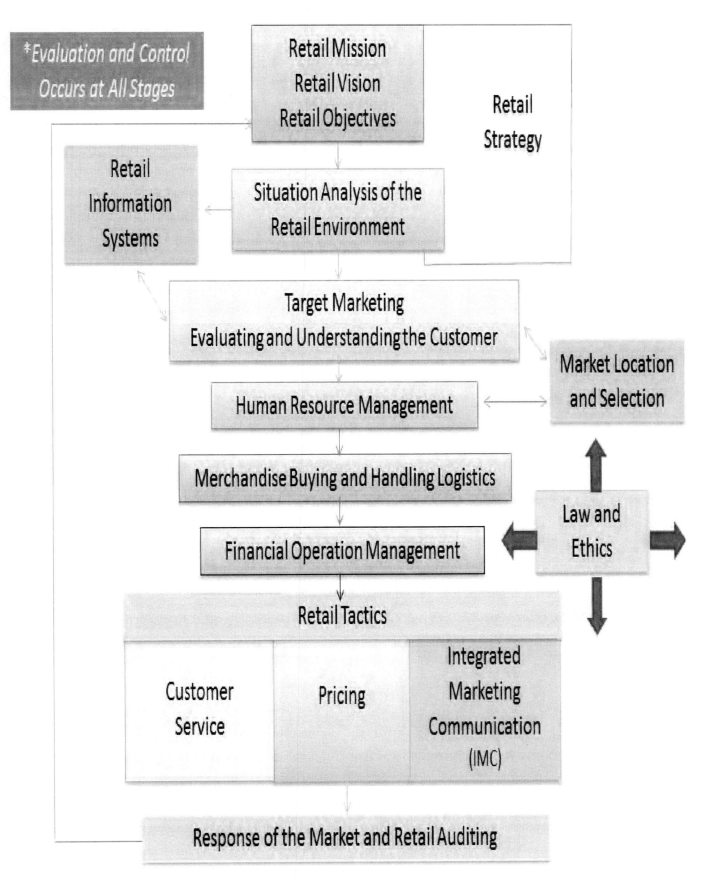

Rite Aid Turnaround

In September 1962, Thrift D Discount Center opened in Scranton, Pennsylvania. In 1968, after tremendous growth, the company went public and officially changed its name to Rite Aid Corporation. Today Rite Aid (www.riteaid.com) is the number three drugstore chain in the United States. The company operates 4,561 stores in the U.S.

In the late 1990s and early 2000s, Rite Aid was investigated by the Securities and Exchange Commission (SEC) for accounting violations. Former chief executive Martin Grass, former chief counsel Franklin Brown, and former financial officer Frank Bergonzi were indicted for orchestrating a fraud that forced Rite Aid to restate $1.6 billion in profit, which at that time was history's largest corporate earnings restatement (Voreacos, 2002). Grass faced thirty-six charges ranging from accounting fraud to witness tampering.

Tapes recorded by Timothy J. Noonan, a former president of Rite Aid, revealed three executives discussing submitting false information to the Federal Bureau of Investigation, backdating documents, and destroying other evidence that would implicate them (Ex-Executive..., 2002). As a result, five executives served jail time including Martin Grass, who spent seven years in prison.

Despite the ethical violations, the company rebounded by installing a new management team and challenging them to create a new course for the company. In addition to the new executive team, the company hired twenty new officers in the hope of stabilizing the firm's financial situation and improving its image in the eyes of its customers and shareholders.

In 2012, under the direction of John T. Standley, Chairman and CEO, the company had its first profitable quarter in five years (Southwick, 2013). To help with the comeback, the company remodeled many stores. Their strategy is to become a neighborhood destination for health and wellness. The company launched a wellness + loyalty program that has helped with their return to profitability (*Rite Aid Annual Report*, 2013). This loyalty program eventually became the wellness+ with Plenti loyalty program. Plenti is a coalition loyalty program where members can earn Plenti points by shopping at Plenti Partner stores, such as Macy's and Exxon Mobil (Annual Report, 2016).

On October 27, 2015, Walgreens Boot Alliance and Rite Aid entered into an agreement to merge. The Federal Trade Commission (FTC) delayed approving the merger due to antitrust concerns. In June 2017, possibly due to the concerns raised by the FTC, the merger fell through and instead Walgreens agreed to buy 2,186 Rite Aid stores for $5.2 billion. This purchase needs regulatory approval before being finalized.

Had Walgreens acquired Rite Aid it would have become the largest drugstore chain in the United States. The FTC was concerned that this would have limited competition, translating into higher prices for consumers (Taulli, 2017).

Introduction

As we can see from the integrated retail management flow chart, laws and ethics affect all the decisions that go into the development of the IRM plan. This chapter discusses the differences between laws and ethics, as well as methods for running an ethical business. The chapter also examines the consequences to retailers for breaking laws and addresses issues in e-tail law. Because numerous company executives have been indicted over the years, businesses and academicians have become more focused on laws and ethical decisions and their influence on corporate behavior. Laws and ethical decisions are intertwined with all aspects of retailing. This chapter provides an overview of the various laws that affect retailers and the ethical issues that management and employees encounter.

The Difference between Laws and Ethics

It can often be difficult to determine the line between right and wrong. Many activities that are unethical are also illegal. However, in some instances an act is legal but unethical and in others an act is illegal but ethical. If you are confused, you are not alone. Consider the following:

• According to the California State Floral Association, many California retail florists have lost business to telemarketers who use the florists' established business names to steal away customers. In defense, telemarketers claim they are introducing more competition. Many Internet florists claim to be local but own no stores. Calls are taken by calling center representatives and sent to local florists, who fulfill the orders. The prices are often more than what would have been paid at a local florist. Many states are considering laws that make it mandatory for florists to disclose whether or not they have a physical location (KSE Focus, 2013).

• As of 2017, a $5 million lawsuit was pending against clothing retailer Zara for deceptive pricing. According to the suit, in their U.S. stores, Zara only list prices on their products in euros. When customers paid, they were allegedly charged more than the conversion rate, sometimes resulting in a markup of 60 percent (Christian, 2016). Zara denies the claim.

• In 2001, human rights groups accused De Beers, a world leader in production and sales of rough diamonds, of buying diamonds from African rebels who used the proceeds to finance their wars. Because of intense pressure, De Beers adopted a code guaranteeing customers that "conflict diamonds" will not be sold by De Beers or De Beers' associates. Unfortunately, the competition did not follow De Beers' lead and today it is difficult for a consumer to know if they are buying conflict diamonds (Perry, 2011).

Source: Perfect Lazybones/Shutterstock.com

Retailers must consider both laws and ethics in running their businesses, but often, as the previous examples show, the "right" answer is not very clear. According to the *Internet Encyclopedia of Philosophy*, the field of ethics involves "systematizing, defending, and recommending concepts of right and wrong behavior" (Fieser, 2001). The concept of what is right or wrong is often based on religious beliefs and moral codes of conduct. In contrast, a law is "a rule established by authority, society, or custom" (International Law Dictionary..., 2002).

Ethics

The study of ethics is divided into three general categories: (1) metaethics, (2) normative ethics, and (3) applied ethics (Fieser, 2001). *Metaethics* is the study of the origin of ethical concepts and theories. *Normative ethics* involves deciding whether certain behavior is right or wrong. It tells us what a person should do when confronted with a particular situation. It also assumes there is only one criterion to guide right and wrong behavior. The criterion could be a single rule, such as the Golden Rule, ("Do unto others as you would have them do unto you"). Alternatively, the criterion could be a set of principles that guides behavior, such as a code of ethics adopted by a retailer. *Applied ethics* involves analyzing specific ethical dilemmas. Retailing examples include deceptive advertising, buying from manufacturing firms that use child labor, recording assets and liabilities improperly, employee theft, inequitable pricing, and unfair competitive practices.

Differences in Ethical Perspectives

One problem in studying ethics is that people may not always agree on what is "right" and "wrong." A person faced with making a judgment about another person's moral conduct bases that decision on his or her own system of ethics; when these systems differ, disagreement arises about whether or not a particular action is moral (Forsyth, 1980). To help explain these perspectives, a classification of ethical ideologies has been developed and is presented in Figure 14.1.

Figure 14.1 Difference in Ethical Perspectives

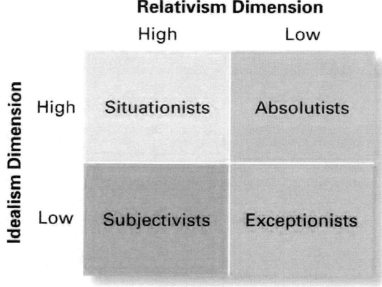

Source: Forsyth, D. R. (1980). A Taxonomy of Ethical Ideologies,
Journal of Personality and Social Psychology, 39:1 (1980) pp. 175-184.

The *relativism* dimension describes the extent to which a person rejects universal moral rules in favor of relativism. On the high end of the relativism dimension, an individual rejects the idea that there are universal codes to which one must adhere. On the low end, an individual believes there are universal rules of conduct that apply to all people. The *idealism* dimension describes the extent to which a person is idealistic in anticipation of outcomes. On the high end of the idealism dimension, an individual believes one can always realize desirable consequences by making the "right" decision. On the low end, a person believes that undesirable actions are often mixed with desirable actions.

Situationists are high in both relativism and idealism. These individuals reject universal moral rules and advocate analysis of moral problems by considering the situation and context in which the behavior occurs. They also believe that with the "right" action, desirable consequences are obtainable. For example, a situationist would be optimistic about the outcome of the Rite Aid scandal if management comes clean. The situationist would also believe that the overall situation and context of the environment must be understood to explain why managers at Rite Aid committed fraud.

Subjectivists are high in relativism but low in idealism. People in this category reject universal moral rules in favor of personal values and perspectives to guide behavior. They also believe that there are bound to be undesirable consequences mixed in with desirable consequences.

Subjectivists would view the Rite Aid scandal in terms of the personal ethics that guided management's behavior. Individuals in this category do not believe there are universal rules of right and wrong. Instead, ethical behavior is guided by a person's perspective. Subjectivists would expect undesirable consequences, even when "right" actions are taken.

Absolutists are low in relativism and high in idealism. People in this category assume the best possible outcome can always be achieved by following universal rules. An absolutist would say that if the Rite Aid executives had followed the laws, the best outcome for the company would have resulted. Such people do not believe that context is important.

Exceptionists are low in both relativism and idealism. These individuals believe that moral universal rules guide conduct but that the consequences of the action must also be considered to determine whether or not the behavior is moral. Exceptionists are pessimistic, believing that undesirable consequences will likely occur even when rules are followed. An exceptionist would say that the Rite Aid executives did not follow laws of behavior, but to determine whether their behavior was ethical, a full examination of the consequences of the behavior would need to be conducted, because even when the rules are followed, there can be undesirable consequences.

Source: ibreakstock/Shutterstock.com

A person's decision as to whether a behavior is right or wrong depends on his or her ideology. For clarification, consider the following retailing example: Is it morally right for a salesperson to lie to a customer? The situationist would say it depends on why the salesperson tells the lie. Perhaps the lie is that the customer looks nice in the outfit he chose when in reality the salesperson thinks it is unflattering. Because the salesperson does not want to hurt the customer's feelings, she tells him a lie.

The subjectivist would also examine the situation to determine what is right or wrong. The subjectivist would most likely believe that undesirable consequences would result from telling a lie. The absolutist would say that a universal moral rule is to tell the truth. People in this category would agree that telling the truth is the best course of action in all circumstances. Finally, the exceptionist would say that moral absolutes guide judgments but that consequences should be considered; if necessary, exceptions should be made to universal standards of conduct. Thus, if telling a lie were the best for all parties concerned, the exceptionist would agree that is the best course of action.

The Profit-Principle Relationship

According to the marketing concept, companies should strive to satisfy customer wants and needs at a profit. Sometimes ethical conflicts arise because the retailer is under pressure from stockholders and other publics to show profits. Four perspectives clarify the relationship between profits and principles (Graafland, 2002). The interplay of profits and principles varies depending on the perspective a company employs.

1. The *win-win perspective* assumes that the more ethically a business operates, the higher the profits for the business. Therefore, no conflict exists between ethics and profits. Instead, profits and principles reinforce each other. This perspective is the most ideal situation.

2. According to the *license to operate perspective*, a company maximizes profits under the condition that the level of principles adhered to by the company is enough for it to receive a "license" from society to operate. The license stands for the acceptance of a company's operations by all stakeholders (i.e., customers, stockholders, government) who can impact the profitability of the company. This perspective recognizes that not all ethical behavior will increase competitive advantage, especially when others are operating unethically. In the license-to-operate perspective, firms strive to maximize profits as opposed to principles.

3. The *acceptable profit perspective* assumes that companies want to maximize principles but are restricted because the market demands that profitability reach a level required by the capital market to ensure financial continuity. In this perspective, firms strive to maximize principles as opposed to profits, but they are restricted by the need to generate a minimum level of profits to ensure the company survives.

4. The *integrated perspective* attaches an optimum intrinsic value to both profits and principles, and the company selects the optimal balance between the two. The optimal balance depends on the relative weights of profits and principles in company operations. This perspective is the most balanced of the four.

These divisions are not clear-cut, because changes in the environment may alter outlooks. But they provide a framework for viewing profit-principle conflicts.

Source: Monkey Business Images/Shutterstock.com

Culture and Ethical Perspectives

A country's culture can have a significant effect on ethical perspectives. More and more retailers are becoming global through both the Internet and global expansion. Therefore, it is increasingly important for retailers to be aware that differences exist. In addition, a retailer must understand the international laws that may affect the company.

Although most companies have policies regarding integrity, relatively few have established practices regarding bribery in the global marketplace. In many countries, bribery is not illegal; thus, ethical questions arise very quickly when a U.S. firm conducts business in those countries. It can be argued that U.S. laws against bribery place U.S. companies at a competitive disadvantage when conducting business in countries where bribery is a common practice.

On February 3, 1975, the chief executive officer of United Brands Company committed suicide. Two months later, the Securities and Exchange Commission discovered that the CEO had bribed the president of Honduras with $1.25 million. The investigation that followed revealed that more than 400 U.S. companies (117 from the *Fortune 500* list) had paid over $300 million in bribes or other illegal payments to foreign officials to gain business opportunities in foreign countries. As a result, the Foreign Corrupt Practices Act was enacted in 1977 to curtail bribery practices. The act makes it illegal for a U.S. company to pay, or offer to pay, a foreign official to gain or maintain business in that country. American corporations claim the act makes it difficult, if not impossible, to compete internationally, especially because bribery is a widespread practice in many countries. In recent years, however, many other countries have recognized the legal and ethical issues surrounding bribery and have developed their own antibribery laws.

Retailers encounter difficulties when it is not clear which standards the company should follow: those of the home country or those of the country in which it conducts business. Thus, the importance of understanding the laws and ethical codes of the country in which the retailer operates cannot be underestimated. Globalization is forcing countries to examine their laws and ethical codes of conduct; in the future, there may be international standards, which will make ethical choices easier.

Running an Ethical Business

Instead of enjoying the appreciation and respect typically experienced by CEOs, executives are increasingly being regarded with hostility and suspicion. There are several ways a retailer can run an ethical business. Table 14.1 (next page) contains suggestions for running an ethical business.

Laws

To facilitate the flow of business while protecting consumers, many local, state, national, and international laws are created. The following sections describe laws that are specific to retailers. Prior to discussing the legal environment of retailing, we will look at some legal issues facing retailers. Keep in mind that many times laws and ethics overlap; although there are laws against theft, for example, ethical perspectives also play a role.

Employee Theft

According to the 2016 National Retail Security Survey (NRSS) internal retail theft accounted for more than one-third of inventory shrinkage in 2015 (Smith, 2016). Employee theft often involves collusion with external sources. Retail theft costs are often passed to the consumer in the form of higher prices. Cash is the number one item stolen by employees, followed by stealing merchandise. One of the ways employees steal cash is by keeping cash collected, but not entering the transaction into the system. Stealing merchandise is often done with the help of another employee or friend. An employee can undercharge a friend, who walks out with more merchandise than was paid for (Robinson, 2017).

According to Dr. Richard Hollinger, conductor of the NRSS, retailers that experience higher than average shrinkage include grocery/supermarket (much comes from spoilage), specialty stores, accessory stores and furniture stores. Those with lower than average shrinkage include supply stores, and entertainment and media gaming stores (Davis, 2011).

Table 14.1 – Suggestions for Running an Ethical Business

Examine the intention. Examine your reasons for implementing ethics policies. Is the retailer implementing ethics policies because it's the "hot topic" or does management plan to make ethics a priority for the long-term? Whose ethical standards will be applied in determining the policies? The rationale behind intentions will help to better communicate policies to employees.

Highlight the company's "legends" that personify the ethics. Celebrate the models of ethical conduct by sharing stories with employees and the public. Employees at Wal-Mart are well versed in stories of Sam Walton, founder, and his appreciation for employees or 'associates', as he called them. Keep these types of stories alive to provide role models to employees.

Make it a company norm-in-action. Every manager must "walk the talk" when it comes to ethical behavior. Employees are watching and will become confused if actions don't mirror words.

Provide parameters and examples. Provide employees guidelines that support the company's standards of ethics. Remember that people see ethical behavior differently. Guidelines will help them to determine the company's standards. Be sure to communicate these standards consistently to all employees.

Incorporate new ways of understanding ethics. It may be beneficial to hire a skilled facilitator to engage your employees in discussions about ethics. If managers feel comfortable enough, they can conduct discussion sessions themselves, but it's important to respect participants' differences, beliefs and insecurities about the subject.

Meld ethics with business. Integrate ethics in all aspects of the operation including hiring new employees, pricing products, implementing standards, and choosing suppliers.

Tie ethics to individual and departmental goals. Incorporate support of the company's ethical standards in performance reviews. Make sure associates understand that they will be rated on ethical behavior and that they understand the consequences of unethical behavior.

Develop safe feedback mechanisms. Make sure employees feel safe in reporting unethical behavior. Some ways to ensure employees are comfortable include anonymous hotlines, suggestion boxes, establishment of an ethics officer, and one on one discussion.

Use an advisor. Get some outside advice from an expert on how to best implement and communicate an ethics policy that fits your organizational culture.

A word of advice. A good rule of thumb is, if your family or friends would think less of you if knowledge of an activity surfaced, then don't do it.

Source: Walter, J. S. (n.d.) Ivy Sea Online . Defining and Communicating Ethics in Your Business.

Employee theft can be extremely costly for retailers, but by taking precautions, retailers can minimize shrinkage and eliminate temptation for employees to behave unethically.

Customer Theft

Although the majority of retail theft is internal, customer shoplifting is also a big concern for retailers. Return fraud occurs when customers take advantage or manipulate a retailer's return policies. Customers may attempt *wardrobing*, which is the return of used, non-defective merchandise, like special event apparel or electronics, after a major sporting event. Others may attempt to return merchandise with a counterfeit receipt. Another type of return fraud occurs when a customer buys goods with counterfeit money or a stolen credit card and attempts to return the product to another location for cash. To curtail return fraud, many retailers are investing in technology, requiring identification and often provide credit instead of cash for items returned without proper documentation (Return Fraud..., 2011).

Although shrinkage has gone down, retailers are reporting increases in *organized retail crime (ORC)* which involves the large-scale theft of consumer items. According to the National Anti-Organized Retail Crime Association, Inc. (naorca.org), ORC costs, in the U.S., amount to $40 - $50 billion/year. Professional shoplifters (called boosters) steal or fraudulently obtain products which are sold or fenced to other people/companies (Finklea, 2012). Many safety and health issues arise when counterfeit goods are sold because the products may contain dangerous chemicals and may not be stored correctly before sale. The rise in ORC has given rise to Organized Retail Crime Associations (ORCA), comprised of companies that share efforts to stop the crime (Robaton, 2013).

Source: think4photop/Shutterstock.com

Ways to reduce shrinkage due to customer theft include supervising the selling floor, making would-be shoplifters feel uneasy, and getting employees involved in the prevention process (ADT, 2013).

Supervise the Selling Floor: It is important that managers be on the sales floor as much as possible during the day. While walking the floor, managers should observe and respond to mismarked merchandise, incorrect prices on signs, unlocked security displays, merchandise concealed for later pickup, fitting room attendants off their posts, inattentive security guards, unpaid-for merchandise under counters, and suspicious activities by customers. Another effective method is to pay plainclothes security personnel to walk the selling floor.

Give Shoplifters an Uneasy Feeling: An effective way to deter shoplifting is to make shoplifting difficult. Methods include the following:

• Train employees to maintain frequent eye contact with customers who insist on browsing on their own.

• Install added security measures in "blind spots" around the store

• Provide personal attention to as many customers as possible.

• Assign zones for staff coverage so that vulnerable areas are not left unattended.

• Instruct employees to give directions to people taking items into the fitting room.

• Use bright lighting, mirrors, video cameras, and anti-shoplifting signs to let customers know the retailer is serious about theft. Let potential shoplifters know that all offenders will be prosecuted.

Get Employees Involved in the Theft Prevention Process: Employees can be very effective in detecting and deterring theft. Given that retailers report $30+ billion in losses yearly due to theft, it is important to get everyone involved in the theft prevention process. There are several ways to ensure employee involvement:

• Do not criticize employees who are overcautious; in fact, employees who report theft should be rewarded.

• Keep employees well informed about what is happening within the company. Informed employees feel like they are part of the company and will be more protective of the company's assets.

• Train employees in how to get assistance when in a security crisis.

• Install silent alarms and educate all employees in company policies and procedures in the event of a theft.

Other Loss Prevention Strategies

Loss prevention strategies are grouped into four categories: pre-employment integrity screening measures, employee awareness programs, asset control policies, and loss prevention systems (Finklea, 2012).

Pre-Employment Integrity Screening Measures: Retailers using these measures most often verify past employment history and check for prior criminal convictions. Other methods include drug screening, driving record checks, credit checks, multiple interviews, education verification, personal reference checks, and surveys that measure honesty. Different measures are undertaken depending on the level of personnel being considered, with greater scrutiny being applied to potential managerial employees than to employees lower in the organizational hierarchy.

Employee Awareness Programs: The most common employee awareness programs involve discussions during new-hire orientation, bulletin board notices and posters, anonymous telephone hotlines, and presentations and lectures. Other programs include codes of conduct, training videos, online training, newsletters, and honesty incentives.

Asset Control Policies: The most widely used retail loss prevention strategies are in the asset control policies category. These policies include refund controls, void controls, employee package checks, point-of-service (POS) exception-based reporting, trash removal controls, inter-store transfer controls, POS bar coding/scanning, price change controls, unobserved exit door controls, inventory bar coding/scanning, web-based management and detailed merchandise receiving controls.

Loss Prevention Systems: The most common programs in this category include burglar alarms and live, visible CCTV (closed-circuit television). Other actions include check approval database screening, hidden CCTV and armored car deposit pickups, cables/locks/chains, digital video recording systems, secured display fixtures, mystery/honesty shoppers, silent alarms, observation mirrors, plainclothes detectives, and merchandise locks and alarms.

Internet Fraud

Fraud committed over the Internet is becoming more prevalent. According to the Department of Justice, *Internet fraud* refers to "any type of fraud scheme that uses one or more components of the Internet to present fraudulent solicitation to prospective victims, to conduct fraudulent transactions, or to transmit the proceeds of fraud to financial institutions or to others connected with the scheme."

Source: David Evison/Shutterstock.com

An example is customer credit card purchases over the Internet. Laws related to customer loss due to fraudulent use of credit cards for purchases at brick-and-mortar retailers or even through direct retailers, such as catalog retail outlets, do not apply to Internet transactions. E-tailers incur the cost of the loss of fraudulent credit card purchases because most credit card issuers and processors require the customer's signature; thus, the e-tailer is unprotected without this signature. If the credit card is not physically present (called CNP for card not present), the e-tailer must assume that the buyer is presenting the information ethically. Many e-tailers will only ship to a verified address. The e-tailer must weigh the cost of potential fraud with the inconvenience experienced by customers by the verification process. People committing fraud take advantage of the fact that small transactions are not caught as often. Investigating Internet fraud is difficult because the thief is often located in a different state or country than the victim. Table 14.2 lists government and nongovernment websites that contain information on fraud.

Table 14.2   Websites with Information on Fraud

Government Websites	Address
Commodity Futures Trading Commission	www.cftc.gov
FirstGov For Consumers	www.consumer.gov
Computer Crime and Intellectual Property Section, Criminal Division, U.S. Department of Justice	www.cybercrime.gov
Federal Bureau of Investigation	www.fbi.gov
Federal Trade Commission	www.ftc.gov
Internet Crime Complaint Center	www.ic3.gov
Securities and Exchange Commission	www.sec.gov
U.S. Customs and Border Protection	www.cbp.gov
U.S. Postal Inspection Service	www.usps.com
U.S. Secret Service	www.secretservice.gov
U.S. Sentencing Commission	www.ussc.gov
Nongovernmental Websites	**Address**
Better Business Bureau	www.bbb.org
Consumer Action	www.consumer-action.org
Consumer Federation of America	www.consumerfed.org
Internet ScamBusters	www.scambusters.org
National Association of Attorneys General	www.naag.org
Financial Industry Regulatory Authority	www.finra.org
National Consumers League	www.nclnet.org
Fraud.org	www.fraud.org
North American Securities Administrators Association	www.nasaa.org

The Internet Crime Complaint Center (www.ic3.gov) accepts online Internet crime complaints from victims and third parties. Since its inception in 2010, there have been about 3.5 million complaints reported. According to the IC3's 2016 annual report there were 298,728 consumer complaints in 2016 resulting in over $1.3 trillion in losses. The center receives on average about 800 complaints per day.

In terms of victim losses, business e-mail compromise (BEC) was the most prevalent, followed by confidence fraud and non-delivery of and nonpayment for merchandise. BEC targets businesses working with foreign suppliers and/or businesses that regularly perform wire transfer payments. Legitimate business email accounts are compromised through computer intrusion techniques to conduct unauthorized transfer of funds. Confidence fraud and romance fraud fall under the BEC umbrella. Victims of these frauds are used to transfer funds to someone who purports to be a family member or romantic interest without knowing that it is a scam. Lastly, non-delivery of and nonpayment for merchandise schemes purport to offer high-value items likely to attract many consumers. The victims send money for the promised items, but either the victims never get the items or receive counterfeit items instead of the promised goods. Other scams included identity theft, get rich quick deals, bogus lottery win notifications, Nigerian scam letters (trick people into sending money with promises of a pay-off; also known as 419 scams), *phishing* (tricking people into disclosing personal information and using it to commit fraud) and the use of intimidation and extortion.

Regulating Bodies

The Federal Trade Commission (FTC) is a regulatory agency of the U.S. government that en-forces federal antitrust and consumer protection laws. The FTC protects consumers and businesses from acts or practices that are unfair or deceptive.

With regulatory powers similar to those of the FTC, the U.S. International Trade Commission (ITC) (www.usitc.gov) provides trade expertise to both the legislative and executive branches of government; determines the impact of imports on U.S. industries; and directs actions against cer-tain unfair trade practices, such as patent, trademark, and copyright infringement.

Other countries have regulatory agencies similar to the FTC and ITC. Examples include the Bangladesh Export Promotion Bureau, Hong Kong trade and Industry Department, Department of Commerce - Government of India, French Ministry for Foreign Trade

Many of the regulations imposed by local, state, federal, and international bodies aim to protect the consumer, give the consumer a broad range of choices, provide the consumer with reli-able, timely information, and prevent unfair trade practices.

Specific Laws that Affect Retailers

Authorities, societies, or custom establish laws. Retailers must abide by the laws imposed by various local, state, and federal authorities. Companies that run global operations must keep in mind that laws in effect in the United States may not apply in other countries. Conversely, other countries have laws that the United States may not have. When a company breaks established laws, it must pay the consequences for illegal activity. Consequences can include paying a fine, providing restitution to affected parties, publicly admitting to crimes, and in severe situations, jail time for the individuals(s) who committed the crime. Frequently the negative publicity generated by law breaking hurls a company into bankruptcy. The investment in a legal department is highly recommended for both national and international companies.

Retailing laws have the greatest effect on retail tactics (pricing, integrated marketing communications, customer service, etc.). For example, truth in advertising Laws make it against the law for retailers to make false or deceptive claims when advertising their products and services.

Let's take a closer look at some other laws that affect retailers.

Trademark Regulations

All businesses must be aware of trademark laws. A *trademark* is a firm's brand name, symbol, or design that is used to identify the company to other businesses and consumers. Trademarks give a business the legal right to use a given design to identify its products. *Servicemarks* are the counterparts to trademarks for services.

Source: niroworld/Shutterstock.com

The Lanham Trademark Act, enacted by Congress in 1946, protects the rights of trademark/servicemark owners. Under the Lanham Act, a company can register its brand name or design with the U.S. Patent Office. A search is conducted to ensure that no other company is already using the mark. Eventually the application to register a trademark is either accepted or rejected. If it is accepted, the company is protected, under federal laws, against unauthorized use of the trademark. If it is declined, the company can file an appeal. There is no single organization that polices trademarks and servicemarks. If a company believes its trademark has been infringed on, it needs to follow up. The courts will decide if an infringement of trademark law has occurred.

In a classic case that occurred in the 1980, the company that owned Domino's Sugar, Amstar, took Domino's Pizza to court over trademark infringement. Domino's Sugar believed Domino's Pizza unfairly used its trademarked name "Domino's." While the case was in court, the owners of Domino's Pizza changed the name to Dominic's Pizza. The court ruled in favor of Domino's Pizza, arguing that a reasonable person would know the difference between sugar and pizza.

Antitrust Laws

Many antitrust laws restrict unfair or unlawful partnerships between retailers. The *Sherman Antitrust Act*, passed in 1890, outlaws monopolies as well as contracts or other forms of conspiracy to restrain or limit free trade. Violation of these laws is a felony. Corporations might be charged up to $100 million for each violation, and an individual breaking these laws might be jailed for up to ten years and fined up to $1 million per violation. Maximum fines can go higher in some instances because the maximum penalty is twice the gain or loss involved.

The *Clayton Act*, passed in 1914, regulates price discrimination, tying contracts, exclusive dealing arrangements, and acquisition of stock of another company. Three revisions to the Clayton act were made that affected trade. The first was the *Robinson-Patman Act*, passed in 1936, which regulates seller-induced price discrimination, buyer-induced price discrimination, and price discounts such as advertising allowances. The second was the *Celler-Kefauver Amendment,* passed in 1950, which regulates acquisition of assets as well as stock of another company. The third was the *Hart-Scott-Rodino Antitrust Improvement Act* (1976), which required large firms to pre-notify the FTC of intentions to merge. Table 14.3 summarizes important sections of various antitrust laws.

Table 14.3   Summary of Antitrust Laws

Antitrust Laws

Antitrust laws describe unlawful practices in general terms, leaving it to the courts to decide what specific practices are illegal based on the facts and circumstances of each case.

• Section 1 of the Sherman Act outlaws "every contract, combination . . . , or conspiracy, in restraint of trade," but long ago, the Supreme Court decided that the Sherman Act prohibits only those contracts or agreements that restrain trade unreasonably. What kinds of agreements are unreasonable is up to the courts.

• Section 2 of the Sherman Act makes it unlawful for a company to "monopolize, or attempt to monopolize," trade or commerce. As that law has been interpreted, it is not necessarily illegal for a company to have a monopoly or to try to achieve a monopoly position. The law is violated only if the company tries to maintain or acquire a monopoly position through unreasonable methods. For the courts, a key factor in determining what is unreasonable is whether the practice has a legitimate business justification.

• Section 5 of the Federal Trade Commission Act outlaws "unfair methods of competition" but does not define unfair. The Supreme Court has ruled that violations of the Sherman Act also are violations of Section 5, but Section 5 covers some practices that are beyond the scope of the Sherman Act. It is the FTC's job to enforce Section 5.

• Section 7 of the Clayton Act prohibits mergers and acquisitions where the effect "may be substantially to lessen competition, or to tend to create a monopoly." Determining whether a merger will have that effect requires a thorough economic evaluation or market study.

• Section 7A of the Clayton Act, called the Hart-Scott-Rodino Act, requires the prior notification of large mergers to both the FTC and the Justice Department.

Source: The Federal Trade Commission http://www.ftc.gov/bc/antitrust/factsheets/FactSheet_AntiTrust.pdf

Horizontal Agreements

According to the FTC, agreements among parties in a competing relationship can raise antitrust suspicions. If agreements hurt competition, they are considered violations of federal law. *Horizontal agreements* are arrangements between a business and its competitors. Following are some of the more common horizontal agreements that retailers must avoid.

Agreements on price. Illegal agreements on price or price-related matters such as credit terms are potentially the most serious violations, because price often is the primary means of competition among retailers. Sometimes retailers appear to be in collusion because their prices are so similar, but to prove illegal activity, the FTC needs evidence of price fixing.

Agreements to restrict output. An agreement to restrict production or output is illegal because when the supply of a product or service is limited its price usually goes up.

Boycotts. A group boycott is an agreement among competitors not to deal with another person or business. If the boycott is used to force another party to pay higher prices, it is illegal.

Market division. Agreements among competitors to divide sales territories or allocate customers are essentially agreements not to compete.

Agreements to restrict advertising. Restrictions on price advertising can be illegal if they deprive consumers of important information. Restrictions on nonprice advertising also may be illegal if evidence shows the restrictions have anticompetitive effects and lack reasonable business justification.

Codes of ethics. A professional code of ethics may be unlawful if it unreasonably restricts the methods by which professionals compete.

Vertical Agreements

Vertical agreements are arrangements occurring in a buyer-seller relationship, such as between a retailer and a manufacturer or wholesaler. The following types of vertical agreements are illegal.

Resale price maintenance agreements. Illegal activity includes price fixing between a supplier and a dealer or between a manufacturer and a retailer. Such activity is illegal because it fixes the minimum resale price of a product, resulting in unfair competition. Although the laws are restrictive, a manufacturer has some latitude to adopt a policy regarding a desired level of resale prices and to deal only with retailers that independently decide to follow that policy. A manufacturer can also cease dealings with a retailer that breaches the manufacturer's resale price maintenance policy.

Tie-in sales. A *tie-in* (also called a *tying agreement*) is an arrangement in which a company tries to sell one product on the condition that the customer purchases a second product. In some cases, the customer does not want the second product or can buy it elsewhere at a lower price. Such a tie-in sale may prevent the consumer from shopping for the product at a competitor; thus, it can potentially harm competition and therefore is illegal.

Consumer Protection Acts

Before the 1900s, merchants followed the *caveat emptor* doctrine: "Let the buyer beware." In the early 1900s, Congress passed a series of laws designed to protect consumers from increasingly exploitive business practices. The slogan for consumers became *caveat vendor*, meaning "Let the seller beware." The Federal Food Drug and Cosmetic Act (passed in 1906 and amended in 1938 and 1997) protects consumers from adulteration of food and misbranding of food, drugs, cosmetics, and therapeutic devices.

In the 1960s and 1970s, as consumers gained more power relative to government and business, a series of laws were enacted that have greatly affected the way businesses interact with their customers. The following sections describe these laws.

Fair Packaging and Labeling Act (1966). This law prevents deceptive product labeling and makes it easier for consumers to make product comparisons due to the required information on product labels.

The FDA Food Safety Modernization Act (FSMA) (2011). The purpose of the FSMA is to ensure the U.S. food supply is safe by shifting the focus of federal regulators from responding to contamination to preventing it.

Truth in Lending Act (1968). This law requires creditors to disclose all costs and terms of credit in a clear manner. Although the disclosure process still confuses some consumers, if you read the terms carefully, you will see that credit agreements must contain information about interest rates.

Fair Credit Reporting Act (1971). This act gives consumers the right to inspect their credit reports and to correct mistakes found in these reports. This act was amended in 1997 to require the major credit reporting agencies to include a toll-free telephone number at which customer service personnel are accessible to answer consumer questions. Under the amendment, consumer credit bureaus must take actions to investigate customer disputes within thirty days.

Credit Accountability, Responsibility and Disclosure (CARD) Act of 2009. The purpose of the act is "to establish fair and transparent practices relating to the extension of credit under an open end consumer credit plan" (HR 627, 2009). The CARD Act includes consumer protections such as limited interest rate hikes, the right to opt out or reject significant changes in terms on accounts, bans on issuing credit cards to anyone under 21 without a co-signer or proof of income to repay debt, reasonable time to pay monthly bills, clearer due dates and late fee restrictions (Prater, 2012). Credit card companies must also give card holders 45 days notice of changes to the account terms.

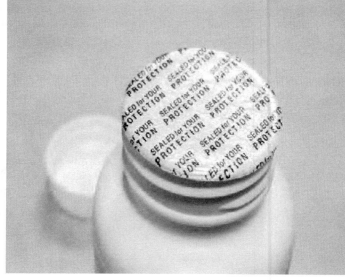

Source: toons17/Shutterstock.com

Consumer Product Safety Act (1972). This act monitors and regulates product safety issues, safety guidelines, and banning and recalling of products.

The Consumer Product Safety Improvement Act (CPSIA) of 2008. This act requires that nearly all children's products comply with all applicable children's product safety rules, are tested for compliance and have permanent tracking information on the product and its packaging.

Fair Credit Billing Act (1975). This law was enacted to help consumers correct mistakes made on their billing statements.

Magnuson-Moss Warranty Act (1975). This act requires that warranties be written in easy-to-understand language.

Equal Credit Opportunity Act (1975). This act makes it illegal to discriminate in any aspect of the credit transaction due to sex, marital status, race, national origin, religion, age, or receipt of public assistance.

Fair Debt Collection Practices Act (1978). This act makes it illegal to harass people when attempting to collect payments. The act also prohibits lying or using unfair tactics to collect payments (amended in 1996).

Patient Protection and Affordable Care Act of 2010. This act aims to increase the quality of healthcare and make health care affordable for all Americans.

Corporate Disclosure Acts

Like all companies, retailers have an obligation to disclose relevant information to the consumer. In general, advertising must tell the truth and claims made about products and services must be substantiated. The FTC has determined that a particular practice is deceptive if it is likely to mislead consumers and affect their behavior or decisions about the product or service.

A practice is deemed unfair if the injury it causes (or is likely to cause) is substantial and not outweighed by other benefits or not reasonably avoidable. Third parties, such as advertising agencies, web designers, or direct marketers, may be held liable for making or disseminating deceptive representations if they participate in the preparation or distribution of such representations, especially if they knew in advance that the practice was deceptive and/or unfair.

Electronic Fund Transfer Act (EFTA). This act requires businesses to adopt practices that protect information transferred electronically. Liability limits are also specified for losses caused by unauthorized transfers. Banks and other financial institutions were affected by this law in 1999 when the Gramm-Leach-Bliley Act (GLBA) amended the EFTA and made it necessary for automated teller machine (ATM) operators to disclose their service fees on or near the ATM. The amendment requires that disclosure of the fee be made before the transaction is completed so the consumer can cancel the transaction if she or he chooses not to pay the fee (Saunders, 2003).

Franchise and Business Opportunity Rule. This rule requires franchise and business opportunity sellers to give detailed disclosure information to help buyers make informed decisions. The disclosure documents should include names, addresses, and telephone numbers of at least ten previous purchasers who live closest to the inquirer, a fully audited financial statement of the seller, the background and experience of the business's key executives, the costs of starting and maintaining the business, and the responsibilities the potential purchaser and the seller will have to each other once the franchise is purchased. Several franchisers have websites containing this information. For example, Dunkin' Donuts has a special website for people interested in starting a franchise (www.dunkinfranchising.com). The website provides the steps to follow to obtain a franchise as well as information about the franchise.

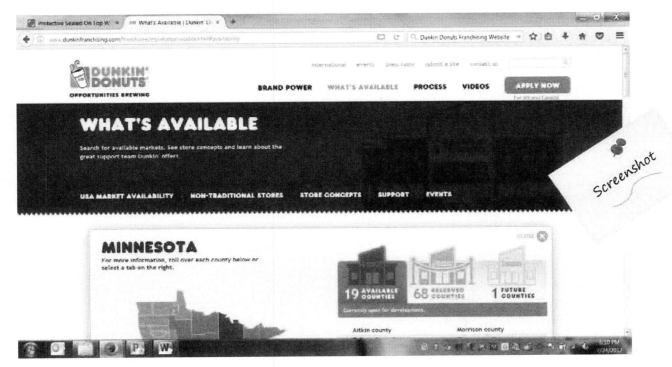

Indian Arts and Crafts Amendments Act of 2010. The new law strengthens the Indian Arts and Crafts Act, which makes it illegal to misrepresent any art or craft product as American-Indian-made, an Indian product, or the product of a particular Indian tribe.

Testimonials and Endorsements. These guides require that testimonials and endorsements reflect typical consumer experiences, unless otherwise clearly and conspicuously stated. The statement has to be more than the typical "not all consumers will get the same results." Also, a testimonial or an endorsement cannot be made unless the advertiser can substantiate the claim and reveals any connections between the endorser and the company. For example, many actors providing testimonials must disclose whether they are getting paid for their testimonials.

Wool and Textile Products Acts. These acts require companies to disclose country-of-origin information in all ads for textile and wool products. In addition, ads that say or imply anything about fiber content must disclose the generic fiber names in order of predominance by weight.

"Made in the U.S.A." To be able to carry the label "Made in the U.S.A.," a product must be "all or virtually all made in the United States."

Regulations Specific to E-tailing

Some laws and regulations apply more to e-tailers than to brick-and-mortar businesses. These are described in the following sections.

Mail or Telephone-Order Merchandise Rule. This rule requires that any business using the telephone or catalogs as a channel ship products as promised or within thirty days. If a business cannot ship when promised, it must notify the customer, who then has the right to cancel the order. The Rule was amended in 2011 to make clear that Internet purchases were included. The FTC frequently files suit against companies that are in violation of this rule. For example, the FTC filed a complaint against *Bargains & Deals Magazine* alleging that the company made misrepresentations over the Internet to sell merchandise and then either failed to deliver the products as promised or, in some cases, did not send the merchandise at all (US FTC…, 2001).

Children's Online Privacy Protection Act (COPPA). This act makes it illegal to collect information from children under age thirteen without parental permission. Any company operating on the Internet that targets children must supply notice of its information collection practices, the type of information it collects, how it is used, parental permission prior to collection of personal information, and information on confidentiality of the information (Davis, 2002). The act was revised in 2013 with stricter rules.

Market Place Fairness Act. Recent laws have been proposed that will force online retailers to collect tax on purchases sold to people in states that collect sales tax. If passed, online retailers will need to make major adjustments to billing practices and consumers will no longer be able to avoid paying taxes.

Sarbanes-Oxley Act

In July 2002, in response to the wave of ethical breaches by both retailers and e-tailers, President Bush signed a law designed to curtail corporate fraud. The Sarbanes-Oxley Act (also called SOX or Sarbox) quadruples sentences for accounting fraud, imposes restrictions on accounting firms that do both consulting work and financial statement audits for the same corporation, requires company executives to personally vouch for the accuracy of their companies' reports, creates a felony for securities fraud that carries a twenty-five-year prison term and places new restraints on corporate officers, and establishes a federal oversight board for the accounting industry. The new law is the greatest overhaul of corporate law since the aftermath of the 1929 stock market crash (Loven, 2002).

As we have seen, there are many laws of which retailers must be aware. Smaller retailers typically monitor local, state, and national laws and determine which ones apply to them. Larger retailers typically have a legal department that handles all legal actions for and against the company.

Summary

Many ethics, rules, and laws pertain to the operation of a retail business. The retailer must be aware of these laws and rules for every geographic area in which it competes. In addition to federal laws, the retailer must abide by regional and local rules and regulations that affect the business, as well as international laws if the retailer has global operations. Retailers engaged in interstate commerce come under the purview of federal laws. Retailers involved in intrastate commerce may also be subject to some federal laws and must answer to the state and locality where they do business.

Although the concepts of laws and ethics are related, they actually differ somewhat. Ethics involve concepts of what is right and wrong and are often based on moral and religious beliefs. Laws are rules established by society. Differences in ethical perspectives explain why different people can have differing views on whether an act is right or wrong. In retailing, ethical conflicts can arise from the conflict between profit and principles. Retailers are often under pressure to show profits, and this can cloud ethical judgments.

Employee and customer theft are the two biggest sources of inventory shrinkage. Retailers can reduce theft by implementing loss prevention strategies such as pre-employment screening, asset controls, supervision of the selling floor, and employing devices to deter theft. Internet fraud is a concern in e-tailing. Customers are especially concerned about the security of their online transactions.

There are several laws that affect retailing. Consequences for breaking these laws range from paying a fine to imprisonment. Retail laws have the greatest effect on retail tactics (pricing, integrated marketing communications, and customer service). Nonetheless, every area in the IRM flow chart has the potential to be affected by ethics and laws. The area where laws and ethics become most apparent is the situational analysis.

The ethical and legal environments have played, and will continue to play, an important role in the retail industry.

Terms

acceptable profit perspective	A perspective on the relationship between profit and principles that assumes companies want to maximize principles but are restricted because the market demands that profitability reach a certain level to ensure financial continuity.
applied ethics	The study of ethics that involves analyzing specific instances of ethical dilemmas.
horizontal agreement	A restrictive agreement between two competitors in the same market.
integrated perspective	A perspective of the relationship between profit and principles stating that firms strive for an optimal balance between profits and principles.

Internet fraud	The use of the Internet to present fraudulent solicitation to prospective victims, conduct fraudulent transactions, or transmit the proceeds of fraud to financial institutions or others connected with the scheme.
license to operate perspective	A perspective on the relationship between profit and principles stating that firms must have a minimum value of principles required by society to obtain a license to operate.
metaethics	The study of the origin of ethical concepts and theories.
normative ethics	The study of ethics using criteria to determine whether certain behavior is right or wrong.
organized retail crime (ORC)	The large-scale theft of consumer items.
phishing	Tricking people into disclosing personal information, usually through e-mail or the Internet, and using the information to commit fraud.
servicemark	A firm's brand name, symbol, or design used to identify the company to other businesses and consumers as the source of a service.
tie-in	A practice in which a company tries to sell one product on the condition that the customer purchase a second product. (Also called a *tying agreement*.)
trademark	A firm's brand name, symbol, or design used to identify the company to other businesses and consumers as the source of a product.
vertical agreement	An agreement, between at least two parties, operating at different levels of the supply chain, that relates to the conditions under which the parties may purchase, sell, or resell goods or services.
wardrobing	The return of used, non-defective merchandise like special event apparel or electronics after a major sporting event.
win-win perspective	A perspective on the relationship between profit and principles that assumes the more ethically a business operates, the higher its profits will be.

Discussion Questions

1. What is the difference between ethics and laws?
2. Explain the profit-principle relationship.
3. What are some ways to reduce the amount of employee theft in a retail outlet?
4. Why do you think there has been such a large increase in Internet fraud? What do you think can be done to reduce this fraud?
5. Explain the concept of a retail price maintenance agreement.
6. Why do you think horizontal agreements in retailing are restricted and sometimes illegal?
7. Do you believe the government should allow vertical agreements for businesses? Why or why not?

Exercises

There are many websites that discuss business and professional ethics. Choose three of the sites below to explore and answer the following questions:

1. Do you think organizations that promote professional ethics are effective? Why or why not?

2. What should employees do when one of their colleagues or a company executive is being investigated for ethical violations?

3. Write your own code of ethics reflecting on what you expect from yourself in terms of ethical behavior.

4. Find a code of ethics for a business. Evaluate the code and make suggestions for improvement.

- **Association for Practical and Professional Ethics** (http://appe.indiana.edu/)
- **Ethics Web (Canada)** (http://www.ethicsweb.ca/)
- **Business for Social Responsibility** (www.bsr.org)
- **E-Center for Business Ethics** (http://e-businessethics.com/)
- **Edmond J. Safra Center for Ethics** (http://www.ethics.harvard.edu/)
- **Ethical Trading Initiative** (www.ethicaltrade.org)
- **Institute for Global Ethics** (http://www.globalethics.org/)
- **International Business Ethics Institute** (http://business-ethics.org/)
- **International Center for Ethics in Business** (https://business.ku.edu/international-center-ethics-business)

Case

Counterfeit Coupon Rings

The sale or transfer of coupons is against most manufacturers' coupon redemption policies. People out to commit fraud usually purchase coupons and attempt to redeem the coupons without purchasing any products. Many times crime rings are involved. When caught, people involved with coupon fraud are charged and often convicted.

In 2012 Robin Ramirez, a 40-year-old woman from Phoenix, AZ, was arrested for running the largest counterfeit-coupon enterprise in U.S. history. She owned 26 vehicles, a boat and three condominiums that she paid for with money obtained from the fraud. Ramirez sold over 240 brands, which totaled $40 million in fake coupons, from her website. Authorities caught her in 2013 and she was sentenced to two years in state prison. In addition she may have to pay up to $5 million in restitution. Her husband was convinced that she was running a legitimate business because the items bought with the money were stored in an airport hangar.

Ramirez started out selling fake coupons on eBay and in 2007 she launched a website called savvyshoppersite.com. Companies affected by the scam joined forces with the Coupon Information Corporation to hire private investigators. The coupons were tracked to Phoenix, AZ. Despite the use of fake identities and addresses, it was eventually proven that Ramirez was the leader of the ring.

To pull off the fraud, Ramirez collected product coupons. She used a foreign printing company to produce the coupons in mass quantities. She then sold these coupons online for half the value, often adding a counterfeit hologram that signaled the coupon was real. Coupons ranged from $2 to $70. The coupons were high quality so retailers accepted them. It was not until the coupon reached the manufacturer that the fake was detected (Gunter, 2013).

The Coupon Information Corporation (CIC) (www.couponinformationcenter.com) lists the following tips to avoid counterfeit coupons:

1. Use the coupons obtained from the newspaper, manufacturer's website or an authorized distributor

2. Never pay money for a coupon

3. Do not download coupons from Internet forums

4. If a friend e-mails you coupons, especially high value or free product coupons, the coupons are most likely counterfeit.

5. Most manufacturers follow common sense practices about Internet Print-at-Home Coupons; for example, the coupon itself should not be visible on your computer screen.

6. Check the counterfeit coupons listed on the CIC website.

Questions:

1. Could you tell the difference between a real and counterfeit coupon?

2. How can retailers and manufacturers prevent coupon fraud?

3. Why would someone attempt coupon fraud?

4. Is two years in prison enough?

5. Why is coupon fraud so prevalent?

Sources: Coupon Information Corporation (2013). Access at www.couponinformationcenter.com; Chan, C. (2013). Phoenix Woman Led Largest Counterfeit-Coupon Enterprise in U.S. History. Retrieved from AZCentral.com at http://www.azcentral.com/business/consumer/articles/20130507phoenix-woman-led-largest-counterfeit-coupon-enterprise-us-history.html; Gunter C. (2013). The Coupon Lady: Counterfeit Coupon Scheme. *The Augusta Chronicle* (June 6). Retrieved from http://chronicle.augusta.com/news/business/smart-shopper/2013-06-06/coupon-lady-counterfeit-coupon-scheme

References

ADT Security Services, Inc. (2013). Retrieved from www.adt.com.

Christian, S. (2016). Zara Is Being Sued for USD5 Million over "Deceptive" Pricing. *Esquire* (Aug 25). Retrieved from http://www.esquire.my/style/Fashion/zara-5-million-pricing-lawsuit

Davis, E. (2011). Dr. Hollinger Shares Preliminary NRSS Findings. National Retail Federation (Jun 14). Retrieved from http://blog.nrf.com/2011/06/14/dr-hollinger-shares-preliminary-findings-from-the-nrss/

Davis, J. J. (2002). Marketing to Children Online: A Manager's Guide to the Children's Online Privacy Protection Act. *S.A.M. Advanced Management Journal*, 67 (Autumn 2002), pp. 11-21.

Ex-Executive of Rite Aid Assisted Prosecutors in Building Fraud Case; Retailing: Timothy Noonan Agreed to Record Sessions with Former Chief Executive and Chief Counsel, Defendants Seek to Have Tapes Banned (2002). *Los Angeles Times*, (Sept 11), p. C3.

Fieser, J. (2001). Ethics. Internet Encyclopedia of Philosophy. Retrieved from www.utm.edu/research/iep/e/ethics.htm.

Finklea, K. M. (2012). Organized Retail Crime. Congressional Research Service (Jun 16). Retrieved from http://www.fas.org/sgp/crs/misc/R41118.pdf

Forsyth, D. R. (1980). A Taxonomy of Ethical Ideologies. *Journal of Personality and Social Psychology*, 39:1 (1980), pp. 175-184.

Graafland, J. J. (2002). Profits and Principles: Four Perspectives. *Journal of Business Ethics*, 35 (Feb), pp. 293-305.

H.R. 627 (111th): Credit Card Accountability Responsibility and Disclosure Act of 2009. 111th Congress, 2009–2010. Text as of Aug 24, 2010 (Passed Congress/Enrolled Bill). Retrieved from http://www.govtrack.us/congress/bills/111/hr627/text

International Law Dictionary and Directory (2002). Retrieved from www.august1.com/pubs/dict/l.htm.

Ivy Sea Online (n.d.). Defining and Communicating Ethics in Your Business. Retrieved from www.ivysea.com.

KSE FOCUS (2013). Deceptive Floral Advertising. Congress.org (July11). Retrieved from http://congress.org/2013/07/11/deceptive-floral-advertising/#sthash.eRMkufWj.dpuf

Loven, J. (2002). Bush Enacts Law Cracking Down on Corporate and Accounting Fraud. Associated Press, (Jul 31). Retrieved from www.yahoo.com.

National Anti-Organized Retail Crime Association, Inc. (2017). Retrieved from http://naorca.org/

Internet Crime Complaint Center (2016). 2016 Internet Crime Report. Prepared by the Federal Bureau of Investigation. Retrieved from https://pdf.ic3.gov/2016_IC3Report.pdf

Perry, A. (2011). The Return of the Blood Diamond. (And We Don't Mean the Movie). Time World (Dec 5). Retrieved from http://world.time.com/2011/12/05/the-return-of-the-blood-diamond-and-we-dont-mean-the-movie/

Prater, C. (2012). Credit Card Act of 2009 into Law May 22, 2009. What the Credit Care Reform Law Means to You (Jun 13). Creditcards.com. Retrieved from http://www.creditcards.com/credit-card-news/help/what-the-new-credit-card-rules-mean-6000.php

Smith A. S. (2016). Retail Inventory Shrinkage Increased to $45.2 Billion in 2015. Press release (Jun 13). Retrieved from the National Retail Federation at https://nrf.com/media/press-releases/retail-inventory-shrinkage-increased-452-billion-2015

Return Fraud to Cost Retailers $3.5 Billion this Holiday Season (2011). National Retail Federation press release (Nov 10). Retrieved from http://www.nrf.com/modules.php?name=News&op=viewlive&sp_id=1243

Rite Aid Annual Report (2013). Retrieved from https://content.riteaid.com/www.riteaid.com/w-content/images/company/investors/anrpts/annual13.pdf

Rite Aid Annual Report (2016). Retrieved from https://content.riteaid.com/www.riteaid.com/w-content/images/company/investors/anrpts/annual16.pdf

Rite Aid homepage at www.riteaid.com.

Robaton, A. (2013). The Growth of Theft, Inc. Shopping Centers Today (May). Retrieved from http://sct.epubxp.com/i/122387/187

Robinson, D. (2017). Outsmarting Employee Theft. *PSN Pool and Spa News* (Jan 24). Retrieved from http://www.poolspanews.com/business/retail-management/outsmarting-employee-theft_o

Saunders S. (2003). The Rising Role of ATMs in Alaska. *Alaska Business Monthly*, 19 (Jan 1), p. 30.

Smith, S. (2011). Can Rite Aid Recover? Many in the Midstate are Depending on It. The Patriot News (May 8). Retrieved from http://www.pennlive.com/midstate/index.ssf/2011/05/can_rite_aid_recover_many_in_t.html

Southwick, R. (2013). Continuing Its Comeback, Rite Aid Expands Online Access to Doctors. The Patriot News, (Mar 2). Retrieved from http://www.pennlive.com/midstate/index.ssf/2013/03/rite_aid_offering_online_acces.html

Taulli, T. (2017). Is Rite Aid Corporation (RAD) Stock Worth the Risk Anymore? MSN Investor Place (Apr 3). Retrieved from http://www.msn.com/en-us/money/topstocks/is-rite-aid-corporation-rad-stock-worth-the-risk-anymore/ar-BBzhywy

The Federal Trade Commission (2013). Fact Sheet. Retrieved from http://www.ftc.gov/bc/antitrust/factsheets/FactSheet_AntiTrust.pdf

U.S. Department of Justice (2013). Retrieved from http://www.justice.gov/atr/public/div_stats/antitrust-enfor-consumer.pdf

US FTC: Bargains & Deals Magazine Charged with Internet Fraud: Company Allegedly Misrepresented Products, Did Not Deliver Merchandise to Consumers (2001). *M2 Presswire*, (Oct 17), p. 1.

Voreacos, D. (2002). U.S. Denies Ethics Violations in Rite Aid Probe. *Los Angeles Times*, (Oct 15), p. C6.

Chapter 15

Retailing Trends and Best Practices

"Progress is impossible without change; and those who cannot change their minds, cannot change anything."

~ George Bernard Shaw

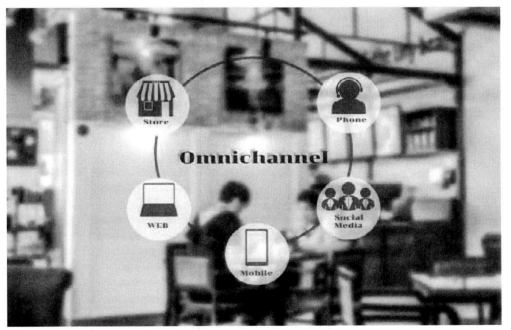

Source: Montri Nipitvittaya/Shutterstock.com

CHAPTER OBJECTIVES

After completing this chapter you will be able to:

- Outline current trends in retailing.
- Describe some best practices in the retail environment.
- Apply the integrated retail management flow chart to a hypothetical retail outlet.

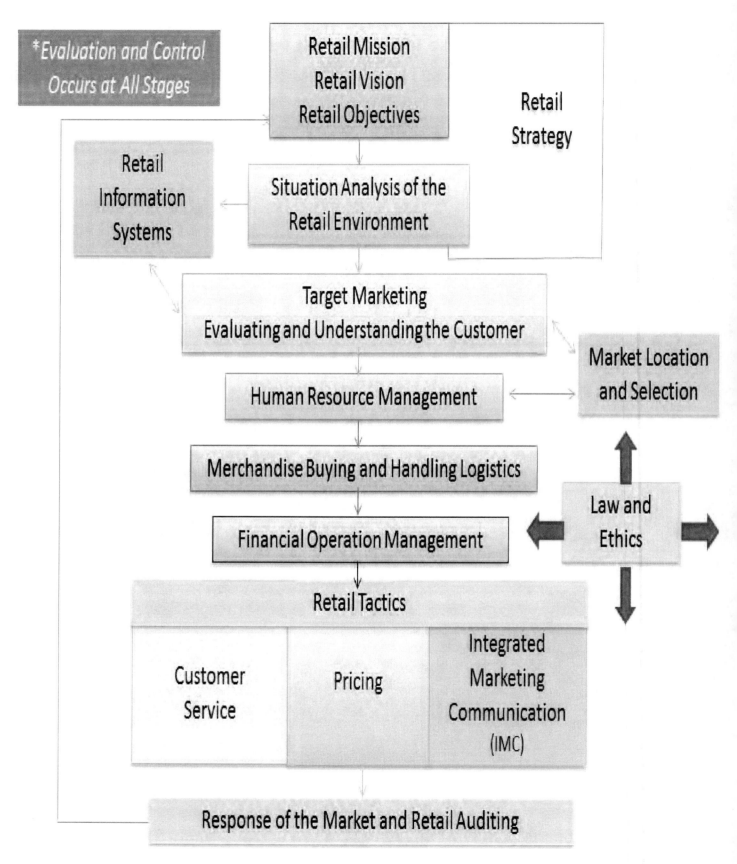

Build-A-Bear Creates Memories

Build-A-Bear Workshop (www.buildabear.com) is a specialty store whose mission is "to bring the Teddy Bear to life." The company was started in 1997 by Maxine Clark, who served as "Chief Executive Bear" until June, 2013. The retailer has more than 400 Build-A-Bear Workshops worldwide and has company and franchise stores. Children of all ages can build their own stuffed animal in stores and through the interactive website (www.buildabearville.com). Since the first bear was made at the St. Louis Galleria mall store, there have been over 125 million more created. People who enter a store are greeted by a Bear Builder associate who guides the process to ensure satisfaction. The price for a stuffed animal is as little as $15. People can customize the toys with voice, a name and clothing. Each bear comes with a heart inserted by the creator before it's sewn up. The retailer also hosts birthday parties and events that increase interactions with their target market. Build-a-Bear Workshop is a leader in creating a retail experience that is unforgettable.

Introduction

The first fourteen chapters of this book covered issues and systems involved in developing an effective IRM plan. This chapter highlights current and future issues that will both challenge and excite retailers in the twenty-first century. Each topic covered affects the situational analysis of the flow chart, as well as the retailer's strategies and tactics.

What should a retailer expect in these changing times? What innovations are on the horizon? Discussed in this chapter are trends in retailing and best practices. This chapter also provides an example of the development and execution of an integrated retail management plan by a hypothetical retailer.

Many environmental issues influence the IRM program. A retailer's effective response to these issues will contribute to its success. One such issue is diversity in the retail environment.

Retail Trends

There are many global trends that will affect the retail industry. Just as demographics are changing the retailing environment, so are these three types of influences. A retailer should keep the following trends in mind when creating and maintaining the IRM flow chart.

According to *Global Powers of Retailing 2017* (Deloitte, 2017), five retail industry trends include less is more, "following" economy, "retailization" of the world, on-demand shopping and fulfillment, and exponential living. Other trends discussed include omni-channel retailing growth, lack of privacy, evolution of brick-and-mortar stores and the sharing economy. Let's look at each.

Less Is More

Instead of accumulating things, people are turning toward quality over quantity. More often people are seeking experiences instead of things. According to a poll of millennials conducted by The Harris Group, 72 percent of those polled would prefer to spend money on experiences or events versus things. Those surveyed believe that experiences increase connections to other people (Saiidi, 2016). Retailers who create experiences that connect with the brand are better positioned to succeed. Customer service will be especially important as a differentiator.

The Following Economy

Social media is increasingly becoming a way for people to expose and reflect on their personal brand. People share consumption experiences on social media including where and what they are eating, where they stay while traveling, what they are wearing, and what they would like to possess. In addition to following celebrities, people are interested in creating their own following and want "sharable" experiences. FoMO (fear of missing out) is a big motivator with social media.

FoMO is "a pervasive apprehension that others might be having rewarding experiences from which one is absent" and, as a result, people want to "stay continuously connected with what others are doing" (Przbylski, Murayama, DeHaan and Gladwell, 2013). Many people who sleep with their cell phones nearby may be suffering from FoMO. According to Dr. Sherry Turkle (2012), Professor of the Social Studies of Science and Technology at Massachusetts Institute of Technology, because of social media, texting and email, we are "getting used to a new way of being alone together." She says we are connected but alone.

Source: Sky Cinema/Shutterstock.com

To capitalize on the following economy, retailers need to create experiences that are sharable such as fashion shows and cooking demonstrations (Macy's); Lady Gaga present at a store opening (H&M); lectures and book signings (Barnes and Noble). It's also important for retailers to be active on social media. Activities such as live broadcasts, engaging customers to post their experiences, and creating exclusivity, such a limited product offering, help to engage people.

The Retailization of the World

It is becoming increasingly difficult to identify a retailer due to the blurring of channels and market fragmentation in the industry. Non-traditional retailing will become more prevalent as new retailers enter the landscape with differentiated offerings. Retailers who adapt and re-invent themselves are more likely to survive. One trend related to the re-tailization of the world is the growth in direct-to-consumer (DTC) sales.

Due to technology advances, manufacturers and wholesalers are bypassing the retailer and selling directly to consumers. The number of manufacturers selling to consumers is growing yearly and includes Tesla Motors, REI, Under Armour and Nike. Nike plans to grow the DTC part of their business by 250 percent in the next five years, projecting sales in DTC will reach $16 billion by 2020 (Hopwood, 2016). Advantages of the direct-to-consumer method include increased sales, increasing touch points with consumers, building the brand relationship, and control over more aspects of the supply chain (Hendell, 2016). For retailers, the DTC trend from manufacturers and wholesalers means even more competition and a different approach to these channel relationships.

On-Demand Shopping and Fulfillment

Customers will become more demanding and expectations of on-demand products will continue to rise. Apparel, grocery, automotive and the service industry are adapting to this trend. Several food retailers have delivery options, and many retailers are offering same-day delivery of online purchases. A study by Temando found that 80 percent of those surveyed want same-day shipping, while 61 percent wanted their packages within one to three hours of placing an order. Unfortunately, many consumers surveyed did not want to pay extra for the faster delivery. The study concluded that customer expectations were higher than what is being provided by retailers (Lindner, 2016).

Retailers will continue to rely on customization to increase sales and gain customer loyalty. For example, Bath Junkie (www.bathjunkie.com), a franchise specialty shop, allows customers to create their own lotions, soaps, and body washes by mixing and matching hundreds of different fragrances. In 2000, Nike, Inc. created NikeiD, which allows users to design their own athletic shoes. In Nike's 2016 Annual Report, the company reports an increased focus on personalization through their Nike+ app. The app offers a personal store, targeted offers, invitations to exclusive events and on-demand coaching.

Personalization also helps retailers create a brand experience and engage the customer in experiential retailing and in a "brand story." According to Interbrand (2013), "Now that the idea of shopping can't be managed as an event, the brand experience is too important—and holds too much promise—to be ignored. It's critical that retailers focus on enhancing brand experiences no matter where they are."

Related to personalization is "subscription commerce" where people subscribe to a service that delivers product(s) monthly. Companies such as Dollar Shave Club (razors), Wittlebee (kid's cloths), JustFab (shoes), Doorganics (organic food), and BREAKbox by blissmo (snack food) have grown in members. Subscription commerce is a reboot from many of the early day subscription clubs like the Columbia Record Club, where members received an album each month (and would have to return it if they didn't like the selection).

Source: Mopic/Shutterstock.com

Exponential Living

Driverless cars, robots, wearable technology and artificial intelligence are all technologies that continue to impact retailing. Technology has changed, and will continue to change, the retailing industry. Smartphone technology will continue to be a major force in multi- and omni-channel approaches. Channels of distribution that are available for selling are colliding. This will change the way consumers interact with retailers. There will be more interactive technology like digital fitting rooms and kiosks in stores that allow customers to order, check inventory and pay. Big Data (large volumes of data) analytics will grow as access to information and analysis of information becomes easier.

An area of growth is facial and emotional recognition programs. Customer service call centers are using speech analysis to detect personalities and emotional states. Facial expression analysis is also linked to detecting emotions. Knowledge of emotions helps retailers improve the customer experience by better understanding reactions at a given time in the buying process (Lawlor, 2017). In the future, consumers might pay through facial recognition programs. Already Uniqul (www.uniqul.com), a Finnish company, has created a process whereby those who sign up can pay by standing in front of a scanner that matches their face to the company's database. The company envisions a day when customers can shop without wallets; they will pay simply by being in a store. Other uses of facial technology are to notify staff that a celebrity or VIP has entered the store and to customize the shopping experience. Facial recognition technology is being tested in the U.S. and U.K. and may someday become commonplace (Fell, 2013). Consumers will be able to pay much faster as radio frequency Identification technology becomes more affordable for retailers. Walmart is also experimenting with Scan & Go technology, which allows Walmart shoppers with iPhones to scan barcodes in a store and see a running total (Silverstein, 2013). In 2016, NEC announced it was conducting trials for cashless payment services using facial recognition technology. Once perfected, retailers will be able to collect money without using cash or credit cards. Some retailers, such as Saks Fifth Avenue, are using facial recognition programs for loss prevention.

Consumers will be able to shop whenever they choose as long as there is an Internet connection. Technology will make it easier to predict what consumers want. For example, Target scans purchases, e-mail activity on Target.com and more to determine when a customer is pregnant. Then it targets specific products to appeal to the expectant families (Duhigg, 2012).

Concerns about data privacy and security will continue to challenge retailers. The trade-off between privacy and convenience for consumers is a concern. Retailers will need to invest in security and educate customers on how information is protected.

Omni-Channel Retailing Growth

Integration of the multiple channels of distribution retailers use will continue to grow and will become a necessity. Retailers will improve technology to track consumers across channels to better communicate with their customers. The amount of data a smartphone can hold is steadily increasing, allowing consumers to store music, books and movies on their mobile devices. Retailers will use consumer data to provide more personalized shopping experiences. The information will be used to segment customers and manage customer relationships. Customers will continue to expect more personalized experiences.

The rise in omni-channel retailing is also related to the increase in mobile payment users. payment by 2020 (Rampton, 2016), and *Business Insider* (2016) predicts that by 2020 mobile payments will increase to $503 billion in sales, reflecting compound annual growth rate of 80 percent between 2015 and 2020.

Lack of Privacy

Although Americans are concerned with privacy, many are willing to share personal information if they can get something in return. According to a Pew research study, whether a person shares personal information in exchange for something depends on the deal and the circumstances. Trust and a knowledge of how their data are/were being used were key factors (Rainie and Duggan, 2016).

According to the International Telecommunication Union (2012), the Internet of Things (IoT) is a global infrastructure for the information society, enabling advanced services by interconnecting (physical and virtual) things based on existing and evolving interoperable information and communication technologies." In other words, it's the idea that everyday objects such as phones, watches and appliances are increasingly transferring data back and forth, often using Internet-enabled technology. As the Internet of Things (IoT) grows, privacy is an area of concern. Cybercriminals and hackers have more entry points to information as we become more connected. IoT makes it easier for companies to keep tabs on customers and for people to spy on each other. The concern about privacy is valid as the amount of information collected on consumers will continue to grow. For example, according to their annual report (2015), Facebook had 1.04 billion daily active users (DAUs) on average in December, 2015. Of those 934 million DAU accessed Facebook from a mobile device. Facebook experiences an incoming daily rate of 600 terabytes (TB) and their warehouse stores over 300 petabytes (PB) of Hive data (Vagata and Wilfong, 2014). A terabyte equals more than one trillion bytes and holds the equivalent of about 1,500 CD-ROM discs. A petabyte equivalent to the content of 1.5 million CD-ROM discs. One PB contains over 1 quadrillion bytes and is equal to about 1,024 TB (Fisher, 2017).

The Sharing Economy

The sharing economy (also known as collaborative consumption) refers to a system that allows shared access to under-utilized assets. Information technology is leveraged to allow individuals, companies, non-profits and governments to share information about rentals or asset trading opportunities. The idea is to increase value of the goods and services for all involved (Sundararajan, 2013). Growth of the sharing economy is expected to grow globally from $14 billion in 2014 to $335 billion by 2025 (Yaraghi and Ravi, 2016). Companies like Airbnb (www.airbnb), Rent the Runway

Source: Georgejmclittle/Shutterstock.com

(www.renttherunway.com) and Task Rabbit (www.taskrabbit.com) match up owners and renters with everything from renting a room to running errands. Technology used includes GPS technology, social networking sites and online payment systems.

Technology reduces the transaction costs, which makes sharing cost effective and easy (The Rise of the Sharing Economy, 2013). Growth in this business model will increase as people get more comfortable with the model; and technology makes the sharing economy easier. For example, Airbnb matches thousands of people with rooms in 192 countries and over 65,000 cities. Beds are provided by private individuals at the prices decided by the renter.

Proponents of the model believe that collaborative consumption promotes environmental sustainability through more efficient use of resources (Hull, 2013). In the future, more companies and individual people will make a living through businesses based on the sharing economy.

The Changing Consumer

In an editorial for the Center for Retailing Studies, two authors looked at trends within the retailing industry. By conducting an in-depth study of these trends, the authors came up with trends occurring with consumers (Scansaroli and Szymanski, 2002). Consumer power, diversity, changing wants and needs, and changes in behaviors will impact retailing.

Consumer Power

The availability of information via the Internet has empowered consumers to demand fairness in their transactions. In addition, consumers are placing more value on their time and thus are increasingly intolerant of retailers that do not respect their time. In general, consumers are more demanding and seek ways to control the shopping situation. As a result, consumers may become less store loyal and more willing to go elsewhere to shop when their demands are not met. Social media has given consumers a platform to display their likes and dislikes of retailers which, in turn, gives them power never before experienced.

Source: Rawpixel.com/Shutterstock.com

Diversity

Understanding the diverse base of consumers is important. Although diversity has always been a part of the environment, its magnitude continues to intensify. Culture, race, and ethnicity as well as the changing composition of the family are just a few aspects of diversity that the retailer must consider. Religious diversity is also an aspect that requires retailers to think about their products and food selections. Many food retailers have aisles of food dedicated to ethnic and religious preferences.

The growth of the world's population and the lengthening lifespans of people in developed countries will also impact retailing. Implications for retailers include growth in the health care industry and a wealth of new products geared toward an increasingly older population. Costs of health care are expected to rise and may create a crisis in health-care financing and services. As the senior population expands, there will be a need for doctors specializing in diseases of the elderly.

Another societal trend deals with gender. According to the National Center for Education Statistics (2013), since 1988, the number of women in post-baccalaureate programs has exceeded the number of men. As more educated women enter the work force and fill higher-level positions, an increase in child-care and other family-care businesses is likely. There will be a greater need than ever before for services and businesses that can accommodate this trend. More women are also becoming the primary earner in households. In 2013, 10 percent of men were stay-at-home dads, the highest percent ever (Peacock and Marsden, 2013). Millennial fathers are increasingly active in shopping activities. Younger fathers are buying 25 percent more groceries than their forefathers (Millennial Dads..., 2016).

Desire for Both Stimulation and Sanctuary

Because consumers have less time, they want to get the most out of the time they do have. In addition, consumers have developed a desire for more speed and excitement. On the other hand, consumers also want to be left alone *when* they choose to be left alone. In other words, consumers will want both greater stimulation and greater sanctuary. It is up to the retailer to satisfy those wants (Scansaroli and Szymanski, 2002).

Behavioral Changes

Because of increasing diversity and the redefinition of households, consumers are creating new "codes" or norms from which to operate. Although some carryover from past norms exists, new norms are slowly replacing many older norms, paving the way for new values. Thus, consumers have new codes of conduct and create norms and behaviors from situation to situation as they reinvent themselves (Scansaroli and Szymanski, 2002). Technology has changed people's behaviors in ways that have never been imagined. Retailers must track these changes and be responsive to the changing behaviors.

Best Practices

Profound changes are taking place, and will continue to occur, in the retail industry. Although the future is difficult to predict, forthcoming trends in retailing will focus on demographics, geographic convenience, time convenience, increased food expenditures away from home, rapid changes in information technology and the evolution of the traditional store. In addition, retailers will find a convergence of all channels of distribution and communication.

In 2012, the customer analytics company Parature listed five best practices in retailing that are still relevant:

1. Simplicity
2. Transparency
3. Accessibility
4. Making Every Experience Count
5. Using Social Media

Let's take a look at each area.

Source: mama_mia/Shutterstock.com

Simplicity

Simplicity means focusing on what's important to the customer. Although there is a lot of technology available, retailers must remember to make the store (online or otherwise) easy to use. Even with technology, it's important to make sure the most basic forms of communication, such as phone support, are also available. The design of the store, website or app is also important and it must be easy for the customer to navigate across channels. An example of simplicity is the trend of consumers demanding more simplified food ingredients. Retailers are highlighting natural and organic products to appeal to this desire.

Transparency

It's important for retailers to be upfront about costs, taxes, inventory, wait time etc. By doing so the customer is more confident in the retailer and trusts the brand more. Customer feedback and satisfaction remain important areas of best practices. Many retailers allow customers to post and access reviews of the products sold. The use of feedback systems will increase the value of customer concerns and allow retailers to better understand their changing customer segments.

Accessibility

Today retailers need to have a *physical or cyber* presence where their customer base is located. This means being innovative in communicating with customers. Accessibility also means becoming more mobile to be physically present where customers gather. Creating a seamless shopping experience across channels is important and related to accessibility. More stores are allowing customers to pick up products bought online from a physical store. The ability to check product availability before going to a store is also important (Accenture Consulting, 2016). Delivery services will continue to grow. One area of growth is seen in online grocery shopping, which will increase as grocery retailers adapt to the demand. According to a Food Marketing Institute/Nielsen report, by 2025 the share of online grocery spending could reach 20 percent, representing $100 billion in sales (Daniels, 2017).

Source: AlexAranda/Shutterstock.com

Making Every Experience Count

Retailers can differentiate themselves from the thousands of options available to consumers by making sure every experience with the brand is relevant. Retailers will have to engage the customer to create a passion for the retail outlet. The marketing concept will need to be modified from satisfying customers to "wowing" customers, which is the basis of the extended marketing concept. *Customer-centric cultures* require the creation of a performance-driven culture that is focused on individual consumers rather than the mass market (Sheth, Sisodia and Sharma, 2002). Many companies measure customer-centric practices. One of the first companies to measure online satisfaction was CustomerRespect.com. The company developed a Customer-Centric Index, a qualitative and quantitative measure of a customer's online experience when interacting with companies via the Internet.

Using Social Media

Social media should be included in all plans. Along with retailers using social media to communicate with customers, there should also be a manager whose job is to monitor and respond to information placed on social media. Many public relations crises have occurred because a customer complained over social media and the complaint went viral. A British Airways passenger used Twitter to complain about lost baggage. In addition to posting on his Twitter account the customer also bought Twitter-promoted tweets to get his complaint out to the company and others. The tweet was retweeted thousands of times and garnered media attention.

What could have been resolved with a little time and money can turn into a nightmare for retailers. Retailers should be proactive to find problems before customers do. When there is a compliment given to a retailer over social media, the customer should receive a thank you. When there is a complaint the customer should be contacted immediately so that the complaint can be addressed. Often people will share the story when companies answer customer concerns or do not address them. Retailers need to be leaders in creating and interacting with the social media communities. This activity helps to strengthen the brand and build consumer trust and confidence.

Five Pillars of Retailing

In an article from the *Harvard Business Review,* Leonard Berry (2001) describes five important actions for retailers. These actions, deemed pillars, sound simple, but are often difficult to implement, especially as the integration of multi- and omni-channel retailing grows:

1. Solve your customers' problems.
2. Treat customers with respect.
3. Connect with your customers' emotions.
4. Set the fairest (not the lowest) price.
5. Save your customers' time.

Source: Rawpixel.com/Shutterstock.com

Information is becoming increasingly available to consumers, which has empowered them to demand fairness in their transactions. As customers place more value on their time they are less likely to give retailers a second chance. Retailers that convey the appropriate level of respect will experience an increase in customer loyalty and sales (Scansaroli and Szymanski (2002).

Retailers should always keep these five pillars in mind when conducting business. As the work force becomes more diverse and the retail environment continues to change, consumers' needs are rapidly changing. Retailers must prepare for the challenges ahead and pay particular attention to this evolving consumer. In addition to following the five pillars, a good grasp of consumer trends is essential for retailer success.

Evolution of Brick and Mortar Stores

Brick-and-mortar stores will have to evolve if they are to survive. As multi-channel and omni-channel retailing grows, the retail landscape is changing. In the first quarter of 2017 several chains announced store closings. These included Macy's, JCPenney, Radio Shack, American Apparel, Office Depot, Aeropostale, The Limited, Bebe, American Eagle, Finish Line, Chicos, Abercrombie and Fitch, Game Stop and Staples. As online and alternative retail formats grow, many traditional retailers are struggling. Malls throughout the U.S. are experiencing high vacancy rates. Green Street Advisors, an analysis firm that tracks real estate investment trusts (REITs), forecasts that 10 percent of the roughly 1,000 large malls in the U.S. will fail within the next 10 years. Many believe the amount will be higher (Jordan, 2012). Green Street Advisors' research (2017) divides malls into categories based on productivity: The "A" players are high quality malls. These malls are evolving with the changing landscape and the trend is to include services and entertainment experiences within the mall. There are over 300 "C" quality malls that are struggling and in danger of closing; especially as anchor stores close in greater numbers.

The trend will be toward very big stores/formats or smaller stores. The West Edmonton Mall (www.wem.ca) in Alberta, Canada is an example of a mall that is combining experiences with traditional retailing. In addition to the typical mall-type stores it contains two hotels, an NHL size hockey rink, bowling alley, indoor amusement park, a water park, and many other entertainment selections. This mall is the province's number one tourist destination with over 30.8 million visitors each year. The Mall of America in Bloomington, MN is another example of a mall turned tourist attraction. According to the website it would take 86 hours to complete a mall visit if you spend just 10 minutes in each store. With so much to do, it is a city within a city.

For retailers and malls to survive they must use *experiential retailing* which is "a retail strategy that transforms products and services into a total consumption experience. It satisfies emotional or expressive (hedonic) desires, as well as rational or functional (utilitarian) needs of the consumer" (Kim, Sullivan and Forney, 2007, p. 3). Leaders in experiential retailing include Cabela's, Build-A-Bear Workshop, American Girl Place, FAO Schwarz and Nike Town. Retailers need to give consumers a reason to come to the store. Events and customer engagement augment the shopping experience.

The new buzzword for experiential retailing is *shoppertainment*; a strategy which focuses on experiences and events to make shopping interesting and fun. When people are engaged they are more likely to buy. By combining shoppertainment with excellent customer service, the retailer is more likely to get repeat business and positive word of mouth. Classes, workshops, cooking demonstrations, celebrity appearances and games all attract customers. Lululemon (www.lululemon.com), the yoga clothes retailer, holds free yoga classes once a week in their stores and provides free yoga videos online.

Formats that combine mixed-use stores and services will increase and replace the traditional mall. Lifestyle centers are an example of a mixed-use format that combines retail with entertainment to provide upscale consumers with many options. If traditional malls are to survive they have to become places that offer more than just shopping.

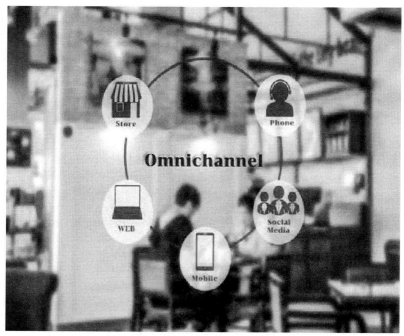

Source: Montri Nipitvittaya/Shutterstock.com

Retailers will reduce their square footage as omni-channel retailing becomes more integrated. Best Buy, Target and Kohl's are examples of retailers that have invested in smaller format stores. Specialized stores will also increase in popularity. According to Interbrand (2013), "The store, as the heart of the brand and its emotional center, cannot be starved of investment and innovation, or appropriate levels of design, media and technology. It needs to be the showcase for interesting new collaborations to keep things exciting, whether it's a luxury jeweler or a humble dollar store." Thus a retailer must create experiences for the customer in order to remain relevant. To keep customers engaged, social media must be managed and integrated into the brand's story.

A small retailer that is using technology in innovative ways is Hointer (www.hointer.com) out of Seattle, Washington. The store combines technology with traditional shopping. Customers use a smartphone to scan a QR code on clothing and the items are delivered to the dressing room within 30 seconds. When the customer is done shopping they slide the credit card through a machine and then the shopper leaves without interacting with a salesperson. Hointer's online site is integrated with the physical shopping experience so that the customer has access to the inventory at all stores. Due to the success of the small store, Hointer expanded to consulting and now helps other sectors and retailers in "building amazing shopping experiences....by merging the best of the physical and digital universe (www.hointer.com).

Source: Razvan Iosif/Shutterstock.com

Pop-up stores will increase in popularity as retailers try to be where their customers are located. These types of stores provide mobility that stationary physical stores don't provide. Pop-up stores also allow online retailers an inexpensive way to increase touch points with customers. Another trend is for online retailers to open small locations to serve as showrooms for products. Clothing retailer Bonobos (www.bonobos.com) and eyeglass retailer Warby Parker (www.warbyparker.com) have showrooms in their New York offices. Consumers can try samples of merchandise and when ready to buy, the order is fulfilled from a warehouse since no inventory is carried at these sites (Jordan, 2012). Even department stores are featuring pop-up formats within a store. For example, in 2017 Lord & Taylor launched The Dress Address, devoted to dress shopping for all occasions and featuring a rotating pop-up format within their stores where clothing or accessory brands are featured.

Augmented reality and artificial intelligence technology will gain in popularity as the online and physical spaces become more intertwined with people's lives. According to Jonathan Chippindale, Chief Executive of Holition, an augmented reality consultancy, "The holy grail now for retailers is creating digital empathy. No one can really guess what the future will look like. But those who are using technology and data to create bespoke shopping experiences that recognize every person is different, and with different needs, are more likely to come out on top" (Paton, 2017).

Market Adaptability

The future of retailing is truly exciting. Many changes will occur in retail institutions. There are indications that the face of retailing as we currently know it will not be around in the future. In addition, trends point toward a dramatic change in the typical retail customer. A key characteristic that separates successful businesses from failures is the capacity to respond to change. The key to retailers in the future is *market adaptability*, which is knowledge about environmental changes and the ability to react to these changes in a way that benefits both the retailer and the consumer. Critical components of adaptability include decentralizing decision making to more quickly adapt to consumer needs, streamlining processes, focusing on core competencies, implementing free exchange of information, and developing reward systems based on responsiveness to customers (H.R. Chally Group, 1998).

Companies that thrive in the face of a volatile environment are adaptive in their infrastructures, processes, and philosophy (The New Business..., 2003). It is imperative that new retail owners and managers develop comprehensive and integrated plans to deal with these issues.

Application: The IRM Flowchart

The IRM flowchart can provide retail managers with tools to create greater efficiency and competitiveness in the retail arena. Thus, the IRM flowchart provides a best-practice tool for current and aspiring retail managers. This section illustrates the use of the IRM flowchart for a new retail store for Z-CoiL (doing business as Z-CoiL). The store is fictitious, but we use information from the real-world company as a basis for the plan's development. While the IRM plan may not be as detailed as typical, it provides a condensed version.

Background

Dean, Don, and Denise (aka "the partners") are seeking to open a retail outlet. After assessing the market area, the partners have decided to sell pain-relief footwear and have chosen Z-CoiL as their supplier. To effectively compete in the marketplace, the partners have will use the IRM flowchart as a planning tool. They have adapted and modified the flowchart to make sure it is a good fit for their operations.

Retail Mission and Vision

The first step is to ascertain that the supplier's (Z-CoiL) and retail partners' mission and vision are synergistic. The partners have decided to use Z-CoiL's "belief statement" as a launching point for their own mission and vision statement, because this statement will guide the overall development of an IRM plan for the shoe store: "We're not interested in being a different kind of Shoe Company. We are interested in helping people enjoy life on their feet: running, walking, working or just standing around. . . . We're on a mission to launch a whole new pain-relief footwear industry."

Using this initial mission and vision statement, the partners created their own:

We're on a mission to change the way our customers walk. We believe in relieving our customers' foot pain; thus, we sell shoes for pain relief. It is our vision that all of our customers will experience more comfort and less pain with their Z-CoiL shoes. We will strive to exceed customer expectations. At the same time, we are committed to providing business partners with a return on their investment.

Situational Analysis and Integration of a Retail Information System

Because retailers operate in a world of constant change and increasingly available technology, the partners will utilize a retail information system (RIS) to facilitate the integration of all areas of retailing. After completing an external environmental analysis, the partners selected Jacksonville, Florida, as the physical site for the retail operation.

Jacksonville was chosen based on a number of criteria. First, there are currently no other Z-CoiL dealers in the Jacksonville area. Second, a number of skilled laborers are available for hire. Third, the demographic profile of Florida, and of Jacksonville in particular indicates a large elderly population. (See Figure 15.1 on the next page for regions of the United States with large elderly populations.) Specifically, according to the U.S. Census Bureau (as of 2010) the total adult population of Jacksonville is over 800,000 and about 11 percent are over age sixty-five. This is an ideal market because the elderly population is a primary segment for the Z-CoiL shoe. Sixteen percent of the adult population of Jacksonville is between ages forty-five and sixty-four. Income levels are steady, with the median household income at about $49,000 per year, slightly higher than the state's median. In addition people living in Jacksonville enjoy walking, playing golf, running or jogging, and exercise and other physical fitness activities. The lifestyle of the Jacksonville population, therefore, makes this segment ideal for the new retail store.

Figure 15.1 Regions of the U.S. Based on Percentage of People Aged 65 and Over

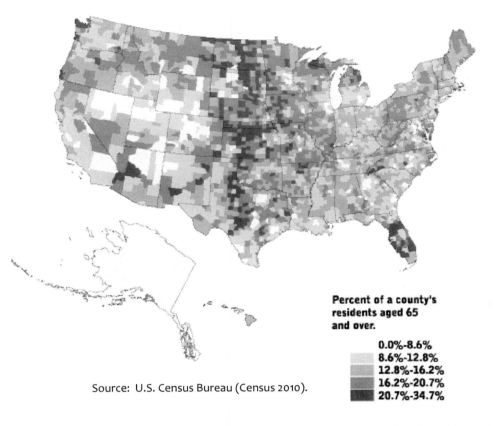

Source: U.S. Census Bureau (Census 2010).

Percent of a county's residents aged 65 and over.

0.0%-8.6%
8.6%-12.8%
12.8%-16.2%
16.2%-20.7%
20.7%-34.7%

An RIS will be used to store and disseminate information that is collected, such as demographic and location statistics, so the decision makers will have the data at their fingertips. The data will also guide the development of the retailer's tactical executions.

Based on the data, the partners have created a strategy for market development. Because the Z-CoiL shoe is a relatively new product, the partners have the added task of more closely defining their target market(s). Utilizing the data from the RIS, the partners have defined their target market, described next.

Target Market

The partners decided to mirror Z-CoiL's target market of people who spend excessive time on their feet. This market can be broken down into the following target segments:

1. Working people (postal workers, restaurant staff, doctors, nurses, other health care providers, etc.)---ages thirty-five to seventy.

2. Runners and sport walkers---age 20+.

3. People with pain or discomfort (heel spurs, plantar fascia, diabetes, arthritis, foot pain, leg pain, back pain caused by the impact of running and/or walking)---all ages.

4. Health care providers such as podiatrists, chiropractors, other MDs, and insurance companies will be used to reach individuals who are under medical care or receiving some type of treatment for pain.

5. Current and retired athletes, in particular local athletes (including the Jacksonville Jaguars), will also be targeted to help relieve their pain and also to be used for product promotion, publicity, and public relations.

Although age is a factor, the target market is more defined by the people experiencing pain or those who want to prevent pain. The partners will develop a database of customers' interests, as well as their demographic, behavioristic, and psychographic characteristics, to assist in the IRM executions.

Market Location and Selection

The partners spent months searching for the perfect Jacksonville location for their retail outlet. Traffic patterns were assessed for automobiles, buses, foot traffic, and main traffic arteries. Based on this research, a freestanding site with plenty of parking was selected in a highly traveled part of Jacksonville. This also allows for additional walk-in traffic.

Financial Operations Management

Because the partners want to establish a new venture and develop their market, they need to generate enough funds to start up the retail outlet. Thus, the partners want to make sure that the variable and fixed costs of running the store will be met. Cash and credit are needed for the physical site and for racks and display units for the products. In addition, the partners want to have enough capital left over to create an effective and balanced integrated marketing communication plan. Although salaries are a concern, the partners are willing to take less money up front to generate sales and revenues.

The partners have developed a five-year plan that will allow them to forecast sales each year for that period. In addition, the partners are planning to sell complimentary items, such as T-shirts, socks, insoles, and additional orthotics, although the majority of the planned sales will come from the shoes themselves.

Because they lack enough capital to create an attractive sales floor, the partners plan to use credit for the first three years to have enough cash on hand to meet changes in the retail environment; thus, they will have a buffer for unplanned events.

The partners developed a breakeven point for their business. When they crunched the numbers, the breakeven point, in units, was 10,000 pairs of shoes per year. Thus, the partners used an averaging method and found they needed to sell 2,500 pairs of shoes per quarter. This figure will be integrated into the evaluation portion of the IRM plan (Response of the Market and Retail Auditing).

Merchandise Buying and Handling

Because the partners will be exclusive dealers of the Z-CoiL product, they will have one supplier, Z-CoiL, for their main product. To supplement their revenue, the partners have decided to include ancillary products. They have found a company that specializes in promotional products such as T-shirts, socks, water bottles, and other items that the partners can use for promotion.

It was decided that all products will be stored at the physical retail location, thus reducing costs associated with

Source: Rawpixel.com/Shutterstock.com

storage. The disadvantage to this approach is that the actual selling space will have to be reduced to provide room for inventory. Inventory will be sold using the FIFO (first in, first out) method of inventory management.

The store will utilize point-of-sale (POS) terminals that allow for automatic reordering and replenishment of supplies. In addition, the POS will allow the partners to maintain control of their inventory levels and to generate financial statements at any point in time, thus integrating this function with the financial operations.

Human Resource Management

Due to the small size of the overall retail operation, two of the partners will be in charge of all retail activities. Denise will run the marketing portion of the business and Don will serve as general manager. Dean is designated as the chief financial officer (CFO) and will be responsible for all financial matters pertaining to the partnership.

The partners estimate that in addition to Denise and Don, they will need four additional sales and service personnel. These employees will be paid on an hourly basis, and their main function will be to provide customer service and follow-up with customers. They will deal with each customer who comes into the retail outlet. Benefits will be offered to each employee based on the financial plan, but the employees will be responsible for paying for a portion of them. This amount will be deducted from their biweekly paychecks.

Laws and Ethics

An attorney will be retained for legal guidance in terms of all laws applicable to the Z-CoiL store. The state of Florida requires that at least one owner of products marketed as "pain relief" devices have certification. It was decided that Dean would undertake the certification process during the first month and the other partners would also certify during upcoming months.

The partners decided they needed a diverse employee base. They themselves are a diverse group, including two employees that are fluent in Spanish as well as English. They want to ensure this diversity in their employee selection as well so that the employees are representative of their client base. This diversity will mirror the diverse customer base developed in the situational analysis.

Ethical business practices are of utmost importance to the partners, so they have designated Dean to be in charge of business ethics for the Z-CoiL store. Checks and balances will be instituted to ensure mistakes are caught early and corrected. The store will follow the ethics of Z-CoiL, the main supplier for the store.

Retail Tactics

Retail tactics include pricing, integrated marketing communication (IMC), and customer services decisions. The following sections outline the tactical executions the partners are planning based on data from the situational analysis, the financial plan, and the product mix. Each area must be integrated with the others to generate as much awareness as possible of the store's targeted markets.

Pricing

For products other than the shoes themselves the partners plan a 100 percent markup on the product's cost. The shoe prices will follow the suggested prices given by Z-CoiL for its complete line of products. By following the Z-CoiL pricing schedule, the partners will be able to better estimate demand and revenue flows.

Each shoe product will be tracked at the current prices, and adjustments to the retail price will be made based on supply and demand for each unit. The store will carry a wide breadth and depth of Z-CoiL shoes. In addition, allowances for the purchase of multiple products will be addressed at a later date. To create and maintain a high-quality product image, the prices of Z-CoiL shoes will be above the industry average for similar products.

The partners foresee that there may be demand for the products from groups of individuals or organizations (e.g., the Jacksonville athletic teams) and will provide prorated pricing and quantity discounts. The partners will also, when possible, use individuals from these organizations as spokespersons for the product or include testimonials from customers as part of the IMC program (discussed next).

Integrated Marketing Communications (IMC).

Because the market is geographically defined (that is, the primary geographic market is Jacksonville, Florida, and surrounding areas), local media vehicles will be used. At present, the partners plan to use local newspapers, local radio and television stations, and outdoor media such as billboards. The major social media sites will also be used to post testimonials and to communicate with customers.

There will be a tie-in with customer testimonials for each piece of IMC offered to the potential market. Testimonials and spokespersons will be vehicles for educating the public about this unique product. Presentations at local activities, festivals, fairs, and sporting events will take place. Presentations to educational institutions will also be a featured execution. The partners are expecting that the unique look of the shoes will generate publicity, which could mean "free" media coverage.

To keep down costs for the IMC tactics, the partners plan to use cooperative advertising with Z-CoiL headquarters, which has produced a number of television advertisements that the store will use. The cost of the ads to the partners is zero; however, there will be an associated cost for media placement. In addition to the TV ads, the store will use Z-CoiL--created print advertisements that feature the store's location, phone number, and website. As a natural element of IMC, the website will include videos, hotlinks to podiatrists; feature stories about the Z-CoiL shoe; Z-CoiL's headquarters in Albuquerque, New Mexico; and any other sites that may be of interest to the store's customer base.

To develop a customer list for the RIS, the partners plan to create contests and sweep-stakes. The contests will require that each entrant supply his or her name, address, phone number, and e-mail address to be eligible to win a free pair of Z-CoiLs or other promotional items. By generating these data, the partners will be able to expand their understanding of the Z-CoiL store customer. This database will be used to generate e-tailing campaigns.

For the future, the partners are planning store expansions and an increase in the amount and types of products they carry. Each of these expansions will be supported with IMC promotions.

Customer Service

The cornerstone for the success of Z-CoiL is outstanding customer service. The store will borrow these success techniques from the main supplier. Each employee will be required to attend a three-day training session at Z-CoiL's headquarters to ensure they have the skills and abilities necessary to promote and sell the products.

In addition to the corporate training, Z-CoiL store employees will be required to attend customer service training seminars offered by a national consulting group. This training focuses on customer satisfaction, but also includes different methods of selling. The Z-CoiL store will utilize the consultative approach to selling.

Employees' performance with regard to customer service will be assessed by evaluating each individual's sales as well as communications received from customers. An evaluation questionnaire will be developed and placed in the box of every pair of shoes sold. In addition, a random telephone survey and/or Internet survey of customers will be made, inquiring about the treatment the customer received from the Z-CoiL staff. This will also allow the store's employees to understand how well they are performing and how well accepted the product is. Any suggestions for product improvement will be forwarded to Z-CoiL. Rewards will be given to high-performing employees. This process will be developed throughout the first year of operation and adapted as the retail outlet thrives.

Source: michaeljung/Shutterstock.com

Response of the Market and Retail Auditing

The partners understand that the only constant in the universe is change. Therefore, they will give a great deal of attention to end-of-year assessments of sales and service. In addition, there will be a quarterly assessment of sales both to identify high-volume selling times and to correct any problems that occurred during the operating quarter.

Each member of the organization will be reviewed twice a year. The first review will be informal. Team members will be informed of their strengths and weaknesses regarding sales and service of the products. The end-of-year review will be a formal process, with raises, job terminations, or promotions based on that review.

Each year the store will undergo a major retail audit. The audit will both be performed in-house and outsourced. The internal audit will show how the partners believe the organization is performing; the external audit will be used to verify or dispute the findings from the internal audit. One important reason for undertaking the retail audit is to make sure all the functions are clearly defined and all the elements are being effectively integrated.

The partners want to ensure that their plan is dynamic and flexible. They know that they need to be able to respond to changes in the retail environment and have developed an environmental scanning process that allows them to identify changes. When coupled with the IRM, the overall plan becomes exciting and adaptable, and will enable the partners to compete at a high level with other shoe retailers in their geographic market.

Summary

As we move further into the twenty-first century, retailers will face many challenges and opportunities. This chapter discussed diversity and other trends in retailing. Many of the issues and trends in retailing focus on technological improvement. Emerging technologies allow for better customer segmentation and give retailers a more comprehensive knowledge of their markets. In addition, the technologies help retailers build relationships with their external customers as well as their internal customers (employees) and retail stakeholders.

The U.S. demographic base is changing. Thus, it is important for retailers to understand how to leverage diversity. In addition, changes in the economy, environment, and society are forcing retailers to look at their operations and how these trends will affect them.

The integrated retail management flowchart developed and presented throughout the text will propel retailers to develop new retail formats. As a dynamic tool, the IRM process allows retailers to make adjustments in their plans. By understanding the IRM plan and how to execute it, a retailer will be in a good position to compete in a saturated market that demands more and more new product and service offerings.

Key Terms

customer-centric culture	An active philosophy within a company that focuses on meeting the needs of individual consumers rather than those of the mass market.
experiential retailing	A retail strategy that transforms products and services into a total consumption experience.
market adaptability	Retailers' knowledge about environmental changes and their ability to react to these changes in a way that benefits both the retailer and the consumer.
shoppertainment	A strategy that focuses on creating experiences and events to make shopping interesting and fun.

Discussion Questions

1. Why is it important for retailers to understand future trends in the retail industry?

2. List and discuss three trends you think are occurring in the retail industry that have not been mentioned.

3. How can experiential retailing differentiate a company?

4. If your future plans involve retailing, what type of retailer would you prefer to be, and why?

5. Do you agree with the IRM plan devised by the Z-CoiL partners? What, if anything, would you change?

Exercises

1. Find three online retailers that use interactivity on their site. Discuss the strategy and whether or not it is effective.

2. Visit the Louis Vuitton website (http://www.louisvuitton.com/front/#/dispatch) and evaluate the website in terms of experiential retailing.

3. Choose a department store and provide recommendations for how to make the shopping experience more enjoyable/memorable.

Case

AT&T on the Forefront of Experiential Retailing

In 2012, AT&T opened a 10,000 square foot flagship store on Chicago's Magnificent Mile. The store is unlike the typical AT&T retail store because it helps create a brand experience. In addition to products and services, the store offers customers options to explore technology of the future. The store attracts over 30,000 people/month. According to AT&T (AT&T Opens..., 2013) customers can:

- Play and learn about apps that interest them in the Explorer Lounge. At the Apps Bar, "app-tenders" serve up one-on-one and group demos, which are also displayed on multiple video monitors on the Apps Wall. An 18-foot high Connect Wall shows interactive content and product information, visible to the entire store and passers-by.

- See products, apps and accessories organized and showcased based on their needs in the Lifestyle Boutiques, including Get Fit, Be Productive, Share Your Life and Chicagoland. Chicagoland includes local apps and Chicago-themed accessories exclusive to the AT&T Michigan Avenue store.

- Use and interact with AT&T products for home security and automation, entertainment, music and automobiles at the Experience Platform. Customers can see how AT&T Digital Life services can enable them to control their home using AT&T wireless devices with a demo in the Family Life area. The Street Smart area features a brand-new Nissan Leaf and shows the future of automotive connectivity, safety and efficiency.

- View artwork from two artists with Chicago ties, Cody Hudson and Dalek, in The Gallery. One-of-a-kind smartphone cases with their designs are available exclusively at the AT&T Michigan Avenue store.

- Check out the latest smartphones, tablets, and other mobile devices in the product runway.

- Discuss new purchases or resolve questions with AT&T store representatives in quiet and comfortable consultation areas.

Salespeople access registers with a biometric fingerprinting technology while sitting on a couch face to face with their customer. In 2015 AT&T expanded the interactive concepts to the Lubbock, Texas location. Customers can engage with AT&T products in three zones: The connected experience zone, highlighting how products can be used every day; the community zone where people can shop and play at interactive community tables; and the explore zone where AT&Ts devices are showcased next to digital monitors that explain how they work. Other AT&T stores are scheduled to adopt the experiential concept.

These stores are designed to encourage engagement and are examples of shoppertainment and experiential retailing.

Questions

1. What are the advantages of investing in a store like the AT&T Store? What about disadvantages?

2. How can retailers create in-store experiences that are integrated with online and other channel activity?

3. What will be the impact of high technology-enabled stores on the retailing industry?

Sources: AT&T Flagship Store's Interactive Tech Going Nationwide, Starting in Texas (2015). Retail Customer Experience (Oct 26) Retrieved from https://www.retailcustomerexperience.com/news/att-flagship-stores-interactive-tech-going-nationwide-starting-in-texas/; Heine, C. (2013). The Store of the Future Has Arrived (and No, It's Not Apple). *Adweek* (Jun3). Retrieved from http://www.adweek.com/news/advertising-branding/store-future-has-arrived-and-no-its-not-apple -149900; AT&T Website – www.att.com; AT&T Flagship Store. Retrieved from http://www.att.com/Common/about_us/ pdf/michigan_ave_store_infographic.pdf; AT&T Opens Flagship Retail Store on Chicago's Famed Magnificent Mile. Press Release from AT&T (Aug 30). Retrieved from http://www.att.com/gen/press-room? pid=23251&cdvn=news&newsarticleid=35277

References

Accenture Consulting (2016). Retail Customers are Shouting-Are You Adapting? Retrieved from https:// www.accenture.com/t20160728T162953__w__/us-en/_acnmedia/PDF-7/Accenture-Adaptive-Retail-Research-Executive-Summary-V2.pdf#zoom=50

Berry, L. L. (2001). The Old Pillars of New Retailing. *Harvard Business Review*, 79 (Apr), pp. 131-137.

Bureau of Labor Statistics (2011), U.S. Department of Labor, *The Editor's Desk*, Occupational Employment by Race and Ethnicity. Retrieved from http://www.bls.gov/opub/ted/2012/ted_20121026.htm

Business Insider (2016). The Mobile Payments Report: Market Forecasts, Consumer Trends, and the Barriers and Benefits that Will Influence Adoption. *Business Insider* (June 3). Retrieved from http://www.businessinsider.com/the-mobile-payments-report-market-forecasts-consumer-trends-and-the-barriers-and-benefits-that-will-influence-adoption-2016-5/?r=AU&IR=T

Colao, J. J. (2012). Five Trends Driving Traditional Retail Towards Extinction. *Forbes* (Dec 13). Retrieved from http://www.forbes.com/sites/jjcolao/2012/12/13/five-trends-driving-traditional-retail-towards-extinction/

Daniels, J. (2017). Online grocery sales set to surge, grabbing 20 percent of market by 2025. CNBC Retail (Jan 20). Retrieved from http://www.cnbc.com/2017/01/30/online-grocery-sales-set-surge-grabbing-20-percent-of-market-by-2025.html

Deloitte LLP (2012). Switching Channels: Global Powers of Retailing 2012. Retrieved from http://www.deloitte.com/ assets/Dcom-Global/Local%20Assets/Documents/Consumer%20Business/dtt_CBT_GPRetailing2012.pdf

Duhigg, C. (2012). *The Power of Habit. What We Do in Life and Business.* New York, Random House.

Facebook Annual Report (2015). Retrieved from https://s21.q4cdn.com/399680738/files/doc_financials/ annual_reports/2015-Annual-Report.pdf

Fell J. (2013). The Future of Retail: Paying with Your Face? *Entrepreneur* (Jul 23). Retrieved from http:// www.entrepreneur.com/article/227529

Fisher, T. (2017). Terabytes, Gigabytes, & Petabytes: How Big are They? *Lifewire* (Feb 4). Retrieved from https://www.lifewire.com/terabytes-gigabytes-amp-petabytes-how-big-are-they-4125169

Green Street Advisors (2017). 2017 Sector Outlook Highlights from Real Estate Analytics (blog). Retrieved from https://www.greenstreetadvisors.com/insights/blog/2017-sector-outlook-highlights-from-real-estate-analytics

H. R. Chally Group (1998). *The Customer-Selected World Class Sales Excellence Research Report.* Dayton, Ohio

Hendell, R. (2016). *Manufacturing Net* (June 2). Retrieved from http://www.manufacturing.net/blog/2016/06/what-manufacturers-need-know-about-direct-consumer-sales

Hointer (2017). Website www.hointer.com

Hopwood, C. (2016). Why Direct-to-Consumer is Becoming an Important Retail Channel. VisionCritical. Retrieved from https://www.visioncritical.com/direct-to-consumer-marketing-channel/

Hull, D. (2013). "Sharing Economy" Moves Mainstream. *San Jose Mercury News* (Aug 8). Retrieved from http://www.mercurynews.com/business/ci_23809325/sharing-economy-moves-mainstream

Interbrand (2013). Experience is Everything. Retrieved from http://www.interbrand.com/en/BestRetailBrands/2013/articlesinterviews/experience-is-everything.aspx

International Telecommunication Union (2012). Overview of the Internet of Things. Retrieved from http://www.itu.int/ITU-T/recommendations/rec.aspx?rec=y.2060

Jordan, J. (2012). The Death of the American Shopping Mall. *Atlantic Cities* (Dec 26). Retrieved from http://www.theatlanticcities.com/jobs-and-economy/2012/12/death-american-shopping-mall/4252/

Kim, Y., Sullivan, P., and Forney, J. C. (2007). *Experiential Retailing*. New York, NY: Fairchild Publications.

Lawlor, T. (2017). Is Facial Recognition in Retail Market Research the Next Big Thing? *Chain Store Age* (Feb 14). Retrieved from http://www.chainstoreage.com/article/facial-recognition-retail-market-research-next-big-thing

Leigh, T. W. and Marshall, G. W. (2001). Research Priorities in Sales Strategy and Performance. *Journal of Personal Selling and Sales Management,* (Spring), pp. 83--93.

Lindner, M. (2016). Shoppers Want Their Online Orders Faster. Digital Commerce 360 (Jan 21). Retrieved from https://www.digitalcommerce360.com/2016/01/21/shoppers-want-their-online-orders-faster/

Millennial Dads Take on Household Grocery Shopping. Convenience Store News (June 22). Retrieved from http://www.csnews.com/product-categories/other-merchandise-services/millennial-dads-take-household-grocery-shopping

National Center for Education Statistics (2013). Fast Facts. Retrieved from http://nces.ed.gov/fastfacts/display.asp?id=98

NEC Trials Cashless Payment by Facial Recognition (2016). (June 21). Retrieved from http://www.nec.com/en/press/201606/global_20160621_01.html

Paton, E. (2017). A Glimpse of our Shopping Future. *The New York Times* (April 13), p. D2.

Parature (2012). White Paper: Five Best Practices to Steal from the Retail Industry. Retrieved from http://www.parature.com/white-papers/Best%20Practices/2012colors-5-Retail-Best-Practices-WP.pdf

Peacock, L and Marsden, S (2013). Rise in Stay-at-Home Fathers Fueled by Growing Number of Female Breadwinners. *The Telegraph* (Jan 23). Retrieved from http://www.telegraph.co.uk/women/9822271/Rise-in-stay-at-home-fathers-fuelled-by-growing-numbers-of-female-breadwinners.html

Przbylski, A. K.; Murayama, K.; DeHaan, C.R.; and Gladwell, V. (2013). Motivational, Emotional, and Behavioral Correlates of Fear of Missing Out. *Computers in Human Behavior*, 29(4); 1841-1848.

PwC/Kantar Retail (2013). Retailing 2020: Winning in a Polarized World. Retrieved from http://uk.kantar.com/media/106221/retailing_2020_kantar_retail.pdf

Rainie, L. and Duggan, M. (2016). Privacy and Information Sharing. Pew Research Center (Jan 14). Retrieved from http://www.pewinternet.org/2016/01/14/privacy-and-information-sharing/

Rampton, J. (2016). The Evolution of the Mobile Payment. Tech Crunch (June 17). Retrieved from https://techcrunch.com/2016/06/17/the-evolution-of-the-mobile-payment/

Saiidi, U. (2016). Millennials are Prioritizing "Experiences" Over Stuff. CNBC (Life, May 5). Retrieved from http://www.cnbc.com/2016/05/05/millennials-are-prioritizing-experiences-over-stuff.html

Scansaroli, J. S. and Szymanski, D. M. (2002). Who's Minding the Future? Center for Retailing Studies, Texas A&M University, *Retailing Issues Letter*, (Jan), pp. 1--8.

Sheth, J. N., Sisodia, R. J., and Sharma, A. (2002). The Antecedents and Consequences of Customer-Centric Marketing. *Academy of Marketing Science*, (Winter), pp. 55--66.

Silverstein, B. (2013). The Future of Retail: Blending the In-Store and Online Experience. *Brand Channel* (Mar 27). Retrieved from http://www.brandchannel.com/home/post/2013/03/27/Retail-Walmart-Amazon-032713.aspx

Silverstein, B. (2013B). The Future of Retail: Reinventing and Preserving the In-Store Experience. *Brand Channel* (March 22). Retrieved from http://www.brandchannel.com/home/post/The-Future-of-Retail-Reinventinge28094and-Preserving-the-In-Store-Experience.aspx

Spotlight on Target's Hispanic Business Council (2013). Target website (July 23). Retrieved from https://corporate.target.com/discover/article/spotlight-on-Target-s-Hispanic-Business-Council

Sundararajan, A. (2013). From Zipcar to the Sharing Economy. *Harvard Business Review* Blog Network (Jan 3). Retrieved from http://blogs.hbr.org/cs/2013/01/from_zipcar_to_the_sharing_eco.html

Target Corporation Website. Retrieved from www.target.com

The New Business Imperative: The Capacity to Respond. *Chief Executive*, (May). Retrieved from Proquest database.

The Rise of the Sharing Economy (2013). *The Economist* (Mar 9). Retrieved from http://www.economist.com/news/leaders/21573104-internet-everything-hire-rise-sharing-economy

Turkle, S. (2012). Connected, But Alone? (Speech). TED2012.

Vagata, P. and Wilfong, K. (2014). Scaling the Facebook Data Warehouse to 300 PB. (April 10). Retrieved from https://code.facebook.com/posts/229861827208629/scaling-the-facebook-data-warehouse-to-300-pb/

Watson, E. (2013). The Future of US Food Retailing: The Pendulum is Swinging Back to Smaller Store Formats. Food Navigator-USA (Aug 8). Retrieved from http://www.foodnavigator-usa.com/Markets/The-future-of-US-food-retailing-The-pendulum-is-swinging-back-to-smaller-store-formats

Yaraghi, N. and Ravi, S. (2016). The Current and Future State of the Sharing Economy. Retrieved from https://www.brookings.edu/wp-content/uploads/2016/12/sharingeconomy_032017final.pdf

Glossary

CH.	Term	Definition
13	1:1 marketing	Using customer response management techniques to personalize products and services.
5	80/20 rule (aka Pareto principle)	A guideline stating that 20 percent of a retailer's customers make up 80 percent of its sales volume. Also known as the Pareto principle.
14	acceptable profit perspective	A perspective on the relationship between profit and principles that assumes companies want to maximize principles but are restricted because the market demands that profitability reach a certain level to ensure financial continuity.
8	accounts receivable (A/R) turnover in days	A measurement of the number of days, on average, it takes to convert accounts receivable into cash.
8	acid test ratio (quick ratio)	Quick assets divided by current liabilities.
8	activity ratios	Ratios used to determine how well a firm manages current assets, pays off current liabilities, and uses assets to generate sales.
11	additional markup	An increase in the retail price of a product in addition to what has already been added as a markup.
12	advertising	A form of either mass communication or direct-to-consumer communication that is nonpersonal and is paid for by an identifiable sponsor to inform or persuade members of a particular audience.
10	advertising allowance	A price concession given by a manufacturer of a product to a retailer to defray the retailer's costs associated with advertising the product.
10	affirmative action	Programs that address conditions that systematically disadvantage individuals based on group identities such as gender or race.
7	airport mall	A community shopping center located in an airport.
9	allowance	A discount offered to retailers that agree to participate in the vendor's marketing efforts.
12	all-you-can-afford method	A method of budgeting in which the retailer allots all the money it can manage to bear toward the IMC functions.
4	anchor	The largest store in a shopping center and serves to draw customers to the center.
2	app	Short for application; Software that can run on computers or mobile devices.
14	applied ethics	The study of ethics that involves analyzing specific instances of ethical dilemmas.
8	assets	Anything of value that a retailer owns.
9	assortment	The collection of products a retailer carries.
13	assurance	A component of quality that addresses a customer's satisfaction with the retailer or its products and services.
12	atmospherics	The attempt to create an overall positive atmosphere in a retail outlet.
8	balance sheet	A financial statement that itemizes the retailer's assets, liabilities, and net worth as of a specific point in time.

7	balanced tenancy	The process of optimizing tenants with each other so that retailers provide greater relevancy to their customers.
9	basic stock method	Inventory planning tool that allows the retailer to include a few more items (*basic stock*) than were forecasted in an order for a given period of time. BOM stock (at retail) = Planned sales (monthly) + Basic stock.
5	behavioristics	The subdivision of a retailer's current or potential markets based on buying responses, product usage patterns, product loyalty, or store loyalty.
12	best-guess method	A method of budgeting in which the retailer makes a subjective guess at how much to allocate to IMC.
11	black market	The illegal selling of goods outside of their authorized channels of trade.
9	bottom-up approach	A method of budgeting in which each retail department supplies data. The budgets are passed up to the next levels of management until all budgets reach an individual who is responsible for the budgeting process.
2	brand associations	Attributes or personality that the owners of a brand wish to convey to their current or potential customers.
5	brand community	A group of consumers with a product or brand attachments.
2	brand equity	The consumer's perceived level of quality for the retailer's product lines.
11	brand or image objectives	Objectives used to establish a clear idea of brand personality and positioning.
9	breadth	The number of different lines of product a retailer stocks. The number of product lines (or categories) the retailer offers. Breadth is often described along a continuum of narrow or broad.
11	breakeven point (BEP)	The level of activity at which income from sales (total revenue) equals total costs.
11	breakeven pricing	A pricing method in which pricing is based on the breakeven point for a given product.
2	bricks-and- clicks	Companies that have both a brick and mortal store and an Internet site.
4	business franchising	A situation characterized by a great deal of interaction between franchisee and franchiser; the franchisor agrees to support all of the business functions while listening to the needs and wants of its franchisees.
1	business sales	Sales from one business organization to another business organization; also called *business to business or B2B.*
9	buyer	The employee whose basic responsibility is to make purchases.
5	Buying power (also known as purchasing power)	The money people have to spend on products/services after paying taxes.
11	cannibalization	A situation in which a company introduces a product that takes away sales from an existing product.
8	carrying costs	The costs of storing and maintaining inventory.
4	cart abandonment rate	Percent of customers will leave their shopping carts (online or instore) prior to check-out.
9	cash conversion cycle (CCC)	A measure of how many days it takes to turn purchases of inventory into cash.
9	cash discount	A discount offered to retailers to encourage them to pay early or pay with cash.
8	cash flow from financing activities	Cash received or disbursed from activities dealing with a company's own debt and capital instruments.

8	cash flow from investing activities	Cash received or disbursed from extending or collecting loans and acquiring or disposing of investments or long-term assets.
8	cash flow from operating activities	Cash received or disbursed from all of the activities involved in a company's operations.
11	cash flow objective	A type of pricing objective in which the retailer attempts to generate money quickly.
9	category captain	A trusted manufacturer who coordinates efforts and makes recommendations for category management.
4	category killer	Sometimes known as a *power retailer or category specialist, a discount specialty store that offers a deep assortment of merchandise.*
9	category manager	The person that coordinates the efforts of the businesses involved in category management.
6	census	A is the process of including *all members of the population for input in a research study.*
7	central business district (CBD)	An unplanned shopping site in the downtown area of any city.
10	centralized organizational structure	An organizational structure in which decisions are made from one central location, often termed "headquarters" or the "home office."
4	chain store	A retailer that operates multiple (more than one) retail stores.
9	channel captain	The company or person that plays the biggest role in the supply chain.
1	channel of distribution	A network that includes all members of a team of businesses and organizations that help direct the flow of goods and services from the producer to the end user, or ultimate consumer.
5	cognitive dissonance (aka buyer's remorse)	A consumer's doubt associated with a purchase.
4	combination store	A retail format in which food items are combined with nonfood items to create a one-stop shopping experience.
9	commercial merchandise	Articles for sale, samples used for soliciting orders, or goods that are not considered personal effects.
8	common size financial statement	A financial statement in which common size ratios are used to compare financial statements of different size companies. For balance sheet items, ratios are typically expressed as a percentage of total assets. For income statement items, ratios are expressed as a percentage of total revenue.
7	community shopping center	A retail center typically between 100,000 and 400,000 square feet in size. Tenants often include smaller stores, branch department stores, and a large discount store.
4	company analysis	An analysis that includes data on sales and profit figures, company mission/vision, company's risk or conservative orientation, corporate resources, level of aggressiveness, market share, sales trends, etc.
8	comparative financial statement	A financial statement that reflects more than one year of financial information, to show changes over time. The information is typically presented in a side-by-side columnar format.
11	competition-oriented pricing	Pricing of products based on the industry leader's prices.
4	competitive analysis	Conducted to gain knowledge about the other retailers competing in the market and determine how competitors will respond to a retailer's own strategy and tactics.

5	compulsiveness	The degree of openness shoppers have to impulse purchases.
11	consignment selling	A method in which the retailer sells goods for the supplier and receives a commission on sales instead of taking title to the merchandise.
5	consumer behavior	The study of how customers buy products.
4	consumer cooperative	A retail establishment owned and operated by a group of consumers.
11	consumer market approach	A method in which a retailer generates data about prices based on controlled store experimentation.
6	consumer research panels	A group of customers who have agreed to participate for a period of time in marketing research
12	consumer-generated marketing	When a consumer gets directly involved with the marketing activities of a company.
12	continuity	One of the attributes of media objectives, indicating a stable level of IMC activity.
3	controllable variables	Those areas of the retail operation that can be effectively controlled and changed by retail managers.
4	convenience store	A retailer that caters to a neighborhood and carries a very limited assortment of products.
7	Core-based statistical areas (CBSA), also known as metropolitan statistical areas (MSA)	A government designation of an area within the United States that has a minimum of 50,000 permanent residents.
2	corporate social responsibility (CSR)	The commitment of business to contribute to sustainable economic development, working with employees, their families, the local community, and society at large to improve their quality of life.
9	cost complement	Total value at cost divided by total value at retail.
8	cost of goods sold (COGS)	The amount a retailer pays for its merchandise.
12	cost per thousand (or CPM)	Refers to the cost of reaching 1,000 people through an identified medium.
11	cost-oriented pricing	A pricing method in which a fixed percentage is added to the cost of products; also called *cost-plus pricing*.
12	creative platform	The creative strategy of a selected IMC tactic; includes the promise, creative objectives, and reasons the customer should buy. Also called *copy platform or creative strategy*.
5	culture	A group's shared beliefs and values which affect their thinking and behavior.
9	cumulative discount	A discount that runs for an entire purchase period and allows the retailer to order several times until the agreed-on discount level is reached.
8	current assets	Cash and other items that can be converted to cash quickly.
8	current liabilities	Financial obligations that must be paid back within the upcoming year.
8	current ratio	Current assets divided by current liabilities.
2	customer equity	The value of the complete set of resources, tangible and intangible, that customers invest in a firm.
13	customer response management (CRM)	The management of databases that assist retail managers in identifying trends and responding to customer characteristics.

2	**customer service**	Activities designed to enhance the level of customer satisfaction.
3	**customer services**	Anything a retailer provides in addition to the core product or service that adds value.
7	**customer spotting**	An observational technique in which the retailer utilizes various types of already-acquired data to try to ascertain where customers are located.
2	**customer-centered retailing**	An approach to retailing that places the customer at the center of all decisions.
15	**customer-centric culture**	An active philosophy within a company that focuses on meeting the needs of individual consumers rather than those of the mass market.
6	**data**	News, facts, and figures that have not been organized in any manner.
6	**data collection instruments**	Devices used to collect data such as the paper that a survey is printed on or the computer used by researchers to record responses.
13	**database marketing**	A form of direct marketing that uses databases with consumer information to create more relevant marketing materials.
5	**deal proneness**	The shopper's propensity to purchase products that are on sale or where some type of "deal" for the product is offered.
8	**debt-to-equity ratio**	Total liabilities divided by total owner's equity.
10	**decentralized organizational structure**	An organizational structure in which decisions are made at the local level, such as at individual stores.
6	**Delphi technique**	A research method used to generate information from a panel of experts.
11	**demand-oriented pricing**	Pricing of products based on consumer demand.
5	**demographics**	Statistics about any given population base.
4	**department store**	Large retailers that carries a wide breadth and depth of product and is organized into departments.
9	**depth**	Consists of the stock keeping units (SKUs) or variety within a category (this could include colors, styles and sizes that the retailer stocks within each line it carries). Depth is often described along a continuum of shallow to deep.
7	**designated market area (DMA)**	A designation developed by A.C. Nielson to describe a particular geographic area that serves a specific market.
4	**differentiation**	A strategy used to distinguish a company and their product from others.
4	**direct marketing**	An interactive system of marketing that uses one or more advertising media to generate a measurable response or transaction at any location.
4	**direct selling**	One-to-one selling directly to the consumer outside of a retail establishment such as in-home and online.
4	**discount store**	A type of department store that offers limited customer services and has merchandise priced below that at department stores.
10	**diversity**	Differences among people, including but not limited to age, gender, ethnicity, race, and ability.
10	**diversity management**	The method of implementing diversity and inclusion strategies to maximize benefits of corporate diversity in the workplace.
4	**divertive competitors**	Retailers that compete by selling the same type of merchandise or services; they do not necessarily specialize in that merchandise.

10	divisional chart	An organizational chart based on the divisions or business units within an organization.
10	downsizing	The planned elimination of a group of employees to increase organizational performance.
4	drug stores (aka pharmacy)	A retailer that sells medicines and other items.
1	e-commerce	The conduct of selling, buying, logistics, or other organization management activities via the Web.
6	economic order quantity	A calculation of how much merchandise to reorder.
9	economic order quantity (EOQ)	A calculation of how much merchandise to reorder.
4	economies of scale	Achieving lower costs per unit through higher-quantity purchases.
12	efficiency	The productivity of a store's selling space.
8	efficiency ratios	Ratios that provide evidence of how effectively management is running the business.
9	efficient customer response (ECR)	Category management strategy devised through joint efforts of retailers and suppliers with the objectives to increase sales and better fulfill customer wants and needs.
9	electronic data interchange (EDI)	A technology that allows retailers to conduct business with vendors electronically.
2	electronic data interchange (EDI),	The exchange of information between businesses using an electronic system.
12	electronic marketing	The use of digital technologies to sell goods and services. Also called digital marketing.
13	empathy	A component of quality that promotes understanding of the customer's needs.
2	encryption system	A system that codes data so that the data can be understood only by the intended user.
3	environmental scanning	A systematic process whereby the retailer acquires and uses information to assist in the management and planning of future actions.
10	Equal Employment Opportunity (EEO) laws	Laws that collectively prohibit discrimination on the basis of color, race, sex, religion, national origin, age, or physical disability.
2	equity	The marketing and financial value that the customer provides for the retailer.
1	e-tailing	A form of retailing utilizing the Internet to take the place of or supplement a physical retail location.
3	ethics	Concepts of right and wrong behavior.
5	ethnic group	Any group defined by race, religion, national origin, or some combination of these categories.
10	evaluation	An area of management that involves assessing an employee's performance in relation to goals and objectives designated for that employee's position.
4	everyday low pricing (EDLP)	A retailing strategy that emphasizes consistently lower-priced merchandise.
6	executive summary	A summary of an entire paper.
10	executive training programs (ETP)	Training available to the company's managers or executives.

10	**exit interview**	An interview conducted when an employee leaves an organization, for the purpose of determining the reasons behind the departure.
15	**experiential retailing**	A retail strategy that transforms products and services into a total consumption experience.
6	**exploratory research**	Research that is conducted when there are no earlier studies available to answer a question and a problem has not been clearly defined.
2	**extended marketing concept**	The concept of exceeding customer wants and needs at a profit.
6	**external secondary data**	Sources of data and information that are external to the firm.
4	**extreme-value retailers**	These retailers offer a very limited assortment of merchandise at very low prices.
10	**extrinsic motivation**	The desire to achieve something that comes from outside the individual (money, acknowledgment, etc.).
1	**facilitators**	External individuals or groups that help the retailer make a sale.
5	**feature proneness**	The tendency of shoppers to use or not to use coupons or other promotional items in their shopping decisions.
9	**FIFO (first in, first out)**	An inventory costing method that assumes older merchandise is sold before newer stock is sold.
4	**flea market**	A retail format in which many vendors sell used as well as new and distressed merchandise.
6	**focus group**	Interviews conducted with small groups of current or potential customers on a particular topic.
12	**follow-the-leader budgeting**	A method of budgeting in which the retailer generates estimates of competitors' IMC budgets from outside sources and attempts to match the industry leader's budget.
4	**food retailers**	Sell food products to consumers as its primary function.
4	**franchise**	A contractual agreement between a franchisor and a franchisee that allows the franchisee to operate a retail establishment using the name and (usually) the franchisor's operating methods.
4	**franchisee**	The owner of a retail establishment who has a contract with the franchisor to use the franchise's name and (usually) methods of operation.
4	**franchisor**	A business that grants the franchisee the privilege to use the franchisor's name and (usually) operating practices.
7	**freestanding sites**	Retailers that are located in a site with no immediate retailers in close proximity.
12	**frequency**	The number of times a target audience is exposed to an advertising message over a particular time period.
10	**functional chart**	An organizational chart based on the company's functional activities.
4	**general merchandise retailer**	A retailer involved in the sale of general, nonfood items.
5	**generational marketing**	The study of age groups and how they behave in the consumer market.
5	**geodemographics**	The combination of geographics and demographics which is used to describe the customer more clearly.
7	**geofence**	Virtual geographic perimeter around a real-word physical area.
7	**geofencing**	Using a **geofence** to deliver marketing communications (text, email, coupon, other promotional material)

7	**geographic information system (GIS)**	A computer-based tool for integrating and analyzing spatial data from multiple sources.
5	**geographics**	Analysis that helps the retailer find out where customers are physically located.
7	**geolocation**	Technology that uses Web geography to determine where an online buyer is located.
7	**Global Positioning System GPS**	A global navigation satellite system owned by the U.S. government and operated by the U.S. Air Force which provides users with positioning, navigation and timing services.
11	**gray market**	The selling of goods outside of their authorized channels of trade. While legal, these sales are unauthorized or unintended by the original manufacturer.
1	**gross margin**	The revenue remaining from the sales of products once the production costs have been subtracted.
11	**gross margin**	The total cost of goods sold subtracted from net sales.
9	**gross margin return on inventory (GMROI)**	A calculation of how much investment is being returned for each type of merchandise purchased.
8	**gross profit**	The difference between the retailer's net sales and the cost of goods sold.
12	**gross rating points (GRPs)**	An advertising measurement taken by multiplying reach by frequency.
10	**group training**	A type of training offered to groups of employees with similar training needs.
4	**hi-lo pricing**	A pricing strategy in which retailers set a higher price on less frequently purchased items and then discounts the price of featured items through sales promotions and couponing.
14	**horizontal agreement**	A restrictive agreement between two competitors in the same market.
8	**horizontal analysis**	An analysis that uses comparative financial statements for two consecutive years.
10	**human resource information system (HRIS)**	Software or online method for systematically gathering, analyzing, storing, and utilizing information and data related to personnel management.
10	**human resource management (HRM)**	Policies, practices, and systems that influence employees' behavior, attitudes, and performance.
10	**human resource recruitment**	The process of identifying and attracting the best potential employees to an organization.
1	**human resources**	A function that ensures that a company has the right mix of skilled people to perform its value creation activities effectively.
4	**hypermarket**	A large retailer that carries many types of products in addition to foods; originated in Europe.
10	**image advertising**	A type of advertising that attempts to enhance the retailer's image.
4	**impulse buying**	The purchase of products and services by consumers that was not planned in advance.
4	**independent retailer**	A type of retailer that operates a single establishment.
7	**index of retail saturation (IRS)**	A formula used to assess the saturation levels of various trading areas.
10	**individual training**	A trial-and-error approach to training in which employees take responsibility for training themselves.

11	industrial market approach	An approach in which the retailer sells its products to other businesses in addition to the final consumer. Prices for products or services may be different for business customers than for nonbusiness customers.
4	industry analysis	An analysis of the industry in which a retailer chooses to operate.
6	information	A meaningful body of facts organized around some specific topic.
11	initial markup	The price set on a product less the cost of the merchandise.
11	initial markup percentage	The initial markup expressed in percentage form.
7	inshoppers	People who tend to shop in their local communities.
1	integrated marketing communication (IMC)	The process and methods used to integrate and coordinate all of a firm's marketing communication activities.
12	Integrated Marketing Communications (IMC) mix	All the communications activities undertaken in an integrated marketing communications approach, including personal selling, advertising, public relations, direct marketing, sales promotions, and electronic/Internet marketing.
14	integrated perspective	A perspective of the relationship between profit and principles stating that firms strive for an optimal balance between profits and principles.
1	integrated retail management	An approach that involves coordinating all functions of a retailer so that different areas deliver consistent messages and service to customers
1	integrated retail management (IRM) flow chart	A chart that provides a framework to guide retail decision making.
3	Integrated retail management planning	The establishment of objectives, policies, and procedures to carry out goals set my retail managers.
1	integration	The condition wherein all parts of the retail organization have the information necessary to carry out their functions and the strategic philosophies are incorporated consistently throughout the plan.
6	internal secondary data	Sources of data and information that are internal to the firm.
14	Internet fraud	The use of the Internet to present fraudulent solicitation to prospective victims, conduct fraudulent transactions, or transmit the proceeds of fraud to financial institutions or others connected with the scheme.
7	Internet malls	Planned shopping centers located on the World Wide Web.
12	Internet marketing	Using the Internet to sell products and services
4	intertype competitors	Different types of retailers that compete by selling the same lines of products and compete for the same household dollars.
4	intratype competitors	Retailers that compete for the same customer bases or households.
10	intrinsic motivation	The desire to achieve something that comes from within the individual (happiness, satisfaction, etc.).
8	inventory (I/V) turnover in days	A measurement of the number of days, on average, from the time a retailer receives inventory to the time the inventory is sold to the customer.
9	inventory turnover	A measure of how many times a store sells its average investment in inventory during a year.
10	job (position)	A general category used by managers to assign responsibility of task performance to members of a retail organization.

10	job description	An explanation of the tasks involved in the performance of a given position in an organization.
11	just noticeable difference (JND)	The price at which consumers believe they are paying more or less than the norm or reference price.
9	just-in-time (JIT) inventory	A process in which a supplier delivers products to a retailer right before they are needed, thus saving the retailer storage costs.
4	kiosks	Small stand-alone structures that are often open on one side or more.
3	law	A rule established by authority, society, or custom.
11	leader pricing	A type of promotional pricing in which products are priced below the usual markup, near cost, or below cost. Also called *loss leader pricing.*
4	leased department	A department in a large retail store in which space is "leased" or rented to an outside vendor that in turn operates under the larger retailer store's policies.
10	leveraging diversity	The practice of seeking out different voices and viewing them as opportunities for added value.
8	liabilities	Financial obligations owed by a retailer.
14	license to operate perspective	A perspective on the relationship between profit and principles stating that firms must have a minimum value of principles required by society to obtain a license to operate.
11	life cycle pricing	Price planning based on the stage of the product (or store) life cycle that the product (or store) has reached.
7	lifestyle center	A planned shopping center targeted to upper-income shoppers. Typically outdoors with a "Main Street" ambience, tenants that sell nonessential items, higher building and landscaping costs than those of other retail developments, and parking in front of the stores.
9	LIFO (last in, first out)	An inventory costing method that assumes newer merchandise is sold before older stock is sold.
4	limited-line store (box store)	No frills food and merchandise discounters that offer a small selection of products.
8	liquidity ratios	Ratios that reflect management's control of current assets and current liabilities.
9	list price	The price given in the vendor's price list.
1	logistics	Every action taken to ensure that products and services get from the point of origin to the final customer.
9	logistics management	Every action taken to ensure that products and services get from the point of origin to the final customer.
8	long-term assets	Property, equipment, and other fixed assets used to operate a business.
1	macro retail environment	The external environments that affect retailers.
4	magalog	A catalog developed in a magazine format.
11	maintained markup	The amount of markup the retailer attempts to sustain for a particular product or product grouping. Calculation: Net sales – COGS.
11	maintained markup percentage	The maintained markup expressed in percentage form.
11	markdown	A decrease in the initial retail price, typically expressed as dollar amounts or a percentage.
15	market adaptability	Retailers' knowledge about environmental changes and their ability to react to these changes in a way that benefits both the retailer and the consumer.

4	market area	The geographical area where consumers that have a demand for the product reside.
11	market penetration objective	A type of pricing objective in which product prices are initially set low to attract large numbers of buyers. The resulting increase in sales volume offsets the lower introductory price.
6	market research	The process of data collection, organization, analysis, and dissemination of data relating to a particular area.
2	market segments	Groups of customers that share one or more characteristics and respond similarly to marketing efforts
11	market share	The proportion of sales of a particular product (or brand) to the total sales of that product (or brand) in a given area.
11	market share objective	A type of pricing objective in which the retailer adjusts price levels based on competitors' changes in price, with the goal of gaining market share.
4	marketbasket	Everything a customer plans on purchasing.
2	marketing concept	The philosophy that an organization should try to satisfy customers' needs through a coordinated set of activities that also allows the organization to achieve its goals.
1	marketing intermediary (middleman)	A business that links producers to other middlemen or to ultimate consumers through contractual arrangements or through the purchase and reselling of products.
6	marketing research	Research conducted to identify and define marketing opportunities and problems; generate, refine, and evaluate marketing actions; monitor marketing performance; and improve understanding of marketing as a process.
11	markup	The dollar amount added to the cost of a product to determine its final price.
12	marquee	A large exterior sign that includes the retailer's name.
3	mass marketing approach	An approach in which the retailer utilizes one unique marketing mix to try to capture the market.
2	m-commerce (mobile commerce)	Technologies that include smart phones and computer tablets that have Internet access and can be leveraged by companies to keep consumers connected.
7	megamall	A mall that is often several times larger than a regional center; also known as a *superregional center.*
10	mentoring	A type of training in which an experienced employee is assigned to train and act as a role model for a new employee.
9	merchandise	The products or services the retailer currently offers, or plans to offer, for sale to customers.
3	merchandise buying and handling	The physical purchase of products and services and how those products and services are brought to the retail outlet, handled, and finally placed ready for sale.
9	merchandise buying and handling	The physical purchase of products and services and how those products and services are brought to the retail outlet, handled, and finally placed ready for sale.
9	merchandise mix	The combination of merchandise variety, assortment, depth, quality, and price points.
9	merchandising	Activities involved in organizing the display of products and services.
14	metaethics	The study of the origin of ethical concepts and theories.
3	mission statement	A statement that explains why the firm is in business, what it does, and what it stands for.
4	mobile POS systems (m-POS)	Mobile systems, typically hand-held, that aid in the completion of a retail transaction.

11	**modified breake-ven pricing**	A method wherein the retailer estimates the market demand for a product and then applies it to the breakeven point.
4	**monopolistic com-petition**	A market in which there is a limited amount of competition from other retailers for consumer dollars.
4	**monopoly**	A market in which there is only one seller selling a specific good or service.
10	**motivation**	A basic drive of all humans; in business, it is usually associated with the need to create personal or job satisfaction.
1	**multi-channel re-tailing**	Retailing through several channels to reach customers where they buy
6	**mystery shopping**	Form of observational research in which retailers hire shoppers to pose as customers to shop at various stores
2	**name equity**	The value of the organization's name.
7	**neighborhood busi-ness district (NBD)**	An unplanned shopping site that provides *shopping for a neighborhood rather than a larger trading area.*
7	**neighborhood shopping centers**	Planned shopping areas with a small anchor store.
8	**net income after taxes**	The difference between net income before taxes and income taxes.
8	**net income before taxes (NIBT)**	The difference between net income from operations and the net effect of other income (expenses).
8	**net income from operations**	Gross profit minus operating expenses.
8	**net sales**	All gross sales a retailer earns during a specified period of time, minus sales discounts given to customers to promote sales and minus returns and allowances given to customers for returned items or defective products.
8	**net worth (owner's equity)**	Assets minus liabilities; represents the net value of a retail business on a cost basis.
6	**netnography**	Thee analysis of online behavior.
6	**nonprobability sampling**	Sampling in which no member of the population has an equal and known chance of being selected for the research study.
7	**non-store retailer**	A retailer that has no physical location but sells via cyberspace, catalogs, vending machines, or other nontraditional places of business, such as a home.
14	**normative ethics**	The study of ethics using criteria to determine whether certain behavior is right or wrong.
4	**North American Industrial Classification System (NAICS**	A business coding system developed by the government that uses a coding system to identify types of businesses for better comparisons.
8	**notes to the finan-cial statements**	A financial statement that provides supplemental information about the balance sheet, income statement, and statement of cash flows.
12	**objective-and-task method**	A method of budgeting in which the retailer specifies the role IMC will play and the outcomes desired in the overall operation.
6	**observational re-search**	A non-intrusive research tool that is used to evaluate consumer behaviors.
11	**odd/even pricing**	The practice of using prices that end in either an odd or even number.
4	**off-price retailer**	A retailer that sells brand-name merchandise, which may include overruns or distressed merchandise, at 40 to 50 percent below traditional retailers.

4	oligopoly	A market characterized by similar products and very few sellers.
1	omni-channel retailing	An integrated approach to multi-channel retailing which strives to create a consistent and seamless shopping experience for the customer across channels.
9	open-to-buy	The amount the buyer has left to spend for a given time period, typically a month. Each time a purchase is made, the open-to-buy amount decreases.
8	operating expenses	The normal costs associated with doing business, not including the cost of the merchandise for sale.
3	operations management	The management of all of the functions necessary in running the retail business.
8	operations management	A planning function dealing with the implementation of store policies, tactics, and procedures.
9	order lead time	The span of time required to fulfill an order.
10	organizational chart	A graphical display that delineates who is responsible for the various areas of the firm.
10	organizational culture	The pattern of shared values and beliefs that helps employees understand how their organization functions and provides guidelines for behavior on the job.
14	organized retail crime (ORC)	The large-scale theft of consumer items.
7	outlet center	A type of community center that brings together retail establishments for manufacturers and retailers of consumer goods. These centers increase drawing power by providing deep discounts on brand-name products.
10	outplacement	A process in which a business hires experts to offer support, personal assessments, and job-search skills training to employees that are being downsized.
7	outshoppers	People who are more likely to shop outside their community.
6	outsourcing	The practice of hiring an individual, a group, or an organization outside the company to perform certain work.
7	overstored	A situation in which too many stores (or too much selling space) are devoted to a product or product line.
9	percentage variation method	Inventory planning tool in which the beginning-of-month planned inventory during any period (typically a month) differs from planned average monthly stock by half of that month's variation from average monthly sales. BOM stock (at retail) = Average stock for the sales period (at retail) x 1/2 [1 + (Planned monthly sales/Average monthly sales)].
12	percentage-of-profit method	A method of budgeting in which the retailer determines a basic percentage amount to be used for IMC based on overall profits.
12	percentage-of-sales method	A method of budgeting in which the retailer allots a basic percentage amount for the store and, in some cases, for each of the store's brands or products (or product lines).
9	periodic inventory system	A cost accounting system in which sales are recorded as they occur but inventory is not updated.
9	perpetual inventory system	A cost accounting system that shows the level of inventory on hand at all times.
12	personal selling	Using face-to-face communication to sell products and services.
14	phishing	Tricking people into disclosing personal information, usually through email or the Internet, and using the information to commit fraud.
7	planned shopping site	Retail site typically planned by a developer. Upfront planning is done to determine which retailers would provide the best mix of products and services to customers.
3	planning	The establishment of objectives, policies, and procedures to carry out goals.

12	**planogram**	A visual map of a store's layout and shows where products and displayed should be placed to maximize sales.
6	**pluralistic research**	The combination of qualitative and quantitative research methods when conducting research.
7	**point of indifference**	The distance at which the choice between two shopping destinations is equal.
12	**point-of-purchase (POP) communications**	A type of sales promotion that includes in-store materials such as posters and displays designed to influence consumer purchases. Also called point-of-purchase advertising.
4	**point-of-sale systems** (POS)	Systems that aid in the completion of a retail transaction.
1	**pop-up retail**	A temporary retail space
7	**power center**	A type of community center that includes at least one category killer with a mix of smaller stores.
11	**prestige pricing**	The practice of selling products at high prices to build a reputation for quality.
1	**Price**	The amount of money set for a product.
11	**price elastic**	A term referring to consumers who are sensitive to changes in price.
11	**price elasticity of demand**	A measurement of the responsiveness of quantity demanded to a change in price, with all other factors held constant; also called *price elasticity.*
11	**price gouging**	A tactic wherein a retailer takes advantage of high demand and limited supply to raise the price of a good or service beyond customary amounts.
11	**price inelastic**	A term referring to consumers who are relatively insensitive to price changes.
11	**price leveling**	The practice of setting prices on products and services so that prices remain stable for a defined period of time. Also called *customary pricing, products are generally priced above, below, or at market prices.*
9	**price points**	The range of prices for a particular merchandise line.
11	**price stability policy**	A practice in which the retailer attempts to create a one-price policy for individual products.
11	**price variability**	The practice of varying price of merchandise or services based on established criteria.
11	**pricing flexibility**	The range of prices consumers are willing to pay for a particular product or service.
11	**pricing policies**	General rules or guidelines for price development based on company strategies.
3	**pricing policy**	Refers to the methods used by a business to guide price setting for products and services that will be sold.
3	**primary data**	Data that have been generated specifically to solve a problem.
6	**primary data**	Data that are gathered for a specific purpose and have not yet been published.
7	**primary market**	The group of people that account for at least 60 percent of the retailer's total business.
6	**probability sampling**	Sampling in which each and every member of the population has an equal and known chance of being chosen for the sample.
1	**Product**	Anything that is produced and sold.
4	**product franchising**	A situation in which the franchisee agrees to sell the franchisor's products or services.
1	**product line**	A group of related products that satisfy a class of need, serve a particular market, have similar methods of distribution, or fall within a specific range of prices.

9	product line	A category of products with similar characteristics.
11	product quality objective	A type of pricing objective that focuses on recouping costs associated with retail research and development or to develop a desired product image.
10	product/brand chart	An organizational chart based on the products or brands an organization carries.
11	profit objective	A type of pricing objective in which the retailer attempts to meet or exceed projected profit levels.
10	programmed learning	A structured, formal training process that allows the employee to study material pertaining to the retailer's operation and then respond to questions about the material studied.
11	promotional pricing	The practice of coordinating pricing with the promotion variable of IMC.
5	psychographics	Lifestyle analysis data used to determine what consumers do over specified time periods.
11	psychological pricing	A method of pricing in which the retail takes into account consumer's perceptions and beliefs.
12	public relations (PR)	The efforts of an organization to win the cooperation of various publics.
12	publicity	A sub functions of public relations in which the organization attempts to attract attention through various media.
8	purchase discount	Reduction in the payment amount a vendor is willing to accept to satisfy the amount due if the payment is made earlier.
5	purchase involvement	The consumer's involvement in the overall shopping experience.
4	pure competition	A market in which there are many different buyers and sellers.
2	QSP	Categorization of customer value by quality, service, and/or price.
6	qualitative research	Collection, analysis, and interpretation of data that cannot be quantified with numbers.
6	quantitative research	Research which uses structured questions in which the response options have been predetermined and the results of which can be summarized with numbers.
9	quantity discount	A discount offered to retailers that purchase in large quantities.
8	quick assets	Assets that can usually be converted quickly into cash (includes cash, accounts receivable, and current notes receivable).
5	race	A group of individuals sharing common genetic traits that determine physical characteristics.
6	radio frequency identification (RFID)	Wireless technology that used radio waves to read product information.
8	ratio analysis	The computation of several financial ratios derived from the financial statements.
12	reach	The percentage of a target audience that is exposed to an advertising message at least one time during an advertising campaign.
5	reference group	Those people to whom an individual compares him/herself to and whose attitudes and values guide the person's decisions.
11	reference pricing	A concept of what the price of a product should be based on the consumers' frame of reference.
7	regional center	A retail site that provides general merchandise and is typically enclosed with parking surrounding the center.

10	regional chart	An organizational chart based on geographic designations.
7	regional shopping centers	Large, planned facilities which appeal to a larger, geographically dispersed market. Each regional center has at least one department store (usually more), and at least 50 smaller retail businesses (usually more).
2	relationship marketing	A type of marketing that focuses on building long-lasting relationships with customers.
13	reliability	A component of quality that addresses the dependability of the retailer or its products and services.
13	responsiveness	A component of quality that tells the customer the retailer is willing to provide high levels of prompt customer service.
3	retail (corporate) objectives	Define actions that the retailer wants to achieve.
8	retail accounting system (RAS)	A method for systematically gathering, analyzing, storing, and utilizing financial information and data.
1	retail audit	A comprehensive evaluation of the retail plan.
3	retail information system (RIS)	A system in which data are gathered and stored, turned into useful information, and disseminated to employees and managers to assist in making retail decisions.
6	retail information system (RIS)	A method for systematically gathering, analyzing, storing, and utilizing valuable retail information and data.
3	retail objectives	Goals that are for a medium-length term and provide measurable statements.
7	retail saturation	The point at which consumers' needs are just being met with the existing retail facilities.
3	retail strategy	A plan that provides the retail decision maker with a framework for current and future actions and dictates how objectives will be achieved.
2	retail technology	Any tool that helps retailers succeed in carrying out strategy.
1	retailer	A company or an organization that purchases products from individuals or companies with the intent to resell those goods and services to the ultimate, or final, consumer.
1	retailing	To sell goods and services in small quantities directly to consumers.
4	retail-sponsored cooperative	A type of retail organization in which several retailers have banded together to create an organization that helps to overcome many of the problems associated with running a small retail operation.
11	return on investment (ROI) objective	A type of pricing objective in which the retailer attempts to meet or exceed stated return on investment figures.
8	return-on-assets ratio	Net income plus interest income, net of its tax effect, divided by average total assets.
8	return-on-equity ratio	Net income available to owners divided by average owner's equity (net worth).
8	return-on-sales ratio	Net income divided by sales.
9	reverse logistics	The development of policies and procedures for the return of merchandise purchased by customers to a store or to a vendor or manufacturer.
9	safety stock	Extra merchandise carried to keep a retailer from running out of a product.
12	sales promotion	A short-term activity that enhances or supports other IMC variables.
6	sampling	The process of choosing a subset of the population of interest to collect problem-specific data.
6	sampling frame	A list of all population members from which a sample will be drawn.

6	scaling technique	A method used to measure attitudes, knowledge, opinions, or perceptions on a given topic or issue.
1	seamless	Functioning as one cohesive unit, with no "seams," or vulnerabilities.
9	seasonal discount	A discount given to retailers for making purchases out of season.
7	secondary business district (SBD)	An unplanned shopping site (smaller than a CBD) that is located around the major transportation intersections of cities. A typical SBD has at least one department store or variety store, coupled with a number of smaller stores.
3	secondary data	Data that have already been collected and analyzed.
6	secondary data	Published data that have already been collected for some other purpose.
7	secondary market	The group of people subordinate to the primary market that accounts for the fifteen to twenty percent (15-20 %) of sales.
3	segmentation	The process of breaking up the target market into more controllable subgroups.
3	segmented approach	An approach in which the retailer breaks up the mass market into submarkets (called *segments*) *and then develops a unique marketing mix for each segment.*
14	servicemark	A firm's brand name, symbol, or design used to identify the company to other businesses and consumers as the source of a service.
2	services retailing	A type of retailing in which the "product" being sold is actually a service; the customer derives value from the "service product" that is provided.
2	servicescape	All the variables of the service operation that are visible to consumers, including facilities, personnel, equipment, and the service's customers.
4	share of wallet	The percentage of a customer's total spending at a particular retailer.
15	shoppertainment	A strategy that focuses on creating experiences and events to make shopping interesting and fun.
2	silo	A term used to describe how different parts of an organization work separately from one another.
11	skimming objective	A type of pricing objective in which the price for a newly introduced product is set high. After competitors enter the market, the price is adjusted down.
9	slotting allowance	An allowance given to retailers to get the vendor's products and/or services on the shelves or in choice locations in the retailer's stores.
12	social media marketing	The use of social media sites to connect with customers and generate traffic.
11	special-event pricing	A type of promotional pricing in which advertised sales, typically coinciding with a major holiday or event, are used to generate store traffic.
4	specialty store	A store that carries a limited number of products within one or a few lines of goods and services.
8	statement of cash flows	A financial statement showing cash receipts and cash payments during a given period.
11	status quo objective	A type of pricing objective in which the retailer attempts to maintain the current situation.
4	stock keeping units (SKU)	Retailer-defined numbers or codes used to identify each unique product sold.
9	stock-to-sales ratio	A measurement that compares a retailer's stock levels to levels of sales.
7	store-based retailer	A retailer that has one or more permanent, fixed physical location(s).
4	strategic clarity	The retailer's commitment to create and achieve an in-depth understanding of their strengths and weaknesses.
3	strategic thinking	Utilization of the retail mission statement, the vision statement, the environmental scanning results, and the situational analysis to understand the environmental forces that affect a retail business.

1	strategy	Planning that provides the total directional thrust of the retail plan.
7	strip (or string) shopping district	An unplanned shopping site with stores that are visible from the road and arranged in a strip.
5	subculture	A group of individuals within a broader culture who share the same morals, beliefs and values, but are distinctive in other ways.
4	super center	A retailer that is a combination of a superstore and a discount store.
4	superstore	A food-based retailer that is larger than a traditional supermarket and carries expanded service deli, bakery, seafood, and nonfood sections.
10	supervision	An area of management in which managers direct employees in various tasks and monitor employees' productivity.
1	supply chain	All the people and companies involved in getting products/services from the manufacturer to the final consumer
3	supply chain management	The coordination of the functions and tactics across business functions within a particular company and across businesses within the supply chain for the purposes of improving the long-term performance of the individual companies and the supply chain as a whole
11	survival objective	A type of pricing objective in which the retailer increases price levels to meet sales expenses.
3	tactical executions	The day-to-day operational activities that implement the strategic plan.
1	tactics	The actual executions of the overall plan; provide for short-term (less than one year) actions.
13	tangibility	A component of quality that involves the physical characteristics of the retail store.
1	target market	All the people toward whom the retailers plans to aim its marketing efforts
3	target marketing	is the process of identifying and attempting to reach people with a company's marketing efforts.
10	task	A duty to be performed in a given job.
10	task analysis	A technique used to facilitate the listing of tasks.
10	termination	The legal dismissal of an employee.
7	tertiary market or fringe market	The group of people subordinate to the primary and secondary markets that account for the remaining sales not represented by these two groups.
14	tie-in	A practice in which a company tries to sell one product on the condition that the customer purchase a second product. (Also called a *tying agreement*.)
9	top-down approach	A method of budgeting in which members of upper management prepare budgets and pass them down to departments to follow.
1	touch points	Contacts between a company and a consumer or group of consumers.
9	trade discount	An offer by a vendor to reduce the price of merchandise if the retailer provides the vendor with a service in return for the discount.
14	trademark	A firm's brand name, symbol, or design used to identify the company to other businesses and consumers as the source of a product.
7	trading area	A geographical area containing the customers of a particular firm or group of firms for specific goods or services.
4	traditional supermarket	A store that offers a full line of groceries, meat and produce with at least $2 million in annual sales and up to 15% of their sales in general merchandise/health and beauty care. The stores carry between 15,000 and 60,000 SKUs (stock keeping units) and may have a deli, bakery and/or pharmacy.
3	typical customer profile	A description of a retailer's most frequent customers.

1	**ultimate consumers**	Families, individuals, and/or households that plan to consume the products or services themselves. AKA end users
3	**uncontrollable variables**	Those areas of the retail operation that cannot be controlled by retail managers.
7	**understored**	A situation in which a trading area has too few stores (or too little selling space).
1	**unified commerce**	An approach to multi-channel retailing that emphasizes the connection of all channels in real time.
11	**unitary elasticity**	A situation in which the percentage change in price equals the percentage change in quantity demanded.
6	**Universal Product Code (U.P.C.)**	A bar code found on many consumer packaged goods that stores all pertinent product information.
7	**unplanned shopping site**	A site that develops when two or more retailers move into the same area or in close proximity to each other. These sites are a function of evolution; they are not planned but develop over time.
9	**usage rate**	Average sales per day of a specific product in units.
2	**value**	An amount, as of goods, services, or money, considered to be a fair and suitable equivalent for something else; monetary worth of something; relative worth, utility, or importance.
2	**value proposition**	A short, clear, simple statement containing the reasons that a customer would choose one brand over another
4	**vending machine**	A non-store retailing format in which consumers purchase products through a machine.
9	**vendor-managed inventory (VMI)**	A technology that allows a vendor to track sales of its products through its various retail outlets using scanner data.
14	**vertical agreement**	An agreement, between at least two parties operating at different levels of the supply chain, that relates to the conditions under which the parties may purchase, sell, or resell goods or services.
8	**vertical analysis**	An analysis that concentrates on the relationships among items within the same set of financial statements.
3	**vision statement**	A statement that focuses on the firm's future goals.
12	**visual merchandising**	An attempt to inspire customers to purchase through the use of design techniques that enhance the overall buying experience.
14	**wardrobing**	The return of used, non-defective merchandise like special event apparel or electronics after a major sporting event.
4	**warehouse club**	A retailer that charges a membership fee to consumers or businesses who buy from the store.
4	**warehouse store**	A retailer that offers a limited assortment of goods and services, both food and merchandise, to both end users and small to midsize businesses at reduced prices.
5	**web community**	Online websites that attract people with similar interests
9	**weeks' supply method**	Inventory planning tool in which beginning of the month inventory equals several weeks' expected sales. BOM (at retail) planned inventory = Average weekly sales (estimated) x Number of weeks to be stocked.
1	**wholesaler**	An individual or organization that facilitates and expedites exchanges that are primarily wholesale transactions.
4	**wholesale-sponsored cooperative**	An organization that is developed, owned, and run by a group of wholesalers.
14	**win-win perspective**	A perspective on the relationship between profit and principles that assumes the more ethically a business operates, the higher its profits will be.

Index

Subject Index

Page numbers in italics indicate illustrations and t indicates tables.

Name Index
Page numbers in italics indicate illustrations and t indicates tables.

Ogden & Ogden

Retailing:
Integrated Retail Management 3e

Denise T. Ogden, Ph.D.
Professor, Marketing
Penn State Lehigh Valley
President, The Doctors Ogden Group, LLC

James R. (Doc) Ogden, Ph.D.
Emeritus Professor of Marketing
Kutztown University of Pennsylvania
CEO, The Doctors Ogden Group, LLC

Textbook *Media*

The Quality Instructors Expect
At Prices Students Can Afford
Replacing Oligarch Textbooks Since 2004

For more information, contact

Textbook Media Press

1808 Dayton Avenue

Saint Paul, MN 55104

Or you can visit our Internet site at

http://www.textbookmedia.com

or write

info@textbookmedia.com

For permission to use material from this text or product, submit a request online at info@textbookmedia.com

Retailing: Integrated Retail Management 3e

Denise T. Ogden, Ph.D.

James R. (Doc) Ogden, Ph.D.

10 Digit ISBN: 0-9969963-6-2

13 Digit ISBN: 978-0-9969963-6-5

Textbook Media Press is a Minnesota-based educational publisher. We deliver textbooks and supplements with the quality instructors expect, while providing students with media options at uniquely affordable prices. *All our publications are made in the U.S.A.*

Brief Table of Contents

Detailed Table of Contents